BANK COLLECTIONS AND PAYMENT TRANSACTIONS

BANK COLLECTIONS AND PAYMENT TRANSACTIONS

Comparative Study of Legal Aspects

BENJAMIN GEVA

OXFORD
UNIVERSITY PRESS

OXFORD

UNIVERSITY PRESS

Great Clarendon Street. Oxford OX2 6DP

Oxford University Press is a department of the University of Oxford.
It furthers the University's objective of excellence in research, scholarship.
and education by publishing worldwide in

Oxford New York

Athens Auckland Bangkok Bogotá Buenos Aires
Cape Town Chennai Dar es Salaam Delhi Florence Hong Kong Istanbul
Karachi Kolkata Kuala Lumpur Madrid Melbourne Mexico City Mumbai
Nairobi Paris São Paulo Shanghai Singapore Taipei Tokyo Toronto Warsaw

and associated companies in Berlin Ibadan

Oxford is a registered trade mark of Oxford University Press
in the UK and certain other countries

Published in the United States
by Oxford University Press Inc., New York

© Benjamin Geva 2001

The moral rights of the author have been asserted
Database right Oxford University Press (maker)

First published 2001

British Library Cataloguing in Publication Data

Data available

Library of Congress Cataloging in Publication Data

Geva, Benjamin, 1946–
Bank collections and payment transactions: comparative
study of legal aspects/Benjamin Geva.
p. cm.
Includes bibliographical references.
1. Banking law. 2. Check collection systems–Law and legislation.
3. Clearinghouses (Banking)–Law and legislation. I. Title.
K1066.G48 2001
346'.082–dc21

ISBN 0–19–829853–6

1 3 5 7 9 10 8 6 4 2

Typeset by J&L Composition
Printed in Great Britain
on acid-free paper by
T.J. International Ltd. Padstow, Cornwall

To Esther

On the Author

Benjamin Geva is a Professor of Law at Osgoode Hall Law School in Toronto. He specializes in commercial, financial, and banking law, particularly in payment and credit instruments, electronic banking, and the regulation of the payment system. He obtained his LL.B. (cum laude) at the Hebrew University of Jerusalem (1970) and his LL.M. and SJD at Harvard. He held visiting positions, in the United States, at the University of Chicago, the University of Illinois and the University of Utah; in Israel at Tel Aviv University; in Australia in Monash, Deakin, and Melbourne Universities; and in France at the Faculté de Droit et de Science Politique d'Aix-Marseille. He practised in Israel and Toronto and under IMF technical assistance programmes, has advised the authorities in Bosnia-Herzegovina, Kosovo, and Haiti. He is a member of the Osgoode law faculty since 1977.

Professor Geva is the author of *The Law of Electronic Funds Transfers*, published in the USA, and *Financing Consumer Sales and Product Defences in Canada and the United States* as well as of a casebook on *Negotiable Instruments and Banking*, both published in Canada. He has written numerous articles in Canadian, American, English, Australian, South African, and Israeli periodicals, primarily in the negotiable instruments and payments area. Professor Geva is the editor-in-chief of the *Banking and Finance Law Review*, a Canadian-based periodical that he founded in 1986. His current research is mainly on funds transfer and payment law.

Professor Geva is currently a member of the International Academy of Commercial and Consumer Law as well as of professional committees dealing with legislation on personal property security and tiered holding of securities. He is Visiting Professorial Fellow and member of the Academic Board of International Scholars at the Centre for Commercial Law Studies, Queen Mary, London, a participating Professorial Fellow of the Institute of International Banking and Finance of Southern Methodist University, Dallas, Texas (USA), a member of the Academic Advisory Board and an External Professorial Fellow of the Asian Institute of International Financial Law of the University of Hong Kong Law Faculty, and a member of the Editorial Advisory Board of Kluwer Law International's Yearbook of International Financial and Economic Law and book series on International Banking, Finance and Economic Law, and of the Editorial Board of the Lloyds of London book series on Banking Law.

Preface

Upon its initiation in 1993, this comparative law project was supposed to lead to the writing of a chapter in the Commercial Transactions and Institutions volume of the *International Encyclopedia of Comparative Law* (published under the auspices of the International Association of Legal Science). It significantly expanded in both scope and depth, so that its inclusion in the Encyclopedia became impractical in terms of both space and timing. The project was then transformed into the present study. I remain grateful to both Professor Ulrich Drobnig of the Max Planck Institute for Foreign & International Private Law in Hamburg, Germany, the Co-editor of the Encyclopedia, and Professor Jacob S. Ziegel of the University of Toronto Faculty of Law, the Chief Editor of the Commercial Transactions and Institutions volume, for their initial support and encouragement.

In carrying out the study, I had to face my own linguistic limitations; I do not speak or read German, Japanese, and Italian. In addition, notwithstanding my interest in comparative law, my point of view might have been coloured by my predominant common law background as well as by my North American base of operation. Accordingly, input from the jurisdictions discussed in the book has been indispensable. The work thus draws heavily on information obtained from jurists in the various countries, whose invaluable help and in some cases, ongoing feedback, I acknowledge with great gratitude. I am particularly grateful to the late Professor Christian Mouly, Professor Jean Stoufflet, Daniel Mainguy, as well as to Professors Jacque Mestre and Alan Ghozi (all five from France); to Professor Guido Ferrarini, Professor Vittorio Santoro, Adele Lorenzoni, as well as to Professor Concetto Costa, Marcello Gioscia, and Massimo Trentino (all six from Italy); to Dean Kiichi Gotoh, Professor Shinsaku Iwahara, Professor Kazuhito Yukizawa, Professor Kasturo Kanzaki, and Hitoshi Kimura (all five from Japan); to Professor Uwe Schneider, Dr Jens Nielsen, Frank Meyer, as well as to Professor Otto Sandrock, Dr Oliver Remien, Horst Ahlers, Martin Lang, Felix Blum, Professor Norbert Reich, and Margrit Detschelt (all ten from Germany); to Professor Mario Giovanoli, Professor Luc Thévenoz, Andrea E. Rusca, as well as Dr Jacques Bischoff, Dr Thalmann, Dr Martin Hess, and Professor Bernd Stauder (all seven from Switzerland); to Professors Denis Cowen, Leonard Gering, Angela Itzkowitz, and Frans Malan (all four from South Africa); Professors Shalom Lerner, Ricardo Ben-Oliel, and Alfredo Mordechai Rabello (all three from Israel); Professor Harold Luntz and Pearl Rozenberg (both from Australia); Paul Turner and Stephanie Heller (both from the USA); Martin Karmel (from the UK) and Robert van Esch (from the

Netherlands). For the historical part of the research, I am also indebted to John Barton of Oxford, Professor Ronald Sweet of Toronto, and Mordechai Adler of Israel. Also, I remain obliged to numerous individuals from central banks, banks, bank associations, and payment services providers and organizations, in the various jurisdictions, for making available to me invaluable information. Needless to say, all errors and misunderstandings are mine.

For financial support in various stages, I am grateful to the Max Planck Institute, the Social Sciences and Humanities Research Council of Canada (SSHRC), and the Foundation for Legal Research of the Canadian Bar Association. Invaluable institutional support was provided by the Osgoode Hall Law School of York University. I am thus grateful to both Deans Marilyn Pilkington and Peter Hogg, as well as to Ross Irwin, Assistant Dean, and Elaine Andrew, Administrative Officer, through whom assistance and support were bestowed on me. For administrative assistance throughout the years I am obliged primarily to Christine Wright, Aleksandra Nesic, and Marilyn Reckord. Invaluable research assistance was provided by various Osgoode students. For the final and decisive stage, including compilation of the subject matter index, I am enormously indebted to Caroline Brennan. At earlier stages, indispensable assistance was provided primarily by Michael Torkin, Mindy Gilbert, Marc Lacoursiere, Sumit Soni, as well as Nathan Aryev and Joanna Obrejanu, to whom all I remain grateful.

Most research was carried out in Toronto, particularly at the Osgoode Hall Law School Library, to whose staff I am most grateful, in all areas of service, particularly for reference help as well as for making available to me extensive interlibrary loan facilities. I am also grateful to librarians at Oxford University, both at the main law library and St John's College, the Max Planck Institute, the Bank of France, and Université d'Aix Marseille III where I conducted some of the research. For hospitality in these institutions, I am grateful particularly to Professor Roy Goode, Professor Ulrich Drobnig, Hervé Le Guen, and Professor Christian Louit respectively, as well as to staff and other colleagues in these institutions.

Research on the book commenced in 1993, and it is only natural that some of its fruit has been presented in professional conferences or published. The following acknowledgements are to be mentioned: 3.C(i) builds on parts of 'International Funds Transfers: Mechanisms and Laws', Chapter 1 in J. J. Norton, C. Reed, and I. Walden (eds.), *Cross Border Electronic Banking —Challenges and Opportunities* (London: Lloyd's of London Press, 1995), 1; 3C.(ii), (x), and (xii) were presented at the 2000 Pennsylvania State University Dickinson School of Law 10th Biennial Conference of the International Academy of Commercial and Consumer Law; 3.C(x) was also presented at the 1998 Tokyo 8th Seminar on International

Finance of the Asian Development Bank and is part of 'Promoting Stability in International Finance—Legislative and Regulatory Reform of Payment and Settlement Systems', in R. Lastra (ed.), *The Reform of the International Financial Architecture* (London: Kluwer Law International, 2000) 248; 3.C(xii) is part of 'Cross-Border Credit Transfers in Euros: Legal and Operational Aspects', in J. J. Norton (ed.), *1998 Yearbook of International Financial and Economic Law* (London: Kluwer, 1999), 173; 3.D is based on an unpublished paper presented at the 1998 Biennial Conference of the Academy of Commercial and Consumer Law, at Bond University, Gold Coast, Australia which draws heavily on a part of 'Study of the Payments Systems of Four Countries: The United States, Australia and the Netherlands, with an Addendum on New Zealand', submitted on 31 July 1997 to the Department of Finance, Canada, in conjunction with the payment systems review; 4.B updates 'Allocation of Forged Cheques Losses—Comparative Aspects, Policies and a Model for Reform' (1998), 114 L.Q.R. 250; 4.C was originally presented at the 1996 Bar Ilan University 8th Biennial Conference of the International Academy of Commercial and Consumer Law, and published in J. S. Ziegel (ed.), *New Developments in International Commercial and Consumer Law* (Oxford: Hart, 1998), 107; 4.D incorporates both 'Conversion of Unissued Cheques and the Fictitious or Non-Existing Payee—Boma v. CIBC', (1997), 28 Can. Bus. L.J. 177 and 'Forged Check Indorsement Losses under the UCC: The Role of Policy in the Emergence of Law Merchant From Common Law' (2000), 45 Wayne State Law Review 1733.

I acknowledge with gratitude the encouragement and support of Oxford University Press, which made the publication of this book possible. Particularly I am grateful to John Louth, Mick Belson, Edwin Pritchard, and Liz Davies.

Last but not least, I acknowledge the support I received from my immediate family, daughters Anat and Dorith, and wife Esther. Particular gratitude is extended to my wife Esther, to whom the work is dedicated. The book would not have been completed but for her endurance, perseverance, endless patience, and constant encouragement.

B.G.
Toronto,
Autumn 2000.

Contents

4. THIRD PARTY'S FRAUD: BREACH OF THE MANDATE AND MISDELIVERY OF FUNDS

Description

A study of the law governing the bank–customer relationship pertaining to the disposition of funds by cheques and credit transfers, covering common law, civilian, and 'mixed' jurisdictions. It integrates a strong analytic perspective, both doctrinal and policy oriented, into a comparative descriptive framework. It discusses the mandate performed in carrying out bank collections and payments as well as loss allocation upon the misuse of payment systems by means of fraudulently initiating or directing payments.

Table of Cases

Table of Legislation

PART 1
Introduction: payments, banking, and laws

A. Payment Transactions and the Overall Book Plan

In the modern economy, the cashless payment system provides a facility for non-cash payments by allowing payors and payees access to funds held in the financial system. A cashless payment transaction consists of the following elements: **[1]**

1. the pre-existing account relationships of customers with account—(or value—) holding institutions. Account-holding institutions may be depository or non-depository institutions that may provide asset, investment, and credit accounts that can be used for payments;

2. the communication of payment instructions by customers;

3. clearing of payment instructions (namely, the processing and exchange mechanism that enables participants to determine their debit and credit positions towards others); and

4. settlement (namely, the process of payment for positions established in the clearing).

Generally speaking, in each domestic payment system, access to clearing and settlement facilities, linking customer accounts throughout the country, is effectively limited, either by law or by practice, to supervised regulated depository institutions, such as banks. Yet, funds may be held by the public in non-depository financial institutions, such as securities brokers or insurance companies. Nevertheless, as outlined in Chapter 1.B below, it is still universally true that the banking system is the backbone of the cashless payment system.[1] **[2]**

A payment transaction is a mechanism facilitating payment other than by means of the physical delivery of coins and banknotes from the payor to the payee.[2] Typically, banks are the conduits for payment transactions, so that in the context of the modern banking system, a payment transaction is initiated by an instruction given to a bank either by the payor or under the payor's authority. The operation of the payment transaction is premissed on the transmission of funds from the payor's account to that **[3]**

---

[1] For the disposition of funds held by non-banks, see 3.D below.
[2] For the legal nature of the payment mechanism see in general, B. Geva, 'The Concept of Payment Mechanism' (1986), 24 Osgoode Hall L.J. 1.

of the payee. In this process, the payor's account is debited and the payee's account is credited. The part of the payment transaction carried out for the payee is known as 'collection'. Where the payor and payee hold their accounts at different banks, a payment transaction further involves interbank clearing of payment instructions, followed by the settlement of resulting interbank obligations.

'Clearing' can be defined broadly as the interbank exchange and processing of payment instructions, which may be in execution of customers' instructions, with the view of calculating and establishing respective bank debit and credit positions available for settlement. 'Settlement' is the payment of the interbank obligations arising from the respective debit and credit positions resulting from the clearing. Settlement may be bilateral or multilateral, gross or net, as determined in conjunction with the debit and credit positions produced in the clearing process.[3]

[4]   In principle, payment instruction may be given orally, in writing, or electronically. When the payor directly instructs the payor's bank to make payment, so that the banking operation commences with a debit to the payor's account, the payment transaction is called a credit transfer, often described as a 'credit push'. Conversely, when payment instructions, either from the payor or under the payor's authority, are first communicated by the payee to the payee's bank, the banking operation commences with a credit to the payee's account, followed by collection of funds from the payor's account; this payment transaction is then called a debit transfer, often described as a 'debit pull'. Cheque collection is a good example for a debit transfer. Generally speaking, a cheque is a written order of the payor, directed to the payor's bank, but issued to the payee, who deposits it for collection to the payee's account at the payee's bank.

(II) THE OVERALL BOOK PLAN

[5]   This book is a study of the law governing payment transactions. The discussion evolves around the bank–customer relationship relating to the disposition of funds by cheques and credit transfers, covering both paper-based and electronic payments. I address, with various degrees of detail, common law, civilian, and 'mixed' jurisdictions: particularly Australia, Canada, England, France, Germany, Israel, Italy, Japan, South Africa, Switzerland, and the United States. Other than a description of the law in

---

[3] See e.g. B. Geva, 'The Domestic Payment System: Policies, Structure, Operation and Risk', in J. J. Norton and M. Andenas, *Emerging Financial Markets and the Role of the International Financial Organizations*, being vol. iv of *International Economic Development Law* (London: Kluwer Law International, 1996), 115 at 120–6.

these jurisdictions, the book contains an in-depth analysis of common issues and responses to them, in light of desired policies. Accordingly, an evaluation of the various rules and proposals for reform is an integral part of the study.

The book is divided into four parts. Part 1 is an overview of the various legal systems and fundamentals of banking and payment law, in an over-all historical context. Part 2 deals with the banking relationship, within which collections and payments occur. It highlights the customer contract, the deposit transaction, the mandate authorizing bank collections and payments, and the debt resulting from entries to the current account. Part 3 covers the performance of the mandate by the bank. It discusses the laws governing the payment and collection of cheques and credit transfers extensively, in the context of actual clearing and settlement mechanisms—particularly, large value transfer systems in developed countries. Part 4 discusses the misuse of payment systems through fraud, which may occur during the initiation of payments or later, in misdirecting them. It focuses on cheque forgery, unauthorized electronic funds transfers, forged cheques indorsements, and misdirected credit transfers.

The book focuses on payment transactions with respect to which substantial law has developed. Space does not permit detailed attention to retail electronic payment systems. Moreover, payment transactions carried out of value stored on cards or computer software, referred to as payment ie. payments in e-money, are not dealt with in this book. Such payments are not performed out of bank accounts, on which this book focuses. Furthermore, the law governing payment in e-money, even as a specific application of general principles regulating payment transactions, is to a large extent, still in the making; it has not matured to the same degree as the law applicable to cheques and credit transfers. Thus, it does not merit a similar comparative analysis.[4]

A major objective of this study is the integration of a cohesive analytic perspective, both doctrinal and policy-oriented, into a comparative descriptive framework. In highlighting fundamentals relating to payment transactions under the various legal systems, I search for a universal 'law merchant' transcending the boundaries of the diverse jurisdictions. Yet, in the final analysis, what constitutes common ground is the universal endeavour to meet the needs of payment transactions participants within the existing legal principles of each jurisdiction.

---

[4] From the voluminous literature on e-money payments, particular mention will be made to Task Force on Stored-Value Cards, "Commercial Lawyer's Take on the Electronic Purse: An Analysis of Commercial Law Issues Associated with Stored-Value Cards and Electronic Money" (1997), 52 Bus. Law. 653, which is quite comprehensive in identifying legal issues.

B. Banking and Payment System Architecture

[1]   The modern payment system has been described as 'a complex set of arrangements involving such diverse institutions as currency, the banking system, clearing houses, the central bank, and government deposit insurance'[1]. Among these institutions, currency refers to cash, or to coins and banknotes; payment with cash is outside the scope of this book.[2] Government deposit insurance is a facility provided to depositors, insuring them against the insolvency of their deposit-taking bank. It is designed to pool the risk of individual bank failures and thus encourage reliance on the banking system as a whole. Clearing houses are designed to facilitate interbank handling of payment instructions with the view of settling resulting obligations. Both deposit insurance and clearing houses are incidents relating to the functioning of the banking system. As for the central bank, it operates in the payment system primarily within its role as the bankers' bank.[3] It is thus the banking system, with the central bank at its head, which serves as the backbone of the cashless payment system.[4]

The payment system has been described as 'an inverted pyramid',[5] with

---

[1] M. S. Goodfriend, 'Money, Credit, Banking, and Payment System Policy', in D. B. Humphrey, *The US Payment System: Efficiency, Risk and the Role of the Federal Reserve* (Boston: Kluwer Academic Publishers, 1990), 247 at 247.

[2] For my perspective on the evolution of coins and banknotes as money, see B. Geva, 'From Commodity to Currency in Ancient History—on Commerce, Tyranny, and the Modern Law of Money' (1987), 25 Osgoode Hall L. J. 115 (hereafter: Geva, 'Commodity').

[3] 'Defining central banking is problematic. In one sense we recognize it when we see it'. See F. Capie, C. Goodhart, and N. Schnadt, 'The Development of Central Banking', in F. Capie, C. Goodhart, S. Fischer, and N. Schnadt, *The Future of Central Banking—The Tercentenary Symposium of the Bank of England* (Cambridge: Cambridge University Press, 1994), 1 at 5. Briefly stated, the central bank is the issuer of the national currency and guardian of its value. As a bank, its main clients are the government and the commercial banks. It may be assigned regulatory powers relating to the financial and payment systems.

[4] Among all enumerated institutions, deposit insurance is not all that indispensable, and does not universally exist. Also, in exceptional circumstances, as for example in connection with a payment system other than in the national currency or in the case of a currency board, a central bank, in the traditional and the usual sense, may not exist. Briefly stated, in a currency board regime, the amount of currency issue, together with other issuer's obligations, is restricted by foreign currency reserve, so that the issuer is not free to exceed this reserve by extending credit to banks and thus providing them with liquidity as may be required. This compromises the issuer's role as a bankers' bank. In general, see e.g. T. Shu-ki, 'Legal Frameworks of Currency Board Regimes', Hong Kong Monetary Authority Quarterly Bulletin, August 1999, Issue No. 20 at 50.

[5] E. G. Corrigan, 'Luncheon Address: Perspectives on Payment System Risk Reduction', in D. B. Humphrey (ed.) above, n. 1, 129 at 130.

'the broad base of economic actors whose daily activity in the market economy gives rise to payment obligations',[6] made through banks, 'with the central bank at the apex'.[7] The evolution of this architecture of the banking system, 'consisting of commercial banks and the central bank', stated to be 'the instrumentality through which payments are made in a developed market economy',[8] is the subject-matter of the present discussion.

'Banking' is a form of financial intermediation for the transmission of surplus economic resources from savers to borrowers. Broadly speaking, such transmission occurs through the bank by means of lending to borrowers the funds deposited by savers. A standard legal definition fully recognizes this economic function. In the European Union, a 'credit institution', effectively a bank, is thus defined to mean 'an undertaking whose business is to receive deposits or other repayable funds from the public and to grant credits for its own account'.[9] In effect, funds lent by banks to borrowers originate primarily from savers' deposits and neither from contributions to capital nor from any other borrowing. [2]

The provision of payment services has emerged as a distinct characteristic of banks. 'To be recognized as a bank . . . an institution is expected to receive deposits of money from its customers; to maintain current accounts for them; to provide advances in the form of loans or overdrafts; and to manage payments on behalf of its customers . . .'.[10] Indeed, as indicated, the cashless payment system operates on the basis of the transfer of funds from one bank account to another. For the most part, transferable account balances consist of deposited funds. According to a classic text,[11] the primary economic function of commercial banks is thus to hold demand deposits and honour payment instructions drawn on them, 'in short, to provide us, the economy, with the largest component of the money supply'.[12] From an economic perspective, the use of the deposited money through profitable lending compensates banks, and provides them with an incentive for deposit taking.

It is in this sense that the lending of money to the public is stated to be,

---

[6] H. J. Blommestein and B. J. Summers, 'Banking and the Payment System', in B. J. Summers (ed.), *The Payment System — Design, Management and Supervision* (Washington: International Monetary Fund, 1994), 15 at 27.

[7] B. J. Summers, 'The Payment System in a Market Economy', in B. J. Summers (ed.), ibid., 1 at 5.

[8] Blommestein and Summers, above, n. 6 at 28.

[9] Art. 1 of the First Council Directive 77/780/EEC of 12 Dec. 1977 and the coordination of laws, regulations administrative provisions relating to the taking up of the business of credit institutions (the 'First Banking Directive'), (1977) OJ L 322/31.

[10] E. Green, *Banking—An Illustrated History* (New York: Rizzoli International Publications, Inc., 1989) at 11.

[11] P. A. Samuelson, *Economics* 11th edn. (New York: McGraw-Hill, 1980) at 275.

[12] The other, more obvious, but economically less significant, component of the money supply is banknotes and coins in circulation.

as an economic function of a bank, secondary in importance, after the deposit taking.[13] It is, however, the profitable moneylending by banks which has facilitated their avoidance of charging fees for the mere safe-keeping of sums held on deposit so as to encourage the public to retain funds with banks. In turn, in each country, this has facilitated the development of a universal domestic interbank payment system—linking all banks by means of correspondent accounts, held by one bank with another, as well as by means of accounts which banks hold with the national central bank.[14]

(II) POLICY CONSIDERATIONS—THE QUEST FOR EFFICIENCY

[3]   The linkage among deposit taking, lending, and the provision of payment services, leading to the architecture of the modern payment system, is economically rationalized by the quest for efficiency gains.[15] At its inception, deposit taking was a safekeeping facility, designed to protect depositors against the risk of loss. Inter-deposit transfers subsequently developed as cashless payment mechanisms, designed to avoid the physical transportation of money, thereby reducing costs as well as the risks of accidental loss and theft. Recognizing the opportunity to profitably invest funds on deposit, depositaries seized the idea, leaving idle at their disposal only adequate amounts of cash necessary to meet the reasonable needs of their customers for cash withdrawals. This increased profit to deposit takers (banks) and reduced costs for customers, thereby ensuring the continuation and growth of this practice.

Further efficiency gains were facilitated by the implementation of transfers between deposits in different depositaries. This required the establishment of correspondent interbank relationships. Accordingly, an efficient interbank system purporting to reduce interbank cash deliveries required that banks extend credit to each other or keep interbank balances, thereby requiring them to monitor each other. Stated otherwise, to support efficient payment services for their customers, banks specialized in information-intensive credit extension with respect to their fellow bankers.

Banks promptly carried over this specialization to non-banks, namely to bank activities outside the payment system. They thus specialized in information-intensive credit extension as the primary method of deriving

---

[13] Samuelson, above, n. 11 at 275.

[14] In some countries, all banks are required to maintain accounts with the central bank. For example, this is the case in Australia. Elsewhere, for example in Canada, it is only the large banks which maintain accounts with the central bank with each of the smaller banks maintaining an account with a correspondent large bank.

[15] For this analysis, see Goodfriend, above, n. 1 at 252–7.

profit from funds held with them on deposit. Non-traded information-intensive loans have become the principal assets of banks. In turn, in the absence of an objective cost-effective mechanism facilitating the ongoing evaluation of non-traded information-intensive loans, banks have been unable to pass on to their depositors a share in the profits from the loans; that is, banks could not operate as mutual funds. Rather, they could pay to depositors an amount determined irrespective of the bank profit (or loss). This is the explanation of the par valuation of bank deposits, that is, of the fact that depositors' return is independent of the fortune of the bank's investment.

With the crystallization of the relationship between payment services, deposit taking, and lending, the design of the payment system continued to evolve. Efficiency generated the establishment of multilateral clearing and settlement arrangements to substitute the numerous bilateral inter-bank correspondent links. The private-sector clearing house introduced central collection, collective settlement, centralized holding of reserves, more extensive interbank lending, and payment finality. Multilateral clearing reduced the number of exchanges and streamlined the domestic banking process. Multilateral settlement, resulting from the multilateral clearing, enabled each bank to set one deposit, held with one central counterparty, in anticipation of its own anticipated debit position vis-à-vis all other banks. This substituted the numerous bilateral relationships, including the myriad interbank balances required to be held to meet anticipated bilateral indebtedness to the various debtor banks. Ultimately, it was the settlement on the books of the central bank, as such a central counterparty, that could provide finality equivalent to that of the physical delivery of money. This is so, since in any domestic system, both the banknote and the deposit held at the central bank are obligations of the central bank, and are thus of equal value. Deposit insurance (where available), bank supervision, and the monetary policy of the central bank have further contributed to the stability and safety of the payment system in its design as it has thus developed.

(III) ORIGINS IN ANTIQUITY

The actual historical development of payment systems was quite consis- **[4]** tent with, and confirms to this evolutionary model. Indeed, ancient Mesopotamia has been identified as the 'cradle of banking operations'.[16]

---

[16] R. Bogaert, *Les Origines antiques de la banque de dépôt—Une mise au point accompagnée esquisse des opérations de banque en Mésopotamie* (Leyde: A. W. Sijthoff, 1966) at 129 (hereafter: Bogaert *Les Origines*)

This particularly applies to deposit taking, and possibly to inter-deposit transfers. However, in ancient Mesopotamia, credit was made available by depositaries out of their own capital and without dipping into deposits, so that deposit-taking had not turned yet to banking. All such operations preceded the emergence of money, in the sense of standardized metallic pieces, in fixed denominations, whose value is certified by the ruler's stamp,[17] and took place in fungible items such as grain or silver. These operations were carried out, as a 'secondary activity' by temples, palaces, merchants, and landowners, 'that is to say, [by] all those in possession of capital'.[18] Thus, the emergence of banking operations in ancient Mesopotamia led to neither the emergence of banking, in the full sense of the word, nor to the appearance of banks as distinct institutions. In short, limited banking activity historically preceded both banking and banks.[19]

The invention of coined money affected banking in opposing directions. On one hand, the Greeks are said to be 'the creators of the bank of deposit';[20] even the other fundamental features of modern banking, namely, lending out of such deposits, as well as transfers from the account of one customer to another, can be traced to them, though only in a rudimentary manner.[21] Conversely, subsequently, during the Roman Empire, the predominance of coins arrested the development of banking[22] and favoured payment in specie, thereby demoting the function of cashless payments.[23] Ironically, 'the honour for the first full and efficient operation' facilitating 'a nation-wide circulation and transfer of credit' developed in connection with grain warehouse banking and 'belongs to the Egypt of the Ptolemies' during the

[17] For a discussion on the process, see Geva, 'Commodity', above, n. 2 at 121–41. The origins of money in the sense described in the text are attributed to Lydia in the seventh century BCE.

[18] Bogaert, *Les Origines*, above, n. 16 at 174.

[19] See Bogaert, ibid., particularly at 65–6, 75–6, 126–9, and 174–5. The summary of G. Davies, *A History of Money from Ancient Times to Present Day* (Cardiff: University of Wales Press, 1994) at 47–50, is generally in line with Bogaert's extensive account, except that Davies is more definitive as to the evolution of deposit receipts into 'transfers to the order not only of the depositors but also to a third party'. Ibid. at 49.

[20] R. Bogaert, *Banques et banquiers dans les cités grecques* (Leyde: A. W. Sijthoff, 1968) at 413.

[21] Bogaert, ibid. at 412–13 and see Davies, above n. 19 at 70–3 and 77–8. Green identified 'safe-keeping', as distinguished to improving methods of payment, as the main concern of Greek banking. Green, above, n. 10 at 12.

[22] Roman temples, which were heavily involved in deposit taking, 'did not lend money at all'. See B. Bromberg, 'Temple Banking in Rome', (1939–40), 10 The Economic History Review 128 at 130.

[23] Davies, above, n. 19 at 86–92. The predominance of coinage is attributed both to the durability of the coin as well as to its use by the Romans to disseminate information and propaganda, a point noted by Toynbee. See Geva, 'Commodity', above, n. 2 at 139. Note however, that Green, above, n. 10 at 12, attributes to the Romans the improvement of methods of payments. Even so, 'qualitative' improvement might have been overshadowed by 'quantitative' insignificance.

last quarter of the fourth century BCE,[24] namely, sometime between the fall of Greece (as a unified empire) and the rise of Rome.

(IV) SUBSEQUENT DEVELOPMENTS IN CONTINENTAL EUROPE

The first banking system, characterized by features still recognizable in the **[5]** modern one, existed in Continental Europe, particularly in Italy, from the end of the Middle Ages, until the Renaissance. It was an outgrowth of money changing, a profession whose roots go back to antiquity.[25]

Indeed, as a distinct type of institution, the bank originally emerged as a successor of the money changer. Money dealing, in which money changers came to specialize, became an economic activity a century or two after the invention of the coined money in the seventh century BCE.[26] While there are documented instances of early money changers becoming bankers by lending out of deposited funds,[27] such an activity was not quick to institutionalize. Instead, gradually, well into the Middle Ages, money changers came to specialize in the transmission of funds between distant parties. To that end, they developed the forerunner of the modern bill of exchange. Such an instrument was typically used in a payment from a debtor to a distant creditor, in connection with a commercial transaction between them, as for example, the sale of goods. To carry out payment, the debtor delivered the amount to be paid to a money changer in the debtor's place, and in coins current to that place. The instrument was then issued and sent to the creditor by the money changer in the debtor's place. It was payable to the creditor through a money changer at the creditor's place, in the creditor's currency. Resulting indebtedness of the debtor's money changer to the creditor's money changer was settled as part of either bilateral or multilateral clearings covering their global dealings, consisting of other similar transactions. Settlement took place in a forthcoming fair, with relatively small amounts required to be paid in specie.

The bill of exchange mechanism was designed to avoid the risk of transport as well as the risk of payment in defective or counterfeit coins, in a currency in which a counterparty may not be familiar, and which the debtor may not have.[28] The bill of exchange machinery thus upheld an international cashless payment system, carried out through professional

---

[24] Davies, ibid. at 52, and in general at 51–4.
[25] The ensuing discussion in s. 5 heavily draws on W. Holdsworth, *A History of English Law*, vol. viii (London: Methuen & Co. Ltd., 1937, repr. 1966) at 177–92.
[26] For the early money changers, see Bogaert, *Les Origines* above, n. 16 at 135–7.
[27] Bogaert, ibid. at 137–44.
[28] For the bill of exchange, see Holdsworth, above, n. 25 at 128–30.

intermediaries. However, this mechanism was not premissed on a transfer between customers' running or current accounts; rather, for each payment to be made, the amount to be transmitted in foreign currency was to
be delivered by the debtor, in local currency, to the local money changer.
Similarly, payment to the creditor was to be made by the money changer
in the creditor's place, in specie, in the currency prevailing in that place.

The transformation of the money changer to a banker, towards the end
of the Middle Ages, involved a process of correcting these limitations, and
taking advantage of the resulting circumstances. Thus, in the words of
Holdsworth, 'somewhere between 1270 and 1318 the money-changers of
Venice were becoming bankers'; in addition for carrying out payments
they received funds on deposit and lent them to others.[29]

On one hand, a merchant who had begun by entrusting a particular sum to a
money-changer for the purpose of transmission in a particular transaction, found
it convenient to keep with him a sum on which he could draw whenever he
needed to transmit money; and others, besides merchants, found it convenient to
deposit money with such a person for safe custody. On the other hand, the money-
changer was only too glad to get this money into his hands, and was willing to
pay something to get it. He could lend it at remunerative rates to needy princes or
to merchants.[30]

For two centuries, these newly emerging banks expanded and played an
important economic role in the transition from the Middle Ages to the
Renaissance. Nevertheless, notwithstanding attempts to regulate and
supervise, these new institutions did not prove to be viable. As of the end
of the sixteenth century, with the establishment of the State Bank of Venice
in 1587, a process under which private banks were largely superseded by
state or public banks had begun. These state or public banks mushroomed
throughout Continental Western Europe. Such a state or public bank, the
most prominent of which was the Bank of Amsterdam, was primarily a
deposit taker and dispenser of exchange facilities to money changers and
merchants. It provided extensive inter-account in-house payment services, but had only restricted lending powers, mainly to the state, and later
to private customers against good security. Its expenses were met by duty
on import, or more generally, as a result of being granted monopolistic
powers by the state, usually in return for assuming state debt. These powers were often related to the transmission of funds in international trade.[31]

Dwelling on the merits and demerits of the newly substituted system is

[29] Ibid. at 178.   [30] Ibid. at 177.

[31] R. D. Richards, *The Early History of Banking in England* (New York: A. M. Kelley, 1965,
repr. of 1929 edition) at 136; Green above, n. 10 at 32–3; Davies above, n. 19 at 548–9; and
Holdsworth, above, n. 25 at 184–9. Yet, there were also state banks with more extensive
lending powers in existence. See e.g. Richards, ibid. at 136 n. 2.

outside the scope of the present discussion. What is noteworthy, from our point of view, is the setback to commercial banking, in the sense of restricting the use of deposits as a source of lending, and arresting of any further development in the payment system. At the same time, the heritage of the Italian private banks, that of creating the first truly private banking system, was to leave an everlasting impression. This heritage was subsequently revived and was re-implanted, in an improved form, in England, thus forming the foundation for the architecture of the banking and payment systems that have survived to this very day.

(v) THE ENGLISH MODEL

The English banking system improved on the Italian model in three fun-   [6]
damental respects. First, it heavily relied on close correspondent relationships among participating banks that provided support to each other. Second, by extending credit to each other, banks became positioned to develop a truly national interbank payment system. Both features facilitated specialization in information-intensive non-traded loans, which became the principal niche for a profitable banking business. Third, the appearance of a central bank provided commercial banks with both a source of liquidity, coming from the central bank as a lender of last resort, and the efficiency of multilateral settlement in reserve accounts held with the central bank. This improved system set the tone for the future design of banking and payment systems all over the world.

The business of banking, namely, borrowing in order to lend, was first   [7]
carried on in England by the Scriveners, who were scribes, and whose original business was to write legal documents. But, neither paper money nor payment mechanisms was instituted by them.[32] English banking, precipitating the current design of the banking system worldwide, goes back to goldsmith banking.[33]

Prior to the Civil War of the mid-seventeenth century, merchants kept their surplus money in the King's mint in the Tower of London. During the course of the seventeenth century, and following Charles I's forcible loan from that money in 1640, merchants began to leave their money in

---

[32] See J. M. Holden, *The History of Negotiable Instruments in English Law* (London: Athlone Press, 1955; repr. Holmes Beach, Fla.: WM. W. Gaunt & Sons, Inc., 1993) at 205–6. For more on the scriveners as the pioneers of banking in England who preceded the goldsmiths, see Richards, ibid. ch. 1. On the early history of English banking, in the framework of the evolution of banking in Europe in general, see Holdsworth, above, n. 25 at 177–92.

[33] The ensuing discussion is from Geva, 'Commodity', above, n. 2 at 145–7, where I explore the origins of English paper money, which lay in the early development of English banking.

the hands of the goldsmiths.[34] Soon, during the Cromwellian period, the goldsmith became a banker. Having acted heretofore as bailee or custodian of money in trust, he was now fully authorized to make use of deposited money by lending it to others.[35]

Goldsmiths issued receipts with respect to moneys deposited with them.[36] A receipt was in favour of a payee or bearer. The instrument contained the goldsmith's undertaking to pay on demand when presented with the receipt. It came to be known as a goldsmith's or banker's note and evolved into an early form of the promissory note,[37] leading the way for the subsequent Bank of England note, namely, to paper money.[38] Alternatively, rather than taking goldsmiths' notes, a depositor was allowed to draw upon the goldsmith various amounts up to the amount of the deposit. Such a draft, payable on demand and made out to a payee or bearer, was the forerunner of the modern cheque.[39]

Goldsmiths' notes and cheques were payment mechanisms, which facilitated the transmission of funds from a debtor to his creditor. Through the use of such machineries, a depositor or debtor could avoid the need of physically delivering coined money to the creditor. Payment could be made by delivering a goldsmith's note or cheque and having the account with the goldsmith debited upon the presentment of the instrument.[40] Soon, goldsmiths' notes and cheques came to serve as money itself; as a new type of money, both were interchangeable and indistinguishable.[41] Being dependent for its acceptance 'not upon containing within itself a substance with a value apart from its value as money, but upon people's belief that a promise to exchange it for other money will be honoured,'[42] the acceptability of paper money depended on the credit of its issuer, irrespective of the form of the instrument.

Gradually, however, goldsmiths' notes superseded cheques as money. In some respects, cheques were more advantageous than such notes, but

---

[34] Holden, above, n. 32 at 70; Richards, above, n. 31 at 35. 'Until the Civil War, the goldsmiths' business had consisted chiefly of the manufacture of gold and silver plate and jewellery and the purchase, mounting and sale of jewels.' Holden, ibid. at 71, n. 2. For the pre-Civil War roots of the practice of goldsmiths' acceptance of 'money and plate in trust', see Richards, ibid. at 35. See also Holdsworth, above, n. 25 at 185. It thus appears that Charles I's forcible loan had merely reinforced a process which was already underway.

[35] Richards, above, n. 31 at 37.   [36] Richards, ibid. at 40–3.

[37] Holden, above, n. 32 at 70–3. For the evolution of the form of the goldsmith's note, see also A. E. Feavearyear, *The Pound Sterling—A History of English Money*, 2nd edn.—rev. E. V. Morgan (Oxford: Clarendon Press, 1963) at 107–8.

[38] For this development, leading to the demise of the goldsmith note itself, see summary in Geva, 'Commodity', above, n. 2 at 149–52. Paper money in China and Sweden preceded that of England but lacked continuity. See e.g. Green, above, n. 10 at 36 and Davies, above, n. 19 at 54–6 and 177–83.   [39] For the development, see Holden, above, n. 32 at 204 ff.

[40] Feavearyear, above, n. 37 at 107–10.   [41] Feavearyear, ibid. at 258.

[42] Feavearyear, ibid. at 99.

their advantage was not absolute. Consequently each instrument developed to satisfy different needs of the financial community. According to Milnes Holden,

... cheques could be drawn for the exact amount of the debt ... they provided a permanent record of settlement; and ... their use made it unnecessary for customer to keep large amounts of notes and coins on their premises. On the other hand, creditors would prefer to receive bankers' notes rather than cheques from debtors whose financial standing was uncertain.[43]

Indeed, cheques were used primarily 'by the nobility and landowning classes, whose signatures were widely known and accepted'.[44] At the same time, inasmuch as the financial standing and the authenticity of the signature were likely to be more certain in the case of a banker than in the case of an unknown depositor, bankers' notes were a more promising and widely used medium of exchange.[45] Their success could further be attributed to an improvement in the original system of receipt issue by goldsmiths. Originally, a goldsmith issued one note for the whole sum deposited with him. If any of it was paid off, the amount so paid was marked on the original note.[46] It was, therefore, impossible either to pay with parts of the deposit or to transfer the note to several different creditors. Ultimately, a more sophisticated system replaced the original one. The gross deposit was subdivided into several receipts in various denominations; instead of one note containing a single promise to pay the entire sum, the goldsmith gave a series of promises to pay a number of smaller sums making up the total of the deposit. Finally, such notes might be given by a goldsmith not against a deposit, but rather as proceeds of a loan.[47]

Goldsmith banking is thus the source of the banknote, cheque, and **[8]** banking itself. Indeed, each such an institution or concept can be traced to an earlier development; yet, the goldsmiths clearly deserve the credit for the combined effect and continuity of these concepts leading to modern banking. Furthermore, during the second half of the seventeenth century, through a tight network of correspondent banking facilitating systemic debt clearing, goldsmith banking allowed interbank customer payments to take place on a regular basis.[48]

---

[43] Holden, above, n. 32 at 214.   [44] Feavearyear, above, n. 37 at 109.

[45] At the same time cheques were more promising payment mechanisms, or devices for the transmission of funds for the purpose of avoiding the need and the risks of carrying money in specie. Holden, above, n. 32 at 213–14.

[46] For this practice, see for example *Cooksey v. Boverie* (1693), 2 Show. K.B. 296 at 296–7; 89 E. R. 949.

[47] For this development, see Holdsworth, above, n. 25 at 190–1.

[48] See, in detail, S. Quinn, 'Balances and Goldsmith-bankers: The Co-ordination and Control of Inter-Banker Debt Clearing in Seventeenth-Century London', in D. Mitchell (ed.), *Goldsmiths, Silversmiths and Bankers: Innovation and the Transfer of Skill, 1550 to 1750* (London: Allan Sutton Publishing Ltd. and Centre for Metropolitan History, 1995), 53.

At its inception, the goldsmith clearing system was strictly bilateral. 'Moreover, the goldsmith-bankers avoided depositing large sums with each other by routinely creating overdrafts.'[49] A goldsmith did not demand from a fellow-goldsmith a positive balance as a precondition for paying an instrument presented to him. Payment was immediately made by the paying goldsmith in reliance on credit extended by him to the presenting fellow-goldsmith. This did not unnecessarily tie funds and facilitated expansion. It improved on the Amsterdam Exchange Bank system, under which a bill presented for payment was paid on the following day and only against an offsetting bill in the opposite direction.[50]

There was no formal institutional structure to the clearing system which was based on trust and credit monitoring. As indicated, fellow-goldsmith credit monitoring appears to have led the way to customer credit monitoring, and hence, to the specialization in information-intensive non-traded loans as bank assets. For its part, the initial trust, without which the system could not have operated, may be explained by the goldsmith trade's earlier specialization in precious metals and the lengthy intensive apprenticeship required to become a goldsmith, which was fully adapted to train the goldsmith to become a banker. 'In exchange of seven years of non-wage skilled labour and often an initial fee, the master taught the apprentice the necessary banking skills, introduced him to established bankers and developed the ground work for a long professional relationship.'[51] In the final analysis, in laying down the foundations for the modern banking system on the basis of concepts and institutions that had already evolved elsewhere, seventeenth-century London bankers took advantage of their goldsmith background and put it into full use.

[9]   As previously indicated, domestic modern banking and payment systems are premissed on a network of commercial banks, linking all customers and each other, primarily through a central bank, and only in small part through correspondent banking. So far as the goldsmith system described above is concerned, the missing element, that of a central bank, was soon to be supplied, following the establishment of the Bank of England at the end of the seventeenth century.

The Bank of England was established in 1694.[52] It was a public or state bank modelled on the goldsmith bank and not on the Continental public or state bank. 'Its chief original function was that of a bank of issue',

---

[49] Ibid. at 54.

[50] For this point see Quinn, ibid. at 55 and Richards, above, n. 31 at 234–5.

[51] Quinn, ibid. at 61.

[52] 5 & 6 Will. & Mar. c. 20, s. XIX. See Holden, above, n. 32 at 87–94. The foundation of the Bank of England and its early transactions are extensively discussed by Richards, above, n. 31 at 132–88.

which never professed to have its issue limited by coin and bullion in its possession, 'whereas the banks of the Continent were essentially banks of deposit and exchange'[53] which 'actually kept in specie all the money deposited with them' and whose 'notes represented actual money in their possession'.[54] Nor did the Bank of England monopolize the London market so as to supersede goldsmith bankers.[55] Rather, right from the beginning, it operated side by side with them, not affecting their financial activities.[56]

It is said that the creation of the Bank of England 'was really the work of an impecunious government striving to borrow money in order to wage a war against France'.[57] Its promoters promised to lend the government a vast amount of money. In return, they received the privilege of forming the first, and for more than a century the only, joint-stock bank in the country, which meant it had a much larger capital than any other bank. Also, the new institution acted as a banker for the government.[58] Arguably, it is this combined economic strength and political power which explains how the Bank of England note entirely superseded the goldsmith note and became paper money.[59] Yet, it is precisely the close connection to government, underlying this economic and political power, which deterred merchants from putting their trust in the Bank of England and enabled the private banks to stay.

Regardless, the Bank of England was less interested in taking the place of private banks than in attracting such banks as its own customers, thereby developing its own role as the bankers' bank. Indeed, the Bank of England did not assume central banking functions until the nineteenth century, at which point it became a bankers' bank, acting as a lender of last resort, or the provider of liquidity to illiquid banks, and in fact, the curator of the banking system.[60] During that period, the banking system significantly expanded, beyond the original 'gold boys network' of the

---

[53] Richards, ibid. at 136. Ironically, neither the Act of Parliament nor its Charter conferred on the Bank an explicit power to issue other than formal notes under seal, which are to be distinguished from the unsealed variety, from which the banknote, or paper money emerged. See Holden, ibid., particularly at 88–90.

[54] Holdsworth, above, n. 25 at 188.

[55] For the state or public bank in the Continent, see s. 5, second last paragraph.

[56] Richards, above, n. 31 at 87.

[57] Holden, above, n. 32 at 87–8. For the Bank and its financing of the Whig government, see in general, Holdsworth, above, n. 25 at 188–9.

[58] R. Roberts, 'The Bank of England and the City', in R. Roberts and D. Kynaston (eds.), *The Bank of England—Money, Power and Influence 1694–1994* (Oxford: Clarendon Press, 1995) 152 at 153.

[59] For this development, leading to the demise of the goldsmith note itself, see summary in Geva 'Commodity', above, n. 2 at 149–52.

[60] A. Cairncross, 'The Bank of England and the British Economy', in Roberts and Kynaston, above, n. 58, at 56–61.

original goldsmiths.[61] Particularly, joint-stock banks, other than the Bank of England itself, were allowed to operate outside London as of 1826, and as of 1833, in London.[62] Interbank bilateral debt clearing, which had set the banking system in motion,[63] became unworkable. Efficiency considerations had been working to establish the London clearing house, to carry out interbank multilateral clearing.[64] Ultimately, balances were to be settled in reserve accounts at the Bank of England, acting as the bankers' bank, maintaining accounts for such customer-clearing banks;[65] with non-clearing banks left to carry out bilateral clearing and settlement with clearing banks. Settlement on the books of the central bank gave the assurance of a central bank's obligation, as if on its banknote, and thus accorded finality to all transactions included in a clearing and settlement cycle. The design of the banking and payment systems had thus been fully established.

(VI) NEW TRENDS

[10]   The process of the exportation or subsequent creation of this architecture in each of the jurisdictions under review here is outside the scope of the present discussion. My purpose here was to highlight the main elements of the evolutionary process leading to the emergence of the payment system architecture whose legal features in the various jurisdictions is the subject matter of the substantive parts of this work.

Regardless, the purity of the model described above has been disturbed by recent developments. With enhanced technology and increasing globalization, as walls separating banks from other financial institutions crumble, providers of payment services other than banks have entered the scene. To a large extent, each such an individual new player has acted on the basis of a bilateral relationship with an individual bank, providing

---

[61] This term is from Quinn, above, n. 48 at 61.

[62] See 'Appendix 1: Chronology', in Roberts and Kynaston, above, n. 58 at 225, 231.

[63] For the original goldsmith clearing system, see s. 8 above. This change in practice took place in 1854. See E. Nevin and E. W. Davis, *The London Clearing Banks* (London: Elek Books, 1970) at 69.

[64] For the establishment of the London Clearing House at the end of the eighteenth century, see Holden, above, n. 32 at 214–15. According to Davies, above, n. 19 at 321–2, 'The private bankers of London first set up their clearing house in 1770, but they did not admit joint-stock banks until 1854, nor any country banks until 1858. . . . The Bank of England was admitted in 1864, greatly simplifying the clearing process.'

[65] Interestingly, 'many goldsmiths opened accounts with the Bank [of England] within a few months of its creation'. Holden, ibid. at 93. However, '[a]s late as 1844 [interbank] balances were still settled in banknotes, but soon afterwards this method was superseded by cheques on the Bank of England'. E. V. Morgan, *The Theory and Practice of Central Banking 1797–1913* (New York: A. M. Kelley, 1943, repr. 1965) at 11.

to it access to interbank clearing and settlement, as outlined below in 3.D). By now, direct access to interbank clearing and settlement facilities is actively sought by such institutions in several countries. Nevertheless, the banking system's role as the main conduit for payments has remained unchallenged, with other institutions effectively seeking increased access on the basis of a claim for competitive equality. In the final analysis, this only confirms the position of banking networks as the lifeline of the cash-less payment system.

C. Payment Law Sources: General Observations

[1] Legal systems explored in this work fall into three broad categories discussed below. It should however be stressed, that, in principle, no one jurisdiction has laws identical to those in the other. Moreover, some countries are federations, so that the law may be different in each of the composing units. Nevertheless, the purpose of the ensuing classification is to address fundamental commonalities and bypass specific distinctions, so that the latter are overlooked intentionally. With the view of addressing the forest rather than the trees, no cites to any piece of legislation are provided for here. Any such cites appear in the discussion contained in the subsequent substantive parts of the work. The three broad groups are as follows:

1. France, Germany, Italy, Japan, and Switzerland have civil codes drawing on the Roman Law tradition. They are generally known as civil law jurisdictions. Each such civil code contains general principles of law and provides for such matters as contract, torts, and property.

2. Australia, England, the United States, and all Canadian provinces other than Quebec are common law jurisdictions. Each such legal system draws on English common law, broadly defined to include equity as well. As a rule, general principles of law in such jurisdictions, governing contract, torts, and property, are not codified, but rather derived from applicable case law. Among these jurisdictions, the United States broke away from the English Crown, and went on a path of its own.

3. Israel, South Africa, and the Canadian province of Quebec are mixed jurisdictions. Israel has been working on its own civil code, adopting whatever is deemed best for the resolution of any given issue, which is thus not specifically linked to any particular juridic tradition. At the same time, thirty years of British administration (between 1917 and 1948), the predominance of English as the principal foreign language, and perhaps other cultural factors, have left a strong common law imprint on the entire legal culture of Israel. South African general law is Roman Dutch law. Yet, unlike the other civil law jurisdictions, it has no civil code and the Roman Dutch law operates on a case-by-case basis, as the common law of South Africa. Also, particularly in the area of commercial, and more specifically, banking, law, there is a strong English influence, obviously related to old colonial

ties. The third mixed jurisdiction, that of the Canadian province of Quebec, has a civil code, modelled on an old French one. Yet, in commercial and banking law matters, more than in any other area of law, court decisions have been strongly influenced by English law, particularly, due to strong historical English dominance over commercial and financial interests. In fact, similar to South Africa, Scotland is also a mixed jurisdiction, with an uncodified civil law, strongly influenced by English law. Nevertheless, other than in passing, the Scottish legal system will not be addressed in this study.

The scope of this work cuts across three principal subject-matters. Thus,   [2]
the work is concerned with the law governing the bank and customer relationship, the law of cheques and their collection and payment, and the law of credit transfers. In the various jurisdictions under consideration, each such area is governed by various sources of law.

The bank and customer relationship is fundamentally a matter for the law of contract. Specific legislation, particularly in relation to consumer or customer protection, may also be applicable. There is also room for mandate or agency, as well as implied terms. With respect to credit transfers, there is a comprehensive statute only in the United States. A statute dealing with some aspects of the transaction exists in Germany. In all other countries, be they common law or civilian jurisdictions, the credit transfer payment is almost entirely governed by general principles of law applicable in the given legal system. Obviously, in civil law countries, such principles are codified.

The law of cheques is predominantly statutory; such statutes fall into   [3]
two broad categories. Some jurisdictions adhere to a statute modelled on, or derived from, the English Bills of Exchange Act (BEA) of 1882. These jurisdictions, other than the USA, are occasionally referred to as BEA jurisdictions. The common law jurisdictions, other than the USA, and the mixed jurisdictions make up this category. Accordingly, South Africa and Israel each have a BEA, while in Canada, the BEA is federal, so as to apply in Quebec also. Among the BEA jurisdictions, Australia adopted a specific statute to govern cheques. Finally, speaking generally, the Americans derived Article 3 of the Uniform Commercial Code (UCC), governing negotiable instruments including bills of exchange and cheques, from the BEA, but significantly departed from its provisions from the outset. Points of departure only increased and gaps deepened throughout the years. Among all jurisdictions dealt with in this work, a statute governing bank collections, supplanted by specific federal legislation, exists only in the USA.

The civil law jurisdictions under discussion all adopted a statute modelled on the Uniform Cheques Law (UCL) of the Geneva Conventions of

1932, which varies in some fundamental concepts from both the BEA and UCC. Unlike both the BEA and UCC, but as in Australia, such a statute is restricted to cheques only.

As a rule, the statute governing cheques is primarily concerned with cheques as instruments rather than payment mechanisms. This opens the door for general principles of law to interact with the specific provisions of the statute, which as a matter of statutory interpretation is quite a challenge particularly in the mixed jurisdictions.

[4]   In the final analysis, in each jurisdiction, the fundamental needs of payment transactions participants are quite the same. The broad question to be answered only implicitly in this work is whether any uniformity can be detected in the way such needs are met by the general principles and specific legislation of the diverse legal systems under discussion. To the extent that solutions are common and pragmatic, so that gaps separating different legal systems are bridged, a governing 'law merchant' can be said to exist. 'Law merchant' can also be said to exist when, in reaching a decision on any given point, a local variation is attributed to giving a different weight to applicable factors, considered by all to be relevant. Ultimately, it is the specific adaptation of existing principles of a given legal system to cover circumstances arising in commercial and financial transactions which creates an applicable 'law merchant' within that legal system.[1] It is this mechanism of adaptation which is universal, transcending the boundaries among the various legal systems.

---

[1] This view of 'law merchant' follows the principal theme of J. S. Rogers, *The Early History of the Law of Bills and Notes — A Study of the Origins of Anglo-American Commercial Law* (Cambridge: Cambridge University Press, 1995), challenging the conventional wisdom under which law merchant is a distinct cohesive body of law, common to the mercantile community in all jurisdictions, but alien to the local legal system of any particular one.

PART 2

The banking relationship

A. The Account Agreement

(I) INTRODUCTION

The relationship between a bank and its customer, known as the banking [1]
relationship, is based on contract.[1] Separate and distinct contracts may
govern various aspects of a banking relationship, such as deposit taking,
lending and credit, security, safe custody of valuables or securities, the
provision of payment services, or the furnishing of investment facilities.
Yet, 'the term "banker-customer relationship" is generally taken to refer to
the specific legal relationship generated by the opening and operation of
a bank account'.[2] It is in the context of this agreement that deposits and
withdrawals of funds, including third party payments, are made. The
present discussion focuses on the framework governing the contractual
incidents of the account agreement in the various jurisdictions under
discussion.

Generally speaking, as provided by contract, and possibly, regulated
by law, a deposit in a bank may be made either by the depositor or by a
third party, may be carried out either in cash or by means of collection
or payment from another account, may be payable either on demand or
at the expiry of a maturity or notice period, and may or may not bear
interest. It may be withdrawable either as a whole or in part, and by
means of an order instructing payment either to the depositor or to a
third party.[3] In each case, the deposit is reflected by a credit to the

[1] For West European jurisdictions, this is the conclusion of R. Cranston, 'Introduction', in
R. Cranston (ed.), *European Banking Law: The Banker–Customer Relationship* (London: Lloyd's
of London Press, 1993), 1. For a comprehensive discussion in the USA, see E. Symons, Jr.,
'The Bank-Customer Relation: Part I—The Relevance of Contract Doctrine' (1983), 100
Bk'ng L.J. 220, and 'Part II—The Judicial Decisions' (1983), 100 Bk'ng L.J. 325. For Canada,
see B. Crawford, *Crawford and Falconbridge Banking and Bills of Exchange*, 8th edn., vol. i
(Toronto: Canada Law Book, 1986) at 741 §3202.
[2] W. Blair, 'England', in R. Cranston (ed.), above, n. 1, 11 at 12. See also M. H. Ogilvie,
Canadian Banking Law, 2nd edn. (Toronto: Carswell, 1998) at 435, and J. L. Rives-Lange and
M. Contamine-Raynaud, *Droit bancaire*, 6th edn. (Paris: Dalloz, 1995) at 171–2 ¶181.
[3] For the types of deposits in the various jurisdictions, see e.g. J. J. Norton and S. C. Whitley,
'A United States Comparison', in Cranston (ed), above, n. 1, 227 at 235–40, classifying
deposits by type, customer, or duration (for the USA); J. L. Rives-Lange and M. Cabrillac,
'Dépôt et compte en banque', *Encyclopédie Dalloz, Rep. dr. commercial* (1974, updated to
1992) at ¶50–62 (for France); D. Guggenheim, *Les Contrats de la pratique bancaire suisse*, 2nd
edn. (Geneva: Georg, 1981) at 77–118, and in general at 78–9 (dealing with the issue for
Switzerland in the broader context of the bank as a depositary also for valuables and securities); M. Hapgood, *Paget's Law of Banking*, 11th edn. (London: Butterworths, 1996) at
167–78 (particularly at 167–8) (for the UK); Z. Kitagawa, *Doing Business in Japan*, vol. iii
looseleaf (Danvers, Mass.: Matthew Bender, 1999) at §4.02 (for Japan); Crawford, above,
n. 1 at 758 §3301.1 (for Canada).

account and the withdrawal is expressed by a debit. The balance on the account, namely, the amount due between the bank and its customer, is that of the difference between the credits and debits to an account. Typically, payment services, facilitating the collection and payment of payment orders instructing payment to a third party, particularly as applied to withdrawals from the accounts, are provided in connection with deposits payable on demand from which also part withdrawals may be made.

The contract governing the account relationship thus provides for the legal framework within which collection and payment services operate. In the context of the various jurisdictions, the discussion will consider the right to enter into an account agreement, the contractual incidents of the account agreement as a banking transaction, freedom of contract and the account agreement as a standard form contract, and country-wide standards and terms for account agreements.

(II) THE RIGHT TO ENTER INTO AN ACCOUNT AGREEMENT

[2]   Invariably, the opening of an account will involve the confirmation by the bank of the customer's identity, the verification by the bank of the customer's creditworthiness and moral integrity,[4] and the deposit of funds by the customer.[5] An account may be misused, either by the account holder or an outsider. Accordingly, banks could not be faulted for undertaking to serve as gatekeepers endeavouring to eliminate or reduce fraud losses by screening those who wish to open an account, and attempting to identify those who are likely either to defraud or to be defrauded. Furthermore, a bank opening an account for a customer incurs risks associated with unauthorized collections and payments into and out of the account, albeit, in many jurisdictions, this may be limited to losses to which the bank's conduct contributed.[6] Understandably, the bank is quite keen on attempting to prevent any fraudulent use of the account, to which it may

---

[4] The standard for carrying out these two tasks is not likely to be identical. The confirmation of identity is typically based on authentic unequivocal documentation to be produced by the customer, and to that extent is thorough. Conversely, at least when no credit obligation is undertaken towards the new customer, and in the absence of suspicion, the verification of creditworthiness and moral integrity is likely to be superficial, if not merely impressionistic.

[5] In principle, an account may be opened even without the actual deposit of funds. However, to avoid misuse, as well as due to the fact that banks' remuneration is in the form of interest on deposited funds and charges related to operations with account balances, banks are likely to decline to open an account absent of an immediate deposit into it. This is of course true with respect to new customers, but is less true for the opening of new accounts for old customers with other pre-existing accounts.

[6] The allocation of fraud losses is dealt with in Part 4 below.

end up being responsible.[7] In a given case, the bank may honestly and reasonably judge that the best means to that end is to refuse altogether the opening of the account.

The starting point is thus, as a matter of contract law, that the bank is free to select its customers. However, banks have increasingly become expected to provide a universal service of safe custody for money, coupled with cashless payment or money-transfer service.[8] Some of the previous pronouncements as to the bank's absolute or unfettered discretion in opening or refusing to open accounts[9] may not be accurate anymore, and where applicable, not in line with human rights legislation precluding arbitrary private sector discrimination.[10]

Nevertheless, in principle, bank discretion remains legitimate. Definitely a bank ought to insist on the proper identification of a prospective customer. Also, the moral and creditworthiness of a customer are reasonable concerns even with respect to an account that will allow limited services, such as cash withdrawals against collected funds.[11] At the same time, the limits of the permissible discretion are more controversial. For example, a refusal to open an account for a customer who is perceived as unlikely to provide an adequate volume of business to the bank is quite a contentious point. Most legal systems have nevertheless not addressed themselves specifically to these issues.[12] France and Israel are an exception. However, as will be seen below, solutions provided in these countries are incomplete. French law leaves a bank exposed to some risk while

---

[7] In the USA, a bank that opens an account when it has reason to be suspicious of the depositor, might be held liable in fraud, by reason of exercising bad faith with respect to the payor bank in connection with the subsequent fraudulent cheque transaction. See *Perini Corporation v. First National Bank of Habersham County*, 553 F.2d 398 at 404–5 (5th Cir. 1977).

[8] Both points of view are discussed, first generally and then in the context of Israeli law, by R. Ben-Oliel, 'Account Opening—Bank's Responsibility and Bank Risk' (1982) 12 Mishpatim 60 [in Hebrew].

[9] Two leading American cases, cited by Ben-Oliel, ibid. at 62 & n. 3 are *Elliott v. Capital City State Bank*, 103 N.W. 777 at 778 (Iowa S.C. 1905) and *Grants Pass & Josephine Bank v. City of Grants Pass*, 28 P. 2d. 879 at 880 (Ore. S.C. 1934).

[10] For example, see Canadian Human Rights Act, R.S.C. 1985, c. H-6 as am., which is a federal anti-discrimination legislation, applying, among other matters, to the provision of services 'customarily available to the general public' by chartered banks, and prohibiting discrimination on the basis of 'race, national or ethnic origin, colour, religion, age, sex, sexual orientation, marital status, family status, disability and conviction for which a pardon has been granted': see sections 5 and 3(1). For the USA, see e.g. New York Executive Law section 296 (McKinney's).

[11] For example, funds actually paid or collected into the account so as to become withdrawable by the customer may be originated by a fraudulent deposit, to which the bank may nevertheless be responsible. See e.g. 4.D, below.

[12] For a discussion and proposal dealing with the exclusion of low-income consumers from payment services provided by banks in the USA, see E. L. Rubin, 'The Lifeline Banking Controversy: Putting Deregulation to Work for the Low-Income Consumer' (1992) 67 Indiana L.J. 213.

Israeli law is not adequately specific in prescribing what 'reasonable' grounds permit the bank's refusal.

[3]   In France, the Banking Law of 24 January 1984[13] settled a fierce controversy[14] and reconciled the bank's right to refuse to open an account with a person's right to have an account.[15] First, section 89 exempted banks from the application of competition law requirements as to the duty not to refuse the sale of goods or the provision of a service.[16] Second, under section 58 of the Banking Law, '[a]ny person whose applications to open a current account[17] have been refused[18] by several credit institutions[19] and who therefore has no account may ask the Banque de France to name a credit institution[20] . . . where he can open such an account'. However, such an account will not necessarily entitle its holder to obtain a broad range of payment services. Rather, the provision goes on to state, the designated institution 'may restrict the services linked with the opening of this account to cash operations'.[21] In the view of the Bank of France, the 'forced'

---

[13] Loi bancaire no. 84-46 du 24 janvier 1984, translated into English by the Bank of France.

[14] Briefly stated, the bank's refusal right was challenged on two grounds. First, certain legal requirements for payment, in specified circumstances, only through accounts, gave rise to a perception of the service provided by banks as 'public'. For such requirements, effectively constituting restrictions on cash payments outside the banking system, see e.g. Loi relative aux règlements par chèques et virements, J.O., 8 Nov. 1940, 5602, D. 1940. Lég. 1660, as am. by Loi no. 88-1149, J.O. 28 Dec. 1988, 16333, D. 1989. Lég.29, art. 80. Second, an objection to the bank's right to refuse relied on a statutory prohibition, imposed on a merchant, to refuse the provision of a service under a law rooted in Ordinance no. 45–1483 of 30 June 1945.

[15] See e.g. Rives-Lange and Cabrillac, above, n. 3 at ¶74; Rives-Lange and Contamine-Raynaud, above, n. 2 at 147–8 ¶158, and 176–7. ¶186; and C. Gavalda and J. Stoufflet, *Droit bancaire*, 3rd edn. (Paris: Litec, 1997) at 102 ¶¶203–4.

[16] More specifically, section 89 limits the application of competition law, other than specific provisions, to non-core banking activities.

[17] This is a rather not well-chosen translation of 'un compte de dépôt', which, in fact, corresponds better to a deposit account, as opposed to the current account or 'le compte courante'. For the various types of accounts under French law see 2.D (ii), below.

[18] According to section 5 of Décret no. 84-708 of 24 July 1984, refusal must be made in a writing delivered to the addressee.

[19] 'Credit Institutions' are defined in section 1 of the Banking Law as 'legal persons carrying out banking operations as their regular business', and are thus referred to throughout this discussion as 'banks'. The provision goes on to state that '[b]anking operations comprise the receipt of funds from the public, credit operations and making available to customers or managing means of payment'. Receipt of funds from the public is elaborated on in Section 2. For a discussion preceding the passage of this Law, see in general, J. Stoufflet, 'Le Nonopole des banques quant à la réception de fonds en dépôt', in *Études de droit commercial à la mémoire de Henri Cabrillac* (Paris: Librairies techniques, 1968), 437.

[20] More specifically, the Banque de France may be asked to name 'a credit institution or one of the persons or services referred to in Section 8 . . .'. The latter enumerates 'the Treasury, the Banque de France, the financial services of the Post Office' and several other institutions. All institutions and services enumerated in section 8 are stated 'not [to] be subject to the present Act'.

[21] The French original of 'cash operations' is 'opérations de caisse' which ought, however, to be distinguished from the broader 'le service de caisse'. The latter encompasses the entire range of payment services provided by the bank. See e.g. Rives-Lange and Contamine-Raynaud, above, n. 2 at 265 ¶280.

opening of an account under such conditions entitles the customer only to minimal services, which do not include chequing as well as card facilities.[22] Presumably, they include the receipt of incoming payments and cash withdrawals. Yet, a bank is not without risk even in such a limited context, unless it is free not only from bad faith but also from negligence.[23]

In Israel, the right to receive a bank service, including the right to have **[4]** a bank account, is governed by the Banking Law (Service to Customer) 1981.[24] Under Section 2(a), a bank will not 'reasonably refuse' to provide the following services: the receipt of the deposit of funds, the opening of a current chequing account where the customer either has a positive balance or complies with the agreement with the bank as to the operation of the account, the sale of bank drafts, and any action which under currency control legislation must exclusively be made by a financial institution. These are quite a limited range of services, and as indicated, the bank is not even absolutely required to provide them. Rather, what the statute mandates, is that the bank's refusal to provide such services in any given case must be 'reasonable' and cannot be arbitrary. There is no obligation whatsoever on a bank to extend credit.

Section 2(b) clarifies that attaching 'unreasonable conditions' to the provision of a service is tantamount to an 'unreasonable refusal' to provide the service in the first place, in violation of the Law. A reasonable refusal may be based on a bank policy advised in advance to, and not objected by, bank supervisory authorities (s. 2(d)). The Law further prohibits banks to mislead customers and exploit a customer's weakness, distress, or lack of knowledge or experience (ss. 3–4). Finally, the Law authorizes the Governor of the Bank of Israel, which is the central bank, to fasten on banks disclosure rules in relation to their services (s. 5).

(III) THE CONTRACTUAL INCIDENTS OF THE ACCOUNT AGREEMENT

In all jurisdictions, the account agreement consists of express as well as **[5]** implied terms. The latter may partly be customary or usage based.[25] The

---

[22] See e.g. Rives-Lange and Contamine-Raynaud, ibid. at 176–7 ¶186.

[23] For the fact that in France, as in other civil law jurisdictions, a collecting bank does not bear forged indorsement losses, only to the extent that it acts in good faith and without negligence, see 4.D (iii), below. Similarly, no risks are associated with incoming credit transfers, only as long as the receiving bank has acted in good faith and without negligence. See below, 4.E (i). By the same token, forged cheques losses are essentially universally allocated between the customer and the paying bank and thus do not fall on the collecting bank. See 4.B below, and similarly, for unauthorized funds transfers, see 4.C, below.

[24] For an overview, see R. Ben-Oliel, *Banking Law—General Part* (Jerusalem: Sacher Institute, 1996) at 67–72 [in Hebrew].

[25] This is particularly true in civil law jurisdictions. See e.g. for Italy, C.C. Campi in *Jura Europae–Droit bancaire et boursier* (Paris: Éditions Techniques Juris Classeurs, 1976) at §10.11.8,

former are typically standard form contracts, which as a rule, tend to favour the bank. This is so not only vis-à-vis small customers, particularly consumers, but potentially, also towards large corporate customers, which by nature of things, deal with the bank not in the context of their main line of business. As such, terms in account agreement are characteristically narrowly construed against the bank.[26]

Bank standard form contracts may reflect an industry-wide formalized consensus for minimum standards, which ought not to preclude an individual bank to do business with customers on better terms. The banking codes in the UK, Canada, and Australia, as well as the General Conditions and comparable documents in Germany, Japan, and Italy fall into this latter category of an interbank agreement setting threshold standards for uniform contractual terms.[27] From a policy point of view, the banking code/general conditions approach can be rationalized on the publicity accorded to the agreed-upon standards, so as to promote transparency, as well as discourage the inclusion of unjustified onerous terms that will put banks in bad light. Country-wide banking codes and general conditions may further require some kind of either formal or informal public scrutiny. They may, however, be limited to a specific aspect or service, as for example, the debit card codes in Australia and Canada.

A system under which standard terms are negotiated between banking and customer organizations, possibly in the context of some oversight by government, may represent a substantial improvement to the contract-making process.[28] The Netherlands adopted such a system.[29] In Australia[30] as well as in Canada[31] the debit card banking code is a product of a similar negotiated mechanism. Generally speaking, however, this is a workable method of producing balanced fair terms only in an environment where customer organizations are effective. For consumer organizations this may well depend on funding.[32] Otherwise, the bank account agree-

§40.02.3; for Switzerland, Guggenheim, above, n. 3 at 25–8, 36; for France, Rives-Lange and Contamine-Raynaud, above, n. 2 at 144–5 ¶155, 146 ¶157, 150–1 ¶165, and 175 ¶185.

[26] See e.g. for Germany, H. Schönle in *Jura Europae*, above, n. 25 at §10.02.3; for Italy, Campi, above, n. 25 at §40.02.3; and for Switzerland, Guggenheim above, n. 3 at 61. For the common law, see 2.C(iii), below.

[27] For more on some of these banking codes and general conditions documents, see below, in 2.A(v).

[28] A strong proponent of this view in the various sectors of the economy, is R. Hasson, 'The Unconscionability Business—A Comment on Tilden Rent-A-Car v. Clendenning' (1978–79) 3 Can. Bus. L.J. 193 at 196–7.

[29] See J. A. Roelvink and L. J. Hijmans van den Bergh, 'The Netherlands', in Cranston (ed.) above, n. 1, 129 at 130.

[30] See in general, M. Sneddon, 'A Review of the Electronic Funds Transfer Code of Conduct' (1995) 6 J.B.F.L.P. 29.   [31] The Canadian code is discussed in (v) below.

[32] For this analysis, in connection with commercial law legislative process, see e.g. E. L. Rubin, 'Thinking Like a Lawyer, Acting Like a Lobbyist: Some Notes on the Process of Revising UCC Articles 3 and 4' (1993) 26 Loyola LA L. Rev. 743.

ment may be regulated by law. Such regulation may provide for threshold principles to be met in each individual contractual arrangement.[33] Alternatively, it may provide for the contents of the agreement in great detail. As will be seen below, for consumer electronic transactions, the USA is the best example for this latter model.

A more modest approach for both public oversight over banking contract terms and interference in the contractual process exists in France, where two components are present. First, under section 59 of the Banking Law, a consultative committee is established, in order 'to study matters concerning credit institutions' relations with their customers and suggest appropriate measures in this sphere'. This mandate is to be carried out 'in particular by putting forward opinions or general recommendations'.[34] Second, under section 33(4) of the Banking Law, contract terms must comply with 'bank conditions' set by decisions of the Committee of Banking Regulation.[35] Nonetheless, the impact of both mechanisms ought not to be overstated. The consultative committee, as its name suggests, has only a non-binding advising power. On its part, the Committee of Banking Regulation, notwithstanding its broad powers, has in practice confined its oversight to ensuring that bank operations do not compromise their

[33] See e.g. the EC Recommendation of 8 December 1987 on a European Code of Conduct relating to electronic payment (87/598/EC No. L 365/72, OJ 24. 12. 87) applicable to consumer transactions. Article III requires contracts to be in writing, in an applicable official language, transparent as to charges, fair, clear, and to contain provisions as to termination.

[34] Section 59(2) of the Banking Law goes on to require the consultative committee, or in the original French, 'Comité consultatif', to report annually to the Conseil National du Crédit et du Titre (CNCT), established under section 24, with no real normative power. In addition to its consultative role on monetary and credit policy, the CNCT is mandated under section 24 to 'study the working of the banking and financial system, particularly as regards customer relations'. With respect to the consultative committee, section 59(3) further states that '[t]he Comité shall be chaired by a prominent person chosen for his competence in banking and financial matters and shall be composed predominantly, and in equal numbers, of representatives of the credit institutions and representatives of their customers'. With respect to the bank and customer relationship, the consultative committee's study or research mandate and advisory role towards government and central bank are further confirmed in Article 7 of Decree no. 84-709 of 24 July 1984. Article 8 of the same decree sets out the membership of the consultative committee, to consist of eight bank representatives, eight representatives of various customer groups such as farmers, manufacturers, merchants, and consumer-depositors and borrowers, three bank trade union representatives, and two persons designated on the basis of their competence in matters of banking and finance, one of whom is to be nominated by the minister as the committee chair. All twenty-one members are to be appointed by the minister charged with the economy and finance for a three-year term.

[35] Under section 33(4) of the Banking Law, the Committee of Banking Regulation (or in the original French, Le Comité de la Réglementation Bancaire), established under section 29, is authorized, as part of its mandate under section 30, among other things, to 'establish the regime governing in particular . . . [t]he conditions of operations that may be carried out by credit institutions, particularly in their relations with customers . . .'. See Rives-Lange and Contamine-Raynaud, above, n. 2 at 142–4 ¶154, and for the Committee of Banking Regulation, ibid. at 75–6 ¶95.

financial stability or public interest, as, for example, in connection with money laundering.

[6]   In practice, the express terms may either be set out in one or more documents signed by the customer, or else, incorporated by reference to another document, possibly an interbank agreement. Reference may be either implicit or explicit.[36] Full disclosure of all applicable terms, whether drawn from a side document or banking practice or usage, may, however, be required by law.[37]

Also, a customer may have a general overall account agreement, side by side with various agreements reflecting specific services.[38] Particularly in civil law, there is a scholarly debate as to whether 'banking contract law' exists as an autonomous body of law governing the entire bank and customer relationship. Within this context, a question arises as to whether the 'account agreement' can be regarded as an umbrella contract, providing for an overall framework for the whole range of bank collections and payments carried out in the context of the account.[39] The alternative approach is to examine each transaction, whether or not occurring as part of the account operation, separately, in light of the civil code special contract covering it. Proponents of this view acknowledge, however, that the tolerance of basic civil law special contracts to variations introduced by the banking or account relationship is quite low, so that such special contracts have been 'deformed' in the banking context.[40]

Regardless, all systems recognize that the basic banking or account relationship, whether it is governed by one overarching contract or a series of separate agreements, may effectively be broken down to three principal components:[41] (i) the deposit transaction and the bank's liability stemming from it; (ii) the operation of the withdrawal and payment services by the bank and the reciprocal duties between bank and customer arising in the course of this operation; and (iii) the debt or monetary relationship

---

[36] For a West European overview see Cranston, above, n. 1 at 1–2.

[37] See e.g. in France, Decree no. 84-708 of 24 July 1984, section 7, requiring full disclosure to customers as well as to the public of all general conditions applicable to services offered. Specifically, according to section 7(2), a disclosure duty, relating to terms, charges, and respective obligations, is fastened on a bank when an account is opened. For the information to be disclosed by the bank to the customer in France, see, in general Gavalda and Stoufflet, above, n. 15 at 107–8 ¶¶222–3. For the mandatory disclosure of statutory terms in the USA see further below.

[38] For the USA with respect to wire transfers, see e.g. P. S. Turner, *Negotiating Wire Transfer Agreements* (Bethesda, Md.: TMA, 1996). The appendix of this work is *Model Funds Transfer Services Agreement and Commentary*, of the American Bar Association, 1994.

[39] For an overview, see e.g. Guggenheim, above, n. 3 at 31–2.

[40] See e.g. G. Ripert and R. Roblot, *Traité de droit commercial*, vol. ii, 13th edn. (Paris: Librarie Générale de Droit et de Jurisprudence, 1992) at 371 ¶2284.

[41] In contrast, the lending aspect of banking is not inherent in the bank–customer relationship, but is rather accessory to it.

between bank and customer arising from deposits and withdrawals. Each of the following three sections in Chapter 2 of the book is dedicated to one of these aspects. It is, however, recognized that banking contracts, even if separate and distinct, share common features.[42] Here the discussion focuses on the account agreement, as reflecting the fundamental characteristics of the banking relationship, whether it is unitary or fragmented. The overall treatment of the contractual relationship between the bank and its customer is thus highlighted in the course of the ensuing discussion.

As part of the treatment given to banking contracts, Italy has an entire **[7]** section, consisting of arts. 1852–1857, dealing with banking transactions in current accounts.[43] They provide for the customer's right to dispose of a positive balance in the account 'at any time', though 'subject to the agreed terms concerning notice' (art. 1852). They further provide for the combination of balances in different accounts of the same customer (art. 1853), for current account in the name of more than one person (art. 1854), and for the withdrawal from the contract (art. 1855). They specifically provide, in art. 1856, that '[f]or the carrying out of instructions . . . the bank is answerable according to the rules concerning mandate . . . '.[44] Finally, art. 1857 refers to three general provisions governing a non-banking current account,[45] and specifies that they apply 'to banking transactions for a current account'. These are arts. 1826, 1829, and 1832, respectively dealing with the right to commissions and reimbursement of expenses, exclusion of uncollected collection claims, and the approval of the account.

The common law deals with the account agreement as a unitary over- **[8]** arching contract that may nevertheless be broken down to its components. It was argued in *Joachimson v. Swiss Bank Corporation*[46] that in connection with the opening of a current account, the contract made between banker and customer 'is a simple contract of loan', to which 'there is added, or superadded, an obligation of the bank to honour the customer's drafts to any amount not exceeding the credit balance at any material time', which nevertheless 'does not affect the main contract'.[47]

---

[42] See e.g. M. Giovanoli, 'Switzerland', in Cranston (ed), above, n. 1, 183 at 183–4.

[43] Section V—Banking Transactions for Current Account, containing Articles 1852–7, is in Chapter XVII—Banking Contracts, which is in Title 3—Specific Contracts, of Book 4— Obligations. A commentary on these provisions is by V. Santor, *Il conto corrente bancairo artt. 1852–1857* (Milano: Giuffré, 1992). The other sections of the banking contract chapter deal with bank deposits, banking service concerning safe deposit boxes, bank advances, and bank discounts. The current account provisions, consisting of Arts. 1823–33, constitute a distinct chapter (Chapter XVI), immediately preceding the banking contract chapter.

[44] The provision further adds, in Art. 1856(2), that '[i]f the instructions are to be carried out in a place in which the bank has no office, it can entrust their performance to another bank or to one of its correspondents . . .' . See further discussion on the point in 3.C(v) ¶¶3–5.

[45] Non-banking current accounts are dealt with in Italy in arts. 1823–33. See further in 2.D (iii), below. [46] [1921] 3 K.B. 110 (C.A.).

[47] [1921] 3 K.B. 110 (C.A.) at 127.

Lord Atkin was 'unable to accept this contention' and summarized the contractual incidents of the account agreement as follows:[48]

'I think that there is only one contract made between the bank and its customer. The terms of that contract involve obligations on both sides . . . They appear . . . to include the following provisions. The bank undertakes to receive money and to collect bills for the customer's account. The proceeds so received are not to be held in trust for the customer, but the bank borrows the proceeds and undertakes to repay them. The promise to repay is to repay at the branch of the bank where the account is kept, and during banking hours. It includes a promise to repay any part of the amount due against the written order of the customer addressed to the bank at the branch, and as such written orders may be outstanding in the ordinary course of business for two or three days, it is a term of the contract that the bank will not cease to do business with the customer except upon reasonable notice. The customer on his part undertakes to exercise reasonable care in executing his written orders so as not to mislead the bank or to facilitate forgery. . . . [I]t is necessarily a term of such contract that the bank is not liable to pay the customer the full amount of his balance until he demands payment from the bank at the branch at which the current account is kept.'

At present, a customer's payment instructions may be given to the bank not only in writing but also electronically, and under some conditions, even orally. Otherwise, the essence of this summary still holds good today. Nevertheless, additional duties, particularly in relation to aspects that were irrelevant to the specific issue addressed in *Joachimson* v. *Swiss Bank Corporation*, have been added. In broad terms, and within certain limits and preconditions, a bank is obliged to comply with the customer's demands for withdrawal or payment to a third party out of the account, to collect incoming payments to the account, to render accounts to a customer,[49] periodically or upon demand, and to maintain secrecy.[50] In return, the customer is obligated to give clear and not misleading instructions[51] and advise the bank of forged or unauthorized instruction he knows.[52] This is usually referred to as the core of the implied contract established by the opening of the bank account.[53] In the common law, however, a term will not be implied into a contract unless it is necessary, so that in its

---

[48] [1921] 3 K.B. 110 (C.A.) at 127.

[49] The leading case is *Devaynes* v. *Noble; Clayton's Case* (1816), 1 Mer. 572, 35 E.R. 781 (H.L.).

[50] The leading case is *Tournier* v. *National Provincial and Union Bank of England*, [1924] 1 K.B. 461 (C.A.).

[51] The leading case is *Young* v. *Grote* (1827), 4 Bing. 253, 130 E.R. 764 (Ct. Common Pleas.), as subsequently confirmed in *London Joint Stock Bank* v. *Macmillan*, [1918] A.C. 777 (H.L.).

[52] The leading case is *Greenwood* v. *Martins Bank Ltd.*, [1933] A.C. 51 (H.L.). In Canada see also *Ewing* v. *Dominion Bank* (1904), [1905] 35 S.C.R. 133 and *Ontario Woodsworth Memorial Foundation* v. *Grozbord* (1966), 58 D.L.R. (2d) 21 (Ont. CA), *aff'd* [1969] S.C.R. 622.

[53] See e.g. Ogilvie, above, n. 2 at 443–9. But notwithstanding Ogilvie, id. at 445, these implied reciprocal duties do not include the one under which the customer *may* be required

absence the whole transaction would become 'inefficacious, futile and absurd'.[54] The terms mentioned appear to be reasonable and comply with both banking practice and the presumed intention of the parties. They may nevertheless, at least in part, not meet this standard. It may thus be more appropriate to consider the account agreement as supplemented by terms originated from the usage of trade. Also, it may be more appropriate to treat the account agreement in its entirety, as a special contract, along similar lines that the bailment or sales agreement are recognized as distinct categories, each importing, by definition, a set of implied terms underlying the essence of the transaction.

In all legal systems, the account agreement is typically of an indefinite duration.[55] Obviously, in the absence of a specific maturity or expiry date agreed upon, the customer is free to terminate the agreement by closing the account at any time,[56] though clearly, without prejudice to the bank's right to recover from him the remaining debit balance of an overdrawn account. Effectively, a customer may achieve termination by the mere withdrawal of all remaining funds in the account, except that until giving advice of closure, he may continue to incur charges. **[9]**

The bank's right to unilaterally modify the agreement is recognized by the common law, where to be effective, any such modification requires a reasonable notice. Common grounds for a permissible modification are changes in banking practices, as, for example, the introduction of cheque processing on the basis of MICR encoding. Prior to this latter practice, a customer could request a bank to charge a cheque to an account other than the one indicated on the cheque form, by noting the request on the cheque itself. Presumably, this was a term, possibly implied, in the account agreement. However, once cheques are automatically processed by MICR reading machines, such instructions would be overlooked by the bank. Hence, it is reasonable for the bank to initiate the unilateral modification of the agreement, so as to preclude the customer from directing payment out of an account other than preprinted on the cheque form,

---

to verify the accuracy of an account rendered. See 4.B below. As she in fact admits, such a duty is fastened on a customer only by contract.

[54] *Liverpool City Council* v. *Irwin*, [1977] A.C. 239 at 262 (H.L.).

[55] See e.g. for Germany, H. Schönle in *Jura Europae*, above, n. 25 at §10.11.8; for Italy, C.C. Campi, ibid. at §40.11.9.

[56] In Italy, under art. 1855 of the civil code, '[i]f a banking transaction for a current account . . . is on an indefinite time basis, either party can withdraw from the contract by giving advance notice of the period established by usage or, in the absence of a customary time limit, *fifteen days*'. This is an exception to the general rule of art. 1833, under which, for non-banking transactions, '[i]f the contract [of current account] is for an indefinite time, either party can withdraw on any closing date . . . by giving at least *ten days* advance notice'. [Emphasis added].

provided adequate notice is given.[57] Unilateral modifications initiated by the bank may refer to service charges.[58]

It should, however, be pointed out that the question of the adequacy of the modification notice is different from the issue relating to the effectiveness of the modification itself. The reasonableness or adequacy of the advice or notice is thus an essential but inadequate element in determining the effectiveness of the modification. To become a term in the contract, the modification, once reasonably notified, must satisfy the same rules governing the effectiveness of any term of the account agreement, as discussed in (iv), below. For example, for a consumer account agreement in the UK, the modified term needs to satisfy the Unfair Terms in Consumer Contracts Regulations 1994 implementing the EU Directive on Unfair Terms in Consumer Contracts discussed below.

Once he is properly advised, the customer is free to reject the modification by closing the account and terminating the agreement. Certainly, the unilateral termination of the agreement by the bank, like any modification, requires a reasonable notice, but only where the account has been in credit. The notice is necessary in order to allow the customer to effectively relocate his account.[59] Upon any termination by whichever party, the bank is further required, for a reasonable time, to honour, against available funds, the customer's payment instructions given prior to termination, and not yet processed.

[10]   In the USA, incidents of the bank–customer relationship, particularly in relation to consumers, are heavily regulated.[60] So far as cheques are concerned, Article 4 of the Uniform Commercial Code (UCC) deals with matters such as the paying bank's right to charge the customer's account, a bank's liability for a wrongful dishonour of a cheque, a customer's right to stop payment,[61] a bank's position with respect to stale cheques, and a customer's duty to discover and report unauthorized signatures and alterations.[62] UCC Article 3 provides for the respective reciprocal obligations of

---

[57] See e.g. *Burnett* v. *Westminster Bank Ltd.*, [1966] 1 Q.B. 742, Mocatta J., holding that notice printed on the chequebook cover was inadequate. Two recent Canadian cases requiring reasonable notice for the effective modification of the account agreement by the bank are *Armstrong Baum Plumbing & Heating* v. *Toronto Dominion Bank* (1994) 15 B.L.R (2d) 84 (Ont. Gen. Div.) aff'd (1997) 32 B.L.R (2d) 230 (Ont. C.A.) and *Rancan Fertilizer Systems Inc.* v. *Lavergne* [1999] W.W.R. 323 (Man. C.A.).

[58] In Canada, notice requirements are set out in the *Disclosure of Charges (Banks) Regulations*, S.O.R./92-324.

[59] The leading case is *Prosperity Ltd.* v. *Lloyd Bank Ltd.* (1923), 39 T.L.R. 372 (K.B.). In the USA, the notice requirement may not be unanimous. See Norton and Whitley, above, n. 3, 227 at 245.

[60] See e.g. J. A. Spanogle, 'Regulation of the Bank–Customer Relationship in the United States' (1993) 4 J.B.F.L.P. 18.

[61] This aspect is also dealt with, though more briefly, by cheque legislation in the UK and jurisdictions deriving their cheque laws from it. See 3.B(iii), below.

[62] See particularly UCC §§4-401 to 407 and discussion in 3.B (iv) and 4.B(iv), below.

bank and customer to prevent forgeries and alterations.[63] In principle, and subject to preclusion of disclaimer clauses in relation to good faith and ordinary care, discussed in 2.C below, variations by contract of the provisions of Article 4 are permissible.[64] Federal legislation and regulation provide for funds availability in favour of the recipient of payment.[65]

All these laws do not distinguish between consumer and business accounts. Conversely, with respect to electronic funds transfers, separate legislation applies to business and consumer payments. The former is governed, in each state, by UCC Article 4A, while the latter is dealt with by the federal Electronic Fund Transfer Act (EFTA)[66] and Regulation E,[67] issued by the Federal Reserve Board, which is responsible for implementing it. Within certain limits, variations by agreements are permitted for business electronic funds transfers,[68] but are absolutely precluded with respect to consumer ones.[69]

Regulation E contains strict disclosure and documentation requirements applicable to a financial institution providing electronic fund transfer services to consumers and thus form part of the account agreement[70] within which these services are offered.[71] Under Regulation E, §205.7(a), initial disclosure by the financial institution must be made either at the time a consumer contracts for an electronic fund transfer service, or before the first electronic fund transfer is made. Under §205.4(a), disclosure must be made in a readily understandable written statement that the consumer may keep.

[11]

Under Regulation E, §205.7(b), disclosure must include the following terms and conditions relating to the EFT service: a summary of the consumer's liability for unauthorized electronic fund transfers;[72] the telephone number and address for the notification of an unauthorized transfer; the financial institution's business days; the type of electronic fund transfers that the consumer may make and (subject to a security

---

[63] See UCC §3-406 and discussion in 4.B(iv), below.

[64] UCC §4-103(a). Under UCC §4-103(b), 'Federal Reserve regulations and operating circulars, clearing-house rules, and the like have the effect of agreements under subsection (a) . . .'.

[65] The Expedited Funds Availability Act, 12 U.S.C. §4001 et seq., and Regulation CC 12 C.F.R. §229, issued by the Federal Reserve Board, which implements it.

[66] 15 U.S.C. §1693 *et seq.*   [67] 12 C.F.R. §205.

[68] UCC §4A-501(a). In addition, the provisions of Article 4A may be superseded by regulations of the Federal Reserve Board and operating circulars of Federal Reserve Banks, as well as overridden by funds transfer system rules. See UCC §§4A-107 (particularly Official Comment 3) and 4A-501(b). For a detailed discussion, see B. Geva, *The Law of Electronic Funds Transfers*, looseleaf (New York: Matthew Bender, 1992–9) at §2.02[6], and ch. 2 in general for UCC Article 4A.   [69] EFTA §914.

[70] 'Account' is defined in both EFTA §903(2) and Regulation E §205(2)(b)(1) by reference to an asset account, such as a demand, saving, or deposit account, rather than a line of credit, even where the latter occasionally has a credit balance.

[71] For formal requirements, see Geva, above, n. 68 at §6.06, and ch. 6 in general for EFTA and Regulation E.   [72] For this right, see discussion in 4.C(iii), below.

exception) any limitations on the frequency and dollar amount of transfers; fees imposed by the institution for electronic fund transfers or the right to make them; a summary of the consumer's right to receive documentation of transfers and notices regarding pre-authorized transfers; a summary of the consumer's right to stop payment of a pre-authorized transfer and the procedure for placing a stop-payment order; a summary of the financial institution's liability for damages proximately caused by its failure to comply with the consumer's instructions;[73] the circumstances under which the financial institution will disclose account information to third parties; and an error resolution notice.[74]

Under Regulation E, §205.8(a), a notice of change of terms and conditions is required to be sent to the consumer for a change in a term or condition required to be disclosed under §205.7(b), but only when the change would result in: increased fees; increased liability for the consumer; fewer types of available electronic fund transfers; or stricter limitations on the frequency or dollar amounts of transfers.

Notice must be written and be mailed or delivered by the financial institution to the consumer at least twenty-one days before the effective date. Prior notice of change is excused where an immediate change in terms or conditions is necessary to maintain or restore the security of an electronic fund transfer system or account.

Under Regulation E, §205.8(b), for each account from or to which electronic fund transfers can be made, an error resolution notice must be mailed or delivered by the financial institution at least once each calendar year. Alternatively, the financial institution may include an abbreviated notice on or with each periodic statement required by Regulation E, §205.9(b).[75]

Documentation of transfers is governed by Regulation E, §205.9. Documentation requirements are of two types: terminal receipts and periodic statements. The requirements are excused for certain foreign initiated transfers. Under EFTA, §906(f), proper documentation of payment to a third party constitutes prima facie proof that the transfer was made.

A terminal receipt is required at any time an electronic fund transfer is initiated by a consumer at an ATM or POS (but not home banking) electronic terminal. At that point of time, the financial institution is required to make available to the consumer a written receipt of the transfer(s) that clearly sets forth: the amount of the transfer; the calendar date the con-

---

[73] Such instructions are either to make payment or to stop payment of pre-authorized transfers. The financial institution's liability to be pointed out to the consumer is provided for in EFTA §910.

[74] A model initial disclosure statement substantially similar to the statement appears in Regulation E 12 C.F.R. §205, App. A. According to §205.4(b), Regulation E disclosures may be combined with additional information or disclosures required by other laws.

[75] Either notice must be substantially similar to a model form set forth in Model Form A3 in Appendix A to Regulation E.

sumer initiated the transfer; the type of transfer and the type of the consumer's account; a number or code that identifies the consumer account or accounts or the access device used to initiate the transfer; the terminal location or an identification such as a code or terminal number; and the name of any third party to or from whom funds are transferred.

Under Regulation E, §205.9(b), the periodic statement requirement applies to any consumer account to or from which electronic fund transfers can be made. With respect to such accounts, the financial institution must mail or deliver a statement for each monthly cycle in which an electronic fund transfer has occurred, but at least a quarterly statement if no transfer has occurred. A quarterly statement suffices also for accounts that may be accessed only by pre-authorized transfers to the account. Periodic statements are excused for passbook accounts where the financial institution updates the passbook on presentation or enters on a separate document the amount and date of each electronic fund transfer since the last presentation of the passbook.

Each periodic statement shall include: (1) for each transfer occurring during the cycle, the amount of the transfer, the date the transfer was credited or debited to the account, and the type of transfer and the type of the consumer's account; for a transfer initiated by the consumer at an electronic terminal (except for a deposit of cash or a cheque or draft or similar paper instrument), the terminal location or an identification such as a code or terminal number, and the name of any third party to or from whom funds were transferred; (2) consumer's account number; (3) fees assessed against the account for electronic fund transfers, the right to make transfers, or account maintenance; (4) opening and closing account balances; (5) address and telephone number for error inquiries (unless included in a yearly notice of error resolution procedures under Regulation E, §205.8(b)); and (6) a telephone number for inquiries on pre-authorized credits (if applicable).

Italy has specific legislation on the transparency of banking transac- [12] tions,[76] to a large extent, superseding an earlier Interbank Agreement of 1978. The legislation governs the transparency of charges, rates, and terms relating to banking and financial services as well as of any modification of such charges, rates, and terms. It further requires each bank to provide a periodic statement of account to each customer. The content of each statement is considered to be approved by the customer if he does not contest it in writing within sixty days after receipt.

---

[76] Particularly Law No. 154 of 2 Feb. 1992, G.U. no. 45 of 24 Feb. 1992, discussed by S. Cotterli, 'Italy', in Cranston (ed.), above, n. 1, 109–13, as further confirmed by Title VI of the Consolidated Banking Act (Decree 1.9.1993, No. 385) governing the transparency of financial transactions.

(IV) FREEDOM OF CONTRACT AND THE ACCOUNT AGREEMENT

[13] The ensuing discussion deals with the effect of onerous express terms in the account agreement in the various legal systems covered. Prima facie, exemption clauses ought to fall within the ambit of the present analysis. However, since the effect of an exemption clause in a banking agreement is particularly to disclaim or restrict bank liability implied by law, the effectiveness of such clauses is dealt with below in 2.C, in the context of the discussion on implied terms.

Extra-legal standards limit the freedom of contract in all modern legal systems. In civil law, they are grouped under 'immorality': '[a]ll the great Europeans codifications . . . contain a general clause declaring immoral contracts and/or those that offend against public policy null and void. These clauses go back . . . to the suppression of transactions "contra bonos mores" by Roman jurists and Emperors.'[77] Contracts offending public policy are thus precluded in civil law jurisdictions.[78] They are also invalidated in the common law,[79] as well as by legislation in Israel.[80] Furthermore, a 'good faith' obligation in the performance of a contract is a fundamental principle, going back to Roman law,[81] and presently codified, and occasionally expanded, in civil codes,[82] the American Uniform Commercial Code,[83] as well as in Israel.[84]

Nonetheless, freedom of contract is a fundamental principle in all mod-

---

[77] R. Zimmermann, *The Law of Obligations—Roman Foundations of the Civilian Tradition* (Cape Town: Juta, 1990) at 706.

[78] See art. 1133 in France; BGB §138(1) in Germany; arts. 1343 and 1354 in Italy; art. 90 in Japan: arts. 1373, 1411, and 1413 in Quebec; and CO art. 20 in Switzerland. For texts in English, see *The French Civil Code Revised Edition* (as am. to 1 July 1994), trans. J. H. Crabb (Littleton, Colo.: Fred B. Rothman, 1995); *The German Civil Code* (as am. to 1 January 1975), trans. I. S. Forrester, S. L. Goren, and H. M. Ilgen (South Hackensack, NJ: Fred B. Rothman, 1975) (with 1981 Supp., trans. S. L. Goren); *The Civil Code of Japan* (translation) (Japan: The Ministry of Justice, 1972); *The Italian Civil Code*, trans. M. Beltramo, G. E. Longo, and J. H. Merryman (Dobbs Ferry, NY: Oceana, 1969); The Swiss-American Chamber of Commerce, *Swiss Contract Law, English Translation of Selected Official Texts* (Zurich: Swiss-American Chamber of Commerce, 1977) (reproducing portions of the Swiss Code of Obligations—CO); and the bilingual edition of the Quebec Civil Code, *Code civil du praticien* (Montreal: DACFO, 1995).

[79] See e.g. M. P. Furmston, *Cheshire, Fifoot and Furmston's Law of Contract*, 12th edn. (London: Butterworths, 1991) at 393.   [80] See s. 30 to the Contracts Law (General Part) 1973.

[81] See in general, Zimmermann, above, n. 77 at 674.

[82] See e.g. art. 1134(3) in France (agreements must be executed in good faith); BGB §242 in Germany (performance according to good faith); art. 1175 in Italy (fair behaviour by debtor and creditor); art. 1 in Japan (the exercise of rights and performance of duties must be done faithfully and in accordance with the principles of trust); art. 1375 in Quebec (creation, performance, and extinction of obligation in good faith); and art. 2(1) in the Swiss Civil Code (good faith requirement in exercising rights and executing obligations).

[83] UCC §1-203, providing that '[e]very contract or duty . . . imposes an obligation of good faith in its performance or enforcement'.

[84] Sections 12 and 39 to the Contract Law (General Part) 1973, requiring good faith in the negotiation, performance, and enforcement of a contract.

ern legal systems, and, as a rule, these limits have been narrowly applied.[85] Typically, one-sided terms in a standard form contract reflect the strong bargaining position of the supplier, but, nevertheless, manifest a legitimate interest of that supplier. This makes 'immorality', 'good faith', as well as 'public policy', at least as it has so far been applied, inappropriate.

Even more refined controls on contract terms have proved to be inadequate. First under the common law, a supplier of a product or service using a standard form contract is required to point out to customers onerous terms;[86] the terms are thus not invalidated if properly explained. Similarly in the civil law, French courts validate terms in standard contracts as long as they have been understood by the customer.[87] Also, Japanese courts focus on the acceptance by one party of standard terms relied upon by the other party as an indication for the incorporation of such terms into the contract between these two parties.[88] In Switzerland, under a view to the contrary, the mere knowledge by a customer of the existence of standard terms puts the onus on the customer to become familiar with those terms, in discharge of the customer's good faith obligation. While the existence of standard terms must be taken as common knowledge, this view is strongly disfavoured.[89] **[14]**

The second means of control developed in the common law is unconscionability. In the USA, unconscionable contracts and clauses are precluded under UCC §2-302, but only in connection with the sale of goods. Regardless, unconscionability is not all that clear a doctrine. According to Official Comment 1 to UCC §2-302, for the section to apply, '[t]he basic test is whether, in light of the general commercial background and the commercial needs of the particular trade or case, the clauses involved are so one-sided as to be unconscionable under the circumstances existing at the time of the making of the contract'. At the same time, '[t]he principle is one of the prevention of oppression and unfair surprise . . . and not of disturbance of allocation of risks because of superior bargaining power'. There is an academic debate in the USA as to whether the proper role of unconscionability ought not to be confined to the contract-making process, so as not to extend to striking down substantive **[15]**

---

[85] For the narrow set of circumstances under the common law, see e.g. Furmston, above, n. 79 at 393, enumerating only the denial of access to courts, prejudice to marriage, and restraint of trade.

[86] See e.g. *Tilden Rent-A-Car Co.* v. *Clendenning* (1978), 83 D.L.R. (3d) 400 (Ont. C.A.).

[87] See Rives-Lange and Contamine-Raynaud, above, n. 2 at 146 ¶157.

[88] See Kitagawa, above, n. 3 at §1.10[2], particularly relying on the leading case of *Liverpool & London & Globe Hoken K.K.* v. *Shimazaki*, Great Court of Judicature, 21 Minroku, 2182, 24 Dec. 1915.   [89] See Guggenheim, above, n. 3 at 59–61.

terms agreed between the parties, no matter how objectionable these terms are.[90]

Generally, in the common law, so far as decided cases are concerned, 'unconscionability' linked to 'unequal bargaining power', may be limited. It may denote what is broadly understood as undue influence exercised in a transaction,[91] leading to the domination or victimization of a party by the other resulting in a transaction that is manifestly or greatly disadvantageous to the former.[92] Alternatively, it may address the use of harsh pressure tactics, amounting to exploitation, inducing a party to enter into a one-sided contract containing unfavourable terms.[93] Unconscionability will, however, not apply where one party 'neither exercised pressure on the [other party] nor unfairly took advantage of social or economic pressures on him' to induce him to enter into the contract.[94]

[16]   Similar principles codified in civil law jurisdictions condemn the exploitation of the weak party to the contract and accordingly are to the same effect.[95] The typical setting for a standard form contract in general, and the bank account in particular, is thus unlikely to be covered by unconscionability in both common and civil law jurisdictions.

[17]   Many jurisdictions have specific legislation dealing with unfair terms in either standard form or consumer contracts. Account agreements are typ-

---

[90] For the argument forcefully made effectively in favour of 'procedural' as opposed to 'substantive' unconscionability, in the context of the desired scope of freedom of contract, subject only to very narrow limits, see R. A. Epstein, 'Unconscionability: A Critical Reappraisal' (1975) 18 J.L. & Econ. 293.

[91] Even under the judgment of Lord Denning MR in *Lloyd Bank Ltd.* v. *Bundy*, [1975] Q.B. 326 (C.A.), disfavoured by Lord Scarman in *Morgan*, below, n. 92, relief will be granted to one who 'without independent advice enters into a contract upon terms which are very unfair' only 'when his bargaining power is grievously impaired by reason of his own needs or desires, or by his own ignorance or infirmity, coupled with undue influences or pressures brought to bear on him by or for the benefit of the other'. Ibid. at 339.

[92] *National Westminster Bank plc* v. *Morgan*, [1985] 1 All E.R. 821 (H.L.), *rvs'ng* [1983] 3 All E.R. 85 (C.A.) and rejecting 'unequal bargaining power' as an organizing principle of various equitable categories including undue influence. See M. H. Ogilvie, 'Undue Influence in the House of Lords' Commentary (1986) 11 Can. Bus. L.J. 503.

[93] See e.g. *Dominion Home Improvements Ltd.* v. *Irmgard Knuude*, unreported, Ont. DC, 16 April 1986, reproduced in J. S. Ziegel, *Sales Transactions*, being vol. i of J. S. Ziegel, B. Geva, and R. C. C. Cuming, *Commercial and Consumer Transactions—Cases, Text and Materials*, 3rd edn. (Toronto: Emond Montgomery, 1995), 75.

[94] See *Dyck* v. *Manitoba Snowmobile Association Inc.* (1985), 18 D.L.R. (4th) 635 at 637 (S.C.C.).

[95] See e.g. BGB §138(2) in Germany, avoiding a legal transaction 'whereby a person exploiting the need, carelessness or inexperience of another' induces that other to enter into a one-sided contract to the latter's disadvantage; art. 1406 in Quebec, dealing with 'lesion' resulting from the exploitation of a party which creates 'a serious disproportion between the prestations of the parties'; and CO art. 21 in Switzerland, entitled 'lesion' (translated to English as 'unconscionability'), and providing for the rescision of a one-sided contract concluded through exploitation. While 'lesion' may better be translated as 'injury' or 'prejudice', 'unconscionability' conveys better the subject-matter of the provision.

ically standard form contracts, and where applicable, namely in connection with non-business personal accounts, may be consumer contracts. To that extent, and other than in countries where relevant legislation is limited to contracts in specific areas that do not include banking,[96] account agreements may be subject to such legislation.[97] The following is an overview of this legislation in the countries under discussion.

Germany passed in 1976 an Act on the Regulation of Standard Condi- **[18]** tions, known as 'AGB-Gesetz'. Drawing on previous jurisprudence, section 9 of the Act renders void '[p]rovisions in standard conditions of contract' which 'unreasonably prejudice the contractual partner . . . in violation of the requirements of good faith'.[98] German courts applied this provision to a number of terms in banking contracts, requiring both transparency and fairness of terms.[99]

The Italian civil code regulates four aspects of standard form con- **[19]** tracts.[100] First, under art. 1341(1), standard conditions prepared by a party to the contract are effective only where 'at the moment of the conclusion of the agreement, the [other contracting party] knew of them or should have known of them by using ordinary diligence'. Obviously, this offers very little control on abusive terms. The only test is that of knowledge, or ability to know; a customer is bound not only by what he knows but also by what he should have known, regardless of whether the term itself is fair or reasonable.

Second, under art. 1341(2), certain types of terms in standard form contracts must specifically be approved in writing, and are otherwise ineffective. Such terms include conditions relating to limitations on liability, the unilateral withdrawal from a contract, and limitations on the power to raise defences. This regulates the form of certain terms, but again, avoids dealing with their contents.

The third and fourth aspects are rules of interpretation of standard form contracts. Under art. 1342, in the case of a conflict between a standard term in a standard form contract and a negotiated clause added to it, it is the latter that prevails. Finally, under art. 1371, standard form terms are interpreted, 'in case of doubt', against the drafter and in favour of the

---

[96] As is the case in Japan, see Kitagawa, above, n. 3 at §1.10[3].

[97] See e.g. E. H. Hondius, 'Standard Form Contracts in the Banking Industry—Some European Experiences' (1991) 2 J.B.F.L.P. 231.

[98] See O. Sandrock and E. Klausing, 'Germany', in Cranston (ed.), above, n. 1, 61 at 69.

[99] See Hondius, above, n. 97 at 238, who quotes a precedent, requiring the bank, in order to meet the transparency requirement mandated by this statutory provision, to 'draft [its] standard form contracts in such a way that legally or commercially not-educated customers may comprehend them without special instructions'. Also, in that case, a term effectively requiring the payment of interest for a non-existent debt was struck down under that statutory provision as 'substantively unfair' and 'unconscionable'. Ibid.

[100] See Cotterli, above, n. 76 at 120–2.

customer. Consistently with the other aspects regulated in Italy, this does not undermine the effectiveness of clearly drafted abusive standard terms that are not in conflict with any negotiated clause.

[20]   In Switzerland, art. 8 of the Law on Unfair Competition 1986[101] covers 'preformulated contractual terms and conditions which are misleading' and which diverge considerably from either applicable statutory rules or the normal risk allocation. Art. 8 declares such terms and conditions to be unfair and facilitates their invalidation by courts. Apart from statute, Swiss courts have interpreted standard terms against their drafter and in favour of the customer, but have recognized the knowing acceptance of objectionable terms by a party to a contract. In providing for the unfairness of 'misleading' terms, the statute is not believed to add much to the standard already pronounced by courts. A clearly drafted contract term is unlikely to be misleading. Objectionable as it may be, it will thus not be invalidated by Article 8; once knowingly accepted by the customer, such a term will further meet the standard set by jurisprudence. The statute makes a difference only in facilitating the invalidation of a 'misleading' (and divergent) standard term knowingly accepted by a customer, which other than under art. 8, would have been effective.[102]

[21]   The civil code of Quebec contains specific provisions applicable to consumer as well as to adhesion contracts. 'Consumer contracts' are defined in art. 1384 broadly enough to cover services provided by an enterprise for a natural person 'for personal, family or domestic purposes', but only within a 'field of application . . . delimited by legislation respecting consumer protection . . .' which may exclude the bank account. Conversely, 'a contract of adhesion', specifically enumerated as a type of contract under art. 1378, is defined in art. 1379 as 'a contract in which the essential stipulations were imposed or drawn up by one of the parties . . . and were not negotiable'. This, indeed, is broad enough to cover the typical account agreement.

    In relation to consumer or adhesion contracts, limitations are set in Quebec for the validity of an external clause, an illegible or incomprehensible clause, as well as of an abusive clause. Thus, an external clause, that is, a term from an outside source, not stated in a contract but to which the contract nevertheless refers, is null, if it was neither pointed out to nor known by the consumer or adhering party (art. 1435). Also a clause 'which is illegible or incomprehensible to a reasonable person', that has not been adequately explained to the consumer or adhering

---

[101] Loi sur le concurrence déloyale (LCD), of 19 Dec. 1986, ref. 241.
[102] See Giovanoli, above, n. 42 at 211–13. See also X. Favre-Bulle, *Les Paiements transfrontalières dans un espace financier européen* (Bruylant, Brussels: Helbing & Lichtenhahn, 1998) at 391–5.

party, and which has caused injury to him is null (art. 1436). Finally, under art. 1437, nullity is also accorded to an abusive term in a consumer or adhesion contract. An abusive clause is defined to be 'a clause which is excessively and unreasonably detrimental to the consumer or the adhering party and is therefore not in good faith'. Particularly, the provision adds, 'a clause which so departs from the fundamental [normal] obligations . . . that it changes the nature of the contract is an abusive clause' (art. 1437(2)). Other than for abusive terms, the validity of any other type of an objectionable clause is thus stated to depend on its clarity and understanding by the customer; no nullity *per se* is provided for.

In Israel, abusive or unfair terms in a standard form contract may be **[22]** invalidated.[103] A unique and original feature[104] under Israeli law is the abstract pre-screening of terms in standard form contracts by a tribunal presided by a judge, by way of an alternative to challenging their validity in a case-by-case litigation.[105] To assist in the determination as to whether a term in a standard form contract is prejudicial or abusive, namely, whether it 'prejudices customers or confers an unfair advantage to the supplier so as to prejudice customers',[106] several factors are listed, each being presumptive so as to lead to the invalidation of the term. Such is the case for an exemption clause, a term conferring on the supplier a unilateral and unreasonable right to avoid, suspend, or modify the contract as well as to transfer the supplier's obligations, and a term providing for unreasonable limitations on the customer's remedies or access to courts.[107] The implementation of the abstract pre-screening feature has, however, not been entirely successful.

Unfair terms in consumer bank agreements fall within the ambit of the **[23]** EU Directive on Unfair Terms in Consumer Contracts.[108] Article 6 requires

---

[103] Section 3 to Standard Contracts Law, 1982. For an overview and critical assessment in the banking law context, see S. Deutch, 'Bank and Customer Relationship—Contract and Consumer Aspects', in A. Barak, I. Englard, A. M. Rabello, and G. Shalev (eds.), *Essays in Memory of Professor Guido Tedeschi* (Jerusalem: Sacher Institute, 1995) at 163, 174–83 [in Hebrew].

[104] According to Hondius, above, n. 97 at 239, in adopting this feature, 'the Israelis were the first to hit on a solution to [the enforcement] problem' so as to pave the way to other jurisdictions.

[105] See in general, S. Deutch, 'Controlling Standard Contracts—The Israeli Version' (1985) 30 McGill L.J. 458.　　　　　　　　　　　　　　　　　[106] Section 3, n. 103 above.

[107] Section 4 to Standard Contracts Law, 1982.

[108] EC Council Directive 93/13 of 5 Apr. 1993 on Unfair Terms in Consumer Contracts, [1993], OJ No. L.95/29 J. Bus. L. For English perspective, see e.g. P. Duffy, 'Unfair Terms and the Draft EC Directive', [1993] J. Bus. L. 67; R. Brownsword and G. Howells, 'The Implementation of the EC Directive on Unfair Terms in Consumer Contracts—Some Unresolved Questions', [1995] J. Bus. L. 243; and A. Padfield, 'The Impact on English Contract Law of the EC Directive on Unfair Terms in Consumer Contracts' (1995) 10 J. In'l. Bank. L. 175. See also Favre-Bulle, above, n. 102 at 226–41.

member states[109] to 'lay down that unfair terms used in a contract concluded with a consumer by a seller or supplier shall . . . not be binding on
the consumer . . .' . 'Consumer' is defined in Article 2(b) as a natural person acting outside his trade, business, or profession. Conversely, 'seller or
supplier' is defined in Article 2(c) to refer to any natural or legal person
acting for purposes relating to his trade, business, or profession. In relation to the provision of banking services, a 'bank' seems to constitute such
a 'seller or supplier' and an individual non-business customer is a 'consumer'. Hence, the Directive applies to any service contract between a
bank and consumer, including the personal account agreement. The
Directive, however, does not apply to an account agreement between a
bank and a businessperson, whether a corporation or an individual. Similarly, the Directive does not cover an interbank agreement.[110]

Article 3 elaborates on the unfairness to which the Directive applies.
Under Article 3(1), '[a] contractual term which has not been individually
negotiated shall be regarded unfair if, contrary to the requirement of good
faith, it causes a significant imbalance in the parties' rights and obligations arising under the contract, to the detriment of the consumer'. For
this purpose, under Article 3(2), '[a] term shall always be regarded as not
individually negotiated where it has been drafted in advance and the consumer has therefore not been able to influence the substance of the term,
particularly in the context of a pre-formulated standard contract'.[111] The
standard account agreement seems to be fully covered.

Several points addressing the centrality of 'unfairness' to the scope of
the Directive should be highlighted. First, regrettably, 'good faith', which
is a key term in the definition of unfairness under Article 3, is not defined.
It is thus unclear whether the standard is merely of honesty in fact, or
whether it also embodies objective elements. Second, under Article 4, 'the
unfairness of a contractual term shall be assessed, taking into account the
nature of the goods or services for which the contract was concluded', as
well as 'by referring, at the time of conclusion of the contract, to all the circumstances attending the conclusion of the contract and to all the other
terms of the contract . . .'. However, it appears that this definition is subject to Article 3. This is so since under Article 2(a), ' "unfair terms" means
the contractual terms defined in Article 3'. It is therefore plausible to
argue that to be covered by the Directive, a term must first meet the con-

---

[109] In the UK the Directive was implemented by the Unfair Terms in Consumer Contracts
Regulations 1994. For a brief discussion on their application to banks, see Hapgood, above,
n. 3 at 313–15.

[110] Obviously, however, the Directive will apply for a term in an interbank agreement
where and as it is incorporated in the bank agreement with the customer.

[111] Article 3(2) goes on to allocate on the seller or supplier the onus of proof that a given
standard term has been individually negotiated.

ditions specified in Article 3, and that Article 4 does not get into play except for in order to shed light on the unfairness test under Article 3. Under this interpretation, the Directive is limited to non-negotiated unfair terms in standard consumer contract, where the unfairness, as defined in Article 3, is further fine-tuned in Article 4. The standard form personal account agreement is typically such a standard consumer contract which may include non-negotiated unfair terms.

Third, Article 5 requires terms offered to consumers in writing to 'always be drafted in plain, intelligible language' and further provides that in the case of doubt as to the meaning of a term 'the interpretation most favourable to the consumer shall prevail'. Presumably, though this is unfortunately not explicitly stated, a contract in violation of this provision is unfair. Conversely, however, as before, this could be so only where the clauses drafted other than 'in plain, intelligible language', meet the conditions specified in Article 3, as illuminated by Article 4.

Fourth, as provided in Article 3(3), the Annex to the Directive contains 'an indicative and non-exhaustive list of terms which may be regarded as unfair'. With regard to the account agreement, relevant terms may refer to unreasonable cancellation, termination, or modification rights. Also, they may refer to a consumer becoming bound by terms without being given a real opportunity to familiarize himself with them before the conclusion of the contract. Other unfair terms set out in the Annex, which may apply to the bank account, exclude or hinder the consumer's right to take legal action or exercise any other legal remedy, or give the seller or supplier the exclusive right to interpret any term of the contract.

Yet, it is specifically recognized in paragraph 2 of the Annex, that for 'a valid reason', a supplier of financial services may reserve the right to unilaterally terminate a contract of indeterminate duration without notice, 'provided that the supplier is required to inform the other contracting party . . . immediately'. Also, and for 'a valid reason', a supplier of financial services may reserve the right to alter 'without notice' the amount of charges or interest, 'provided that the supplier is required to inform the other contracting party . . . at the earliest opportunity and that the latter [is] free to dissolve the contract immediately'.[112] It follows that the reservation of such rights is not unfair under the Directive.

Finally, Article 7 of the Directive requires Member States, 'in the interests of consumers and competitors', to ensure that 'adequate and effective means exist to prevent the continued use of unfair terms in contracts concluded with consumers by sellers or suppliers'. Adequate legal remedies may provide for administrative, as well as individual, collective or repre-

---

[112] Restrictions further do not apply to unilateral changes by virtue of indexation clauses as well as to transactions with derivatives.

sentative, whether private or public, enforcement, though no particular avenue is mandated.

[24]   In Australia, a contract or contract provision may be invalidated as 'unjust in the circumstances relating to the contract' under state legislation such as section 7 of the NSW Contracts Review Act 1980, No. 16. In so invalidating a term or contract, the Court is mandated, by section 9, to 'have regard to the public interest and to all the circumstances of the case', and to take into account circumstances such as disparity in bargaining power, economic resources or knowledge, whether the contract has been negotiated and its terms explained, the utility of the contested term, the intelligibility of the contract language, the availability of independent legal or other expert advice, and the existence of undue influence.

Also, in Australia, aspects of the account agreement are extensively regulated by the Securities and Investments Commission Act 1989 (Cth) ('ASICA'). Several important provisions are included in Division 2 of Part 2, entitled Unconscionable conduct and consumer protection in relation to the supply of financial services.[113] 'Financial service' is defined in section 12BA as a service either consisting of providing a financial product or otherwise supplied in relation to a financial product. 'Financial product' is broadly defined by the same provision to include 'a facility for taking money on deposit . . . made available in the course of conducting a banking business'. This covers the bank account. Arguably, the operation of payment services is a service supplied in relation to the bank account so as to constitute a financial service governed by the ASICA.

Subdivision C of Division 2 precludes a corporation, including a bank,[114] from being engaged in unconscionable conduct in relation to financial services.[115] Unconscionability is defined either by reference to 'the unwritten law' (section 12CA) or in terms of several alternative factors, such as disparity in bargaining power or knowledge, the objective utility of the conduct to protect the corporation's legitimate interests, undue influence, and the availability of a reasonable alternative to the customer (section 12CB).

---

[113] In general, for these provisions, as well as for section 74 of the Trade Practices Act 1974, No. 51 (Cth) which they superseded for payment services (other than those not linked to a bank accounts), see A. Tyree, 'Section 74 of the Trade Practices Act and Payment Services' (1998) 9 J.B.F.L.P. 304 and A. Tyree, 'Regulation of the Payment System—Part 2—Consumer Protection' (1999) 10 J.B.F.L.P. 161.

[114] 'Corporation' is defined to include 'financial corporation' which is defined to include a bank. See section 12BA.

[115] The preclusion is stated to apply to a corporation engaged 'in trade or commerce' which is broad enough to encompass banking. See *Bank of NSW* v. *Commonwealth* (1948), 76 C.L.R. 1 at 381 (H.C.A.). It was held in *Larmer* v. *Power Machinery Pty. Ltd.* (1977), 29 F.L.R. 490 at 493 (Fed. C.A.) that the expression 'is intended to cover the whole field in which the nation's trade is carried on'.

Subdivisions D and E are limited to consumer transactions. 'Consumer' is defined in section 12BC by reference to price and type of services. Subdivision D, dealing with consumer protection, enjoins false or misleading misrepresentations as well as harassment and coercion, and regulates specific types of conduct, such as the offering of gifts and prizes, bait advertising, and referral selling.

Subdivision E deals with conditions and warranties in consumer transactions. Particularly noteworthy are the warranty under which services will be rendered with due care and skill, as well as the warranty for fitness for any known purpose (section 12 ED). Both may not be disclaimed (section 12 EB), though liability for consequential losses may be excluded (section 12EC).

(V) COUNTRY-WIDE BANKING CODES AND GENERAL CONDITIONS

In some countries, the account agreement may be governed or inspired, at least in part, by terms derived from an interbank agreement. Such an interbank agreement is in the form of either a banking code or general conditions. Broadly speaking, while the former establishes guidelines for banks as to standards to be met in their various customer agreements, the latter is a set of specific terms, designed to form, either in whole or in part, each individual customer banking agreement. Such a banking code or set of general conditions may cover either the basic banking relationship or be limited to a specific type of transaction. For example, both Australia and Canada have banking codes governing debit cards. Conversely, the UK banking code encompasses the overall relationship of a bank with personal customers, namely, consumers. Germany has both a set of general conditions underlying the basic banking relationship as well as several sets of special conditions covering various standardized banking transactions. Japan has several sets of standard terms, each covering a specific type of transaction. One of such sets governs the account relationship.

Obviously, an interbank agreement fastens reciprocal rights and duties on banks parties to the agreement. A question then arises as to how such an agreement may either bind or benefit a customer non-party to that agreement. Frequently, an interbank agreement may not be intended by its parties to bind or benefit customers. Typically, such is the case with regard to interbank agreements governing the clearing of cheques and other customers' payment instructions. Whether such an interbank agreement nevertheless binds or benefits customers is discussed under various legal systems in 3.B, below. Here, with regard to banking codes and general conditions, the customer's position, at least to benefit from the

[25]

interbank agreement, appears to be stronger, since the purpose of the interbank agreement is to provide for standards and rules governing bank relations with customers.

Indeed, a banking code or general conditions may be drafted in a process involving not only banks and other depository institutions providing banking services. Customer organizations and even government may be consulted, be involved in the drafting-negotiation process, and even be parties to the agreement itself. Such is the case, for example, for the debit card code in both Australia and Canada. Regardless, however, a customer is not a party to an interbank agreement providing for a banking code or general conditions, even where organizations purporting to protect his interests have been actively involved in the negotiating process and are parties to the interbank agreement. Neither being the subject of the interbank agreement nor having his interest protected in the drafting process make the customer either liable on or entitled under the banking code or general conditions. From the individual customer's point of view, there is no difference whether an outside document reflects an interbank agreement, with or without the agreement of customer organizations, or whether such an outside document reflects the particular bank's own standard terms and conditions. Either way, as long as the document has not been incorporated somehow into the banking agreement, it is not binding on the customer.

Indeed, as indicated,[116] there is a view premissed on the supposition that the mere knowledge by a customer of the existence of standard terms under which a given bank does business must be taken as common knowledge. Accordingly, this view continues, the onus is on the customer to become familiar with those terms, in discharge of the customer's good faith obligation. Consequently, the terms bind the customer irrespective of the customer's actual familiarity with them. This view is, however, strongly disfavoured.[117]

There are various ways in which the terms of such an interbank agreement may nevertheless bind each subscribing bank vis-à-vis each individual customer. A straightforward approach is taken in Germany where in each instance of a banking contract, the customer specifically agrees to adhere to the applicable conditions, as in fact required by section 2 of the 1976 Act on the Regulation of Standard Conditions. Stated otherwise, in opening an account with a bank, the customer expressly signs a written agreement accepting the binding effect of the general conditions, which thus become specifically incorporated into the individual customer agreement.[118] In Japan, each bank drafts its own rules, based on model rules

---

[116] See (iv), above.   [117] See Guggenheim, above, n. 3 at 59–61.
[118] Sandrock and Klausing, above, n. 98 at 72.

adopted by the Federation of Bankers' Association of Japan, and issues them to the customer at the time the customer opens the account.[119]

A customer in Italy does not specifically adhere to the interbank agreement on business terms. However, a bank not specifically incorporating the terms of the interbank agreement into a customer contract, and thus deviating from a guideline as to what constitutes fairness, is in breach of the good faith obligation, under Article 1375 of the civil code. In an appropriate case, '[n]on-observance of the rules provided for in the [interbank] agreement could be used . . . by a customer to support his cancelling a banking contract due to an error caused by a lack of information about the terms applied to the contract', an error which is known to the bank.[120] As will be seen below, under the common law, a banking code, to which a customer does not specifically adhere, may be binding on the bank vis-à-vis the customer either as an implied term or on the basis of a preliminary or collateral contract. The collateral contract is formed by the customer's acceptance of the bank's engagement to abide by the code; this acceptance is expressed by the customer entering into the banking contract with the bank.

Regardless, a customer bound by a banking code or general conditions, is not precluded from challenging any included objectionable term, under any ground recognized in contract law.[121] This is so, notwithstanding any official approval given to the interbank agreement in a public process, which may have involved customer organizations, in particular, as long as the process was designed merely to ensure that the interbank agreement does not violate competition or antitrust laws.[122] In principle, such is the case, for example, in Germany.[123] While the openness of the negotiating as well as approval process is bound to minimize the inclusion of

---

[119] Kitagawa, above, n. 3 at §4.02[2][c], who further added, that '[i]n the past, a bank would have its customer sign a form with the rules printed on it, but today this step is omitted'.

[120] Cotterli, above, n. 76 at 109, 110, and see also Cranston, above, n. 1 at 1–2.

[121] Such grounds are discussed in (iv), above.

[122] It is noteworthy that in Switzerland, such a public process may have precluded altogether the promulgation of such country-wide standard terms and conditions for banking contracts. According to Giovanoli, above, n. 42 at 183, 212, following criticism by the Federal Commission on Cartels (Antitrust Commission) in its 1989 report of some aspects of a 1966 standard terms and conditions developed by the Swiss Bankers' Association, banks in Switzerland have abandoned a project designed to develop such country-wide standard terms and conditions to be recommended for banking contracts. For the lack of common country-wide standard terms and conditions for banks in Switzerland, see Guggenheim, above, n. 3 at 58.

[123] But, in theory, not in Israel, to the extent that the agreement was pre-screened under the Standard Contracts Law, 1982, discussed in (iv) above. It appears, however, neither an interbank agreement, nor in fact, any standard account contract, has been submitted to such a pre-screening process.

objectionable terms, it neither precludes it altogether nor bars any challenge to such a term.[124]

[26] Space does not permit a detailed exposition of country-wide banking codes and standard conditions in all jurisdictions under discussion. The ensuing analysis is limited to selected countries, each representing a specific model. Accordingly, and as already indicated, the Canadian debit card code is a banking code governing consumer debit card transactions. The UK banking code is a banking code applying to virtually the entire banking relationship between banks and consumers. Both banking codes are sets of principles that subscribing banks undertake to introduce into their customer agreements. Conversely, the German General Business Conditions are specific terms governing the overall relationship between a bank and each business customer. The Japanese Current Account Regulations govern the overall account relationship between a bank and each of its customers. Two variants exist for these Regulations; one applies to business customers and the other to consumers.

[27] On 1 May 1992, a voluntary *Code of Practice for Consumer Debit Card Services* (the Code) was launched in Canada. It was slightly revised in 1996.[125] Following precedents in New Zealand and Australia, it was developed through consultation among representatives of organizations of consumers, retailers, and financial institutions as well as federal and provincial governments. The Code outlines industry practices. Organizations endorsing it undertake to adhere to standards not lower than provided by it. The Code is designed to provide consumer protection in domestic debit card transactions at point-of-service terminals incorporating a card reader and PIN pad, such as automated banking machines (ABMs; also known as automated teller machines, ATMs), point-of-sale (POS) terminals, and home terminals. It does not preclude higher protection given by existing laws and standards.

'Debit Card Transactions' are defined in section 8 as '[d]eposits, withdrawals, payments, or other funds transfers made at point-of-service terminals'. They enable consumers to access their bank accounts for various banking transactions or purchase of goods or services by means of debit cards and personal identification numbers (PINs). The PIN is defined in section 8 as 'a secret code intended for the sole use of the cardholder'. It

---

[124] However, I am advised that in effect, the 2000 General Business Conditions, currently in effect in Germany, have not been under attack. It seems that the openness of the process leading to their drafting enhanced their fairness and facilitated their acceptance.

[125] The ensuing discussion updates B. Geva, 'Canadian Code of Practice for Consumer Debit Card Services' (1993) 4 J.B.F.L.P. 78. The present 1996 revised text, prepared by the Electronic Funds Transfer Group, is preceded by an overview of the code as well as a discussion on the process under which it was developed.

'is used in conjunction with a debit card to confirm the identity of the cardholder and to authorize debit card transactions'.

It is recognized that a debit card and its associated PIN may be issued by two organizations. The responsibilities of the PIN and card issuer are outlined in section 2. The PIN issuer is required to

(a) commence the debit card services only on receipt of a signed request from an applicant;

(b) enable the consumer to choose eligible accounts the card will access;

(c) inform the consumer of fees, purposes, and functions of the PIN, cardholder's responsibility for PIN security and possible consequences of its breach, and how to contact the PIN issuer in case of a problem;

(d) ensure that the PIN is only disclosed to (or selected by) the cardholder; and

(e) advise the cardholder in connection with the avoidance and consequences of unauthorized use.

Similar disclosure and advice responsibilities are fastened on the card issuer. In addition, the card issuer is required to provide the cardholder with a copy of the cardholder agreement.

Standards for cardholder agreements are required, under section 3, to be written in plain language and include terms covering definitions, dispute resolution, liability, lost or stolen cards, PIN confidentiality, service charges, and termination. A copy of the agreement is required to be provided to the consumer when a card is issued or a PIN is initially issued or selected, or when requested. The consumer is to be informed of any change in the agreement and where to obtain a copy of it.

Transaction records, periodic statements (or passbook entries), and transaction security are governed by section 4. For each transaction, the cardholder is to be offered a printed transaction record containing the transaction amount, date, and type; type of account; card number; transaction number; identity of card acceptor; and terminal identification. Similar information is to be provided in periodic statements or passbook update entries. In general, information provided in transaction records and periodic statements (or passbook entries) 'will contain enough information to enable cardholders to check account entries'. The information may be in the form of abbreviations or codes, as long as the meanings of the codes are clearly set out in the document in which the codes are used.

So far as transaction security is concerned, section 4 further provides that terminals will give access to account information only when used with that cardholder's card and PIN. Also, 'sufficient privacy to enable a cardholder to enter a PIN with minimum risk of it being revealed to others' is to be assured when terminals in a public place are installed or replaced.

Liability for loss is governed by section 5. Cardholders are responsible for all authorized use of valid cards, for erroneous entries or fraudulent or worthless deposits, as well as for loss incurred 'when a cardholder contributes to unauthorized use'.

A cardholder contributes to unauthorized use by:

(a) voluntarily disclosing the PIN, including writing the PIN on the card, or keeping a poorly disguised written record of the PIN in proximity with the card; and

(b) failing to notify the issuer, within a reasonable time, that the card has been lost, stolen, or misused, or that the PIN may have become known to someone other than the cardholder.

Usually, liability for loss resulting from unauthorized use 'will not exceed the established debit card transaction withdrawal limits'.

At the same time, cardholders are not liable for 'losses resulting from circumstances beyond their control' such as losses resulting from:

(a) technical problems, issuer problems, and other system malfunctions;

(b) unauthorized use of a card and PIN where (i) the card has been reported lost or stolen, (ii) the card is cancelled or expired, (iii) the cardholder has reported that the PIN may be known to others, or (iv) in other circumstances 'where the issuer was responsible for preventing [the] use'; or

(c) unauthorized use unintentionally contributed to by the cardholder, 'provided the cardholder co-operates in any subsequent investigation'.

This last exception to liability for loss resulting from unauthorized use contributed to by the cardholder may prove to be extremely important.

A framework for resolving disputes is outlined in section 6. Regrettably, only minimal standards are set out. Issuers are required to have clear, timely procedures for dealing with debit card transaction problems which provide for review at a senior level with their organizations. Problems with merchandise or retail service are explicitly excluded. The issuer is required to provide information on the dispute resolution process whenever a problem cannot be settled when the cardholder first complains. A cardholder whose problem cannot be settled by the issuer will be informed of the issuer's reasons and advised whom to contact. During the dispute resolution process, 'cardholders will not be unreasonably restricted from the use of funds that are the subject of the dispute'.

The Code does not purport to freeze consumer protection on the level attained by it. It 'will be reviewed regularly', with a view to ensuring 'its relevance to current technology and business practices, and its effectiveness in promoting of consumer protection . . .'.

The UK Banking Code is a voluntary code, adhered to by banks and building societies, and followed by them in their relations with consumers.[126] It covers all banking transactions but not the selling of investment or investment activities. For subscribers that are members of the Council of Mortgage Lenders, mortgage transactions are superseded by a more detailed Code of Mortgage Lending Practice.

[28]

The current edition of the UK Banking Code is of 2001. The document sets standards of good banking practice which are followed as a minimum by deposit-taking institutions subscribing to it. It does not preclude the adoption of higher standards by subscribing institutions.

The Code consists of six parts. These are (1) ten key commitments of the Code subscribers, (2) provisions as to the availability of information relating to the bank and customer relationship, (3) conditions relating to account operations, (4) a commitment for confidentiality and guidelines as to protecting accounts, (5) policies for dealing with various difficulties, and (6) some useful information relating to the Code.

In their ten commitments, the subscribing deposit-taking institutions promise to (i) act fairly and reasonably in all their dealings with customers; (ii) ensure compliance of all services and products with the Code, 'even if they have their own terms and conditions'; (iii) provide information on services and products in plain language and offer help to facilitate further understanding as needed; (iv) help a customer to make an informed choice of a service or product fitting the customer's needs; (v) have secure and reliable banking and payment systems; (vi) ensure the procedure followed by the institution employees follow and reflect the Code commitments; (vii) consider cases of financial difficulty sympathetically and positively; (viii) correct errors and handle complaints speedily; and (ix) ensure that all services and products comply with relevant laws and regulations, and (x) advise of available alternative access to products and services.

---

[126] The code was originally promulgated in response to the recommendations of the Banking Services Review Committee contained in ch. 16 of its report. See R. B. Jack (chairman), *Banking Services: Report by the Review Committee* (London: Her Majesty's Stationary Office, 1989) at 139–44. Appendix J of the Report (at 377) is a Code of Good Practice Proposed by the Office of Fair Trading. Appendix L (at 389) is an Illustrative Non-statutory 'Code of Banking Practice' prepared by the Review Committee. Appendix S (at 433) is an Outline of Supporting Legislation if Needed for a Statutory Code of Banking Practice. All these appendices were not acted upon due to the prompt compliance of banks with the Review Committee's recommendation to promulgate the code.

Subscribers undertake to provide 'clear information' on key features of principal services (Section 3.1). Account information available to customers ought to pertain to stop-payments instructions, debits, funds availability, unpaid cheques, out-of-date cheques, and the availability of account details to credit reference agencies, as well as to charges and rates. Subscribers undertake that all written terms and conditions 'will be fair' and set out the customer's rights and responsibilities 'clearly and in plain language', with legal and technical language used only 'where necessary' (section 6.1). Conditions relating to account operations concern statements, pre-notification of charges and interest rates, and the safe-keeping of paid cheques. They also deal with cards and PINs, lending and foreign exchange services.

Account protection refers to customer identification and customer's reciprocal duty to take care of chequebooks and access devices.[127] With regard to the misuse of cards, the customer's liability is limited to £50 loss occurring prior to loss notification, unless the customer 'acted fraudulently or without reasonable care', in which case no ceiling applies to the customer's exposure (section 14.8).

The Code was already treated as evidence of good banking.[128] Banks may specifically include its provisions in contracts with customers,[129] and otherwise, may be held bound by it as an implied term of a banking contract.[130] Regardless, banks may be treated as bound by the code on the basis of the representation by them as to their adherence to the Code, as well as possibly, as to their treatment of it as even controlling any express contract term to the contrary, which they seem to do in the commitments.[131] A customer led to enter into a banking contract under such a representation or statement may accordingly regard his entrance to that specific banking contract as an acceptance of the bank's engagement contained in the Code, so as to create a binding contract between them. The customer may thus be holding the misstating bank liable for any damages

---

[127] Introducing customer's obligations, reasonable as they may be, into a document purporting to provide for standards for good banking services to customers, may be regarded as inappropriate. Moreover, from a strict legal point of view, such reciprocal obligations may not be binding on a customer, other than as terms in the contract, which, by itself, the Banking Code is not.

[128] *Barclays Bank plc.* v. *O'Brien*, [1993] 4 All E.R. 417 at 430–1 (H.L.).

[129] According to Hapgood, above, n. 3 at 111 '[m]any banks agree with their customers to observe the Code'.

[130] See Cranston, above, n. 1 at 1. See also Blair, above, n. 2 at 11 and 26, who, by analogy to s. 63C of the Financial Services Act 1986 which empowers the issue of codes of practice, speaks of the contravention of the Banking Code as establishing liability.

[131] From the eleven commitments set out above, see particularly the second one.

suffered by virtue of the bank's breach of promise.[132] Presumably, however, the bank is to be held liable only subject to compliance by the customer with any precondition, as for example, the standards set out by the Code for the protection by the customer of chequebooks and access devices.[133]

In Germany, the current General Business Conditions (GBC) became **[29]** effective at the beginning of 2000.[134] Subject to the application of Specific Conditions to a given transaction, the document purports to govern 'the entire business relationship between the customer and the bank's domestic offices' (para. 1(1)). The GBC document further provides a framework for amending the agreement (para. 1(2)), regulates the bank's duty of secrecy (para. 2), and recognizes that, in principle, the allocation of losses between the bank and its customer is governed by the degree in which each party's fault contributed to the loss (para. 3). The document further provides for limitations on the customer's right of set-off (para. 4), as well as for the legal consequences arising upon the customer's death (para. 5). Applicable law and place of jurisdiction are provided for in paragraph 6.

Specific provisions govern the operation of accounts (paras. 7–10) and the customer's obligation to cooperate (para. 11). For a current account, the bank is required to issue quarterly balance statements. A customer is obligated to raise objections in writing within a month of the receipt of each statement and otherwise is deemed to approve of the balance. Prior to the issue of a periodic statement, the bank may unilaterally reverse an incorrect credit entry, but only to the extent it has a valid claim for reimbursement against the customer. After the issue of the statement, no correction entry may be posted by the bank against the objection of the customer, though the bank is free to sue its customer for the amount of the disputed entry. For calculating interest due to the customer on the

---

[132] For such a collateral or preliminary contract, 'the consideration for which is the making of some other contract', under *Heilbut, Symons & Co.* v. *Buckleton*, [1913] A.C. 30 at 47 (H.L.), see e.g. Furmston, above, n. 79 at 65. For a possible alternative theory of liability by a bank, on a negligent statement inducing the misrepresentee to enter into a bad contract, see judgment of Lord Denning MR in *Esso Petroleum Co. Ltd.* v. *Mardon*, [1976] 2 All E.R. 5 (C.A.).

[133] While such a condition may not be binding as a term on a customer sued by the bank (see n. 127 above), it may be regarded as a condition-precedent to an action against the bank. Stated otherwise, the bank's statement on which it is bound could be regarded as pertaining to compliance by it with certain standards, provided the customer reciprocally complies with others.

[134] The 1993 text is reproduced as Appendix I in Cranston (ed.), above, n. 1 at 289. There are three types of banks operating in Germany: commercial banks, savings banks, and cooperative banks. Each group has its own General Business Conditions, except that, in practice, the General Business Conditions of all three groups are quite similar. The ensuing discussion draws on the GBC of the commercial banks.

balance, reverse and correction entries may be backdated to the date of the erroneous credit entry. Credit posted for cheques and other debit entries deposited or input to the account is provisional and conditional pending collection. Further provisions govern the time of payment of cheques and direct debits and risks relating to foreign currency accounts and transactions.

In turn, the customer is mandated to cooperate fully with the bank. The customer is thus required to advise the bank promptly of all changes in the customer's name, address, or power of representation towards the bank. Orders given by the customer must be clear, and special reference must be made to any urgency in connection with the execution of an order. Also, paragraph 11(4) restates the customer's duty to immediately examine statements of accounts and any other information 'as to . . . correctness and completeness' and is required to 'immediately raise any objection relating thereto'. Further duty is fastened on the customer to advise the bank in case of non-receipt of statements.

Cost of bank services is governed by paragraph 12. Unless specifically agreed upon, interest and charges are to be set by the bank 'at its reasonable discretion'. Customer's right of termination upon changes in interest and charges is specifically provided for.[135] Expenditure made by the bank in carrying out customer's instructions, as well as in acting 'in the presumed interest of the customer,' is to be borne by the customer.

Other provisions deal with security for the bank's claim against the customer and the bank's lien (paras. 13–17) and termination rights (paras. 18–19). In the absence of a specific agreement, and otherwise, for a reasonable cause, the customer's right of termination may be exercised 'without notice'. Conversely, and other than for 'reasonable cause', in exercising its termination right, the bank must observe 'an adequate notice period', which in connection with current accounts, is no shorter than one month. Finally, paragraph 20 governs deposit protection.

[30]   In Japan, the Federation of Bankers' Association has adopted model rules governing current accounts.[136] These rules provide for items for deposit, receipt of instruments for deposit, remittance by depositor, deposits by a third party, and dishonour of received instruments (arts. 1–5). They further deal with procedure for face-value recognition, pay-

---

[135] However, strictly speaking, under para. 12(4), '[i]nterest adjustments and changes in charges' are stated by reference to para. 12(3), which is limited to 'variable interest loans'.

[136] In fact, two parallel sets exist, the one entitled 'Current Account Regulations' and the other 'Current Account Regulations (For Use for a Personal Account)'. There is a third relevant document, entitled 'Agreement on Overdraft in Current Account'. Overdrafts are further governed by a fourth document, entitled 'Agreement on Bank Transactions'. For all four documents, there is an unofficial English translation. The ensuing discussion evolves around the first document, to which the second closely corresponds. For the Current Account Regulations see Kitagawa, above, n. 3 at §4.02[2][c].

ment of cheques, cheque forms, payment limits, inadequate funds and excessive drawing, debits for bank charges, and the issue of Manager's Cheques, a specie of the Bank Draft replacing cheque certification which is not practised in Japan[137] (arts. 6–13). The rules go on to provide for the filing with the Bank of the depositor's seal impression or signature specimen, as well as of required notices on matters such as lost instruments or blank forms (arts. 14–15). The depositor undertakes to be bound by payment of any instrument, whether forged, altered, or misused, for which the bank has verified the signature 'in good faith' and with 'reasonable care'. The depositor further undertakes to draw instruments with care so as not to facilitate any alteration (arts. 16–17). Also, the rules govern the bank's responsibilities for crossed cheques. They further exonerate the bank from any responsibility as to an internal approval for the authorization of a duly signed instrument, and deal with the bank's obligations to pay interest and provide information on balances (arts. 18–21). The depositor is precluded from transferring or pledging the deposit (art. 21).

The right to terminate the account agreement is accorded to each party at that party's discretion. The notice of termination by the depositor must be in writing. Upon termination, the bank is not responsible for items 'which may have been drawn or accepted prior to the termination'. The depositor is required to return all blank forms and 'settle the Current Account'. With respect to a personal account, the bank may terminate the account agreement unilaterally only on enumerated grounds, which include a long period of inactivity in the account, repeated delay by the depositor in making deposits necessary for outgoing payments, suspension of payment of the depositor, 'or other cause which has resulted in loss of mutual trust' (arts. 23–4).

Clearing house rules are stated to be binding on the customer 'in addition' to these rules (art. 24). Finally, a provision exists as to adverse information which may be recorded at the Credit Information Centre (art. 26).

(VI) CONCLUSION

The account agreement is the foundation of the bank and customer rela- **[31]** tionship. Within the framework of this agreement banks provide collection and payment services to their customers. To a large extent, the account agreement is governed in each jurisdiction by general contract law, as may have been adapted to cover standard form contracts. A common issue for most jurisdiction evolves around the fairness of the account agreement, particularly in light of the typical unequal bargaining power

---

[137] For the latter point, see 3.B (vi) s. 10.

inherent in the contracting process leading to the conclusion of the agreement. Other common issues are the balance between implied and express terms and the role of legislation, or any other form of regulation, in determining the contents of the account agreement.

There are no substantial variances as to the role of courts as the ultimate arbiters for the validity of terms in an account agreement. At the same time, rules underlying the discretion of courts are not uniform. In some jurisdictions the principal ground for invalidating an objectionable term is a defect in the process leading to the conclusion of the contract, whether in the form of undue influence or inadequate disclosure. In other jurisdictions, terms may be invalidated on the basis of unfairness *per se*. Also, among the various jurisdictions, there are different levels of involvement by government, bank organizations, and customer groups in the drafting of, or providing for governing underlying principles for, standard form banking agreements, including the one pertaining to the bank account.

In each jurisdiction, and in the context of its own contract law, cohesive principles govern the account agreement. Yet, and notwithstanding the possible unitary nature of the banking and even the account agreement, reciprocal duties and rights between a bank and its customer are determined, to a large extent, by reference to the particular act in question. It is to that end that the banking contract or relationship is broken down to its principal components, namely, the deposit of funds, the provision of payment services, and the monetary relationship. Each of the ensuing three sections of this book deals with one of these components.

B. The Deposit of Funds

From an economic point of view, the bank deposit is the customer's enti- **[1]**
tlement from his bank in the sum of outstanding credit to the customer's
account. From a legal perspective, the bank deposit is constituted by the
delivery or remittance by or for a customer to a bank of a sum of money,
against the bank's obligation to return this sum upon demand or according to specified terms agreed upon.[1] A deposit not payable on demand
may be payable by the bank either at the expiry of a specified period or
upon advance notice at an agreed time. The bank's repayment obligation
may be either with or without interest, either as agreed, or as regulated by
law.

The bank deposit may be created by either the physical delivery of
money in specie to the bank or the receipt or collection by the bank of
incoming cashless payments. It can be made either by the customer himself or a third party. It is usually made for the purpose of safekeeping. The
ensuing discussion on the juridical nature of the bank deposit will focus
on the physical deposit of money in specie by one person ('depositor') to
another ('depositary').

Modern banking practice universally permits the bank an unrestricted **[2]**
right to mix and use deposited money, while fastening on it a debt obligation towards the customer, by whom or to whose benefit the deposit
was made. There may not however be a similar consensus on, or even
understanding of, the entire legal subtlety underlying the money deposit
transaction and its juridical nature accommodating the current understanding of this modern banking practice. The ensuing discussion
responds to this gap and purports to highlight the evolution of legal doctrine governing this transaction.

The deposit of money for safekeeping, made by a depositor to a depositary, gives rise to two issues as to the effect of the deposit transaction. The
first issue is whether the depositary has a right to mix the depositor's
money with that of other depositors, or even with the depositary's own
money. The second issue is whether the depositary has a right to use the
depositor's money. This must be taken to include the right to the use of
the value, namely, the right to use the money without the corresponding
obligation to promptly replace the amount used or constantly replenish

---

[1] See in general e.g. J. L. Rives-Lange and M. Contamine-Raynaud, *Droit bancaire*, 6th edn.
(Paris: Dalloz, 1995) at 267–8 ¶282. While this text concerns France, it is generally true for
all other jurisdictions.

the deposit. The existence of an obligation to replace or replenish, or keep an actual reserve in the amount of the deposit, effectively means a bare right to mix only, without any effective right to use the economic value of the deposit.

The juridical nature of the depositary's obligation to return the money to the depositor depends on the determination of these two issues. In this context, several questions arise. The first question is whether the depositary is obligated to return the funds in specie or an equivalent amount. Obviously, the mixture of the money will preclude restitution in specie. The second question is to whose benefit accrues the use of the money; that is, must the depositary account to the depositor for any profits made with the money? The third question arises where the use of the money is for the benefit of the depositary. In such a case, the question is whether the depositary owes interest, namely a fixed return, for money delivered to him for deposit. Fourth and last, a question arises as to the depositary's defences against the depositor, particularly in connection with loss of the money.

[3]   The present discussion examines the juridical nature of the bank deposit in historical as well as doctrinal contexts. The historical evolution of doctrine applicable to the deposit of funds will be considered in Roman, Jewish, civil and common law so as to shed light on the response to the issues and questions raised above. On this basis, conclusions as to the juridical nature of the bank deposit under modern legal systems will be drawn.

(II) ROMAN LAW

[4]   In Roman law, the legal ramifications of the deposit of money transaction are extensively discussed in the broader context of the law of obligations arising from contracts.[2] In general, Roman law distinguishes among Real, Verbal, Litteral, and Consensual contracts. In a real contract, obligations arise from the delivery of a thing (*res*). In a verbal contract, it is the form of the words which give rise to an obligation. A litteral contract creates obligations only on a basis of a special kind of writing. Finally, in a consensual contract, obligations arise on the basis of the mere agreement.

Regardless, each contract is either (i) unilateral or bilateral, (ii) *stricti juris* or bona fide, and (iii) formal or informal. A unilateral contract is one in which the duty to perform is only on one party. Conversely, in a bilateral (or 'synallagmatic') contract there are reciprocal obligations. Such a contract may be either perfectly or imperfectly bilateral. In the former

---

[2] In general on obligations arising from contract under Roman law, see R. W. Lee, *The Elements of Roman Law*, 4th edn. (London: Sweet & Maxwell, 1956) at 285–9.

case, each side is under a duty from the moment the contract has been concluded. In the latter case, one party's obligation is only contingent upon the occurrence of some circumstance.

A *stricti juris* contract binds the promisor to the very thing he has promised, neither less nor more. Conversely, good faith is a factor in the enforcement of a bona fide contract. All unilateral contracts are *stricti juris* while all bilateral contracts are *bonae fidei*. Effectively, this allows a broader range of defences, not raised in the pleadings, to be introduced in *bonae fidei* contracts.

Finally, contracts are formal or informal. A contract is formal when its validity depends on its form; it is the form which makes the contract. At the same time, an informal contract derives its effectiveness exclusively from the intention of the parties. Being self-contained, namely, confined to the contours of the formula and not to any outside event, a formal contract may be referred to as abstract.

In Roman law, the irregular deposit (or the *depositum irregulare*) is **[5]** defined as a deposit of an object, subject to a condition of restitution in genre, namely in equivalent amount, and not in specie. It entails the transfer of ownership in the object of the transaction to the depositary, and not merely of physical control or right of detention.[3] In terms of its classification, it is an informal real contract, giving rise to the depositary's obligation upon the delivery of the object.[4] Yet, the precise nature of this obligation, and the other legal features of the transaction, require further analysis.

In fact, the irregular deposit combines elements derived from three types of real contracts.[5] All such real contracts are informal. They are the loan for the consumption (or *mutuum*), loan for use (or *commodatum*), and deposit (or *depositum*).[6]

The *mutuum* is a loan for consumption of money or any other *res* **[6]** *fungibiles*, namely, interchangeable things that are weighed, numbered, or measured. Delivery vests title and right to use on the recipient (the

---

[3] In Roman law, the depositary's 'detention' is consistent with the depositor's continuous 'possession', as long as it purports to be on the depositor's behalf and not in challenge to the depositor's right. See in general, Lee ibid. at 179.

[4] In general for the irregular deposit see Lee, above, n. 2 at 295 and R. Zimmermann, *The Law of Obligations—Roman Foundations of the Civilian Tradition* (Cape Town: Juta, 1990) at 215–19.

[5] In South Africa, this is the conclusion of D. V. Cowen and L. Gering, *Cowen on the Law of Negotiable Instruments in South Africa*, 4th edn. (Cape Town: Juta, 1966) at 368, where earlier (at 367) the irregular deposit is described as an 'anomalous category'.

[6] In general for the real contracts in Roman law see Lee, above, n. 2 at 290–7; B. Nicholas, *An Introduction to Roman Law* (Oxford: Clarendon Press, 1962) at 167–71; and in more detail, Zimmermann, above, n. 4 at 153–229. A fourth category of real contracts is the pledge (or *pignus*), under which a corporeal thing is handed over by one person to another as security for a debt.

'borrower') who becomes liable to return to the transferor (the 'lender') an equal amount of same quality objects at the agreed-upon time or upon demand. It is a unilateral *stricti juris* contract fastening on the borrower an absolute duty. Liability to pay interest on money lent requires, however, an incidental verbal formal contract, in the form of a stipulation (*stipulatio usuranum*).[7]

Unlike the *mutuum*, both the *commodatum* and *depositum* are *bonae fidei* and imperfectly bilateral contracts, conferring on the transferee merely detention and not ownership in the object delivered to him, and an obligation to return the object in specie. The *commodatum* is a gratuitous loan for use of an object, usually a chattel.[8] It might relate to fungible things, as long as the obligation to return is in specie. The borrower is bound to exercise the highest degree of diligence, and is thus liable even for slight negligence (*culpa levis in abstracto*). He is however not absolutely liable, and is released when loss has been caused by *force majeure*. On his part, the lender is required to allow the borrower to use the thing as agreed, to indemnify him for extraordinary expenses, and to indemnify him for damage caused by the thing lent owing to some defect of which the lender was aware.

Finally, the deposit is a contract under which one person, the depositor, gives to another, the depositary, a thing to be kept for him gratuitously and returned on demand. The depositary is not entitled to use the thing and is liable in its safekeeping for *dolus*, namely intentional wrongful act or bad faith, but not *culpa*, that is fault or negligence. He is also liable for *culpa lata*, or gross negligence, 'scarcely to be distinguished from dolus'.[9] In turn, the depositor is required to compensate the depositary for expenses as well as to indemnify him for all damage attributed to the depositor's *dolus* or *culpa*.

[7]   Technically, the irregular deposit is a subcategory of deposit. Accordingly, the depositor in the irregular deposit could recover from the depositary under the same action available to a depositor who seeks recovery in specie under a regular deposit. Yet, fundamental differences exist which make the features of the irregular deposit closer to those of the *commodatum* or *mutuum*. Unlike the ordinary deposit, but like the *commodatum* and the *mutuum*, the irregular deposit allowed the depositary to use the thing. Furthermore, as in *mutuum*, ownership of the thing passed to the depositary whose liability has been fastened in terms of the return of an equivalent amount of the thing.

---

[7] On the stipulation as a formal, verbal, unilateral and *stricti juris* contract, consisting essentially of a formal question and answer, see Lee, above, n. 2 at 298–304.

[8] Where the loan of the chattel is for remuneration rather than gratuitous, the contract is for hire (or *locatio conductio*), which is classified as a consensual rather than real contract. See e.g. Lee, above, n. 2 at 320.   [9] Lee, above, n. 2 at 294.

At the same time, unlike the *commodatum*, the irregular deposit conferred title on the transferee and required restitution in genre rather than in specie. Also, two fundamental distinctions existed between the *mutuum* and the irregular deposit. First, the economic rationale of each transaction is different. Unlike the *mutuum*, the irregular deposit 'was a deposit made with a capitalist not a loan made by a capitalist'.[10] Its principal objective was the safekeeping of money, rather than the economic gain from lending. Second, there are a few legal distinctions. Historically, particularly noted was the ability of the depositor to recover interest on the basis of a bare agreement, made at the time of the deposit, without the need to invoke to that end a formal stipulation.[11] Presumably, the latter difference stems from the bilateral and bona fide nature of the deposit that bypassed the necessity of a formal obligation without which nothing could be added to a unilateral *stricti juris* contract such as the *mutuum*.[12]

It is thus not surprising that the exact juridical nature of the irregular **[8]** deposit in Roman law has been a subject of a major scholarly controversy.[13] Even the process of its introduction from the Hellenistic East[14] and its recognition as a distinct concept are not entirely clear. In the final analysis, however, a learned discussion supports the existence of the irregular deposit as a subcategory of the deposit already before the codification by Justinian.[15] Accordingly, a distinction is made between the deposit of money in a sealed bag and the 'open deposit', namely the deposit of money not sealed in a bag. In the former case we have an ordinary deposit, giving rise to an obligation to return the sealed bag in specie. In the latter case we have the irregular deposit.

There is some controversy as to the precise point in which the deposi- **[9]** tary in an irregular deposit assumes the obligation of a borrower. Some suggest the time the use of the money has begun. Others regard the mere

[10] Lee, above, n. 2 at 295.

[11] For the general validity of the *pacta adjecta*, namely, a simple agreement or pact annexed to some principal contract, intended to form part of it and to modify it, see Lee, above, n. 2 at 343. For the inapplicability of this rule to a 'bare pact' attached to a *mutuum*, see text at the footnote which follows. A 'pact' or 'bare pact' is an agreement which does not conform to any recognized category, and which in the absence of any recognized exception (such as the *pacta adjecta*), does not give ground to an action. Ibid. at 342.

[12] For this explanation, see Zimmermann, above, n. 4 at 217 and 218.

[13] For a comprehensive overview see e.g. W. Litewski, 'Le Dépôt irrégulier', Part I (1974), 21 RIDA 215, and Part II (1975), 22 RIDA 279. See also W. M. Gordon, 'Observations on "Depositum Irregulare" ' in *Studi in Onore di Arnaldo Biscardi*, vol iii (Milano: Instituto Editoriale Cisalpino–La Goliardica, 1982) at 363. Litewski opens his study stating that 'the irregular deposit constitutes one of the most controversial institutions in the science of Roman law'. Part I at 215 (my translation).

[14] See e.g. R. Vigneron, 'Résistance du droit romain aux influences hellénistique: le cas du dépôt irrégulier' (1984), 31 RIDA 307.

[15] See summary of Litewski, above, n. 13 Part II at 312.

delivery by the depositor as the turning point.[16] It seems though, that transfer of ownership, giving full authority to the depositary to use the money, occurs at the time of the 'open deposit', without any need to invoke specific authorization.[17] Conversely, for a deposit of money in a sealed bag to turn into an irregular deposit, a specific authorization must be given by the depositor to the depositary, upon which ownership in the money, together with the right to use it, passes to the depositary.

In any event, so far as the allocation of risk is concerned, it seems to be accepted that as the owner of the money, the depositary under an irregular deposit 'would naturally carry the risk of the money getting lost'.[18] In other words, he is under an absolute obligation to repay the amount of the deposit. Accordingly, 'in modern law there is no practical difference' between the views treating the depositary's liability under the irregular deposit either as a subcategory of deposit or as a species of *mutuum*.[19]

[10]   Pothier, an eighteenth-century French jurist, concluded[20] that from a strictly legal point of view, other than for the different motive or economic rationale underlying each transaction, the only remaining difference between the *mutuum* and the irregular deposit is the inability of a lender, in contrast to that of the depositor in an irregular deposit, to demand the money back immediately after delivering the money. He recognized that both the irregular deposit and the money loan passed on the right to use the money together with the inherent risk of its loss. He however was of the view that in the irregular deposit, both the depositary's right to use the money, as well as the resulting transfer to him of the entire risk of loss or theft, are by-products of the fungibility of the money; that is, they both stem from the readiness of the depositor to be satisfied by the return in genre rather than in specie, and not from the basis of the transaction as in the money loan. He thus recognized the existence of both common and distinguishing elements between the irregular deposit and the money loan. Nevertheless, his overall conclusion was that other than in theory, the depositary's liability in the irregular deposit is subject, in principle, to the same rules governing the money-borrower's liability.

[11]   In hindsight, the choice made in Roman law to regard the obligation of the depositary under an irregular deposit who has been authorized to use the deposited money to his own benefit, at least effectively, as that of a

---

[16] For the diverse views on this point, see Litewsky, above, n. 13 Part I at 218 and Part II at 280–1.

[17] Cf. e.g. in South Africa, *Ex parte Smith*, 1940 OPD 120, 126–7, *per* De Beer J., in effect rejecting 'the subtle distinction' between implicit and explicit authorization to use the money given to the depositary.   [18] Zimmermann, above, n. 4 at 216.

[19] Ibid at 219 n. 231.

[20] R.J. Pothier, 'Traité du contrat du dépôt', in M. Bugnet (ed.), *Œuvres de Pothier*, 2nd edn., vol. v (Paris: Henri Plon, Cosse et Marchal, 1861) at ¶¶ 82–3.

borrower on a loan, looks superficially convincing. It is however submitted that there is a subtle flaw in Pothier's reasoning leading to this conclusion. Fungibility of money, and hence the depositor's readiness to be satisfied with restitution in genre, rather than in specie, explains the depositary's right to mix the deposited money instead of keeping it separate. It does not necessarily explain the depositary's right to use the money. Presumably, a depositor of money for safekeeping will be prepared to concede to the depositary the right to use the money only where the depositor is satisfied that there is no risk of the depositary's insolvency. Otherwise, the deposit is not for safekeeping; rather, its effect is to substitute one risk (depositary's insolvency) for another (theft or physical loss). A depositor for safekeeping, who is content with restitution in genre, and hence with the mixture of the deposited money, may nevertheless insist on the physical safekeeping of the money, whether in the form of an equivalent amount to be physically set aside, or in the form keeping in specie all money deposited by diverse depositors.

One may speculate that the use of the irregular deposit also as a deposit of money with a friend rather than necessarily with a financial intermediary[21] facilitated the view that no insolvency risk was contemplated. Accordingly, the depositor, having been indifferent to the identity of the actual coins to be returned to him and not being concerned with the depositary's solvency, was taken to be prepared to allow the depositary the unrestricted use of the deposited money. Yet, paradoxically, it is precisely this legal conclusion as to the effect of the irregular deposit which facilitated its application as the basis for the legal regime underlying the deposit of money with a bank as a financial intermediary.

(III) JEWISH LAW

Logically, notwithstanding the irregular deposit in Roman law, the **[12]** depositary's right to use deposited money should not be regarded as inseparable from the right to mix it. As the preceding discussion demonstrates, the right to mix need not necessarily be taken to produce the right to use. Arguably, to a similar end, though in the opposite direction, developments in Jewish law demonstrate that a depositary of money may have the right to use the deposited money without the right to mix it, so that the depositary remains a custodian, as in an ordinary deposit, at least

---

[21] For the fact that in Rome the irregular deposit was not exclusively linked to the bank deposit, see Gordon, above, n. 13 at 364. See also Pothier, ibid. at para. 82, referring to the irregular deposit as made by the depositor with 'one of his friends'.

until he commences to use the money. Stated otherwise, the right to use may exist separately from, and in the absence of, the right to mix.

Indeed, as in Roman law texts, the Babylonian Talmud[22] distinguishes[23] between the deposit of money in an open bag, and the deposit of money in a sealed bag.[24] However, in a first departure from Roman law, the distinction is effective only where the depositary is a money changer.[25] A person other than a money changer[26] is not allowed to use the money, irrespective of whether it was deposited in a sealed or open bag. Conversely, the money changer is allowed to use money deposited in an open bag but not money deposited in a sealed bag. Regardless, the money changer, as any other person to whom money has been deposited, is treated as a custodian of the money.[27] However, depending on the right to

---

[22] The Talmud is the summary of the oral law that evolved after centuries of post-biblical scholarly effort by sages who lived in Eretz-Yisrael (Palestine) and Babylonia. It has two complementary components; the Mishnah, a book of law and the commentary known as Gemara. In principle, each Mishnaic law is followed by the corresponding Gemara commentary, so that both form the Talmudic text on the given point. There are two versions for the Gemara, between which the one completed in Babylonia in the fifth century is the foundation of Jewish law. For an introduction, see e.g. A. Steinsaltz, *The Talmud—The Steinsaltz Edition—A Reference Guide* (New York: Random House, 1989). Other than indicated otherwise, the ensuing discussion is on the basis of the Hebrew-Aramaic original text.

[23] The principal text, on which the ensuing discussion draws, is Baba Metzia, ch. 3, at 43:a. A Hebrew-English edition of the tract containing this text (by I. Epstein, ed.) was published in New York by MP Press in 1983.

[24] More specifically, the Mishnaic text speaks of bound-up coins, namely, of money in a bound-up bag. It is however explained in the accompanying Gemara text that the money, that is, the bag, must be bound up and sealed. It is then questioned, but not determined in that Gemara, whether money in a bound-up bag with an unusual knot is to be treated as money in a bound-up and sealed bag. For the distinction between the Mishnah and Gemara, as the two complementary components of the Talmud, see n. 22 above. For an early post-biblical (from a Jewish point of view) but pre-Mishnaic account, probably involving the deposit and return, against a document issued to the depositor, of money sealed in bags, see the Book of Tobith (or Tuvia), 1:14, 4:1, 4:20, 5:1-3, 9: 1-4. This book, apparently written in the fourth century, BCE, belongs to the *Apocrypha*, namely, books included in the Septuagint and Vulgate but excluded from the Jewish and Protestant cannons of the Old Testament. (Translation to Hebrew by A.S. Hartom, (Tel Aviv: Yavneh, 1969).)

[25] A comprehensive exposition of the money changer's business is by A. Gulak, 'The Money Changer's Business According to Talmudic Law' (1931), 2 Tarbitz 154 [in Hebrew]. His primary business was money changing from one metal and denomination to another metal and denomination. The more precious was the metal the higher was the denomination, and during this pre-deposit banking and pre-paper money era, people needed low-denomination coins for everyday transactions and high-denomination coins for saving or large value transactions. The money changer charged fees for his exchange services.

[26] It is further disputed, and not settled, in the text cited in n. 24 above, whether, in this context, a shopkeeper is in the same position of a money changer.

[27] Talmudic law has three categories of custodians with a varied degree of responsibility for loss or theft. Briefly stated, an unpaid custodian is liable only where he was grossly negligent, a paid custodian is responsible unless loss occurred in circumstances beyond his control (namely, by *force majeure*), and a borrower of a chattel for use who is not obliged to pay for the use is responsible also for loss caused by *force majeure*. For these categories and a succinct summary of each one's responsibility see the compilation of Halakhic Concepts in Steinsaltz, above, n. 22 at 262–3.

use the money, the degree of the custodian's responsibility varies. A custodian who is not allowed to use the money, namely, any depositary of a sealed bag and a non-money changer to whom money in an open bag has been deposited, is regarded as an unpaid custodian[28] who is not responsible for loss and theft, unless he is grossly negligent. Where the custodian is allowed to use the money, namely, where he is a money changer to whom money was deposited in an open bag, his responsibility increases, but there is controversy as to its exact scope.

According to one view, a custodian who has permission to use the money, namely a money changer to whom money was deposited in an open bag, is to be treated as a paid custodian.[29] As such, he is responsible for loss or theft, other than when caused by *force majeure*. A more stringent view regards him as a borrower of a chattel for use who is not obliged to pay for its use,[30] and who, in the case of loss or theft, may not plead *force majeure* as a defence to his liability. This controversy exists only as long as the money changer has not actually used the money. It is agreed that once the money has been used, the money changer falls into this latter category of a borrower of a specific chattel who is not obliged to pay for its use[31] and who is also responsible for losses caused by *force majeure*. It was left for a post-Talmudic authority[32] to draw what seems to be an inevitable

[28] However, the text does not clarify why a money changer will undertake the custody of money without receiving any remuneration for it.

[29] The money changer's remuneration is in the form of his ability to use the money in his money-changing business. The text (above, n. 24) further suggests that he may use the money for an opportune profit-making transaction. But according to one modern view, the text refers, rather, to the depositor's ability to make profitable use of the deposited money, as long as it has not been in actual use by the depositary. According to this view, the depositary is to be regarded as a paid custodian due to the common enjoyment shared between him and the depositor prior to the actual use of the money by the depositary. See Y.M. Margaliot, (1942), 16 Hapardes 2: 23–4 and 4: 34–6 [in Hebrew].

[30] The depositary uses the money without being obliged to pay for its use since under Jewish law, no interest may be charged. See n. 36 below. Nonetheless, it is less obvious why the safekeeping of the money is not a remuneration to the depositor. According to one modern view, this is so since as in the case with any borrower of a specific chattel for use who is not obligated to pay for the use, the entire use enjoyment, from which liability stems, is in the depositary's hands. See Margaliot, ibid.

[31] Indeed, while the money is in actual use, there is no question that the entire use enjoyment is that of the depositary, so as to render him a borrower of a specific chattel for use who is not obligated to pay for its use.

[32] Maimonides, *Mishné Tora*, vol. vi, Book 13: Laws, Laws of Borrowing and Deposit, ch. 7, rule 7 [in Hebrew]. Further controversies, referred to above, are determined in this text as follows: (i) a shopkeeper is allowed to use money deposited with him on an equal footing with the money changer; (ii) the use of the money is forbidden (to both the money changer and the shopkeeper) when the money is either bound up and sealed or bound up in an unusual knot; and (iii) up to permissible actual use, the money changer (as well as the shopkeeper) is a paid custodian (rather than a borrower of a specific chattel who is not obliged to pay for its use) who is thus not responsible for losses caused in circumstances which are beyond his control (namely, by *force majeure*). Ibid. rules 6–7. In rule 8 Maimonides determines that to avoid liability for gross negligence, an unpaid custodian, other than a money

conclusion that once the money has been used, the money changer becomes absolutely liable for the return of the sum so used as a borrower under a money loan.[33]

[13]   Treating a depositary who is allowed to use the money as a custodian appears to constitute a fundamental difference between Jewish and Roman law. It seems to me, however, that at the root of the matter is not so much an alternative jurisprudential outlook, but rather a different interpretation as to the effect of the money deposit transaction. It appears that Roman law supposes that what is conferred on the depositary is not only the right to use the money, but also the right to mix it. Conversely, arguably, the Talmud does not allow any mixture, so that even the right to use does not undermine the basic depositary's obligation with respect to the specific coins deposited. Stated otherwise, as long as it has not been used, each depositor's money remains separate and thus identified. Also, possibly, during the time money is actually lawfully used by the depositary, namely before the use bears fruit, a duty to return may nevertheless be fastened on the depositary in Roman law but not under the Talmud.[34] Yet, under both systems, once the money has been used, the depositary's duty to return cannot be in specie and is accordingly in genre.

Also, under both systems, the depositary's use is to his own benefit. This is so irrespective of whether the depositary is regarded as a borrower under a money loan or a borrower of a specific chattel without an obligation to pay for its use. Accordingly, there is no duty on the part of the depositary to account for profits. Nor can the depositary raise defences based on the loss of the money through a bad investment. In both systems, a borrower under a money loan is under an absolute obligation to repay. Similarly, in Jewish law, a borrower of a chattel for use who is not obliged to pay for its use is not released for losses caused in circumstances which are beyond his control, namely, by *force majeure*, not to mention those created by his own negligence. His obligation is thus virtually absolute.[35] On his part, in both systems, a borrower of money is absolutely

---

changer or shopkeeper, must bury the money in the ground. Maimonides lived in various Mediterranean countries during the twelfth century.

[33] Nevertheless, while under the Talmud *force majeure* is a defence which is unavailable to both a borrower under a money loan and a borrower of a chattel for use who is not obligated to pay for its use, there are still subtle differences, providing for tenuous qualifications, at least in theory, on the absolute nature of the liability of each type of borrower. For example, a borrower of a chattel for use is not responsible if the article is destroyed during normal use by the borrower. Arguably, however, this will not apply to the loss of money through a bad investment. Conversely under Jewish law, technically, a money loan may be released in a seven-year cycle of abandonment of debts.

[34] As to Jewish law, see Margaliot, above, n. 29.

[35] For subtle qualifications in Jewish law on the absolute nature of the liability of a borrower under a money loan as well as of a borrower of a specific chattel who is not obliged to pay for its use see n. 33 above.

liable to return the principal. In turn, liability for interest is determined differently by each system. We already saw that in Roman law interest has to be specifically agreed upon; yet, historically, the adequacy of a bare pact rather than a stipulation, to form such an agreement, actually depended on the classification of the irregular deposit as a subcategory of the deposit rather than a simple loan. At the same time, Jewish law prohibits to charge interest,[36] so that in this context, no particular issue arises with respect to the deposit of money.

(IV) CIVIL LAW JURISDICTIONS

Generally speaking, Civil law jurisdictions[37] regard the bank deposit as an **[14]** irregular deposit. They thus inherited the ambiguity originated from Roman law and vary as to the categorization of the transaction, particularly as to whether it is a subcategory of a deposit or a money loan. Occasionally, however, particularly in jurisdictions where the irregular deposit is not provided for by statute, proponents of the loan classification reject altogether even the position that the bank deposit is an irregular deposit.[38] Several principal models should be noted:

1. In Switzerland, the irregular deposit is dealt with in CO art. 481, located among the provisions governing the deposit (CO arts. 472–91). Under CO art. 481, a depositary who agrees, whether expressly or by implication, to return a sum of money and not money in specie, becomes entitled to any profit and bears all risks. That is, he becomes strictly liable to pay the agreed sum. Such an agreement is presumed to exist whenever money is given in an open unsealed bag. No application of the provisions governing money loans is specifically mentioned. It is however disputed in doctrine whether the bank deposit should not be classified as a loan for

---

[36] Prohibition is based on three biblical cites and exists for any transaction where a party is obligated to deliver or pay in genre. These biblical verses are Exodus 22: 24, Leviticus 25: 36–7, and Deuteronomy 23: 20.

[37] In the ensuing discussion, quotes of statutory provisions in English are from *The French Civil Code Revised Edition* (as am. to 1 July 1994), trans. J. H. Crabb (Littleton, Colo.: Fred B. Rothman & Co., 1995); *The German Civil Code* (as am. to 1 Jan. 1975) trans. I. S. Forrester, S. L. Goren, and H. M. Ilgen (South Hackensack, NJ: Fred B. Rothman & Co., 1975) (with 1981 Supp. trans. S. L. Goren); *The Civil Code of Japan* (translation) (Tokyo: Ministry of Justice, 1972); *The Italian Civil Code*, trans. M. Beltramo, G. E. Longo, and J. H. Merryman (Dobbs Ferry, NY: Oceana, 1969); and the bilingual edition of the Quebec Civil Code, *Code civil du practicien* (Montreal: DACFO, 1995). *Swiss Contract Law, English Translation of Selected Official Texts—Swiss Code of Obligations* (Zurich: Swiss-American Chamber of Commerce, 1997) does not contain the deposit provisions.

[38] A strong proponent of this view is G. V. V. Nicholls, 'The Legal Nature of Bank Deposits in the Province of Quebec' (Part I) (1935), 13 Can. Bar Rev. 634, at 644–54.

consumption (governed in Switzerland by CO arts. 312–18).[39] It should be noted that under CO art. 481, with respect to fungibles other than money, an authorization as to the depositary's right of disposition (that is, the right to use) must expressly be given. Moreover, under CO art. 484, unless specifically authorized, a warehouseman is not allowed even to mix fungible things given to his custody. Whenever a mixture occurs, each depositor has a proportional proprietary right in the entire mixture. It appears that the depositary of money has both the right to mix and to use and that therefore he incurs all risks. This is in line with the consensus underlying the irregular deposit in civil law; yet, the attention given to the distinction between the right to mix and to use, though with respect to chattels other than money, is noteworthy.

2. In both Germany and Japan the irregular deposit is dealt with, as in Switzerland, in the context of the general deposit provisions. However, in both civil codes, the irregular deposit is explicitly classified as a loan for consumption. In Germany, under BGB §700, '[i]f fungibles are deposited in such manner that the ownership is to pass to the depositary, and he is to be bound to return things of the same kind, quality and quantity, the provisions relating to loan for consumption apply. . . .' Furthermore, '[i]f the depositor permits the depositary to consume deposited fungibles, the provisions relating to loan for consumption apply as from the time the depositary takes over the thing.' Yet, classification as a loan for consumption is not for all intents and purposes: in case of doubt, 'the time and place of return is determined . . . according to the provisions relating to the contract of deposit.' Similarly in Japan, under art. 666 of the civil code, the provisions relating to loans for consumption 'shall apply with necessary modifications' to the case where the depositary is allowed to consume the deposited thing. However, 'if no time for . . . return has been fixed by the contract', the depositor 'may at any time' demand the return of the deposited thing. In Germany loans for consumption are governed by BGB §§607–10. In Japan loans for consumption are governed by arts. 587 –92 of the civil code.

3. In both France and Quebec, the civil code does not contain any specific provisions governing the irregular deposit.[40] In France, it is disputed whether the transaction is governed by the deposit provisions

---

[39] See in general, D. Guggenheim, *Les Contrats de la pratique bancaire suisse*, 2nd edn. (Geneva: Georg, 1989) at 77–84.

[40] In France, art. 1932 requiring the depositary of 'minted sums' to return in specie is an example of an ordinary deposit, conferring on the depositary neither the right to mix nor to use. Hence, it is not an exception.

(arts. 1915–54), whether it is a simple loan for consumption (governed by arts. 1892–1914), or if it is a contract *sui generis*. There is however unanimity that the determination of this issue is of no practical importance.[41] The consensus is that the basic features of the transaction are well understood, and that anyway it does not fit completely into any of the statutorily recognized categories. For example, those who argue that the irregular deposit is a specie of deposit, concede that art. 1930, precluding a depositary from using the deposited chattel, does not apply to irregular deposit. The same is true with regard to art. 1943 providing for the place where the deposit was made as the default place of return. Similarly, the payability on demand, an inherent default feature of the irregular deposit, does not easily fit the repayment provisions applicable to a loan for consumption. This particularly applies to art. 1900 which accords discretion to the judge as to the maturity of a loan for which the agreement does not provide time for restitution. In Quebec, the view is that under the provision of the civil code, the bank deposit, effectively as an irregular deposit, is not a 'deposit' governed by arts. 2280–311. Rather, it is a 'simple loan', that is, a loan for consumption, defined in art. 2314 and governed by arts. 2327–32.[42]

4. In Italy, art. 1782 of the civil code, located in the deposit chapter, defines the irregular deposit as 'the deposit ... of an amount of money or other fungible things [under which] the depositary is authorized to make use of it'. Thereunder, the depositary 'acquires ownership thereof and is bound to return an equal number of things of the same kind and quality'. As in Germany and Japan, 'the rules applicable to loans', that is, arts. 1813–22 governing loans of money or other fungibles, 'are observed, insofar as applicable'. Yet, in departure from all other jurisdictions under discussion, Italy specifically regulates the bank deposit, albeit as a specie of an irregular deposit, as a banking contract.[43] Thus, under art. 1834, '[b]y the deposit (1782) in a bank of a sum of money the bank acquires ownership of it and is bound to repay it in the same kind of money at the extension of the

---

[41] See e.g. J. L. Rives-Lange and M. Cabrillac, 'Dépôt et compte en banque', *Encyclopedie Dalloz, Rep. dr. commercial* (1974, updated to 1992) at ¶¶9–10; Rives-Lange and Contamine-Raynaud, above, n. 1 at 267–71 ¶¶282–5; and G. Ripert and R. Roblot, *Traité de droit commercial*, 13th edn. (Paris: Librairie Général du Droit et de Jurisprudence, 1992) at 420–6.

[42] See in general, N. L'Heureux & E. Fortin, *Droit bancaire*, 3rd edn. (Cowansville, Que: Les Éditions Yvon Blais, 1999), at 41–4; and in detail, Nicholls, above, n. 38 & (Part II) (1935), 13 Can. Bar Rev. 720.

[43] Other banking contracts dealt with by the Italian civil code concern safe deposit boxes (arts. 1839–41), bank advances (arts. 1842–51), current accounts (arts. 1852–7) and bank discounts (arts. 1858–60). The provisions governing current accounts are discussed in 2.D below.

agreed term or on demand of the depositor, observing the period of advance notice established by the parties or by usage'. Art. 1834 further states that '[i]n the absence of contrary agreement, all deposits and withdrawals shall be made at the same office of the bank at which the relationship was established.'[44]

5. As in France and Quebec, Israel and South Africa have no specific provisions governing the irregular deposit. These two jurisdictions do not have all inclusive civil codes and are thus treated here separately. In Israel, the Custodians Law, 1967, governing the ordinary deposit, specifically applies only to the custody of an asset 'other than by ownership' (s. 1); this appears to exclude the irregular deposit, under which ownership and unrestricted right to use passes to the depositary.[45] According to case law, the depositor is to be regarded as a moneylender to the bank.[46] In South Africa, following English law further discussed below, the bank deposit is stated by case law to create between the bank and the customer a debtor and creditor relationship.[47]

(V) THE COMMON LAW

[15] The common law has not recognized the irregular deposit as a distinct concept. The classic statement on the nature of the bank deposit in the common law is from *Foley* v. *Hill*.[48] In that case, the House of Lords dealt with the characterization of the 'common position of a banker . . . receiving money from his customer on condition of paying it back

[44] The ensuing provisions dealing with bank deposits, namely, arts. 1835–8, cover passbooks, including those issued to the bearer or to a minor, and deposits of securities.

[45] It was pointed out that it is not mere ownership which excludes the application of the Law. Rather, the Law does not apply to an owner who is in possession solely on the basis of his ownership. Thus, an owner in possession for the benefit of another (such as where the owner temporarily holds property for a buyer or hirer under a contract requiring a subsequent delivery), though an owner, may nevertheless be a custodian under the Custodians Law. At the same time, under the bank deposit, the bank is not only the owner; it is allowed the use of the money, so as to hold it for its own benefit (subject to an obligation to return an equivalent sum, either with or without interest). The bank's possession is solely on the basis of its newly acquired ownership and, hence, it is not a custodian. See G. Tedeschi, 'On the Nature of the Bank Deposit' (1983), 22 Banking Quarterly 14, 19 [in Hebrew]. See also M. Cheshin, 'Custody and Custodians—On the Interpretation of Section 1 of the Custodians Law, 5927–1967' (1971), 3 Mishpatim 137, 157 [in Hebrew].

[46] A leading case is *Estate of Nathan Williams* v. *Israel British Bank*, SP 32/84 PD 44(2) 265, 272–3 (SC), *per* Barak J. For an overview and earlier authorities, see R. Ben-Oliel, *Banking Law: General Part* (Jerusalem: Sacher Institute, 1996) (hereafter: Ben-Oliel, *Banking Law*), at 149–50 [in Hebrew].

[47] See Cowen and Gering, above, n. 5 at 365–8. A leading case to that end is *Duba* v. *Ketsikile*, 1924 EDL 332, 341, *per* van der Riet J.   [48] (1848) 2 HLC 28; 9 E.R 1002 (HL).

when asked . . .'[49] In this context, Lord Cottenham held that 'the banker is not an agent or a factor, but he is a debtor'.[50] More specifically, the banker has the right to mix and use money deposited with him, subject to a repayment obligation of an equivalent sum, either with or without interest:

Money, when paid into a bank, ceases altogether to be the money of the principal; . . . it is then the money of the banker, who is bound to return an equivalent by paying a similar sum to that deposited with him when he is asked for it. The money paid into the banker's, is money known by the principal to be placed there for the purpose of being under the control of the banker. It is then the banker's money; he is known to deal with it as his own; he makes what profit of it he can, which profit he retains to himself, paying back only the principal, . . . or the principal and a small rate of interest.[51]

Stated otherwise,

The money placed in the custody of a banker is to all intents and purposes the money of the banker, to do with it as he pleases; he is guilty of no breach of trust in employing it; he is not answerable to the customer if he puts it into jeopardy, if he engages in a hazardous speculation; he is not bound to keep it or deal with it as the property of the principal, but he is, of course answerable for the amount, because he has contracted, having received that money, to repay to the principal, when demanded, a sum equivalent to that paid into his hands. . . .[52]

In his concurring judgment, Lord Brougham pointed out that 'even a banker who does not pay interest could not possibly carry on his trade if he were to hold the money, and to pay it back, as a mere depositary of the principal'. In his view, it thus follows, that a banker receives the deposit of money, 'to the knowledge of the customer, for the *express purpose* of using it as his own'.[53] The inevitable conclusion is then, that in his trade, a banker becomes a 'debtor of the person who has *lent* or deposited with him money to use as his own . . .'[54] While the relationship is characterized, in general, as of a debtor and creditor, it is thus strongly flavoured with specific allusions to a loan transaction.

The common law evolution that culminated in these conclusions will **[16]** now be examined. The earliest writs for the recovery of a specific sum of money as well as a specific chattel were modelled on the *praecipe* writs, namely the Writs of Right for the recovery of land. Around the close of the

---

[49] Ibid., at 43 (HLC), 1008 (ER), *per* Lord Brougham.

[50] Ibid., at 37 (HLC), 1006 (ER). The particular issue to be determined was whether the depositor (referred to in the excerpts from the judgment as 'principal') could bring a bill of equity against the banker in a Court of Equity, on the basis of a relationship other than that of a mere debtor and creditor. The bill was accordingly dismissed.

[51] Ibid., at 36 (HLC), 1005 (ER).   [52] Ibid., at 36–7 (HLC), 1005–6 (ER).

[53] Ibid., at 44 (HLC), 1008 (ER); emphasis added.

[54] Ibid., at 44 (HLC), 1008 (ER); emphasis added.

twelfth century, in Glanvill's time, they formed a composite writ originally encompassing Debt and Detinue. The ultimate split occurred
towards the end of the thirteenth century. Debt had come to provide for
the recovery of a specific sum of money, while Detinue had come to provide for the recovery of specific goods.[55]

Money enclosed in a chest, bag, or other receptacle so as not to be used
as current coin, was recoverable in Detinue. In such a case, the recoverable
object was not a sum of money, but the container enclosing the money.
Such a 'box under seal', rather than the sum of money, was conceived as
the specific chattel to be recovered in Detinue.[56]

The 'bailment of money' gave rise to some difficulties. In its simplest
sense, the term means delivery of money. Case law was concerned with
the failure of the purpose for which the money was delivered to the
bailee. Hence, as a legal concept, the bailment of money denotes the delivery of money for a particular, or in effect, any given purpose.[57] Where the
purpose was not carried out, being not obligated to keep the specific coins
separately, the bailee was not liable to the bailor for the money in Detinue.
At the same time, Debt was originally perceived to lie either on an Obligation, namely a sealed deed, or on a Contract, namely on a 'real transaction' like sale or loan, where the defendant-debtor had received a material
benefit, technically called *quid pro quo*.[58] Unlike in Roman law, where a
'real' contract resulted from the mere delivery of a *res*, such as money in
a loan or chattel in the deposit, a 'real transaction' in the common law further required the *res* to confer a tangible benefit on the recipient.

Account was also originally unpromising. To be accountable for prop-

---

[55] See in general, S. F. C. Milsom, *Historical Foundations of the Common Law*, 2nd edn.
(Toronto: Butterworths, 1981) at 262–5; C. H. S. Fifoot, *History and Sources of the Common
Law: Tort and Contract* (London: Stevens & Sons, 1949) at 25–8 and 217–18. See also T. F. T.
Plucknett, *A Concise History of the Common Law*, 5th edn. (London: Butterworths, 1956) at
363–5. Recovery of a specific amount of fungible (i.e. unascertained) goods fell under Debt.

[56] *Luffenham* v. *Abbot of Westminster* (1313), Y.B. Hil. 6 Ed. II (43 s.s.), 65. See Fifoot, Ibid. at
27–8. Accidental loss of 'money delivered in keeping under seal . . . which could not be
changed' is a defence in the bailee's hands. See *Anon.* (1339), Y.B. 12 & 13 Ed. III (R.S.), 245,
245–6.

[57] The term is used in numerous authorities. See e.g. the anonymous 1368 case cited
below in n. 60, *Core's Case* cited below in n. 71, *Doige's Case* cited below in n. 88, and the 1505
anonymous case cited below in n. 91. For a partial definition see R. M. Jackson, *The History
of Quasi-Contract in English Law* (Cambridge: Cambridge University Press; Toronto: Macmillan, 1936) at 24.

[58] See in general, Fifoot, ibid. above, n. 55 at 223, 225–6. But see *Anon.* (1294), Y.B. 21 & 22
Ed. I (R.S.), 598: on a seller's failure to convey land fully paid for by the buyer Metingham
CJ would allow the buyer to 'demand the money by writ of Debt', as an alternative to his
remedy to enforce the seller's Covenant. Ibid. at 600. For the discontinuation of such
' "equity" jurisdiction' by common law courts in the earlier part of the fourteenth century,
see Jackson, ibid. at 20, relied on by Fifoot, at ibid 222 n. 33.

erty committed to his charge, the defendant must have acted as plaintiff's guardian in socage, bailiff, or receiver.[59]

The breakthrough occurred in 1368. In a case decided that year,[60] the bailor was allowed to bring either Debt or Account against the bailee. In that case, 'the plaintiff bailed to the defendant £10 on condition that, if the defendant made him an assurance of certain land, the defendant should keep the £10, but that, if he did not make the assurance by a certain day, he should bail them back to the plaintiff'.[61] Claiming that the defendant had acted as his 'receiver' and that he had not made the assurance by that day, the plaintiff brought a writ of Account. Arguing for the defendant, Cavendish denied a receiver status, and thought that the proper Action should have been Debt.[62] Belknap, for the plaintiff, responded that '[w]e cannot have a writ of Debt, for there is no contract on which we can count . . .'.[63] Thorpe CJ conceded that the plaintiff might have brought Debt, but nevertheless allowed Account: 'Inasmuch as he may have an action of Debt or an action of Account, he may choose which of them to bring. Wherefore, albeit he may have a writ of Debt, this will not oust him from the action of Account.'[64]

The bailee's Account liability should be looked upon as part of the expansion of the receiver category, by which Account ultimately was transformed into a general quasi-contract remedy.[65] Nevertheless, Account was a cumbersome proceeding. In general, a judgment in Account established the defendant's accountability and provided for the appointment of auditors to work out its detail. To enforce the auditors' award, the plaintiff was then required to bring a separate and subsequent Debt action.[66] Where the amount in which a defendant was 'accountable' to the plaintiff was in a sum certain and did not require any calculation, as was the case in the bailment of money,[67] such lengthy proceedings served no useful purpose. Courts were hard pressed to avoid the

---

[59] See in general e.g. J. H. Baker, *An Introduction to English Legal History*, 3rd edn. (London: Butterworths, 1990) at 410.

[60] *Anon.* (1368), Y.B. Pasch. 41 Ed. III, f. 10, pl. 5, Fifoot, above, n. 55 at 285.

[61] Ibid.

[62] Ibid. Perhaps he had in mind the 1294 case cited in n. 11, above. It is more likely that he made this argument in order to oust plaintiff's case from court. Insofar as medieval procedure did not allow for alternative counts, the dismissal of Account would have forced the plaintiff to bring a fresh Debt action where he was required to start all objections, including as to the propriety of the writ.   [63] *Anon.* (1368) above, n. 60.

[64] Ibid.

[65] For this process, see in general e.g. Baker, above, n. 59 at 301–2, and in greater detail, S. J. Stoljar, 'The Transformations of Account', (1964) 80 L.Q.R. 203.

[66] See e.g. Fifoot, above, n. 55 at 273–4.

[67] According to Jackson, '[t]here is good reason to think that . . . the [bailor's] remedy was limited to the recovery of the sum paid to [the bailee]'. Above, n. 57 at 26. For yearbook authorities, see Baker, above, n. 59 at 303 n. 11.

duplication and redundancy, and permit the bailor to sue the bailee directly in Debt.[68] The fact that wager of law[69] could more easily be defeated in Account than in Debt[70] did not reverse this trend.

[17]   The disadvantages of Account may explain the pressure to introduce Debt to the bailment of money. Ultimately, a firm demarcation line was drawn. It corresponded to the line noted above, differentiating claims for a specific sum of money from claims for a specific chattel, and distinguished between two categories of cases involving the liability of one to whom money was delivered. The first category is typified by the mid-sixteenth-century judgment given in *Core's Case*,[71] where money was delivered to the bailee to purchase merchandise for the bailor. Upon the bailee's death prior to the purchase, the bailor sought to recover the money. In that and other cases of the first category, the bailee 'had liberty by the bailment to make an exchange' of the money delivered to him.[72] Consequently, liability was in terms of the sum of money, not the coins themselves, and hence in Debt or Account. This was true even where the money delivered to the bailee was 'sealed up in a bag', provided of course that the bailee was free to open the bag and use the money, and was liable to the bailor only in terms of its amount.[73]

Usually, however, delivery of money sealed up in a bag constituted the second category of cases. Money in a bag which the bailee was not free to use, or the bag itself, became the subject of a Detinue action 'to recover the thing it self.'[74] The Detinue category also covered cases involving 'money that may be known',[75] namely coins 'valued for their rareness or their aesthetic or archaeological interest'[76] and not used as current money. The second category thus encompassed cases where a bag of money or coins were treated as specific goods. Strictly speaking, only the first category where liability lay in terms of the sum of money and not in any specific chattel, involved the bailment of money. It was to be contrasted with the

---

[68] Baker, ibid. at 303.

[69] Under medieval law, a defendant could defend an action on an informal contract by waging his law, namely, by denying his liability on his oath, supported by the oaths of eleven compurgators or oath-helpers (rather than witnesses). See e.g. W. M. McGovern, 'Contract in Medieval England: Wager of Law and the Effect of Death' (1968), 54 Iowa L. Rev. 19.   [70] For this point, see Fifoot, above, n. 55 at 273.

[71] (1537), Dyer, 20a, 73 E.R. 42, Fifoot, above, n. 55 at 285.

[72] Ibid. at 22a (Dyer), 46 (E.R.), 287 (Fifoot).

[73] See e.g. *Anon.* (1573), 3 Leon 38, 74 E.R. 526 (money sealed in a bag given to the bailee to be used by him to purchase goods for the bailor).

[74] *Sir George Walgrace's Case* (1606), Noy 12, 74 E.R. 983.

[75] See e.g. *Bretton* v. *Barnet* (1599), Owen 86, 74 E.R. 918.

[76] For this definition of coins which are not treated as fungible chattels, see F. H. Lawson and B. Rudden, *The Law of Property*, 2nd edn. (Oxford: Clarendon Press; Toronto: Oxford University Press, 1982) at 25.

bailment of a bag of money or specific coins, falling under the second category.

Responsibility for the loss or theft of money varied and depended on whether liability was to return money lent (in Debt), to account for money delivered (in Account), or to return a specific chattel (in Detinue).[77] Responsibility in Debt was absolute, and was not excused by *force majeure* or even lack of negligence.[78] Whether the same applied to Account was not settled.[79] In Detinue, originally as in Debt, no defence was available to a defendant.[80] Subsequently, however, following the treatment of the liability under deposit in Roman law,[81] a custodian sued in Detinue could raise a defence based on his due diligence or lack of any fault.[82] However, in the course of the fifteenth century the defence disappeared and responsibility tightened. It became excused only where two cumulative conditions existed. Loss must have thus occurred, first, in circumstances beyond the custodian's control, and second, so that no cause of action or remedy over, even theoretical, arose against a wrongdoer.[83] Ultimately, as the seventeenth century closed, with Detinue having partly been superceded by Case, the custodian's responsibility relinked to due diligence or duty of care.[84]

The delivery of money by one person (hereafter the 'bailor') to another (hereafter the 'bailee') to deliver to a third person (hereafter the 'beneficiary'), is a specific type of 'bailment of money'.[85] In such a case, the delivery of money to the beneficiary, is the particular purpose to be carried out

---

[77] In Detinue, the development is best outlined by Milsom, above, n. 55 at 228–31.

[78] Though in the late thirteenth century, 'Britton, knowing no Roman law and misunderstanding Bracton's point' on the liability of the custodian for safekeeping discussed below, thought that an accidental loss would excuse a money debtor. See Milsom, above, n. 55 at 229.

[79] For a non-conclusive discussion on the point, see Hil. 38 Eliz. (1596), Owen 57; 74 E.R. 897, where it was debated whether as in Detinue (see immediately below), a plea based on loss in circumstances beyond control so as not to provide the defendant with a cause of action, even theoretical, against a wrongdoer, cannot be raised before the auditors.

[80] This view, attributable to Glanvill at the beginning of the thirteenth century, may be explained on the basis of the common ancestry of Debt and Detinue. See Milsom, above, n. 55 at 229.   [81] See (ii) above.

[82] This was Bracton's position in the middle of the thirteenth century, which subsisted through the fourteenth century as well. See Milsom, above, n. 55 at 229 and Fifoot, above, n. 55 at 159–60.

[83] This is following *The Case of the Marshalsea* (1455), YB. Hil. 33 Hen. 6, f.1. pl. 3; Fifoot, above, n. 55 at 168, where the Court, which dealt with the liability of the Marshal of the King's Bench upon the escape of a prisoner, was prepared to accept a plea based on loss caused by 'the King's enemies or . . . sudden tempest', but not by an act of any of the King's subject, including one unknown, against whom the Marshal had an action. See also *Southcote* v. *Bennet* (1601), Croke Eliz. 815, 78 ER 1041; 4 Coke Rep 83b, 76 ER 1061; Fifoot, above, n. 55 at 169.

[84] A leading case, in which Holt CJ specifically followed Roman law, is *Coggs* v. *Bernard* (1703), 2 Ld. Raymond 909; 92 ER 107; Fifoot, above, n. 55 at 173.

[85] See in general, Jackson, above, n. 57 at 24.

by the bailee. The machinery does not require the delivery to the beneficiary the same coins originally delivered to the bailee.

[18]   Two prominent dicta[86] came to support the proposition that a bailee who has failed to deliver the money to the beneficiary is chargeable to the bailor, not only in Account, but also in Debt. First, in 1442, Newton CJ[87] stated in *Doige's Case*,[88] that '[i]f I bail a certain sum of money to *Paston* to bail over to *Fortescue*, now, if *Paston* does not do this, he will be liable to me in an action of Account and also in an action of Debt'.[89] As to the relationship between these two liabilities, the plaintiff-bailor may choose which action to bring, and having 'brought the one, the other is extinguished'.[90] Secondly, in a 1505 Anonymous case,[91] Frowicke CJ stated that 'if I bail money to one to bail over and he converts it to his own use, I can have action of Account [or] Debt . . .'[92] Also in *Core's Case*, the majority of the court thought that 'if money be delivered . . . to be bailed over, if the bailee break his trust, [Debt or Account] lies for the bailor.'[93] Indeed, the bailee's liability to the bailor in Debt or Account, arising upon the bailee's failure to hand over the money to the beneficiary, is in line with the 1368 Anonymous case.[94] As recalled, this case held in general for the bailee's liability to the bailor in Debt or Account upon the bailee's failure to carry out the particular purpose of the bailment. The failure to deliver the money to the beneficiary is just one instance of such a bailee's failure.[95]

[19]   The nature of the liability of a custodian of money for safekeeping, whether in Debt or Account, 'was never really clarified in medieval law'.[96] As he was allowed to mix the money, such a custodian was not

---

[86] Other yearbook authorities are cited by J .B. Ames, 'Account' in *Lectures on Legal History and Miscellaneous Legal Essays* (Cambridge, Mass.: Harvard University Press, 1913), 116 at 120 n. 4.

[87] But note that a year earlier, Newton CJ thought that only Account was available. *Anon.* (1441), Y.B. 19 Hen. VI, 5, pl. 10. See Jackson, above, n. 57 at 25 n. 1, and Ames, ibid. at 120 n. 3.   [88] (1442), Y.B. Trin. 20 Hen VI, f. 34, pl. 4, Fifoot, above, n. 55 at 347.

[89] Ibid. at 348, Fifoot.   [90] Ibid.

[91] *Anon.* (1505), Y.B. Mich. 20 Hen. VII, f. 8, pl. 18, Fifoot, above, n. 55 at 351 (Also reported in Keilwey 69 and 77, 72 E.R. 229 and 239 as (1506), Mich. and Hil. 21 Hen. VII. See Fifoot, ibid. at 351 n. 54).

[92] Fifoot, ibid. at 352. Frowicke CJ. (who was in minority as to the principal holding of that case) would allow also an action on the Case. Case was introduced to facilitate the bailor's remedy for wrongful dishonour. *Id*. at 352, 353. In the Keilwey 77 report, *id*., the same judge is reported to mention Account and Case only. Debt is surprisingly omitted.

[93] *Core's Case* above, n. 71 at 22a (Dyer), 46 (E.R.), 287 (Fifoot) *per* Spilman, J., Portman, J., and Fitzjames CJ. For opposing counsels' views, see *id*. 20a and 20b (Dyer), 43 and 44 (E.R.).

[94] *Anon* (1368) above, n. 60. The case is explicitly relied upon by the majority of the Court in *Core's Case*, ibid.

[95] According to Ames, above, n. 86 at 120, the bailor 'might have account, and afterwards debt' against the bailee, also where the bailee's failure to deliver the money was caused by the beneficiary's refusal to accept it.

[96] A. W. B. Simpson, *A History of the Common Law of Contract: The Rise of the Action of Assumpsit* (Oxford: Clarendon Press, 1975) at 183, citing at n. 1 yearbook authorities.

liable in Detinue. Whether he was also entitled to use the money is another question. Regardless, safe custody appears to be a possible purpose for a bailment of money, so as to charge the bailee in Debt, on the same footing as with regard to any bailee of funds. In retrospective, the origins of the law governing the bank deposit can thus be traced in the common law to the medieval legal doctrine governing the bailment of money.

Indeed, the bailee–bailor debt relation was pronounced in the 1368 Anonymous case[97] and established in *Core's Case*;[98] it is the ancestor of the rule under which the relationship between a banker and customer as to deposited money is that of a debtor and creditor. The connection is supplied at the end of the sixteenth century by *Bretton* v. *Barnet*.[99] The case dealt with the situation where '[a] man delivers money to J.S. to be redelivered to him when he should be required: which J.S. refused'.[100] Plaintiff-bailor brought a Debt action against J.S. Particular emphasis was given to the distinction between Debt and Detinue, namely between an action for a sum of money, and an action for the return of specific coins. Explicitly citing a case with similar facts to *Core's Case*,[101] the court held for the plaintiff. The judges were not concerned with the question whether the bailee had been free to use the money. Rather they agreed that 'if money be delivered, it cannot be known, and therefore the property is altered'.[102] Stated otherwise, the bailee's freedom to 'make an exchange'[103] of the money deposited with him and pay the depositor a sum equivalent thereto, namely the right to mix the deposited money, had given adequate grounds for Debt.

It is submitted that the bailor's Debt remedy is best explained by an [20] analogy to the remedy of a moneylender. Since a bailee of money is free to use the specific coins and his liability is in terms of the sum of money delivered to him, he is to be treated very much like a borrower. This is true with respect to every bailment of money, whether to be delivered to a third party beneficiary, for safe custody, or for any other purpose. The money loan has always been a transaction giving rise to Debt. True, unlike a loan, the bailment of money does not necessarily involve an explicit

---

[97] *Anon* (1368), above, n. 60.   [98] *Core's Case* above, n. 71.   [99] See above, n. 75.

[100] *Id.* Notwithstanding the ambiguity in this settlement of facts, the report unequivocally suggests (and so it was understood by Simpson, above, n. 96 at 183) that the case dealt with the deposit of money for safekeeping, and not with a demand loan. It is unlikely that a borrower's Debt liability would have been disputed in 1599.

[101] Under the cited judgment, where 'a man delivers money to another to buy certain things for him, and he does not buy them, the party may bring an action of debt . . .'. *Bretton* v. *Barnet* above, n. 75. *Core's Case* is cited above, in n. 71, and its fact situation is summarized in the text thereafter.

[102] *Bretton* v. *Barnet*, above, n. 75.

[103] *Core's Case*, above, n. 71 at 22a (Dyer), 46 (ER), 287 (Fifoot).

repayment undertaking on the bailee's part.[104] Also, unlike a loan, the objective of the bailment of money is not to provide the bailee with the use of the money, but rather to carry out a specific purpose. In the absence of the right to use, the bailment does not appear to confer on the bailee a quid pro quo, in the form of any material benefit. Nevertheless in the final analysis, every bailment of money contains a strong element of a loan. Inasmuch as any bailee actually receives the *specific coins* to his own use and benefit, subject to his accountability for their *specific amount*, his Debt liability to the bailor is in line with a borrower's Debt liability to his lender.

In any event, during the seventeenth century, by lending to others the money delivered to him, the depositary of money had transformed the nature of his business. From a custodian of money for safekeeping he had turned to a banker.[105] Being free to use the money, he truly became a borrower from the customer-depositor[106] so as to be liable to him in Debt. Any doubts as to the banker's absolute liability for loss or theft of deposited money, even occurring in circumstances which are beyond his control or regardless of any lack of negligence on his part, have thus been removed.

(VI) THE JURIDICAL NATURE OF THE BANK DEPOSIT

[21]   It seems that there is a basic consensus, transcending boundaries between legal systems, as to the principal features of the bank deposit. At the same time, however, no corresponding consensus has emerged as to its legal characterization. In the course of the previous discussion, the bank deposit was examined as an (i) ordinary deposit; (ii) irregular deposit as a subcategory of the deposit; or (iii) money loan, whether by itself, or as the proper characterization of the irregular deposit. However, each characterization has been fraught with difficulty.

The typical ordinary deposit, precluding both the mixture and use of the money by the depositary, has been applied only in connection with the deposit of money in a sealed bag, or in other circumstances where the law has disallowed mixture and use. This is however the antithesis of the

---

[104] For example, an explicit undertaking to repay, or to 'bail . . . back' existed in the 1368 anonymous case, above, n. 60. No repayment undertaking was involved in *Core's Case*, above, n. 71.

[105] See e.g. R. D. Richards, *The Early History of Banking in England* (New York: AM Kelley, 1965) at 37 and in more detail, D. Mitchell (ed.), *Goldsmiths, Silversmiths and Bankers: Innovation and Transfer of Skills, 1550 to 1750* (London: Alan Sutton Publishing and Centre for Metropolitan History, 1995), particularly an article by S. Quinn, 'Balances and Goldsmith-Bankers: The Co-ordination and Control of Inter-banker Debt Clearing in Seventeenth-Century London' at 53.

[106] See e.g. *Pott v. Clegg* (1847), 16 M&W 321, 153 E.R. 1212 (Exch.).

bank deposit; it thus explains what the bank deposit is not. Alternatively, the discussion of the Talmud demonstrates that the rules governing the ordinary deposit may apply to the deposit of money which the depositary is allowed to use, though not to mix. This discussion facilitated the understanding of the distinction between the depositary's right to use and mix the deposited money. However, otherwise, it was unhelpful in highlighting the juridical nature of the bank deposit, since underlying the latter are both the right to use and mix.

At the same time, the legal ancestry of the irregular deposit has not particularly been helpful in settling the issue; on the contrary, its effect has been to reintroduce the old controversy as to the juridical nature of the irregular deposit itself. Indeed, as evolved in Roman law, the irregular deposit is inherently faulted and cannot properly explain the juridical nature of the bank deposit. As indicated, the basic conceptual flaw underlying the irregular deposit is the assumption that it necessarily gives the depositary not only the right to mix but also the right to use the money, thereby making the depositary a mere debtor as if he were a borrower in an unsecured money loan. Consequently, the depositor's motive to physically safeguard deposited money is undermined. Had the depositary been given a right to mix subject to a duty to retain the mixture, so as to confer on each depositary a proprietary right in the mixture, the irregular deposit would have made sense as a species of deposit for safekeeping, at least juridically, albeit obviously not from the perspective of modern banking. Once it is determined that in fact it is not a subcategory of the deposit, the irregular deposit becomes redundant. Whether the transaction is a type of loan can be examined by the direct examination of its features, so that the intermediation of the 'irregular deposit' becomes unhelpful.

An argument repeatedly made in support of the preference of the [22] deposit over the loan is the transaction motive.[107] Thus, the argument goes, the deposit transaction is initiated by the depositor, seeking to safeguard his money, and is thus, primarily to his benefit. Conversely, in a loan transaction, it is the borrower, being in need of money, who initiates the transaction which is thus primarily to his benefit. Accordingly, concludes the argument, it is the classic deposit, and not the money loan, that must be taken to provide the appropriate explanation.

In analysing the motive for the transaction, this argument is nonetheless quite dated, or at least, overstated. In a contemporary financial intermediation environment, the bank is actively seeking to attract deposits, much needed for its own financial activity. Similarly, an investor with

---

[107] See e.g. Pothier, above, n. 20 at ¶83; Ripert and Roblot, above, n. 41 at 422; and Ben-Oliel, *Banking Law* above, n. 46 at 155.

excess funds may be on the lookout for lending opportunities, designed to enhance his own welfare. Not surprisingly, whether a modern financial product is a traditional deposit or loan is, quite often, not easy to determine. In the final analysis, both the bank deposit and the ordinary loan are financial transactions directed towards the benefit of both parties.

At the same time, this is more to point at a grey area between the bank deposit and the ordinary loan than to deny the predominant safekeeping, or better security, motive of the typical bank depositor. The point is, however, that taking into account the risk allocation, as intended by both the depositor and the bank, the depositor's motive is not a strong enough reason to overlook the objective features of the bank deposit as a loan. This is, of course, not to say that the depositor's predominant motive is to be ignored by the law. For example, intending to achieve security and having confidence in the depositary's solvency,[108] consistently with the economic though not strictly legal view of the matter, a depositor may regard the bank deposit as a real asset, rather than a mere enforceable claim. Also, in a demand deposit, the depositor is not likely to make a demand unless a need arises.

[23]   This may justify substantial adjustments to rules governing prescription or statutory limitations. First, in the context of a scheme governing dormant accounts, a longer prescription or limitation period[109] for the claim on the bank deposit, or even its abolition altogether,[110] may be justified. Also, it may be unfair to have prescription or statute of limitations running against a depositor from the day of the 'advance' he made to the bank;[111] it is more appropriate to have the period running against him from the last demand or other activity in the account.[112] It is thus a mere

---

[108] The depositary's solvency may further be strengthened by applicable deposit insurance in the jurisdiction.

[109] For example, in France, a bank deposit in an account that has not been subject to any activity is to be transferred to the state after thirty years, though already after it has been dormant for ten years, which is the standard prescription period, it may be transferred by the bank (under Law no. 77 of 3 Jan. 1977) to a 'Caisse des dépôts', specifically designated by law for that purpose, where it is held, for the benefit of the depositor, until the original 30-year period expires. See Ripert and Roblot, above, n. 41 at 426.

[110] For example, in Canada, a bank deposit in an account that has not been subject to any activity is to be transferred to the Bank of Canada after ten years, where, subject to a $100 floor, it is kept indefinitely for the benefit of the depositor. See s. 438 of the Bank Act, S.C. 1991, c. 46 (Part VIII) as am. by S.C. 1992, c. 27, s. 90(1)(a) and s. 22 (1) of the Bank of Canada Act, R.S.C. 1985, c. B-2 (Part XVI), as am. by S.C. 1997, c. 15, ss. 94–110.

[111] Which is the usual common law rule for an obligation payable on demand. See *Norton v. Ellam* (1837), 2 M. & W. 461; 150 E.R. 839 (Exch. of Pleas).

[112] In the common law, a leading case on the point, in connection with the deposit of money for safekeeping, is *Tidd v. Overll* [1893] 3 Ch. 154, specifically relying on *Pothier on Contracts* (Evans' trans., vol. ii, p. 126), which is a civilian source. The case, together with the extract from Pothier, was followed in South Africa in *Ex parte Smith*, above, n. 17, where (at 127) De Beer J. regarded the position to 'be in accordance with the principles of the Roman-Dutch law'.

coincidence that the latter rule corresponds to the rule governing the running of prescription or limitation against a depositary in an ordinary deposit.[113] In the ordinary deposit, such a rule is based on the lack of adverse possession[114] in the depositary's hands until the demand for return and its denial. In the bank deposit a similar rule is premised on other grounds; it is designed to accommodate the nature of the transaction and the expectations of the parties.

Such solutions do not undermine the objective character of the bank deposit as a loan transaction. They merely provide adjustments. Nor are they inherent in the nature of the bank deposit. They are policy choices for the law to make in providing rules to govern the bank deposit and fine-tune its features as a special type of loan.

Several other arguments have been put forward to explain the deficiencies in characterizing the bank deposit as a loan.[115] First, it is argued, unlike the typical loan, the bank deposit does not necessarily bear interest. Sometimes, payment of interest is even precluded.[116] Second, even a loan payable on demand ought to be understood as allowing the borrower a reasonable time to use its proceeds[117] as well as to respond to a demand of payment.[118] Conversely, it is argued, the return of a demand deposit may be insisted upon immediately after the deposit is made,[119] and the bank is required to respond to the demand promptly.[120] Third, it is argued, a depositary may raise defences that are inconsistent with the borrower's absolute obligation to repay a money loan. **[24]**

Nevertheless, and notwithstanding their superficial attraction, these objections do not withstand a rigorous examination. As a specific type of loan, the bank deposit may be subject to specific rules governing interest and demand. For example, in the common law, in addition to the scenarios outlined in the second objection, a bank may pay on a demand deposit **[25]**

---

[113] For the prescription in ordinary deposit as of demand and refusal (rather than as of the deposit), see Pothier, above, n. 20 at ¶68.

[114] In Roman law, the distinction is between the depositary's 'detention' which is consistent with the depositor's continuous 'possession', as long as it purports to be on the depositor's behalf and not in challenge to the depositor's right. See in general, Lee, above, n. 2 at 179.

[115] For a summary see e.g. Ben-Oliel, *Banking Law*, above, n. 46 at 151–6.

[116] See e.g. *Foley* v. *Hill*, above, n. 48 at 36 (HLC); 1005 (ER), *per* Lord Cottenham; and Rives-Langes and Contamine-Raynaud above, n. 1 at 269.

[117] For a judicial authority, from Israel, see e.g. SP 32/84 *Estate of Walter Nathan Williams* v. *Israel British Bank (London) (in Liquidation)*, PD 44(2) (1990) 265 (SC) at 279 *per* Barak J.

[118] A leading Canadian case on this point is *Ronald Elwyn Lister* v. *Dunlop Canada Ltd.* [1982] 1 S.C.R. 726, (1982) 135 D.L.R. (3d) 1, *rev'g* 105 D.L.R. (3d) 684, *aff'g* 85 D.L.R. (3d) 321.

[119] See e.g. Pothier, above, n. 20 at ¶83.

[120] Though for large cash payments, possibly, this is subject to availability at the bank of cash in specie. See e.g. *Libyan Arab Foreign Bank* v. *Bankers Trust Co.* [1988] 1 Lloyd's Rep. 259 (QB Com. Ct.). In France, the banking agreement may provide that for a withdrawal over an agreed sum, an advance notice, at a specified time, must be given. See Rives-Lange and Cabrillac, above, n. 41 at ¶41.

only upon demand made at the branch where the account is kept,[121] and is precluded from making payment unless demand was properly made;[122] as long as the banking contract has not been terminated, a borrower-bank may neither prepay nor seek its creditor.[123] However, this does not undermine the nature of the bank deposit as a loan; after all, it is not argued that the bank deposit is a typical loan. Rather, on the basis of the objective manifestations of the transaction as reflected in the risk allocation between the bank and its depositor, the argument is that the bank deposit ought better to be analysed as a specific type of loan of money and not as a specific type of deposit of a chattel for custody.

Also the third objection, based on the bank's defences, is unconvincing. Indeed, a bank is discharged towards the depositor upon the lawful[124] seizure[125] of the deposit by the state.[126] In some cases, it may further be discharged where funds did not reach the lender-depositor or his nominee,

---

[121] Though in the circumstances of modern international banking, the task of identifying in each case only one branch as the designated payment place may be illusive. See e.g. *Wells Fargo Asia Ltd.* v. *Citibank NA*, 936 F.2d 723 (2nd Cir. 1991), *cert. denied*, 112 S. Ct. 2990 (1992) dealing with a foreign currency deposit whose applicable law, also governing the place of payment, was held to be the law of the currency; as well as *Garcia* v. *Chase Manhattan Bank NA*, 735 F. 2d 645 (2nd Cir., 1984) dealing with the effect of assurances given by the bank's officers as to the place of payment. Compared to their American counterparts, English courts may adhere more closely to principle. See e.g. *Libyan Arab Foreign Bank* ibid. where Staughton J. stated at 270 that '[i]n the age of the computer it may not be strictly accurate to speak of the branch where the account is kept. Banks no longer have books in which they write entries; they have terminals in which they give instructions; and the computer itself with its magnetic tape, floppy disc or some other device may be physically located elsewhere. Nevertheless, it should not be difficult to decide where an account is kept . . .'. Even the existence of a managed account arrangement between two separate accounts held in different locations did not alter the distinct location of either one.

[122] The limitation to payment at the branch of deposit does not seem to exist in France where it is stated that the debt is payable where the debtor-bank is domiciled or in one of its branches. See e.g. Rives-Lange and Cabrillac, above, n. 41 at ¶42. Nevertheless, according to the report of the case cited in support of this proposition, Req. 11 juin 1929, *Gaz. Pal* 1929. 2, 479, following the taking by the Turks of Smyrne, the place of the depositor's branch, the depositor's credit was transferred to his account in the Paris head office of the bank anyway, where the demand was actually made.

[123] The leading case as to the demand requirement and rules is *Joachim* v. *Swiss Bank* [1921] 3 KB 110.

[124] Perhaps the *ipso facto* illegality of the seizure by Italian authorities of bank deposits of Jews during the Second World War, mentioned by R. Ben-Oliel, 'Banker's Liability in the Bank Deposit Relationship' (1979), 14 Israel L. Rev. 164, (hereafter: Ben-Oliel, 'Banker's Liability'), at 166–7, explains the inconsistency of the treatment of the seizure by post-War Italian courts. But according to Tedeschi, these cases actually involved the confiscation of bank assets backing these deposits, in which case, as discussed in text & n. 130 below, the liability of the bank is anyway not affected. See Tedeschi, above, n. 45 at 24.

[125] In principle, temporary suspension should not be distinguishable from seizure, notwithstanding the result to the contrary in both Req. 11 juin 1929, *Gaz. Pal* 1929. 2, 479 in France and *Wells Fargo Asia Ltd.* v. *Citibank NA* above, n. 121 in the USA.

[126] The leading case is *Arab Bank* v. *Barclays Bank*, [1954] A.C. 495 (H.L.). See also *Perez* v. *Chase Manhattan Bank NA*, 61 NY 2d 460, 474 N.Y.S. 2d 689, 463 NE 2d 5 (N.Y. C.A., 1984), *cert. denied*, 105 S. Ct. 366 (1984).

notwithstanding compliance with the lender-depositor's instructions,[127] or even upon payment over unauthorized instructions.[128] It was stated that, undermining the typical lender-borrower risk allocation, such rules are irreconcilable with the characterization of the bank as a borrower under a money loan.[129]

Nonetheless, in my view, this criticism is misplaced. Absolute liability by a borrower of money means only full responsibility for loss or theft of the money, irrespective of *force majeure* or lack of any negligence. Indeed, consistently with this principle, banks were held to remain liable to their depositors, notwithstanding loss of all assets backing such liability on the bank's books.[130] At the same time, the borrower's absolute liability to the lender does not mean full responsibility in case of the lawful seizure of the lender's right. Also, it does not necessarily mean lack of discharge in case of the borrower's compliance with either the lender's instruction or what appears to be the lender's instruction, even though payment has not reached the lender or somebody nominated by him. Generally speaking, the standard for compliance with instructions is a matter governed by the law of mandate, and the instructions given by a customer to a bank, or any lender to a borrower, in pursuance with their agreement, is no exception.[131] Accordingly, the bank's discharge in the case of either deposit seizure or compliance with instructions need not necessarily be viewed as inconsistent with its absolute liability as a borrower.

Nevertheless, the inadequacies of any of the known categories to pro- **[26]** vide a complete explanation to all features of the bank deposit, has led to a search for an alternative. As the predominant feature of the bank deposit, Ben-Oliel highlighted[132] its 'double disposition',[133] namely, the simultaneous availability of the same funds to both bank and depositor. This led him to conclude that 'the depositor, having placed his money in

---

[127] Such could be the case, in most jurisdictions, in the absence of any negligence by the bank. See throughout 3.C below. [128] See 4.C below.

[129] See e.g. Ben-Oliel, *Banking Law*, above, n. 46 at 148–56, particularly, at 152–4.

[130] See e.g. Req. 11 juin 1929, *Gaz. Pal*. 1929. 2, 479 in France (though in the facts of this case funds were actually physically transferred to France and were not lost when Smyrne fell in the hands of the Turks) and *Vishipco Line* v. *Chase Manhattan Bank NA* 660 F. 2d 854 (2nd. Cir. 1981) in the USA. *Quaere*, however, if in the facts of this case, the confiscation order was not broad enough to cover the deposits as well (in which case, the case should have been governed by *Arab Bank* and *Perez*, above, n. 126, except that arguably, in the facts of the case, what was surrendered by the bank was its own funds, rather than those of the depositors). On *Vishipco* and related subjects, see J. S. Ziegel, 'Canadian Perspectives on Banking Transactions and the Conflict of Laws' (1990), 4 BFLR 201, at 209–17. See also Tedeschi's discussion on the Italian confiscation of funds backing deposits owned by Jews during the Second World War, above, n. 45 at 24. [131] Discussed in 2.C below.

[132] R. Ben-Oliel, 'The Juridical Nature of the Bank-Depositor Relationship' (unpublished Doctoral Thesis, Hebrew University of Jerusalem, 1977) [in English].

[133] On this point, he purports to develop an idea he attributes to the Italian jurist G. Molle, whose position is outlined in the thesis, id. at 65–75.

the bank still retains ownership in the fund: the bank acquires possession and may dispose of the customer's money, thus showing part ownership.' Stated otherwise, 'a deposit in a bank implies a contractual fragmentation of the depositor's ownership between the customer and the bank'. Consequently, both depositor and bank 'maintain converging real rights in the fund, thus giving rise to a peculiar *real relationship*'.[134]

While every loan can equally be said to generate two assets, one in the form of money placed in the borrower's hands, and the other in the form of a debt or receivable owned by the lender, Ben-Oliel's emphasis on the 'double disposition' of the money in the bank serves to highlight the function of money deposited in a bank as actual money, at least from the economic point of view. Yet, without entering into the scholarly debate as to the jurisprudential merit of Ben-Oliel's innovative position,[135] two reservations should be pointed out. First, Ben-Oliel relies strongly on the inadequacy of the loan to explain the entire range of the banking relationship. This, however, overlooks the fact that the deposit is but one facet of that relationship, consisting also of the mandate, as well as of implied and express contract terms. Second, in departing from the view regarding the deposit as a loan, Ben-Oliel may downgrade the importance of assigning to the deposit the loss allocation features of the loan. After all, it is the predominance of these features that underlies the conclusion that the bank deposit is a specific type of loan.

[27]   Upon reflection, 'loan' relates to the bank deposit in a similar manner 'bailment' of a chattel relates in the common law to distinct but related concepts such as borrowing, hire, and the deposit for custody of a chattel.[136] It effectively provides for the basic risk allocation while recognizing variations, based on implied contract, drawn on the particular features of each transaction.

---

[134] Ben-Oliel, 'Banker's Liability', above, n. 124 at 164; emphasis in the original. For a succinct summary see also Ben-Oliel, *Banking Law*, above, n. 46 at 151–6.

[135] For a critical discussion, see Tedeschi, above, n. 45, *passim*.

[136] For 'bailment' as an organizing concept in the common law, covering various contract categories, recognized in Roman law, involving the control of another's goods (including 'real' contracts enumerated in (ii) above), see judgment by Chief Justice Holt in *Coggs* v. *Bernard*, above, n. 84.

C. Management of Customers' Payments: Mandate, Agency, and Implied Terms

In both common law[1] and civil law[2] jurisdictions[3] the cheque, as a pay-   [1]
ment instruction, is discussed in terms of a mandate, given by the customer as a mandator to his bank as mandatary. Furthermore, under the
civil law, the entire relationship between a customer and a bank, under
which the latter is to carry out the former's payment instructions, may be
regarded as a mandate.[4] In both common law[5] and civil law[6] the mandate
is also considered applicable to the collection and receipt of payments by
banks for customers. Along these lines, the Italian civil code specifically
provides in art. 1856(1) that in executing customers' instructions 'the bank
is answerable according to the rules concerning mandate'. Not surprisingly then, in both major legal systems, the law of mandate plays a cardinal role in providing for the rules governing the management by a bank
of incoming as well as outgoing customers' payments.

In Roman law, the mandate was broadly defined as 'a contract whereby   [2]
one person (mandator) gives another [mandatary] a commission to do
something for him . . .'[7] In principle, this definition was adopted by the
various civil codes.[8] Originally, the service to be performed under the

---

[1] See e.g. *London Joint Stock Bank* v. *Macmillan and Arthur*, [1918] A.C. 777 at 789 (H.L.), and in general, H. Luntz, 'Cheques as Mandates and as Bills' (1997), 12 B.F.L.R. 189.

[2] See e.g. J. L. Rives-Lange and M. Contamine-Raynaud, *Droit bancaire*, 6th edn. (Paris: Dalloz, 1995) at 287 ¶300.

[3] In the ensuing discussion, quotes of statutory provisions in English are from *The French Civil Code Revised Edition* (as am. to 1 July 1994), trans. J. H. Crabb (Littleton, Colo.: Fred B. Rothman & Co., 1995); *The German Civil Code* (as am. to 1 Jan. 1975) trans. I. S. Forrester, S. L. Goren, and H. M. Ilgen (South Hackensack, NJ: Fred B. Rothman & Co., 1975) (with 1981 Supp. trans. S. L. Goren); *The Civil Code of Japan* (translation) (Tokyo: Ministry of Justice, 1972); *The Italian Civil Code*, trans. M. Beltramo, G. E. Longo, and J. H. Merryman (Dobbs Ferry, NY: Oceana Publications Inc., 1969); *Swiss Contract Law, English Translation of Selected Official Texts—Swiss Code of Obligations* (Zurich: Swiss-American Chamber of Commerce, 1997); and the bilingual edition of the Quebec Civil Code, *Code civil du practicien* (Montreal: DACFO, 1995).

[4] See e.g. in Switzerland, D. Guggenheim, *Les Contrats de la pratique bancaire suisse*, 2nd edn. (Genéva: Georg Éditeur, 1989) at 256.

[5] See M. Hapgood, *Paget's Law of Banking*, 11th edn. (London: Butterworths, 1996) at 407.

[6] See e.g. Rives-Lange and Contamine-Raynaud, above, n. 2 at 303 ¶310 and 312 ¶317.

[7] See e.g. R. W. Lee, *The Elements of Roman Law*, 4th edn. (London: Sweet & Maxwell, 1956) at 334.

[8] See e.g. Swiss CO art. 394(1), French CC art. 1984 (where the mandatary's action must be in the mandator's name), Italian CC art. 1703, Japanese CC art. 643 (in conjunction with art. 656), Quebec CC art. 2130 and BGB §662 (in conjunction with §675) in Germany. In Italy

mandate must have been performed gratuitously. Indeed, under Roman law, services could have been performed for a reward, in which case, the contract was for hire and not a mandate. However, a contract for hire, whether for services (*locatio conductio operarum*) or work (*locatio conductio operis*)[9], was quite limited in its scope: '[i]t was generally limited to services which were commonly rendered by slaves'. Conversely, '[m]embers of what are called the liberal professions were supposed to do their work for nothing'.[10] Hence, the inappropriateness of the contract for hire, the need for another type of contract, namely, the mandate, as well as the gratuitous nature of the mandate.

While in principle the service performed under a mandate might be of any kind, it commonly consisted of entering into a contract or some other legal transaction with a third party.[11] With the passage of time, the gratuitous nature of the mandate became a matter of mere form, with the mandatary becoming entitled to an agreed honorarium, which he could claim under a separate action, without being allowed to raise that entitlement by way of defence to the mandator's action.[12] At present, most civil codes do not define the mandate as a gratuitous contract,[13] or at least, eliminate any practical implication from such a characterization.[14] Also, most civil codes do not restrict the task or service to be performed by the mandatary.[15]

While the word 'mandate' suggests a 'command', the mandate may not be created by the mandator unilaterally. Rather, it is a bilateral contract.[16] As for the mutual obligations of the parties, '[m]andate was imperfectly bilateral, the [mandatary] being bound to perform the service, and the

---

and Quebec the mandate is limited to the accomplishment of a legal transaction or the performance of a juridical act. Arguably, the payment of the drawer's or originator's debt falls into this category.

[9] Briefly stated, the distinction between these two types of the contract for hire is as follows: while the subject-matter of the former (*operarum*) is the services themselves, the subject-matter of the latter (*operis*) is the result accomplished by the services. See e.g. R. Zimmermann, *The Law of Obligations: Roman Foundations of the Civilian Tradition* (Cape Town: Juta & Co. Ltd., 1990) at 394. A third category of the contract for hire was the hire of a thing (*locatio conductio rei*). For all three categories see Lee above, n. 7 at 320–1.

[10] Lee, ibid. at 321. See also at 320 and 335, as well as Zimmermann, ibid. at 390 and 413.

[11] B. Nicholas, *An Introduction to Roman Law* (Oxford: Clarendon Press, 1962), at 187.

[12] See ibid. at 188.

[13] Though remnants from the original rule may still be quite visible. For example, under art. 1986 in France, in the absence of an agreement to the contrary, the mandate is gratuitous.

[14] For example, in Germany, while the mandate is gratuitous (BGB §662), most provisions relating to it are stated to apply to a contract of service or a contract for work (BGB §675) under which performance is for remuneration (BGB §611) and which is broad enough to cover the role of a bank in paying or receiving payments for customers.

[15] But see n. 8 above.

[16] D. J. Joubert and D. H. Van Zyl, 'Mandate and Negotiorum Gestio', in W. A. Joubert, *The Law of South Africa*, vol. xvii (Durban, Pretoria: Butterworth, 1983), at ¶2.

[mandator] being contingently bound to indemnify him for his expenses. The [mandatary] was also bound to account to the [mandator] for any incidental benefits he derived from the performance of the service'.[17] This remains true under present civil codes.

Mandate doctrine has not fastened on the parties' reciprocal duties of care. In the classical law, the mandatary was liable only for *dolus*,[18] namely, an intentional wrongful act,[19] or breach of good faith.[20] In the course of the years, the mandatary's liability had been expanded,[21] in the current civil codes, the mandatary is held to a duty of care.[22] As for the mandator's liability, at present, other than in Switzerland,[23] the prevailing view is that it is not limited to negligence. Rather, the mandator's liability extends to all losses and damages incurred by the mandatary in connection with the execution of the mandate,[24] and arises even in the absence of any negligence on the part of the mandator.[25]

In Roman law, the exclusion of liability for *dolus*, that is, an intentional wrongful act or the breach of good faith, was disapproved of as being contrary to the good morals.[26] Most civil codes extended this policy by also precluding the exclusion of liability for gross negligence.[27] Generally speaking, liability for light negligence may effectively be disclaimed.

The following is an outline of the principles governing the mutual obligations in a mandate, as supplemented by principles of general contract law, particularly in relation to liability to the mandator for the breach of mandate, in the various jurisdictions under discussion. The specific application of such principles to payment and collection operations in each country may be touched upon here and is further discussed in 3.C and 4, below. Quite frequently, in order to complete tasks relating to both customer's incoming and outgoing payments, a bank is required to engage   [3]

---

[17] See Nicholas, above, n. 11 at 187.   [18] Lee, above, n. 7 at 335.   [19] Ibid. at 287.

[20] Zimmermann, above, n. 9 at 210.

[21] See discussion by Zimmermann, ibid. at 426–30.

[22] See Swiss CO art. 398 (with references to arts. 321a(1) and 321e(1)); French CC art. 1992; Japanese CC art. 644; Italian CC art. 1710; BGB §276 in Germany (for any debtor in general); and Quebec CC art. 2138.   [23] Swiss CO art. 402(2).

[24] See French CC art. 2000; Italian CC art. 1720; Japanese CC art. 650 and Quebec CC art. 2154. In Germany BGB §670 reads to entitle the mandatary to claim from the mandator only expenses or outlays (and not losses or damages) incurred by the mandatary in the course of carrying out the mandate. However, '[these] narrow confines . . . were soon left behind by courts and legal writers. The principle of a liability (not based on fault) for risks arising from and connected with activities undertaken by another person in the debtor's interest, is widely acknowledged today'. See Zimmermann, above, n. 9 at 432.

[25] For this development see Zimmermann, ibid. at 430–2. In fact, both the narrow scope of the *original* mandatary's liability and the *modern* broad scope of the mandator's liability are reminiscent of the original gratuitous nature of the mandatary's undertaking.

[26] See Zimmermann, ibid. at 712. See also Lee, above, n. 7 at 287.

[27] For the proximity between gross negligence (*culpa lata*) and *dolus*, see Nicholas above, n. 11 at 170; Lee above, n. 7 at 294 and Zimmermann ibid. at 209.

the services of one or more banks. This is particularly true whenever two parties to a payment transaction have accounts in different banks. In such a case, the mandate agreement ought to be taken as authorizing, or in fact requiring, the mandatary to engage others in the performance of the mandate, so that any presumption as to an obligation fastened on the mandatary to carry out the mandate personally[28] is rebutted. The mandatary may thus engage in the performance of the mandate one or more employees, sub-mandataries, or substitute mandataries. As the ensuing discussion demonstrates, not every statutory scheme provides for a comprehensive treatment for all such situations. Regardless, subtle differences among the various jurisdictions exist as to liability in connection with losses caused by those engaged by a mandatary.

[4]   For each country, the ensuing discussion thus focuses on three aspects of the mandatary relationship, not necessarily dealt with in the following order. First are the rules governing the mutual obligations of the parties. The second aspect is the application of these rules to situations where, for the execution of the mandate, the mandatary bank requires the services of third parties. Third, there is the question of the power of the mandatary bank to disclaim liability fastened on it by law through the use of an effective exemption clause. In the latter context, the discussion primarily revolves around the power to disclaim liability for loss or damage caused by negligence. In countries where the mandator-customer's liability arises only upon his negligence, there is the additional question as to whether, under circumstances where the mandatary bank would have been liable other than on the basis of fault, an exemption clause may effectively pass on responsibility to a non-negligent mandator-customer. It should be pointed out that in Member States of the European Union, an exemption clause must satisfy the EU Directive on Unfair Terms in Consumer Contracts[29] discussed above, in 2.A.

(II) CIVIL LAW JURISDICTIONS

[5]   In France, a mandatary 'is required to accomplish [the mandate] as long as he remains responsible, and responds in damages which may result from its inexecution' (FCC art. 1991). He answers 'not only for [intentional

---

[28] The mandatary's personal obligation to perform, and its exceptions, are dealt with in Swiss CO art. 398(3); French CC art. 1994; Japanese CC art. 104; Italian CC art. 1717; German BGB §664; and Quebec CC art. 2140. From South Africa, see Joubert and Van Zyl above, n. 16 at ¶9. See also s. 16 of the Israeli Agency Law, 1965. For the common law position under the law of agency see S. J. Stoljar, *The Law of Agency* (London: Sweet & Maxwell, 1961), at 276–80. For the relation between agency and mandate see further below.

[29] 93/13/EEC, OJ L 095 pp. 0029 (21 April 1993). From the countries under discussion, EU jurisdictions are France, Germany, Italy, and the United Kingdom.

wrongful acts],[30] but also for faults which he commits in his management' (art. 1992), and 'is required to render accounting of his management' (art. 1993).

In turn, vis-à-vis the mandator, and irrespective of the success or failure of the task undertaken, provided it acted without fault, the mandatary is entitled to be reimbursed 'for advances and expenses . . . made for the execution of the [mandate]' and to be paid promised wages (art. 1999). It is also entitled to be indemnified for losses 'sustained during the course of his management without negligence which is imputable to him' (art. 2000).

The general rule under FCC art. 1994 is that a mandatary is not answerable for a substituted mandatary, except for where substitution was unauthorized or where '[substitution] was conferred on him without designation of a person, and the one of whom he made choice was notoriously incapable or insolvent'. Nonetheless, '[i]n all cases the principal may act directly against the person whom the [mandatary] substituted for himself'.

French jurisprudence renders ineffective disclaimer clauses purporting to exonerate liability for an intentional wrongful act ('une faute dolosive') as well as gross negligence ('une faute lourde').[31]

In Germany, 'a debtor [that is, a party liable on a contract, including a [6] mandatary] is responsible . . . for wilful misconduct and negligence. A person who does not exercise ordinary care acts negligently'. And liability for wilful misconduct cannot be disclaimed (BGB §276). A mandatary is bound to provide the mandator with information, render an account to him, hand over to him all that he received in connection with the mandate, and pay interest on money for which he is accountable and which he spent to his benefit (BGB §§666–8). He is entitled to receive advances from the mandator for the execution of the mandate as well as to obtain reimbursement for any outlay which he regarded necessary under the circumstances (BGB §§669–70). While as a debtor, a mandatary is liable for the fault of an assistant or employee (BGB §278), 'he is responsible only for fault imputable to him' in making a permitted transfer of the mandate but not otherwise for the fault of the transferee (BGB §664).

In Switzerland, the mandatary is obligated to render an account to the [7] mandator and transfer to him rights acquired in the course of carrying out the mandate (CO arts. 400–1). A mandatary is responsible to the mandator for the faithful and careful performance ('bonne et fidèle exécution') of the mandate (CO art. 398(2)). In general, the mandatary is bound by the

---

[30] Or 'dol' in the original French, which is translated by Crabb, above, n. 3, less accurately in my view, as 'deceit'.
[31] *Civil Code 1992–3* (Paris: Litec) at 548 ¶¶ 39–40, annotation to art. 1147.

same standard of care as that of an employee ('travailleur') (art. 398(1)). This standard contains an obligation of diligence and faithfulness (art. 321a). Treated as an employee, the mandatary is answerable to damage caused to the mandator intentionally or by negligence. The standard of care is determined by contract and circumstances (art. 321e). Also, any person is liable for damage caused by his employee/assistant ('auxili-aire') during the exercise of the latter's function in performing the for-mer's obligation (art. 101(1)).

Further, in Switzerland, a mandatary is required to carry out his obli-gations in person. He may, however, be authorized to transfer perform-ance to a third person, whether by contract or under the circumstances (CO art. 398(3)).[32] He is also responsible for the acts of a substitute improp-erly appointed, as well as for the careful selection and instruction of a properly appointed sub-mandatary, but not for the latter's acts and omis-sions if carefully selected and instructed. A substitute, whether properly appointed or not, is directly responsible to the mandator (art. 399).

For his part, the mandator is bound to reimburse the mandatary for advances the latter made for the performance of the mandate (CO art. 402(1)). At the same time, the mandator is obligated to compensate the mandatary for damage caused by the performance of the mandate only where the mandator is unable to prove that he was not negligent (CO art. 402(2)). With respect to this latter point, as already indicated, Switzerland deviates from Roman Law doctrine (as accepted by other civil law coun-tries) in effectively establishing reciprocal duties of care between the mandator and the mandatary. In Roman law, the mandator's exposure to losses and damages incurred by the mandatary in connection with the performance of the mandate is irrespective of any negligence on the mandator's part.

Under Swiss law, a contractual waiver of liability for an intentional tort ('dol') or gross negligence ('faute grave') is ineffective (CO art. 100(1)). This means that liability for simple negligence can usually be contracted out of. However, liability for damage caused by an employee/assistant ('auxiliaire') can be contractually excluded (art. 101(2)); this is broad enough to cover any type of fault, including gross negligence and inten-tional tort, and not only simple negligence. Nevertheless, these rules are modified and liability is tightened where liability arises from the exercise of an occupation for which a public licence is necessary ('la responsabilité résulte de l'exercice d'une industrie concédée par l'autorité'), as well as where the waiving party was employed by the other ('se trouvait à son service'). In these two cases, namely, of liability arising under either

---

[32] Cf. CO art. 68, under which '[a]n obligor is only bound to perform personally where performance depends on his person'.

public licence or employment, and notwithstanding art. 100(1), a judge may also hold void any waiver of liability for simple, namely slight, negligence ('faute légère'), and not only gross negligence (art. 100(2)). Also in these two cases, namely, of liability arising under either public licence or employment, and notwithstanding art. 101(2), liability for damage caused by an employee/assistant ('auxiliare') may be excluded contractually only for slight negligence ('faute légère') (art. 101(3)), but not for an intentional tort or gross negligence. At the same time, there is nothing in Swiss law to preclude a mandatary, not liable for his own fault, from passing on responsibility, by contract, to a mandator who has not been at fault.

In Italy, the mandatary is required to perform the mandate with dili- [8] gence (art. 1710(1) cc.). He is further bound to make known to the mandator 'any supervening circumstances which might cause the revocation or modification of the mandate' (art. 1710(2) cc.). Also, the mandatary is under a duty to render an account for its activities (art. 1713 cc.).

Upon the substitution of a mandatary, the original mandatary remains responsible to the mandator for instructions the former gives the substitute (art. 1717(3) cc.). However, where substitution was either necessary or authorized, the mandatary is not responsible for the activities of the substitute (art. 1717(1) cc.). This is true as long as the original mandatary was not at fault in selecting that substitute (art. 1717(2) cc.). Vicarious liability for default by a properly selected substitute is thus excluded. Under art. 1856(2), substitution for a bank acting as a mandatary, by 'another bank or one of its correspondents,' is explicitly permitted whenever 'the instructions are to be carried out in a place in which the bank has no office'.

In turn, the mandator is bound to furnish the mandatary with the means necessary to perform the mandate, reimburse the mandatary for expenses and pay him the remuneration to which he is entitled, and 'compensate the mandatary for damages incurred by [the mandatary] by reason of his undertaking' (arts. 1719–20 cc.).

Art. 1229 cc. in Italy precludes the exclusion or limitation of liability for fraud, malice, or gross negligence as well as for any liability for the violation of a duty arising from rules of public policy.

In Japan, a mandatary is bound to manage the affairs entrusted to it [9] 'with the care of a good manager in accordance with the tenor of the mandate' (art. 644 cc.). Namely, the mandatary's liability is for the breach of a duty of care and is not absolute or strict. He is further under a duty to make full disclosure (art. 645 cc.) and account (arts. 646–7 cc.) to the mandator. He is entitled to advances or reimbursement for expenditures (arts. 649–50 cc.) as well as to the specially agreed remuneration (art. 648).

Under Japanese law, the mandate may create an agency relationship (governed by arts. 99–118 cc.) between the mandator (as principal) and mandatary (as agent).[33] Where the commission of the mandate involves tasks carried out by subagents, the Japanese civil code appears to suggest that usually the original mandatary, as agent, is not vicariously liable for the default of a subagent, and that each subagent is liable directly for its own default to the mandator. Thus, according to art. 104 cc., an agent created by mandate may not appoint a subagent, except where the agent has obtained the principal's consent or an unavoidable reason exists. Under art. 105(1) cc., where the agent has duly appointed a subagent, the agent 'shall be responsible to the principal in respect of *the appointment and supervision*' but not otherwise (emphasis added); that is, vicarious liability for the default by a properly appointed and supervised subagent is excluded. Under art. 105(2) cc., this limited liability for the appointment and supervision of a subagent is excluded altogether where the agent has appointed a subagent 'as designated by the principal', unless the agent actually knew the designated subagent 'to be unfit or untrustworthy' and has neglected to act on the basis of this knowledge. Finally, under art. 107(2) cc., '[a] sub-agent has the same rights and duties as the agent towards the principal and third persons'. Thus, the subagent is, in effect, a substituted agent.

Under art. 709 cc. '[a] person who violates intentionally or negligently the right of another is bound to make compensation for damage arising therefrom'. In the absence of any direct provision to the point, case law in Japan has nevertheless precluded any effective disclaimer of liability for gross negligence and intentional wrongful act in both torts and contract.[34] Conversely, disclaimer for ordinary negligence is effective.

[10]   Under the Quebec civil code, a mandatary is bound to fulfil the mandate and act 'with prudence and diligence in performing it'. It must further 'act honestly and faithfully in the best interests of the mandator' (art. 2138 cc.). In turn, a mandator, is bound to cooperate with the mandatary and cover his costs (arts. 2149–51).

In principle, under art. 2140(1) cc., '[t]he mandatary is bound to fulfill the mandate in person unless he is authorized by the mandator to appoint another person to perform all or part of it in his place'. The appointment of a substitute by the mandatary is also permitted 'where unforeseen circumstances prevent [the mandatary] from fulfilling the mandate and he is unable to inform the mandator in due time' (art. 2140(2) cc.). Upon an unauthorized substitution, the mandatary remains liable to the mandator for any default by the substitute. At the same time, where substitution has

---

[33] Not every mandate creates agency. However, where agency is created by mandate, the mandatary as agent acts in the name of the mandator/principal. For the distinction between mandate and agency see below, in the discussion on the common law.

[34] I am advised that a leading authority to that effect is a Supreme Court decision of 25 March 1980 Hanreijihou No. 967 at 61.

been authorized, the mandatary 'is accountable only for the care with which he selected his substitute and gave him the instructions' but not for the default of a properly selected substitute. In any case, regardless as to whether his appointment has been authorized, the substitute is directly liable to the mandator for its own default (art. 2141 cc.).

Substitution of a mandatary, under the Quebec civil code, ought however to be distinguished from the appointment of an assistant to whom powers are delegated by the mandatary. The latter is permissible in the performance of the mandate, 'unless prohibited by the mandator or usage'. The mandatary remains liable to the mandator for any default by such an assistant (art. 2142 cc.).

Liability limitation or exclusion 'for material injury caused . . . through an intentional or gross fault' is precluded in Quebec under art. 1474 cc. The provision goes on to define 'gross fault' as 'a fault which shows gross recklessness, gross carelessness, or gross negligence'.

In South Africa, in the absence of any statutory provisions, the mandate [11] is governed by Roman-Dutch law,[35] which recognizes that the mandate is not limited to the one contained in the payment instruction. Rather, it extends to the entire banking relationship governing the execution and collection of payment and is supplemented by mutual good faith and due care obligations fastened on the parties in carrying out the mandate.[36] In general, a mandatary is required to act without negligence and in good faith as well as to render accounts. For his part, the mandator is obligated to compensate the mandatary for expenses and pay the agreed remuneration. Regardless of his lack of negligence, the mandator is further responsible to compensate the mandatary for all losses caused by dangers inherent in the performance of the mandate and which the mandatary could not avoid. A mandatary who employs another to perform the mandate is not responsible to the mandator for losses caused by a substitute-mandatary, but is fully responsible for any breach of duty by a sub-mandatary. A substitute is directly liable, as a mandatary, to the mandator. Conversely, there is no privity between the mandator and sub-mandatary, who is responsible to the mandatary, and not liable to the mandator. Under general South African contract law, public policy precludes the enforcement of a term exonerating a party from liability for fraud.[37]

---

[35] See Joubert and Van Zyl, above, n. 16, particularly at ¶¶9–15.

[36] See F. R. Malan and J. T. Pretorius, 'Bills of Exchange, Cheques and Promisssory Notes', §7 around n. 55, in *ABLU '96 (Annual banking Law Update, 1996)*.

[37] A leading authority to that effect in *Wells v. SA Alumenite CO.*, ([1927] A.D. 69 at 72; *per* Innes CJ.

(III) MANDATE AND IMPLIED TERMS IN THE COMMON LAW

[12]   While being a civil law concept, the mandate has been considered as providing the foundation for the cheque drawer–drawee relationship also in
the common law.[38] By extension, this applies to the relationship under any
type of payment instruction.[39] Unlike the civil law, where the mandate has
been broadly perceived as commission to do something for the mandator,
the common law views the mandate as merely 'a direction or request',[40] or
an instruction.[41] Accordingly, in the common law, the mandate did not
attract such vast scholarship, doctrine, and jurisprudence as in the civil
law. Perhaps it is against this background that the modern trend in the common law is to analyse the banker and customer relationship on the basis of
an implied contract, irrespective of any general mandate doctrine. At the
same time, the content of this implied contract has strongly been affected
by early court decisions specifically applying mandate doctrine.

[13]   It seems that the application of the mandate doctrine to the banker and
customer relationship goes back in the common law to the authority of
Young v. *Grote*,[42] as fully re-established in *London Joint Stock Bank* v. *Macmillan*.[43]
It was thus recognized in *Greenwood* v. *Martins Bank Ltd*.[44] that '*Macmillan* had
laid stress on the relations of banker and customer as giver and executor of a
mandate', under which 'the duties . . . are . . . mutual, to use reasonable care
. . .'.[45] Hence, in limiting the customer's responsibility as mandatary to negligence, thereby effectively adopting the minority civil law position (departing on this point from Roman law classic doctrine), the common law came to
treat the banker and customer as owing mutual duties of care. With the passage of time, and in the absence of a general common law mandate theory,
such reciprocal or mutual duties have been characterized as implied terms
in contract, irrespective of any mandate doctrine.[46]

     In the common law, the duty of a bank to its customer to exercise 'rea-
sonable care and skill' in the performance of its banking service[47] was

---

[38] See Malan and Pretorius, n. 36, above.
[39] For a possible extension of the mandate relationship to the entire account relationship
(as indeed in Switzerland and South Africa), see *Greenwood* v. *Martins Bank, Ltd*. [1932] 1 K.B.
371 at 381–2, *per* Scrutton L.J., *aff'd* [1933] A.C. 51.
[40] J. Burke, *Jowitt's Dictionary of English Law*, 2nd edn. (London: Sweet & Maxwell, 1977)
at 1140.
[41] See e.g. *National Westminster Bank Ltd*. v. *Barclays Bank International Ltd*., [1975] Q.B. 654
at 666; and *Barclays Bank Ltd*. v. *W.J. Simms Son & Cooke (Southern)*, [1980] Q.B. 677 at 699.
[42] (1827), 4 Bing. 253; 130 E.R. 764. Mandate doctrine was earlier cited in argument but not
referred to by the Court in *Hall* v. *Fuller* (1825), 5 B. & C. 750; 108 E.R. 279.
[43] *Young* v. *Cote*, ibid. at 792 and 799, *per* Lord Finlay, LC.   [44] Above, n. 39.
[45] Ibid. at 380–1, *per* Scrutton LJ.
[46] See M. H. Ogilvie, *Canadian Banking Law*, 2nd edn. (Toronto: Carswell, 1998) at 443–9.
[47] *Hilton* v. *Westminster Bank Ltd*. (1926), 135 L.T. 358 at 362 (C.A.), where the duty was
stated by Atkin LJ to exist in relation to 'communications which the customer sends', is a

characterized as '[t]he most significant implied term' in the banking contract.[48] Nevertheless, the extent under which banks may disclaim responsibility for breach of this duty is not entirely settled. Generally speaking, a businessperson using a standard form contract is required to point out disclaimers and other onerous terms to customers.[49] At the same time, under current jurisprudence, exemption clauses are not unconscionable *per se;*[50] rather, they are enforceable according to their terms.[51] They may however be contained by 'an impressive array of interpretive devices', including their interpretation *contra proferentem*, or more generally, their narrow interpretation; they may also be construed not to disclaim liability for negligence, where only general words of exclusion are used.[52] There is, however, some Canadian case law purporting to preclude,[53] or at least restrict,[54] banks from contracting out of their liability in negligence.[55] Yet,

leading authority. See also *Selangor United Rubber Estate Ltd.* v. *Cardock*, [1968] 2 All E.R. 1073 (Ch.D), at 1118 and 1119, where Ungoed-Thomas J., after finding that reasonable care and skill is an objective standard applicable to bankers, state that a '. . . a bank should normally act in accordance with the mandate–but not if reasonable skill and care indicate a different course'.

[48] B. Crawford, *Crawford and Falconbridge, Banking and Bills of Exchange*, 8th edn. vol. (Toronto: Canada Law Book, 1986) at 746.

[49] See e.g. *Tilden Rent-A-Car Co.* v. *Clendenning* (1978), 83 D.L.R. (3d) 400 (Ont. C.A.).

[50] Even if such doctrine exists in cases of 'inequality of bargaining power', as put forward by Lord Denning MR in *Lloyds Bank Ltd.* v. *Bundy* [1975] Q.B. 326 (C.A.), since thereunder, relief will be granted to one who 'without independent advice enters into a contract upon terms which are very unfair' only 'when his bargaining power is grievously impaired by reason of his own needs or desires, or by how own ignorance or infirmity coupled with undue influence or pressures brought to bear on him by or for the benefit of the other'. *Id.* at 339. Such is unlikely to be the case in connection with the standard account agreement governing the execution of payment transactions.

[51] The leading case is *Photo Production Ltd.* v. *Securicor Ltd.* ([1980] A.C. 827 (H.L.) where the doctrine of fundamental breach as to the limits to the reach of exclusion clauses under *Suiss Atlantique Société d'Armement Maritime SA* v. *NV Rotterdamsche Kolen Centrale* [1967] 1 A.C. 361 (H.L.) was rejected.

[52] See B. Coote, 'The Effect of Discharge by Breach on Exception Clauses' [1970] Cam. L.J. 221 at 238. For the consistency between this and *Photo Production id.*, see *Darlington Futures Ltd.* v. *Delco Australia Pty. Ltd.* (1986), 161 C.L.R. 500 (H.C. of Australia) where the Court (at 509) '[did] not understand [*Photo Production*] to deny the legitimacy, indeed the necessity, of construing the language of . . . [an exemption] clause in the context of the entire contract of which it forms part'. An exemption clause was nevertheless held to cover negligence (in connection with a snowmobile race accident) in *Dyck* v. *Manitoba Snowmobile Ass'n Inc.* (1985), 18 D.L.R. (4th) 635 (S.C.C.).

[53] *CIBC* v. *Schweitzer* [1976] W.W.D. 9 (Alta. Dist. Ct.), holding that a bank may not contract out of its liability to its customer for the consequences of negligently failing to perform a statutory duty to serve notice.

[54] *CIBC* v. *Haley* (1979), 100 D.L.R. (3d) 470 (N.B. C.A.), holding that an exemption clause purporting to release a bank regardless of its fault, did not cover bank's negligence.

[55] This line of cases was well received by Ogilvie, above, n. 46 at 448–9. For an adverse view see Crawford, above, n. 48 at 748, who recognizes 'the obvious imbalance of bargaining power between [banks in Canada] and the majority of their customers' but notes that 'traditionally, Canadian banks have not been found . . . to have dealt unfairly or unreasonably with customers . . .'.

jurisprudence on this point has not been fully settled, and so far, there is no unequivocal common law authority precluding exemption clauses aimed at either exonerating a bank from its own negligence or passing on liability to a non-negligent customer.

(iv) LEGISLATION IN COMMON LAW JURISDICTIONS

[14]	In the USA, the Uniform Commercial Code marks a departure from the common law position. The power of a bank to disclaim responsibility under an implied undertaking, is explicitly dealt with, at least partially, in UCC §4–103(a). Regarding cheques, the section provides that 'parties to [an] agreement cannot disclaim a bank's responsibility for its lack of good faith or failure to exercise ordinary care or limit the measure of damages for the lack or failure'. At the same time, 'the parties may determine by agreement the standards by which the bank's responsibility is to be measured if those standards are not manifestly unreasonable'. As will be seen below in 4.B (iv), the UCC fastens on a bank and its customer reciprocal duties of care in connection with cheques. Yet, the UCC does not have a stated position as to the power of a non-negligent bank to pass on, by contract, responsibility for a breach of duty, to a non-negligent customer. Indeed, under the UCC, the statutory preclusion against unconscionable contract terms is stated in such a way so as not to apply to bank deposits and collections.[56] There are, however, strong views in the professional literature,[57] to the effect that, primarily by reference to the good faith requirement, and as against a non-negligent customer, a bank may not disclaim liability for wrongfully dishonouring a properly payable cheque, for paying either a forged cheque or a cheque whose payment has been stopped, or for deposits made in a night deposit box.[58] Conversely, according to the proponents of these views, a bank may set by contract

---

[56] Unconscionable contracts and clauses are precluded under UCC §2–302 in connection with the sale of goods. According to Official Comment 1, for the section to apply, '[t]he basic test is whether, in light of the general commercial background and the commercial needs of the particular trade or case, the clauses involved are so one-sided as to be unconscionable under the circumstances existing at the time of the making of the contract'. At the same time, '[t]he principle is one of the prevention of oppression and unfair surprise . . . and not of disturbance of allocation of risks because of superior bargaining power'.

[57] See e.g. J. J. White and R. S. Summers, *Uniform Commercial Code*, 4th edn. (St Paul, Minn: West, 1995), at 652–9 and B. Clark, *The Law of Bank Deposits, Collections and Credit Cards*, rev. edn. (Boston: Warren, Gorham & Lamont, 1970–95), at ¶3.01[3][b].

[58] For the latter point see e.g. *Hy-Grade Oil Co.* v. *New Jersey Bank*, 350 A. 2d 279 (N.J. App. Div. 1975), *cert. denied*, 361 A. 2d 532 (N.J. S.C. 1976), where the decision against the bank was nonetheless premised on its inability to disclaim responsibility for its lack of good faith and failure to exercise ordinary care.

reasonable time and format requirements for communications from its customer.[59]

At the same time, as will be seen below in 3.C(x) and 4.C, in the USA, loss incurred in carrying out electronic funds transfers is not allocated between the bank and the customer on the basis of fault. Nor can it be reallocated by agreement other than as specified by law.

In Australia, as indicated in 2.A(iv) s. 24 above, a disclaimer clause may **[15]** be invalidated as 'unjust in the circumstances relating to the contract' under state legislation such as section 7 of the NSW Contracts Review Act 1980 No. 16. Also, aspects of the account agreement are extensively regulated by the Securities and Investments Commission Act 1989 (Cth) (SICA). Several important provisions are included in Division 2 of Part 2, entitled Unconscionable Conduct and Consumer Protection in relation to the supply of financial services. 'Financial service' is defined in section 12BA as a service either consisting of providing a financial product or otherwise supplied in relation to a financial product. And 'financial product' is broadly defined by the same provision to include 'a facility for taking money on deposit . . . made available in the course of conducting a banking business'. This covers the bank account. Arguably, the operation of payment services is a service supplied in relation to the bank account so as to constitute a financial service governed by the SICA.

Subdivision E deals with conditions and warranties in consumer transactions. Particularly noteworthy is the warranty under which services will be rendered with due care and skill as well as the warranty or fitness for any known purpose (section 12 ED). Both may not be disclaimed (section 12 EB), though liability for consequential losses may be excluded (section 12EC).

In the UK, disclaimer clauses for liability under both implied and **[16]** express terms are governed by the Unfair Contract Terms Act 1977.[60] Under s. 2(2), a person may not exclude or restrict his liability for negligence causing loss or damage[61] except in so far as the term . . . satisfies the requirement of reasonableness'. For consumer contracts,[62] this extends, under s. 3, to any exclusion or restriction of liability for the breach of a standard form contract, as well as to the reservation of any right to render either a performance materially different or no performance at all.

---

[59] See cites in n. 57 above.

[60] For a brief overview, in the banking context, see M. Hapgood, *Paget's Law of Banking*, 11th edn. (London: Butterworths, 1996), at 312–13.

[61] This applies to liability for both economic and property losses or damages but not for death or personal injury for which any exclusion or restriction of liability resulting from negligence is precluded under s. 2(1).

[62] 'Consumer' is defined in s. 12 as one making the contract outside the course of business with someone making the contract in the course of business.

Furthermore, under s. 2(3), a person's agreement to or awareness of any exclusion or restriction of liability for negligence 'is not in itself to be taken as indicating his voluntary acceptance of any risk'. Under s. 11(1), to satisfy the reasonableness requirement, 'the term shall have been a fair and reasonable one to be included having regard to the circumstances which were, or ought reasonably to have been, known to or in the contemplation of the parties when the contract was made'. Under s. 11(4), in determining the reasonableness of a term restricting liability to a specified sum of money, 'regard shall be had in particular' to the availability of both resources and insurance to cover the liability. Guidelines for the application of the reasonableness test, set out in Schedule 2,[63] include the relative bargaining positions of the parties, any inducement given to the customer to agree to the term, the availability of an alternative with another person, the customer's knowledge of the term or whether the customer should have known it, and, in the case of an exclusion or restriction of liability which is conditional, whether it was reasonable that the fulfilment of the condition would be practicable. It should however be pointed out that no clear-cut preclusion from either disclaiming liability for negligence or from passing responsibility to a non-negligent party is included. Rather, it is specifically stated that a 'reasonable' term excluding or restricting liability for negligence is valid.

(V) THE ROLE OF AGENCY

[17]   In the USA, both the reciprocal duties of a bank and customer and the effectiveness of exemption clauses are thus matters of statutory law. In the UK, it is only the latter point which is dealt with by statute. Australian legislation provides for the bank's duty of care and regulates the effectiveness of exemption clauses. Under English law, the reciprocal duties, together with the responsibility for an act or omission by a third party engaged in carrying out a task, have essentially been left to be determined under the common law. With the exception of issues regarding the bank's duty of care, the same holds true for Australia. In both England and Australia, as in the other common law jurisdictions, the inadequacy of mandate doctrine to explain remaining gaps may well explain the recurring characterization of the bank, in carrying out payments and collec-

---

[63] The guidelines are stated to be applicable only to contracts relating to goods. They are, however, regarded as being of general application. See *Singer Co. Ltd. (UK)* v. *Tees and Hartlepool Port Authority* [1988] 2 Lloyd's L.R. 164 at 169; *Flamar Interocean Ltd.* v. *Denmac Ltd.*, [1990] Lloyd's L.R. 434 at 438–9; and *Stewart Gill Ltd.* v. *Horatio Meyer & Co. Ltd.*, [1992] Q.B. 600 (C.A.) at 608 and 609. In the common law, the reasonableness on an exemption clause to disclaim liability for negligence was upheld in *Dyck*, above, n. 52.

tions on behalf of its customer, as an agent acting for the latter as principal.[64]

Indeed, agency and mandate are related but not identical institutions. The distinction as well as the commonality are explained by Lee, where '[i]n the law of contract agency implies a contractual relation established [by the agent] between . . . the principal and a third person . . .', so that the law of agency is particularly concerned with this relation. At the same time, 'mandate is essentially a contract of employment and its rules are concerned only with the reciprocal rights and duties of the mandator . . . and the [mandatary]'.[65] Yet, he acknowledges, the law of mandate played an important role in the development of the law of agency;[66] more to the point, agency law has not been restricted to the relationship between the principal and the third party. Rather, the internal relationship between the principal and agent also bears relevance to the law of agency. It is this aspect of the law of agency that in the common law has become applicable to the banker and customer relationship as if it were interchangeable with mandated doctrine.

In the common law, an agent owes a duty of care to the principal. Also, he is required to keep accurate accounts of all transactions and be prepared to produce them to the principal. The agent is entitled to be reimbursed by the principal for all expenses, liability, and losses incurred in the course of carrying out his tasks as well as, when agreed, to a remuneration.[67] On this latter point, so far as the scope of the principal's obligations is concerned, in not restricting the principal's liability to negligence, the common law of agency follows the Roman law of mandate, as codified and followed by most civil law jurisdictions. Yet, it should be pointed out, so far as the banker and customer relationship is concerned, this is superseded in the common law by the customer's contractual implied and reciprocal duty of care to the banker.

Where the agent appoints a subagent, the latter's responsibility is only **[18]** to the agent and not to the original principal. There is neither agency relationship between the principal and subagent nor a privity of contract

---

[64] See e.g. *Selangor United Rubber Estates Ltd* v. *Cradock et al. (No 3)*, [1968] 2 All E.R. 1073 (Ch.D) (in respect of the payment of the customer's cheques); *Royal Products Ltd* v. *Midland Bank Ltd.*, [1981] 2 Lloyd's L.R. 194 at 198 (Q.B.) (in respect of the payment of a credit transfer); and *Bank of Nova Scotia* v. *Sharp*, [1975] 6 W.W.R. 97 (B.C. C.A.) at 99 and 103 (in respect of the collection of cheques).   [65] Above, n. 7 at 336.

[66] In fact, as recognized in the civil code of Japan discussed above, the agency relationship is established by mandate, though of course, not every mandate, as a contract of employment and management, creates agency; indeed, a mandate 'may be given without conveying any power to represent legally'. See Joubert and Van Zyl, above, n. 16 at ¶2. Obviously, this is less true in those jurisdictions, indicated on n. 64 above, where mandate is linked to an authority to perform a juridical act.

[67] *Halsbury's Laws of England*, 4th edn. reissue (London: Butterworths, 1990), vol. i (2) Agency, particularly, ¶¶92, 96, 115, and 123.

between them. The agent remains responsible to the principal for the due execution of the transaction which he has undertaken, whether he had authority to delegate to a subagent or not.[68] Stated otherwise, the agent is vicariously liable to the principal for the negligence of the subagent[69] and the latter is not liable to the principal.[70]

At the same time, substitution results in the replacement of the original agent by a new one so as to create direct privity between the principal and the substitute-agent. The original agent's authority terminates upon the substitution and he is not responsible for any loss created by the substitute. Yet, substitution is not a unilateral act by the original agent. It is a novation requiring an agreement, to which the principal must be a party. Effectively, substitution is created whenever 'the substitute agrees to act as [the principal]'s agent in consideration of [the principal]'s withdrawal of authority from [the original agent]'.[71]

[19]   In Israeli legislation, the mandate is not recognized as a distinct institution. Yet, in the literature and in the context of agency law, the mandate is referred to as the internal relationship between a principal and agent under which the agent's authority is given.[72] It is thus agency law which may determine the nature of duties owed by a bank acting on a customer's behalf. Under the Israeli Agency Law, 1965, the agent must act faithfully, comply with the principal's instructions, account to the principal for profits and assets coming to his hands in the course of the agency, and is entitled to be indemnified for reasonable expenses.[73] Under general law, the agent owes the principal a duty of care.[74] In principle, a substitute agent is liable directly to the principal, as his own original agent. Conversely, the subagent is the agent's agent, and there is no direct agency relationship, or in fact, any privity, between him and the principal.[75] However, under s. 14 of the Torts Ordinance [New Version], as the principal of the subagent, the original agent is vicariously liable to his own (namely, the original) principal for the subagent's wrongs.[76]

Section 11 of the Israel Agency Law requires the agent to indemnify the

---

[68] See e.g. R. Powell, *The Law of Agency*, 2nd edn. (London: Pitman, 1961) at 309.

[69] But see doubts expressed by Atkin LJ, in *Cheshire & Co.* v. *Vaughan Bros. & Co.*, [1920] 3 K.B. 240 at 259, particularly as applied to the case where the agent had used reasonable care in selecting the subagent.

[70] *Calico Printers' Association* v. *Barclays Bank and Anglo-Palestine Co., Ltd.* (1931), 145 L.T. 51 at 55, *per* Wright J. But see doubts as to the absolute nature of this rule in Powell, above, n. 68 at 309.   [71] Powell, ibid. at 308.

[72] See A. Barak, *The Law of Agency*, vol. i (Tel-Aviv: Nevo, 1996) [in Hebrew] at §§11, 12, and 202.   [73] Ss. 8, 10, and 11.

[74] Barak, above, n. 72, vol. ii, at §§733 and 738.

[75] For a comprehensive discussion on subagency, including the distinction with the substitution of an agent, see Barak, *id.* vol. ii at §§1000–39

[76] This is similar to the employer's vicarious liability for the wrongs of his employee, but usually, not to that of his independent contractor. See ss. 13 and 15 of that Torts Ordinance.

principal for his reasonable expenses and obligations reasonably incurred due to the agency. This may not be broad enough to cover liability for losses incurred in connection with the agency. It is however recognized, as a matter of the law of torts, and similarly to the minority civil law position, that the agent owes a duty of care to the principal and may thus be liable to him in negligence.[77]

Regardless, and following the common law position, Israeli law fastens on a bank a duty of care towards the customer, either as an implied contract term or in tort,[78] and further recognizes a limited reciprocal duty of care owed to a banker by the customer.[79] There is neither a specific statutory preclusion against contracting out liability for an intentional or negligent breach, nor any prohibition against contractually passing on responsibility to a non-negligent customer. However, as indicated in 2.A (iv) s. 13 above, under general law, contracts which are contrary to public policy,[80] as well as abusive or unfair terms in a standard form contract,[81] may be invalidated.

(VI) CONCLUSION

In the final analysis, in all jurisdictions mandate doctrine underlies the **[20]** bank's duty, as a mandatary, to both act with care and account to the customer. Where mandate doctrine is not prevalent, these duties are reinforced by implied contract, agency, and at least in part, by tort. Regardless, no express terms are required to fasten such duties on a bank. In turn, as may infrequently be provided by statute, express terms have only a limited power, which may differ from one jurisdiction to another, to disclaim liability for negligence.

---

[77] Barak, above, n. 72, vol. ii, at §834.

[78] See R. Ben-Oliel, *Banking Law—General Part* (Jerusalem: Sacher Institute, 1996), at 86–91 [in Hebrew]. [79] Ibid. at 328.

[80] S. 30 to Contracts Law (General Part), 1973.

[81] S. 3 to Standard Contracts Law, 1982. On the banking contract as a 'standard contract' under this Law, see Ben-Oliel, above, n. 78 at 72–5 and discussion in 2.A above.

D. The Current Account

(I) INTRODUCTION

[1] A bank deposit may be made either in cash or by means of a cashless payment, and either by the customer or by a third party for the customer. Similarly, a withdrawal out of a bank deposit may be made by the customer or under the customer's authority, either in cash or in the form of a cashless payment, and either for the customer himself or in the form of payment to a third party. In 2.B the bank deposit was treated as an isolated transaction, followed by either one full withdrawal or a series of withdrawals of the entire amount. Obviously, as may be observed from 2.C, the situation is typically[1] more dynamic, as a succession of deposits and withdrawals, or of incoming and outgoing payments, may occur in no particular sequence. The framework within which the bank–customer deposit and withdrawal activity, and hence, payment operations, take place, so as to establish their respective monetary positions, is the bank account. Where the account governs successive reciprocal operations it is generally known as a current account.

[2] It is generally recognized that the bank account is more than a framework for posting deposits and withdrawals of the customer to and from the bank. Rather, the account is viewed as a mechanism for the settlement of multiple reciprocal debts between the two parties. With each entry to the account, resulting from either a deposit or withdrawal, a new balance, reflecting new indebtedness, between the counterparties, is created. It is with regard to the entire legal implication of this balance, and its impact on the various transactions to which the account applies, that views may vary.

[3] At first blush, in each legal system, novation and 'compensation' or set-off ought to underlie the nature of the current account. The following is an explanation of these concepts, followed by a demonstration of their inadequacy as a complete explanation. Stated otherwise, they are essential but insufficient concepts to wholly explain the nature of the current account.

In the common law, '[n]ovation is a transaction by which, with the consent of . . . the parties . . ., a new contract is substituted for the one that has

---

[1] This, of course, is not to deny the possibility of a simpler 'static' relationship, of one ad hoc deposit made for a specific purpose, to be withdrawn either as a whole or in parts, until fully exhausted. Such will be the case, for example, where a non-customer deposits a sum of money to be transmitted by a credit transfer, as well as where a customer draws on a fixed-amount line of credit given to him by the bank. Such however is not the typical bank account relationship.

already been made'.[2] It 'amounts to the extinction of [an] old obligation, and the creation of a new one'.[3] Substantially, this is also the position under the civil codes of Germany, Japan, France, Italy, and Quebec as well as under the Swiss code of obligations.[4] It however appears that while novation explains the replacement of each individual debt entered to the account by the overall debt for the entire account balance, it fails to set out the terms of the contract underlying the novated debt. It further omits to provide for a complete explanation underlying the process of replacement and the entire implication of all its incidents. In fact, novation may be no more than a recognition that the current account is created by contract.

Both 'compensation' and set-off[5] are concerned with the adjustment of **[4]** mutual (that is, reciprocal) debts between counterparties. Under the civil codes of both France and Quebec, as well as of Italy, the effect of 'compensation' is to extinguish mutual debts automatically, as soon as they exist, namely, merely by operation of law, without any act by the debtor.[6]

---

[2] M. P. Furmston, *Cheshire, Fifoot and Furmston's Law of Contract*, 12th edn. (London: Butterworths, 1991) at 518.

[3] P. S. Atiyah, *An Introduction to the Law of Contract*, 5th edn. (Oxford: Clarendon Press, 1995) at 387.

[4] See art. 513 in Japan; art. 1271(1) in France; art. 1230 in Italy; and art. 1660 in Quebec. Cf. §364 in Germany; and art. 116 in Switzerland which assume the validity of an effective novation to substitute a new debt for an old one.

[5] In principle, as outlined immediately hereafter, 'compensation' is a civil law concept, and 'set-off' is a common law term. Unfortunately, this linguistic distinction, underlying a substantive one, has not always been respected by the translators to English. Thus, only for Quebec and Italy 'compensation' is used in the English translation. For France, 'compensation' is translated to 'extinguishment' which correctly describes the effect of 'compensation' but is too broad. However, for Switzerland, translation of 'compensation' (in the official French language text) is to 'set-off'. Similarly, 'set-off' is employed in the translation of the German and Japanese provisions. Confusion is further increased, since as outlined immediately below, the extinguishing effect of 'compensation' is automatic in France, Quebec, and Italy, which is not the case for the Swiss 'compensation' as well as for the Japanese and German 'set-off'. I am advised that while in Germany, the original for 'set-off' is 'Aufrechnung', the original in the German language official text for the Swiss 'compensation' (in the original French language text) is 'Verrechnung'. At the same time, the French 'compensation' is translated to German as 'Kompensation'. While purporting to adhere to the terminology of each English translation, I prefer the use of 'compensation' in English, *per* the translations for the Quebec and Italian codes. See *The French Civil Code Revised Edition* (as am. to 1 July 1994), trans. John H. Crabb (Littleton, Colo.: Fred B. Rothman & Co., 1995); *The German Civil Code* (as am. to 1 Jan. 1975) trans. I. S. Forrester, S. L. Goren, and H. M. Ilgen (South Hackensack, NJ: Fred B. Rothman & Co., 1975) (with 1981 Supp. trans. S. L. Goren); *The Civil Code of Japan* (translation) (Tokyo: Ministry of Justice, 1972); *The Italian Civil Code*, trans. M. Beltramo, G. E. Longo, and J. H. Merryman (Dobbs Ferry, NY: Oceana, 1969); *Swiss Contract Law, English Translation of Selected Official Texts—Swiss Code of Obligations* (Zurich: Swiss-American Chamber of Commerce, 1997); and the bilingual edition of the Quebec Civil Code, *Code civil du practicien* (Montreal: DAFCO, 1995).

[6] See arts. 1289–90 in France (where it is further stated that 'compensation' occurs even without the knowledge of the debtor as to the existence of the debt owed to him by the creditor); arts. 1672–3 in Quebec; and arts. 1241–2 in Italy. For 'compensation' in general see M. E. Tigar, 'Comment—Automatic Extinction of Cross-Demands: *Compensatio* from Rome to

Conversely, in common law jurisdictions, the right to set off mutual debts[7] 'is generally characterized as being, not a modification of an obligation, but an incident of its enforcement'.[8] It is 'merely a convenient mode of settling mutual accounts or preventing multiplicity of actions between the same parties'[9] and 'not an incident or an accompaniment of the debt'.[10] More specifically, in the common law, the right of set-off 'is not a defense, but a cross action [which] concedes the validity of the plaintiff's claim, and is founded upon an independent cause of action in favor of the defendant, who may at his election assert it by way of set-off, or enforce it by a separate suit'.[11] By statute, however, it may be asserted against a plaintiff as part of the statement of defence.[12] Nevertheless, its effect to extinguish the mutual debts and replace them with a new debt in the amount of the resulting balance is only from the time judgment is given.[13]

'Compensation' under the Swiss code of obligations and 'set-off' under the civil codes of Germany and Japan reflect an intermediate position.[14] Similarly to the common law, each operates only by the assertion, by means of declaration or advice, by the debtor to his creditor. Yet, once the debtor takes the initiative, the effect of the resulting debt adjustment, namely, of extinguishing the old mutual debts and their replacement by a new debt for the balance due, is retroactive to the time when mutuality first arose, as in France, Quebec, and Italy. Thus, unlike the common law set-off, whose effect is merely procedural, the Swiss 'compensation' and the Japanese and German set-off, once asserted, have the same substantive effect as that automatically achieved by 'compensation' in France, Italy, and Quebec.

California' (1965), 53 Cal. L. Rev. 224, as well as P. J. Omar and A. Sorensen, 'Set-off: The French Perspective of a Universal Institution' [1997] 10 J.I.B.L. 409.

[7] The right is invariably known as statutory, legal, independent, court, or procedural set-off. See P. R. Wood, *English and International Set-off* (London: Sweet & Maxwell, 1989) at 7. It is provided for by statute.

[8] B. Crawford, *Crawford and Falconbridge Banking and Bills of Exchange*, 8th edn., vol. ii (Toronto: Canada Law Book, 1986) at 1730.

[9] A. W. Rogers, *Falconbridge on Banking and Bills of Exchange*, 7th edn. (Toronto: Canada Law Book, 1969) at 671. This quote does not appear in the current (8th) edition. Instead, the author states, '[t]o prevent circuity, mutual debts taking the form of liquidated demands may be set off, the one against the other, with judgment being rendered for the net balance'. See Crawford, *id.* vol. i, at 786.

[10] *Lincoln* v. *Grant*, 47 DC App 475 (1917–18) at 483.　　　　[11] Ibid.

[12] See e.g. currently in Ontario, s. 111 of the Courts of Justice Act, R.S.O. 1990, c. 43. In England the right of set-off exists by statute since the Act for the Relief of Debtors with Respect to the Imprisonment of their Persons', 1729, 2 Geo. II, c 22, s. 13.

[13] Wood, above, n. 7 at 84–6.

[14] See arts. 120–4 in Switzerland; arts. 505–6 in Japan; and §§ 387–9 in Germany. In Japan, the former Japanese civil code of 1890 adopted French style 'compensation' provisions which extinguished mutual debts (ss. 519 et seq.). Subsequently, in 1899, the current Japanese civil code adopted German style 'Aufrechnung' provisions requiring a party's declaration which nonetheless has a retroactive effect.

Since its effect is not automatic to extinguish debts, the right of set-off under the common law does not appear to provide an adequate explanation to the automatic effect of the current account to establish a binding balance between the counterparties. The same seems to apply to the right of set-off in Germany and Japan and 'compensation' in Switzerland. Also, in all jurisdictions, including in France, neither set-off nor 'compensation' explains the creation of a new debt by increasing the balance due rather than reducing it by a counter-debt. Thus, as indicated, as an explanation underlying the current account, both 'compensation' and set-off are inadequate.

(ii) France

Special thought to the current account has been given in France,[15] where in fact, it acquired a precise legal meaning.[16] In contrast, in common law jurisdictions, the current account has not attracted substantial doctrinal discussion, and it usually denotes a bank account used for payment operations, and from which withdrawals can be made on demand. As such it differs from a deposit account with respect to which the procedure for withdrawals is more onerous.[17] Both current and deposit accounts are said to 'possess the essential characteristics of running accounts of "deposits" of money by customers'.[18] Current account may however be often loosely used interchangeably with running account to denote any type of account recording successive reciprocal operations. In banking, such operations are the deposit and withdrawal of funds.

[5]

French law distinguishes among the deposit account, the current account, and the special account provided for by specific law.[19] According to a common definition prevailing in France, a current account agreement

[6]

---

[15] The ensuing discussion particularly draws on G. Ripert and R. Roblot, *Traité de droit commercial*, 13th edn. (Paris: Librairie Générale de Droit et de Jurisprudence, 1992) at 391–418, as well as on C. Gavalda and J. Stoufflet, *Droit bancaire*, 4th edn. (Paris: Litec, 1999) at 139–61 and (the less orthodox account in) J. L. Rives-Lange and M. Contamine-Raynaud, *Droit bancaire*, 6th edn. (Paris: Dalloz, 1995) at 220–61 ¶¶227–75. See also M. T. Calais-Auloy, 'Compte courant', Fascicule 210, *Bank and Credit*, Editons Techniques—Juris Classeurs, 1992 and see e.g. J. L. Rives-Lange and M. Cabrillac, 'Dépôt et compte en banque', *Encycl. Dalloz, Rep. dr. commercial* (1974, updated to 1992).

[16] For the Quebec conception of the current account, effectively endorsing the essence of French doctrine, see M. Duval, 'Le Compte courant en droit commercial au Quebec' (1997), 57 Revue du Barreau 455.

[17] See M. Hapgood, *Paget's Law of Banking*, 11th edn. (London: Butterworths, 1996) at 160 and 167–8.

[18] *United Dominion Trust v. Kirkwood* [1966] 11 E.R. 968 (C.A) at 986, Diplock LJ.

[19] See Gavalda and Stoufflet, above, n. 15 at 103–72 and Rives-Lange and Contamine-Raynaud above, n. 15 at 171–264 ¶¶ 181–279. It is generally said that the less sophisticated deposit account is usually held by consumers.

(or in the original, 'la convention de compte courant') is created by two parties, or counterparties, who decide to include their reciprocal monetary transactions in an account, whose balance successively and continuously adjusts with each transaction, and which is to be settled only upon the closure of the account. It is the successive recording or posting of each transaction which characterizes the account as 'current' or 'running'. While the current account is not limited to the bank and customer relationship, and in fact, may exist between any pair of counterparties with mutual dealings, its centrality to the banking relationship makes it a 'banking instrument'.

In each transaction included in the current account, the creditor is the 'sender', while the debtor is the 'receiver'. Each transaction entered into the account is often described as a 'remittance' from the sender to the receiver. Accordingly, in connection with the bank deposit or an incoming payment, the customer is the sender and the bank is the receiver. Conversely, in a withdrawal or outgoing payment, the bank is the sender and the customer is the receiver.

In fact, the above-mentioned definition is too broad. A current account must be created by agreement. It must cover liquid and certain claims, whether current (that is, presently due)[20] or deferred,[21] but not conditional.[22] Three features are essential: generality, reciprocity, and alternance.[23] It is the combined effect of these three features which in fact sets aside the current account as a distinct category of account under French law.

[7]   Generality means that all liquid and certain claims arising from transactions falling into the designated category, and not specifically excluded, are to be automatically covered. That is, while a customer is not required to deal exclusively with one bank, all transactions dealt with the bank, unless specifically agreed otherwise, must be settled through the account. Generality further means that even deferred claims are automatically affected by and brought into the framework of the account, though obviously, they are not to be posted and merged into the balance until they fall due.

---

[20] Technically, each claim must be liquid, certain, presently due and fungible (or in French, 'liquide, certaine, exigible, et fongible').

[21] A deferred claim ('un différé') meets all the qualifications noted above, other than that it is not presently due.

[22] While deferred claims will not enter into the calculation of the balance until their due date, they immediately become covered by the agreement, so as, for example, to be netted with the counterparty's claims due on the same day. Conversely, claims to be collected are not included. All this is irrelevant for the regular payment activity. Technically, deferred claims (or in French, 'différés') 'enter' to the account (or become governed by its underlying agreement) as they arise, but are 'posted' to it only on their due date when they become 'available' (or in French, 'disponibles'). 'Availability' is thus a function of 'exigibility'.

[23] Some view the alternance as an aspect of reciprocity. See e.g. Ripert and Roblot, above, n. 15 at 394 and Rives-Lange and Contamine-Raynaud, above, n. 15 at 233 ¶242.

Reciprocity means mutuality, that is, the existence of transactions going in both directions, so as to generate for each counterparty debits and credits. Reciprocity is regarded as an objective element, in the sense that regardless of the intention of the parties, only dealings capable of generating reciprocal debts may be brought into a current account agreement.

Alternance means entanglement (or in French, 'enchevêtrement'). Essentially, it means that mere reciprocity will not suffice. For example, such mere reciprocity, which will not suffice, exists in the case of a one-shot deposit, followed by either a full withdrawal, or a series of partial withdrawals to the full amount. This will not create the required alternance or entanglement even if the operation is repeated, and even on a continuous basis. Stated otherwise, there is no current account as long as the contract requires that remittances by one party do not commence until the other's terminate. What is required is the continuous and unstructured exchange of remittances in both directions, which creates the alternance or entanglement. It is however not required that alternance or entanglement will necessarily occur in fact; it is required, rather, that alternance or entanglement will be within the purview of the agreement. Also, alternance or entanglement does not necessitate a right to an overdraft, the latter being consistent with the current account, but not an indispensable part of its underlying theory.

Following each transaction giving rise to a remittance, the respective [8] sender's claim against the receiver becomes an item in the account, which passes as a credit to the sender and debit to the receiver. According to one view, the process of fusion is that of novation. Yet, novation requires the extinction of an old claim and its substitution by a new one. Here, however, while the old claim extinguishes, it is not substituted by the creation of a new claim; rather, the old claim merges into another, namely the balance, so that the overall existing balance between the parties changes, but no new claim is created. Accordingly, it may be more appropriate to talk of a 'quasi-novation'. But even then, no explanation is provided as to the legal nature of this new provisional balance.

Others view the process of fusion as a continuous netting or 'compensation' of mutual claims in opposite directions, under which each claim is paid to the extent of a counter-claim. Indeed, as indicated, under the civil code, 'compensation' is a mode of extinguishing a debt, by the mere operation of law, by means of a counter-debt, namely, a debt in the opposite direction, owed by the creditor (of the debt to become extinguished) to the debtor, and to the extent of that counter-debt.[24] In the context of the current account, however, this overlooks the contractual foundation of the

---

[24] French civil code, arts. 1289–99. See above for the distinction between compensation under the civil law and the right of set-off under the common law.

account, which is inconsistent with the extinction, under compensation, by the mere operation of law. Further, as indicated, this overlooks the fact that in a current account a claim extinguishes also by means of merely increasing the balance due, and not necessarily by its reduction due to the rise of a counter-claim. Stated otherwise, while each remittance is automatically paid as it is posted to the account, payment occurs by virtue of its fusion into the balance, rather than effected by a counter-debt as under compensation. The other side of the same coin is that a new remittance pays neither the old balance nor counter-debts of which the old balance consists; rather, the new remittance merges into the old balance so as to create a new one.

[9]   The current account has accordingly been described as a particular financial mechanism to whose particular items the civil code does not apply. It is a melting pot into which all transactions are thrown and merged so that from the fusion a residue is created which is the balance of the account. 'The settlement of credits put into the account is realized by a phenomenon of agglomeration which amalgamates and reduces them into a homogeneous bloc, with the view of global liquidation at the closure of the account.'[25]

[10]   It is said that the credit which passes through the account is extinguished and not transformed. This results in the loss of security interests securing the original obligation, as well as possible changes in the prescription period and the interest to be charged. For example, a remittance posted to an account creates a new balance which becomes subject to the prescription period applicable to the account and which recommences to run for each new balance created by the new remittance.[26] Yet, not all connection with the past disappears; if the original obligation is invalidated, a counter-entry ('contre-passation') in the account is justified.

The general rule is, however, that of the unity or indivisibility of the current account. Its different items become part of a whole, so that a sender may not declare himself a creditor to any individual remittance. Nor can any such remittance be individually discharged.[27] In the classic conception of the current account, 'indivisibility' has served to explain the

---

[25] Ripert and Roblot, above, n. 15 at 401. My translation.

[26] In France, a bank deposit in an account for which no demand has been made for thirty years is to be transferred to the state, though already after it has been dormant (namely, has been the object of no operation or demand) for ten years, which is the standard prescription period, it may be transferred by the bank (under Law no. 77 of 3 Jan. 1977) to a 'Caisse des dépôts', specifically designated by law for that purpose, where it is held, for the benefit of the depositor, until the original thirty-year period expires. See Ripert and Roblot, above, n. 15 at 426.

[27] Accordingly, the civil code provisions governing the debtor's right to impute payments to any of the several debts owed by him to the creditor (arts. 1253–6) do not apply to remittances covered by the bank account.

effect of the novation, carried out with each remittance to the account, to create a new provisional balance, that until the closure of the account, is neither available ('disponible') nor presently due ('exigible'); hence, until closure, each provisional balance is at least, 'indivisible'. It is only a global 'compensation', occurring at the closure of the account, which turns the final balance into a presently due debt owed by the counterparty in debit to the counterparty in credit.[28] The conventional wisdom has thus been that it is only upon the closure of the account that we truly have a creditor and a debtor, and only to the entire balance.

In a sense, it is the fusion of all entries to the account which provides the basis for the indivisibility. Fusion further explains why 'compensation' does not work as an underlying theory for the current account, in the course of its operation and prior to its closure, even in connection with a counter-claim, or a transaction in the opposite direction. Once put into the account, the earlier transaction extinguishes, so as to be incapable of being 'compensated' or 'paid' by a transaction coming from the other direction. Accordingly, the inclusion of a transaction in an account constitutes its 'payment' only in the sense of its extinguishment and fusion into a new balance, but not in any other sense, including that of compensation by a counter-entry (namely a transaction in the opposite direction). Stated otherwise, a debt that is already extinguished (upon its merging into a new balance) cannot (and need not) be extinguished again by a counter-debt.

Fusion, however, does not explain the gap between 'indivisibility' and   [11]
'availability' or 'exigibility'. While the 'global compensation' occurring upon closure purports to close the gap and provide the necessary link, it does not appear to be entirely consistent with the earlier 'fusion' leading to the 'indivisibility'.

Furthermore, while there is no enforceable debt between the parties to an account prior to its closure, there are, nevertheless, various implications for a counterparty, not precluded by mere 'indivisibility', in having either an overall credit or debit position, in the course of the operation of the account prior to its closure. A few examples relating to a positive or credit balance of a customer with a bank will be given. First, a customer with a credit position is permitted to draw on a positive balance with his bank. Second, the credit balance constitutes an asset in the customer's hands in terms of his balance sheet. Third, a third party creditor of the customer may seize a credit balance in an account in satisfaction of a debt owed by the customer to that creditor.

According to the orthodox view, the tension between the mere indivisibility of the balance and its availability to the counterparty with a credit   [12]

---

[28] For a good summary, see e.g. Calais-Auloy above, n. 15 at ¶14.

balance is thus not irreconcilable.[29] At the same time, this tension led to a challenge against 'indivisibility' as a useful concept. It is thus stated that since each provisional balance is certain, liquid, and available (or in French, 'certaine, liquide et disponible'), it is better to regard it as a truly subsisting debt owed by the counterparty in debit to the counterparty in credit, whose enforcement *inter se* is nevertheless postponed until the closure of the account.[30] The key to this feature of the current account is the fusion of each remittance into a new balance. In this context, 'indivisibility', as the 'novation' allegedly leading to it, is either redundant or misleading, as it obscures the nature of each provisional balance as a debt owed by one counterparty to the other.

[13]   According to one summary, the essential character of the current account has been described as tripartite. The current account is thus (i) a simplified mechanism for the settlement of reciprocal debts eliminating the multiplicity of individual cash payments, (ii) a mechanism facilitating between counterparties the guarantee of incoming debts by the creation of debts in the opposite direction, and (iii) a mechanism supporting credit operations by the mere delay conferred on the payment of each individual debt.[31]

With regard to these features, no disagreement appears to exist, however, as to the nature of any type of account, and not only as to the current account, as a mechanism for the settlement of mutual (or reciprocal) debts. Similarly, the third feature, that of a mechanism supporting credit operations, does not seem to be unique to the current account, and anyway, may not be as central to the nature of the account.[32]

[14]   Different views exist, however, as to what separates the current account from any other type of account. While there is no disagreement as to the ensuing rules, there seem to be different opinions as to the relative importance of each rule as the most characteristic of the current account. According to one view, alternance or entanglement constitutes the most distinctive feature of the current account which distinguishes it from any other type of account.[33]

---

[29] Ripert and Roblot, above, n. 15 at 405.

[30] See Rives-Lange and Contamine-Raynaud, above, n. 15 at 221, 225–6 ¶234, and 244–7 ¶¶ 260–1. The authors specifically stop short of arguing that a provisional balance is presently due (or in French, 'exigible'), though they maintain there is nothing in the concept of 'current account' to preclude the counterparties from agreeing to the availability of a cause of action to a counterparty even for the payment of a provisional balance. Ibid. at 247.

[31] Alfred Jauffret and J. Mestre, *Droit commercial*, 20th edn. (Paris: Librairie Générale de Droit et de Jurisprudence, 1991) at 344.

[32] For example, it is not enumerated by Rives-Lange and Contamine-Raynaud, above, n. 15 (e.g. at 222–3, where the two other features, that of mechanism for settlement and guaranty, are specifically enumerated).

[33] Riper and Roblot, above, n. 15 at 399.

Others view its feature as a mechanism of guaranty, which is a by-product of the generality of the current account, as the essential differentiating mark.[34] Thus, the general application of the current account to all transactions means that no specific decision by a counterparty is required as to whether a mutual dealing is to be included. The generality feature further precludes any option of excluding a mutual dealing. The combined effect of this automatic application is thus to provide a mechanism of guaranty applying not only to existing counter-debts, but also to deferred claims, and even to merely anticipated ones. True, no posting to the account, leading to a fusion into the balance, will take place until maturity or due date. Nonetheless, each counterparty incurs debts owed to the other, on the basis and anticipation of counter-debts owed or to be owed by the other to him.

(III) OTHER CIVIL LAW JURISDICTIONS

The current account is provided for, though not fully dealt with, in the civil code of Italy,[35] the code of obligations of Switzerland,[36] and the commercial codes of Germany[37] and Japan.[38] In all four jurisdictions the current account is not limited to claims[39] arising in connection with the banking relationship, though in the two commercial codes (that is, in Germany and Japan) the account must be with a merchant,[40] broadly defined to also cover a bank.[41] **[15]**

Italy has provisions applicable exclusively to banking transactions for current account (arts. 1852–7). There is no consensus in Italy as to the application of the general current account provisions, namely, arts. 1823–33, to the banking current account, other than arts. 1826, 1829, and 1832, explicitly stated in art. 1857 to apply to banking transactions for a

---

[34] Rives-Lange and Contamine-Raynaud, above, n. 15 at 222–3 ¶¶ 230–1. But see at 262–3, where the authors concede another difference, namely, that other than in a current account, settlement of claims posted to an account is by mere 'compensation'. Cf. ¶¶8 and 10, above.   [35] Articles 1823–33.

[36] Article 117.

[37] See §§355–7. See English translation by S. L. Goren, 2nd edn. (Littleton, Colo.: Fred B. Rothman & Co., 1998).

[38] Articles 529–34. An English translation appears in Z. Kitagawa, *Doing Business in Japan* (New York: Matthew Bender, 1980–99). Vol. DBJ App. 5-A.

[39] Only the Italian provisions elaborate on the nature of claims to be included. They must be claims subject to 'compensation', and may include expenses and commissions for transactions from which a remittance originates. See arts. 1824 and 1826.

[40] More specifically, in Germany, under §355(1), a current account may exist between a merchant and someone standing in business relations to him. In Japan, under art. 529, a current account may be created between merchants or a merchant and a non-merchant.

[41] See §1(2)(4) in Germany. In Japan, 'merchant' is broadly defined in art. 4(1), to mean 'a person who, as a business, engages in commercial acts . . .'.

current account. These articles 1826, 1829, and 1832 respectively deal with the right to commissions and reimbursement of expenses, exclusion of uncollected collection claims, and the approval of the account. In fact, arts. 1852–7 to the Italian civil code focus on contractual aspects of the banking current account, as set out in 2.A¶7 above, more than on the mechanism of the current account and its impact on the reciprocal entries posted to it, dealt with in arts. 1823–33, governing the general current account. This lends support to the position that arts. 1823–33, and not only 1826, 1829, and 1832, apply to banking transactions for current accounts, as long as they are not inconsistent with arts. 1852–7.

[16]   In Italy (art. 1823) and Japan (art. 529), the current account is stated to exist by reference to an agreement providing for it. Conversely, in Germany (§355(1)) and Switzerland (art. 117), the current account is described as actual activity or practice of posting remittances, rather than an agreement providing for such an activity or practice. In Japan and Germany, but not in Italy and Switzerland, a regular course of dealing between the counterparties is required for the establishment of a current account.

In Switzerland, art. 117 specifically delays the novation, namely the extinction of the individual remittances and their replacement by the balance, to the point in time where 'the balance is drawn and acknowledged'. Stated otherwise, no continuously running novation takes place with each provisional balance, occurring with each posting of an entry to the account. In a further departure from French legal doctrine, unless otherwise agreed, security interests securing individual transactions do not extinguish in Switzerland even upon 'the drawing and acknowledgment of the balance' (art. 117(3)). On this latter point, Switzerland is in line with Germany (§356) and Italy (art. 1828).[42]

'Set-off' is stated in both Germany (§355(1)) and Japan (art. 529) as the principle under which the current account operates. In Japan, the 'set-off' takes place at the expiration of the current account, which unless otherwise agreed, is at the end of six months (art. 531). In Germany, a distinction is made between the '[t]he closing of the account', which in the absence of an agreement to the contrary, will take place annually (§355(2)), and the 'regular intervals' in which the account is balanced by setting off the mutual claims (§355(1)). Either way, in not providing for a continuously running novation with each posting of a remittance to the account, this appears to be in line with Switzerland and contrary to France. Interest on the balance due runs, in Germany as well as in Japan, from the closure of the account.[43]

---

[42] In Italy, art. 1827 further provides for the survival of any right of action or defence to the original transaction, as well as for the striking from the account of any entry corresponding to a transaction declared void, annulled, rescinded, or dissolved.

[43] See §355(1) in Germany and art. 533(1) in Japan, where, however, under art. 533(2), this 'shall not hinder the right to claim interest on each item from the day on which the item was

In Italy, the provisions are silent as to whether each remittance resulting in a new provisional balance effects a novation as to the amount due. At the same time, the 'understanding that . . . claims [entered into the account] are uncollectible and untransferable until the closing of the account' is stated, in art. 1823(1), to be fundamental to the contract of the current account. Also, the account is to be closed and the balance is to be liquidated 'at the expiration of the terms stipulated in the contract or set by usage', and otherwise, 'in the absence of such term, at the end of each semester, computable from the date of the contract' (art. 1831).

Both Italy (in art. 1829) and Japan (in art. 530) provide for the striking out of uncollected collection claims entered to the account. Italy (in art. 1830) as well as Germany (in §357) specifically recognize the effectiveness of a third party creditor seizure of an account balance and the resulting inability of the account counterparties to undermine it by conducting transactions subsequent to such an effective seizure.

The effectiveness of an acknowledgement of a statement of account is [17] provided for in Japan (in art. 532) and Italy (in art. 1832). In Japan, an acknowledgement is binding 'except in the case of error or omission'. In Italy, merely forwarding a statement is considered approved, unless contested within the agreed or usual time. However, in any case, '[a]pproval does not preclude the right to attack the account for errors in writing or calculations, omissions or duplications'. This is so, provided the action is brought 'within six months from the date of receipt of the statement of account rendered in connection with the closing liquidation . . . which statement shall be sent by registered mail'.

Japan (in art. 534), Germany (in §355(3)), and Italy (in art. 1833) provide [18] for the early closure of the account by the unilateral act of any party. In Germany, however, this right to accelerate account closure is stated to exist only '[i]n case of doubt'. In Italy, a ten-day advance notice is required. Also in Italy, termination may further occur upon mental infirmity, disability, insolvency, or death. Regardless, in Italy, termination bars entry of new remittances, but does not accelerate the payment of the balance, which 'can only be demanded at the expiration of the [original] term'. Conversely, in both Japan and Germany, payment of the balance may be demanded upon the unilateral early account closure.

Doctrine, however, has not always followed the letter of the law and some of the distinctions noted above have been overlooked, de-emphasized, or reconstructed. For example, German doctrine[44] seems to require an

entered in the account current'. In Germany, interest from account closure 'even insofar as the account includes interest'. (Ibid.) In Italy, art. 1825, '[r]emittances bear interest at the rate established by the contract or by usage or, in their absence, at the legal . . . rate'.

[44] See e.g. H. Schönle, 'Allemagne', in *Jura Europae—Droit bancaire et boursier* (Munich: Verlag C. H. Beck and Paris: Éditions Techniques Juris-Classeurs, updated to 1976), at 10.11, particularly at 10.11(4), (5), and (13).

agreement to underline the current account and does speak of novation occurring with the posting of each remittance to the account.[45] This is in conjunction with a view which, in line with the express provision in Italy on the point, regards each remittance becoming individually unenforceable as it is posted to the account. Possibly then, as seems to be recognized by doctrine in Italy,[46] the actual distinction is between, on the one hand, the novation, that with each new remittance, nonetheless creates an unavailable (and not presently due) provisional balance, and on the other hand, enforceability of the final balance, or its becoming due, which is delayed to the closure of the account. Obviously, even without specifically mentioning the 'indivisibility' of each provisional balance, such distinction echoes the position of French classic doctrine on the point.

(iv) COMMON LAW JURISDICTIONS

[19]   Neither set-off nor the medieval writ of Account provides the doctrinal foundation for the current account in the common law. As indicated, in the common law, set-off does not generate a novation substituting the balance due for each remittance; rather, set-off facilitates a step taken by a debtor resulting in a novated debt. On its part, the medieval Account had two drawbacks.[47] First, to be accountable for property committed to his charge, the defendant must have acted as plaintiff's guardian in socage, bailiff, or receiver.[48] While 'receiver' expanded to cover commercial relations so as to facilitate the transformation of Account into a general quasi-contract remedy,[49] thereby alleviating the first drawback, the second obstacle remained insurmountable. This second obstacle was that Account was a cumbersome proceeding; a judgment in Account established the defendant's accountability and provided for the appointment of auditors to work out its detail. To enforce the auditors' award, the plaintiff was then required to bring a separate and subsequent Debt action.[50] Stated otherwise, the medieval Account was a mere framework for recording mutual transactions, even without the facility of keeping a

---

[45] For the importance of the acknowledgement of the balance as acknowledgement of a debt, which subject to rights in unjust enrichment may preclude recourse for any substantial discrepancy, see ibid. at 10.11(5)–(6).

[46] See e.g. CC Campi, 'Italie' in *Jura Europae—Droit bancaire et boursier*, ibid. at 40.11, particularly at 40.11(3).   [47] See further in 2.B(v), above.

[48] See in general e.g. J. H. Baker, *An Introduction to English Legal History*, 3rd edn. (London: Butterworths, 1990) at 410.

[49] For this process, see in general, e.g. Baker, above n. 47 at 301–2, and in greater detail, S. J. Stoljar, 'The Transformations of Account', (1964) 80 L.Q.R. 203.

[50] See e.g. G. H. S. Fifoot, *History and Sources of the Common Law* (London: Stevens & Sons, 1949) at 273–4.

running account monitoring the respective positions of the counterparties, with both calculations and novation occurring only subsequently, upon the auditors' award. This indeed is a far cry from the modern account.

Any effect of each remittance, whether on the entire debt owed or on a remittance occurring in the opposite direction, must thus be attributed to the agreement of the counterparties. The nature and limits of this agreement, particularly in the context of its impact on a third party attempting to trace an asset through the bank account,[51] is ably dealt with by Lionel Smith,[52] who analysed the account balance under four alternative models. According to Smith, in connection with a bank account, the account balance is either (i) a single asset, in the form of a monolithic debt, acquired through a mixed substitution, (ii) a mixture of indistinguishable intangible assets, (iii) a series of debts 'stacked' one on the top of the other, or (iv) a series of debts 'queued' one after the other in the order of each deposit.

These models can be explained in connection with the following example. Suppose an account consists of a $200 balance made by one deposit. This deposit is followed by a $100 deposit and subsequently, by a $50 withdrawal. Under the first view, that of the single asset, the second deposit generated a mixed substitution, under which the previous $200 debt and the new $100 deposit are both given in exchange for a new asset, which is a debt of $300. One monolithic debt in the sum of $200 is thus replaced by a new monolithic debt of $300. Following the $50 withdrawal, a new monolithic debt of $250 is created. From this perspective, the withdrawal cannot be attributed to any of the two deposits; rather, it decreased the monolithic debt created following the second ($100) deposit. In fact, this strongly echoes the French views as to the novating effect and 'indivisibility' of the account balance, under the orthodox position, or the 'fusion' of its components, under the heterodox one.

Under the second model, the bank account is viewed as a mixture of indistinguishable intangible assets, of one cent each, the latter being the smallest unit for withdrawal or deposit. Accordingly, following the original $200 deposit, the fund consisted of 20,000 units. Following the $100 deposit, the fund expanded to consist of 30,000 units, all mixed and indistinguishable. In the aftermath of the $50 withdrawal, the fund consisted

[20]

---

[51] Briefly stated, in connection with the substitution of assets, 'following' is concerned with the original substituted object, 'tracing' focuses on the identification of a substituting asset as the proceeds of the original one, while 'claiming' is the assertion of a right based on either 'following' or 'tracing'. For example, where B steals A's chattel, sells it and deposits the proceeds in B's bank account, A may attempt to trace the proceeds into B's bank account and seize them. Having already withdrawn some funds from the account, and perhaps deposited others, B will argue that the proceeds of A's chattel are no longer in the account. See, in general, L. D. Smith, *The Law of Tracing* (Oxford: Clarendon Press, 1997) at chapter 1.

[52] In his book, ibid. at chapter 5, particularly at 183–218.

of 25,000 indistinguishable units. As under the first model, the $50 withdrawal cannot be out of any specific deposit; rather, it was out of the mixture as a whole. In fact, this model also strongly echoes the French views as to the novating effect and 'indivisibility' of the account balance, under the orthodox position, or the 'fusion' of its components, under the heterodox one.

Under the first two models, each deposit has lost its identity in the increased balance. The first model views a debt created by the deposit of funds as a single asset. The second model views such a debt as the sum of small debts, each in the sum of its smallest component, namely, one cent. Accordingly, with any change in the balance, the first model entails the replacement of the asset by a new asset in the new amount. At the same time, under the second model, any change in the balance results in a change of quantity rather than replacement of assets. In effect, under the second, but not the first, model, the first deposit had no separate identity from its inception, as it originally consisted of indistinguishable intangible assets.

Conversely, under the two other models, each deposit retains its identity throughout the life of the account. The balance is seen as a series of individual and separate debts with no novation taking place. That is, under each model, by reference to the previous example, the balance of $300, consisting of the two deposits, is seen under the third and fourth models as two separate and distinct debts, one for the original $200 deposit and the other for the second $100 deposit. From this perspective, there is no difference between these third and fourth models.

[21]   To the extent that each deposit retains its identity under the third and fourth model, each withdrawal may be attributed to a specific deposit. Here lies the dissimilarity between the third and fourth model. The difference between them is in the metaphor; it is between 'stacking' debts one on the other and queuing them one after the other. The former is the third model and the latter is the fourth one. Under the third model, the debt (namely, deposit) added most recently to the stack is the first one to be removed; that is, the rule is 'last in first out', or LIFO. In our example, the $50 withdrawal is thus attributed to the subsequent $100 deposit. Conversely, under the fourth model, the one which has been longest in the queue is the first one to be removed; that is, the rule is 'first in first out', or FIFO. In our example, the $50 withdrawal is thus attributed to the initial $200 deposit.

Presumably, all four models recognize the existence as well as effectiveness of counterparties' agreement to delay the enforceability of each transaction posted to the account until the account is closed. Stated otherwise, the nature of each remittance as well as each provisional balance as not a presently due debt must be taken to be a universal and fundamental element of the current account. Similarly to the French position, this however, has not precluded the seizability of funds deposited in a bank account. In the common law, the service of the garnishee notice to the bank is regarded as a valid demand for withdrawal, as if made on the depositor's behalf.[53]

Conversely, the effect of posting a remittance to an account on collateral securing it is not specifically dealt with in connection with any of the models. Arguably, the security survives the posting at least under the third and fourth models. In fact, neither the third nor the fourth model appears to contemplate novation at any point of time, including at the closing of the account. Stated otherwise, under these two last models and unlike, for example, under the Swiss code of obligations, even the final balance does not represent a monolithic debt. Rather, under the third and fourth models, the balance consists of all outstanding deposits, each forming a separate and distinct debt. Such debts are, however, all discharged upon payment in full of the balance. In fact, this is consistent with the view that even an account stated, striking a balance between counterparties, is no more than a calculation adjusting their mutual positions,[54] rather than novating their respective obligations, so that the final payment effectively discharges the various remittances and not any one novated debt.[55]

Case law is not decisive in its choice of the preferable model. The leading authority is that of *Clayton's Case*.[56] In his judgment, Sir William Grant MR distinguished 'the case of a banking account' from 'cases of distinct insulated debts'; rather, he characterized it as a situation 'where all the sums paid in the form of one blended fund, the part of which have no longer any distinct existence'. Yet, he ruled, '[i]n such a case there is no room for any other appropriation than which arises from the order in which the receipts and payments take place, and are carried into the account'. Accordingly, in his view, the presumption is that 'it is the sum first paid in, that is first drawn out'.[57] In effect, while speaking of 'one blended fund' which sounds consistent with the second (or even the first) model, in applying the FIFO rule, Sir William Grant appears to apply the fourth model. The two limbs of his position as quoted above, **[22]**

---

[53] *Joachimson* v. *Swiss Bank Corporation* [1921] 3 K.B. 110 at 115 *per* Bankes LJ.

[54] See e.g. *Camillo Tank SS Co. Ltd.* v. *Alexandria Engineering Works* (1921), 38 T.L.R. 134 (H.L.) at 138, *per* Viscount Cave; and *Siqueira* v. *Noronha* [1934] A.C. 332 at 337 *per* Lord Atkin.

[55] See *Laycook* v. *Pickles* (1863) 4 B & S 497, 122 E.R. 546, (Q.B.) *per* Blackburn J. (cited in approval by Lord Atkin in *Siqueira id.* at 338), except that he expressly equated the effect of the discharging payment to that of novation.

[56] *Devaynes* v. *Noble; Clayton's Case* (1816), 1 Mer. 529 at 572; 35 E.R. 767 at 781 (Rolls Ct.)

[57] Ibid. at 608 (Mer.); 793 (ER).

namely, the principle and what purports to be its application, thus appear to be irreconcilable.

As pointed out by Smith, '[a]lthough Sir William Grant MR said that the sums paid in had 'no longer any distinct existence', in the sense that they were not wholly distinct debts, the very idea that withdrawals extinguish the oldest deposits entails a view that the bank account is made up of a series of debts, which are essentially arranged in a queue'.[58]

[23]   Ultimately, Smith settled the contradiction by resolving that as it is based on the presumed intention of the counterparties, the rule in *Clayton's Case* is limited to the appropriation of payments between debtor and creditor.[59] He concluded however[60] that tracing into and through bank accounts is to be governed by analogy to the rules of following through physical mixtures so that the account is to be regarded as an indistinguishable mixture of value. He thus endorsed the second model. Accordingly, in his view, '[t]racing through bank accounts is subject to the limitation of the lowest intermediate balance',[61] simply by resolving the impossibility of linking any withdrawal to any deposit against the wrongdoer.[62] Evidential complexity, particularly in the case of tracing by multiple claimants, may nevertheless lead courts to prefer the distribution in proportion to respective contributions, regardless of the timing of each contribution and withdrawal.[63]

[24]   It should however be noted that under the common law, limitation against both the customer's claim for a credit balance[64] and the bank's claim for a debit balance[65] commences to run as of the creditor's demand.

---

[58] Smith, above, n. 51 at 188.   [59] Ibid. at 185–94.   [60] Ibid. at 194–5.

[61] This effectively means that the money to be traced is the last to be withdrawn. Suppose in our example, the tracing claim is for the original $200 deposit. Under the FIFO rule, once $50 were withdrawn, they are deemed to be taken out of this original $200 deposit, so that only $150 can be traced into the final $250 balance. Conversely, under the lowest intermediate balance rule, since at no point in time the balance was reduced below the $200 claim, the entire $200 claimed may be traced. Under the LIFO rule, the $50 were withdrawn out of the second $100 deposit, so that the original $200 remained intact. In this numerical example, this is the same result as under the lowest intermediate balance.

[62] Smith, above, n. 51 at 201.

[63] For a critical discussion, see Smith, ibid. at 265–70. A leading case is *Barlow Clowes Int'l* v. *Vaughan* [1992] 4 All E.R. 22 (C.A.), followed in Canada in *Law Society of Upper Canada* v. *Toronto Dominion Bank* (1999), 42 O.R. (3d) 257 (Ont. C.A.), where the Court (Blair J.), having recognized the bank account to be a whole blended fund, which is in line with Smith's second and favoured model, nevertheless disfavourly treated the lowest intermediate balance rule. While applauding Blair J.'s methodology, Smith 'found fault with his reasoning'. See L. Smith, 'Tracing in Bank Accounts: The Lowest Intermediate Balance Rule on Trial' (2000), 33 Can. Bus. L.J. 75 at 91.

[64] For the necessity of demand and its role in commencing the limitation period for the customer's claim, see *Joachimson* v. *Swiss Bank Corp.*, above, n. 53 at 130 and 131, *per* Atkin LJ, and Hapgood above, n. 17 at 117.

[65] For the modern view as to the necessity of demand and its role in commencing the limitation period for the bank's claim, notwithstanding some earlier case law focusing on the

In connection with the customer's claim, this indeed is quite consistent with the nature of the claim as one for funds deposited with the bank.[66] At the same time, as it pertains to the bank's claim for an overdraft, this rule seems to differ from the general one applicable to a loan payable on demand and thus seems to be unique to an advance posted to an account.[67]

Either way, effectively then, other than as may be provided for by a specific statute,[68] a claim for a dormant account balance, for which no demand was made by the creditor, remains indefinitely available. This is true regardless of whether the creditor is the customer or the bank.[69] This indeed is quite consistent with the lack of enforceability of any individual remittance posted to the account. It appears that this is also consistent with viewing the account balance as either a monolithic debt or consisting of a series of debts.

In South Africa, each advance made by the bank to the customer and [25] posted to the account retains its individual identity as a separate debt. More specifically, the account consisting of the various overdrafts is viewed, as under the fourth model put forward by Smith, as a series of debts 'queued' one after the other in the order of each advance. For each such advance, as it is the rule for each loan payable on demand, prescription commences to run as of the moment the advance is made.[70] It thus follows that South Africa rejects the monolithic debt or mixture approaches embodied in Smith's first two models. However, it does not exclude the possibility that for a credit balance, prescription against the customer runs only as of the demand;[71] this would still be consistent with the nature of

---

centrality of the creation of the overdraft (rather than the demand for its repayment), see Hapgood, ibid. at 118; and E. P. Ellinger and E. Lomnicka, *Modern Banking Law*, 2nd edn. (Oxford: Clarendon Press, 1994) at 111.

[66] A leading case is *Tidd* v. *Overell* [1893] 3 Ch. 154. See 2.B(iv), above.

[67] The usual common law rule for an obligation payable on demand is that the limitation period runs as of the advance. See *Norton* v. *Ellam* (1837), 2 M. & W. 461; 150 E.R. 839 (Exch. of Pleas).

[68] For example, as indicated in 2.B(iv) s. 22, in Canada, a credit balance in an account that has not been subject to any activity is to be transferred to the Bank of Canada after ten years, where, subject to a $500 floor, it is kept indefinitely for the benefit of the depositor. See s. 438 of the Bank Act, S.C. 1991, c. 46 (Part VIII) as am. by S.C. 1992, c. 27, s. 90(1)(a) and s. 22 (1) of the Bank of Canada Act, R.S.C. 1985, c. B-2 (Part XVI), as am. by S.C. 1997, c. 15, ss. 94–110 and S.C. 1999, c. 28, s. 97.

[69] In Israel, at least so far as the bank's claim on an overdrawn account is concerned, to preclude the commencement of the limitation period, the demand must be made within a reasonable time. See S.P. 32/84, *Estate of Walter Nathan Williams* v. *Israel British Bank (London) (in Liquidation)* (1990), 44 PD(2) (SC), 265, per Barak J.

[70] See *Standard Bank of SA Ltd* v. *Onenate Investments (Pty) Ltd* 1995 (4) S.A. 510 (Cape PC) at 546 and 551, *per* Selikowitz J.

[71] Which is the rule in South Africa under *Ex Parte Smith* 1940 O.P.D. 120 at 126–7, *per* De Beer J.

the customer's claim to a deposit of funds, and would not offend the previous position of the common law which was not symmetric. In providing that the limitation period runs against the customer as of the demand, but against the bank as of the advance,[72] the common law accommodated such lack of symmetry,

[26]   In the final analysis, as a distinct concept, the current account has not been the subject of an extensive doctrinal discussion in the common law. It is therefore not surprising that solutions to specific issues have not been made by reference to a consistent theory, as such a theory simply does not exist. Alternatively, tracing into bank accounts is a common law concept; for example, it is not recognized in France.[73] Accordingly, on this point, the need to reconcile conflicting policies may be unique to the common law.

At the same time, the lack of a doctrinal attention to the current account in the common law does not necessarily entail the failure to recognize the existence of its distinct features. For example, it does not follow that the common law rejects altogether the French conception of viewing the account as a double mechanism for settling and guaranteeing mutual debts. Yet, in the common law, the practical implications of such functions have not led to the emergence of a comprehensive and cohesive doctrine.

---

[72] For the irrelevance of the demand under previous law see e.g. *Par Banking Co. Ltd.* v. *Yates* [1898] 2 Q.B. 460 (C.A.), specifically considered by Hapgood, above n. 17 at 118 as not representing the law today.

[73] See e.g. Cass. civ. 1, 20 avril 1983, Bull. civ. 1983.I.n. 127.

PART 3

The performance of the mandate

A. Orders for the Dispositions of Funds

Executing and receiving payments on the customer's behalf is an impor- [1]
tant bank function under the banking contract. Payment could be made
from one account into another either at the same bank or at two different
banks. In the latter case, the two banks may settle either bilaterally over a
correspondent account each holds with the other, or multilaterally, over
the books of a common correspondent, possibly the central bank. Alternatively, the two banks may be linked through more banks, with each link
being either a bilateral or multilateral settlement.

An inter-account transfer is initiated by payment instructions communicated by a customer to a bank and is carried out by means of a debit to
the payor's account and a credit to that of the payee. Depending on the
manner in which payment instructions are communicated to the payor's
bank, which affects the sequence of the banking operations in debiting the
payor's account or crediting the payee's account, inter-account transfers
are divided into debit and credit transfers. As a rule, the communication
flow and the movement of funds are in opposite directions in a debit
transfer but in the same direction in a credit transfer.

In a debit transfer, the payor's instructions are communicated to the
payor's bank by the payee through the payee's bank. Such instructions
may be initiated by the payee pursuant to the payor's authority; as, for
example, in connection with recurring mortgage or insurance premium
payments. When the instructions are first communicated by the payee to
the payee's bank, the payee's account is credited. When the instructions
ultimately reach the payor's bank, the payor's account is debited; that is,
in a debit transfer, the credit to the payee's account precedes the debit to
the payor's account. The credit to the payee's account, however, is initially provisional and is subject to reversal if the payor's bank dishonours
the payor's instructions, e.g. for lack of funds, and communicates its rejection to the payee's bank. Credit to the payee's account is final only when
the debit to the payor's account becomes irreversible. In a debit transfer,
funds credited to the payee's account are collected or 'pulled' from the
payor's account.

In contrast, in a credit transfer, such as a direct deposit of payroll, benefit, interest, pension or dividend, the payor's instructions are communicated to the payor's bank directly by him, without the mediation of a
credit to the payee's account at the payee's bank. When the instructions
are communicated, the payor's account is debited. As such, in a credit
transfer, unlike in a debit transfer, the first impact of the payor's instructions on the banking system is a debit to the payor's account with the

payor's bank. Having received the payor's instructions and debited the payor's account, the payor's bank forwards the instructions to the payee's bank which then proceeds to credit the payee's account. Thus, in a credit transfer, the debit to the payor's account precedes the credit to the payee's account, and is not subject to reversal, for example for lack of funds. In a credit transfer, funds debited to the payor's account are 'pushed' to that of the payee.

In both debit and credit transfers, whenever the payor's and payee's accounts are at the same bank, no interbank communication is required. Nonetheless, the sequence of banking operations, as set out above, is unaffected.

[2]   Customer and interbank payment instructions may be written, electronic, or even oral. The ensuing discussion will focus on two payment mechanisms: the cheque and the credit transfer. The cheque is a written instruction initiating a debit transfer, pulling into the payee's account funds from the payor's account. However, cheque payment also may be made in cash rather than to the payee's account. A credit transfer, pushing funds from the payor's account to that of the payee, may be initiated by written, electronic, or even oral instructions. Particular attention will be given below to the wire or large value credit transfer. Pre-authorized debit and credit transfers will not be dealt with.

[3]   The Swiss Code of Obligations (CO) contains provisions applying to 'orders' (arts. 466–71), initiating both credit and debit transfers. In contrast, the German civil code (BGB) provisions covering 'orders' (ss. 783–92) are limited to written instructions initiating debit transfers. Other countries do not have any identifiable body of law covering payment instructions in general.[1] Even in Switzerland[2] and Germany[3], the provisions governing 'orders' are superseded by a specific law applicable to cheques.

Nevertheless, a payment instruction may be an 'order', regardless of its further classification according to the specific payment mechanism it initiates. Accordingly, the provisions governing the 'order' in Switzerland and Germany merit a preliminary consideration.

Under both Swiss CO art. 466 and German BGB s. 783, an order constitutes a double authority from the order giver (the drawer in Germany), directed first to the recipient of the order (the drawee in Germany) to pay[4]

---

[1] See, in general, B. Geva, 'The Concept of Payment Mechanism' (1986), 24 Osgoode Hall L.J. 1.   [2] Swiss CO art. 471(2).

[3] In the absence of a specific provision to that effect in Germany, this is a straightforward application of the principle under which a law of special application (law of cheques) supersedes or defers a law of general application (law of orders).

[4] Under the provisions, the order directed to the recipient/drawee may be to remit to the payee money, securities or other fungibles. We are concerned here only with the remittance (namely payment) of money.

the payee for the account of the order giver/drawer. Second, the order is directed to the payee, authorizing him to collect in his own name from the recipient/drawee. In Germany, the order must be contained in 'an instrument' and delivered by the drawer to the payee. Hence, the 'order' must initiate a paper-based debit transfer. No such limitation exists in Switzerland where consequently, the payment order may initiate both electronic and paper-based, as well as both credit and debit, transfers.

In both Switzerland (CO art. 467(1)) and Germany (BGB s. 788), where the order is intended to discharge a debt of the order giver/drawer to the payee, the debt is discharged only upon payment by the recipient/drawee to the payee. In Switzerland, under CO art. 467(2), 'the payee who has agreed to the order can only renew his claim against the order giver if, having demanded payment from the recipient of the order, he was unable to obtain it at the expiration of the term stated in the order'. Under art. 467(3), to avoid liability for damages, in connection with a debit transfer, the payee who receives the order directly from the order giver must, if he does not intend to abide by it, notify the order giver of his refusal promptly.

In both Switzerland (CO art. 468(1)) and Germany (BGB s. 784(1)), acceptance of the order by the recipient/drawee binds him towards the payee, who can enforce the acceptance free from defences available to the recipient/drawee against the order giver/drawer. In Switzerland (ibid.), acceptance is to be notified by the recipient to the payee 'without reserve'. In Germany, under BGB s. 784(2), the acceptance is made 'by a written notation on the order'. Where that notation has been made before the delivery of the order to the payee, the acceptance becomes effective upon delivery.

The drawee's position in Germany is further governed by three rules. First, under BGB s. 786, the payee's claim against the drawee arising from the acceptance, 'is barred by prescription in three years'. Second, under BGB s. 785, the drawee is bound to pay 'only on presentation of the order'. Third, under BGB s. 789, upon the drawee's refusal to accept or pay, 'the payee shall give notice to the drawer without delay'.

The latter provision has a counterpart in Switzerland. Under CO art. 469,

If the recipient of the order refuses the payment demanded of him by the payee ... or he declares in advance that he will not pay, [the payee][5] must immediately advise the order giver of such refusal, in order to avoid liability for damages.

---

[5] While the wording (in the French original as well as in the English translation) is not unambiguous, it is undisputed in Switzerland that the duty to give notice rests, as in Germany, on the payee (and not the recipient).

It is however quite difficult to imagine what damages may be caused to the order giver due to the payee's default.

In Switzerland, under CO art. 468(2), 'to the extent that the recipient is indebted to the order giver', he is liable, vis-à-vis the latter, to pay to the payee, 'provided his position is not prejudiced thereby'. However, '[e]ven in such a case, he is not obligated to notify his acceptance prior to payment, unless so agreed with the order giver' (CO art. 468(3)). Conversely, in Germany, under BGB s. 787(2), '[t]he drawee is not bound as against the drawer to accept the order or to make payment . . . to the payee merely because the drawee is a debtor of the drawer'. However, upon payment to the payee, the drawee is discharged from the debt he owes to the drawer (CO s. 787(1)).

In both Switzerland (CO art. 470(2)) and Germany (BGB s. 790), vis-à-vis the recipient/drawee, the order is revocable by the order giver/drawer until acceptance or payment. In Switzerland, under CO art. 470(1), the revocation against a payee is wrongful, where the order 'has been made to extinguish a debt owed [by the order giver] to the payee or otherwise has been made for the benefit of the latter'. In Switzerland, under CO art. 470(3), '[t]he bankruptcy of the order giver entails the revocation of an order which has not yet been accepted'. Conversely, in Germany, under BGB s. 791, an order is not extinguished 'by the death of one of the parties or by one of the parties becoming incompetent to enter into legal transactions'.

Finally, in Germany, under BGB s. 792, the payee may transfer the order by agreement in writing and the physical delivery of the instrument, unless transferability has been excluded by the drawer. To be effective against the drawee, the exclusion must either be noted in the instrument, or communicated to the drawee before acceptance for payment. Upon acceptance in favour of the transferee, the drawee may not raise defences available to him against the payee. 'For the rest, the provisions applicable to assignment of a claim apply *mutatis mutandis* to the transfer of the order'. In Switzerland, CO art. 471(1) recognizes the effectiveness of '[w]ritten orders to pay the respective bearer of the document'.

B. Payment and Collection of Cheques

In principle, a cheque is a written unconditional order, addressed to a **[1]** bank, to pay on demand a sum certain in money. In practice, it is drawn by a bank customer on funds (or against a line of credit) available to the drawer/customer with the drawee bank. As a rule, the cheque is a negotiable instrument, transferable by delivery, with indorsement where it is not payable to the bearer. A cheque is presented for payment to the drawee bank by the holder, either directly, or by a collecting bank acting as the holder's agent. The cheque collection machinery is a paper-based debit transfer payment system. The current form of the cheque as an instruction or mandate, as well as the contemporary interbank cheque collection machinery, have their origins in the seventeenth-century goldsmith system in England.[1]

In civil law countries, cheques are governed by statutes modelled on the 1931 Geneva Uniform Law of Cheques. This is currently so in France, Germany, Italy, Japan, and Switzerland. The various national statues are nonetheless not identical. In common law jurisdictions, including jurisdictions that have been under strong British influence, the model statute is the 1882 English Bills of Exchange Act, which treats the cheque as a specie of a bill of exchange. This is the case in the United Kingdom (where a specific statute concerning cheques supplements the Bills of Exchange Act), Canada (where the Bills of Exchange Act is federal so as to be applicable also in the civil law province of Quebec), South Africa, and Israel. Australia has a specific statute governing cheques, which is nonetheless drawn on the English model. National statutes in all such common law jurisdictions contain local variations. In the various jurisdictions of the United States, cheques, as negotiable instruments, are governed by Article 3 of the Uniform Commercial Code. Cheque deposits and collections are further governed by Article 4 of the Uniform Commercial Code, as pre-empted or supplemented by federal law, particularly dealing with the availability of funds.

Much of cheques law is concerned with the instruments themselves[2] but the ensuing discussion in this chapter will focus on those aspects of

---

[1] See e.g. M. Vasseur and X. Marin, *Le Cheque* (Paris: Sibey, 1969) at 9–11. For the origins and early development of cheques in England, see e.g. J. M. Holden, *The History of Negotiable Instruments in English Law* (London: The Athlone Press, 1955; repr. 1993, Wm. W. Gaunt & Sons Inc., Holmes Beach, Fla.) at ch. VII (pp. 204–43).

[2] For a comparative study, as part of the law of bills and notes in general, particularly see E. P. Ellinger, 'Negotiable Instruments', being ch. 4, vol. ix of J. S. Ziegel (chief editor),

cheques law concerning the banker–customer relationship. Both the drawer and the depositor of a cheque are bank customers. Both their respective banks participate in the cheque collection and payment process. Hence, both the drawer–drawee bank and the holder–collecting bank relationships form the basis of our investigation. However, the law of cheques as instruments is not always easily separable from the law governing the banking relationship as it applies to cheques. For example, vis-à-vis its customer, the drawee bank will not be discharged unless it pays the cheque to the one entitled to obtain payment, as determined under the law governing cheques as instruments.

[2]   The following is a concise overview of the common as well as the distinguishing features of cheques under the various national laws. Principal features of national laws are set out in the ensuing sections of this chapter.

1. A cheque is universally defined as an unconditional order in writing, of a drawer, directed to a drawee bank, to pay on demand a sum certain in money. There may be local variations, the most important of which is the requirement under the Uniform Cheques Law that the term 'cheque' be included. According to the Uniform Cheques Law, a cheque must be drawn on a banker holding funds at the drawer's disposal, but is nonetheless a 'cheque', notwithstanding the violation of this requirement.

2. In the United States and common law jurisdictions, except for Australia, cheques are governed by the same statute that deals with bills of exchange (or drafts) and promissory notes. In contrast, in Australia and in civil law countries, there is a separate statute dealing with cheques. Selected cheque aspects are dealt with in the United Kingdom under a specific statute. Statutes in common law jurisdictions are modelled on the English Bills of Exchange Act. Statutes in civil law countries follow the Uniform Cheques Law of the Geneva Convention.

3. Specific legislation dealing with the collection and payment of cheques exists only in the United States, and nowhere else.

4. Specific legislation dealing with the revocation of chequing privileges to overdrawing customers exists in France, Israel, and Italy. An interbank voluntary measure in Japan is to a similar effect. Besides, specific civil or criminal sanctions for issuing cheque(s) without cover are prescribed in Switzerland, Italy, and Japan.

Commercial Transactions and Institutions, International Encyclopedia of Comparative Law—Under the Auspices of the International Association of Legal Science (Dordrecht: J.C.B. Mohr, Martinus Nijhoff Publishers, 2000), pp. 160–75.

5. In France, as well as in Scotland, but not elsewhere, the issue and each subsequent transfer of a cheque constitutes an assignment to the holder of the drawer's funds in the drawee's hands.

6. Short periods within which a cheque must be presented for payment are prescribed in civil law countries but not others. Presentment of a cheque at a clearing house is specifically provided for in civil law countries. Electronic presentment, and hence, cheque truncation, is authorized by statute in the USA, UK, and Australia, Arguably, however, off-paying branch presentment, including electronic, is not precluded in common law jurisdictions.

7. Certification of cheques is recognized in the United States, Canada, France, Italy, and Japan. It was recently recognized in South Africa. Certification is also recognized in Germany but only for cheques drawn on the central bank. In Canada, the practice is not backed by any specific statutory provision. In both Canada and the United States, cheque certification is analysed as a form of acceptance of the cheque. In line with the provisions of the Geneva Uniform Cheques Law, this mode of analysis is precluded in France, Italy, Japan, and Germany. In Canada and the United States, certification involves the actual withdrawal of funds from the drawer's account and their placement in a suspense account, pending presentment for payment. Elsewhere, certification may involve the holding or blocking of funds by the drawee bank in the drawer's account for the short period within which a cheque must be presented. In fact, cheque certification is not practised in Japan and Italy.

8. Universally, cheques are defined as unconditional payment orders drawn on a bank and payable on demand. Accordingly, post-dating is ignored in civil law countries, except for determining the end of the statutory mandated period within which cheques must be presented. Post-dating is not recognized in the United States, but could be given effect by temporary stop-payment orders. Cheque post-dating is recognized in common law jurisdictions where payment by the drawee bank prior to the ostensible date of the cheque is wrongful.

9. Countermand of payment (namely, ordering stop payment) of cheques is recognized in common law jurisdictions and in the United States. It is generally precluded in France. Limited recognition, only following the expiry of the statutory period for presentment, exists in civil law countries. In the common law jurisdictions and the United States, the countermanded cheque must be identified in the stop-payment order with reasonable certainty. In all jurisdictions, restitution law governs the position of a drawee bank

that mistakenly paid a countermanded cheque. Only in Australia does the statute specifically invalidate altogether any agreement purporting to negate the right to countermand payment.

10. Notice of the customer's death revokes the drawee bank's duty and authority to pay cheques in common law jurisdictions as well as in the United States. In both Australia and the United States, revocation does not become fully effective until ten days after the receipt of the notice of death by the bank. The drawee bank's duty and authority to pay a cheque drawn by its customer comes to an end also upon receiving notice of: the customer's bankruptcy in Israel; of the customer's mental incapacity in Australia; and of the customer's adjudication of incompetence in the United States. Similar events terminate the bank's authority to pay in South Africa. In contrast, in civil law countries, neither the death of the drawer nor his incapacity, occurring after the issue of the cheque, have any effect as regards the cheque.

11. The wrongful dishonour of a cheque by the drawee bank, notwithstanding the availability of cover in the customer's account (either in the form of credit balance or due to an overdraft facility), is actionable by the customer in all jurisdictions. In the United Kingdom, substantial damages for injury to credit may be awarded to the customer without proof of actual damage.

12. Cheques are universally recognized as negotiable instruments. This means that (i) they are transferred by delivery, with or without any necessary endorsement, and that (ii) the transferee may acquire a better title to the cheque than that of the transferor. Cheque negotiability and even transferability can be curtailed, in varying degrees, in civil as well as in common law jurisdictions, but not in the United States.

13. In principle, cheques are payable to the holder by the drawee bank either in cash, over the counter, or to the holder's bank account. Restrictions on payment either in cash or to non-customers, can be imposed by using either 'payable in account' or crossed cheques. Both forms are recognized in the Uniform Cheques Law. Only cheque crossing is provided for by legislation in common law jurisdictions. Neither payable in account cheques nor cheque crossing exist in the United States. In fact, crossed cheques (as well as, obviously, payable in account cheques) are not used in Canada. In civil law countries, crossed cheques are not recognized in Germany, while cheques payable in account are not provided for in Japan and France. In Switzerland and Italy, both forms exist.

14. A short six-month limitation period, running from the expiration of the time limit prescribed for presentment, is provided for by the Uniform Cheques Law. In the United States, an action to enforce liability on a cheque is barred three years after the dishonour of the cheque or ten years after its date, whichever comes first. No limitation period is prescribed under cheque or negotiable instrument legislation in common law jurisdictions, and the matter may be governed, in each jurisdiction, by general law. In Canada and the United States, the holder's action against the drawee of a certified cheque is not barred by any limitation period, until presentment for payment. Thereafter, the holder's action is barred in the United States after three years, and one year in Japan.

15. A cheque may be collected for a holder by a collecting bank, acting as a mandatary, or agent, for the depositor. Upon the dishonour of the cheque, the collecting bank, that has provisionally credited the holder's account, may pursue its recourse against the holder, its own customer, either as an indorser of the cheque, or on the basis of the account or mandate agreement. Alternatively, the collecting bank may recover from the drawer of the dishonoured cheque. In such a case, in some jurisdictions, and under some conditions, the collecting bank may enforce payment irrespective of the drawer's defences against the original payee of the cheque.

16. The collection and payment of cheques into a bank account held at a bank other than the drawee bank is universally governed by interbank clearing rules. Such rules constitute an interbank agreement, binding and benefiting subscribing participating banks. The degree in which clearing rules indirectly bind or benefit bank customers, namely, the drawer and depositor of a cheque, is not uniform. In the United States only, clearing rules are stated by statute to bind as well as to inure to the benefit of parties not specifically assenting to them such as bank customers.

17. Other than in the United States, there are no statutory rules dealing with the time a cheque is 'paid'. Particularly unclear, as well as non-uniform, is the treatment of the effect of the failure by the drawee bank to return dishonoured cheques within the time limits prescribed by clearing rules. Namely, the question whether such a delay constitutes 'payment' of the cheque is particularly controversial.

(II) CHEQUING ACCOUNT LEGISLATION

[1] France, Israel, and Italy have specific statutory provisions dealing with banks' duties in connection with their customers' use of cheques. In principle, such provisions are aimed at the prevention and deterrence of the use of cheques without cover.[3]

[2] In France,[4] the bank's position is governed by the provisions of the Cheques Law,[5] which forms part of the Code of Commerce. Specific provisions govern the bank's obligations in issuing a chequebook (or blank cheque forms in general) to its customer. The statutory scheme applies to the delivery by a bank to its customer of standard blank cheque forms, other than those restricted to either withdrawals by the customer for his own use or to being certified.[6]

In principle, a bank has complete discretion whether or not to issue a chequebook to a customer. Once a positive decision with respect to a customer has been reached by the bank, each blank cheque delivered to a customer must bear the customer's name and address. Crossed cheque forms, specifying transferability only to a bank,[7] must be given to the customer (to whom the bank chose to give a chequebook or blank forms) free of charge. The use of other standard cheque forms is discouraged; they may be given to the customer only upon request, for a charge, and are subject to a stamp duty. The tax authorities are entitled to have those requesting forms of uncrossed cheques identified to them.

The bank is responsible to the holder for any cheque of 100 F or less, regardless of the availability of cover in the drawer-customer's account, provided the cheque was written on a form supplied by the bank to the customer, and was presented for payment within a month of its issue by the customer. Obviously, this promotes diligence by banks in according chequing privileges to customers.

Whenever a cheque is dishonoured for insufficiency of funds, the dishonouring bank must, at the holder's request, issue to him a certificate of non-payment, permitting a simplified execution against the overdrawing customer. Furthermore, upon such dishonour, an 'incident of payment' takes place. The dishonouring bank ought then to report the occurrence to the Bank of France. Subject to reinstatement and the payment of a fine by

---

[3] Other measures to the same end, whether statutory or voluntary, are dealt with as part of the discussion on the specific cheque legislation in the various countries. In particular, see (vi) s. 9 below.

[4] G. Ripert and R. Roblot, *Droit commercial*, vol. ii, 13th edn. (Paris: Librairie Général de Droit et de Jurisprudence, 1992) at 257–95, 283–5, and 292. See also, J. L. Rives-Lange and M. Contamine-Raynaud, *Droit bancaire*, 6th edn (Paris: Dalloz, 1995) at ¶¶301–4.

[5] Decret-loi of 30 October 1935, as am., particularly arts. 65–75.

[6] For cheque certification in France, see (vi) s. 10 below.

[7] For crossed cheques under the UCL, see (vi) s. 4 and (vi) s.12 below.

the defaulting drawer-customer, the dishonouring bank must then require him to return all blank cheque forms, and may not issue to him new ones for ten years. The fine is excused where no similar incident involving the same customer has taken place during the preceding twelve months and reinstatement occurred within a month. Conversely, the fine doubles upon the third such an incident within the twelve-month period.

In the absence of rectification, a customer subject to the restrictions must return blank cheque forms and may not issue new cheques on any bank. Against a non-complying customer, the restrictions can be supported by a court order. Violations are punishable under criminal law.

The ten-year restriction is not limited to the dishonouring bank. Rather, it applies to each bank that knows, or that should have known, of such an incident of payment involving the customer and any bank. Before issuing blank cheque forms to a new customer, a bank must consult the Bank of France as to the status of that customer, with the view of determining that customer's right to draw cheques.

The violation by a bank of its duties in relation to restrictions imposed on a customer upon the occurrence of an incident of payment entails the bank's responsibility to a holder for the amount of each cheque drawn by the customer on a form supplied by the bank. The holder may further recover from the violating bank damages and interest. Liability for breach of each of these duties, namely, the delivery of blank cheque forms to a new customer without consulting the Bank of France, the delivery of cheque forms to a customer with knowledge (actual or presumed) of a prohibition to issue cheques, or the failure to demand the return of blank forms from a defaulting drawer-customer, is strict and absolute; accountability to the holder by the bank for the amount of each cheque arises regardless of any fault by the holder.

Also, under the general law, a bank that has not violated any of these duties, but that nevertheless was negligent in delivering blank cheque forms to a customer, may find itself liable to a holder for the resulting loss the latter incurred. However, in this context, the holder's fault is relevant in assessing the bank's liability. Whether upon the breach of a statutory duty and negligence by the bank, the holder has a choice between suing on the statute or under general law, has not been settled yet.

In Israel, the opening of a chequing account, the issue of chequebooks [3] (or blank cheque forms) to bank customers, and the position with respect to customers issuing cheques dishonoured for lack of cover are dealt with by the NSF Cheques (or Cheques Without Cover) Law of 1981, as subsequently amended in 1990 and 1992.

The Law prohibits a bank from opening a chequing account unless the identity of the account holder is properly recorded. Similarly, the identity of each signatory to the account must be recorded by the bank.

Furthermore, particulars of identity relating to the account holder must be recorded on each blank cheque delivered to the customer. Upon the dishonour of a cheque, for any reason, the drawee bank is specifically required to provide the holder, at the latter's request, with the drawer's or account holder's identity.

Where, within twelve consecutive months, ten cheques drawn on an account have been dishonoured for lack of adequate cover, and an appropriate warning was sent to each account holder and signatory, both the account and its holder become 'restricted'. The 'restriction' is however not triggered where the ten cheques have been dishonoured within a fifteen-day period. Further, a cheque dishonoured due to the seizure of the account by means of a creditor process is not to be counted among the ten cheques, as long as it was presented for payment within sixty days after the bank had been served with notice of the seizure. Conversely, a cheque dishonoured because payment on it was countermanded, or for any other reason other than of lack of cover, is nonetheless counted among the ten, if the cheque would have been anyway dishonoured for lack of cover. Mistake by the bank in dishonouring a cheque, side by side with a reasonable mistake by the customer as to the availability of either cover or overdraft facility, are grounds for seeking a court order to exclude the relevant cheque from being included in the count.

Where during the period of the 'restriction' or within three years of its expiry, the chain of events leading to 'restriction' recurs for the same customer, either with respect to the same[8] or any other account, the customer becomes classified as 'severely restricted'. All the accounts of a 'severely restricted' customer become 'restricted'.

All 'restrictions', including 'severe' ones, are to be advised by the bank to the account holder, any signatory, to the Superintendent of Banks, and to the Bank of Israel. The regulatory authorities[9] are required to pass on the information to all banks. Particulars identifying 'restricted' accounts as well as 'severely restricted' customers, together with pertaining expiry dates, may be publicized by the Bank of Israel.[10]

A 'restriction' lasts one year. The duration of a 'severe restriction' is effective for two years. A bank will not honour a cheque drawn on a 'restricted' account,[11] will not provide blank cheque forms for drawing

---

[8] In which case, recurrence must have taken place only within three years after the expiry of the original 'restriction', and not throughout its duration.

[9] Thus, the Superintendent is required to advise all banks of any restricted customer, restricted account, or a severely restricted customer. See s. 3A(c). On its part, the Bank of Israel must provide each bank 'particulars pertaining to the restrictions, as prescribed by the Superintendent'. See s. 13. The distinction is not all that self-explanatory.

[10] Also, a bank and the Bank of Israel may reveal any 'restriction', as necessary for the conduct of any criminal investigation.

[11] Though within fifteen days of the commencement of the 'restriction', a bank may honour a cheque bearing an earlier date.

from a 'restricted' account, and will not open a chequing account to a 'restricted' customer. As for bank customers, a 'restricted' customer will not open a chequing account; no person will draw a cheque on a 'restricted' account; finally, a 'severely restricted' customer will not draw any cheque on any chequing account.

Drawing a cheque contrary to a 'restriction' is punishable as a criminal offence. In addition to any punishment, the Court may impose up to a five-year 'restriction' and turn a 'restricted' customer into a 'severely restricted' one. Dishonour of a cheque by a drawee bank in compliance with this Law does not affect the holder's right against the drawer. Enforcement against banks is in the Superintendent's hands. The Superintendent may further substitute a bank not carrying out the provisions of this Law and take any action required to execute a 'restriction' with respect to any account or an account holder.

In Italy,[12] where a cheque is dishonoured for lack of cover, the drawee [4] bank is obligated to revoke the drawer-customer's authority to issue cheques and to require him to return all blank cheque forms in his possession. No new authorization can be granted until after three months, or where the sum of the dishonoured cheque(s) exceeds L.20,000,000, until after six months. Where authorization to draw cheques is nevertheless granted to the customer earlier, namely, in violation of the three/six-month restriction, the drawee bank must pay each cheque issued by the drawer, irrespective of the availability of cover, up to L.10,000,000, until the restriction expires.

Notice of revocation of authority to draw cheques must be communicated to the drawer by the drawee bank by means of registered mail or telegram. Having failed to send such notice within twenty days of the dishonour, the drawee bank becomes obligated to pay each of the drawer's cheques issued thereafter, up to L.10,000,000, irrespective of the availability of cover.

New authorization to draw cheques may be given by the drawee bank to the customer simply by payment of his cheques. Accordingly, payment of cheques within the three/six-month restriction period, other than cheques paid with adequate available cover within ten days after the notice of revocation of authority to draw cheques was sent, has the effect of giving a premature new authorization, obligating the bank to pay each cheque, up to L.10,000,000, irrespective of the availability of cover, until the expiry of the three/six-month restriction period.

It is quite apparent that the three national legislative schemes govern- [5] ing the chequing account relationship are, to a large extent, dissimilar in their treatment. Thus, in Italy, contrary to the situation in both France and

[12] Law of 15 Dec. 1990, number 386 (Official Gazette 20 Dec. 1990).

Israel, there is no duty on the dishonouring bank to report the ensuing revocation of the drawer's authority to draw cheques to bank regulators. Accordingly, the revocation sanction is a matter between the revoking bank and its customer and does not extend to the relationship between the overdrawing customer and other banks. Unlike their French counterparts, Israeli and Italian banks are not encouraged to issue to their customers crossed cheque forms specifying transferability only to banks. Israeli banks, unlike their French and Italian counterparts, even when violating the statutory requirements pertaining to 'restricted' accounts or customers (or to the issue of blank cheque forms in general), do not risk accountability to the holder for any amount of a cheque drawn by a customer without adequate cover. In turn, the restriction period is longer in France than in Israel as well as in Italy, where it is the shortest. Finally, in both France and Italy, a single cheque without cover triggers the statutory prescriptions. Conversely, in Israel, 'restrictions' become effective only after ten occurrences of cheques dishonoured for lack of sufficient funds. At the same time, a timely reinstatement of a bad cheque may exonerate an overdrawing customer in France but not in Israel and Italy.

(III) CHEQUE LEGISLATION IN COMMON LAW JURISDICTIONS

[1]   In the United Kingdom, cheques are governed by the Bills of Exchange Act (hereafter, the BEA or 'Act'),[13] as supplemented by the Cheques Act.[14] As a rule, statutes in common law countries, and hence, their laws of cheques, are modelled on the BEA, though local variations may exist. A statute modelled on the BEA is in force in Israel[15] and South Africa.[16] Both are not pure common law jurisdictions.[17] In Canada, cheques are governed by the federal Bills of Exchange Act,[18] modelled on its English predecessor, which is in force also in the province of Quebec. In Australia, cheques were excluded from the coverage of the Bills of Exchange Act,[19] and are currently governed by a specific Cheques Act.[20] In turn, the provisions of the latter statute are not substantially different

---

[13] 1882, 45 & 46 Vict., c. 61.   [14] 1957, 5 & 6 Eliz. 2, c. 36.

[15] The Bills of Exchange Ordinance [New Version] 1957, Laws of the State of Israel, New Version 1957 2, p. 12 (hereafter: BEO).

[16] No. 364 of 1964. Recently, changes were made by the Bills of Exchange Amendment Act, 2000 (Act No. 56 of 2000) Govt Gazette 21846, 6 December 2000, prolaimed in force on 1 March 2001 (hereafter: SA Bill)

[17] In fact, Scotland, which is also a constituent of the United Kingdom, falls into this category.

[18] R.S.C. 1985, c. B-4.   [19] Bills of Exchange Act 1909.

[20] No. 145 of 1986. Most recently, the Act was amended by Act No. 77 of 1998. For the principal features of the amendment, see n. 24 below.

from the former. For the purpose of the present discussion, all such legal systems having a statute modelled on the BEA can be characterized as common law jurisdictions.

In a common law jurisdiction, the applicable statute effectively[21] defines a cheque to be an unconditional[22] order in writing,[23] addressed (or drawn) by one person (the drawer) on a banker (or bank)[24] (the latter being the drawee), payable on demand,[25] in a sum certain[26] in money,[27] to or to the order of a specified person, or to the bearer.[28] A cheque is a species of a bill of exchange,[29] so as to be governed in the BEA by the provisions applicable both to cheques specifically and to bills of exchange in general.[30] This,

[21] BEA ss. 3(1) and 73 in the UK, ss. 16(1) and 165(1) and (2) in Canada, ss. 1 and 2(1) in South Africa, ss. 3(a), and 73(a) in Israel, and s. 10(1) in Australia. Unless otherwise indicated, all ensuing statutory references are to the BEA in the UK, South Africa, and Canada, to the BEO in Israel, and to the Cheques Act in Australia. With regard to cheques in Australia, BEA provisions are superseded by the Cheques Act and thus are not to be taken into account or referred to.

[22] For some elaboration see ss. 3(2) and (3) and 11 in the UK, to which correspond ss. 16(3) and 17(1) in Canada, ss. 2(3) and 9 in South Africa, and ss. 3(c) and 10(b) in Israel. In Australia, see s. 12.

[23] In the UK, the BEA clarifies in s. 2 that 'written' includes printed.

[24] In the UK (s. 2) and Israel (both in s. 1), a banker is effectively defined as someone carrying on the business of banking. Australia (s. 3(1)) and Canada (s. 2) opted for an institutional definition, initially effectively referring to regulatory legislation governing banks. The SA Bill, above, n.16 (expected to be proclaimed 1 March 2001), departs from the original position that was (in s.1) like that of the UK and Israel and combines the two definitions. In Canada, for the purpose of the provisions dealing with cheques, 'bank' was effectively broadened to mean (s. 164) any regulated depository financial institution, not necessarily under 'banking' legislation. In Australia, where the drawee is a non-bank financial institution, the instrument was originally called 'payment order' rather than 'cheque'. The distinction, together with the 'payment order' category, was eliminated in 1998, and currently, under s. 10, a cheque must be drawn on a 'financial institution', broadly defined in s. 3(1) to cover domestic as well as foreign banks, the Reserve Bank of Australia, building societies, credit unions, and special services providers to credit unions and building societies.

[25] Normally, a cheque does not express time for payment, which makes it payable on demand in the UK (s. 10(1)(b)), Canada (s. 22(1)(b)), Israel (s. 9(a)(2)), South Africa (s. 8(1)(b)) and Australia (s. 14(1)(b)). Post-dated cheques are not payable prior to the date they bear in Israel (s. 73(b)) and Australia (ss. 16(1) and 61(2)). Cheque post-dating is not prohibited in the UK, South Africa, and Canada. Cf. s. 13(2), 11(2), and 26(d) respectively. That provision validates the post-dated cheque but is silent as to whether it is payable on demand prior to the date it bears. The current judicial position is that it is not.

[26] As elaborated in s. 9(1) in the UK, s. 27 in Canada, s. 8(a) in Israel, s. 7(1) in South Africa, and in s. 15 in Australia. In practice, a cheque states a fixed amount, without interest or any other charge.

[27] A foreign currency cheque may express or indicate a rate of exchange. See s. 9(1)(d) in the UK, s. 27(1)(d) in Canada, s. 8(a)(4) in Israel, s. 7(1)(d) in South Africa, and s. 15(3) in Australia.

[28] See ss. 7 and 8 in the UK, ss. 6 and 7 in Israel, ss. 18, 20, and 21 in Canada, ss. 4 and 5 in South Africa, and ss. 19–24 in Australia.

[29] For an early authority to that effect see judgment of Byles J. in *Keene* v. *Beard* (1860), 8 CB (NS) 372 at 381; 141 ER 1210 at 1213 (C.P.), conceiving of a cheque to be 'in the nature of an inland bill of exchange . . .', differing from the latter only in being 'an appropriation of so much money of the drawer's in the hands of the banker' and usually in not being discharged by a delay in the presentment. [30] See cites in n. 21, above.

however, is not so in Australia, where the BEA does not apply to cheques anymore.

[2]　　Except for in Scotland, a cheque, by itself, 'does not operate as an assignment of funds in the hands of the drawee available for payment thereof, and the drawee of a [cheque] . . . is not liable on the instrument'.[31] In the absence of acceptance,[32] a drawee is not liable on a bill of exchange.[33] Accordingly, upon the dishonour[34] of the cheque, regardless of the availability of funds in the drawer's account, the depositor has no remedy against the drawee bank; the depositor's sole recourse is against the drawer of the cheque.[35]

Three exceptions exist. First, as indicated, a different rule applies to Scotland. Thereunder, 'where the drawee of a [cheque] has in his hands funds available for payment thereof, the [cheque] operates as an assignment of the sum for which it is drawn in favour of the holder, from the time the [cheque] is presented to the drawee'.[36] That means that in Scotland, contrary to the general rule under the BEA, the depositor, namely, the payee-holder, is entitled to the funds in the drawer's account, as against the drawee bank itself.

Second, in Canada, a drawee bank that dishonoured a cheque notwithstanding the availability of funds in the drawer's account, may be found liable to the payee-holder for inducing the drawer-customer's breach of

---

[31] S. 53(1) in the UK, to which correspond s. 126 in Canada, s. 53(a) in Israel, s. 51 in South Africa, and s. 88 in Australia.

[32] The acceptance of a bill of exchange (which other than in Australia includes a cheque: see text at n. 30, above) is defined as 'the signification by the drawee of his assent to the order of the drawer'. See s. 34(1) in Canada, s. 17(1) in the UK, s. 15(1) in South Africa, and s. 16(a) in Israel. No cheque acceptance is provided for in Australia under the Cheques Act.

[33] The acceptor's engagement to honour a bill of exchange (which other than in Australia includes a cheque: see text at n. 30, above) 'according to the tenor of his acceptance', is provided for in s. 54(1) in the UK, s. 127 in Canada, s. 52(a) in South Africa, and s. 54(1) in Israel (though 'tenor' replaces 'tenour' in both Canada and South Africa). The general principle is that no person is liable on an instrument without having signed it. See s. 23 in the UK, s. 130 in Canada, s. 22(a) in Israel, s. 21 in South Africa, and s. 31(1) in Australia. The Australian Cheques Act does not provide for the acceptance of a cheque.

[34] A cheque is dishonoured by non-payment when it is duly presented for payment and payment is refused or cannot be obtained, or when presentment is excused. See s. 47(1) in the UK, s. 45(1) in South Africa, s. 94(1) in Canada, and s. 46(a) in Israel, Cf. s. 69 in Australia providing that a cheque is dishonoured 'if the cheque is duly presented for payment and payment is refused by the drawee [bank], being a refusal that is communicated by the drawee [bank] to the holder . . .' Presentment is further discussed in s. 4, below.

[35] As well as against any other party who has signed the instrument. See s. 47(2) in the UK, s. 45(2) in South Africa, s. 94(2) in Canada, s. 46(b) in Israel, and s. 70 in Australia. For the drawer's engagement to compensate the holder upon the dishonour of the cheque, see s. 55(1)(a) in the UK, s. 53(1)(a) in South Africa, s. 129(a) in Canada, s. 55(a)(1) in Israel, and s. 71 in Australia. Since under the Cheques Act 'dishonour' does not include circumstances where presentment is excused (see n. 34, ibid.), the drawer's undertaking to compensate the holder is stated to cover the case where the presentment of the cheque for payment is dispensed with.　　[36] S. 53(2) in the UK.

contract with the payee-holder. This rule is derived from *Thermo King Corp.* v. *Provincial Bank of Canada*,[37] where a bank unilaterally terminated its banking relationship with its customer without giving adequate notice, and with knowledge of the consequences pertaining to the contract between the customer and its creditor.

Third, in theory, under the BEA, a cheque, as a species of a bill of exchange, may be accepted, so as to trigger the drawee bank's liability towards the payee-holder.[38] However, while only the Cheque Act in Australia seems to preclude the acceptance of a cheque,[39] the acceptance of a cheque is not recognized in common law jurisdictions,[40] except for Canada, where cheque certification has been practised for quite a long time.

'Certification' is the name given to the marking of a cheque by the drawee bank to show that (1) the cheque is drawn by the person purporting to draw it, (2) it is drawn upon an existing account with the drawee, and (3) that there are funds sufficient to meet it. Certification is demonstrated by some physical marking on a cheque, normally by stamping on its face the word 'certified'. Certification may be procured either by the drawer prior to the delivery of the cheque to the payee, or by the holder. In either case, certification is invariably accompanied by transferring the sum of the cheque from the drawer's account into a special suspense account.[41]

Certification is not explicitly provided for in the Canadian BEA. Rather, it has developed and become well established without a clear legal theory underlying the obligations which it imposes. While certification procured by the holder discharges the drawer,[42] as well as any other prior party, certification procured by the drawer leaves him liable.[43] The binding effect of certification on the drawee bank towards the holder is currently explained

[37] (1981), 130 D.L.R. (3d) 256 (Ont. C.A.). The case is characterized as 'extraordinary' and 'exceptional' by B. Crawford, *Crawford and Falconbridge Banking and Bills of Exchange*, 8th edn. (Toronto: Canada Law Book, 1986) at 1004 and 1005 (vol. i).

[38] For the acceptor's statutory engagement, see n. 33, above.

[39] This is done simply, as indicated in n. 32, above, by omitting any reference to the acceptance of the cheque.

[40] Indeed, old English authorities recognized the practice existing among bankers of marking cheques presented by a collecting bank after 4 o'clock p.m., so as to bind the drawee bank in the next-day clearing. The leading authority is *Robson* v. *Bennet* (1810), 2 Taunt. 389; 127 E.R. 1128 (C.P.). See also *Goodwin* v. *Robarts* (1875), L.R. 10 Exch. 337 at 351–2. The practice was however discontinued so that '[n]o usage in favour of the holder of a marked cheque has ever been established in [England]'. See F. R. Ryder and A. Bueno, *Byles on Bills of Exchange*, 26th edn. (London: Sweet & Maxwell, 1988) at 310.

[41] Upon the insolvency of a bank, and subject to the rights of secured parties, certified cheques drawn on that bank are accorded first priority, followed by bank drafts and money orders. See s. 31 of the Canadian Payments Association Act, R.S.C. 1985, c. C-21.

[42] See *Boyd* v. *Nasmith* (1889), 17 O.R. 40 (CPD).

[43] See *Gaden* v. *The Nfl'd Savings Bank*, [1899] A.C. 281 (P.C.).

in Canada[44] on the basis of acceptance,[45] rather than contractual novation.[46] On an unpresented certified cheque, the claim based on certification is of unlimited duration, as it is not subject to any limitation of actions.[47] 'Certification' is now specifically provided for, as a distinct statutory contract of the certifying bank, under the most recent amendment (proclaimed March 1, 2001) in South Africa.[47a] Under s. 72A(1), a cheque is certified where 'the drawee signs it and adds words to the cheque that indicate that the cheque will be paid or that funds are available for its payment.' According to s. 72A(2)(a), a certifying drawee 'undertakes that he will pay the holder, or the drawer or an indorser who has been compelled to pay the cheque . . . according to the tenor of his certification.'

[3]   The duty and authority of a drawee bank to pay a cheque drawn on it by its customer 'are determined', namely, terminated or come to an end, by the countermand of payment, or notice of the customer's death.[48] The duty of the drawee bank to comply with the drawer's countermand, or stop-payment order, irrespective of the merits of the drawing customer's claims and defences against the holder, can be rationalized on viewing the

---

[44] In contrast to the prevailing view in other common law jurisdictions that disfavour certification, as expressed e.g. in *Bank of Baroda, Ltd.* v. *Punjab National Bank, Ltd.*, [1944] A.C. 176 (P.C.).

[45] For 'acceptance' and acceptor's liability, see nn. 32 and 33 above. Nonetheless, while an acceptance, as any statutory contract on an instrument (see cites in n. 32, above), must be *signe*d by the drawee (s. 35(1)(a) in Canada, s. 17(2)(a) in the UK, s. 15(2)(a) in South Africa, and s. 16(b)(1) in Israel), one case held that certification does not require a signature since it is not strictly an acceptance but rather its equivalent. See *Bank of Nova Scotia* v. *Canada Trust Co.* (1998), 78 A.C.W.S. (3d) 774 (Ont. Gen. Div.).

[46] See e.g. *Re Maubach and Bank of Nova Scotia* (1987), 60 O.R. (2d) 189 (H.C.J.), aff'd. (1987) 62 O.R. (2d) 220; and *A.E. Le Page Real Estate Services Ltd.* v. *Rattray Publications* (1991), 5 O.R. (3d) 216 (Gen. Div.), aff'd. (1995), 21 O.R. (3d) 164 (C.A.). See in general, B. Geva, 'Irrevocability of Bank Drafts, Certified Cheques and Money Orders' (1986), 65 Can. Bar Rev. 107 at 123–30.

[47] This is so with respect to Canadian funds cheques, of $500 or more, certified by chartered banks. See s. 438 of the Bank Act, S.C. 1991, c. 46 (Part VIII) and s. 22(1) of the Bank of Canada Act, R.S.C. 1985, c. B-2 (Part XVI) as am. by S.C. 1991, c. 46, ss. 582 and 583; S.C. 1991, c. 48, s. 494; S.C. 1997, c. 15, s. 100; and S.C. 1999, c. 28, s. 97. See B. Geva, 'Lost Cheques, Certification and Countermand—Is the Law Satisfactory?' (1987–8), 2 B.F.L.R. 357.

[47a] See SA Bill, above, n. 16.

[48] S. 75 in the UK, and s. 167 in Canada, to which correspond s. 73 in South Africa, s. 75 in Israel, and s. 90(1) in Australia. Under the Israeli and South African provisions, notice of the customer's bankruptcy (in Israel) or until recently, insolvency (in South Africa) has the same effect. The SA Bill, above, n. 16 (proclaimed 1 March 2001), added notice of the customer's incapacity and replaced insolvency by the coming into effect of specified regimes under which the assets of an insolvent debtor are administered. The Australian section adds (to countermand and notice of death) notice of mental incapacity. In Australia, under s. 90(2), notice of the customer's death does not terminate the bank's duty and authority to pay a cheque if not more than ten days have elapsed after receiving notice of death and the bank has not received a countermand of payment from a successor of the drawer's title.

payment instruction embodied in a cheque as a mandate[49] which does not inure to the benefit of the payee-holder and is thus revocable.

As indicated above, there are three exceptions to the rule providing that the cheque does not entitle the holder vis-à-vis the drawee bank. These exceptions cover the assignment of funds, the inducement to break a contract, and the cheque certification.[50] I will now examine the viability of the countermand of payment as against the holder's right in each of these situations.

First, in Scotland, under s. 53(2) of the UK BEA, the cheque operates as an assignment of funds in the holder's favour. However, on the countermand of payment of a cheque, 'the banker shall be treated as having no funds available for the payment of the cheque',[51] so as not to be indebted to the holder, and hence, is obliged to comply with the customer's countermand.[52] As for the second exception, it seems obvious that compliance by the bank with countermand of payment will relieve the bank from liability to the holder for inducing the drawer's breach of contract; after all, it is the countermanding drawer who has initiated the breach. Countermand thus defeats the holder's right against the drawee in these two situations. Conversely, with respect to the third exception, in Canada, the certification of a cheque, insofar as it results in the withdrawal of funds from the drawer's account and in fastening liability on the drawee, defeats a stop-payment order and renders it ineffective.[53] Presumably, the certifying bank's newly created statutory liability defeats countermand in South Africa as well.

No particular form is required for an effective countermand. It may be given either orally, whether by phone or in person, or in writing. It must be communicated to the appropriate bank officer so as to enable the bank to act on it prior to payment. Under the contract with the customer, the bank may require a written confirmation for an oral countermand and perhaps impose other preconditions. The Cheques Act in Australia specifically invalidates (in s. 6(2)) any agreement purporting to negate the right of countermand altogether. No corresponding provision exists in other common law jurisdictions.[54]

---

[49] See e.g. *Barclays Bank Ltd.* v. *W. J. Simms Son & Cooke (Southern) Ltd.* [1980] Q.B. 677.

[50] See s. 2, above.

[51] S. 75A(1) of the UK Act, applicable to Scotland only.

[52] The effect of s. 53(2) to the BEA thus appears to be quite limited, for example, to the determination of priorities to funds among competing claims.

[53] See e.g. *A.E. Le Page Investment Ltd.* v. *Rattray Publications Ltd.* (1995), 21 O.R. (3d) 164 (C.A.).

[54] For disclaimer clauses in the various jurisdictions in general, as applied to bank's duties to customers, see 2.C(ii) and (iv), above. For freedom of contract and the account agreement, namely, for the effect of onerous express terms, in the various jurisdictions, see 2.A (iv), above.

It was held that the bank to whom a countermand is addressed is entitled to have an unambiguous description of the cheque set out in the countermand.[55] Accordingly, it was acknowledged in Canada that an effective countermand 'must not be expressed in ambiguous terms'; rather, it 'must unequivocally refer to the particular cheque which it stopped'.[56] This strict description standard was subsequently found to be qualified by 'the bank's duty to its customer . . . to use ordinary diligence to enlist the assistance of the customer before making the decision to pay the cheque'.[57] Ultimately, it was held, a minor discrepancy with respect to the amount of the cheque does not undermine its clear identification in the countermand.[58] Perhaps, even the English test is that of no more than identification with sufficient certainty.[59]

The position of a drawee bank that mistakenly overlooked a stop-payment order and thus paid a cheque over an effective countermand is controversial. A leading authority stands for the proposition that such a drawee bank, having acted in breach of contract with its customer, the drawer of the cheque, is universally not entitled to debit the drawer's account, and may thus recover the payment made by mistake from the recipient.[60] However, under another view, pursuant to principles of equity, particularly the doctrine of subrogation, the relative position of the parties to the cheque must be assessed.[61] Accordingly, the mistaken bank may, depending on the circumstances, either debit the countermanding customer's account on the basis of the discharge obtained from the holder, or, having declined to do so, pursue the holder on the basis of the drawer's claim against him.

[4]   By statute, and unless excused,[62] presentment of a cheque is required in

---

[55] *Westminster Bank, Ltd.* v. *Hilton* (1927), 43 T.L.R. 124.

[56] *Shapera* v. *Toronto Dominion Bank* (1970), 17 D.L.R. (3d) 122 at 127 (Man. Q.B.).

[57] *Giordano* v. *Royal Bank of Canada* (1973), 38 D.L.R. (3d) 191, 196 (Ont. C.A.). See also *Bank of Montreal* v. *H&M Chan's Enterprises Ltd.*, (30 June 1999) Saskatoon 2222/98 (Sask. Q.B.); 1999 Sask. D. LEXIS 318 on-line: LEXIS (Canada, ALL CANADIAN DIGESTS) in connection with a pre-authorized payment plan.

[58] *Remfor Industries Ltd.* v. *Bank of Montreal* (1978), 21 O.R. (2d) 225 (Ont. C.A.).

[59] A.G. Guest, *Chalmers and Guest on Bills of Exchange, Cheques and Promissory Notes*, 15th edn. (London: Sweet & Maxwell, 1998) at 618. The facts of *Hilton*, above, n. 55, may be consistent with this test. The SA Bill, above, n. 16, proposes to add to s. 73 of the BEA a requirement to the effect that a 'countermand . . . identifies the cheque . . . and customer with reasonable particularity and gives the drawee a reasonable opportunity to act on it'.

[60] *Simms*, above, n. 49.

[61] The leading case is *B. Liggett (Liverpool), Ltd.* v. *Barclays Bank, Ltd.* [1928] 1 K.B. 48, followed in Canada in *Shapera*, above, n. 56.

[62] Presentment is dispensed with, *inter alia*, when there are no funds in the account (nor is an overdraft facility available), and when it was waived. See s. 46(2) in the UK, s. 44(2) in South Africa, s. 91 in Canada, s. 45(b) in Israel, and s. 59 in Australia. See also, under ss. 70A–70B in Australia, the 'deemed dishonour' of a cheque drawn on a financial institution which failed prior to presentment.

order to charge its drawer, as well as any indorser, with liability thereon.[63] Its objectives are twofold. First, presentment is aimed at achieving certainty as to the moment of demand of payment addressed to the drawee, so as to force the drawee to respond unequivocally, either by paying the cheque or dishonouring it. Second, presentment purports to ensure that demand for payment be made by the holder or on his behalf, that is, by the one to whom the cheque is payable and who is in possession of the cheque.[64] This twofold objective eliminates ambiguity as to rights and duties arising in the collection and payment process. Presentment thus serves the interests of the drawer and the holder, as well as their banks.

Accordingly, in addition to being a term in the statutory engagement of the drawer vis-à-vis the holder,[65] adequate presentment is a term in the contract between the holder and the depositary bank,[66] between the drawer and the drawee bank, as well as in the interbank agreement, whether bilateral or multilateral, and whether or not embodied in clearing rules. The drawee bank's authority and duty owed to its customer,[67] to honour, that is to pay, a cheque, is thus upon the presentment of the cheque. Obviously, the duty to the customer does not arise from the cheque; nor is it absolute. Rather, it is a contractual duty, which is subject to the availability of either funds in the drawing customer's account or of an overdraft facility to him.

Presentment must be made, within reasonable time after the issue of the cheque,[68] by the physical exhibition of the cheque, by the holder or on

---

[63] See e.g. s. 45 in the UK, s. 43(1) in South Africa, s. 84 in Canada, s. 44(a) in Israel, and s. 58 in Australia.

[64] 'Holder' is defined in s. 2 in the UK and Canada, s. 1 in Israel and South Africa, and s. 3 in Australia. Payment in due course that discharges the cheque must be made by or on behalf of the drawee and to the holder. See s. 59 in the UK, s. 57 in South Africa, s. 138 in Canada, s. 60 in Israel, and ss. 78–9 in Australia. For further discussion, see s. 7, below.

[65] The drawer's statutory engagement to have the cheque paid upon presentment (made by the holder to the drawee), and compensate the holder upon the dishonour of the cheque (which occurs at the drawee's refusal to pay upon presentment) and the ensuing dishonour proceedings, is set out in s. 55(1)(a) in the UK, s. 53(1)(a) in South Africa, s. 129(a) in Canada, s. 55(a)(1) in Israel, and s. 71 in Australia (which, nevertheless, does not render the drawer's engagement conditional on the occurrence of all the requisite dishonour proceedings).

[66] The 'deposit institution's' presentment duty, presumably owed to its customer, the holder, is provided for specifically in s. 66(1) in Australia.

[67] In Canada, upon certification procured by the holder, but not by the drawer, see *Gaden* v. *Nfl'd Savings Bank*, above, n. 43; the drawer's is discharged, see *Boyd* v. *Nasmith* (1889), above, n. 42, so that the only remaining engagement is towards the holder.

[68] Delay is excused where caused by circumstances beyond the control of the holder. See s. 46(1) in the UK, s. 44(1) in South Africa, s. 90 in Canada, and s. 45(a) in Israel. To a similar effect, see s. 66 in Australia. Furthermore, specifically in connection with cheques (but not any other bill of exchange), unreasonable delay does not discharge the drawer except for the damage suffered (e.g. due to the insolvency of the drawee bank after the expiration of the reasonable time). See s. 74 in the UK and Israel, s. 166 in Canada, and s. 60(1) in Australia.

his behalf, to the drawee bank, usually at its branch, as indicated on the cheque.[69] In Canada and Israel, neither clearing house nor electronic presentment is authorized.[70] An interbank agreement, whether or not embodied in clearing rules, will not suffice to provide for a valid alternative to the statutory requirement of physical presentment at the branch upon which the cheque is drawn.[71] However, an agreement to that effect between the drawer and the holder is adequate;[72] it is arguable that such an agreement can be implied from the existence of an interbank agreement, to whose terms both the drawer and payee/holder agreed in their respective agreements with their banks.[73] Presentment by electronic means as well as in places designated by the drawee bank other than at the branch are specifically provided for in the UK[74] and Australia,[75] and recently added in South Africa.[75a]

[5]   A drawee bank could mistakenly dishonour a cheque, notwithstanding the existence of funds available at the drawer's account, or of the availability of an overdraft facility to the drawer. In such a case, wrongful dishonour has taken place, in breach of the drawer–drawee banking contract, so that the drawee bank becomes liable to its customer, the drawer,[76] for damages.[77]

As to the scope of damages, a distinction was drawn between a customer who was a 'trader', and any other customer. Accordingly, '[t]he customer will always be entitled to nominal damages'; however, 'a trader,

---

[69] Ss. 45 and 52(4) in the UK; ss. 44 and 51(d) in Israel; ss. 43 and 50(4) in South Africa; ss. 84(3), 85(1)(b), 86(1), and 87(b) in Canada; cf. ss. 61–65A in Australia, which are more detailed.

[70] For a general discussion, see e.g. J. Vroegop, 'The Legal Implications of Cheque Truncation', [1990] LMCLQ 244.

[71] *Barclays Bank* v. *Bank of England* [1985] 1 All E.R. 385 (Bingham J.).

[72] As between the drawer and holder, presentment may be waived. See s. 46 (2)(e) in the UK, s. 44(2)(e) in South Africa, s. 91(1)(e) in Canada, s. 45(b)(5) in Israel, and s. 59(b)(ii) in Australia. Inasmuch as presentment serves the interests of both the drawer and the holder, waiver of physical presentment at the drawee branch is likely to be accompanied by an agreement as to a substituting procedure, such as clearing house or electronic presentment, which will confer upon participants similar benefits to those present by the statutory presentment.

[73] See B. Geva, 'Off-Premises Presentment and Cheque Truncation under the Bills of Exchange Act' (1986–7), 1 B.F.L.R. 295.

[74] Ss. 74A–74C, added in 1996.   [75] Ss. 62–65A, particularly, ss. 62(1)(c), (3)–(12).

[75a] S. 43A, added by the SA Bill, n. 16, above (proclaimed 1 March 2001), further allowing presentment at a place designated by clearing house rules.

[76] Under some circumstances, liability may be fastened against the holder as well. See three exceptions (to the limitation of the drawee, liability to the drawer alone) set out in s. 2, above.

[77] For the contractual nature of the customer-drawer's action against the drawee bank, see *Marzetti* v. *Williams* (1830), 1 B. & Ad. 415 at 424; 109 E.R. 842 at 845, where Lord Tenterden CJ stated that an action for wrongful dishonour 'is, in fact, founded on contract, for the banker does contract with his customer that he will pay checks drawn by him, provided he, the banker, has money in his hands belonging to that customer'.

will be able to recover substantial damages for injury to his credit without proof of special damages'.[78] This rule is regarded[79] as exception to the principle requiring damages for breach of contract to be assessed,[80] but not to the requirement that damages recovered in contract are to be foreseeable.[81] 'Trader' is not a term of art; it loosely refers to any businessperson or professional.

In any event, the rule as to unique position of a 'trader' was not followed by the English Court of Appeal in *Kpoharor* v. *Woolwich Building Society*.[82] It was specifically held there that history had changed the social factors that moulded the rule in the course of the nineteenth century. Inasmuch as credit rating has become important to individuals for their personal transactions, a presumption of substantial damage arises in every case, not only one involving a trader.[83]

In the absence of an overdraft facility, the unavailability of funds in the drawer's account justifies the dishonour of a cheque by the drawee bank. A question as to the unavailability of funds in the drawer's account arises where the drawee bank is faced with competing claims to limited funds in the customer's account. Such claims may be cheques, garnishment orders, as well as debts owed by the customer to the bank itself. In *Bank of British North America* v. *Standard Bank of Canada*,[84] Middleton J. expressed his view that '[w]hen a customer draws a cheque upon his bank, and there are funds to answer it when presented . . . the bank [would not] be at liberty to refuse to honour it, retaining the money to meet some demand of its own which has not yet matured, or to pay some other cheque drawn by the customer . . .'. Presumably, this is a 'first in time first in right' rule, subject only to the bank's liberty to satisfy first a mature debt owed to itself by the customer, by exercising the right of set-off.

In presenting a cheque for payment, or in fact, throughout the entire **[6]** collection and payment process, the depositary bank acts as an agent for its customer, the depositor, or cheque holder. In carrying out its mandate, usually through the interbank clearing system, the depositary bank may

---

[78] See Baxter, *The Law of Banking and the Canadian Bank Act*, 2nd edn., 19–20, as quoted with approval in *Smith* v. *Commonwealth Trust Co.* (1969), 10 D.L.R. (3d) 181 (B.C. S.C.).

[79] *Smith* v. *Commonwealth Trust Co.*, ibid.

[80] Recognition of the wrongful dishonour exception, with two others (breach of promise of marriage, and breach of condition of title by vendor of land), go back to *Sikes* v. *Wild* (1861), 1 B. & S. 587 at 594; 121 E.R. 832 at 835, *per* Lord Blackburn, as quoted in *Smith* v. *Commonwealth Trust*, ibid.

[81] For the consistency between the 'trader rule' for wrongful dishonour and the 'forseeability' rule under *Hadley* v. *Baxendale* (1854), 9 Ex. 341 at 354, 156 E.R. 145 at 151, see *Smith* v. *Commonwealth Trust*, ibid.   [82] [1996] 4 All E.R. 119 (C.A.).

[83] However, in the facts of the case, the customer whose cheque was wrongfully dishonoured was held to be a trader.

[84] (1917), 26 D.L.R. 777 at 782 (Ont. S.C.), *aff'd.* 35 D.L.R. 761 (Ont. S.C. A.D.).

use intermediary bank(s), acting as subagent(s) for the depositor.[85] Any such depositary or intermediary bank is known as a collecting bank.[86] No funds availability legislation, setting specific time limits for a depositary bank to provide its customer, the depositor and cheque holder, with irrevocable credit, or other means of final payment, for the deposited cheque, is in place in any of the common law jurisdictions.

Normally, the depositor's account is provisionally credited with the amount of a cheque deposited for collection. Upon the dishonour of such a cheque, the depositary bank has recourse against the customer, and may debit the account with the amount of the returned cheque. The recourse is either on the basis of the depositor's engagement as an endorser[87] or 'the common law and [the depositary bank's] position as a collection agent,'[88] namely the banking contract.

Alternatively, upon the dishonour of the cheque, rather than pursuing its recourse against its customer, the depositary bank, in possession of the returned dishonoured cheque, may choose to exercise its remedies on the cheque, against any prior party, usually the drawer.[89] As a holder in due course, the depositary bank may enforce the drawer's obligation to pay the cheque free from most drawer's defences against the payee, including those arising from the transaction for which the cheque was issued.[90]

In principle, and provided the cheque is regular on its face and not properly marked 'not negotiable' or to a similar effect,[91] a depositary bank can be a holder in due course where it took the cheque from its customer by negotiation, for value, in good faith, and without knowledge of any

---

[85] For these well-established propositions, see e.g. *Barclays Bank* v. *Bank of England*, above, n. 71.

[86] The SA Bill, above, n. 16 (expected to be proclaimed 1 March 2001), added to BEA s. 1 a definition stating that ' "collecting bank" means a bank collecting payment of a cheque . . .'.

[87] An indorser engages that on due presentment the cheque will be paid, and if it is dishonoured, he will compensate the holder or any subsequent endorser who is compelled to pay it, provided that the requisite proceedings on dishonour (that is, the sending of notice of dishonour, and where necessary, protest) are duly taken. See s. 55(2)(a) in the UK, s. 53(2)(a) in South Africa, s. 132(a) in Canada, and s. 55(b)(1) in Israel. Cf. s. 73 in Australia which (in conjunction with s. 70) does not condition the indorser's liability on the receipt of a notice of dishonour.

[88] *Bank of Nova Scotia* v. *Sharp* [1975] 6 W.W.R. 97 at 103 (B.C. C.A.).

[89] For the alternative nature of these causes of action, see e.g. *Royal Bank of Canada* v. *Wild* (1974), 51 D.L.R. (3d) 188 at 190 (Ont. C.A.). For the drawer's statutory engagement, see above, n. 87.

[90] Rights of a holder in due course are governed by s. 38(2) in the UK, s. 73(b) in Canada, s. 37(2) in Israel, s. 36(b) in South Africa, and s. 49(2) in Australia.

[91] 'Not negotiable' cross, precluding a holder in due course status on the cheque, is provided for in s. 81 in the UK and Israel, s. 80 in South Africa, s. 174 in Canada, and s. 55 in Australia. Cf. 'account payee' cross under s. 81A in the UK (added in 1992) and the nontransferable cheque under s. 75A in South Africa (see SA Bill, above, n. 16, proclaimed March 1, 2001), as well as s. 8(1) in the UK, s. 6(5) in South Africa, s. 20(1) in Canada, and s. 7(a) in Israel, dealing with curtailing the negotiability of a bill of exchange by

adverse information.[92] Typically,[93] the taking in good faith and without adverse notice conditions are fulfilled by a depositary bank acting in the ordinary course of its business.[94] Difficulties may arise primarily with respect to the taking for value as well as by negotiation requirements. This is so since merely provisionally crediting the depositor's account with the proceeds of a deposited cheque does not constitute compliance by the depositary bank with the taking for value requirement,[95] at least as long as such credit has not reduced or eliminated an overdraft. On its part, 'negotiation' of a cheque payable to order is by indorsement, which requires the customer-indorser's signature.[96] Further, the negotiation to a holder in due course may not be by means of a restrictive indorsement, such as 'for collection'.[97]

There is no uniform response to these difficulties in the various common law jurisdictions. Thus, Israel does not provide for any modifying conditions for holding in due course by a depositary bank.[98] The other extreme is represented by Canada, where neither taking for 'value' nor by indorsement and hence through the depositor's signature is required for a depositary bank crediting the account. Nor will a restrictive indorsement affect the position of a depositary bank collecting a cheque.[99] In the UK, Australia, and South Africa, to be a holder in due course, the depositary bank need not take the cheque by indorsement, and hence signature; it must nonetheless, take the cheque for value.[100] Presumably also in Israel

words prohibiting transfer, all further discussed in ss. 7–8, below. Neither cheque crossing nor any other means for curtailing the negotiability of cheques is practised in Canada.

[92] General holding in due course conditions are set out in s. 29(1) in the UK, s. 27(1) in South Africa, s. 55(1) in Canada, s. 28(a) in Israel, and s. 50(1) in Australia.

[93] But not always. See e.g. *Toronto Dominion Bank* v. *Jordan* (1985), 61 B.C.L.R. 105 (B.C. C.A.).

[94] It is worth mentioning though that the knowledge of each branch is separate and not attributable to another branch of the same bank. See e.g. *Bank of Nova Scotia* v. *Gould* (1977), 79 D.L.R. (3d) 473 at 476 (Ont. Co. Ct.).

[95] See e.g. *A.L. Underwood Ltd.* v. *Bank of Liverpool* [1924] 1 K.B. 775, 885.

[96] See ss. 31–2 in the UK, ss. 29–30 in South Africa, ss. 59 and 61 in Canada, 30–1 in Israel, and ss. 40–1 in Australia. The Canadian spelling is 'endorsement' rather than 'indorsement'.

[97] For restrictive indorsement, see s. 35 in the UK, s. 32 in South Africa, s. 67 in Canada, and s. 34 in Israel. There is no corresponding provision in Australia.

[98] For a discussion on the depositary bank as a holder in due course under Israeli law, see S. Lerner, *The Law of Bills and Notes*, 425–42 (Tel-Aviv, Israeli Bar, 1999) [in Hebrew]. For the position in Israel of the depositary bank, which holds the cheque as a restrictive indorsee, as holder *not* in due course, see Lerner, ibid. at 233.

[99] Canadian s. 165(3) broadly states that '[w]here a cheque is delivered to a bank for deposit to the credit of a person and the bank credits him with the amount of the cheque, the bank acquires all the rights and powers of a holder in due course of the cheque'. Notwithstanding the breadth of this language, courts insist on the compliance of the depositary bank with the good faith and without notice requirements. See e.g. *Royal Bank of Canada* v. *Ryan* (1993), 107 Nfld. & P.E.I.R. 1 (Nfld. S.C. T.D.).

[100] See s. 2 to the UK Cheque Act 1957, s. 84 in South Africa, and s. 96 in Australia. The latter is stated to be limited to a depositary bank collecting a cheque for the *payee*, rather than for any holder.

'value' is given by a depositary bank mainly by allowing the depositor to withdraw against the provisional credit.[101] In Australia, the Cheques Act contains no provision for the restrictive indorsement of a cheque.

[7]   A cheque may be presented for payment by or on behalf of someone other than the original payee. This is so due to the transferability or nego-tiability of the cheque. A cheque payable to bearer is transferred by deliv-ery.[102] A cheque payable to order is transferred by delivery and indorsement.[103] The bearer of a cheque payable to bearer, and the payee or indorsee in possession of a cheque payable to order is a 'holder'.[104] The transfer of a cheque from one holder to another is 'negotiation'.[105] The negotiation of the cheque to a holder in due course, that is, to a holder who acquires the cheque in good faith and for value,[106] passes title free from adverse claims as well as prior parties' defences,[107] including those of the drawer against the payee. However, a transferee of a crossed cheque[108] marked 'not negotiable' can neither obtain nor give a better title to the cheque than that of the transferor.[109]

Except for in Australia, under a specific provision in the BEA, a cheque containing words prohibiting transfer, or indicating an intention that it should not be transferable, 'is valid as between the parties thereto' but 'is not negotiable'.[110] Such an instrument cannot be negotiated to another holder.[111] A majority of the Supreme Court of Israel held that a cheque payable to order but crossed 'to the payee only' is governed by

---

[101] See Guest, above n. 59 at 716–19.

[102] S. 31(2) in the UK, s. 29(2) in South Africa, s. 59(2) in Canada, s. 30(2) in Israel, and s. 40(3) in Australia.

[103] S. 31(3) in the UK, s. 29(3) in South Africa; s. 59(3) in Canada, s. 30(3) in Israel, and s. 40(2) in Australia.

[104] S. 2 in the UK and Canada, s. 1 in Israel and South Africa, and s. 3 in Australia.

[105] S. 31(1) in the UK, s. 29(1) in South Africa, s. 59(1) in Canada, s. 30(1) in Israel, and s. 40(1) in Australia.

[106] These holding in due course conditions are elaborated in s. 29(1) in the UK, s. 27(1) in South Africa, s. 55(1) in Canada, s. 28(a) in Israel, and s. 50(1) in Australia.

[107] Or in the statutory language, a holder in due course holds the instrument 'free from any defect of title of prior parties, as well as from mere personal defences available to prior parties among themselves'. See s. 38(2) in the U.K., s. 36(b) in South Africa, s. 73(b) in Canada, s. 37(2) in Israel, and almost *verbatim*, s. 49(2) in Australia.

[108] For cheque crossing, see s. 8, below.

[109] Ss. 81 in the UK and Israel, s. 80 in South Africa, s. 174 in Canada, and s. 55 in Australia. All these provisions are limited to cheques and do not apply to other bills of exchange and promissory notes.

[110] S. 8(1) in the UK, s. 6(5) in South Africa, s. 7(1) in Israel, and s. 20(1) in Canada. The provision applies to bills and exchange, including cheques, as well as to promissory notes. According to *Hibernian Bank* v. *Gysin and Hanson* [1939] 1 K.B. 483 (C.A.), a bill of exchange marked on its face 'not negotiable', though drawn payable *to the order* of a designated payee 'only', is governed by that provision; not being a cheque, the instrument was not governed by s. 81 cited in n. 91, above. No corresponding provision exists in the Australian Cheques Act, where under s. 20, '[a] cheque is either payable to order or payable to bearer'.

[111] *Hibernian Bank*, ibid.

that provision. The majority was of the view that an instrument governed by the provision can neither be negotiated, nor otherwise transferred.[112] However, it was held in Canada that the provision does not preclude the transferability of the debt embodied in the instrument other than by negotiation, so that debts due in respect of instruments governed by that provision are nonetheless assignable under general principles of law.[113] It is not common in Canada to insert restrictions on the negotiability or transferability of a cheque.

The position in Australia is opposed to that in other BEA jurisdictions. Under s. 39 of the Australian Cheques Act, '[e]very cheque may be transferred by negotiation . . .'. This is true notwithstanding anything written or placed on the cheque. Accordingly, a cheque crossed 'account payee only' is not only transferable; it also passes by negotiation and may fall into the hands of a holder in due course. A cheque so crossed merely requires the bank of deposit in Australia to make inquiries when it collects the cheque for someone other than the named payee.[114]

In one case, the UK went beyond the common position precluding negotiability in connection with words prohibiting transfer. It thus deviated from the common position in a direction reversed to that of Australia. Rather, the BEA was amended in 1992 to include s. 81A, stating that a crossed cheque bearing across its face the words 'account payee', or 'a/c payee', with or without the word 'only', 'shall not be transferable, but shall only be valid as between the parties thereto'.[115] South Africa followed UK s. 81A in recently passing a new s. 75A (proclaimed March 1, 2001). Contrary to the UK provision, the South African counterpart applies to a 'cheque [bearing] boldly across its face the words "not transferable" or "non transferable", either with or without the word "only" after the payee's name.'[115a] Similarly to the cheque governed in the UK by s. 81A, the cheque governed in South Africa by s. 75A 'shall not be

---

[112] See CA 1560/90, *Zitayat* v. *First International Bank of Israel*, (1994) 48 PD (Pt. IV) 494. The dissent did not dispute the interpretation of the provision given by the majority but disagreed as to its applicability to a cheque payable to order crossed 'to the payee only'. In his view, such a cheque is transferable by negotiation but incapable of passing to a holder in due course.For cheque crossing, see s. 8 below.

[113] See *Chandler* v. *Edmonton Portland Cement Co. Ltd.*, [1917] 1 W.W.R. 1408 (Alta. S.C. A.D.). The judgment dealt with promissory notes, each made out on an ordinary printed form, with the words 'or order' deleted, and payable to a designated person 'only'. Promissory notes are governed by each of the provisions cited in n. 110, but not to those cited in n. 109, above.

[114] See A. L. Tyree, *Australian Law of Cheques and Payment Orders*, ¶¶ 18.57–18.68 (Sydney: Butterworths, 1988). For cheque crossing, see s. 8, below.

[115] For a critical analysis, see J. K. Macleod, 'The Plight of the Unbanked Payee' (1997), 113 L.Q. Rev. 133.

[115a] See SA Bill, above, n.16. Such a language cannot be cancelled and the cheque containing it is stated to "be deemed crossed generally, unless it is crossed specially".

transferable but shall be valid as between the parties thereto'. Presumably, in precluding transferability, and not only negotiability as under UK s. 81 and its counterparts elsewhere,[116] the language of both UK s. 81A and SA s. 75A purports to impede any means of transfer and not only by negotiation. There is however a Canadian authority, pointing at the scope of the BEA as a statute 'dealing with mercantile instruments not debts' and thus concluding that 'transferable' must 'import a physical delivery'.[117] Under this reasoning, assignability is not precluded even under UK s. 81A. In any event, in South Africa, under recently added s. 84(2) (proclaimed March 1, 2001), in some circumstances, a non-transferable cheque governed by s. 75A is assignable to a collecting bank to whom the holder was indebted; upon its delivery to the bank for collection, '[t]he bank shall be deemed to be the holder thereof taking the cheque in pledge for such indebtedness with the same rights and subject to the same liabilities as the holder had'.[117a]

To discharge the drawer (as well as other signatories) from liability on the cheque, so as to be entitled to debit the drawer's account with the amount of the cheque, the drawee bank must pay the cheque to the person designated by the drawer. In the usual case of a cheque payable to order or to bearer, such designated person is the 'holder'. Payment to the holder 'in good faith and without notice that his title . . . is defective' is such an effective or discharging payment.[118] Where the transferability of the cheque has been effectively curtailed, as indicated above, payment must be made to the original payee, or his agent for collection, such as the bank of deposit or any other properly appointed collecting bank. Arguably, however, where not precluded, payment could effectively be made to a transferee other than by negotiation, except that in the context of the mass cheque collection system, a bank ought to be excused for declining to act for, or pay to, anyone other than the holder, and where applicable, the payee only, or someone on his behalf. Stated otherwise, where permitted, a transfer by assignment, other than by negotiation, may be good enough to confer title to the assignee vis-à-vis the transfer-

---

[116] Provisions are cited in n. 91, above.

[117] *Chandler*, above, n. 113 at 1410 (dealing with the meaning of 'transferable' in connection with Can. s. 20(1), above, n. 91), where in the Canadian Constitutional context, the Court even questioned the power of federal Parliament to affect the assignability of debts represented by instruments. In Canada, legislative jurisdiction relating to the assignment of debts, being a matter of 'property and civil rights' belongs to the various Provinces, while 'bills and notes', including cheques, fall under federal jurisdictions.

[117a] See SA Bill, above, n. 16.

[118] S. 59(1) in the UK, s. 57(1) (in conjunction with definition of 'payment in due course' in s. 1) in South Africa, s. 60(a) in Israel, s. 138 in Canada, and almost *verbatim*, ss. 78–9 in Australia.

ring holder and parties liable on the instrument; it may nevertheless not be recognized by the drawee in the ordinary course of business.

Regardless, the transfer of a cheque whose negotiability has been curtailed, whether to a purchaser or to a collecting agent, may not confer on the transferee a better title than that of the transferor; ordinarily, without 'negotiation', even a collecting bank taking such a cheque under modified conditions as set out in s. 6 above may not be a holder in due course.[120]

In common law jurisdictions, 'payment' is not defined by legislation. **[8]** Obviously, payment in cash, over the counter, is 'payment'.[121] However, payment over the counter is effectively precluded where the cheque is crossed.[122] Crossing could be either general or special. A cheque bearing on its face the addition of two parallel traverse lines (with or without the words 'and company' inserted between such lines) is generally crossed. Where a name of a banker is added, crossing is specially to that banker. 'Not negotiable' marking can form a part of general as well as of special crossing. A drawee bank incurs liability to the true owner of a cheque unless it pays a generally crossed cheque only to a banker and a specially crossed cheque only to the designated banker. In Australia, special crossing is effectively excluded by the Cheques Act. While recognized by the Canadian BEA, crossing is not practised in Canada.

Obviously, an uncrossed (i.e. 'open') cheque may also be collected and paid through the interbank clearing system. Where a cheque is so collected and paid, some case law in Canada speaks of the completion of the internal payment process at the drawee branch as the point of 'payment'.[123] In any event, as a rule, interbank clearing rules impose strict time limits on a drawee bank, within which it must return a dishonoured cheque to the depositary bank. A question may arise as to whether the failure to return a cheque in the prescribed time frame constitutes 'payment', so as to finalize the provisional credit in the depositor's account with the depositary bank. There is no consensus on this point.

---

[120] It is uncertain whether this broad statement is correct in relation to s. 165(3) in Canada under which the mere *delivery* of a cheque to a bank for deposit, followed by a credit posted to the account, confers on the bank a holder in due course status. Whether this provision applies to cheques whose negotiability has been curtailed has not been determined. However, the question may be entirely academic, since no practice of curtailing negotiability exists in Canada in relation to cheques.

[121] See *Chambers* v. *Miller* (1862), 13 C.B. (N.S.) 125; 143 E.R. 50.

[122] Cheque crossing is governed by ss. 76–81A in the UK, ss. 75–82 in South Africa, ss. 76–83 in Israel, ss. 168–75 in Canada, and 53–7 in Australia. Crossing may be made either by the drawer or holder (or person in possession in Australia). The SA Bill, above, n. 16, specifically permits crossing by a collecting bank as well (see s. 76, proclaimed March 1, 2001). Cheque crossing in the context of forged indorsements is dealt with in 4.D(i) ss. 15–16, below. Specific features of s. 81 in South Africa, in the context of forged indorsements, are dealt with in 4.D(iv)(d) (South Africa), below.

[123] See e.g. *White* v. *Royal Bank of Canada* (1923), 53 O.L.R. 543 (A.D.).

In principle, clearing rules constitute an interbank agreement, binding participating banks,[124] but to which customers are not privy. Nonetheless, a leading Australian case[125] concluded that 'payment' occurred by the expiration of times prescribed for 'returns' under the clearing rules. In thus holding that at that point of time, credit given to the depositor upon the deposit of the cheque at the depositary bank became final and irrevocable, the Court reasoned as follows:

The [depositary] bank dealt with the cheque . . . in the capacity of agent for the [depositor] . . . In discharge of its duty to make a prompt presentation of the cheque . . . the bank was entitled to use the ordinary machinery of the clearing . . . The [depositor] could not complain of any delay involved in the clearing house practice . . . On the other hand he was entitled as between himself and his agent to have the benefit of any advantage arising from the use of the machinery of the clearing.[126]

One appellate authority in Canada reached a similar result,[127] rationalizing it on the depositary bank's duty to exercise reasonable diligence for the protection of the depositor's interests. However, another leading appellate judgment in Canada went the other way,[128] declining to see how a contract to which the depositor is not a party could benefit him.[129] Further reliance was put on the broad language in the account agreement allowing the bank to debit the customer's account for all returned items. In the view of the Ontario Court of Appeal, the agreement 'entitled [the bank] to debit the [customer's] account, even though the cheque was returned in a manner not strictly in accord with the clearing house rules'.[130]

[9]   Australian law provides for a unique category of agency cheque. This instrument can broadly be described as a cheque drawn on the account of

---

[124] See e.g. *National Bank of Greece (Canada)* v. *Canada Permanent Trust Co.* [1987] R.J.Q. 607 (Que. S.C.); *Banque nationale du Canada* v. *Caisse centrale Desjardins du Québec* [1997] AQ no. 3783 (Que. Sup. Ct), on-line: QL (QL); *National Bank of Greece (Canada)* v. *Bank of Montreal* [1999] Fed. Ct. Trial LEXIS 1168 (Fed. Ct. T.D.), on-line: LEXIS (Canada, ALL CANADIAN DIGESTS).   [125] *Riedell* v. *Commercial Bank of Australia Ltd.* [1931] V.L.R. 382 (S.C.).

[126] Ibid. at 384.

[127] *Stanley Works of Canada Ltd.* v. *Banque Canadienne Nationale* (1981), 20 B.L.R. 282 (Que. CA). See also *Royal Bank of Canada* v. *Blinn*, [1999] A.J. No. 1380 (Alta. Prov. Ct.), on-line: QL (AJ); 1999 A.B.P.C. 121, where *Stanley Works* was regarded (in para. 7) as legal authority for the argument that the depositary bank 'had a duty to enforce a due observance of the clearing rules on behalf of its customers'.

[128] *National Slag* v. *Canadian Imperial Bank of Commerce* (1983), 140 D.L.R. (3d) 473 (Ont. H.C.), aff'd. (1985), 19 D.L.R. (4th) 383 (Ont. C.A.), cited with approval in *Bank of Nova Scotia* v. *Regents Enterprises* (1997), 157 Nfld. & P.E.I.R. 102 at para. 37.

[129] However, *National Slag*, ibid. was distinguished and not followed where the depositary bank attempted to return cheques several months after presentment. See *Toronto Dominion Bank* v. *Reeser*, unreported, 4 Nov. 1987, 238131/85, Ont. Dis. Ct. Civ. Div.

[130] *National Slag*, ibid. at 384.

a financial institution (typically a non-bank),[131] held in a depository institution (typically a bank),[132] and carrying out payment by a customer of the financial institution. The financial institution, on whose account the agency cheque is drawn, is typically either a credit union or building society, namely, a non-bank depository institution.[133] It could however also be a provider of services to credit unions and building societies or a financial intermediary that lends to and borrows from the public, though not necessarily a deposit taker.[134]

Agency cheques occur in Australia in two forms. First, at the request of a customer, a credit union or building society may issue its own cheque, drawn on its own account with a correspondent bank, to the order of the payee and for a sum as instructed by the customer. Second, under a more sophisticated variation, the customer receives a chequebook with blank cheque forms of the credit union or building society, drawn (once filled in and signed) on its account at the correspondent bank. The customer is given authority to draw such cheques, which are presented for payment at the drawee bank. However, payment of such cheques by the drawee bank requires referral to and receipt of confirmation from the credit union or building society. Technically, such an agency cheque is the cheque of the credit union or building society, drawn on the bank, by the customer as an agent for the credit union or building society. The Cheques Act, however, expressly releases the credit union or building society from any liability for a dishonoured agency cheque signed by the customer. Such

[131] Under s. 100 in Australia, an agency cheque is to be drawn either by an FIC institution or an FCA institution. According to definitions in s. 3(1), and as explained below, such an institution is a building society, credit union, special services provider, or registered corporation under the Financial Corporations Act 1974.

[132] Under s. 10 in Australia, a cheque must be drawn on a financial institution, the latter being broadly defined in s. 3(1) to cover domestic as well as foreign banks, the Reserve Bank of Australia, building societies, credit unions, and special services providers.

[133] Until the end of 1998, an instrument drawn on a credit union or building society and payable on demand was not a 'cheque'; rather, it was called a 'payment order'. In comparison to the cheque, the payment order was less familiar and less popular. In response, building societies and credit unions facilitated the use of agency cheques by their customers.

[134] A special services provider (SSP) is a provider to member institutions of settlement services, treasury management services, loans or other financial accommodation facilities, and investment facilities for deposits. In practice, member institutions are non-bank depository financial institutions, namely, credit unions and building societies. The term is not defined, but is specifically referred to, in the Cheques Act. The financial institution, on whose account the agency cheque is drawn, could also be a registered corporation within the meaning of the Financial Corporations Act 1974, ch. 2, as am. ('FCA'), as may be prescribed. In addition to credit unions and building societies which are depository institutions, the FCA covers financial intermediaries, which borrow from and lend to the public. However, borrowing need not necessarily be made by taking deposits. Issuing long-term debt instruments such as debentures will also qualify. In any event, to date, no non-depository financial institution falling within the FCA has been prescribed, so that in practice, the agency cheque is one drawn on the account of a non-bank depository institution kept at a bank.

agency cheques are visibly distinguishable from cheques actually drawn by the credit union or building society which constitute an obligation of that institution rather than of its customer.[135]

(IV) CHEQUES UNDER THE AMERICAN UNIFORM COMMERCIAL CODE (UCC)

[1]   In the various jurisdictions of the USA, cheques are governed by the provisions of Article 3 of the Uniform Commercial Code, as supplemented by Article 4.[136] A cheque ('check' in the American spelling) is defined in UCC §3–104(f) to be essentially[137] an unconditional[138] order,[139] other than a documentary draft,[140] to pay a fixed amount of money,[141] payable on demand[142] and drawn on a bank.[143] It may, but is not required to, be payable to bearer or to order.[144] An instrument that complies with all these requirements is

---

[135] Agency cheques are governed in Australia by s. 100. See also s. 68(2A).

[136] UCC Article 3, Negotiable Instruments, and Article 4, Bank Deposits and Collections. The current text of Article 3 is from 1990. Previously, Article 3 was entitled 'Commercial Paper'. Conforming and miscellaneous amendments to Article 4 were made in 1990. In case of conflict, Article 4 governs Article 3. See UCC §3–102(b). As applied to the payment and collection of cheques Article 4 is further discussed in (v) below.

[137] The provision further specifies that a draft (see n. 139, below) drawn by a bank, whether on itself (in which case it is a 'cashier's check' under §3–104(g)) or on another bank (in which case it is a 'teller's check' under §3–104(h)), is also a 'check'. For these two types of bank instruments, see n. 164, below.

[138] See UCC §3–106. For the possibility that a separate agreement may nevertheless affect the instrument see §3–117.

[139] An instrument which constitutes an order is a 'draft'. See §3–104(e). A 'draft' under the UCC is thus a 'bill of exchange' elsewhere. A cheque is a species of a draft.

[140] Under UCC §4–104(a)(6) 'Documentary draft' is stated to mean 'a draft to be presented for acceptance or payment if specified documents . . . are to be received by the drawee or other payor before acceptance or payment of the draft'.

[141] Broadly defined in §1–201(24) to mean 'a medium of exchange authorized or adopted by a domestic or foreign government and includes a monetary unit of account established by an intergovernmental organization or by agreement between two or more nations'. UCC §3–107 specifically deals with instruments (including cheques) payable in foreign money. The amount of money payable on an instrument may be 'with or without interest or other charges', see UCC §3–104(a). In practice, cheques do not contain provisions for interest or other charges.

[142] According to UCC §3–108(a), an order (including a cheque) is 'payable on demand' if 'it (i) states that it is payable on demand or at sight, or otherwise indicates that it is payable at the will of the holder, or (ii) does not state any time of payment'.

[143] Broadly defined in UCC §4–105(1) as 'a person engaged in the business of banking, including a saving bank, saving and loan association, credit union, or trust company'. This effectively covers any type of a depositary financial institution.

[144] This is a specific exception, applicable exclusively to cheques. See UCC §3–104(c). All other types of negotiable instruments must be 'payable to bearer or order', as set out in §3–109, at the time of issue or delivery to the first holder. See §3–104(a)(1). In any event, the words 'to the order of' are almost always preprinted on the cheque form. According to §3–109(b), a cheque is payable to order if it is payable '(i) to the *order* of an identified person or (ii) to an identified person or *order*' (emphasis is added). The drafters rationalized the

a 'check' and a 'negotiable instrument'[145] under the UCC even where 'it contains a conspicuous statement, however expressed, to the effect that the . . . order is not negotiable or is not an instrument governed by . . . Article [3]'.[146] Effectively then, restrictions on the transferability or negotiability of a cheque are to be disregarded.[147]

Cheques payable to bearer are transferred by delivery.[148] Cheques payable to order are transferred by delivery accompanied by signature, called an 'indorsement'.[149] The person in possession of a cheque payable to bearer and the payee or indorsee in possession of a cheque payable to order is a 'holder'.[150] The transfer to a holder, other than by the initial issuer, is 'negotiation'.[151] The negotiation of a cheque to a holder in due course, that is, to a holder who acquires the cheque in good faith and for value,[152] passes title free from adverse claims as well as prior parties' defences,[153] including those of the drawer against the payee. A cheque is paid to the extent payment is made by the drawee bank to the holder, and subject to enumerated exceptions, even when the drawee is aware of a third party's claims to the instrument.[154]

A cheque is a species of 'item', the latter being defined in UCC §4–104(a)(9) to mean 'an instrument or a promise or order to pay money

---

§3–104(c) cheque exception by explaining that holders of cheques may overlook the omission of the usual 'order' language, and ought nevertheless to be protected. The omission of the required words from the cheque may either be in the original form of the cheque, as was some credit unions' practice, or caused by the drawer striking out the 'payable to order' language from the preprinted form. See Official Comment 2 to UCC §3–104. A cheque payable to an identified person, while technically not 'payable to order', is thus nevertheless a 'check' and 'negotiable instrument' governed by UCC Article 3.

[145] See definition in UCC §3–104(a). Other than an 'unconditional . . . order', namely a draft (including cheque), a negotiable instrument may be an 'unconditional promise', in which case it is, under §3–104(e), a 'note'.

[146] See UCC §3–104(d), further providing that for instruments other than cheques, the rule is to the contrary, namely, that language disclaiming negotiability effectively excludes the instrument from the coverage of Article 3.

[147] In fact, Article 3 is silent as to restrictions on transferability other than by the omission of the word 'order', which is to be disregarded. Arguably, however, the combined effect of §§3–104(c) and (d), at least by implication, is that in connection with cheques, any restriction on transferability, and not only on negotiability (in the sense of passability free of any defence or adverse claim into the hands of a holder in due course), is ineffective.

[148] UCC §3–201(b).   [149] UCC §§3–201(b) and 3–204.   [150] UCC §1–201(20).

[151] UCC §3–201(a).

[152] Holding in due course requirements are set out in UCC §3–302

[153] UCC §§3–305(a) and (b) and 3–306.

[154] UCC §3–602. More specifically, a discharging payment is to be made under that provision 'to a person entitled to enforce the instrument', who is stated in UCC §3–301 to include, besides the holder, a non-holder in possession who has rights of a holder (such as successor in title of a deceased ex-holder), as well as in some circumstances, a non-holder out of possession, as for example, of a lost cheque. Payment by the drawee with knowledge of injunction against payment or theft of the cheque is stated in §3–602(2) not to be a discharging payment.

handled by a bank for collection or payment' except for a payment order governed by UCC Article 4A[155] or a credit or debit card slip. In general, Article 3 deals with 'negotiable instruments' while Article 4 is concerned with rights and obligations in connection with 'items'. The 'check' is both a 'negotiable instrument' and an 'item', so as to fall under both UCC Articles 3 and 4.

The relationship between the drawee-payor bank[156] and its customer, usually the drawer, in connection with cheques (in fact, all 'items'), is governed by Part 4 of Article 4 (that is, UCC §§4–401 to 407). The bank's principal duties are to honour 'properly payable' cheques and not to wrongfully dishonour them.[157] The bank is not obligated to pay a cheque more than six months old.[158] In clear departure from previous law in the USA, UCC §4–401(c) provides that the drawee bank may ignore postdating and pay a cheque before its date, unless the drawer has specifically ordered it to stop payment on the cheque until the date it bears.[159]

[2]   Under UCC §4–401(a), a cheque is 'properly payable', 'if it is authorized by the customer and is in accordance with any agreement between the customer and bank'. Hence, a bank may charge to the customer's account any 'properly payable' cheque, even though the charge creates an overdraft. Accordingly, under §4–401(b), a customer who neither signed a cheque nor benefited from its proceeds, is not liable for the amount of an overdraft.

According to UCC §4–402(a), the wrongful dishonour is constituted by the dishonour of a 'properly payable' cheque. The provision goes on to state that a bank may dishonour a cheque that would create an overdraft unless it has agreed to pay the overdraft.[160] Indeed, inasmuch as overdraft has not been agreed upon, the cheque creating it is not 'properly payable' under §4–401(a). While under §4–401(a) the bank may nevertheless honour such a cheque and still be entitled to be reimbursed by the overdraw-

---

[155] Extensively dealt with in 3.C(x) below.

[156] In connection with cheques, these terms are interchangeable. See UCC §4–105(3).

[157] See UCC §§4–401 and 402. For disclaiming responsibility in connection with such duties under the UCC see 2.C(iv) s. 14 above. For freedom of contract and the account agreement under the UCC see 2.A(iii) s. 10 above. See also unconscionability under the UCC in 2.A(iv) s. 15 above.

[158] See UCC §4–404 which further states that nevertheless, the drawee bank 'may charge its customer's account for a payment made thereafter in good faith'. The provision is limited to cheques, other than certified, and does not apply to other 'items'.

[159] Official Comment 3 explains the change on the basis that 'the automated check collection system cannot accommodate postdated checks'.

[160] The agreement need be neither in writing nor express and where the bank 'had a longstanding policy of honoring [uncleared] checks' can arise from the 'implied . . . obligation of good faith and fair dealing' under UCC §1–203. See e.g. *Spencer Companies Inc.* v. *Chase Manhattan Bank*, 81 B.R. 194 (U.S. D. Mass 1987), course of dealing.

ing customer, under §4–402(a) the bank is under no duty to so honour the overdrawing cheque.

The measure of damages for wrongful dishonour is governed by UCC §4–402(b):

A payor bank is responsible to its customer for damages *proximately caused* by the wrongful dishonor ... Liability is limited to *actual damages* proved and may include damages for an arrest or prosecution ... or other *consequential damages*. Whether any consequential damages are proximately caused by the wrongful dishonour is a question of fact to be determined in each case. [Emphasis added]

Punitive damages appear to be excluded, even when the bank has acted intentionally. Also, the provision does not retain the 'trader rule', under which substantial damages in defamation were presumed, and ought not to have been proved, in the case of a customer in business, trade, or profession.[161]

Under UCC §3–408, a cheque 'does not of itself operate as an assign-   [3] ment of funds in the hands of the drawee available for payment ...'. Accordingly, the drawee-payor bank is not liable on the cheque until it accepts it.[162] A payee-holder has rights against an *obligated* bank,[163] incurring liability either as an issuer of a cashier's or teller's cheque,[164] or on the certification of a personal cheque[165] which amounts to acceptance.[166] The obligated bank's liability is of indefinite duration, though it becomes

---

[161] For both points, that is, punitive damages and the 'trader rule', see Official Comment 1 to UCC §4–402. Note however that as for the first point, the Comment is less categorical: 'Whether a bank is liable for non-compensatory damages, such as punitive damages, must be decided by Section 1–103 and Section 1–106 ("by other rule of law")'.

[162] See UCC §3–408. The acceptor's obligation is governed by §3–413. Inasmuch as 'acceptance' is constituted by 'the drawee's *signed* agreement' (§3–409(a); emphasis added), §3–408 is consistent with s. §3–401(a), under which liability on an instrument requires signature.

[163] Against whom consequential foreseeable damages may be recovered for the wrongful refusal to pay under UCC §3–411.

[164] Under UCC §3–104(g), a cashier's cheque is 'a draft with respect to which the drawer and drawee are the *same* bank or branches of the same bank'. Under §3–104(h) a teller's cheque is 'a draft drawn by a bank (i) on *another* bank, or (ii) payable at or through a bank'. [All emphasis added.] For an item payable through or at a bank, designating that bank either as a collecting or a drawee bank, see UCC §4–106. Under the quoted definitions, both the cashier's and teller's cheques are not required to be payable on demand. They are, nevertheless, specifically stated to fall within the definition of a 'check' under UCC §3–104(f). See n. 137, above. In practice, cashier's and teller's cheques are commonly payable on demand. The obligation of the issuer of a cashier's cheque is governed by §3–412. For the obligation of the drawer of a draft, including that of a teller's (but not cashier's) cheque see §3–414.

[165] 'Personal cheque', which is not defined, is loosely taken to mean a cheque issued by a bank customer, on which (unless certified) a bank is not liable.

[166] For cheque certification as acceptance, see UCC §3–409 which further provides (in subsection (d)) that '[t]he drawee of a check has no obligation to certify the check, and refusal to certify is not dishonor of the check'. The acceptor's obligation (including that of the certifying bank) is provided for in §3–413.

subject to a limitation of actions three years after demand for payment is made to the obligated bank.[167]

Upon the issue or certification of a cheque by its obligated bank, the customer's account is promptly debited. Certification thus discharges the drawer, 'regardless of when or by whom [it] was obtained'.[168] Otherwise, in a case of a personal uncertified cheque, namely, a cheque neither issued nor certified by an obligated bank, the drawer-customer may order the drawee-payor bank to stop payment on the cheque, as long as it has not been paid. Prior to payment, the drawer-customer's obligation to pay the cheque, derived from his signature, is triggered upon the dishonour of the cheque, and irrespective of any stop-payment order, may be enforced by an action commenced within three years after the dishonour or ten years after the date of the draft, whichever period expires first.[169] Obviously, in such an action, the drawer may raise defences available to him against the plaintiff.[170]

[4]   Under UCC §4–405, '[n]either death nor incompetence of a customer revokes the authority to accept, pay, collect or account until the bank knows of the death or of an adjudication of incompetence and has reasonable opportunity to act on it'. Furthermore, '[e]ven with knowledge, a bank may for 10 days after the date of death pay or certify checks drawn on or before that date unless ordered to stop payment by a person claiming an interest in the account'.

The customer's right to stop payment of any cheque drawn on his account, as well as to close the account, is provided by UCC §4–403(a). The right may be exercised by the customer[171] giving 'an order to the bank describing the [cheque] or account *with reasonable certainty*' (emphasis added). To be effective, the customer's order must be received by the bank,[172] at the branch where the account is kept,[173] 'at a time and in a man-

---

[167] UCC §3–118(d) and Official Comment 3.   [168] UCC §3–414(c).

[169] See §§3–401(a), 3–414(b)(together with Official Comment 2, characterizing the drawer's liability, in departure of former law, as primary), and 3–118(c)(together with Official Comment 3).

[170] Defences to an action on a cheque are governed by §3–305. In general, defences under the transaction for which the cheque was paid are not available against a holder in due course, who has taken the instrument for value, in good faith, and without notice of any defence or adverse claim §3–302).

[171] More specifically, an order may be given by a customer, 'or any person authorized to draw on the account if there is more than one person. . . . If the signature of more than one person is required to draw on an account, any of these persons may stop payment or close the account.'

[172] Under UCC §1–201(27), '[n]otice, knowledge or a notice or notification received by an organization is effective for a particular transaction from the time when it is brought to the attention of the individual conducting the transaction, and in any event from the time when it would have been brought to his attention if the organization had exercised due diligence'. In this context, due diligence means the maintenance of reasonable routines for communicating significant information, usually as one's regular duties.

[173] Under UCC §4–107, a branch or separate office is a separate bank, *inter alia*, for the purpose of determining the place to which notices and orders are to be given under Articles 3 and 4.

ner that affords the bank a reasonable opportunity to act on it' before any 'milestone' in dealing with the cheque has been passed. Under §4–303, such milestones are the acceptance or certification of the cheque by the bank, payment of the cheque in cash by the bank, the occurrence of irreversible settlement of the cheque, the accountability of the bank by the failure to make a timely provisional settlement, and a prescribed cut-off hour during the next banking day[174] after the banking day on which the bank received the cheque.[175]

As indicated, the stop-payment order must describe the cheque or account 'with reasonable certainty'; no strict accuracy is required.[176] It must be given in a timely manner to the appropriate branch employee. No formal requirements as to the stop-payment order are otherwise stated. However, under §4–403(b), an oral, unconfirmed in writing, stop-payment order lapses after fourteen calendar (that is, neither 'banking' nor 'business'; weekends and holidays are included) days. Once confirmed in writing, or initially given in writing, a stop-payment order is effective for six months. It 'may be renewed for additional six-month periods by a writing given to the bank within a period during which the stop-payment order is effective'.

In principle, under §4–403(c), a bank which mistakenly paid a cheque **[5]** 'contrary to a stop-payment order or order to close an account' is liable to the customer for his loss. The loss, as well as its amount, must be established by the customer. The customer's loss from payment of a cheque contrary to a stop-payment order 'may include damages for dishonor of subsequent items'. However, under UCC §4–407, a drawee-payor bank sued for improper payment may exercise its right of subrogation. The bank may thus defend the drawer-customer's action by pleading that the mistaken payment effectively discharged the drawer-customer's debt, either to the payee-holder, or to a holder in due course,[177] as the case may be. Under such circumstances, no actual loss has in fact been incurred by the drawer-customer. In the shoes of a holder in due course, the subrogating payor bank may have the benefit of discharge, notwithstanding the availability to the drawer-customer against the original payee of defences

---

[174] 'Banking day' is defined in UCC §4–104(a)(3) to mean 'the part of the day on which a bank is open to the public for carrying on substantially all of its banking functions'.

[175] For the 'milestones' under UCC §4–303, see text and note at 203, below.

[176] See e.g. *First State Bank of Warren* v. *Dixon*, 728 S.W. 2d 192 (Ark. C.A. 1987), where the effectiveness of a stop-payment order giving 'the correct account number, check number, date and payee of the check but [slightly] misstat[ing] the amount of the check' was upheld.

[177] Alternatively, under that provision, the payor bank may compensate its customer and subrogate to the customer's rights against the payee (or any other holder) with respect to the transaction out of which the cheque arose. Practically, this authorizes the payor bank to recover the mistaken payment from the payee on the basis of the customer's claim against the payee for the breach of their underlying contract.

arising from their underlying transaction, for which the improperly paid cheque was given. Such defences may not have been raised by the drawer-customer against a holder in due course, to whom the drawer-customer would have remained liable on the cheque.[178] A collecting bank[179] is likely to be such a holder in due course.[180] Hence, the subrogation plea is quite potent in the hands of the payor bank that mistakenly paid a cheque contrary to its customer's instructions.

(V) COLLECTION AND PAYMENT OF CHEQUES IN THE UNITED STATES

[1] In the USA, rights of the depositor (a customer of the bank of deposit) as well as of the drawer (a customer of the drawee bank) in the process of the collection and payment of cheques are governed, in the various jurisdictions, by Article 4 of the Uniform Commercial Code,[181] as pre-empted or supplemented by federal law, particularly[182] Regulation CC—Availability of Funds and Collection of Checks.[183] The effect of the provisions of UCC Article 4 may further be varied by agreement.[184] Federal Reserve regulations and operating circulars, as well as interbank clearing rules, 'whether or not specifically assented to by all parties' have the effect of such agreements, binding and inuring to the benefit of all parties inter-

---

[178] For the right of the holder in due course (who, under §3–302, must have acquired the instrument for value, in good faith and without notice of any adverse claim or defence to it) to recover from the obligor over contractual defences and claims in recoupment (other than 'real' defences rendering the instrument void, rather than voidable), see UCC §3–305.

[179] Broadly defined in §4–105(5) as any bank handling a cheque for collection except the drawee-payor bank. The 'depositary bank', being effectively defined in §4–105(2) to mean the bank where the cheque is deposited for collection, is a 'collecting bank'.

[180] Provided credit it gave for the cheque has been withdrawn, applied, or made available for withdrawal as of right. See UCC §§4–205, 210, and 211. See in general, n. 209, below.

[181] UCC Article 4—Bank deposits and Collections, most recently amended in 1990.

[182] But see also Subpart A of Regulation J, 12 C.F.R. 210, dealing with cheque collection by Federal Reserve Banks.

[183] 12 C.F.R. 229, implementing the Expedited Funds Availability Act, Title VI of Pub. L. 100–86, 12 U.S.C.S. 4001 et. seq. A project designed to incorporate the substantive provisions of Regulation CC into the Uniform Commercial Code is currently being undertaken by the Drafting Committee to Revise Payment Article of the UCC.

[184] See UCC §4–103(a), which further provides that 'the parties to the agreement cannot disclaim a bank's responsibility for its lack of good faith or failure to exercise ordinary care or limit the measure of damages for the lack or failure'. Standards by which the bank's responsibility is to be measured, which are not manifestly unreasonable may, nonetheless, be determined by agreement. 'Agreement' is broadly defined in UCC §1–201(3) to mean 'the bargain of the parties in fact as found in their language or by implication from other circumstances including course of dealing or usage of trade or course of performance . . .'. Under UCC §1–201(11), 'the total legal obligation which results from the parties' agreement . . .', is a 'contract'.

ested in the cheque collection, including customers, not parties to such agreements.[185]

Funds availability upon the deposit into a bank account is the subject-matter of Regulation CC. Section 229.10 which accords next-day availability to cash deposits made in person to an employee of the bank of deposit, to electronic payments for which the bank has received both payment in actually and finally collected funds and relevant amount and account information, and to certain cheque deposits. In general such deposits are of cheques drawn on the US Treasury or a Federal Reserve Bank and other government cheques, postal orders, cheques issued or certified by banks, cheques drawn on another branch of the same bank of deposit in the same state or same cheque-processing region, and up to the first $100 of any other cheque deposit. To benefit from next-day availability, all such cheques must be deposited to the payee's account, usually to an employee of the bank of deposit, and in some cases, with a deposit slip or deposit envelope. Availability of funds for such cheques not deposited in person is delayed for one day.

The availability schedule in other cases is provided for in Reg. CC, s. 229.12. In principle, for local cheques deposited into an account, the bank of deposit must make funds available for withdrawal not later than on the second business day following the banking day of the deposit.[186] This time schedule applies also to some instruments dealt with by s. 229.10 whose deposit did not conform to the conditions specified in that provision. For non-local cheques, as well as deposits made at non-proprietary ATMs, funds are to become available not later than on the fifth business day after the banking day of deposit. A local cheque is generally defined in s. 229.2 as a cheque drawn on a bank in the same cheque-processing region.

The bank of deposit may extend the availability schedule under s. 229.12 by one business day for interstate cheques deposited in branches located outside continental USA, as well as for any amount over $400 in connection with withdrawal by cash, electronic payment, or an instrument on which the bank is irrevocably liable.

In principle, under Reg. CC, s. 229.13, new accounts during the first thirty days after establishment, large deposits in excess of $5,000, redeposited cheques, as well as situations involving repeated overdrafts, reasonable cause to suspect collectability, or emergency conditions, are exempted either in full or in part from the above-mentioned availability schedules.

[2]

---

[185] UCC §4–103(b).

[186] 'Banking day' is defined in Reg. CC, s. 229.2 as 'that part of any business day on which an office of a bank is open to the public for carrying on substantially all of its banking functions'. 'Business day' is effectively defined there as any calendar day other than Saturday, Sunday, or specified holidays.

The civil liability of a bank which did not comply with any requirement of Reg. CC in relation to funds availability is provided for in s. 229.21. In each case, liability to the depositor covers actual damages, costs of the action together with a reasonable attorney's fee, and at the discretion of the Court, additional damages. In the case of an individual action, such additional damages ought to be between $100 and $1,000. No individual minimum recovery applies to a class action, in which case, total recovery, for the additional damages for all members of the class, will not exceed the lesser of $5,000 or 1 per cent of the net worth of the bank involved.

[3]   Funds availability for deposited cheques not governed by Regulation CC remains subject to Article 4. The relevant provision is UCC §4–215(e).[187] In principle, funds availability under Article 4 is dependent on 'final settlement' or 'final payment'. 'Final payment' is also central to the delineation of the drawer's rights. Also, neither credit to the depositor's account nor funds availability to him is irrevocable and unconditional until finality of settlement is achieved. Hence, pertinent terminology must first be established.

[4]   A cheque is either paid or dishonoured in response to its presentment, whether physical or electronic[188] to the drawee bank ('payor bank').[189] A drawee bank is under no obligation to the drawer-customer to pay a cheque, other than certified, which is presented for payment more than six months after its date.[190] A holder presenting a cheque for payment more than thirty days after the date of the cheque incurs the risk of loss occurring due to the suspension of payment by the drawee bank.[191]

A cheque may be presented for payment by the holder to the drawee either directly, for payment in cash over the counter, or through the holder's bank, for collection and payment into the holder's account. Neither crossed cheques nor cheques payable in account are provided for in

---

[187] See also UCC §4–215(f) providing for next-day availability for cash deposits.

[188] Electronic presentment, if agreed upon, is authorized under UCC §4–110. For an outline of a Federal Reserve system committee setting out a series of cooperative steps the Federal Reserve and the private sector can take to remove the barriers to the developments of electronic cheque presentment in the United States, see Federal Reserve press release, 7 Sept. 2000: 'Next Steps by the Payments System Development Committee to Address Barriers to Electronic Check Presentment' (available online at www.federalreserve.gov), where it is further stated that currently, the Federal Reserve presents electronically 25 per cent of the cheques it collects.

[189] In connection with cheques, 'presentment' is defined in UCC §3–501 to mean a demand for payment. Where it is not electronic, presentment usually involves the exhibition of the cheque. UCC §3–502 defines 'dishonor' in terms of non-payment in response to an effective presentment.

[190] UCC §4–404 which further states that the bank may nevertheless 'charge its customer's account for payment made thereafter in good faith'. A drawee of an uncertified cheque is not liable to the holder (UCC §3–408, discussed in (iv) s. 3, above; this is why UCC §4–404 refers solely to the drawee bank's liability to the drawer-customer.

[191] UCC §3–414(f) and Official Comment 6.

the United States. Where the payor bank is not the bank of deposit, the cheque is presented to it through the interbank collection system, either directly by the bank of deposit ('the depositary bank'), or indirectly, through an intermediary bank. A depositary or intermediary bank is called a 'collecting bank'.[192]

In the interbank collection process, each disposition of the cheque, from the depositary bank onward to the payor bank, entails payment to the disposing collecting bank by its receiver. In the terminology of Article 4, such payment is 'settlement', whether made 'in cash, by clearing-house settlement, in charge or credit or by remittance, or otherwise as agreed'.[193] However, under UCC §4–201(a), with respect to a cheque, a collecting bank is normally an agent or subagent of the depositor, so that any settlement given for the cheque is provisional.[194]

In principle, under UCC §4–215(c), interbank provisional settlement becomes final upon final payment of the cheque by the payor bank. Under §4–215(a), final payment occurs when the payor bank has paid in cash, settled without having a right to revoke the settlement, or failed to revoke a provisional settlement in the time and manner permitted by statute, clearing house rule, or agreement.

In fact, UCC §4–302 makes a payor bank 'accountable', namely, strictly liable,[195] where it retained the cheque without settling for it (that is, even provisionally) within specified deadlines.[196] Where the payor bank is not the depositary bank, the cut-off point is the midnight of the banking day of receipt.[197] Otherwise, the deadline is postponed to the following midnight. Usually, however, the payor bank will settle for the cheque before the midnight of the banking day of receipt, so as not to fall into UCC §4–302. Under §4–301(a), such a settlement is provisional and revocable if the bank returns the cheque (or sends written notice of dishonour if the

---

[192] In terms of their respective roles, participating banks are defined in UCC §4–105.

[193] UCC §4–104(11). The medium and time of settlement by bank are governed by UCC §4–213.

[194] Conversely, the terminology of Regulation CC does not distinguish between provisional and final settlement. However, recovery for timely and properly returned cheques is equally authorized.

[195] Liability under the 'accountability' of UCC §4–302 is on the dishonour of the cheque and thus does not constitute 'payment'. See UCC §3–502(b)(1) and Official Comment 4 to the latter provision.

[196] Delay caused by circumstances beyond the control of the bank may be excused under UCC §4–109. But cf. *Blake* v. *Woodford Bank and Trust Co.* 555 S.W. 2d 589 (Ken. C.A. 1977) for a narrow interpretation of that provision. Circumstances causing delay involving an increased volume, breakdown of two posting machines, and temporary absence of a bookkeeper due to illness were regarded as foreseeable and hence inexcusable.

[197] But note that under UCC §4–108 a bank may fix an afternoon hour of 2 p.m. or later as a cut-off hour. A cheque received after that cut-off hour or after the close of the banking day may be treated as being received at the opening of the next banking day. All calculations for such afternoon cheques are thus to be made as of the day following receipt.

cheque is unavailable for return) before its midnight deadline, defined in UCC §4–104(a)(10) as the midnight of the next banking day following the banking day of receipt of the cheque.

Effectively then, 'final payment' takes place under UCC Article 4 when, upon presentment, the payor bank either pays the cheque in cash or, having originally settled for the cheque provisionally, fails to act before its midnight deadline.[198]

[5]   The midnight deadline requirement of UCC §4–301(a) is modified by the 'expedited delivery' extension of Reg. CC, s. 229.30(c). Briefly stated, the latter provision waives the UCC return deadline for a payor bank that used a means of delivery designed to expedite delivery to the next banking day, or even beyond it, presumably as long as the return deadlines of Regulation CC are met. Under Reg. CC, s. 229.30(a) these deadlines are determined under either two-day/four-day test for local/non-local banks, respectively, or under a forward collection test. There is also a specific non-payment notice requirement, under Reg CC, s. 229.33(a), with respect to a cheque of $2,500 or more. The payor bank must advise the depository bank of the return of such a cheque. The notice must reach the depository bank by 4.00 p.m. on the second business day following the banking day of the presentment for payment to the payor bank.[199]

Non-compliance with the return requirements of Regulation CC does not constitute 'payment'. Rather, it gives rise to damages payable by the breaching bank.[200] Where neither the midnight deadline rule of UCC §4–301(a) nor its modification by Reg. CC, s. 229.30(c) is met, final payment results from the violation of the UCC as not corrected by Regulation CC, and not from the mere breach of the modifying conditions outlined in the Regulation. On its part, the large-dollar notice requirement of Reg. CC, s. 229.33(a) neither satisfies nor modifies the return by midnight deadline rule of UCC §4–301. Rather, it is in addition to it.

In practice, the depository bank is quite keen on the speedy return of dishonoured cheques, and hence on the compliance by the payor bank with Regulation CC expeditious return requirements. This is so in order to minimize the risk of making available to depositors funds for would-be returned dishonoured cheques. Obviously, there is no duty to make

---

[198] Note however that both 'finality of payment' under UCC §4–215 and 'accountability' under §4–302 are subject to the payor bank's rights against the recipient for breach of presentment warranties under UCC §§3–417 and 4–208, for payment by mistake under §3–418, and as a drawer's subrogee under §4–407.

[199] The notice may be given by phone but must be delivered to a responsible person at the depository bank. It must be specific, precise, unequivocal, and certain. See *FDIC* v. *Lake Country National Bank*, 873 F.2d 79 (5th Cir. C.A. 1989).

[200] For damages (and civil liability in general) under Regulation CC see s. 2, above.

funds available for cheques known to be dishonoured and timely return or notice will protect the depositary bank from the risk of making payment for which recourse is available only against the receiving customer.

Under UCC §4–215(e), for cases not governed by the funds availability [6] schedules of Regulation CC,[201] a depositary bank that has received a provisional settlement for a cheque, must make funds available to the depositor 'when the settlement becomes final and the bank has had a reasonable time to receive return of the [cheque] and the [cheque] has not been received within that time'. However, when the depositary bank is also the payor bank, and the cheque is finally paid, funds must be made available to the depositor by the bank 'at the opening of the bank's second banking day following receipt of the [cheque]'.

At the payor bank, acceptance or certification of a cheque, final pay- [7] ment either in cash or by means of an irrevocable settlement (but not by other means), 'accountability' for a cheque that was retained under UCC §4–302 without even provisionally settled for,[202] and the close of the banking day following the day of receipt of the cheque,[203] by the payor bank (unless earlier hour as of one hour after opening of that banking day is fixed) are 'milestones'. Each milestone competes for priority, under UCC §4–303(a), with any of the following 'four legals': knowledge or notice received by the bank, stop-payment order received by the bank, legal process served on the bank, and set-off exercised by the bank. In principle, as between a 'milestone' and a 'legal', priority is accorded to the first in time. For example, a stop-payment order that reaches the bank in the banking day following the day of receipt, but after the cut-off hour that has been fixed, comes too late to be effective. In contrast, so far as finality of payment has not been achieved for a cheque, an intercheque competition is determined at the sole discretion of the payor bank.[204] It is noteworthy that the last 'milestone', that of a fixed or closing hour in the banking day following the day of receipt, substitutes for the completion of the process of posting,[205] which has been abandoned by the drafters as inappropriate for the automated cheque collection.[206] In any event, both milestones, that of an hour up to the close of the banking day, as well as

---

[201] See ss. 2 and 3, above. [202] See s. 3, above.

[203] This final 'milestone'—that of a fixed hour or the close of the banking day—provided for under UCC §4–303(a)(5), is specifically limited to 'checks', contrary to the other 'milestones', dealing with 'items', which is broader. See (iv) s. 1 above.

[204] See UCC §4–303(b).

[205] Under old UCC §4–109 (deleted in 1990), the process of posting meant 'the usual procedure followed by a payor bank in determining to pay a [cheque] and in recording [its] payment' so as to include signature verification, funds sufficiency ascertainment, affixation of a 'paid' or other stamp, or error correction or reversal.

[206] Official Comment 4 to UCC §4–303.

its predecessor, the completion of the process of posting, precede the midnight deadline where finality of payment occurs.

[8]   In sum, finality of payment is relevant to the determination of funds availability under UCC Article 4. In contrast, finality of payment does not determine funds availability under Regulation CC; it, however, marks the irreversibility of that funds availability, namely the point from which the depositor (to whom funds have been made available) is not subject to recourse for lack of funds in the drawer's account. While a 'legal' may be defeated even earlier than finality of payment of a cheque, finality forecloses any question of priority, whether of a competing 'legal' or any other cheque.

[9]   The position of a depositary bank that has made provisional settlement with its customer for a cheque but 'fails by reason of dishonour, suspension of payments by a bank, or otherwise to receive [final] settlement' for that cheque is governed by UCC §4–214. Having received a returned dishonoured cheque, the depositary bank is required, under Reg. CC, s. 229.32(b), to pay the returning or paying bank for the amount of the cheque prior to the close of business on the banking day on which it received the cheque. Under UCC §4–214, the depositary bank may then charge back the amount of the credit given for the cheque to the customer's account, or otherwise obtain refund from the customer. Recovery is thus on the basis of the banking relationship and not of an action on the cheque. Where 'by its midnight deadline or within a longer reasonable time after it learns the facts' the depositary bank neither returns the cheque to the customer nor sends him notification of the facts, it is liable for any loss resulting from the delay.

Alternatively, rather than pursuing its recourse against its customer (the depositor) on the basis of the banking relationship, the depositary bank, in possession of the returned dishonoured cheque,[207] may choose to exercise its remedies on the cheque, usually against the drawer. Under UCC §4–205, a depositary bank may be a holder of a cheque it received from a customer for collection even where the cheque is unendorsed.[208] Where credit originally given to the depositor has been withdrawn by him or applied in payment of his indebtedness, the depositary bank is regarded as having given value for the cheque for the purpose of determining its status as a holder in due course.[209] As a holder in due course,

---

[207] In fact, recourse is available to the depositary bank also when it is out of possession of the cheque, as long as it is actually entitled to such possession. See, in general, UCC §§3–301 and 309 and recall the agency status of each collecting bank under §4–201.

[208] The Official Comment acknowledges this rule to be an exception to the general rule of UCC §3–201(b), providing that negotiation of an instrument payable to order requires indorsement by the holder.

[209] UCC §§4–210 and 211. Holding in due course requirements are set out in UCC §3–202. Basically, a holder in due course is a holder who took a regular and complete instrument for value, in good faith, and without notice of any defect.

the depositary bank may enforce the drawer's obligation to pay the cheque[210] free from most drawer's defences against the payee, including those arising from the transaction for which the cheque was issued.[211]

Where a finally paid cheque is nevertheless returned, each paying and returning bank is in breach of the warranty under Reg. CC, s. 229.34(a). Each breaching bank is liable onward, up to the depositary bank, as well as to the latter's customer, the depositor. In such as a case, inasmuch as final payment occurred, no dishonour has taken place.[212] Under UCC §4–215(d), having received final settlement for the cheque, the depositary bank becomes 'accountable to its customer for the amount of the [cheque] and any provisional credit given for [it] . . . becomes final'. The customer is thus fully protected.

(VI) CHEQUES IN CIVIL LAW COUNTRIES: THE GENEVA UNIFORM LAW FOR CHEQUES

The Geneva Uniform Law for Cheques (hereafter: the ULC)[213] is the basis **[1]** of cheque legislation in civil law countries, including France, Germany, Italy, Japan, and Switzerland. An outline of the ULC should thus precede a discussion of particular issues with regard to which the law in any of these countries departed from the Uniform Law.

Under art. 1, to be a 'cheque', an instrument must comply with six for- **[2]** mal requirements. First, it must contain 'in the body of the instrument and expressed in the language employed in drawing up the instrument' the term 'cheque'. Second, the instrument must contain 'an unconditional order to pay a determinate sum of money'.[214] Third, the instrument must name the drawee, that is, the person who is to pay. Fourth, a statement of the place where payment is to be made ought to be included.[215] Fifth, the instrument must state the date and place where it is drawn.[216] Sixth, the

---

[210] Under UCC §3–414.

[211] UCC §3–305(b).

[212] See e.g. UCC §3–502(b)(1) defining the dishonour of a cheque in terms of the failure by the payor bank to return it (or send notice) within the required statutory deadlines.

[213] Adopted on 11 Mar. 1931, by the Second Geneva Convention, as part of an international effort which also generated the Geneva Uniform Law for Bills of Exchange and Promissory Notes (agreed upon in 1930). For the latter, in the context of the overall international effort in which it was concluded, see M. O. Hudson and A. H. Feller, 'The International Unification of Laws Concerning Bills of Exchange' (1931), 44 Harv. L. Rev. 333.

[214] Under art. 7, any stipulation in a cheque to pay interest shall be disregarded. Foreign currency cheques are governed by art. 36.

[215] This requirement is further elaborated on in art. 2. In general, even in the absence of an indication, the place of payment is deemed to be that of the drawee.

[216] Under art. 2, a cheque which does not specify the place at which it was drawn is 'deemed to have been drawn in the place specified beside the name of the drawer' and is nevertheless a cheque.

cheque must contain the drawer's signature. Under art. 3, a cheque must be drawn on a banker[217] holding funds at the drawer's disposal and in conformity with their agreement, 'express or implied', as to the drawer's entitlement to dispose of those funds by cheque.[218] The maturity of a cheque is stated in art. 28 to be 'at sight', so that '[a]ny contrary stipulation shall be disregarded.' Accordingly, a post-dated cheque is not recognized; a cheque presented for payment before its stated date of issue, 'is payable on the day of presentment'. Finally, under art. 5, a cheque may either designate a specified payee,[219] or be made payable to bearer.

[3]   UCL art. 4 prohibits the acceptance of a cheque. 'A statement of acceptance on a cheque shall be disregarded.' Stated otherwise, the drawee-banker may not be made liable on the cheque to the holder. Under art. 31, 'presentment of a cheque at a clearing house is equivalent to presentment of payment', namely, effective. This, however, falls short of authorizing an electronic presentment or cheque truncation. Strict presentment time limits are provided for in art. 29. Accordingly, a cheque payable in the country in which it was issued must be presented for payment within eight days from the date stated on the cheque as the date of issue.[220] Otherwise, a cheque payable in the continent of its issue[221] must be presented within twenty days. A cheque payable in a continent other than of its issue, must be presented within seventy days.[222] Under art. 52(1), the holder's action on the cheque against a party liable thereon is barred 'after six months as from the expiration of the limit of time fixed for presentment'.

Under art. 32, a cheque that has not been countermanded may be paid by the drawee bank even after the expiration of the time limit for presentment. On its part, the countermand of a cheque comes to force only after the expiration of this time limit. Stated otherwise, as against the drawee bank, payment of a cheque may not effectively be countermanded by the drawer within the time period for presentment. However, as a rule,

---

[217] Broadly defined in art. 54 to include 'the persons or institutions assimilated by the law to bankers'.

[218] Art. 3 goes on to conclude, that '[n]evertheless, if [its] provisions are not complied with, the instrument is still valid as a cheque'.

[219] In which case, it may be with or without the express clause 'to order', or with the words 'not to order'.

[220] Accordingly, while, as indicated in s. 2 above, a post-dated cheque is not recognized, post-dating is not without significance. This is so since the time limit for presentment, and hence, as explained below, the limitation period, as well as the time for an effective countermand of payment, are calculated according to the ostensible (namely, the delayed) date of issue indicated on the cheque.

[221] It is however stated that cheques issued in Europe and payable in a non-European country, bordering on the Mediterranean, or vice versa, are to be regarded as payable and issued in the same continent.

[222] As for the time calculation under art. 29, the provision concludes by stating that '[t]he date from which the abovementioned periods of time shall begin to run shall be the date stated on the cheque as the date of issue'.

the drawee bank incurs no liability whatsoever to the holder; accordingly, that bank is, in effect, free to comply with the countermand order of its customer, the drawer of the cheque, even within the presentment period. Since under art. 32, the drawee may anyway pay an uncountermanded cheque, even after the expiration of the time period for presentment, the practical implications of the time limits prescribed in art. 29 are quite limited. Implications are confined, first, to the calculation of the limitation period and, second, to the drawee bank's freedom, though strictly speaking, not duty, to overlook its customer's countermand instructions communicated within the prescribed presentment period.[223]

While as indicated, under art. 32, countermand has a limited effect on the drawee's duty to pay, the drawer's death or incapacity, occurring after the issue of the cheque, are of no effect altogether. Under art. 33, '[n]either the death of the drawer or his incapacity taking place after the issue of the cheque shall have any effect as regards the cheque'.

A person presenting a cheque for payment may be (i) the bearer of a **[4]** cheque payable to bearer, (ii) the payee or indorsee of a cheque payable to a specified person, or (iii) the payee or assignee of a cheque payable to a specified person, in which the words 'not to order' have been inserted.[224] Under art. 19, '[t]he possessor of an endorsable cheque is deemed to be the lawful holder if he establishes his title to the cheque through an uninterrupted series of endorsements . . .'. The negotiability or free circulation of cheques (other than those marked 'not to order') is further enhanced by protecting good faith possession in an indorsable cheque on the same footing as in a cheque payable to bearer. This is done by art. 21, providing that '[w]here a person has, in any manner whatsoever, been dispossessed of a cheque (whether it is a cheque to bearer or an endorsable cheque to which the holder establishes his right in the manner mentioned in Article 19), the holder into whose possession the cheque has come is not bound to give up the cheque unless he acquired it in bad faith or unless in acquiring it he has been guilty of gross negligence'.

To discharge the drawer (as well as other signatories) from liability on

---

[223] Whether a bank is free to disclaim responsibility for complying with a countermand of a cheque even after the expiration of the presentment period depends on local law outside the UCL. For disclaimer clauses in the various civil law jurisdictions in general, as applied to bank's duties to customers, see 2.C(ii), above. For freedom of contract and the account agreement, namely, for the effect of onerous express terms, in the various jurisdictions, see 2.A(iv), above.

[224] According to art. 14, a cheque payable 'to a specified person, with or without the express clause "to order", may be transferred by means of an endorsement'. Under art. 16, an indorsement 'must be written on the cheque or on a slip affixed thereto' and must be signed by the indorser. Art. 14(2) provides that a cheque payable 'to a specified person, in which the words "not to order" or any equivalent expression have been inserted, can only be transferred according to the form and with the effects of an ordinary assignment'. A cheque payable to bearer is transferred by delivery alone, without indorsement.

the cheque, so as to be entitled to debit the drawer's account with the amount of the cheque, the drawee bank must pay the cheque to the person entitled to receive payment, determined under the above-mentioned rules. Under art. 35, with respect to an indorsable cheque, the drawee bank 'is bound to verify the regularity of the series of endorsements, but not the signatures of the endorsers'.[225]

Under art. 34, '[t]he drawee who pays a cheque may require that it shall be given up to him receipted by the holder'. Partial payment is not precluded, in which case, 'the drawee may require that the partial payment shall be mentioned on the cheque and that a receipt shall be given to him'. Presumably, the partially paid cheque is to be retained, properly marked, by the holder.

The UCL does not preclude the payment of a cheque to the holder by the drawee bank, over the counter, in cash. However, payment in cash can be restricted, or even eliminated altogether, by either the crossing of the cheque or designating it as 'payable in account'. These procedures are governed by arts. 37–9.

A crossing may be made by the drawer or holder of a cheque. It consists of two parallel lines drawn on the face of the cheque. It is 'general' where it contains nothing else, or if between the lines the term 'banker', or some equivalent, is inserted. The crossing is 'special' where the banker's name is written between the two lines. Similarly, the drawer or holder may write transversely across the face of the cheque the words 'payable in account' ('à porter en compte') or a similar expression. A general crossing may be converted to a special one, but a special crossing may not be converted to general. The unauthorized obliteration of a crossing, of the name of the banker in a crossing, or of the words 'payable in account' is to be disregarded.

A crossed cheque may be paid by the drawee only to a banker or to the customer of the drawee. Where the cheque is crossed specially, the banker to be paid must be the one named, though payment could be carried out through a collecting bank nominated by the bank named in the crossing. A bank may neither acquire a crossed cheque except for, nor collect it for the account of, one of its customers or another bank. A 'payable in account' cheque can only be settled by the drawee bank by means of a book-entry, such as credit in account, transfer from one account to another, set-off, or clearing house settlement. Settlement by book entry is equivalent to payment.

---

[225] The entire implications of the scheme under arts. 19, 21, and 35 to the allocation of forged indorsement losses, and the differences between that scheme and others (namely, those applicable in common law jurisdictions, United States, and Canada) will be examined in 4.D below.

Liability for resulting damage, up to the amount of the cheque, is fastened on a drawee and any collecting bank not observing the crossing obligations, as well as on a drawee in breach of the requirements imposed in connection with cheques payable in account. Implications of such a wrongful payment are further explored below in connection with the allocation of cheque forged indorsement losses.[226]

According to art. 22, '[p]ersons sued on a cheque cannot set up against **[5]** the holder defences founded on their personal relations with the drawer or with previous holders, unless the holder in acquiring the cheque has knowingly acted to the detriment of the debtor'.[227] Unlike under Anglo-American law,[228] the holder's freedom from the drawer's defences does not depend on the higher standard of good faith acquisition of the cheque for value and without any adverse notice. Rather, acquiring the cheque while not 'knowingly [acting] to the detriment of the [drawer]' will suffice to purge the acquiring holder's title from the drawer's defences based on the drawer's 'personal relations' with the payee. Effectively, this means that under the UCL, having *acquired* the cheque (rather than having taken it merely for collection), upon its dishonour, the bank of deposit may recover from the drawer (that is, the drawee bank's customer), irrespective of the drawer's defences against the payee/holder. This is true, unless of course, in acquiring the cheque, the bank of deposit 'has knowingly acted to the detriment of the [drawer]'.

However, rather than acquiring a cheque payable to a specified person (and not marked 'not to order') by indorsement,[229] the bank of deposit is likely to take the cheque for collection. This may be reflected in the form of the indorsement. Thus, according to art. 23, an indorsement may contain words implying a simple mandate, such as 'value in collection' ('valeur en recouvrement'), 'for collection' ('pour encaissement'), or 'by procuration' ('par procuration'). A holder taking a cheque under such an indorsement 'may exercise all rights arising out of the cheque, but . . . can endorse it only in his capacity as agent'.[230] Furthermore, he takes the cheque subject to defences available against his indorser. The freedom

---

[226] See 4.D(ii) ss. 15–17.

[227] This provision ought not to be read as benefiting a plaintiff claiming on an undorsable, though assignable, cheque payable to a specified person in which the words 'not to order' have been inserted. Such a cheque is governed by arts. 5(1)(b) and 14(2). The 'holder' in art. 22 must be that of either bearer or indorsable cheque.

[228] For holding in due course requirements in common law (BEA) and under the American UCC see B(iii) s. 7 and (iv) s. 1 respectively.

[229] For the transferability of a cheque payable to a specified person by indorsement, see n. 224, above.

[230] Under art. 23(3), 'the mandate contained in an endorsement by procuration does not terminate by reason of the death of the party giving the mandate or by reason of his becoming legally incapable'.

from prior parties' defences under art. 22 is thus inapplicable. As an indorsee for collection from the payee, the bank of deposit is then subject to the drawer's defences against the payee-depositor.

In Germany,[231] and possibly also in Japan,[232] the defence-free position of the bank of deposit, indorsee for collection, against the drawer may nonetheless be established upon acquiring a security interest in the cheque, by giving value to the customer, usually by allowing him to withdraw funds prior to their collection. This is not so in Switzerland, nor France, nor Italy. In Italy, an indorsement for collection is rare. In any event, both in Switzerland and Italy, the prevailing view in connection with cheques is that a bank of deposit is deemed to be an agent for collection, irrespective of the form, or even the absence, of an indorsement.[233] In all five civil law countries under discussion, merely crediting the depositor's account will not suffice to acquire the cheque.

[6]   Obviously, whether it acquired the cheque or took it for collection from its customer, upon the dishonour of the cheque, the bank of deposit holder is not restricted to remedies against the drawer. Rather, the common course of action for a bank of deposit is against its customer, the depositor of the cheque. In the case of a cheque payable to a specified person the bank of deposit may sue its customer on the latter's indorsement.[234] Being a cheque rather than a bank deposits and collections law, the UCL does not provide for, nor does it preclude, the bank of deposit's action against its customer on the dishonour of the cheque, either as customer, under their account agreement, or, where the cheque was taken for collection, as a mandator under their mandate contract, and not necessarily as indorser of the cheque.

In fact, it is universally agreed in the civil law jurisdictions that adopted a statute modelled on the UCL that in collecting a cheque for a customer, the bank of deposit acts as mandatary. In Roman law, the mandate was broadly defined as 'a contract whereby one person (mandator) gives

---

[231] Under para. 15 of the General Business Conditions (GBC) in Germany a bank of deposit 'acquires ownership by way of security of any cheques . . . deposited for collection . . .' as well as all 'claims underlying the cheque . . .'. In general for the GBC, see 2.A(v) s. 29 above.

[232] I am advised that in Japan there may be doubts as to whether an indorsee 'by procuration' may even sue, due to a statutory provision (Article 72 of the Attorney at Law Act) limiting the right to sue as an agent to lawyers.

[233] In Italy, the bank of deposit, as any holder, may further have, under s. 59 of the Cheque Law, an action in unjust enrichment against a drawer who has not provided funds. However, such an action is not defence-free, since the existence of defences in the drawer's hands, precludes unjust enrichment.

[234] Under art. 18, the indorsement usually guarantees payment. No indorsement may exist where a cheque payable to a specified person contains the words 'not to order' (art. 14(2)), as well as in the case of a cheque payable to bearer, though under art. 20, by indorsing a cheque payable to bearer, the indorser incurs liability on the cheque.

another [mandatary] a commission to do something for him . . .'[235] In principle, this definition was adopted by the various civil codes,[236] and is indeed, broad enough to describe the bank of deposit's role in the cheque collection. Where as a mandatary, the bank of deposit is unable to collect the cheque, it is thus entitled to be reimbursed by its customer, as its mandator, for the advance given to the customer following the deposit of the cheque in the form of provisional credit to the customer's account.[237] There are further implications to the mandate relationship between the bank of deposit and the customer. Most notably, the bank must act for the customer, its mandator, with care.[238] This applies to the bank duties in connection with the proper and timely presentment of the cheque, as well as where applicable, the maintenance of proper procedures upon dishonour.

Obviously, as a mandatary, the bank of deposit must account for, and make available to its customer, the mandator, all sums collected on the cheque.[239] However, the law of mandate is not specific enough to address questions relating to the timing of funds availability as well as to the incorporation of interbank clearing rules into the agreement between the customer and bank of deposit. At the same time, no specific legislation is available to fill these gaps. Thus, as in common law jurisdictions, but contrary to the United States, the civil law countries have no specific funds availability legislation, requiring the bank of deposit to make funds available to the depositor/customer within strict time limits after the deposit,

---

[235] See e.g. R.W. Lee, *The Elements of Roman Law*, 4th edn. (London: Sweet & Maxwell Ltd., 1956) at 334.

[236] See e.g. CO art. 394(1) in Switzerland; CC art. 1984 in France (where the mandatary's action must be in the mandator's name); CC art. 1703 in Italy; CC art. 643 (in conjunction with art. 656) in Japan; and BGB s. 662 (in conjunction with s. 675) in Germany. See also CC art. 2130 in Quebec. In Italy and Quebec the mandate is limited to a legal or juridical act. Arguably, the collection of a cheque leading to the discharge of the drawer's debt falls into this category. For texts in English see: *The French Civil Code Revised Edition* (as am. to 1 July 1994), trans. J. H. Crabb (Littleton, Colo.: Fred B. Rothman & Co., 1995); *The German Civil Code* (as am. to 1 Jan. 1975) trans. I. S. Forrester, S. L. Goren, and H. M. Ilgen (South Hackensack, NJ: Fred B. Rothman & Co., 1975) (with 1981 Supp. trans. S. L. Goren); *The Civil Code of Japan* (translation) (Tokyo: Ministry of Justice, 1972); *The Italian Civil Code*, trans. M. Beltramo, G. E. Longo, and J. H. Merryman (Dobbs Ferry, NY: Oceana, 1969); *Swiss Contract Law, English Translation of Selected Official Texts—Swiss Code of Obligations* (Zurich: Swiss-American Chamber of Commerce, 1997); and the bilingual edition of the Quebec Civil Code, *Code civil du practicien* (Montreal: DACFO, 1995).

[237] For the mandatary's reimbursement rights against the mandator for expenses the mandatary incurred in the course of carrying out the mandate see CO art. 402(1) in Switzerland; CC art. 650 in Japan; CC art. 1999 in France; BGB s. 670 in Germany; CC art. 1720 in Italy. See also CC arts. 2154 and 2155 in Quebec.

[238] See CO art. 398 (with references to arts. 321(a)(1) and 321(e)(1) in Switzerland; CC art. 1992 in France; CC art. 644 in Japan; CC art. 1710 in Italy; and BGB s. 276 in Germany (for any debtor in general). See also CC art. 2138 in Quebec. Contractual exemption clauses purported to be relied on by banks were held inapplicable in the case of gross negligence.

[239] See CC art. 1713 in Italy; CC art. 646 in Japan; BGB §§666 and 667 in Germany; CO art. 400 in Switzerland; and CC art. 1993 in France. See also art. 2146 in Quebec.

irrespective of the actual payment of the cheque and the collection of its proceeds.[240]

Nor do civil law countries have specific statutory provisions governing the payee-holder's possible entitlement under interbank clearing rules dealing with the collection of cheques.[241] Such rules usually provide for strict time limits for the return of dishonoured cheques by the drawee bank. Where the bank of deposit nevertheless agreed to a delayed return, a question may arise as to whether the payee/holder/depositor's rights have thereby been broken. It is universally agreed that clearing rules constitute an interbank agreement; but may they also benefit or bind customers? Again, the statutory silence in civil law countries follows the similar position in common law jurisdictions but is contrary to the specific treatment of the subject in the United States.

There is a precedent in France supporting the proposition that in the absence of an agreement to the contrary, in depositing the cheque for collection, the depositor is deemed to have adhered to the clearing rules.[242] The case thus allowed the customer to invoke directly a clearing rule requiring a timely return of a dishonoured item. It further did not hold the customer to be bound by the waiver of his mandatary in accepting a late return of a dishonoured item. Thereby the case went beyond earlier jurisprudence in France. But even the latter was occasionally prepared to regard the delayed return of a dishonoured cheque as 'payment' by virtue of either fact or usage.[243]

There is authority in Japan in the same direction of the current French position. Similarly, in Germany, the non-timely return of a dishonoured cheque may be viewed as 'payment', which as such, benefits the depositor. In Switzerland, the depositor may be viewed as a third party beneficiary to the interbank clearing agreement under CO art. 112(2). Conversely, in Italy, a contractual clause in the standard form agreement which governs the deposit of the cheque releases the bank of deposit from any liability to its customer, the depositor, for accepting the return of a dishonoured cheque outside the time limits prescribed in the clearing rules.

---

[240] Not only that, but the bank–customer agreement may specifically entitle the bank to withhold the disbursement of funds to the depositor until collection of the proceeds of the cheque has actually been completed. See e.g. art. 3 of the Current Account Regulations in Japan. For such provisions in Japan see, in general 2.A(v) s. 30, above.

[241] But cf. model rules governing current accounts in Japan, providing in art. 24 that clearing house rules are binding on the customer. See 2.A(v) s. 30, above. Model rules are the basis for rules each bank in Japan issued to the customer at the time the contract is concluded. See 2.A(v) s. 25.

[242] Com. 28 Nov. 1995, BECM c/Ste' Philipps.

[243] For a commentary, see Cabrillac, RTD com. 49(1), Jan.–Mar. 1996.

Cheque legislation in Germany,[244] Italy,[245] Japan,[246] Switzerland[247] and **[7]** France[248] follows the UCL closely, though relatively minor deviations exist in each country. Pertinent deviations fall into five general categories: time limits for presentment, cover, certification, countermand, and restrictions on the transferability or mode of payment of cheques.

As already indicated,[249] under art. 29 of the UCL, the presentment dead- **[8]** lines are eight days for domestic cheques, twenty days for same-continent cheques, and seventy days for intercontinental cheques. However, in Japan, under art. 29(1) of the Law on Cheques, domestic cheques must be presented within ten days. In Italy, under art. 32(1), the presentment period for a domestic interregional cheque is fifteen days. For intercontinental cheques the presentment period in Italy is sixty days. As discussed, the practical implications of the presentment time limits are generally confined to the calculation of the limitation period, as well as to the drawee's freedom to overlook its customer's countermand instructions communicated within the prescribed presentment period.

Specific provisions relating to cover exist in Italy, Japan, Switzerland, **[9]** and France. Thereunder, funds available for withdrawal in the customer/drawer's account are absolutely required for each cheque drawn.[250] Stiff criminal penalties are fastened on violators in Italy. In addition, a violator in Italy may incur civil liability for 10 per cent of any uncovered amount, as well as be subject to the withdrawal of chequing privileges.[251] In Switzerland, a person drawing a cheque without cover becomes liable to the holder, in addition to the damage caused, for 5 per

---

[244] The Cheques Act, 14 Aug. 1933 (RGB1. I 597). See in general, *Jura Europae—Droit bancaire et boursier* (Munich: Verlay C. H. Beck; Paris: Editions Techniques Juris-Classeurs, 1976), *Germany* para. 10.31 (by H. Schonle); and B. Ruster (founding ed.), *Business Transactions in Germany* (New York: Matthew Bender, updated to 1993), s. 12[2] (by D. Schneider and T. Verhoeven).

[245] R. D. 21 December 1933, n. 1736, as supplemented by L. 15 December 1990, n. 386 See in general, *Jura Europae*, ibid., *Italy* para. 40.31 (by C. C. Campi).

[246] Law on Cheques, Law No. 57, 29 July 1933. See, in general, Z. Kitagawa (general ed.), *Doing Business in Japan* (New York: Matthew Bender, updated to 1999), vol. iii, ss. 3.03 and 3.04 (by K. Tani), and ch. 4 (by J. Eguchi). See also *The Banking System in Japan* (Tokyo: Federation of Bankers' Association of Japan-Zeginkyo, 1989), 94–6.

[247] Arts. 1100–44 of the Code of Obligations.

[248] The UCL was introduced in France by the Cheque Law, Decret-lois of 30 Oct. 1935. As subsequently amended from time to time, this is still the current governing law. While consumer use of cheques is well established and recognized, the Cheque Law forms a part of the Code of Commerce. In particular, see G. Ripert and R. Roblot, above, n. 4 at 257–95 (as well as 532–6). See also, J. L. Rives-Lange and M. Contamine-Raynaud, above, n. 4 at 287–311 ¶¶ 300–15 (as well as 311–19 ¶¶. 316–22). For specific provisions dealing with customers' use of cheques, aimed at the prevention and deterrence of the use of cheques without cover in France, see (ii) s. 2, above.   [249] In s. 3, above.

[250] Arts. 2–3 of L. 15 Dec. 1990, n. 386 in Italy; art. 3 in Japan; art. 1103 in Switzerland; and art. 3 in France.

[251] For the scheme for the removal of chequing privileges in Italy, see, (ii) s. 4 above.

cent of the uncovered amount. A non-penal fine not exceeding 5,000 yen
is exacted from a violator in Japan (art. 71). Also, in Japan, under an interbank voluntary system, a two-year suspension is imposed on an account
holder issuing two bills of exchange or cheques that have been dishonoured for lack of cover within six months. The suspension applies to all
banks belonging to the regional clearing house of the bank where the
account is held and extends to all current account transactions as well as
loans.

French law has a unique position as to cover. In principle, cover
includes either available funds or available credit facility. As indicated,
the dishonour of a cheque for lack of cover entails restrictions on the
cheque-issuing right of the overdrawing drawer. Repeating similar incidents may entail penalties and may be punishable.[252] The withdrawal of
cover after the issue of a cheque, with the intention of prejudicing the
rights of a third party, is specifically punishable.

In connection with either the absence or the existence of cover, and
compared to other countries, French cheque law is quite favourable to the
holder. First, the drawee bank is responsible to the holder for the payment
of each cheque of 100 F or less. Second, a drawee bank that overlooked its
responsibilities in providing a customer with blank cheque forms is
responsible to the holder for the amount of cheques issued by that customer. In both cases, the drawee bank's liability arises irrespective of the
availability of cover, and is only for cheques issued on bank supplied
forms.[253] Third, a holder acquires the right to the cover of a cheque.[254]
Stated otherwise, the cheque and each transfer constitutes the assignment
to the holder of funds in the drawee's hands.

Germany does not have specific provisions relating to cover. However,
lack of cover disables the drawer-customer from performing his reimbursement obligation under his mutual contract with the drawee bank. In
circumstances for which the drawer-customer is responsible, this is a situation governed by BGB s. 325(1), allowing the drawee bank to 'demand
compensation . . . or withdraw from the contract'. Further, under para.
19(3) of the General Business Conditions, 'if there is a reasonable cause
which makes it unacceptable to the bank to continue the business relationship', such as where 'a substantial deterioration occurs or threatens to
occur in the customer's financial status, jeopardizing the discharge of
obligations towards the bank', the bank may terminate a banking relationship even without notice.[255] Obviously, not every instance of a dis-

---

[252] See (ii) s. 2, above.
[253] Ibid.
[254] With respect to indorsement, see art. 17 of the French Cheque Law.
[255] In exercising this right, as well as in determining the notice period for terminating the
relationship other than under para. 19(3), due consideration ought to be given by the bank
to the legitimate concerns of the customer.

honoured cheque for lack of cover would automatically fall within the purview of para. 19(3) but extreme circumstances, such as repeated cases, may be covered.

In France, where adequate cover is available, the drawee bank is bound towards its customer, the drawer of the cheque, to pay a cheque drawn on the customer's account, when duly presented.[256] The wrongful dishonour charges the drawee bank with liability to the drawer for any resulting damage.[257] It further subjects the bank to criminal penalty.[258] Such criminal liability is a unique feature of French law; otherwise, this scheme of responsibility for the wrongful dishonour of a cheque for which adequate cover has been provided, exists in the other civil law jurisdictions as well. As a rule, the wrongfully dishonouring bank's liability to the drawer-customer is premissed on breach of contract. None of the civil law countries has specific rules as to the scope of damages recoverable from the wrongfully dishonouring drawee bank.

Grounds for liability by the wrongfully dishonouring bank, not only to the drawer-customer, but also to the holder, may be found in Japan, France, and perhaps Italy. In Japan, and also according to a minority view in Italy, such grounds are in torts. In France they are premissed on the holder's entitlement to the cover towards the drawee.

In Germany, cheques, other than those drawn on the central bank, may   **[10]** not be certified. Nor may a drawee bank incur liability on a cheque by endorsing or guaranteeing payment on it. German banks may 'mark' a cheque, thereby advising the availability of cover at the moment of marking, but without incurring any payment liability.[259] Certification by the German central bank (the Deutsche Bundesbank) and its binding effect are provided for by statute. Thereunder, certification may take place only after cover has been provided, and is effective for eight days from the day the cheque was drawn. Certification is not repudiated by the drawer's bankruptcy. The claim on a certified cheque that was presented in a timely manner for payment is subject to a two-year limitations period after the expiry of the time for presentment.[260] Under its General Business Conditions, in certifying a cheque, the Bundesbank withdraws its amount from

---

[256] For the drawee bank's liability in France, vis-à-vis the holder to pay 100 F cheques as well as cheques written on forms supplied to the customer in breach of 'incident of payment' procedures see (ii) s. 2, above. Under s. 73–1 of the Cheque Law, the customer and the bank are taken to have agreed on the opening of an irrevocable credit facility in the customer's favour for each cheque of 100 F or less which the bank is required to pay notwithstanding the absence of cover in the account.   [257] S. 65 (2) of the Cheques Law.

[258] S. 65–1 A of the Cheques Law.

[259] In Germany, the prohibition to certify cheques is considered as derived from art. 4 of the Cheque Act, modelled on art. 4 of the UCL, precluding the acceptance of a cheque. The endorsement and guarantee of payment by a drawee bank are precluded under arts. 15(3) and 25(2) of the Cheques Act.

[260] See s. 23 of the Deutsche Bundesbank Act of 26 July 1957, BGBI. I745.

the drawer's account. Where the certified cheque has not been presented for payment, the amount is credited to the drawer's account fifteen days after certification.

Cheque certification for all banks is recognized in Italy, Japan, and France. In Italy, under art. 4(2), the effect of 'certification, confirmation, visa' or a similar expression written on the cheque and signed by the drawee is to certify the existence of funds and preclude the withdrawal of funds prior to presentment for payment. While no liability on the cheque is triggered by the act of certification, there is case law allowing the holder to recover damages from a drawee bank that subsequent to certification permitted the withdrawal of funds by the drawer. In addition, Italian banks may issue to their customers blank cheque forms, each bearing a notation for the maximum amount for which it may be issued by the drawer, and for which the bank is responsible. For each such a cheque, the bank is taken to guarantee the existence and permanence of cover, though in the absence of signature, it is not liable as a party on the cheque itself.

In Japan, cheque certification is governed by arts. 53–8. Thereunder, certification ought to be signed by the drawee and must be unconditional. While not releasing the drawer and any other prior party, certification binds the drawee to make payment, 'but only when the cheque is presented before the expiration of the limit of the time fixed for presentment'.[261] Under art. 29, for domestic cheques, the presentment period is ten days, rather than eight, as under the UCL. For a claim on a cheque against a certifying drawee that declined payment, there is a one-year prescription, running from the expiration of the presentment period.

In fact, and notwithstanding its legal foundations in both countries, certification is practised neither in Italy nor in Japan. This may be attributed to the lack of an explicit statutory basis for debiting the drawer's account prior to presentment for payment. In Italy it may further be attributed to the absence of statutory provision characterizing the certification as a binding obligation of the certifying drawee bank. Be it as it may, the Italian Cheque Law provides in ss. 82–3 for circular cheques issued by banks, each carrying with it the issuing bank's 'unconditional promise' to pay. In Japan, art. 13 of the Current Account Regulations effectively precludes banks from certifying cheques. 'The Bank, instead, will issue Manager's Checks upon request, deducting the amount of the Manager's Checks issued from the Current Account.[262] In both Italy and Japan, such instruments, which in fact are the equivalent of bank drafts or cashier's cheques in Canada and the United States, serve as substitutes for certified cheques.

---

[261] Art. 55(1).

[262] In Japan, a bank in one region may further draw a 'remittance' on its correspondent in another region, thereby facilitating an interregion transfer of funds by means of a cheque drawn by one bank on another.

In France, art. 4 authorizes the drawee bank to 'mark' ('viser') a cheque, thereby stating the availability of cover at that time. In any event, this does not require the bank to set aside or block funds and no liability is fastened on it if funds are subsequently removed from the account. The better security is afforded to the holder by the certification of the cheque by the drawee bank, as envisioned in art. 12(1). Where cover is available, and at the request of either the drawer or the holder, the drawee bank must certify the cheque, except that it has the option of issuing instead its own cheque drawn by itself.[263] The certifying bank must block the cover and make it available for payment upon the presentation by the holder, until the expiry of time for such presentation. Under art. 29, for domestic cheques, this period lasts eight days. Unlike in the United States and Canada,[264] certification is not necessarily accompanied by the actual withdrawal of the funds from the drawer's account, and the effectiveness of the certification towards the holder is not premised in France on acceptance.[265] Rather, certification may be carried out by putting a 'hold' on corresponding funds in the drawer's account, for the duration of the presentment period, and is regulated as a method for the settlement of the right to the cover in the drawer's account. Also, unlike in the United States and Canada, where the duration of the certification may be indefinite, but in line with the laws of Italy, Japan, as well as Germany with respect to cheques drawn on the central bank, certification in France is effective to convey rights to the holder for a short period only.

In Italy, Japan, and France (as well as in Germany in connection with cheques drawn on the central bank), the provisions as to cheque certification discussed above coexist with a provision modelled on art. 4 of the UCL, precluding altogether the acceptance of a cheque.[266] Stated otherwise, contrary to the prevailing theory in the United States and Canada,[267] the certifying bank's liability to the holder in civil law jurisdictions is other than as an acceptor, or more generally, other than as a party on the cheque itself.

No specific jurisprudence dealing with the standard of the description [11] or identification for a cheque to be countermanded exists in any of the

---

[263] For this option, as well as for the manner of certification, by means of signature accompanied by indications as to the certification, its date, and the name of the drawee bank, see art. 31 of Decret no. 92–456 of 22 May 1992.

[264] For cheque certification in the United States and Canada see (iv) s. 3 and (iii) s. 2, respectively, above.

[265] In 1941, when certification was first introduced in France, it was done outside the Cheque Law, so as not to demonstrate nonconformity with the UCL prohibition on the acceptance of cheques. As of 1972, the measure has nonetheless been incorporated into the Cheque Law, on the theory that it does not undermine the anti-acceptance rule, fully recognized in art. 4 of the Cheque Law.   [266] See art. 4 in Italy, Japan, as well as in France.

[267] See (iv) s. 3 and (iii) s. 2, respectively, above.

civil law jurisdictions under discussion. In some of these jurisdictions, there are variations in the countermand statutory provisions. Thus, Switzerland and Italy provide for the drawer's right to promptly countermand payment on a lost cheque.[268] This supersedes the general rule which precludes the countermand of payment before the expiry of the time limit for presentment.[269] In Italy, a specific procedure is provided for the cancellation of a lost, stolen, or destroyed cheque. It involves: the communication of the incident to the drawee bank; request for a court order pronouncing the cancellation of the cheque; advice of the court order to the drawee; and its publication in the Official Gazette, thereby allowing objections to be made within fifteen days.

Under French law, contrary to all other jurisdictions, the cheque is irrevocable. This stems from the transfer of the cover from the drawer to the payee/holder in the course of the issue of the cheque.[270] The payment of the cheque thus cannot be countermanded by the drawer. However, in exceptional circumstances, the drawer may object to the payment of a cheque. This is so only in the case of loss, theft, or fraudulent use of the cheque, or in the case of the holder's insolvency.[271] Objection must be promptly confirmed by the drawer to the drawee bank in writing. A holder disputing the existence of an appropriate ground in a given case must seek a court order removing the objection.

As a rule, in civil law jurisdictions, the drawee bank that mistakenly paid an effectively countermanded cheque may not debit the drawer-customer's account and may further be liable to its customer for any resulting damage. Where the bank suffers loss, it has a recourse in restitution or unjust enrichment. Depending on the circumstances, such a remedy is available to the drawee bank against either the holder or the drawer. Thus, where the holder is not entitled to payment from the drawer, the drawee bank's recourse is from the holder.[272] Alternatively, where the mistaken payment has effectively discharged the drawer's debt to the holder, recovery by the mistaken bank is from the drawer.

[12]   As discussed in s. 4 above, the UCL provides for (i) cheques payable to bearer (transferable by delivery), (ii) indorsable cheques payable to a specified person, and (iii) unindorsable but assignable cheques payable to a specified person in which the words 'not to order' have been inserted. All such cheques are payable either in cash or into a bank account. Pay-

---

[268] Art. 1119(3) in Switzerland and art. 69 in Italy.

[269] Incorporated in art. 1119(1) in Switzerland and art. 35(1) in Italy, each modelled on art. 32(1) of the UCL, discussed in s. 3, above.

[270] See s. 9, above.   [271] See Cheque Law, art. 32.

[272] However, in Japan, there is authority dealing with a credit transfer, which suggests that the restitutionary remedy against the holder is not precluded also where the holder was actually entitled to receive payment from the drawer.

ment in cash can be restricted, or even eliminated altogether, by either crossing a cheque, or designating it 'payable in account'.

In addition, Italy provides, in art. 43(1), for cheques marked 'non-transferable'. Such a cheque is payable solely to the payee, whether in cash, or to his bank's account. The payee may indorse a cheque so marked only to a bank for collection. Payment other than indicated gives rise to liability for damage incurred.

In Germany, the provisions relating to crossed cheques, while included in the Cheques Act, are not in force.[273] At the same time, cheques payable in account, marked 'only for settlement' ('nur zur Verrechnung') or similarly, so as to preclude payment in cash, are fully recognized, and in fact, widely used. Conversely, Japan recognizes crossed cheques (arts. 37–8), but does not provide for domestic cheques payable in account. Under art. 74, a cheque payable in Japan drawn abroad, marked 'payable in account' or similarly, is to be treated as a generally crossed cheque.

For its part, Switzerland adheres (in arts. 1123–5) to the UCL provisions relating to crossed cheques and cheques payable in account, discussed in s. 4 above. However, with regard to the settlement cheque (namely, the cheque payable to account),[274] Articles 1126–7 provide for the holder's right to demand payment in cash upon the drawee's insolvency, as well as to exercise its recourse rights, against the drawer and any preceding endorser, upon the dishonour of the cheque.

French law provides for crossed cheques, but not for cheques payable in account. Foreign cheques payable in account are treated as crossed cheques.[275] In general, cheques may be paid by the drawee bank either in cash, over the counter, or to the payee-holder's bank account, through the interbank cheque collection system. Like any other negotiable instrument, a cheque may be taken from a holder/customer by a bank either by purchase or for collection. A cheque payable to a specified payee (or to his order) is typically taken by a bank by endorsement.[276] Standard cheque forms in France indicate that they are indorsable only to banks or similar institutions.

---

[273] According to art. 1 sentence 2 of the Introductory Act on the Cheques Act of 14.8.1933, RGBl. I 605, 'articles 37, 38 [of the Cheques Act] on the crossed cheque enter into force only at a later point of time which will be determined by the Imperial Minister of Justice'. So far, the provisions have not been proclaimed in force. Nor is such proclamation expected to take place in the foreseeable future. A crossed cheque issued outside Germany is treated as a cheque payable in account. Whether a domestic crossed cheque is to be treated either similarly, or like an ordinary cheque, payable in cash, has not been settled.

[274] Unfortunately, the French Official Text uses two terms (*cheque à porter en compte* and *cheque de compensation*) for what appears in both the German and Italian Official Texts as one term.

[275] See arts. 37–9 of the Cheques Law and compare with ss. 4 and 11, above.

[276] See art. 13 of the Cheques Law.

C. Credit Transfers

(I) OVERVIEW: MECHANISMS AND LAWS[1]

(a) Large value credit transfers: the itinerary

[1]   In a credit transfer, such as a direct deposit of payroll, benefit, interest, pension, or dividend, the payor's instructions are communicated to the payor's bank directly by the payor, without the intermediation of a credit to the payee's account at the payee's bank. When the instructions are communicated, the payor's account is debited. As such, in a credit transfer, unlike in a debit transfer, the first impact of the payor's instructions on the banking system is a debit to the payor's account with the payor's bank. Having received the payor's instructions and debited the payor's account, the payor's bank forwards the instructions to the payee's bank which then proceeds to pay the payee, typically by crediting the payee's account. Thus, in a credit transfer, the debit to the payor's account precedes the credit to the payee's account, and is not subject to reversal, e.g. for lack of funds. In a credit transfer, funds debited to the payor's account are 'pushed' to the payee. Generally, large value international payments and many large value payments in financial transactions are credit transfers.

As a rule, large value credit transfers may be processed and/or settled separately from small value ones. In principle, large value credit transfers are communicated and processed individually. Their settlement mechanism is quite responsive to credit risks associated with the large values involved. At the same time, all credit transfers, large and small value, are usually subject to the same legal regime. Nevertheless, particularly modern legislation governing credit transfers has been passed principally in order to regulate large value transfers, so that coverage of small value transfers is somewhat incidental. The ensuing discussion, particularly in relation to mechanisms, is thus primarily concerned with large value credit transfers.

In a credit transfer, the payor is called the originator, and the payee is the beneficiary. Accordingly, the payor's bank is the originator's bank and

---

[1] The ensuing discussion is adapted from B. Geva, 'International Funds Transfers: Mechanisms and Laws', in J. J. Norton, C. Reed, and I. Walden, *Cross-Border Electronic Banking: Challenges and Opportunities* (London: Lloyd's of London, 1995) [Now in 2nd ed., by Reed, Walden and Edgar, 2000], 1. For more detail on large-value mechanisms and risks, see B. Geva, *The Law of Electronic Funds Transfers* (New York: Matthew Bender, 1992–2000), chs. 3–4.

the payee's bank is the beneficiary's bank. Any other bank participating in the transaction is an intermediary bank. Payment instructions are the subject-matter of a 'payment order'. Each payment order is transmitted by a sender to a receiving bank.[2]

A credit transfer is initiated by the issue of a payment order by the originator to the originator's bank. The transaction is ultimately carried out by debiting the originator's account at the originator's bank and crediting the beneficiary's account at the beneficiary's bank. Where these are separate banks, the originator's bank executes the originator's payment order by issuing its own payment order, either to the beneficiary's bank or to an intermediary bank. An intermediary bank will issue its own payment order either to the beneficiary's bank or to another intermediary bank, that will do the same, until a final payment order is issued to the beneficiary's bank. Each interbank payment order must be paid by the sender to the receiving bank. Interbank communication thus corresponds to the interbank payment or settlement facilities; namely, each bank will issue a payment order only to a receiving bank with which such settlement facilities are available. Typically, such facilities are either bilateral, in the form of a correspondent account, namely an account one bank has with the other,[3] or multilateral, in the form of accounts several banks hold at a central counterparty, which could be the central bank.

Accordingly, a credit transfer may be in-house, correspondent, or complex.[4] Where the originator's and the beneficiary's accounts are in the same bank, the transaction is in-house. No interbank payment order is required to execute the originator's payment order. Otherwise, the transfer is interbank. Where the originator's and beneficiary's accounts are in different banks, which are correspondents, meaning one of them has an account with the other, the interbank transaction is a correspondent transfer, and requires an interbank payment order between the two correspondent banks. Payment of the payment order is then carried out at this account.

Otherwise, the interbank transaction requires the participation of

[2] This terminology is borrowed from Article 4A of the American Uniform Commercial Code—Funds Transfers and from UNCITRAL Model Law on International Credit Transfers.

[3] In banking language, we are concerned with the *vostro* or 'due to' account, held on the books of the funds-holder bank, rather than with its shadow, the *nostro* or 'due from' account administered by the depositor bank. In general, as between two domestic correspondents, one small and one large bank, the former is likely to be depositor and the latter, the funds-holder. Vis-à-vis an overseas or cross-border correspondent, a bank is likely to be funds-holder for its own domestic currency and depositor for the overseas or cross-border currency.

[4] This terminology is borrowed from *Libyan Arab Foreign Bank* v. *Bankers Trust*, [1988] 1 Lloyd's L.R. 259 (Q.B.).

intermediary banks and is classified as a complex transfer. In its simplest pattern, a common correspondent, that is, a third bank having bilateral correspondent relationships with both the originator's and beneficiary's bank, will intermediate between them. One or more intermediary banks may be required in the absence of such a common correspondent. In its most sophisticated pattern, a complex transfer will involve a clearing house facilitating multilateral interbank communication and settlement on the books of a central counterparty, with whom they all hold accounts, such as a central bank. For each country or currency, the domestic Large Value Transfer System (LVTS) linking all major banks is such a facility.

[2]   Broadly speaking, an international credit transfer is from an originator's to a beneficiary's bank where at least one of these banks is located in a country with a different currency.[5] Depending on the location of the originator's and beneficiary's banks in relation to the country of the currency, an international transfer is either onshore or offshore.[6]

Whenever one of these two banks is located in the country of the currency, the transfer is onshore; it could be either incoming or outgoing. While an incoming onshore transfer is originated at an overseas/crossborder originator's bank and its destination is a local beneficiary's bank (at the country of the currency), an outgoing onshore transfer is originated at a local originator's bank (in the country of the currency), and its destination is an overseas/crossborder beneficiary's bank.

Conversely, whenever both the originator's and the beneficiary's banks are located outside the country of the currency, the transfer is offshore. It does not matter whether the two banks are situated in one or two countries, as long as neither of them is located in the country of the currency. In any event, it is quite common for an offshore transfer to 'pass through' one or more intermediary banks in the country of the currency, so as to become an offshore 'passing through' transfer.[7]

Where the originator's and beneficiary's banks are not correspondents,

---

[5] By definition, an international transfer cannot be 'in-house' and must be 'interbank'.

[6] This definition and classification, as further developed below, originally appeared in B. Geva, *The Law of Electronic Funds Transfers*, above, n. 1, at §4.02, and subsequently followed in M. Hapgood, *Paget's Law of Banking*, 11th edn. (London: Butterworths, 1996) at 272–6.

[7] Alternatively, transfers exchanged offshore, and not 'passing through' the country of the currency, may be multilaterally netted offshore into balances that are settled onshore (in the country of the currency). In such a case, each individual transfer can be classified as an 'offshore intermediated outside' transfer. For large value transfer, the only machinery facilitating an offshore intermediate clearing establishing such balances for offshore transfers is that of the Tokyo US dollar clearing operated by Chase Manhattan Tokyo. In the further alternative, an offshore transfer may be settled in a correspondent account outside the country of the currency, in which case it can be classified as a 'passing outside' transfer, as for example, where the originator's and beneficiary's banks are small banks holding US dollar accounts at one large London bank which acts as their common correspondent. See in general H. S. Scott, 'Where are the Dollars?—Off-Shore Funds Transfers' (1989) 3 B.F.L.R. 244.

onshore incoming and outgoing transfers as well as offshore 'passing through' transfers are likely to go in part over the LVTS of the currency of the transfer. Thus, a typical incoming onshore transfer involving non-correspondent originator's and beneficiary's banks will be routed by the originator's bank to its correspondent in the country of the currency which will act as an intermediary bank and transmit its payment order to the beneficiary's bank over the domestic LVTS. Similarly, a typical outgoing onshore transfer involving non-correspondent originator's and beneficiary's banks will be routed by the originator's bank, over the domestic LVTS, to the local correspondent of the overseas or cross-border beneficiary's bank, for further transmission to that beneficiary's bank. For its part, an offshore transfer will usually pass through one or more intermediary banks in the country of the currency. The transfer will thus be routed by the originator's bank to its correspondent in the country of the currency. Where the latter does not have a correspondent relationship with the beneficiary's bank, it will transmit its payment order to the correspondent of the beneficiary's bank in the country of the currency over the LVTS of that currency. Ultimately, the correspondent of the beneficiary's bank will transmit its payment order to the beneficiary's bank.

In each of these settings, a small bank without access to the domestic LVTS and/or without an overseas/cross-border correspondent will use a domestic correspondent having the required facility. This will increase the number of intermediary banks participating in the credit transfer.[8]

In a credit transfer, each payment order, whether from the originator to the originator's bank or from one bank to another, can be given in writing, orally,[9] or by electronic means. A payment order is given electronically whenever it is embodied in a cable or telex ('wire'), initiated through a magnetic tape or diskette that may be physically delivered, or sent from

---

[8] Consider the following example of an offshore 'passing through' transfer. Suppose a customer instructs a small French bank to pay US dollars into an account at a small Spanish bank. Typically, the small French bank will pass on the instruction to its correspondent (large French bank) which will further instruct its New York correspondent. The latter will utilize a US dollar LVTS, probably CHIPS, to carry on a transfer to the New York correspondent of a large Spanish bank which is the correspondent of the destination small Spanish bank. The transaction is completed by onward transmission to the large Spanish bank and onto the destination small Spanish bank which credits the destination account. Altogether, in this scenario, six banks participate: small and large French banks, two New York banks, and large and small Spanish banks. Except for the two New York banks utilizing an LVTS, all other banks utilize correspondent links. Obviously, if one New York bank is a correspondent for both the large French and Spanish banks no LVTS is needed and the total number of participating banks is reduced to five. Either way, inasmuch as the originator's and beneficiary's banks are outside the USA, the transfer is offshore; inasmuch as it passes through the USA, it is an offshore 'passing through' transfer.

[9] Usually by telephone, subject to a security procedure such as involving a secret code or call back. But see *El-Zayed* v. *Bank of Nova Scotia* (1988), 87 N.S.R. (2d) 171 (T.D.), dealing with an oral payment order given over the counter of the destination bank.

a terminal over a dedicated communication network. Communication by wire or over a dedicated network is 'on-line'; when transmission immediately follows input it is also in 'real time'. An electronic funds transfer (EFT) occurs whenever a payment order is given by any electronic means.

Domestic interbank communication for large value domestic currency payment orders is usually over the local LVTS. In major currency countries local LVTSs utilize communication networks for the transmission of interbank payment orders. In the past, overseas/crossborder interbank communication was either by air letter or by means of cable or telex ('wire'); the large value credit transfer has thus been called, in fact, to this day, a 'wire transfer'. However, in overseas/crossborder interbank communication, the wire has increasingly lost ground to the dedicated communication network of SWIFT.

The Society of Worldwide Interbank Financial Telecommunication (SWIFT) is a non-profit cooperative society organized under Belgian law, and owned by numerous banks throughout the world. The SWIFT system operated by the society is a computerized telecommunications network that operates a global data-processing system for transmitting financial messages over dedicated lines about its members and other connected users.

In its current SWIFT II configuration, SWIFT is a central switch system[10] linking numerous and diverse bank terminals all over the world. The central switch currently consists of two slice processors, one situated in the Netherlands and the other in the USA, each functioning as an independent and ad hoc network, linking SWIFT access points. Each country is assigned to a SWIFT access point. Interbank communication is via the SWIFT access points mediated by a slice processor. A system control processor monitors and controls functions of the system but is not involved in routing messages.

More specifically, each SWIFT message travels first on a domestic circuit from the sending bank's terminal to the SWIFT access point for that country. From there, it continues on an international circuit to the slice processor and onward to the SWIFT access point for the receiving bank's country. At that point it is routed on the domestic circuit of that country to the ultimate destination of the receiving bank's terminal. Each message is validated and processed under heavy security.

Advice of credit by the beneficiary's bank to the beneficiary can be given orally, in writing or by electronic means. It can be given individually or in batches, possibly as part of a periodic statement.

[3]   A foreign exchange transaction involves the concurrent deliveries of two currencies between two counterparties. In practice, the transaction

---

[10] For the term, see s. 5, below.

involves the exchange of two credit transfers, one in each currency, between two banks.[11] Both transfers are to be carried out on the same day as determined by contract. In principle, each bank's delivery obligation is concurrent with that of the other bank. However, in the absence of a delivery against payment (DVP) mechanism, each transfer is carried out separately on the payment date, usually over the LVTS for the respective currency. Where for a given currency, the originator's and/or the beneficiary's banks are located outside the country of the currency, SWIFT communication and correspondent transfer(s) are further utilized, from the originator's bank to its correspondent in the country of currency, and/or the beneficiary's bank from its correspondent there.[12]

Inasmuch as both transfers of the foreign currency transaction are separate, a bank that has transferred funds in discharge of its own obligation incurs the risk that its counterparty might fail to carry out the transfer of the consideration. This risk is known as the 'Herstatt risk', following the collapse of the German bank Herstatt on 26 June 1974.[13]

The degree of the Herstatt risk may be measured by the delivery lag (in hours) between the two currencies,[14] multiplied by the value of the

[11] For a discussion on the legal nature of the foreign exchange transaction, as sale of goods, exchange of goods, or exchange of payments, see A. Wardrop, 'The Dual Personality of Money and the Legal Nature of Foreign Exchange Transactions Settled by Wire Transfers' (1999), 15 B.F.L.R. 61. An authority, under American law, for the application of the law of sale of goods to the transaction, specifically criticized by Wardrop, is *In re Koreag, Controle et Revision S.A.*, 961 F. 2d 341 (C.A. 2nd Cir., 1992).

[12] For example, suppose a foreign exchange transaction of Japanese yens and Canadian dollars is to be carried out between banks in Singapore and Hong Kong. The yen transfer is to be originated from Singapore and destined for Hong Kong while the Canadian dollar transfer is to be originated from Hong Kong and destined for Singapore. Accordingly, the yen transfer will travel over SWIFT from the Singapore bank to its Japanese correspondent. Where that Japanese correspondent is not acting also as a correspondent for the Hong Kong bank (namely where it is not a common correspondent), the transfer from the Japanese correspondent of the Singapore bank to that of the Hong Kong Bank will be carried out over a Japanese LVTS. Ultimately, the Japanese correspondent of the Hong Kong bank will transmit its own message to Hong Kong over SWIFT. Likewise, the dollar transfer will travel from Hong Kong to Canada over SWIFT. The Canadian correspondent of the Hong Kong Bank, if it is not a common correspondent, will then carry on the transfer to the Canadian correspondent of the Singapore bank over the Canadian LVTS. The Canadian correspondent of the Singapore bank will then pass on its own message to Singapore over SWIFT.

[13] As documented in two landmark cases, each from the other side of the Atlantic: *Momm v. Barclays Bank International*, [1976] 3 All E.R. 588 (Q.B.) and *Delbrueck & Co. v. Manufacturers Hanover Trust Co.* 609 F. 2d. 1047 (2d. Cir, 1979), *aff'g* 464 F. Supp. 989 (S.D.N.Y. 1979).

[14] For the view that for a foreign currency trader, exposure may actually extend from the input of an irrevocable payment order in the currency to be settled first, until the obtainment of confirmation of receipt of the currency to be settled last, see the New York Foreign Exchange Committee, *Reducing Foreign Exchange Settlement Risk* (Oct. 1994). For a comprehensive study, see Committee on Payment and Settlement Systems of the central banks of the Group of Ten Countries (CPSS), *Settlement Risk in Foreign Exchange Transactions* (Basle, Bank for International Settlement, Mar. 1996), known as the Allsopp Report after the chairman of the Steering Group.

transfer yet to be made. The delivery lag stems from the counterparties' inability to control the precise time (by hour and minute) for carrying out a transfer, as well as from global time difference. For example, the Herstatt risk is particularly significant for a receiver of US or Canadian dollar payment who has already parted with the consideration in a European currency, not to mention in Japanese yen.[15] Around the clock operation for major currency LVTS, already practised by the Swiss SIC and shortly to be implemented by the American Fedwire, may be a step towards the control of the Herstatt risk. However, the total elimination of the risk may require the development of a DVP mechanism involving either a coordinated operation of major currency LVTS, or a joint offering of a multicurrency settlement service provided by central banks through a common agent.[16]

The planned CLS (Continuous Linked Settlement) system is a private sector initiative designed to respond to central banks' concerns for controlling foreign currency risks.[17] This is a variant of a DVP system, under which a debit position of a counterparty resulting from an obligation to pay one currency is secured by this counterparty's entitlement, or credit position in, another currency. More specifically, a bank's intraday short position in one currency is secured by its long position in others. Settlement members are to hold accounts with the CLS Bank, a special purpose bank to be formed under US Federal Law and to be supervised by the Federal Reserve. For each currency, the CLS Bank is to have a settlement account with the relevant central bank, and access to the pertinent RTGS (real-time gross settlement system). Each account with a central bank is in the amount of that currency deposited by settlement members with the CLS Bank. Stated otherwise, settlement on the books of the CLS Bank is always in central bank money. Each settlement member will have a single account with the CLS Bank, for all currencies, valued in US dollars, with sub-accounts for each currency. The operation of the system is premissed on the requirement that for each transaction to be processed, the single

[15] Accordingly, in the example set out in n. 12 above, the Herstatt risk will be borne by the Singapore counterparty. Having paid the yen part of the transaction in the course of the banking day in Tokyo, it must wait to receive the Canadian dollars during the banking day in Toronto. In general, the Tokyo banking day closes before the opening of the same-date banking day in Toronto.

[16] For possible options for central banks to improve efficiency and reduce risk in the settlement to cross-border and multi-currency interbank transactions, see Committee on Payment and Settlement Systems of the central banks of the Group of Ten countries, *Central Bank Payment and Settlement Services with Respect to Cross-Border and Multi-Currency Transactions* (Basle: Bank for International Settlements, Sept. 1993), known also as the Noël Report after the Chairman of the Working Group on Central Bank Payment and Settlement Services Established by the Committee on Payment and Settlement Systems.

[17] See R. Dale, 'Controlling Foreign Exchange Settlement Risks' (1999), 14 B.F.L.R. 329, and CLS Services, *An Introduction to Continuous Linked Settlement* (May 1998).

account, as distinguished from any individual sub-account of which it consists, must always have a positive balance. Overdrafts in sub-accounts will however be strictly controlled.

Funds in accounts of settlement members with the CLS Bank and of the CLS Bank with central banks are to be deposited each morning and all balances are to be withdrawn at the end of the day. Settlement members are to settle for themselves, as well as for their correspondents ('user members') on the single accounts each holds with the CLS Bank. The settlement process runs on the books of the CLS Bank continuously during the settlement period. Transactions input are to be queued and then settled on the books of the CLS Bank. Each transaction is settled only simultaneously in both currencies. It is settled only if, upon completion, each counterparty's account to be transferred from: (1) meets 'the net positive value test', namely, as long as it remains in an overall positive balance, measured in US dollars, and (2) as long as the account does not fall below a 'short position limit' in the particular currency as well as an 'aggregate short position limit' in all currencies. Effectively then, for each participant, an overdraft in one currency is secured by surplus in another, with each overdraft being repaid in the course of the day. This procedure eliminates the Herstatt risk and facilitates the smooth flow of funds so as to enhance liquidity and reduce gridlocks. Where a settlement member defaults in one currency, a liquidity facility is available to cover short positions resulting from transactions which have settled on the CLS Bank's books and which are thus fully collateralized.

(b) Large Value Transfer Systems: components, risks, and models

As indicated, in an international credit transfer, where the originator's [4] and beneficiary's banks have neither a correspondent relationship nor a common correspondent, the LVTS for the transferred currency is usually an important link in carrying out the transmission of funds. The ensuing discussion presents the essential components of an LVTS, reviews large value payment system risk incurred in the course of transfer over LVTS, as well as risk control measures, and provides a brief outline of existing major currency LVTS.

Broadly speaking, a machinery facilitating the multilateral exchange [5] ('clearing')[18] of obligations and their payment ('settlement') is a clearing

---

[18] 'Clearing' is commonly defined to cover not only the exchange of obligations but also their offsetting (or netting). See e.g. *Webster's Ninth New Collegiate Dictionary* (Markham, Ont.: Thomas Allen & Sons, 1984). However, offsetting (or netting), as a prelude to settlement, is not carried out in connection with gross settlement systems (discussed below). Perhaps 'clearing' should thus be understood to cover the exchange of obligations and any preparatory action towards settlement.

house. In any given country, so far as cashless payments are concerned, the national payment system consists of nationwide clearing house arrangements for the multilateral interbank clearing and settlement of payment orders. The payment orders exchanged could be embodied in pieces of paper or in electronic messages. Settlement could be for each payment order individually ('gross' settlement), or for resulting balances ('net' or 'net net' settlement). Ultimately, the nationwide interbank settlement is usually completed on the books of the central bank. Indeed, for each currency, 'central bank money', in the form of credit in an account held at the central bank, is as good as cash, i.e. bank notes and coins.

The segment of the national payment system for the exchange and settlement of large value credit transfers is referred to as Large Value Transfer System (LVTS). For some LVTSs, the threshold or floor value for payment orders is specifically prescribed; others allow participants to decide for themselves what payments should be subjected to the more individualized, and hence more expensive, treatment of the LVTS.

There is no uniformity in direct accessibility of local banks to LVTS facilities. In some systems (e.g. the American Fedwire or the Swiss SIC), access is broadly based. In others (e.g. the English CHAPS), only large banks utilize the facility, with each of the small ones benefiting from its service indirectly through a correspondent large bank direct participant. Furthermore, for some LVTS, strict geographical limitations may apply so that banks outside the geographical area need establish correspondent relationships with banks within the territory. Originally, such was the case for both the American CHIPS and the German EAF. Finally, access to the communication facility may not be identical with access to the settlement facility; one may be broader than the other, in which case agency and/or correspondent relationships must be established for indirect participation. For example, the American CHIPS facilitates broadly based accessibility to the communication facility but gives a quite restrictive access to the direct settlement facility at the Federal Reserve Bank of New York. Conversely, one could envisage a system where there is a limited access to communication but broad participation in the multilateral settlement.

In the past, the operation of the LVTS has invariably been premissed on the interbank exchange of paper vouchers and settlement of resulting balances either separately or as part of the overall daily settlement at the national payment system. Until its closure in February 1995, the London Town Clearing in England was an example of a paper-based facility utilizing special same-day settlement. The Canadian predecessor of the previous IIPS system was a paper-based system whose settlement merged into the overall daily settlement at the Bank of Canada.

Today, all major currency countries have computerized (or automated) facilities for the exchange of messages. Also, they either have adopted or are moving towards the adoption of special settlement arrangements for large value credit transfers.

A technologically advanced LVTS (or 'wire transfers system') is characterized by a communication system linking participating banks by means of dedicated lines capable of providing on-line communication in real time. According to one commentator, '[t]he virtually instantaneous transfer of payment data by a two-way telephone-line communication network shapes the prominent economic operations characteristics' of an LVTS. These characteristics are 'speed, single transaction focus and . . . security', facilitating a relatively expensive individualized handling, confirmation, and notification for each payment.[19]

Some LVTSs utilize the SWIFT network for the exchange of domestic bank-to-bank payment orders. France and Canada fall into this category. SWIFT transmittal of domestic messages does not bypass the international circuit; that is, each message travels between two domestic banks via the SWIFT access point for that country, onward to the slice processor in the Netherlands or the USA, and back to the country SWIFT access point.[20]

Other have developed domestic dedicated networks. This is true, for example, for the USA, England, Germany, Switzerland, and Japan, as well as Australia, Hong Kong, and Singapore.

Computerized LVTSs are either central switch or gateway networks. In the former, interbank communication is intermediated through a central switch. In the latter, interbank communication is facilitated by means of a direct computer-to-computer communication. The American CHIPS is an example of a central switch network while the English CHAPS is a gateway system.

In general, a central switch system facilitates participation by a large number of banks of diverse size and computer capabilities, since only communication to the central switch, and not to each participating bank, is required. A central switch system is thus consistent with an open access policy imposing minimum bilateral compatibility requirements between each participant and the central computer, so as to accommodate a fragmented banking system. A central switch system further requires a centralized organization structure to accommodate the broad range of diverse bank systems.

A gateway architecture, on the other hand, requires a higher degree of multilateral compatibility among all participants, facilitating direct

---

[19] B. K. Stone, 'Electronic Payment Basics', (1986) 71 *Economic Review: Fed. Res. Bank of Atlanta* 3, pp. 9–10. The wire transfer is relatively expensive compared to other payment mechanisms but not necessarily in relation to the size of the payment.

[20] For SWIFT see s. 2, text around n. 10, above.

communication between each participant and any other,[21] and is more decentralized in its organization. For each bank it facilitates a better interface between its gateway and payment system. A gateway system is more responsive to technological enhancements and is likely to accommodate a banking system dominated by a small number of large banks.

LVTS settlement usually takes place on the books of a central counterparty where all direct participants hold accounts. Typically, and in all major currency countries, this central counterparty is the central bank.

As a rule, settlement is conducted either on a net net (multilateral net) or gross basis. In the former, settlement occurs only periodically, usually daily, at the end of each clearing cycle, for payment orders exchanged during the clearing period. In the latter, settlement for each payment occurs on a real-time basis, as each individual order is communicated and processed. The common abbreviation for a transfer system facilitating real-time gross settlement is RTGS.

This means that in a net net settlement system, payment orders are exchanged among participating banks during a clearing cycle, usually one day. At the end of the cycle, multilateral (often preceded by bilateral) netting takes place, sometimes as the conclusion of an accounting process which has taken place throughout the entire daily exchange. Balances are then adjusted on the books of the central bank, usually shortly after the end of the day operations,[22] by means of credit transfers from net net debtor banks to net net creditor banks. Conversely, in a gross settlement system, each transfer is settled individually on the books of the central bank as it is communicated to the receiving bank.

In the USA, CHIPS is a net net settlement system while Fedwire operates on a gross settlement basis.

Where the central switch is operated by the central bank, or any other central counterparty holding accounts for all participants, gross settlement can be facilitated in the course of the transmission of each payment order without further communication. The American Fedwire is a good example for this configuration. Otherwise, in a gateway system, as well as in a central switch system of which the central switch is operated by someone other than the central counterparty, gross settlement requires further communication of each payment order to the central counterparty. Such further communication takes place in both the English gateway network CHAPS and the French central switch system TBF.

[6]   Gross settlement requires individual payment for each obligation. Net-

---

[21] Or at least between each participant and some others, so that ultimately, each participant could communicate to any other either directly, or via another participant.

[22] In which case, the system is 'same-day net net system'. Otherwise, where balances are booked only next day, the system is 'next-day net net system'.

ting reduces the number of actual payments; payment is made solely for netted amounts of obligations rather than for each one individually. In bilateral netting, one payment is made between each pair of counterparties for a series of bilateral obligations; whereas in multilateral netting ('net nettings'), one payment is made by or to each of the counterparties, to or from a central counterparty, for a series of multilateral obligations.[23]

Netting leads to a payment for amounts sent less amounts received. Consequently, compared to a system where payment is made only for amounts sent, netting reduces insolvency losses, provided netting withstands insolvency. In common law jurisdictions, bilateral netting withstands insolvency of a counterparty due to the effectiveness of the right of set-off in insolvency. However, effective set-off requires pre-insolvency mutuality; only debts between the same counterparties can be set off against each other. For multilateral netting to withstand insolvency, therefore, mutuality between each counterparty and the central counterparty, effectively representing all others jointly, must be established prior to insolvency. Stated otherwise, prior to the insolvency, bilateral debts between all pairs of counterparties must be substituted by bilateral debts between each counterparty and the central counterparty.[24]

The effectiveness of netting arrangements to withstand a counterparty's insolvency can further be enhanced contractually, by continuously integrating each individual bilateral obligation, as it is created, into the overall multilateral net net, so that at any point in time throughout the clearing cycle there is one constantly updated obligation of each counterparty to or from the central counterparty. Such 'netting by novation and substitution' is carried out, for example, by CHIPS in the USA.

Specific legislation, such as in the United States,[25] England,[26] and Canada[27] may further reinforce the effectiveness of financial netting arrangements. In contrast, doubt as to the legal strength to withstand

---

[23] For a comprehensive survey, see e.g. Group of Experts on Payment Systems of the central banks of the Group of Ten countries, *Report on Netting Schemes* (Basle: Bank for International Settlements, Feb. 1989), known also as the Angell Report, after the chairman of the Group of Experts.

[24] The leading common law case is *British Eagle International Airlines Ltd.* v. *Compagnie Nationale Air France* [1975] 2 All E.R. 390 (H.L.). See also B. Geva, 'The Clearing House Arrangement' (1991) 19 Can. Bus. L.J. 138. For a French perspective, see H. Le Guen, 'Financial Risks and Legal Problems of International Netting Schemes Seen from a French Point of View', in W. Hadding and U. H. Schneider, *Legal Issues in International Credit Transfers* (Berlin: Ducker & Humblot, 1993), 393. For an American perspective see an article by E. T. Patrikis and D. W. Cook, ibid. at 363.

[25] Federal Deposit Insurance Corporation Improvement Act (F.D.I.C.I.A.) 1991, 12 U.S.C. § 1811 *et seq.*

[26] Company Act 1989, (U.K.), c. 40, Part VII, particularly s. 159.

[27] S.C. 1996, c. 6, s. 162.

insolvency of netting arrangements in some European countries have persuaded European central bankers to recommend the real-time gross settlement model for adoption in each of the European Economic Community countries.[28] In such a gross settlement system, each payment order is paid as it is processed so that no insolvency risk is borne by the receiving bank. While each Member State of the European Union has established and operates a real-time gross settlement system, any remaining doubts as to the effectiveness of multilateral netting to withstand insolvency of a payment system participant have been put to rest by the Settlement Finality Directive.[29]

Obviously, in a net net settlement system, while legal means can bolster the effectiveness of netting arrangements to withstand insolvency, they do not eliminate the loss created by settlement failure, namely the default of a net net debtor that fails to meet its multilateral settlement obligation (whether due to insolvency or temporary liquidity problems). The risk of settlement failure may turn into a 'systemic risk' where one or more net creditors of the failing participant default as a result of their inability to absorb the loss generated by the original settlement failure.

The risk of settlement failure can be reduced, if not eliminated altogether, by prudential measures restricting access to LVTS, as well as by means of a series of risk reduction measures. Overall, under what came to be known as the 'Lamfalussy standard', '[m]ultilateral netting systems should, at a minimum, be capable of ensuring the timely completion of daily settlements in the event of an inability to settle by the participant with the largest single net-debit position'.[30] Specific risk control measures are: bilateral credit limits, multilateral debit caps, collateralization of anticipated amounts in default, and loss-sharing arrangements.

For each counterparty vis-à-vis another, a bilateral credit limit sets the maximum bilateral credit, in the amount of total received less sent that the *other* counterparty may extend to it at any point throughout the exchange. At the same time, for each counterparty vis-à-vis all others, the multilateral debit cap represents the maximum net net debit balance that it may be allowed; it is the maximum credit, in the amount of total received less

---

[28] See Working Group on EC Payment Systems, *Minimum Common Features for Domestic Payment Systems* (Report to the Committee of Governors of the Central Banks of the Member States of the European Economic Community, November 1993), particularly Principle 4 and p. 24. This document is known as the Padoa-Schioppa Report after the chairman of the Working Group.   [29] 1998 OJ L166 pp. 0045.

[30] *Report of the Committee on Interbank Netting Schemes of the Central Banks of the Group of Ten Countries* (Basle: Bank for International Settlements, Nov. 1990) at 26. This document is known as the Lamfalussy Report after the chairman of the Committee. The 'Lamfalussy standard' was specifically approved of in Principle 5 of the Padoa-Schioppa Report, note 28, above, for same-day net net LVTS settling at the central bank and operating parallel to real-time gross settlement systems.

sent, that *all* counterparties are prepared to extend to it at any point throughout the exchange. While the bilateral credit limit measures bilateral debit positions, the debit cap measures the multilateral or overall debit position of a counterparty. A counterparty may have absolute discretion in establishing bilateral credit limits or must act under guidelines. Debit caps are established either on the basis of the total bilateral credit limits or under guidelines, usually referring to capital adequacy standards.

Collateralization is usually in the form of liquid securities. Loss sharing is likely to be based on credit extended (or extendable) by counterparties to the failed counterparty. The size of collateral required may be determined in relation to the total exposure of a counterparty, taking into account its debit cap and anticipated share under the loss-sharing scheme. In the USA, CHIPS employs all four risk-reducing measures.

Inasmuch as it requires the instantaneous (i.e. real-time) settlement of each payment order as it is processed, a gross settlement system does not involve the risk of settlement failure. Nevertheless, liquidity difficulties of counterparty/ies may cause a gridlock and bring operations to a halt.[31] An intraday funds market, facilitating same-day borrowing and repayment, as in Japan, is one means towards the resolution of the issue. Another means to that end is circles processing facilitating the simultaneous settlement of queued payment orders positioned in opposite directions and thus largely setting off each other.

At present, no major currency country, has an LVTS consisting exclusively of a pure gross settlement facility, relying on effective liquidity management by each participant. To bypass liquidity problems, the national payment system does not have a gross settlement facility (e.g. Canada), does not limit itself to a gross settlement LVTS (e.g. Japan, Germany, and the USA), permits bilateral netting operations (resulting in one payment which is instantaneously settled) to occur in designated hours (e.g. Japan until the end of 2000), provides for collateralized intraday liquidity (e.g. TBF in France), as well as introduces circles processing (optimization) facility (e.g. CHAPS in the UK), or allows a counterparty to overdraw on its account with the central bank (e.g. Switzerland as of 1999 and the USA).

The latter practice, namely allowing a counterparty to overdraw on its account with the central bank in order to allow real-time gross settlement

---

[31] Indeed, compared to real-time gross settlement systems, multilateral net settlement systems require participants to have less central bank money in hand so as to lead them to economize on the use of central bank money and, effectively, substitute intrabank intraday credit for central bank money. For this observation, see J. C. Marquard, 'Monetary Issues in Payment System Design', in B. J. Summers (ed.), *The Payment System* (Washington: International Monetary Fund, 1994), 41 at 44.

even in the absence of funds in the account, gives rise to daylight over-drafts. A daylight overdraft is an overdraft in a settlement account with the central bank, generated in the course of the daily payment activity and settlement by the end of the day. The practice facilitates the smooth oper-ation of the gross settlement system, but not without generating a risk of its own, that of end of the day settlement failure (namely the failure to provide cover) by the bank that incurred a daylight overdraft. Unlike in a net net settlement system, the settlement risk in a gross settlement system that allows daylight overdrafts is borne by the central bank and not by the other counterparties. This is so since in a gross settlement system, pay-ment is made to the receiving bank by the central bank as each payment order is processed and settled.

Settlement risks in a gross settlement system providing for a daylight overdraft facility can be reduced if not eliminated altogether by the employment of a series of risk reduction measures. Measures available are a multilateral debit cap (but not bilateral credit limits), collateraliza-tion, and intraday overdraft pricing. Such devices are currently employed by Fedwire in the USA.

A relatively new development is the emergence of net net systems incorporating key elements of gross settlement procedures. Both the EAF in Germany and the PNS in France fall into this category. In such a system intraday bilateral as well as multilateral settlement operations of payment orders are performed periodically. Intraday finality is thus conferred on outgoing payments against incoming payments, in accordance with lim-its set by participants, as well as against the balance held by the sending bank at the central bank, as designated by the sending bank. In connec-tion with each intraday settlement cycle, unsettled payment orders are left in a waiting queue for a subsequent settlement operation.

[7]   The ensuing discussion (current for summer 2000), highlights the prin-cipal features of the automated LVTS of seven major currency countries: the United States, Switzerland, the United Kingdom, Japan, Canada, France, and Germany.[32] It concludes with an overview of the mechanisms available for cross-border transfers in the European Union.

---

[32] For some information see Committee on Payment and Settlement Systems of the cen-tral banks of the Group of Ten Countries, *Payment Systems in the Group of Ten Countries* (Basle: Bank for International Settlements, Dec. 1993), known as the 'Red Book' after the colour of its cover, which is now in the fourth edition. Also, see European Monetary Insti-tute, *Payment Systems in the European Union* (Frankfurt: European Monetary Institute, 1996). I remain responsible for any error or misunderstanding and wish to alert the reader to the fact that in this dynamic area details change constantly and concepts keep evolving.

(c) United States

The United States has two LVTSs. One, Fedwire, is a broadly based nationwide gross settlement system. The other, CHIPS, is a New York-based net net settlement system. The bulk of the foreign exchange activity is carried over CHIPS.

Fedwire is owned and operated by the central bank, namely the Federal Reserve System. It is a nationwide gross settlement system utilizing an electronic communication network linking banks throughout the United States. Each participating bank maintains an account, as well as a communication link, with one of the twelve Federal Reserve Banks throughout the country. The link is either on-line or off-line. On-line access to Fedwire is either by means of computer interface connection or Fedline terminal. Off-line connection is usually by telephone, with security features such as an identification code or call-back procedures. Communication among the Reserve Banks is over FEDNET. FEDNET is a national communication network linking all twelve Reserve Banks into three consolidated data centres, managed by Federal Reserve Automation Services (FRAS). Effectively, these data centres form the central switch of the system, and further run the processing for each Federal Reserve Bank. Payment application is processed for all twelve Federal Reserve Banks in one such centre, so that in fact, an on-line bank communicates directly with the centralized data centre, bypassing its own Reserve Bank. An off-line bank, as well as an on-line, non-dial bank communicates with its respective Reserve Bank, which passes on the communication over FEDNET. The accounts of all banks are maintained by a single application residing in the data centres.

An intra-district transfer is between sending and receiving banks that have their respective accounts in one Federal Reserve Bank. Otherwise, where each bank holds its account in another Federal Reserve Bank, the Fedwire transfer is inter-district. In theory, and unlike the former, the latter involves transmission over the FEDNET. However, in effect, in the FRAS/FEDNET environment, there is no difference between the processing of inter- and intra-district transfers, since there is no real payment order from a sending to receiving Reserve Bank. Regardless, in each Fedwire transfer, the sending bank's account is debited and the receiving bank's account is credited instantaneously as soon as the transfer is processed.[33] Same-day completion is usually achieved.

Daylight overdraft is accommodated in Fedwire, but is not given as of

---

[33] Inter-district settlement among the twelve Federal Reserve Banks consists of a daily reconciliation of inter-district settlement accounts, followed by an annual settlement in Treasury gold certificates and securities accounts.

right. Risk control devices are debit caps, daylight overdraft pricing, and collateral.

CHIPS (Clearing House Interbank Payments Systems) is a New York-based automated private sector clearing facility for large value transfers. It is jointly owned by a subsidiary of the New York Clearing House Association and the participating banks and is operated by another subsidiary of the New York Clearing House. It is a central switch communication and net net settlement system where participating banks exchange same-day irrevocable payment orders over dedicated communication lines linking each onto the CHIPS central computer. Credit risks are controlled by bilateral credit limits, net debit caps, collateral, and a loss-sharing arrangement among all participants, effectively providing for settlement finality.

CHIPS settlement takes place at the end of each day's banking activity. A relatively small number of settling participants settle both for themselves and for their respective correspondent non-settling participants for which they agree to settle.[34] Multilateral balances of settling participants, incorporating also those of represented non-settlement participants, are settled between net net debtor banks and net net creditor banks over Fedwire at the Federal Reserve Bank of New York. Failure to complete the overall daily settlement, notwithstanding the collateralized loss sharing obligation of all banks, may result in unwinding the settlement. This, however, is quite a remote possibility.[34a]

(d) Switzerland

The Swiss SIC (Swiss Interbank Clearing) system is a central switch gross settlement facility. Communication is via a host computer owned and operated on behalf of the central bank, the Swiss National Bank by Telekurs AG, a private company jointly established by Swiss banks. The central bank is responsible for the account management. A relative large number of banks participate in the system.

SIC operates on a twenty-four-hour schedule on bank working days. It does not allow daylight overdrafts in reserve accounts; an unfunded transfer is held pending in a queue until arrival of cover. Payment messages are processed in the sequence of their input, though a participant may attach a priority code to a payment message.

---

[34] Until settlement, a settling participant is under no obligation to settle for a represented non-settlement participant. Where the former walks out, the latter must find another settling participant, in which case 'abnormal settlement' follows. Otherwise, resort to the loss-sharing rule and collateral is made.

[34a] As of January 2001, CHIPS substituted a continuous intraday settlement over a prefunded balance with the Federal Reserve Bank of New York, for the end-of-the-day net settlement procedure, thereby relinquishing credit limits, debit caps, collateral, and loss sharing.

Early entry of payment orders by participants is encouraged by a transaction price structure. A five-day post-dated input facility operates by means of storage in a 'pre-value date file'. Prior to settlement, a payment order can be revoked by the sending bank. Enhanced inquiry options are available to participants and assist forecasting the availability of cover for outgoing payments. A participant may split large-size outgoing payments so as to preclude small size payments from being 'blocked' by large size payments which cannot be settled, due to lack of adequate cover.

For years, SIC has operated as a gross settlement system without resorting to overdraft facilities (as in the USA) or designated hour transfers (as in Japan, until the end of 2000) or optimization (as in the UK). Despite the fact that it operated smoothly and settled timely, the central bank started to offer interest-free intraday liquidity in October 1999, particularly in order to accommodate the planned introduction of CLS for settling foreign exchange transactions. Also, by linking it to SECOM, the computerized facility of SEGA, which handles security transfer, SIC facilitates a truly delivery versus payment (DVP) system.

(e) United Kingdom

In the United Kingdom, the automated LVTS is CHAPS (Clearing House Automated Payment System). It is operated by the CHAPS Clearing Company Limited which is part of the Association for Payment Clearing Services (APCS), an umbrella organization for the UK payment industry.

CHAPS originated as a same-day net net settlement system but has completed its transformation to a real-time gross settlement (RTGS) system. It is a gateway facility in which large banks ('settlement members') exchange irrevocable same-day payment orders. The central bank, the Bank of England, itself is a settlement member. Gateways used for sending and receiving payment orders may be proprietary or shared. A non-settlement member may participate in the exchange and settlement only indirectly by establishing a correspondent relationship with a settlement member, outside the system.

Under the current RTGS mode of operation, each CHAPS payment order is settled at the Bank of England prior to its dispatch to the receiving bank. Thus, a settlement request, derived from each payment order, is initially sent to the Bank of England. The main payment order is automatically released by the sending to the receiving bank only on the basis of settlement confirmation transmitted by the Bank of England to the sending bank in response to the settlement request. For each payment order, settlement takes place in real time, against sufficient funds at the sending bank's account. Nonetheless, to avoid gridlocks, a circles-processing (optimization) facility is provided, so as to allow the simultaneous settlement of payments queued on behalf of different banks which would largely set off each other. Collateralized intraday liquidity is provided by the Bank of England to a participating bank by purchasing from it high-quality securities under a same-day sale and repurchase agreement.

(f) Japan

Japan has two LVTSs. The BOJ-NET Funds transfer system is a gross settlement facility. The Gaitame-Yen is a central switch same-day net net settlement system. While the former is comparable to the American Fedwire and the Swiss SIC, the latter is comparable to the American CHIPS.

The BOJ-NET is managed by the central bank, the Bank of Japan, whose computer centre is its central switch. The system primarily handles domestic payments. In order to avoid competition with the Zengin electronic retail payment network, there is a high floor limit of 300 million yen for third-party transfers.

The BOJ-NET accommodates both on-line electronic and off-line paper-based access. At present, it allows both real-time instantaneous transfers and transfers at designated hours. Once input, real-time payment orders cannot be revoked. On their part, designated-hour payment orders can be booked one day in advance and are revocable up to execution. They constitute the bulk of the funds transfer activity. Under current plans, by the end of 2000, BOJ-NET will process only real-time gross-settlement transfers. Designated-hour transfers will be abolished. The plan to abolish designated hour transfers was prompted by the excessive use of this facility and with the view of thereby reducing systemic risk.

Under the current mode of operation of the BOJ-NET, and unlike in the US Fedwire but like in the Swiss SIC, daylight overdrafts are not permitted. Each transfer must be funded by a credit balance at the sending bank's account with the central bank. An unfunded payment order is immediately rejected; unlike in SIC, there is no queuing mechanism. Designated-hour transfers are processed simultaneously, so that only net net positions are transferred; sending banks are to delete outgoing payment orders in the amount of an uncovered net net debit position. The flow of funds is facilitated by private half-day interbank credit markets for reserve funds. On the planned abolition of the designated-hour transfer facility, intraday liquidity will be provided to participants by the Bank of Japan in the form of a fully collateralized interest-free intraday overdrafts.

The Gaitame-Yen ('foreign exchange') System is a central switch same-day credit-driven net net settlement facility for foreign exchange and other overseas payments. It is managed by the Tokyo Banker's Association but processed and settled over the BOJ-NET.

Participating banks connect their computers directly with the Bank of

Japan's host computers. Payment orders can be input as early as three days prior to transaction date. No revocation facility is available. Credit risks are reduced by optional bilateral net credit limits as well as a loss-sharing rule.

(g) Canada

At present, the Canadian Payment Association (CPA)[35] operates the LVTS under By-law No. 7 Respecting the Large Value Transfer System.[36] In contrast with its predecessor, IIPS (Interbank International Payment System), which was a nationwide next day[37] net net settlement system, LVTS is a same-day net net settlement system. In the footsteps of IIPS, LVTS utilizes SWIFT communication network for the interbank exchange of messages.

Risk control mechanisms in the Canadian LVTS are multilateral debit caps, bilateral credit limits, collateral, and a loss-sharing agreement. To ensure compliance, parts of each outgoing payment message are copied to a central LVTS facility for authorization before the message is released to the receiving participant and a notification is sent to the sending participant. Only a payment message that passed the risk-control tests is authorized and released by the LVTS for further transmission to the receiving participant. Accordingly, for each incoming payment message, settlement is guaranteed by the Bank of Canada and payment is final and irrevocable, as soon as the payment message is received by the receiving participant. A message that does not pass the risk-control tests may either be placed in a queue or returned to the sending participant and is not advised to the receiving participant.

There are two separate streams of payment messages, referred to as tranche 1 and tranche 2, to be selected for each payment message by the sending participant. Tranche 1 is the 'defaulter pay' stream while tranche 2 is the 'survivor pay' stream. Both are equally secure and guaranteed

---

[35] This entity was established by the Canadian Payments Association Act, RSC 1985, c. C-21. Its members are depository financial institutions including the central bank. Its statutory mandate is to establish and operate a national clearing and settlement system as well as to plan the evolution of the national payments system.

[36] The By-law was passed by CPA Board of Directors in Nov. 1997 and was approved by the Governor in Council on 2 Apr. 1998. See PC 1998–568. The LVTS was designated by the Bank of Canada (on 19 Jan. 1999) as a clearing and settlement system under the Payment Clearing Settlement Act, S.C. 1996 c. 6, s. 162. See Canada Gazette Part 1 vol. 133 No. 7 p. 415 (13 Feb. 1999). Particularly, this designation allows the Bank of Canada to provide the system with a guarantee of settlement and liquidity, as well as confirms the validity of its settlement rules and the effectiveness of its default provisions to withstand insolvency.

[37] In fact, on the books of the central bank, i.e. the Bank of Canada, the ultimate position for each bank, which was finalized next day, and incorporated in the overall balance of the bank for the *entire* daily activity over the national payment system, was backdated to the banking day of the exchange. Obviously, this did not eliminate the risk of overnight failure.

payment messages. They differ solely in the method in which they are supported by collateral. In principle, a tranche 1 payment message is supported by the sender's own collateral. At the same time, a tranche 2 payment message is supported by collateral provided by counterparties, with each non-defaulting participant supporting its share as determined by the agreed loss-sharing formula, and having recourse against the defaulting sender. Thus, each outgoing tranche 1 payment message must be against either an incoming tranche 1 payment message or the sending participant's own collateral, up to a fully collateralized tranche 1 net debit cap. Each tranche 2 outgoing message must be within applicable bilateral credit limits and tranche 2 debit cap, as supported by counterparties' collateral.

(h) France

France has two LVTSs. TBF is an RTGS facility operated by the central bank, the Bank of France. PNS is a private sector real-time irrevocable net settlement system, that was launched in 1999 as a successor to SNP, which was an end of the day net net settlement system.

TBF stands for 'Transferts Banque de France'—Bank of France Transfers. It utilizes the SWIFT communication network and provides a real-time gross settlement on the books of the Bank of France. For each payment order, as part of the transmission procedure, the sending bank copies to the central bank those parts of the message directed to the receiving bank needed for the settlement. The central bank advises the sending and receiving banks promptly if the payment order is accepted or rejected. Upon acceptance, the central bank debits and credits the sending and receiving banks' accounts. Upon rejection, the payment order is put in a pending queue. Two FIFO queues are managed by the TBF: queue for priority 1 operations (high) and queue for priority 0 operations (low).

To facilitate the smooth movement of funds, a special 'optimization' procedure is realized. Thereunder, payment orders in the pending queue are settled on a multilateral basis. Overdrafts are not permitted on settlement accounts. However, TBF members can obtain intraday liquidity from the central bank through intraday repurchase agreements of securities as well as through intraday secured loans. For the latter, eligible collateral may consist of banks' entitlements from selected high-quality private debtors.

PNS stands for Paris-net settlement system. It is a private sector real-time irrevocable net settlement system purporting to improve on its predecessor SNP, which stood for 'Système Net Protégé'—Protected Net System and was an end of the day net net settlement facility. In PNS, each outgoing payment order is input into a waiting queue and settled either in central bank money or against an incoming payment. This latter feature has been known as PVP—payment versus payment facility. Accordingly, each outgoing payment order is executed throughout the day in PNS only against either (i) a positive balance in the account with the central bank, as such balance is made available, or (ii) an incoming payment from a counterparty. Throughout the daily cycle, finality is accorded to payments continuously, by means of 'optimization' procedures, in the form of bilateral and multilateral (or global) netting operations. Thus, for each participant, outgoing payment orders are settled against incoming payment orders, either bilaterally or multilaterally, in accordance with sender limits, set by participants both bilaterally as well as multilaterally, and to the extent cover is available in a balance set aside from its account at the central bank, and to which liquidity could be provided against unused collateral available to the participant in TBF. PNS operations closely follow those of the German EAF discussed below, but run more continuously so that more frequent batch settlements are conducted during the day.

In both TBF and PNS, unexecuted payment orders remaining in pending queues at the end of the day are returned to respective senders.

(i) Germany

In Germany, the central bank, i.e. the Bundesbank, operates two large value transfer systems for the transmission of funds from one account to another over its inter-branch network: electronic clearing (EAF) and local and intercity account transfers (ELS). EAF is a same-day net net facility integrating key elements of a gross settlement procedure. ELS is a gross settlement facility for both local (intra-branch) and intercity (inter-branch) transfers. EAF is fully electronic. ELS accommodates both an end-to-end electronic transmission and paper-based access by participating banks. It consists of Prior1 (originally telegraphic and afterwards P-1) and Prior2 (originally express and afterwards P-2) payments. For Prior1 payments, processing is on a single transaction basis with gross settlement in real time. For Prior2 payments, there is a cyclical batch processing leading to gross settlement carried out every thirty minutes to one hour. In ELS, intercity communication is electronic. For both local and intercity transfers, processing is carried out on the EIL-ZV, which is the proprietary telecommunication system of the central bank. Paper access is available to ELS participating banks only for Prior1 (but not Prior2) payments.

No credit risk is incurred by the central bank in connection with providing the ELS services. Daylight overdrafts are not permitted and no transfer will be carried out unless there is adequate cover in the sending bank's account, or an intra-day overdraft secured by prime securities is available to it under a giro Lombard facility. Unexecuted payment orders are put in a queue and for each participant, information is available for queued incoming payments.

In its current enhanced configuration, EAF is a two-phase daily procedure. Phase 1 is the delivery phase which takes place between 7.00 a.m. and 4.00 p.m. In its course, payment orders are input by participants and entered into queues. At regular intervals, finality is accorded by means of bilateral as well as multilateral clearing and settlement operations. That is, at each interval, for each participant, outgoing payment orders are settled either bilaterally or multilaterally, in accordance with the sender limits set by participants both bilaterally and multilaterally, and to the extent cover is available in an EAF 'working balance' set aside from its giro account at the central bank. Any payment order for which cover is not provided remains in the queue for the next processing cycle. Phase 2 is the concluding stage. It takes place between 4.00 and 4.30 p.m. It consists of two multilateral clearing and settlement operations. The first covers all payment orders that were not settled and remained in the queue at the conclusion of Phase 1. For each participant, the resulting balance is settled against its entire available balance at the giro account and collateralized overdraft facility with the central bank. Outgoing payment orders for which no cover is available are excluded from the first settlement and their sender may procure funds over the ELS in a money market for the second and final clearing and settlement. Uncovered payment orders are then deleted (or withdrawn) and returned to the sender.

(j) The European Union: cross-border transfers

In principle, the introduction of the euro as the currency of member states of the European Union[38] has not affected the operation of domestic large value transfers. Within each member state, such payments are processed by existing mechanisms, as described in each of the previous sections applicable to such a member state.[39] Conversely, new mechanisms have been introduced to handle cross-border transfers within the European Union. They operate in the context of the European System of Central Banks (ESCB) consisting of a newly established European Central Bank (ECB) and existing national central banks (NCBs) of the various member states.

---

[38] Under the Maastricht Treaty, Commission of the European Communities, *Treaty Establishing the European Union*, and *Protocol on the Transition to the Third Stage of Economic and Monetary Union*, as well as *Protocol on the Statute of the European System of Central Banks and the European Central Bank*, 1992 OJ C 191, pp. 1, 68 and 87 (7 Feb. 1992). For the denomination of the European single currency as 'euro' in a meeting of the European Council of 15 and 16 Dec. 1995, in Madrid, see 1996 OJ C 32, pp. 82 (5 Feb. 1996) and 1996 OJ C 369, pp. 10 (7 Dec. 1996).

[39] Member states covered in the previous discussion that adopted the euro are Germany and France. The UK is a member state that has not adopted the euro, at least, so far.

One such facility, focusing on, but not limited to, cross-border transfers, is the Euro clearing and settlement service (EURO-1), provided by the Euro Banking Association (EBA). EBA is a private sector organization owned and operated by banks. EURO-1 is a multilateral cross-border clearing and settlement system providing same-day value with Pan-European coverage.

Participants in the EBA euro clearing and settlement service transmit and receive messages over the SWIFT network. Risk-management features are bilateral credit limits, multilateral net debit caps, loss sharing, collateral arrangements, and the single obligation structure. The latter is designed to ensure that multilateral netting withstands the insolvency of a participant in a debit position. Thereunder, multilateral netting by novation is continuously employed with each payment transmitted over the system, so that for each participant, at any time throughout the daily exchange, there is only one debt, in the multilaterally netted amount, between itself and all other participants. Gridlocks are to be avoided by the employment of circles processing.

Each participating bank maintains an account at an NCB. EBA has a central settlement account at the ECB. Each day, after close of clearing, each participating bank in a debit position sends, out of its account with its NCB, the amount of its multilateral debit position, to the EBA's account held at the ECB. The EBA distributes payments so received to participating banks in credit positions. Each participating bank in a credit position thus receives the amount of its multilateral credit position in its account held in its own NCB. The mechanism for transmitting funds within the ESCB, from an account in one NCB to an account in another NCB, as well as between an account in the ECB and an account held in the NCB and vice versa, is TARGET, to be outlined immediately below.

TARGET is the gross settlement system designed by the ESCB exclusively for the cross-border Euro transfers.[40] It includes the national RTGS systems of member states[41] and their linkages. It also includes the ECB's own payment mechanism (EPM). Within TARGET, the infrastructures and procedures which are used to process cross-border transfers within as

---

[40] For TARGET information, provided first by the European Monetary Institute (EMI), the forerunner of the ECB and subsequently by the ECB, see Working Group on EU Payment Systems, *Report to the Council of the Monetary Institute on the TARGET System* (Frankfurt: EMI, May 1995); Working Group on EU Payment Systems, *First Progress Report on the TARGET Project* (Frankfurt: EMI, Aug. 1996); EMI, *Second Progress Report on the TARGET Project* (Frankfurt: EMI, Sept. 1997); and ECB, *Third Progress Report on the TARGET Project* (Frankfurt: ECB, Nov. 1998).

[41] Each member state has an RTGS System, thereby implementing Principle 4 of the report, *Minimum Common Features for Domestic Payment Systems*, prepared by a Working Group on EC Payment Systems, chaired by T. Padoa-Schioppa (and known as 'the Padoa-Schioppa Report'), endorsed in Nov. 1993 by the Committee of Governors of the Central Banks of the Member States of the European Economic Community.

well as outside each RTGS system are called the Interlinking System. The latter consists of a telecommunications network linked in each country to a local interface, called the national Interlinking component. The network provider for the Interlinking System is SWIFT. Only the ECB and the NCBs, as settlement agents of national RTGS systems, are able to access the Interlinking System, whether for their own purposes, or on behalf of their customer banks.

The TARGET System is designed to be able to process cross-border transfers almost as smoothly as if they were domestic. Under a minimum approach, three areas of harmonization were identified: the provision of intraday liquidity, operating hours, and pricing policies. Otherwise, each national RTGS system is free to keep its specific features in processing domestic payments. TARGET thus does not operate under a single set of rules and does not use common or identical infrastructures.

At present, the UK is outside the euro area. In order to cater to euro-denominated payments, CHAPS developed a new LVTS, called CHAPS Euro, which operates side by side with the sterling denominated CHAPS, discussed above, in (e). Access to CHAPS Euro is over SWIFT, and settlement is carried out in the Bank of England, on a gross basis, using the same central settlements systems as CHAPS sterling.[42]

(k) The Law of Credit Transfers: selected comparative aspects

[8]   In the United States, most jurisdictions have adopted Article 4A of the Uniform Commercial Code (hereafter, 'Article 4A') as the law governing credit transfer. In turn, the statute strongly influenced the content of the Model Law on International Credit Transfer, prepared by UNCITRAL (hereafter: 'Model Law'). So far, no jurisdiction has adopted the Model Law. In the ensuing discussion, those enacting either Article 4A or the Model Law may be referred to as 'special statute jurisdictions'.

Elsewhere, credit transfers are currently primarily governed by general principles of law. Attention is given below to the laws of France, Germany, Switzerland, Italy, Japan, and Quebec, all of which are civil law jurisdictions, to Israel and South Africa, as well as to the common law of England, whose principles govern credit transfers also in the nine common law provinces of Canada and Australia. All such civil and common law countries may be referred to as 'general law jurisdictions'.

Among these jurisdictions, Germany's case is special. On 21 July 1999,

---

[42] For CHAPS Euro see e.g. the series of publications of the Bank of England, *Practical Issues Arising from the Introduction of the Euro*, particularly issue Nos. 5–8 and 10, of Aug. 1997, Dec. 1997, Mar. 1998, Sept. 1998, and Dec. 1998, respectively, *Practical Issues Arising from the Euro* (June 1999).

Germany passed a statute, as part of its civil code, which specifically governs credit transfers (hereafter: 'the German statute').[43] It is influenced by the EU transparency directive to be discussed below, but goes further than it, and is not limited to cross-border transfers. From this perspective, Germany may be seen as becoming a 'special statute jurisdiction'. However, unlike Article 4A and the Model Law, the German statute is not a comprehensive code, and the general provisions of the civil code, governing the law of obligations and particularly the mandate, continue to apply to credit transfers, other than as specifically provided in the statute. In the final analysis, Germany is thus still to be regarded as a 'general law jurisdiction', though obviously, it occupies a unique and intermediary position between the two categories.

The European Union adopted a directive governing the transparency, and minimum standards for the performance, of Pan European cross-border credit transfers not exceeding 50,000 euro (hereafter: 'the transparency directive').[44] It addresses issues relating to the obligation to perform, the time of performance, charges, and liability for loss. In general, banks' obligations are excused if non-performance is attributed to *force majeure*. The directive affects the relationship between the originator and the originator's bank as well as that between the beneficiary and the beneficiary's bank.

The ensuing discussion outlines cardinal aspects of the law of credit transfers in special statute as well as general law jurisdictions. No comprehensive comparative study has been undertaken. Emphasis is rather given to salient features which highlight common as well as district elements. A more detailed discussion for each country can be found below.

In principle, the credit transfer can be regarded either as a single and [9] global transaction, or as a segmented one, consisting of a series of successive bilateral operations, each involving a receiving bank. French doctrine, and perhaps all general law jurisdictions, follow the former view. At the same time, Article 4A, followed by the Model Law, opted for the latter approach. The principal practical difference should have been reflected in the choice of law rules. Thus, one could expect to see one unitary law applicable to the entire single and global transaction, in contrast to an individual law applicable to each bilateral relationship under the segmented view of the transaction. Indeed, Article 4A and the Model Law confirm this expectation and follow the latter ('segmented') approach, at least so far as when it was not agreed otherwise. At the same time, it is far from certain whether French law truly adheres to the former ('unitary')

[43] Credit Transfer Law, Überwiesungsgesetz vom 21.7.1999, BGB1. I 1999, s. 1624ff.
[44] 1997 OJ L 43, p. 0025 (14 Feb. 1997).

view. Overall, segmentation according to the location of each receiving bank is a predominant conflict of laws approach in all jurisdictions.

In general law jurisdiction, the originator's payment order is analysed as an authority conferred upon the originator's bank. As such, the entire operation is governed by the law of agency or mandate. In contrast, special statute jurisdictions regard the contract governing the payment order as *sui generis*. Article 4A is explicit in rejecting altogether the notion that a receiving bank may be the agent of its sender.

According to Article 4A and the Model Law, the completion of a credit transfer may be marked by payment to the beneficiary's bank, even prior to crediting the beneficiary's account with it. This was said to conflict with French doctrine, under which it is the credit to the beneficiary's account which marks completion. Nonetheless, inasmuch as Article 4A and the Model Law provide for the post-completion duties of the beneficiary's bank, particularly for its duty to pay the beneficiary by crediting the beneficiary's account, the point may appear to be quite academic, possibly except for the allocation of risk upon the default (particularly insolvency) of the beneficiary's bank, between payment to it (by its sender) and payment by it (to the beneficiary).

A broad range of views applies to the irrevocability of the credit transfer, namely to the identification of the point from which payment cannot be countermanded by the originator. Under French law, for in-house and correspondent transfers, irrevocability is marked by the debit posted to the originator's account by the originator's bank. However, in a complex transfer, namely whenever intermediary bank(s) are involved, irrevocability under French law is postponed to the point where funds become available to the beneficiary's bank. Under Article 4A and the Model Law, the originator may countermand payment as long as the originator's bank has not acted on the originator's payment order. Other that in an in-house transfer, this would mean that countermand is available until the originator's bank has issued its own payment order in executing the originator's instructions. Nonetheless, where an executing bank chooses to cooperate, countermand can be effectuated onward, until payment to or by the beneficiary's bank.

At common law, irrevocability is marked by the receipt of funds by the beneficiary's bank, presumably as long as this point has preceded payment to the beneficiary (or decision to pay him). Payment to the beneficiary, usually by crediting the beneficiary's account, marks irrevocability in Germany, Switzerland, Quebec, and Japan. It is unclear in Italy, South Africa, and Israel whether revocability is available until execution by the originator's bank or payment to the beneficiary. In all countries, rules governing LVTS may provide for the irrevocability of payment orders input thereto even prior to payment to or by the beneficiary's bank.

There may be a universal consensus as to identifying the point of the discharge of the debt paid by credit transfer with the accrual in favour of the beneficiary of an unconditional right against the beneficiary's bank. However, there is no uniformity in determining when such right accrues.

Under Article 4A and a suggestion put forward by the Model Law, this point is reached whenever the beneficiary's bank has been paid by its sender, or has paid to (or advised) the beneficiary, whichever event comes first. Civil law systems regard the credit posted to the beneficiary's account as the crucial point. The common law vacillates; prior to payment by the sender to the beneficiary's bank, a 'decision' to credit the beneficiary's account may suffice. In Israel and South Africa the position is unclear.

The ensuing analysis deals with the treatment by the various laws of the allocation of risks in case of default by a participating bank.

Default by a beneficiary's bank may include delay or loss, as where the **[10]** bank delays payment to the beneficiary, misdirects the funds to an account of an unintended beneficiary who may become insolvent, or where the beneficiary's bank itself becomes insolvent. Under Article 4A, default does not include payment to the designated bank account where the beneficiary's bank does not know that this account does not belong to the named beneficiary. Default may cause interest or exchange losses, dishonour of outgoing payment items, opportunity costs, as well as the loss of discharge causing the termination of a favourable contract. Additionally, loss of funds takes place whenever funds have not reached the beneficiary at all. There is no uniformity among the various laws as to who, as between the originator and beneficiary, bears the risk of delay or loss incurred at the beneficiary's bank.

In special statute jurisdictions, the risk of delay or loss occurring at the beneficiary's bank, is allocated to the beneficiary, as of the point when the beneficiary's bank received payment for the payment order. Article 4A specifically allows the beneficiary to recover from the beneficiary's bank the amount of the credit transfer with interest, as well as consequential but foreseeable damages. Such damages are recovered provided relevant specific circumstances have been advised by the beneficiary to the beneficiary's bank.

In general law jurisdictions, the beneficiary's bank is universally regarded as employed by the beneficiary. It would seem to follow that as between the originator and the beneficiary the risk of delay or loss occurring at the beneficiary's bank must fall on the beneficiary. Nonetheless, in some general law jurisdictions the beneficiary's bank is regarded as acting in double capacity. It is thus looked upon as acting also for the originator or the originator's bank, and not only for the beneficiary. In fact, wherever the originator's debt to the beneficiary is not discharged until the beneficiary's account is credited by the beneficiary's bank, it may be tempting to argue that until that point the entire risk rests with the originator.

Indeed, a defaulting beneficiary's bank may be sued by the originator in Switzerland, Italy, Japan, Quebec, and France. However, French law acknowledges that inasmuch as the beneficiary is the principal of the beneficiary's bank, the beneficiary is answerable to the originator for the default of the beneficiary's bank. This put the ultimate risk on the beneficiary. In fact, insofar as the risk of loss is concerned, French law specifically allocates the risk to the beneficiary. A similar scheme may exist in Quebec. Conversely, except where the loss has been caused by *force majeure*, Swiss law allocates the risk of loss incurred at the beneficiary's bank to the originator. The risk of delay, however, is borne under Swiss law by the beneficiary. In Italy, most beneficiary's bank risks seem to fall on the originator. In Japan, one view seems to suggest that insofar as the originator designates the beneficiary's bank in the payment order, vis-à-vis the beneficiary, the originator bears the entire risk of default by the beneficiary's bank which is to be regarded as the originator's direct agent. However, others in Japan allocate the entire risk of default by the beneficiary's bank to the beneficiary.

In my view, inasmuch as the beneficiary's bank is selected by the beneficiary, the beneficiary ought to bear the entire risk of delay or loss occurring at the beneficiary's bank. This is the state of law in special statute jurisdictions. In general law jurisdictions this is the law in Germany, probably in England, Israel, South Africa, and Quebec and ultimately in France but not in Switzerland or Italy. There is no consensus on this point in Japan.

In principle, in situations where vis-à-vis the beneficiary, the risk of default by the beneficiary's bank is allocated to the originator, the originator has a cause of action against the beneficiary's bank based on the breach by the beneficiary's bank of its duties in acting for the originator. In Japan, under one view, the beneficiary's bank is a subagent of the originator's bank, so that the originator's bank may be liable to the originator for the default of the beneficiary's bank. In turn, in all jurisdictions, where the risk of default by the beneficiary's bank is allocated to the beneficiary, the liability of the beneficiary's bank to the beneficiary for the amount of the credit transfer is based on accountability. However, liability of the beneficiary's bank to the beneficiary for consequential loss, where recognized, is based on the breach of duties by the beneficiary's bank to the beneficiary.

[11]   As between the originator and the beneficiary, the risk of loss incurred at a bank other than the beneficiary's bank (namely an originator's or intermediary bank) is universally allocated to the originator. Except for in

Germany, this is also true for the risk of delay incurred at a bank other than the beneficiary's bank. In Germany, the risk of delay (but not the loss) incurred at a bank other than the beneficiary's bank is allocated to the beneficiary, except where provided otherwise by contract or special law.

Under both Article 4A and the Model Law, the originator may shift the risk of loss incurred at a bank other than that of the beneficiary to the originator's bank. This is the 'money-back guarantee rule' of both statutes, protecting the originator from the non-completion of the credit transfer, particularly due to the insolvency of an intermediary bank not selected by the originator. In turn, the originator's bank may pass the loss onwards, up to the bank that sent its payment order to the insolvent intermediary. Similarly, under Article 4A and the Model Law, the originator may recover interest losses incurred by the originator by virtue of loss of funds or delay incurred at a bank other that of the beneficiary.

Other than such principal or interest losses, the damage caused by delay or loss incurred at a bank other than that of the beneficiary is entirely borne under Article 4A and the Model Law by the originator. That is, the originator may not recover consequential loss incurred by the non-completion of the credit transfer or by the delay in carrying it out. Under the Model Law, but not under Article 4A, there is a narrow exception, under Article 18, where the bank acted either 'with the specific intent to cause loss' or 'recklessly and with actual knowledge that loss would be likely to result', in which case, consequential damages may be recovered under the general law in that jurisdiction. In general, consequential damages may include exchange losses and the termination of a favourable contract by virtue of the default in making a timely payment.

A limited 'money-back guarantee rule' exists under the German statute, limiting the amount to be refunded to 12,500 euro, plus expenses and fees. Elsewhere, no similar 'money back guarantee rule' fastening absolute liability for the benefit of the originator is recognized in general law jurisdictions, possibly with the exception of Japan. Rather, in order to recover in general law jurisdictions, the originator must prove fault or breach of duty by an originator's or intermediary bank, such as in delaying the credit transfer, varying its content, or selecting an incompetent correspondent for onward transmission. Further in contrast with Article 4A and the Model Law, consequential damages may be recovered in all general law jurisdictions, provided they were foreseeable. Nonetheless, there may be difference of opinion as to the extent of liability for consequential damages.

Another, and in fact earlier, limited 'money-back guarantee rule', appears in the EU transparency directive, applicable to Pan European cross-borders transfers not exceeding 50,000 euro. Such a rule, though subject to a 12,500 euro ceiling for the refund, was incorporated into the German statute, which covers also domestic transfers, and does not contain any restriction as to the amount of the transfer. At the same time, the transparency directive, unlike the German statute, does not affect existing rules as to liability for bank breach of duties. Privity rules are not provided for by the directive, but as will be seen below, are dealt with by the German statute.

In principle, recovery under Article 4A and the Model Law is exclusively from a bank in immediate privity. Recovery from a *breaching* bank in immediate privity is universally recognized in all general law jurisdictions. However, with respect to recovery in connection with the default by an intermediary bank no consensus exists in the various general law jurisdictions. In each jurisdiction, the choice between direct liability of the breaching intermediary or vicarious liability of the originator's bank may depend in part on the classification of the intermediary bank as a subagent, substituted agent or an employee/assistant as well as on other aspects of the general law in the particular jurisdiction. In general, there is vicarious liability for an employee/assistant but not a substituted agent. Usually, only a substituted agent is directly liable.

The intermediary bank is a subagent of the originator at common law, in South Africa and probably in Israel. It is a substituted agent in France, Italy, and possibly in Japan. It is an employee/assistant in Switzerland and Quebec.

In Switzerland, direct recovery by the originator from the intermediary bank as an employee/assistant of the originator's bank is precluded. However, under Swiss law, the originator's bank is vicariously liable to the originator for loss caused by the intermediary bank's fault or breach of duty. The same is true under Quebec law.

At common law, as the originator's agent, the originator's bank is responsible to the originator-principal for breach by the intermediary bank subagent. However, in the absence of privity, the intermediary bank subagent is not liable to the originator. This is also the position in South Africa and probably Israel.

In Italy, under the mandate to pay theory, the intermediary bank is a substituted agent directly liable to the originator. The originator's bank, as the original agent, is not vicariously liable for the default of the substitute, as long as it has not been at fault in selecting it. Conversely, under the mandate to issue a corresponding payment order view, default by the intermediary bank is no ground for awarding damages to the originator whether from the originator's bank of from the defaulting intermediary bank.

In France, as long as it was not charged (expressly or tacitly) with a duty to supervise substituted agents, as an agent with power of substitution, the originator's bank is not liable to the originator for breach by the intermediary bank—substituted agent of the originator. This is so provided the originator's bank did not select a notoriously incapable or insolvent intermediary bank. Conversely, as a substituted agent of the originator, the intermediary bank is directly liable to the originator.

No uniformity of opinion exists in Japan. Some regard the originator's bank as liable to the originator either for the absolute completion of the credit transfer; or at least for its fault in the selection of an incompetent intermediary bank, even in the absence of vicarious liability. There are those who speak of the restitution and tort, though no contractual, liability of the intermediary or beneficiary's bank to the originator. Others regard an intermediary or beneficiary's bank designated by the originator as a direct agent of the originator, to whom such a defaulting intermediary or beneficiary's bank is directly liable.

In Germany, the execution of each payment order may give rise to 'protective duties' by the receiving bank. On this basis, the beneficiary may recover directly from the breaching originator's or intermediary bank. By the same token, with respect to the risk of loss as well as in those exceptional circumstances where the risk of delay in Germany is allocated to the originator, the originator may recover directly from the breaching intermediary bank.

At the same time, the prevailing view prior to the adoption of the German statute, was that an intermediary bank was in the position of a substituted agent and was not an employee/assistant. Accordingly, in Germany, the originator's bank was not responsible for the default of an intermediary bank properly selected by it. This, however, was changed by the German statute which effectively classifies the intermediary bank as an employee/assistant, for whose default or breach the originator's bank is fully responsible to the originator. Liability covers consequential (but foreseeable) loss; it is in addition to the liability of the originator's bank under the money-back guarantee rule. Other than for wilful default and gross negligence, as well as for interest losses and risks particularly assumed, liability may be limited to 25,000 euro for inter-state transfers, and 12,500 euro otherwise. It is unclear under the German statute whether an originator's bank, which is found liable to the originator for breach by an intermediary bank, has a recourse against that breaching intermediary bank.[45] Arguably in Germany, prior to the German statute, the originator could recover from an intermediary bank as an assignee of the

---

[45] The question is discussed, so I am advised, by Uwe H. Schneider, 'Pflichten und Haftung der erstbeauftragten Kreditinstitute bei grenzüberschreitenden Überweisungen, *Wertpapier-Mitteilungen 1999*, p. 2189–2198 [in German]. The problem is that the correspondent bank may not be liable under the contract with the originator's bank.

originator's bank. Yet, as indicated, it is not clear under the German statute whether such an assignable action against the intermediary bank is even available to the originator's bank. From the originator's point of view, this however is unlikely to be crucial, at least in usual circumstances, since, as indicated, in departure from prior law, the German statute accords the originator a direct action against the originator's bank for the default of the intermediary bank.

(II) GERMANY[46]

[1] Pursuant to §611 of the German Civil Code (BGB), the contract underlying the credit transfer is a contract for service, under which the bank is bound to carry out the customer's instructions embodied in the payment order, and the customer is bound to pay the agreed upon remuneration.[47] At the same time, the originator's payment order is not an 'order' within the meaning of BGB §783. Under that provision, an order 'to pay or deliver money' must be contained in an instrument and delivered by the payor to the payee, so as to authorize the payee to collect from the drawee. Stated otherwise, German law provides only for an 'indirect order'. Conversely, the originator's payment order is direct; it is issued directly to the originator's bank. Its effect is to 'push' payment to the beneficiary rather than to initiate collection by him. Nor is a payment order necessarily embodied in an instrument.[48]

As 'a contract of service or a contract for work[49] which has for its object

---

[46] The ensuing discussion draws heavily on chapters by W. Hadding and U. Huber in W. Hadding and U. H. Schneider (eds.), *Legal Issues in International Credit Transfers* (Berlin: Duncker & Humblot, 1993) as well as *Jura Europae—Droit bancaire et boursier* (Munich: Verlag C. H. Beck; Paris: Éditions Techniques Juris-Classeurs, 1976), §10.31 (by H. Schönle).

[47] Under BGB §611(1), '[b]y the contract for service, the person who promises service is bound to perform the service promised, and the other party is bound to pay the remuneration agreed upon.' Under BGB §611(2), '[s]ervice of any kind may be the object of the contract for service'. In connection with the credit transfer, the remuneration by the customer could be either in the form of an explicit fee, or in making of deposited funds available for use. All quotes are from translation by I. S. Forrester, S. L. Goren, and H. L. Ilgen (South Hackensack, NJ: Fred B. Rothman & Co., 1975).

[48] It follows that the freedom of the beneficiary's entitlement (from the beneficiary's bank) from defences available (to the originator's bank) against the originator does not emerge directly from BGB §784, the latter being confined to an 'order' governed by §783.

[49] Under BGB §631, '[b]y a contract for work the contractor is bound to produce the work promised . . .'. Its object is 'the production . . . of . . . any . . . result to be brought about by . . . performance of service'. Presumably, until the 1999 Credit Transfer Law discussed below, inasmuch as the bank did not undertake to produce the result, namely, it did not guarantee the completion of the funds transfer, its contract was not of 'work' but rather of 'service'. However, with the introduction under the Credit Transfer Law of a limited 'money-back guarantee rule' discussed below, the contract had come to introduce elements of 'work' into what until then had been a pure contract for 'service'.

the taking care of a matter', the contract underlying the credit transfer is also governed by most provisions relating to the mandate (BGB §675).[50] For example, the originator's obligation to provide cover for a payment order to be executed by the originator's bank is provided for by BGB §669, under which '[t]he mandator shall on demand make advances to the mandatary for the expenses necessary for the execution of the mandate'.

A 1999 German statute, passed as an amendment to the BGB (hereafter: 'the German Credit Transfer Law'),[51] provides for specific rules applicable to three types of contracts of which a credit transfer consists. Each such a contract, is treated as a species of the mandate, to which the general rules of mandate, insofar as they are not inconsistent, apply. The first is the credit transfer contract between the originator and the originator's bank, governed by BGB §§676a–676c. The second is the payment contract between the originator's and an intermediary bank, governed by BGB §§676d–676e. The third is the giro contract, governed by BGB §§676f–676g, applicable to the account, from and to which payments are directed, between a customer, whether the originator or the beneficiary, and a bank. Disclosure requirements are fastened on banks by BGB §675a.

The credit transfer contract is stated to obligate the originator's bank to transfer a sum of money to the beneficiary.[52] The credit transfer chapter provides for the time of execution, the revocability of the payment order, the originator's right to a refund for a transfer that has not been executed, and for bank's liability for defective performance. Its provisions may be contracted out to the originator's detriment only where the originator is itself a bank, the amount of transfer exceeds 75,000 euro, or when the beneficiary's bank is located outside the European Union and European Market Area.[53] Perhaps other than for revocability, all the chapter provisions introduce innovations into German law.

'Execution' is defined in terms of carrying out the entire transfer, and not merely carrying out the originator's payment order. Depending on the distance between the originator's and beneficiary's banks as well as on the currency of the transfer, the time of execution is stated to extend between one and five working days. That is, for a transfer within the European Union, either in euro or in the currency of the destination

---

[50] Under BGB §662, 'by the acceptance of a mandate the mandatary binds himself *gratuitously* to take care of some matter for the mandator entrusted to him by the latter' (emphasis added). That is, the mandate is a gratuitous undertaking, not for valuable consideration. Therefore, the bank's undertaking cannot be characterized as mandate. Mandate provisions inapplicable to the contract of services are referred to in nn. 55 and 65 below. Note 77, below, refers to a mandate provision applicable to the contract of service.

[51] Credit Transfer Law, Überwiesungsgesetz vom 21.7.1999, BGBl. I 1999, s. 1624ff. In writing this section of the book, I used an unofficial translation of the statute.

[52] BGB §676a(1) (under Credit Transfer Law).

[53] BGB §676c(3) (under Credit Transfer Law).

country, the time of execution is five days. For a transfer in domestic currency within Germany the execution time is three days, and for an in-house transfer in domestic currency the execution time is either one day, if within the same office, or two days for an inter-office in-house transfer. Regardless, and in the absence of an agreement to the contrary, the time of execution commences at the end of the day during which the originator's bank has both cover and all necessary beneficiary information necessary to carry out the transfer.[54]

[2]   Prior to the Credit Transfer Law in Germany, both the irrevocability of credit transfer[55] and the discharge of the originator's debt to the beneficiary paid by means of the credit transfer had been marked by the crediting of the beneficiary's account by the beneficiary's bank.[56] As against the originator's bank, revocation was available to the originator as long as the originator's bank had not acted on the payment order. But even if the originator's bank had acted on the payment order, it was obliged to transmit the revocation order onward. Ultimately, the revocation was effective if it reached the beneficiary's bank prior to the latter crediting the beneficiary's account.

This framework has essentially remained intact and fully effective under the Credit Transfer Law. The Law recognizes that usually an originator's bank is not free to unilaterally decline to follow payment instructions for no good reason, such as the unavailability of cover. It further acknowledges that a payment order may be made irrevocable under a funds transfer system rule.[57] Otherwise, an originator is entitled to 'terminate the transfer contract' prior to its completion.[58]

A major innovation of the Credit Transfer Law is the introduction to German law of a limited 'money-back guarantee rule', entitling an originator to obtain at least a partial refund when the transfer has not been completed, for any reason, regardless of the lack of fault by any bank in the chain. Accordingly, the originator is entitled to compensation for interest losses for any delay caused neither by the originator nor the beneficiary. Further, the originator is entitled to a refund of the entire amount

---

[54] BGB §676a(2) (under Credit Transfer Law).

[55] Note that also BGB §671, providing for the revocation (by the mandator) and termination (by the mandatary), is not enumerated in BGB §675 among the mandate provisions applicable to the contract of service (and hence to the credit transfer). See text around n. 50, above.

[56] Under BGB §788, debt paid by order is discharged only upon payment by the drawee to the payee and not previously, upon the earlier acceptance by the drawee of the drawer's order. However, under BGB §790, either acceptance or payment by the drawee marks the irrevocability of the drawer's order. Both provisions do not apply to the originator's payment order initiating the credit transfer. See text around n. 47, above.

[57] BGB §676a(3) (under Credit Transfer Law).

[58] BGB §676a(4), as well as §676d(2) (under Credit Transfer Law).

of a debit wrongfully posted to the originator's account, namely, without the originator's authority, and in breach of contract. At the same time, for a transfer the originator authorized but that has not been completed, notwithstanding the complete and correct beneficiary information provided by the originator, the guaranteed amount to be refunded on no fault basis is 12,500 euro, plus expenses and fees.[59]

Major changes were introduced by the Credit Transfer Law in some **[3]** areas of liability based on fault, which is in addition to the limited strict liability described above. Under general law, as a debtor to the originator for the performance of the payment order,[60] the originator's bank 'is responsible for the fault of his legal representative and of persons he employs in performing his obligation' (BGB §278).[61] Vicarious liability by a bank performing its obligations for 'any negligence on the part of its staff and of those persons whom it may call in for the performance of its obligations' is also recognized in Article 3(1) of the current (2000) General Business Conditions (GBC).[62] Until the Credit Transfer Law, the general view, notwithstanding a high authority to the contrary, was that an intermediary bank was not such a person employed in, or called in for, the performance of obligations of the originator's bank, so as to charge the latter with responsibility to its default.[63]

Furthermore, under GBC Article 3(2) where the order given by a customer requires a bank to entrust 'a third party with its further execution' the bank performs the order 'by passing it on to the third party in its own name,' in which case the bank's liability 'shall be limited to the careful selection of the third party'. Indeed, the originator's payment order is not explicit in requiring the originator's bank to entrust 'a third party with . . . further execution'. Nonetheless, such requirement may be implicit in any payment order initiating other than an in-house transfer.[64] The better view was thus that the position of a sending bank issuing a payment order to a

[59] BGB §676b (under Credit Transfer Law).

[60] Under the BGB, 'debtor' and 'creditor' are parties to any obligation and not merely to a monetary debt (Cf. §241).

[61] In assessing the bank's liability the customer's own contributory negligence will be taken into account. See BGB §254.

[62] GBC art. 3(1) further recognizes the effect of the customer's contributory negligence. It thus echoes the scheme of the BGB outlined above. Under art. 25 of the pre-1986 version of the GBC, bank's liability was limited to gross negligence.

[63] For this point, see Huber above, n. 46 at 55–8, who nonetheless supports the minority view to the contrary.

[64] The alternative is to treat the originator's payment order not as instructing the originator's bank to entrust other bank(s) with further execution, but rather as instructing it to carry out the entire transfer, employing whoever necessary, including other bank(s). Cf. Huber, above, n. 46 at 57, discussing the issue under Article 9 of the pre-1986 version of the GBC, that stated that '[t]he bank may charge in its own name third parties with the execution in full or in part of any transactions entrusted to it if it deems this expedient, also considering the interest of the customer'.

receiving bank, in performance of the order given by the sending bank's customer, was governed by this provision. Otherwise said, the originator's bank has not been regarded to be responsible for the default of any successive bank in the chain, except for the default of an intermediary bank not carefully selected by it.[65]

The Credit Transfer Law specifically departed from this framework, and effectively demoted the intermediary bank to that of an employee/assistant of the originator's bank, for whose default the originator's bank is answerable. In principle, the originator's bank is responsible to the originator for consequential losses caused by the fault of an intermediary bank, other than one selected by the originator. The originator's bank may however contractually limit its liability up to 25,000 euro for the default of a cross-border intermediary bank, and up to 12,500 euro otherwise. However, such limitations are inapplicable 'to wilful default and gross negligence, to interest damages and to risks which the [bank] particularly took over'.[66] An intermediary bank selected by the originator, for whose default the originator's bank is not responsible, is liable directly to the originator.[67]

[4]   Loss and delay at the beneficiary's bank is the beneficiary's responsibility. That is, being employed by the beneficiary, the beneficiary's bank is authorized to receive payment on the beneficiary's behalf, and its default is within the beneficiary's scope of risk. Loss incurred by the insolvency of the beneficiary's bank is thus allocated to the beneficiary. In that regard, some specifics are now provided by the Credit Transfer Law. Thus, the beneficiary's bank is usually required to credit the beneficiary's account on the banking day after the beneficiary's bank received payment, and unless the beneficiary is responsible for the delay, the beneficiary's bank is liable to the beneficiary for interest losses.[68] Under the Credit Transfer Law, the beneficiary's bank is further responsible to the beneficiary for loss caused by an intermediary bank selected by the beneficiary's bank. Upon the default of such an intermediary bank, and

---

[65] In fact this is consistent with BGB §664 (which was incorporated into article 9 of the pre-1986 version of the GBC, ibid.) under which a mandatary who was permitted to transfer the execution of the mandate to a third party is responsible 'only for fault imputable to him in making [the] transfer' as well as for the fault of an assistant under §278. BGB §664 is not enumerated in §675 among the mandate provisions applicable to the contract of service (and hence to the credit transfer). See text at n. 50, above.

[66] BGB §676c(1) (under Credit Transfer Law). In general, the recourse of the originator's bank from the intermediary bank is provided for in §676e, but difficulties persist. The question is discussed, so I am advised, by Uwe H. Schneider, 'Pflichten und Haftung der erstbeauftragten Kreditinstitute bei grenzüberschreitenden Überweisungen', *Wertpapier-Mitteilungen 1999*, pp. 2189–98 [in German]. The problem is that the correspondent/intermediary bank may not be liable under the contract with the originator's bank.

[67] BGB §676c (2) (under Credit Transfer Law).

[68] BGB §676g (1) (under Credit Transfer Law).

irrespective of fault, the beneficiary's bank is required to credit the beneficiary's account in the amount of the transfer, but only up to 12,500 euro.[69] The beneficiary's bank is also responsible to the beneficiary for consequential loss caused to the beneficiary by fault. Such liability may be limited by contract to 25,000 euro for cross-border transfers, and to 12,500 euro otherwise, other than 'to wilful default and gross negligence, to interest damage and risks, which the [bank] particularly took over'.[70] As in connection with the credit transfer contract discussed above, these provisions may be contracted out to the beneficiary's detriment only where the beneficiary is itself a bank, the amount of transfer exceeds 75,000 euro, or when the beneficiary's bank is located outside the European Union and European Market Area.[71]

Otherwise, the risk of loss is borne by the originator. That is, vis-à-vis [5] the beneficiary, the originator is responsible for loss caused by the insolvency of the originator's or an intermediary bank. With respect to the allocation of the risk of delay between the originator and the beneficiary, the question is much more complex. In connection with each risk, there is the further question as to whether the risk can be passed on to a bank.

The initial allocation of the risk of delay between the originator and the [6] beneficiary requires an examination of the scope of the obligation to pay under German law.

The general rule under the German civil code is that in the absence of special circumstances or agreement, an obligation is to be performed by the debtor at the debtor's residence or place of business (BGB §269). This holds true also for the performance of a monetary obligator, even though 'in case of doubt' money must be remitted by the debtor 'at his own risk and expense' to the creditor's residence or place of business (BGB §270).

Accordingly, a debtor may perform a monetary obligation by *sending* the money, though at the debtor's risk and expense; the debtor is not required to *deliver* or *bring* the money to the creditor.[72] A debtor may thus timely perform the monetary obligation by placing in the mail, by payment due date, a stamped envelope addressed to the creditor and containing cash. This will suffice as an act of complying performance, even though the obligation will not be discharged until the arrival of the money to the creditor. However, while the risk of loss of the money in transit is thus incurred by the debtor, the risk of delay is borne by the

---

[69] BGB §676g (3) (under Credit Transfer Law).

[70] BGB §676g (4) (under Credit Transfer Law).

[71] BGB §676g(5) (under Credit Transfer Law), specifically refers to BGB §676c(3) (under Credit Transfer Law).

[72] The payment obligation is said to be *Schickschulden*, that of 'sending', rather than *Bringschulden*, that of 'bringing'. An obligation to be performed entirely at the debtor's residence or place of business is *Holdschulden*.

creditor. Stated otherwise, where the money has not arrived to the creditor, the debtor is required to make a second payment. At the same time, all losses associated with delay, whether interest, exchange, or others, are allocated to the creditor.

There is some controversy as to the application of this scheme to payment by credit transfer. According to one view, the discharging dispatch of the money by the originator occurs where the originator's bank debits the originator's account. Others think that only the subsequent transmittal of the payment order by the originator's bank is the equivalent of the dispatch of cash by the debtor. Yet others go further and opine that only the receipt of funds by the beneficiary's bank, or according to another view, the crediting of the funds to the beneficiary's account, would qualify as the required act of performance by the debtor.

Nonetheless, under the prevailing view, the complying performance by the debtor takes place earlier than all these events. It occurs upon the initial issue of the payment order by the originator to the originator's bank. This is so, provided the originator's bank is obligated to carry out the order, by virtue of cover or credit available to the originator. Stated otherwise, the issue of a payment order to an originator's bank holding funds for the originator is the equivalent of sending cash in the mail.

It follows that a debtor who issues a covered payment order by payment due date fulfils his obligation in a timely manner. The risk of delay is borne by the beneficiary. No participating bank is a 'legal representative' of, or a person employed by, the originator, for whose fault the debtor is responsible under BGB §278.

[7]   As indicated, the risk of loss other than at the beneficiary's bank is allocated to the originator. If the funds do not reach the beneficiary's bank within a reasonable time, the debtor must issue a new payment order, or otherwise send payment to the creditor. The originator thus bears the risk of insolvency by the originator's as well as an intermediary bank, though subject to a limited 'money-back guarantee' by the originator's bank, and potentially more extensive liability by the originator's bank for loss caused by the fault of either the originator's or intermediary bank. At the same time, under no circumstances does the originator bear the risk of loss caused by the beneficiary's bank.

[8]   Damages incurred by the beneficiary due to the fault of any receiving bank may be recovered by the beneficiary from the defaulting bank. With respect to injury caused by the originator's or an intermediary bank this is so, irrespective of lack of privity of contract between the beneficiary and the defaulting bank. Indeed, inasmuch as it does not confer upon the beneficiary an independent *right* to demand performance, the payment order issued to the originator's bank is not a contract for the benefit of a third party, within the meaning of BGB §328. It is however a contract for the

benefit of a third party in a different sense. According to Huber,[73] the agreement between the originator and the originator's bank, and in fact, between each successive sender and receiving bank, may be viewed as providing for 'protective *duties*'. It thus requires the receiving bank to carry out the sender's payment order in the beneficiary's interest. Viewed as a contract with protective effect on the beneficiary, each successive payment order imposes duties whose breach giving rise to damages may be actionable by the beneficiary from the defaulting breaching bank.

Nonetheless, there are situations where under German law a debtor is **[9]** required to perform a monetary obligation by delivering the money to the creditor and not only merely by sending it.[74] For example, the debtor–creditor agreement may specifically require the arrival of funds to the creditor's account by a designated date.[75] Otherwise, performance by delivery of the money (and not by merely sending it) may sometime be required by law. For example, under the United Nations Convention on Contracts for the International Sale of Goods,[76] the buyer must pay the purchase price 'at the seller's place of business' (Art. 57(1)(a)).

In such cases, the originator's responsibility extends up to the receipt of funds by the beneficiary's bank. Stated otherwise, the originator is responsible also to delays caused by the originator's and intermediary banks. Where the delay was caused by the fault of the originator's bank, the originator may sue it for breach of contract. The originator may sue a defaulting intermediary bank as a 'protected party' under the contract between this bank and its own sender. Also the beneficiary may sue the defaulting originator's or intermediary bank on the same basis; this right is, of course, in addition to the beneficiary's right against the originator. The originator may have an alternative route to recover from the defaulting intermediary bank under the legal theory of 'recovery of third party damages'. Such recovery is based on the assignment to the originator of the claim of the originator's bank against the defaulting intermediary (with which it is in privity) to the damages suffered by the originator. This right is available to the originator on the basis of BGB §667 providing for the mandatary, namely the originator's bank, 'to hand over to his [principal] all that he receives for the execution of the mandate and all that he

---

[73] In Huber, above, n. 46 at 65.   [74] As discussed in text around n. 72, above.

[75] This is quite common in charter party contracts. It is important to note that a mere designation of the bank account in the debtor–creditor contract, side by side with an indication of a payment date, will not amount to such a contract requiring the arrival of funds to the account by payment date.

[76] Annex I of the Final Act of the UN Conference on Contracts for the International Sale of Goods, 1980 (A/CONF.97/19). Official Records 178–90 (New York: United Nations, 1981) (Sales No. E.82. V.5). For its application under German law, see Huber, above, n. 46 at 32 and n. 63 *et seq.*

obtains from the charge of the matter'.[77] Yet, as indicated, there are difficulties with the availability of an assignable action to the originator's
bank against the intermediary bank. Regardless, from the originator's
point of view, this is unlikely to be crucial, at least in usual circumstances,
since, as indicated, in departure from prior law, the Credit Transfer Law
accords the originator a direct action either against the originator's bank
for the default of the intermediary bank or against an intermediary bank
selected by the originator.

[10]   The extent of the liability of the originator's bank to the originator is
indirectly provided for by GBC art. 11(3). Thereunder, the customer is
required to advise the bank wherever 'the customer feels that an order
requires particularly prompt execution' as for example where 'a money
transfer must be credited to the payee's account by a certain date'.[78] Presumably, in the absence of such specific advice, the damages recovered
from the originator's bank will be reduced. Under the pre-1986 version of
the GBC where the customer did not notify the bank of specific circumstances, where the bank had not been grossly negligent, or where the
order related to the customer's trade, liability of the originator's bank was
limited to interest losses.[79] Otherwise, liability was not thus limited.

The scope of the intermediary bank's own liability to the originator
may depend on the contents of the intermediary bank's own contract with
the originator's bank. Where specific advice was actually given by the
originator to the originator's bank as to the former's prompt execution
requirement, the scope of the intermediary bank's liability to the originator may further depend on the intermediary bank's knowledge of this
advice.[80]

---

[77] For the application of this provision to the credit transfers under BGB §675 see text
around n. 65, above.

[78] Article 7 of the pre- 1986 version of the GBC provided as follows: 'The customer shall
notify the bank in each particular case—for *orders* given on a printed form this must be done
separately from the form—that payments are *subject to time limits* and that *delay* or *misdirection* of an order or of an advice thereof might cause a loss exceeding the loss of interest. If
no such advice has been given, the bank shall only be liable for any loss exceeding loss of
interest if it has been grossly negligent; however, the liability shall be limited to loss of interest if the order relates to the customer's trade'. Emphasis in the original.

[79] The advice must be communicated by the customer to the bank 'separately'. For example, '[f]or orders given on a printed form, [advice] must be [given] separately from the
form'. Ibid.

[80] See text around nn. 77 and 78, above.

(III) FRANCE[81]

There is a universal consensus in France that pursuant to Article 1984 of [1]
the French civil code (FCC) the originator's payment order initiating the
credit transfer is a mandate, namely 'an act whereby one person [the orig-
inator] gives to another [the originator's bank] the power to do something
for the principal in his name'.[82] In turn, being regarded as the transfer of
a credit balance from one account to another, the credit transfer itself was
treated in the past as either a transfer of a right or a delegation of a duty.[83]

The transfer theory regarded the credit transfer as the transfer to the [2]
beneficiary of the originator's right against the bank[84] to the credit balance
in the account. However, under FCC art. 1690, the completion of a transfer requires either notice by the transferee to the debtor, or acceptance of
the transfer in the form of a certified instrument ('un acte authentique')
made by the debtor. Such formalities are not observed in the case of the
credit transfer, where the bank as the debtor neither certifies its acceptance, nor is notified by the beneficiary as the transferee. Furthermore,
adherence to the transfer theory would mean that the bank, as a debtor,

---

[81] The ensuing discussion draws heavily on M. Cabrillac and J. L. Rives-Lange, *Encycl.
Dalloz*, Rep. de Cour v. Virement; J. L. Rives-Lange and M. Contamine-Raynaud, *Droit ban-
caire*, 6th edn. (Paris: Dalloz, 1995); G. Ripert and R. Roblot, *Traité de droit commercial*, 13th
edn., vol. ii (Paris: Librairie Générale de Droit et de Jurisprudence, 1992); J. Hamel, G.
Lagarde, and A. Jauffret, *Traité de droit commercial*, vol. ii (Paris: Librairie Dalloz, 1966); A.
Jauffret, *Droit commercial*, 20th edn. by J. Mestre (Paris: Librairie Générale de Droit et de
Jurisprudence, 1991); C. Gavalda and J. Stoufflet, *Droit bancaire*, 4th edn. (Paris: Litec, 1999);
Jura Europae—Droit bancaire et boursier (Munich: Verlay C. H. Beck; Paris: Éditions Tech-
niques Juris-Classeurs, 1976), §30.31 (by C. Gavalda et J. Stoufflet); M. Vasseur, 'Law and
Practice of Foreign Funds Transfers in France', in W. Hadding and U. H. Schneider (eds.),
Legal Issues in International Credit Transfers (Berlin: Duncker & Humblot, 1993), 237; and D.
Martin, 'Aspects juridiques du virement', 1989 Rev. de droit bancaire 149. For comparative
perspectives see M. Vasseur, 'Les Principaux Articles de la loi-type de la CNUDCI sur les
virements internationaux et leur influence sur les travaux de la Commission de Bruxelles
concernant les paiements transfrontaliers', 1993 R.D.A.I./I.B.L.J. 155; and B. Geva and M.
Lacoursière, 'Les Virements bancaires sous la loi-type et le droit français—étude comparative', 2 *Mélanges Christian Mouly* 362 (Paris: Litec, 1998).

[82] The provision further states that '[t]he contract is formed only through acceptance by
the [mandatary].' For the present discussion I used *Code civil* (Paris: Litec, 1992–3), with
comments. However, all quotes are from the English translation by J. H. Crabb, *The French
Civil Code* (South Hackensack, NJ: Fred B. Rothman & Co., 1977), except that where I had
reservations as to chosen words, I replaced them with my own, inserted in sequare brackets. Most notably, I replaced 'agency' and 'agent' (respectively denoting 'mandat' and 'man-
dataire') by 'mandate' and 'mandatary'. For rationale, see above, 2.C.

[83] Or in the original French, 'le transport d'une créance' (or 'la cession'), and 'la délégation', respectively. In English, it is appropriate to speak of 'assignment of right' as well as of
'assignment of duty'. Accordingly, the translation of the French 'délégation' to 'assignment'
in English, by Crabb and others, is unfortunate. It is preferable to speak of 'delegation' in
English as well.

[84] As will be indicated in s. 4, below, the theory had superficial appeal primarily in the context of an 'in-house' transfer where one bank acts for both the originator and the beneficiary.

would be able to invoke against the beneficiary, as the transferee, all defences the bank has against the originator, as the original creditor. For these two reasons, the transfer theory has been abandoned.

[3]   Alternatively, the credit transfer was regarded as the delegation by the originator to the bank[85] of the duty to pay the debt owed by the originator to the beneficiary. Such delegation is followed by the bank's assumption of the originator's debt to the beneficiary and is perfected by the beneficiary's acceptance of the bank as a debtor substituting the originator. Delegation is governed by FCC art. 1275. Thereunder, a delegation occurs where 'a debtor gives to the creditor another debtor who obligates himself to the creditor'. It operates as a novation wherever 'the creditor has . . . expressly declared that he intended to discharge the [delegating] debtor'. That is, novation or 'perfect delegation', requires the express acceptance by the creditor of the assumption of debt by the new delegated debtor in discharge of the delegating debtor's debt to the creditor. The effect of the perfect delegation is to substitute the new delegated debtor for the old delegating debtor. Stated otherwise, the perfect delegation operates as novation by discharging the original delegating debtor towards the creditor who has recourse solely against the delegated new debtor.[86]

According, as applied to a credit transfer, a delegation takes place where the originator as debtor gives to the beneficiary as creditor, the bank as another (substituting) debtor, who obligates itself to the creditor. A novation replacing the debtor-creditor's debt by bank-creditor's debt occurs upon the express declaration of the beneficiary as creditor.

According to jurisprudence, upon delegation, the delegated debtor may not raise against the creditor defences available to the former against the delegator. As applied to the credit transfer, this means that the beneficiary is entitled to recover from the bank irrespective of defences available to the bank against the originator. This bypasses the second problem associated with the previously discussed transfer theory. However, several objections have been raised against the application of the delegation theory to the credit transfer so as to lead to its rejection as well:

(1) Delegation does not explain the transfer of funds other than between a debtor and creditor. However, a transfer of funds could take place between two accounts belonging to the same person, or even between the accounts of two persons, other than in the discharge of a debt (e.g. by way of gift).

---

[85] As will be indicated in s. 4, below, the theory had superficial appeal primarily in the context of an 'in-house' transfer where one bank acts for both the originator and the beneficiary.

[86] Under FCC art. 1271(2), one of the three ways in which novation operates is '[w]hen a new debtor is substituted for the old, who is discharged by the creditor'.

(2) In connection with the funds transfer between a debtor and creditor, the delegation theory does not explain well the discharge of the originator. As indicated, art. 1275 requires the *express* declaration by the beneficiary-creditor of the assumption of debt by the bank in discharge of the originator-debtor. Indeed, this objection is often met by interpreting 'expressly' in art. 1275 merely to mean 'in an unequivocal manner' so as to cover any implicit unequivocal acceptance by the beneficiary. However, this explanation overlooks the automatic discharge produced by the completion of the credit transfer, independent of any discharge given explicitly or implicitly by the beneficiary-creditor.

(3) The delegation theory does not explain the transformation of the original ordinary debt owed by the originator-debtor to the beneficiary-creditor into a debt by the bank to the beneficiary which becomes part of the bank account or deposit and governed by all special rules applicable to it.

(4) According to recent jurisprudence the credit transfer has been premissed on the effectiveness of the debit and credit posted to bank accounts and not on the exchange of consents as directed by the delegation analysis.

Finally, both the transfer and delegation theory do not work well other [4] than in an 'in-house' transfer. Thus, it is the originator's bank which serves as the debtor under the transfer theory and as the instructed or delegated party under the delegation theory. At the same time, it is the beneficiary's bank which ultimately becomes indebted to the beneficiary. Indeed, in attempting to establish the beneficiary's right towards the beneficiary's bank solely on the basis of the originator's payment order given to the originator's bank, both theories are undermined where the beneficiary's bank is not the originator's bank.

In the final analysis, the credit transfer is now universally viewed in [5] France as the transfer of 'bank credit money' or 'deposit or cashless money' ('monnai scripturale') which is not amenable to any categorization under the civil code. It is a 'double account transaction' under which credit to one account (that of the originator) extinguishes and is replaced by credit to another account (that of the beneficiary). The legal relationship underlying the latter credit is unaffected by defences based on the legal relationship underlying the former credit. The beneficiary's claim against the beneficiary's bank is further unaffected by defences the beneficiary's bank may have against its sender so that credit to the beneficiary's account is final and irreversible. The credit transfer is thus an abstract transaction, like the delivery of cash. In this respect, the jurisprudential reality is said to surrender to the economic perspective that has always regarded money deposited at a bank, namely credit at a bank account or 'bank credit', as 'money'.

(a) Discharge and irrevocability

[6]   In French banking practice, the originator usually submits his payment order directly to the originator's bank. However, the originator may deliver a payment order to the beneficiary. Some forms of payment orders may even circulate.[87] Ultimately, each payment order is issued by its submission to the originator's bank, whether by the originator or by the ultimate beneficiary acting on behalf of the originator.

By itself, the issue of the originator's payment order does not affect the underlying transaction between the originator and the beneficiary. Being a mandate given to the originator's bank, the issue of the originator's payment order does not confer upon the beneficiary any right to the funds in the originator's account. In French law, the payment order is dissimilar to the cheque, whose issue transfers the funds to the beneficiary.[88] Consequently, in the case of a simultaneous presentment of a cheque and payment order made out by the originator, the originator's bank is required to honour the cheque first.

Where it is paid by credit transfer, the originator's debt to the beneficiary is discharged only when the amount of the credit transfer is ultimately credited to the beneficiary's account. However, posting credit to the beneficiary's account does not have a definitive effect of payment except where it is accepted as payment by the beneficiary. Usually such acceptance cannot conclusively be inferred until after advice of credit has been given to the beneficiary. In any event, the time and place of payment are determined by the posting of credit to the beneficiary's account, at which point the credit transfer is completed. Acceptance by the beneficiary serves as a mere ratification of the general mandate conferred upon the beneficiary's bank to collect payment for the beneficiary.

[7]   Like any other mandate, the originator's payment order is revocable. The prevailing view appears to be that the originator's power to revoke the payment order (as well as the seizability of the amount transferred by the originator's creditors) is lost as early as when the originator's bank debits the originator's account. At this point, the beneficiary is said to

---

[87] According to Hamel, Lagarde, and Jauffret, above, n. 81, §1741 payment orders in negotiable form are rare. The most common form in circulation is that of 'le mandat rouge' on an account at the Banque de France which circulates (like an instrument payable to bearer) with the beneficiary's name blank. The name is filled in only by the person who wishes to submit it for payment (who must have an account at the same branch of the Banque de France as the originator).   [88] See 3.B(vi) s. 9, text at n. 254.

acquire rights with respect to the funds, even prior to their arrival at his disposal.

Nonetheless, this principle is seriously compromised whenever an intermediary bank is involved. In such a case revocability (as well as seizability by the originator's creditors) is lost only upon payment by the last intermediary bank to the beneficiary's bank. In turn, the explanation to this exception appears to undermine the entire principle.

Thus, this exception is rationalized on the intermediary bank's status as a substituted mandatary for the originator.[89] However, if revocability is linked to the mandatary status of the funds holder, debit to the originator's account should have marked irrevocability only in an in-house transfer and not in a correspondent account transfer between the originator's and beneficiary's banks. Indeed, this objection is met by the assertion that in a correspondent account transfer debit to the originator's account by the originator's bank is anyway immediately followed by credit to the account of the beneficiary's bank at the originator's bank.[90] Nonetheless, this response effectively concedes that revocability is marked by payment to the beneficiary's bank,[91] the latter, and not the debit to the originator's account, being the crucial event.

In the final analysis, both milestones, namely debit to the originator's account and payment to the beneficiary's bank, even where they coincide in an in-house and correspondent account transfers, are conceptually different. Between these two milestones only payment to the beneficiary's bank serves as a common denominator marking irrevocability for all types of credit transfers.[92] However, several leading authors refer to the debit to the originator's account as the milestone marking irrevocability, without adding any explanation or qualification.[93] The resulting ambiguity is rather unfortunate.

(b) Duties and chain of liability

As a mandatary, the originator's bank 'is required to accomplish [the mandate] as long as [it] remains responsible, and responds in damages **[8]**

---

[89] See s. 8, below.

[90] See e.g. Cabrillac and Rives-Lange, *Encycl. Dalloz*, above, n. 81, t92.

[91] In fact, the above-mentioned explanation overlooks the fact that even in a correspondent account transfer payment to the beneficiary's bank can be carried out otherwise than by a credit to the account of the beneficiary's bank at the originator's bank, e.g. by means of a debit to the account of the originator's bank at the beneficiary's bank or through a clearing house settlement.

[92] Cf. Gavalda and Stoufflet, *Droit bancaire*, above, n. 81, §§240, 241, and 243 (pp. 117–19), vacillating between payment to the beneficiary's bank and credit to the beneficiary.

[93] See e.g. Rives-Lange and Contamine-Raynaud, *Droit bancaire*, above, n. 81, s. 296, and Vasseur in Hadding and Schneider, above, n. 81 at 251 and 253.

which may result from its inexecution' (FCC art. 1991). It answers 'not only for [intentional wrongful acts][94], but also for faults which [it] commits in [its] management' (art. 1992), and 'is required to render accounting of [its] management' (art. 1993).

In turn, vis-à-vis the originator-principal, and irrespective of the success or failure of the task undertaken, provided it acted without fault, the originator's bank-mandatary is entitled to be reimbursed 'for advances and expenses . . . made for the execution of the [mandate]' and to be paid promised wages (art. 1999). It is also entitled to be indemnified 'for losses . . . sustained during the course of [its] management without negligence imputable to [it]' (art. 2000).

Where more than one bank is involved in carrying out the credit transfer the chain of liability becomes more complex. French law characterizes the originator's payment order as a mandate given to a bank, which may be substituted by other banks, which are, legally speaking, substituted mandataries. The general rule under FCC art. 1994 is that a mandatary is not answerable for a substituted mandatary, except for where substitution was unauthorized or where '[substitution] was conferred on him without designation of a person, and the one of whom he made choice was notoriously incapable or insolvent'. Nonetheless, '[i]n all cases the principal may act directly against the person whom the [mandatary] substituted for himself.'

Other than in an in-house transfer, the power of substitution by the originator's bank is essential for the completion of the credit transfer. Accordingly, in a credit transfer, an originator's bank which is not also the beneficiary's bank ought to be regarded as given the authority to substitute other banks for itself. Consequently, under FCC art. 1994, the originator's bank is responsible only for acts of an intermediary bank it selected where the selected intermediary bank 'was notoriously incapable or insolvent'. In any event, each bank subsequent in the chain to the originator's bank is answerable to the originator directly as a substituted mandatary.

Nonetheless, there is nothing in legal doctrine which precludes a principal from charging his primary (namely, original) mandatary with the duty to supervise substituted mandataries. This can be done by the principal implicitly. According to one view, the originator's payment order typically includes such an implied stipulation. Its effect is to charge the originator's bank, as the primary mandatary, with vicarious liability, inuring to the benefit of the originator-principal, for any wrongdoing of any subsequent bank in the chain acting as substituted mandatary. This vicar-

---

[94] Or 'dol' in the original French, which is translated by Crabb, above, n. 82, less accurately in my view, as 'deceit'.

ious liability of the originator's bank is without prejudice to the direct liability to the originator-principal, of any such a subsequent bank acting as substituted mandatary, under FCC art. 1994.[95]

(c) Risk allocation: delay and loss

In executing a payment order, a receiving bank must act promptly. Case law provides some guidance in determining the speed at which a receiving bank is required to act. For example, while a delay of three days was held to be acceptable, delays of more than a week and of twenty-four days were held to be excessive.[96] **[9]**

As between the originator and the beneficiary the risk of delay or loss occurring at a bank other than that of the beneficiary falls on the originator. Indeed, in the case of delay, there is some case law to the contrary, under which a payment due date requirement prescribed by law may be met by an originator's payment order issued prior to that date.[97] Nonetheless, this jurisprudence has not led to the view that any payment deadline requirement can be met by the issue of the originator's payment order prior to that deadline.[98] **[10]**

Upon the occurrence of delay or loss at a bank other than that of the beneficiary, the originator may sue directly the defaulting bank, the latter being either his primary mandatary, in the case of the originator's bank, or his substituted mandatary in any other case. The originator may further recover from the originator's bank, damages caused by the default of any notoriously incapable or insolvent intermediary bank selected by the originator's bank. According to one view, the originator may also sue the originator's bank for damages caused by the default of any subsequent bank not properly supervised by it.[99] However, there is no 'money-back guarantee rule' charging the originator's bank with liability under any other circumstances, that is, without some fault on its part.

As a mandatary, any sending bank is liable 'in damages which may result from its inexecution' (FCC art. 1991). The general rule under the French civil code is that 'inexecution' includes 'delay in fulfilling [the] obligation' (art. 1146). In general, 'damages are to include, with regard to the loss incurred by the creditor and the gain of which he has deprived, only what is an immediate and direct consequence of the inexecution of **[11]**

---

[95] For this view, see e.g. *Encycl. Dalloz*, above, n. 81, t77–8.

[96] For cites, see Vasseur in Hadding and Schneider, above, n. 81 at 253, and *Encycl. Dalloz*, above, n. 81, t§63–4.

[97] For cites concerning datelines for tax and social security debts, see Vasseur in R.D.A.I./I.B.L.J., above, n. 81 at 191–2.

[98] Cf. *Encycl. Dalloz*, above, n. 81, §47; the issue of the payment order does not affect the debt paid by it.   [99] See s. 8, above.

the agreement' (art. 1151). For a breach committed unwillingly, a debtor is limited 'only to damages which were foreseen or which could have been foreseen at the time of the contract' (art. 1150).

It follows that an originator is entitled to recover damages only to the extent that they constitute 'an immediate and direct consequence of the inexecution'. Except in connection with wilful breach, damages must have been either foreseen or foreseeable. Nevertheless, case law allowed the recovery of consequential damages, such as for loss of an option, even where the bank had not been advised of special circumstances, namely where damages were unforeseeable. This measure of damages was criticized as 'too high and legally unfounded'.[100]

[12]   The allocation of the risk of delay and loss incurred at the beneficiary's bank requires a close examination of that bank status. On one hand, the beneficiary's bank is considered a mandatary for the beneficiary for the purpose of receiving payments on the beneficiary's behalf, or at least as 'one [who] voluntarily manages the affairs of the [beneficiary]' so as to be 'subject to all the obligations which would have resulted had the [beneficiary] given [it] an express [mandate]' (FCC art. 1372). As such, the beneficiary's claim against the beneficiary's bank is based on the latter's duty as mandatary to accomplish the mandate, to respond in damages arising from inexecution, and to render accounting, as provided in FCC articles 1991–3. The beneficiary's bank thus appears to act within the sphere of action of the beneficiary.

Furthermore, the beneficiary's bank is selected by the beneficiary and it is only fair that the risk, delay, or loss incurred at the beneficiary's bank would be allocated to the beneficiary and not to the originator.

Nonetheless, this may not convey the whole picture. In carrying out the originator's instructions to credit the beneficiary's account, the beneficiary's bank is regarded as acting also for the originator. More specifically, it is also a substituted mandatary, liable directly to the originator under FCC art. 1994. Indeed, inasmuch as the beneficiary's bank is not designated by the originator's bank, that provision does not render the originator's bank liable to the originator for the default by the beneficiary's bank. Nonetheless, the direct liability of the beneficiary's bank to the originator under art. 1994 is not thereby shattered.[101]

Furthermore, as indicated, the credit transfer is not completed and the debt paid by it is not discharged as long as the beneficiary's bank has not credited the beneficiary's account. It is thus tempting to argue that until that point, all risks lie with the originator.

In the final analysis, more weight is put on the fact that the beneficiary's

---

[100] Vasseur in Hadding and Schneider, above, n. 81 at 261.
[101] For the direct liability of the substituted mandatary see s. 8, above.

bank was selected by the beneficiary so as to render him responsible for the default by the beneficiary's bank. Accordingly, while conferring on the originator a cause of action against the beneficiary's bank, French law recognizes that this action can be brought by the originator against the beneficiary, in his capacity as the principal for the beneficiary bank who invited the originator to make payment into an account maintained at that bank.[102]

Also, once paid for the payment order, the beneficiary's bank is regarded as a depositary for the beneficiary who must then bear the risk of the subsequent insolvency of the beneficiary's bank.[103]

(IV) SWITZERLAND[104]

Swiss law distinguishes between the general funds transfer contract [1] (namely the giro agreement, or 'le contrat de giro') and each individual payment order. The funds transfer contract governs the traffic of cashless payments into and out of the customer's account and is separate from, though related to, the account agreement. The payment order is an instruction based on the funds transfer contract, initiating the individual funds transfer ('le virement').

The funds transfer contract is concluded implicitly between the bank [2] and the customer at the time a current account relationship is established. It is a service contract, encompassing both the active and passive sides of the cashless movement of funds, namely outgoing as well as incoming payments from and into the account. While complementing the current account agreement, and viewed by some as merely one element in an overall banking relationship, the funds transfer contract is regarded as conceptually separate and distinct.[105]

Under the Swiss code of obligations (CO),[106] the funds transfer contract is a general mandate for a long duration. Under CO art. 394(1), '[b]y accepting a mandate, the [mandatary] is obligated to carry out the con-

---

[102] See e.g. *Encycl. Dalloz*, above, n. 81, §74.   [103] Ibid. §123.

[104] The ensuing discussion draws heavily on I. Billote-Tongue, *Aspects juridiques du virement bancaire* (Zurich: Schulthless Polygraphischer Verlag, 1992); D. Guggenheim, *Les Contrats de la pratique bancaire suisse*, 2nd edn. (Geneva: Librairie de l'Université-Georg et Cie S.A., 1981; Georg Éditeur S.A., 1989); and J. Bischoff, 'Factual Significance and Legal Regulation of International Funds Transfers in Switzerland', in W. Hadding and V. H. Schneider (eds.), *Legal Issues in International Credit Transfers* (Berlin: Duncker & Humblot, 1993), 319.

[105] Under the Swiss Code of Obligations (CO), each contract requires the 'manifestation of the parties' mutual assent'. This agreement 'may be either express or implied' (CO art. 1). I used *Code des obligations* du 30 mars 1911, État le 1er Janvier 1993, Édité par la chancellerie fédérale, 1993. Quotes are generally from a translation by the Swiss-American Chamber of Commerce, except that where I had reservations as to chosen words I replaced them with my own, inserted in square brackets.   [106] Ibid.

tractually agreed business transactions or services with which he has been entrusted'. Under art. 394(2), '[c]ontracts regarding the performance of work[107] which cannot be classified as a special type of contract under other parts of this Code of Obligations are subject to the mandate law (arts. 394–406)'. Being an umbrella agreement for the entire payment traffic, and for an indefinite period, the funds transfer contract is therefore classified as a 'general' mandate concluded 'for a long duration'.[108]

It is well established in Switzerland that a mandatary undertakes to provide means for achieving a result but does not guarantee the attainment of that result. This is the basic distinction between a mandate and a contract for work and labour ('le contrat d'entreprise') defined in CO art. 363 in terms of an undertaking to produce a result or work. It is recognized that under a funds transfer contract, the bank undertakes to provide services but does not guarantee payment. For example, insolvency by an intermediary bank or account closure by the beneficiary may be events which are outside the control and responsibility of the originator's bank. Accordingly, the funds transfer contract is not classified as a contract for work and labour.

Further, the bank's undertaking on the funds transfer contract is not regarded as generating an obligation for the benefit of the beneficiary so as to constitute a contract for the benefit of a third person under CO art. 112. In fact, the funds transfer contract, as distinguished from each individual payment order, is hardly amenable to such a construction. Furthermore, for a contract for the benefit of a third person to be 'perfect', that is to entitle the third person to claim performance on it, either intention of the contracting parties or custom must be shown. This is unlikely to be possible in the case of a funds transfer. Last but not least, CO art. 112(3) precludes the creditor from releasing the debtor, once the debtor has been notified by the third party of his intention to claim. If applied to a payment order, this would mean that the originator ('creditor') may not release the bank ('debtor') once the beneficiary ('third party') advised the bank ('debtor') of his intention to claim. Effectively, this would deprive the originator of his right to revoke the payment order, contrary to the current understanding of this point.[109]

Finally, the funds transfer contract is not regarded as an assumption of obligations ('une reprise de dette'), dealt with by CO arts. 175–83. Under

---

[107] Or 'travaux' in the original French. 'Work' is used here notwithstanding the fact that 'le contrat d'entreprise' under art. 363 is translated as 'a *work* contract' (emphasis added). The 'work' to be produced under the contract governed by art. 363 is 'ouvrage' in the original French.

[108] Unless it is in connection with a 'one-time transfer' ('un virement unique') not in connection with a pre-existing account relationship, Cf. Billote-Tongue, above, n. 104 at 13 and 37.   [109] Discussed in s. 5, below.

CO art. 175, an assumption of obligation is a promise by a person to a debtor to assume his debt, *inter alia* 'by making himself the obligor of the obligee with the consent of the latter'. On its part, the funds transfer contract, as an overall umbrella agreement, does not require the beneficiary's consent. Nor does the bank substitute itself for the originator in the underlying debt.

As indicated, the payment order is an instruction, based on the funds **[3]** transfer contract, initiating the individual funds transfer.[110] It is not a separate contract,[111] but rather an instruction governed by the terms of the funds transfer contract, designed to carry out its provisions. Not being 'a contract', the payment order is thus not a 'mandate' within the meaning of CO art. 394(1).[112]

Nonetheless, the payment order constitutes a direction or an instruction by the principal to the mandatary for the carrying out of the mandate as set out in CO art. 397(1). Furthermore, where it instructs payment other than to another account of the originator, the payment order also constitutes an 'order' defined in CO art. 466 and governed by arts. 466–71. Under CO art. 466, 'By an order, the recipient of the order is authorized . . . to remit to the payee for the account of the order giver, money[113] . . . and the payee is authorized to collect it in his own name from the recipient of the order.' Given directly to the person to whom it is addressed, by the person giving it, and not through the hands of the person authorized to receive payment, the payment order is classified as a direct order.[114]

The official French text of art. 466 speaks of the 'order' as a contract ('un contrat').[115] Nonetheless, the majority view is that the 'order' governed by CO art. 466 is not 'a contract', at least within the meaning of CO art. 1(1).[116] Rather, following the German and Italian official texts, the order ('l'assignation') under art. 466 is regarded as a double authority given by the order giver ('l'assignant') to the order recipient ('l'assigné') to pay, and to the payee ('l'assignataire') to receive payment.

For the purpose of applying the CO provisions to an in-house transfer, the originator is the order giver, the bank is the order recipient, and the

---

[110] See s. 1, above.

[111] Within the meaning of CO art. 1. See text around n. 105, above.

[112] For the mandate under art. 394(1) as 'contract' see text which follows n. 107, above.

[113] As well as 'securities or other fungible . . . items'. Ibid.

[114] This is contrary to Germany when the civil code does not recognize a direct order. Consequently, the originator's payment order could not be classified in Germany as 'order'. See [Germany] text around n. 46, above.

[115] It reads in full as follows: 'L'assignation est un contrat par lequel l'assigné est autorisé à remettre à l'assignataire, pour le compte de l'assignant, une somme d'argent, des papiers-valeurs ou d'autres choses fongibles, que l'assignataire a mandat de percevoir en son propre nom.' [116] Cf. text around n. 111, above.

beneficiary is the payee. In other types of funds transfers, the application of the CO provisions is not all that straightforward.

According to the dominant theory, in a correspondent transfer, the originator's bank is the order giver, acting as a mandatary of the originator. The beneficiary's bank is the order recipient and the beneficiary is the payee. Nonetheless, this view may not accommodate a complex account transfer involving intermediary bank(s). Furthermore, it does not deal satisfactorily with the originator's payment order.

Another view regards the interbank funds transfer as a series of operations, each initiated by an order. For each order, the sender is the giver, the receiving bank is the recipient, and the subsequent participant, whether the next receiving bank or the beneficiary, is the payee. Nonetheless, this view appears to be inconsistent with the intention of the parties. For example, the originator instructs his bank to make payment to the beneficiary and not to the receiving bank of the originator's bank. That is, so far as the originator's order is concerned, the intended payee is the beneficiary.

According to a third view, the originator's payment order, being an order under CO art. 466, is also a mandate under art. 394(1). This order is addressed to the originator's bank as a recipient and designates the beneficiary as the payee. As a mandatary with a power of substitution, the originator's bank, and each subsequent receiving bank up to the sender to the beneficiary's bank, is then authorized to entrust its receiving bank with performance. That is, for the purposes of CO art. 466 the entire funds transfer is viewed as one operation, initiated by one order, addressed to one recipient with a power of substitution.[117] Nonetheless, this solution is generally rejected, since it regards each payment order as a distinct contract or particular mandate, and not an instruction governed by the funds transfer contract or the general mandate.

Purporting to meet the objections to all these views, Billote-Tongue focused on the intention of each issuer of a payment order and proposed to regard the funds transfer as a series of operations, each initiated by a distinct order, as follows:

> (1) The originator's payment order initiating the funds transfer is an order designating the beneficiary as payee. The order is addressed to the originator's bank, but other than in an in-house transfer, it instructs this bank to transfer some of its tasks as a mandatary to the beneficiary's bank. Upon such a transfer, the beneficiary's bank becomes a substituted mandatary.[118] In the final analysis, the

---

[117] This would be reminiscent of the French view of the transaction. See s. (iii) 8, above.
[118] Or according to one view, the transfer relates to carrying out the order, and not the mandate in relation to the payment order. Under that view, the mandate transfer provisions

originator's payment order must be viewed as designating both the originator's and beneficiary's bank as the recipient, with the beneficiary's bank assuming its role by transfer from the originator's bank.

(2) The payment order issued by the originator's bank is an order addressed to the intermediary bank as recipient and designating the beneficiary's bank as payee.

Billote-Tongue does not expand on the payment order of the intermediary's bank as well as on situations involving more than one intermediary banks. One could speculate, on the basis of Billote-Tongue's own reasoning, that any payment order addressed to the beneficiary's bank designates that bank as the recipient and the beneficiary as payee. At the same time, any payment order issued by a sending bank (other than that of the originator) up to the sender to the beneficiary's bank ought to be an order designating the beneficiary's bank as payee, and both the receiving bank and the sender to the beneficiary's bank as the recipient.

(a) Legal relationships

With respect to the originator and the beneficiary, Swiss law analyses the **[4]** funds transfer as generating the following relationships: (i) the cover relationship ('le rapport de couverture') between the originator and the originator's bank, (ii) the payment relationship ('le rapport de paiement') often also called, somewhat inappropriately,[119] the order relationship ('le rapport d'assignation'), between the beneficiary and the beneficiary's bank, (iii) the basic transaction or value relationship ('le rapport de base ou de valeur') between the originator and the beneficiary, and (iv) the indirect relationship, of either the originator or the beneficiary, vis-à-vis a bank with which that party is not in privity, usually an intermediary bank. These relationships will be explored below, starting from that of the underlying transaction and the ensuing payment. As indicated, the principal sources of law are that governing the mandate and the order under the CO.

(b) Basic transaction and payment: discharge and irrevocability

The effect of the relationship created by an order on the order giver and **[5]** the payee, is governed by CO art. 467 which provides that a debt paid by

would apply to our case only by analogy. This view is outlined, but not adhered to, by Billote-Tongue, above, n. 104 at 46.

[119] This is so since this relationship does not pertain to the giving of an order, but rather, to the carrying out of an order previously given. See Billotte-Tongue, ibid., at 55.

means of an order is discharged upon the actual payment to the payee. This principle is then qualified by the provision in two respects. First, a creditor accepting payment by order may not enforce payment against the debtor as long as the order has not expired. Second, a creditor refusing payment by order is obligated to advise promptly the debtor of his refusal. Overall, the effect of CO art. 467 is to produce the following results in connection with the relationship between the originator (as the order giver) and the beneficiary (as the payee):

(1) A beneficiary who does not agree to be paid by credit transfer must advise the originator of his refusal without delay. However, art. 467(3) speaks of an order received by the creditor from the debtor. It thus appears that the provision may not be applicable to the direct order, given by the order giver directly to the recipient, and not through the payee, which is the subject-matter of our investigation.[120]

(2) The creditor who has accepted the order may not demand payment from the debtor until the expiry of the term stated in the order. This provision appears to be limited to an order designating a term. Furthermore, its language accommodates the indirect order (given by the order giver to the payee so as to be accepted by him) more easily than the direct order.

(3) A debt paid by credit transfer is discharged only when payment is effected by the beneficiary's bank as the recipient of the order. This provision clearly governs the direct order such as the one initiating the credit transfer. Its effect is to state that only credit to the beneficiary's account discharges the originator's debt to the beneficiary.[121]

[6] Rights acquired by the mandatary/beneficiary's bank in its name but for the account of the principal/beneficiary become the latter's property (art. 401(1)). Furthermore, the obligation of the beneficiary's bank to pay the beneficiary is that of a mandatary who is required under CO art. 400 to account to his principal of anything realized in the performance of the mandate. This will cover payment received by the beneficiary's bank from its sender.

Alternatively, pursuant to CO art. 468(1), the beneficiary's bank may incur liability to the beneficiary on the basis of its acceptance as a recipient of an order. Such liability is stated to be free from defences available to the order recipient against the order giver.

---

[120] See text around n. 114, above.
[121] For the credit to the beneficiary's account as marking the completion of the credit transfer see BGE/ATF 119 II 232 (1993) and BGE/ATF 124 III 112 (1998).

Acceptance generating liability from the order recipient to the payee is stated in art. 468(1) to be constituted by notice to the payee. Credit to the beneficiary/payee's account by the beneficiary's bank/recipient is considered adequate notice. A recipient indebted to the order giver is usually required to pay the payee (art. 468(2))[122] though not to notify in advance (art. 468(3)). The payee is required to advise the order giver promptly of the recipient's refusal to make payment (art. 469).

Revocation of an order is governed by CO art. 470. Art. 470(1) appears to suggest that an order issued to discharge a debt owed by the order giver to the payee is irrevocable. However, the subsection is regarded as limited to the indirect order sent by the order giver to the payee before its subsequent transmittal to the order recipient. It does not apply to the direct order initiating a credit transfer.[123]   **[7]**

Under art. 470(2), revocation can effectively be made as long as the payee has not been notified of the recipient's acceptance under art. 468(1). As discussed, acceptance by the beneficiary's bank (as recipient) is marked by notice to the beneficiary (as payee), which can be expressed either by specific advise or credit to the beneficiary's account. It however seems that it is only credit posted by the beneficiary's bank to the beneficiary's account, and neither the mere notice given by the beneficiary's account to the beneficiary, nor the receipt of funds for the beneficiary by the beneficiary's bank, which marks both discharge and irrevocability.[124]

The prevailing view in Switzerland is that in order to revoke payment, the originator must address his instructions to the originator's bank. This is for practical reasons and notwithstanding the position of the beneficiary's bank as substituted mandatary; only the originator's bank is in a position to confirm the authenticity of the originator's revocation instructions.

An unaccepted payment order is automatically revoked by the bankruptcy of the order giver (art. 470(3)). On the other hand, the termination of the funds transfer contract, which operates like a revocation of mandate order art. 404, does not revoke outstanding unaccepted payment orders. The same is true with respect to death and legal incapacity; under art. 405(1), they do not terminate a mandate when so implied by the circumstances or nature of business.

---

[122] As to why the payee does not acquire under this provision rights against the originator's bank (where it is other than the beneficiary's bank) see s. 8, below.

[123] For the distinction, see text around n. 114, above.

[124] See X. Favre-Bulle, *Les Paiements transfrontières dans un espace financier européen* (Basle: Helbing & Lichtenhahn, 1998), at 387–91.

(c) The cover relationship

[8] As indicated, the funds transfer contract is regarded in Swiss law as a mandate. Its active side relates to outgoing payments from the originator's account at the originator's bank.[125] The mandate entitles the originator's bank, as a mandatary, to compensation from the principal/originator (CO art. 394(3)), whether in the form of bank charges, or use of funds in the account. The mandate further entitles the originator's bank to a reimbursement for all costs incurred in carrying out the mandate (art. 402(1)), including advances made in executing the originator's payment orders.[126] In fact, it is this obligation to provide cover for payments made (or to be made) on the originator/customer's behalf, which gave the relationship between the originator and the originator's bank the name 'cover relationship'.

Being an instruction or direction regarding the performance of the mandate, the payment order is governed by art. 397(1).[127] It thus requires the originator's bank, as a mandatary, to comply with it. Deviation is excused only where circumstances prevent the obtainment of further instructions and to the extent that the customer/principal's confirmation could have been expected.

As an order recipient, whenever the bank is indebted to the customer/order giver, namely, whenever the account is adequately funded, the bank becomes obligated to pay the payee, though in the absence of an agreement with the order giver, it is not obligated to notify its acceptance in advance (art. 468(2) and (31)). Nonetheless, the order recipient's obligation to pay the payee under art. 468(2) arises only where 'his position is not prejudiced' by the substitution of the payee for the order giver/debtor. Thus, irrespective of whether the subsection inures to the benefit of the payee, it cannot benefit a payee/beneficiary who has an account at a bank other than at the originator's bank. This is so since for the originator's bank/order recipient, payment to such a payee/beneficiary will be more burdensome than payment to the originator/order giver who has an account with that bank. Arguably then, so far as the originator's bank is concerned, the provision is limited to establishing the bank's obligation to the order giver/originator, whose content is to carry out payment to the payee/beneficiary as instructed in the payment order.[128]

[9] As a mandatary, the originator's bank is responsible to the

---

[125] For the distinction between the active and passive side of the contract see s. 2, above.

[126] Notwithstanding the language of the provision, the originator's bank is entitled to demand cover in advance. See Billote-Tongue, above, n. 104 at 42. On this point, BGB §669 is more explicit. See s. (ii) 1, text that follows n. 50, above.   [127] See s. 3, above.

[128] For the effect of this provision to establish the obligation of the beneficiary's bank to the beneficiary, see text around n. 122, above.

originator/principal for the faithful and careful performance of the mandate (CO art. 398(2)). In general, it is bound by the same standard of care as that of an employee ('travailleur') (art. 398(1)). This standard contains an obligation of diligence and faithfulness (art. 321a).

A mandatary is required to carry out his obligations in person. He may, however, be authorized to transfer performance to a third person, whether by contract or under the circumstances (CO art. 398(3)).[129] He is responsible for the acts of a substitute improperly appointed, as well as for the careful selection and instruction of a properly appointed submandatary,[130] but not for the latter's acts and omissions if carefully selected and instructed. A substitute, whether properly appointed or not, is directly responsible to the principal (art. 399).

Transfer to and substitution by the beneficiary's bank are permitted to the originator's bank, by the circumstances if not by agreement, whenever the beneficiary's account is at a beneficiary's bank other than that of the originator. In carrying out its part of the instruction and order, the beneficiary's bank thus substitutes the originator's bank. Not having selected the beneficiary's bank, the originator's bank is accordingly not responsible for any act or omission of the beneficiary's bank. In turn, as a substituted mandatary, the beneficiary's bank is responsible directly to the originator. This is without undermining the position of the beneficiary's bank as a mandatary of the beneficiary responsible directly to him.[131] For the resolution of issues emerging from this double capacity of the beneficiary's bank see s. 11, below.

Whether an intermediary bank is a substituted mandatary for the originator's bank, or its employee/assistant for whose acts and omissions the originator's bank is fully responsible, is discussed in s. 10, below.

(d) Indirect relationships: the position of the intermediary bank

In an interbank transfer, an indirect relationship exists between the originator or the beneficiary and any bank with which he is not in privity. In principle, such would be the relationship between the originator and any bank other than the originator's bank, that is, an intermediary or the beneficiary's bank. Such would also be the relationship between the beneficiary and any bank other than the beneficiary's bank, namely, an intermediary or the originator's bank.

[10]

---

[129] Cf. CO art. 68, under which '[a]n obligor is only bound to perform personally where performance depends on his person'.

[130] While the provision speaks of 'sub-mandatary' ('sous-mandataire'), under our terminology, the transferee may more properly be characterized as a substituted mandatary. See s. (iii) 8, above.   [131] See s. 6, above.

We have seen, however, that by virtue of the transfer of tasks to it from the originator's bank, the beneficiary's bank is in fact not in indirect relationship with the originator.[132] As well, neither a payment order issued to, nor acceptance by, any bank other than that of the beneficiary, inures to the benefit of the beneficiary.[133] Consequently, the indirect relationship of most interest is that between the originator and an intermediary bank. In dealing with this relationship, the principal question is that of classifying the intermediary bank either as a substituted/submandatary[134] or as an employee/assistant.

We already saw that a substitute mandatary is responsible directly to the principal and that the original mandatary is responsible to the principal only for acts of a substitute improperly appointed or not carefully selected or instructed (CO art. 399).[135] On the other hand, under CO art. 101, a person is liable for damage caused by his assistant/employee ('auxillary person' or 'auxiliaire') during the exercise of the assistant/employee's employment function. As there is no privity between the party that incurred damage and the assistant/employee, the latter is not liable to the former.

As applied to our setting, this means that if it is a substitute/submandatary, the intermediary bank is directly responsible to the originator/principal, while the originator's bank is usually relieved from liability to the originator for the intermediary bank's acts or omissions. Conversely, if the intermediary bank is an assistant/employee of the originator's bank, it is not responsible to the originator, who has recourse against the originator's bank for acts or omissions of the intermediary bank.

Under Swiss law, a substitute/sub-mandatary is distinguished from an assistant/employee by meeting two separate and cumulative tests. First, the substitute/sub-mandatary must have a legal, economic, and technical independence. Second, it must act predominantly at the interest of the principal and not at that of the original mandatary. The prevailing view is that the intermediary bank meets the first test but not the second. That is, insofar as it acts predominantly at the interest of the originator's bank, and not of the originator, the intermediary bank is an assistant/employee of the originator's bank rather than a substitute/sub-mandatary acting for the originator/principal.

In this respect, the intermediary bank's position is fundamentally different from that of the beneficiary's bank. The latter, acting predominantly at the originator's interest, is therefore a substitute/sub-mandatary. While the act of the beneficiary's bank is crediting the beneficiary's account is

---

[132] See text around n. 131, above.   [133] See s. 8, above.   [134] Cf. n. 130, above.
[135] See s. 9, above.

predominantly at the originator's interest, the intermediary bank's act, in issuing its payment order, is predominantly in carrying out the undertaking of the originator's bank incurred upon acceptance of the originator's payment order.

Consequently, for acts or omissions of an intermediary bank, the originator has recourse against the originator's bank, but not against the intermediary bank itself.

(e) Allocation of risk and damages

As indicated, under Swiss law, a debt paid by credit transfer is discharged [11] only where the beneficiary's account is credited by the beneficiary's bank.[136] Thus, and insomuch as the duty to pay is characterized as a 'bringing' obligation under which the debtor is required to *bring* payment and not merely to *send* it[137], the starting point is that both risks of delay and loss fall on the originator/debtor.

Indeed, this is so with respect to a default by the originator's bank or an intermediary bank. The originator's bank is a mandatary for the originator.[138] On its part, the intermediary bank is an employee/assistant of the originator's bank.[139] It is thus natural that vis-à-vis the beneficiary the risk of delay or loss ought to be borne by the originator.[140]

With respect to default by the beneficiary's bank, the question is more complex. The general rule under CO art. 91 is that the creditor defaults by his improper refusal to accept a duly tendered performance or to carry out preliminary acts without which the debtor cannot fulfil his obligations. Upon such default by the creditor, the debtor is entitled to be discharged (art. 92).[141] Accordingly, inasmuch as the beneficiary's bank acts for the beneficiary in accepting payment,[142] its default in crediting the beneficiary's account is, so far as the originator is concerned, tantamount to default by the beneficiary himself. Thus, vis-à-vis the originator, the risk of delay at the beneficiary's bank is borne by the beneficiary.

At the same time, the beneficiary's bank also acts for the originator in carrying out the originator's obligation to pay.[143] Accordingly, all risks

---

[136] See s. 5, above.

[137] For the distinction between 'bringing' and 'sending' obligations and the contrary characterization, in usual circumstances of the duty to pay as 'sending' obligation in Germany, see s. (ii) 6, above.   [138] See s. 8, above.

[139] See s. 10, above.

[140] But cf. BGE/ATF 124 III 147 (1998), where risk of delay was fastened on the beneficiary on the basis of the term in his contract with the originator instructing the latter to make payment at the post office as was actually done by the originator.

[141] According to CO art. 92(1), 'Where an obligee is in default . . ., the obligor is entitled to discharge his obligation by depositing the object which he is bound to deliver at the obligee's risk and expense'.   [142] See s. 6, above.

[143] See text around n. 131, above.

other than that of delay at the beneficiary's bank fall on the originator. Loss occurring at the beneficiary's bank is such a risk borne by the originator.[144]

The originator's responsibility for delay other than at the beneficiary's bank and for loss at all banks may be mitigated by three factors. First, the beneficiary is under a duty to inform the originator of any significant delay.[145] Second, the originator is exempted from liability in the case of delay or loss caused by *force majeure*. Third, in a case of delay in crediting the beneficiary's account not caused by the beneficiary's bank, it must be taken into account that even a cash payment would not have necessarily generated interest promptly.

[12]   Loss borne by the beneficiary, could be recovered by him from the beneficiary's bank, when caused by breach of the funds transfer contract by that beneficiary's bank. By the same token, loss borne by the originator, caused by breach of his funds transfer contract by either the originator's bank or the beneficiary's bank could be recovered by the originator from the respective breaching bank.[146] At the same time, loss caused by an intermediary bank and borne by the originator may be recovered by the originator from the originator's bank but not from the intermediary bank. The originator's bank could then seek reimbursement from the breaching intermediary bank.

This scheme is premissed on the characterization of the originator's bank as a mandatary for the originator,[147] of the beneficiary's bank as a mandatary for both the originator and the beneficiary,[148] and of the intermediary bank as an employee/assistant for the originator's bank.[149]

No 'money bank guarantee' is provided by the originator's bank. Stated otherwise, its liability to the originator is based on default by itself or by an intermediary bank and is not absolute. This is consistent with the general rule in Switzerland, under which the debtor who fails to perform his obligation or does not fulfil it properly is liable for damages, unless he proves that there is no negligence ('faute') on his part (CO art. 97(1)). That is, liability is linked to negligence and fault.[150]

More specifically, the mandatary's responsibility is subject to the same rules that govern that of an employee ('travailleur') (CO art. 398(1)).[151] As

---

[144] This division between risks of loss and delay occurring at the beneficiary's bank, between the originator and the beneficiary respectively is advocated by Billotte-Tongue, above, n. 104 at 86–7. Logically however, this particular is not the only possible resolution of the double capacity of the beneficiary's bank as a mandatary for both the originator and the beneficiary.

[145] So as to avoid an abuse of right, in contravention of art. 2(2) of the Swiss civil code.

[146] For the direct liability of a negligent benificiary's bank to the originator, see e.g. BGE/ATF 18 II 239 (1964) as well as BGE/ATF 121 III 310 (1996).

[147] See s. 8, above.   [148] See text around n. 131 and s. 6, above.
[149] See s. 10, above.   [150] See also CO arts. 41 and 99.   [151] See s. 9, above.

such the mandatary is answerable to damage caused to the principal intentionally or by negligence. The standard of care is determined by contract and circumstances (art. 321e). Also, any person is liable for damage caused by his employee/assistant ('auxiliaire') during the exercise of the latter's function in performing the former's obligation (art. 101(1)).

Under Swiss law, a contractual waiver of liability for an intentional tort **[13]** ('dol') or gross negligence ('faute grave') is ineffective (CO art. 100(1)). In contrast, liability for damage caused by an employee/assistant ('auxiliaire') can be contractually excluded (art. 101(2)). However, these rules are modified and liability is tightened where liability arises from the exercise of an occupation for which a public licence is necessary ('la responsabilité resulte de l'exercise d'une industrie concédée par l'autorité') as well as where the waiving party was employed by the other ('se trouvait à son service').

In these two cases, a judge may hold void any waiver of liability also for simple, namely slight negligence ('faute légère'), and not only gross negligence (art. 100(2)). Also, liability for damage caused by an employee/assistant ('auxiliare') may be excluded contractually only for slight negligence ('faute légère') (art. 101(3)), but not for an intentional tort or gross negligence.

It is widely recognized now that the originator's bank operates under such a public licence.[152] It is also well established that the intermediary bank is an employee/assistant of the originator's bank. All this means that the originator's bank may not exclude its liability for its own negligence and may exclude its liability for an intermediary bank only where the latter's negligence was rather slight. However, to the extent that the employees of the originator's bank are its employees/assistants, the originator's bank may exclude its liability for their slight negligence; only liability for acts of an organ of the originator's bank, as opposed to that of a mere employee, may not be excluded altogether under CO art. 100(2).[153]

In the final analysis, the originator's bank may effectively exclude liability, for slight negligence, whether of an intermediary bank or of its own employee, but not for that of its organs. Other than that, disclaimer of liability by the originator's bank is ineffective.

A debtor in default is liable in damages (CO 103(1)) which must be **[14]** proved by the person seeking to recover them (art. 42(1)). It is recognized that such damages may be indirect; that is, consequential loss is recoverable. As applied to the default by the originator's bank in carrying out a

---

[152] This recognition goes back to 1986. For this development, see Favre-Bulle, above, n. 124 at 396, and in general for CO arts. 100–1, ibid. at 395–8.

[153] Presumably, this is so since the bank, as corporation, acts through its organs. Cf. art. 55 of the Swiss Civil Code, and see Billote-Tongue above, n. 104 at 164–5.

funds transfer, in person as well as by obtaining the assistance of inter-mediary bank(s), resulting recoverable damages may include those stem-ming from the loss to the originator of a favourable contract, where the latter has been terminated by the beneficiary upon the originator's failure to meet a punctual payment obligation.

Nonetheless, foreseeability is not thereby excluded.[154] That is, to be liable to the full extent of a consequential loss, the originator's bank must become cognizant of pertinent special circumstances. Stated otherwise, to hold the originator's bank liable for consequential loss, the originator must advise it specifically of such special circumstances. Damage of the type not advised to the originator's bank may be viewed as contributed by the originator, so as not to hold the originator's bank responsible for it (CO art. 44(1)). Also, the contract between the originator and the origina-tor's bank may limit the latter's liability to loss of interest, unless the bank was put on notice as to special circumstances that may increase loss.

However, according to Billote-Tongue, the originator's failure to com-municate special circumstances will not dissolve the originator's bank from responsibility for consequential loss where the bank was grossly negligent. Furthermore, these are situations, particularly in the case of an electronic link between the originator and the originator's bank, where communication of special circumstances may not be feasible. According to Billote-Tongue, having failed to furnish to the originator the means to advise of special circumstances, the originator's bank may not rely on the absence of such advice as a basis for release from consequential loss. Stated otherwise, the bank may be liable to the full extent of the conse-quential loss not only where it was notified of special circumstances; even where it was not so advised, it would be fully liable where it was grossly negligent, or it had failed to furnish the originator with the means of advice.[155]

(V) ITALY[156]

[1]   The characterization of credit transfer under Italian civil law has long been debated. Specific possibilities include the assignment of claims

---

[154] Cf. CO art. 44(1) which reads as follows: 'The judge may reduce or completely deny any liability for damages if the [injured] party consented to the act causing the damage, or if circumstances for which he is responsible have caused or aggravated the damage, or have, otherwise adversely affected the position of the person liable.'

[155] See Billotte-Tongue, above, n. 104 at 254–5.

[156] The ensuing discussion draws heavily on C. Costa, 'The Actual Significance and the Law Relating to Foreign Funds Transfers in Italy', in W. Hadding and U. H. Schneider (eds.), *Legal Issues in International Credit Transfers* (Berlin: Duncker & Humblot, 1993), 267, as well as *Jura Europae—Droit bancaire et boursier* (Munich: Verlag C. H. Beck, Paris: Editions Techniques Juns-Classeurs, 1976), §40.31 (by C.C. Campi).

(art. 1260 cc.),[157] a contract for the benefit of a third party (art. 1411 cc.),[158] and the delegation of payment (art. 1269 cc.).

The Court of Cessation adhered (on 2 August 1956) to the delegation of payment theory, governed by art. 1269(1) cc. Under that provision, 'If the debtor has delegated a third person to make payment, such person can bind himself to the creditor, unless the debtor has forbidden it.' As applied to a credit transfer, the delegation of payment theory means that the originator is discharged from his obligation to the beneficiary (on the underlying transaction) following the posting of credit to the account of the beneficiary (the originator's creditor) at the beneficiary's bank.[159] In this context, it remains debatable whether discharge is effected by virtue of the acceptance by the beneficiary/creditor of the credit posted to his account or due to the obligation of the beneficiary's bank to the beneficiary reflected in this credit.[160]

None of these controversies has been settled. Recently however, the search for an accurate classification has been replaced by an 'atomistic approach' which concentrates on the analysis of the individual 'segments' of the contractual relationships.

So far as the relationship between the originator and his bank, as well as the one between each sending and receiving bank, is concerned, the underlying contract is that under the payment order or instruction. Such a relationship is legally analysed using the concept of the mandate (art. 1703 cc.). This approach is supported by art. 1856(1) cc., providing that, 'For the carrying out of instructions received from those having current accounts or from other customers, the bank is answerable according to the rules concerning mandate' (1703 ff.). The mandate is defined in art. 1703 cc. as 'a contract whereby one party binds himself to accomplish one or more legal transactions for the account of another'. As applied in the context of the credit transfer, this definition refers to the originator's bank binding itself as a mandatory to carry out a legal transaction for the originator.

[2]

---

[157] Under Art. 1260(1) cc., 'A creditor can assign his claim . . . even without the consent of the debtor . . .'. In an in-house credit transfer, the originator (creditor of the bank) would be taken to assign his claim against the bank to the beneficiary.

[158] Under Art. 1411(d) cc., 'A stipulation in favour of a third person is valid when the stipulator has an interest therein'. In turn, '[t]he third person acquires a right against the promisor as a result of such stipulation . . .' (Art. 1411(2) cc.). In an in-house credit transfer, the bank (promisor) would be taken to stipulate, vis-à-vis the originator, in favour of the beneficiary.

[159] Cf. Art. 1268(1) cc., under which '[i]f the debtor assigns to the creditor a new debtor, who binds himself to the creditor, the original debtor is not discharged from his obligation, unless the creditor *expressly declares* that he discharges him' (emphasis added). As applied to the credit transfer, the originator is the debtor, the beneficiary's bank is the new debtor, and the beneficiary is the creditor. Obviously, the difficulty is in finding an express declaration of discharge by the beneficiary-creditor. But cf. s. 10, below.

[160] For more on the controversy as to the adequacy of the credit posted to the beneficiary's account to complete the credit transfer see s. 8, below.

As a mandatory, vis-à-vis its principal, i.e. the originator, the originator's bank is required to perform the mandate with diligence (art. 1710(1) cc.).[161] It is further bound to make known to its principal (the originator) of 'any supervening circumstances which might cause the revocation or modification of the mandate' (art. 1710(2) cc.), such as the closing of the beneficiary's account or the beneficiary's bankruptcy.[162] Also, the originator's bank is under a duty to render an account for its activities (art. 1713 cc.).

[3]   At this point, two issues arise. The first relates to the source of the mandate. The second to its scope or content.

First, as to the source of the originator's mandate given to the originator's bank, a distinction is made between the situation involving an originator without a giro account at the instructed bank, and the situation where the originator holds an account with that bank. In the former case, the originator's payment order itself constitutes the mandate. Conversely, in the latter scenario, the mandate is given to the bank with the current account agreement, and the credit transfer is part of that original mandate, in effect, carrying it out.

Second, when more than one bank is involved in carrying out the credit transfer, the scope or content of the mandate is debatable. According to one view, the mandate of the originator's bank under the originator's payment order is to carry out payment of the designated amount to the beneficiary (hereafter: 'the mandate to pay view'). Conversely, under a second view, the mandate of the originator's bank under the originator's payment order is only to issue a corresponding payment order to a subsequent bank in the chain, whether to an intermediary or the beneficiary's bank (hereafter: 'the mandate to issue a corresponding payment order view'). The determination of the scope of the mandate is crucial to resolving the chain of liability as well as the irrevocability of the transaction.

[4]   Under the first view, that of a mandate to pay, the originator may sue directly a defaulting subsequent bank, the latter being regarded as substitute for the mandatory (art. 1717(4) cc.). As a substitute, the subsequent bank is charged towards the originator directly with all the mandatory's duties, namely to act diligently, to advise of emerging adverse circumstances, and to render an account.[163]

---

[161] Under some circumstances, this may require compliance with a specific time schedule under funds transfer system rules. Thereunder, an urgent transfer must be carried out within one day and normal transfers within four days. Violation of these limits entitle the originator to the return of the transfer fee. See Costa, above, n. 156 at 287.

[162] Stated otherwise, the bank is not free to continue to carry out payment instructions where it knows of changing circumstances. Rather, it must stop acting on the instructions and advise the originator of the adverse change.

[163] For these duties, see s. 2, above. Practically speaking, the duty to render an account is not relevant in the context of the originator-subsequent bank relationship.

As the original mandatory, the originator's bank remains responsible to the originator for instructions it gives the substitute (art. 1717(3) cc.) However, inasmuch as substitution is necessary for the task, if not authorized anyway, the originator's bank is not responsible for the activities of the substitute (subsequent bank) (art. 1717(1) cc.). This is true as long as the originator's bank was not at fault in selecting that substitute (art. 1717(2) cc.). Vicarious liability for default by a subsequent bank properly selected is thus excluded.

In fact, in banking practice, the originator always designates the beneficiary's bank and typically, based on the recommendation of the originator's bank, also the intermediary bank(s). That excludes any liability on the part of the originator's bank for the default of the beneficiary's bank and possibly also for the activities of an intermediary bank even improperly recommended by the originator's bank to the originator.[164]

Under the second view, that of a mandate to issue a corresponding payment order to a subsequent bank, the originator's bank is responsible solely for accurate transmission to the subsequent bank. Neither vicarious liability for the default by a subsequent bank nor broader liability for its own default (e.g. in the selection of a subsequent bank) is fastened on the originator's bank. Furthermore, in the absence of privity, no right of action is available to the originator against an intermediary or the beneficiary's bank.

It should however be pointed out that according to art. 1856(2), '[i]f the instructions are to be carried out in a place in which the bank has no office, it can entrust their performance to another bank or to one of its correspondents.' That other bank or correspondent is then to be considered as a substitute mandatary governed by art. 1717. Under 'the mandate to pay view' art. 1856(2) addresses the responsibility for the activity of that other bank or correspondent. Conversely, under 'the mandate to issue a corresponding payment view, art. 1856(2) may be regarded as simply outlining the contents of the mandate embodied in the instructions as provided in art. 1856(1). Nevertheless, the explicit reference in art. 1856(2) to art. 1717 may be more consistent with 'the mandate to pay view'. Alternatively, under 'the mandate to issue a corresponding payment view', the effect of the reference in art. 1856(2) to art. 1717 may be to render an intermediary (but not the beneficiary's) bank as a substitute mandatary even

---

[164] This (i.e. exclusion of liability for the activity of an intermediary bank) seems to be the view of Costa, above, n. 156 at 278 around n. 62. On the other hand, inasmuch as an intermediary bank is selected by the originator in *total* reliance on the recommendation of the originator's bank, *quaere* as to whether this is not a case where the substitute is *effectively* selected by the mandatary so as to render the latter responsible to the principal for an improper selection under art. 1717(2) cc.

within that view, so far as the communication of the instructions (as opposed to payment) is concerned.

[5]   So far as revocability is concerned, under the first view, that of a mandate to pay, the originator may cancel his payment order directly against each bank, whether as the original mandatory in the case of the originator's bank, or as a substituted mandatory in the case of any subsequent bank, until the credit transfer is completed. As will be discussed below, completion of the credit transfer coincides with the posting of credit to the beneficiary's account.

Conversely under the second view, that of a mandate to issue a corresponding payment order, no direct relationship may exist between the originator and any bank other than the originator's bank. Consequently, the originator may exercise his right of cancellation only with respect to the originator's bank, and only as long as this bank has not transmitted its corresponding payment order to a subsequent bank.

[6]   The second view, that of a mandate given to the originator's bank to issue a corresponding payment order, has been linked to the characterization of the credit transfer as a delegation.[165] This link has been premissed on the designation of intermediary and the beneficiary's banks in the originator's payment order. Accordingly, it was argued, the duty of the originator's bank is confined to the transmittal of the originator's delegation order, designating the role for each subsequent bank in making the payment to the beneficiary. On the other hand, it was contended that the 'true intent' of the originator and the originator's bank is that the credit transfer be carried out by the latter 'through' other banks 'with the result that these other banks should be viewed as agents of the first bank'. It was said on the latter position that it 'appears to most closely do justice to the economic bases of this banking operation,' so that ultimately, the first view, that of the mandate to pay, is 'preferable' over the second view, i.e. that of a mandate to issue a corresponding payment order.[166]

[7]   In an in-house credit transfer, namely a transfer involving one bank only, the controversy as to the scope or content of the mandate is inapplicable. In such a case the mandate under the originator's payment order is to pay the beneficiary. Obviously there is a direct privity between the originator and the bank. Cancellation is available until the transfer is completed, that is, when the beneficiary's account is credited.

[8]   The beneficiary's bank is responsible to its immediate sender for carrying out the credit transfer. Under the mandate to pay view, where more than one bank is involved in the transfer, the beneficiary's bank may further incur liability to the originator, as a substitute mandatory. The

---

[165] For the application of the delegation theory, see s. 1, above.
[166] See Costa, above, n. 156 at 278 and 283.

beneficiary's bank may be liable to the beneficiary only where the latter has an account with that bank.

When the transferred amount has been credited to the beneficiary's account, the beneficiary acquires the right to dispose of the funds credited (art. 1852 cc.).[167] At that point, the banking operation has been completed. It is however disputed whether, vis-à-vis the beneficiary's bank, the beneficiary did not acquire the right to payment even earlier, namely upon receipt of the payment order by that bank. Also, it is debated whether the legally binding completion of the credit transfer is not dependent also on the beneficiary's knowledge of the credit posted to the beneficiary's account.

As for the first question, the prevailing view is that no right to payment from the beneficiary's bank accrues in the beneficiary's favour prior to his account being credited. Stated otherwise, prior to the credit, the beneficiary is entitled only to damages for failure to credit or undue delay in crediting the account.[168]

With regard to the second question, one opinion is that the beneficiary's knowledge of the credit posted to his account is necessary for the completion of the credit transfer. This opinion is premissed on the view that posting the credit to the account ought to be treated as a legal transaction in the form of either an offer or unilateral act. Each becomes binding or effective only when it comes to the knowledge of the person to whom it is directed (arts. 1333–4 cc.). In our case, this person is the beneficiary.

Nevertheless, while the characterization of the credit posted to the beneficiary's account as an offer or unilateral act is not contested, the prevailing opinion is to the contrary, namely that crediting the account alone is adequate to complete the credit transfer. Hence, the advice of credit sent to the beneficiary by the beneficiary's bank is for information only. The reason given to this departure from the general theory relating to agreements, as reflected in arts. 1333–4 cc., is the priority accorded to the private contractual autonomy of the parties. Thus, the authority given by the beneficiary to his bank to collect payment is construed as allowing completion of the transaction embodied in the offer or unilateral act before and irrespective of coming to the knowledge of the beneficiary.

In sum, crediting the account marks both the beneficiary's entitlement to receive payment from his bank as well as the completion of the credit transfer.

[167] Under art. 1852 cc., 'When a deposit (1834), opening of credit (1842) or other banking transaction is made for a current account, the customer can dispose at any time of the balance in his favour, subject to the observance of any agreed terms concerning notice'.

[168] Under case law, the bank is not free to post credits without any time limits but must instead credit amounts as quickly as technical means permit. Under a recent anti-money laundering law, the beneficiary has the right to receive payment by the third day after acceptance by his bank. See Costa, above, n. 156 at 280 and 286.

[9]		Credit posted to the beneficiary's account is final. Recovery from the beneficiary of an amount credited *or refusal to credit* his account can be based by the beneficiary's bank on grounds arising from the relationship between the beneficiary and his bank. In an in-house transfer, recovery by the bank may also be based on the cover relationship between the originator and the bank, on defences arising from the underlying transaction between the originator and the beneficiary, as well as on defects in the originator's payment order. Other than in an in-house transfer, objections based on the originator's payment order, and perhaps others except those based on the relationship between the beneficiary and his bank, may not generally be raised by the beneficiary's bank against the beneficiary.[169] The 'abstraction' of the transaction between the beneficiary and his bank may thus be recognized in credit transfers other than in-house.

[10]		Where the parties agree to payment by credit transfer, the credit to the beneficiary's account is an indirect fulfilment of the payment obligation. It thus marks the discharge of the originator's debt to the beneficiary.[170] Where the beneficiary does not hold an account with the beneficiary's bank, the discharge of the originator's bank is marked by the actual payment by the beneficiary's bank to the beneficiary.

In the absence of agreement between the originator and the beneficiary as to payment by credit transfer, discharge of the originator's debt to the beneficiary does not occur upon the mere posting of credit to the beneficiary's account. Rather, it takes place thereafter, either where the creditor (namely the beneficiary) approves or derives a benefit from the payment (art. 1188(2) cc.),[171] or where he expressly consents to the substitution of the original debtor (namely the originator) by his own bank (art. 1268(1) cc.).[172] However, under the latter view, so far as express consent by the beneficiary to the substitution is required, the beneficiary's use of the transferred amount, his approval of the credit posted to the account, or his failure to make objection to the bank for a long period of time, have generally been construed as providing for the required consent.

[11]		It seems that the risk of delay or loss occurring at a bank other than that of the beneficiary falls on the originator. The latter may be able to pass the

---

[169] This is consistent with art. 1271 cc., (if applicable), under which in delegation, the delegee-creditor relationship is independent of and not subject to defences arising from the delegor/debtor-creditor as well as delegor/debtor-delegee relationships. For the credit transfer as delegation, see s. 1, above.

[170] Under a recent anti-money laundering law, discharge may occur earlier, if and where the debtor (originator) advises the creditor (beneficiary) of the acceptance of the payment order by a bank. See Costa, above, n. 156 at 287.

[171] Under art. 1188(2) cc., 'Payment made to a person not entitled to receive it frees the debtor if the creditor ratifies it or has profited thereby'.

[172] The provision (dealing with delegation) is reproduced in s. 4, above.

risk to the defaulting bank, if the mandate to pay view[173] applies. In any event, no 'money-back guarantee rule' exists and recovery from a defaulting bank depends on breach by that bank of its duties as a mandatory.

Loss occurring after the crediting of the beneficiary's account by the beneficiary's bank, such as where the beneficiary's bank becomes insolvent, falls on the beneficiary. As for the risk of delay or loss occurring at the beneficiary's bank prior to crediting the beneficiary's account the situation is less clear. Under the mandate to pay view, the beneficiary's bank is responsible for its default to both the originator and the beneficiary. This does not tell us who, as between these two, bears the risk where recovery from the beneficiary's bank is unavailable.[174] Presumably, the risk falls on the originator whose debt to the beneficiary is not discharged until the amount is credited to the beneficiary's account. Arguably this is also true under the mandate to transmit a corresponding payment order view,[175] notwithstanding the originator's possible lack of right to recover from the defaulting beneficiary's bank.

There seem to be no specific rules as to the scope of damages recover- **[12]** able from a defaulting bank.

In general, recoverable damages from a defaulting party ('debtor') shall include lost profits 'insofar as they are a direct and immediate consequence of non-performance or delay' (art. 1223 cc.). For a pecuniary obligation, damages include interest ('even if the creditor does not prove that he has suffered any damage') and additional compensation for proven losses (art. 1224 cc.). In general, recoverable damages must have been foreseeable, but only as long as 'the non-performance or delay is not caused by fraud or malice of the debtor . . .' (art. 1225 cc.). Stated otherwise, foreseeability limits damages for default based, for example, on negligence, but not on fraud or malice. Within these boundaries, consequential damages may thus be recoverable.

---

[173] Discussed in ss. 3–6, above.
[174] Recovery from the beneficiary's bank is unavailable where the latter is insolvent or has not breached any of the mandatory's duties. [175] Discussed in ss. 3–6, above.

(VI) JAPAN[176]

[1]　In the past, it was thought that under the Japanese civil code the payment order underlying a credit transfer was a contract for the benefit of a third person (art. 537 cc.).[177] In this context, it was said that the beneficiary acquired direct rights against the beneficiary's bank, either on the basis of the contract between the originator and the originator's bank, or the contract between the originator's bank (acting as an agent of the originator) and the beneficiary's bank.

This view is currently disfavoured. Rather, some maintain that the undertaking of the originator's bank towards the originator is that of an independent contractor under a contract for work. Thereunder, the originator's bank 'has agreed to accomplish a certain work', namely to carry out the credit transfer, in return for an agreement by the originator 'to pay . . . remuneration for the result of such work' (art. 632 cc.).

However, at present, the prevailing view discusses the credit transfer in the context of a mandate. Thereunder, the originator has commissioned the originator's bank 'to do a juristic act' or has entrusted that bank with the 'commissions of [the originator's] affairs' and the bank 'has consented thereto' (arts. 643 and 656 cc.). In fact, some view the account agreement itself, insofar as it authorizes the bank to credit the account for incoming payment orders, and to honour payment instructions and collect cheques, as a 'mandate' for the 'commission of the [depositor's] affairs' (*per* art. 656 cc.). Under Japanese law, the mandate creates an agency relationship (governed by arts. 99–118 cc.) between the originator and the originator's bank.

Under both the contract for work and mandate theories, the beneficiary's rights in the credit transfer are based on the beneficiary's contract with the beneficiary's bank. This contract requires the bank to credit the beneficiary's account after the bank has received cover.[178]

---

[176] The ensuing discussion draws heavily on S. Iwahara, 'The Practical Execution and Legal Framework of International Funds Transfers in Japan', in W. Hadding and U. H. Schneider (eds.), *Legal Issues in International Credit Transfers* (Berlin: Duckers & Hamblot, 1993), 289. See also O. Saito, 'New Developments in Arguments on Legal Liability of Financial Institutions', 11 B O J *Monetary and Economic Studies*, 2: 97, 113–17 (1993). A current project aimed at the passing of an Electronic Funds Transfers Act has not been brought yet to full fruition.

[177] Under art. 537(1) cc., '[w]here a party to a contract has agreed therein to effect an act of performance in favour of a third person, such third person is entitled to demand such act of performance directly from the obligor'. The third person's right accrues, under art. 537(2) cc., 'when he declares to the obligor his intention to accept the benefit of the contract'. Under art. 538 cc., as of that time, the two contracting parties may not 'effect [the] alteration or . . . extinction' of the third person's right. However, the obligor may set up his contract defences against the third person (art. 539 cc.). All civil code quotes are from *The Civil Code of Japan* (translation) (Tokyo: Ministry of Justice, 1972).

[178] On the beneficiary's rights towards his bank, see s. 9, below.

Completion of the credit transfer is marked by crediting the beneficiary's [2] account by the beneficiary's bank. At that point, the originator's debt paid by the means of the credit transfer is discharged. Also, the originator's payment order becomes then irrevocable. In practice however, revocability is severely curtailed under the funds-transfer system rules of both the BOJ-NET and the Gaitame-Yen System. In fact, in the Japanese electronic transfer systems,[179] revocation after input is permissible only in Zengin (until the beneficiary's account is credited) as well as for designated-hour transfers on the BOJ-NET (until execution by the System.).

The contract under a payment order becomes effective when a notice of [3] acceptance is sent by the receiving bank to the sender (art. 526 (1) cc.).[180] Otherwise, no notice of acceptance may be necessary 'either by reason of a declaration of intention ... by the offeror or by reason of business usage,' in which case, the contract is concluded 'when any event takes place which can be taken as a declaration of intention to accept' (art. 526(2) cc.). Presumably, carrying on the transaction, or even debiting the sender's account, would qualify as such 'any event' concluding the contract. A funds-transfer system rule, pre-existing agreement, as well as business usage may advance the point where a binding contract is created to the receipt of the payment order by the receiving bank, whether or not subject to the latter's right to reject it.[181]

The scope of the receiving bank's liability for the breach of its obliga- [4] tions in the credit transfer transaction is governed by general principles of law. Under art. 416 cc., damages should compensate the obligee for 'such damage as would ordinarily arise from the non-performance of an obligation'. However, damages that have arisen through special circumstances may also be recovered 'if the parties had foreseen or could have foreseen such circumstances'.

In the context of a credit transfer, this provision was interpreted to afford the originator damages for consequential loss. This included the loss of a profitable contract, due to the breach of a punctual payment obligation, caused by an error of the originator's bank in its payment order

---

[179] For the three Japanese electronic transfer systems, see s. (i) above.

[180] Under that provision, 'A contract *inter absentes* comes into existence at the time when notice of acceptance is [dispatched]'. It is currently debated in Japan whether the originator may raise against the originator's bank defences based on the invalidity of the *payment order* such as disability, duress, or mistake. Such defences based on the invalidity of the *underlying transaction* may not be raised by the originator against the originator's bank. See Iwahara, above, n. 176 at 302–3.

[181] Under Article 509 of the Commercial Code of Japan, a merchant who has received an 'offer to enter into a contract which falls within his areas of business, from a person with whom he has regular business relations' and who has not dispatched promptly notice of acceptance or rejection, shall be deemed to have accepted the offer. Accordingly, the failure of a bank to promptly reject a payment order sent by a person with whom the bank has regular business relations, constitutes acceptance leading to a binding contract.

purporting to carry out that of the originator. That error on the part of the originator's bank resulted in the misidentification of the beneficiary which caused the originator to miss a payment deadline under his contract with the beneficiary. Consequently, the beneficiary effectively terminated that contract, to the detriment of the originator. The Court held that the originator's potential loss (on his failure to meet payment due date) should have been foreseen by the originator's bank. On this basis, the Court awarded the originator approximately 3 million dollars in damages.

[5]   A breaching receiving bank is thus liable to its sender. What constitutes a breach, whether liability runs also in favour of a participant preceding the immediate sender, and whether liability covers a breach by a subsequent bank in the chain as well, are not entirely settled. The ensuing discussion will deal with these questions from the originator's perspective.

The nature of a receiving bank's liability to the originator is quite controversial in Japan. Those who regard the obligation of the originator's bank on the contract emanating from its acceptance of the originator's payment order as a contract for work governed by arts. 632–42 cc.[182] would argue for extensive liability of the originator's bank. This is so since art. 633 cc. (in conjunction with art. 624 cc.) makes the remuneration of the independent contractor (i.e. in our setting—the originator's bank), dependent on the completion of the work (namely, the crediting of the beneficiary's account) for the other party (that is, the originator). Stated otherwise, the originator's bank assumes full liability in case of the non-completion including incomplete completion of the credit transfer. In principle, under the orthodox view, it would not matter if non-completion occurred due to the fault of the originator's bank, of an intermediary bank, or of the beneficiary's bank, or even if no bank defaulted. Such absolute liability goes further than a 'money-back guarantee rule', since it fastens strict liability on the originator's bank not only with respect to the sum of the payment order (and lost interest) but also with respect to the foreseen or foreseeable consequential loss incurred by the originator.

Conversely, in the case of improper completion, such as delay, the traditional and still prevailing view is that no absolute or strict liability is fastened on the originator's bank. Rather, under such circumstances, the liability of the originator's bank must be based on its fault.

But even with respect to non-completion, some adherents to the 'contract for work' theory are less orthodox. They recognize that the beneficiary's bank is universally designated by the originator and not selected by the originator's bank. Likewise, an intermediary bank may also be

---

[182] For this view see s. 1, above.

selected by the originator. Accordingly, they argue, the originator's bank should be immunized from responsibility for default by a bank it did not select. Another approach restricting the full application of the 'contract for work' theory would exempt the originator's bank from liability for any consequential loss caused by any third party, namely, by anyone other than by itself. This would set the responsibility of the originator's bank to that under a 'money-back guarantee rule' plus for foreseen or foreseeable consequential loss only for its own default.

However, as indicated, the prevailing view regards the credit transfer **[6]** in a context of a mandate and not of a contract for work.[183] As a mandatary, the originator's bank is bound to manage the affairs entrusted to it 'with the care of a good manager in accordance with the tenor of the mandate' (art. 644 cc.). Namely, the mandatary's liability is for the breach of a duty of care and is not absolute or strict. As a mandatary, the originator's bank is further under a duty to make full disclosure (art. 645 cc.) and account (arts. 646–7 cc.) to the mandator. It is entitled to advances or reimbursement for expenditures (arts. 649–50 cc.) as well as to the specially agreed remuneration (art. 648).

Where the commission of the mandate involves tasks carried out by subagents, the Japanese civil code appears to suggest that usually the original mandatary is not vicariously liable for the default of a subagent, and that each subagent is liable directly for its own default to the mandator. Thus, according to art. 104 cc., an agent created by mandate may not appoint a subagent, except where the agent has obtained the principal's consent or an unavoidable reason exists. Under art. 105(1) cc., where the agent has duly appointed a subagent, the agent 'shall be responsible to the principal in respect of *the appointment and supervision*' but not otherwise (emphasis added); that is vicarious liability for the default by a properly appointed and supervised subagent is excluded. Under art. 105(2) cc., this limited liability for the appointment and supervision of a subagent is excluded altogether where the agent has appointed a subagent 'as designated by the principal', unless the agent actually knew the designated subagent 'to be unfit or untrustworthy' and has neglected to act on the basis of this knowledge. Finally, under art. 107(2) cc., '[a] sub-agent has the same rights and duties as the agent towards the principal and third persons.' Effectively, the subagent is a substituted agent.

Except for in connection with an in-house credit transfer, the mandate created by the originator's payment order would require the appointment of subagent(s). An originator instructing payment held at an account other than that of the originator's bank must be taken to provide consent to the appointment of a subagent. Alternatively, where the destination

---

[183] For this view see s. 1, above.

account is not held at the originator's bank, 'an unavoidable reason exists' for the appointment of a subagent by the originator's bank (the original agent). Either way the requirements of art. 104 cc. have been satisfied and the appointment of any further bank as a subagent in carrying out the credit transfer is thus effective.

As applied to the credit transfer, the statutory scheme of the civil code of Japan would mean that the originator's bank is not vicariously liable for the default by an intermediary or the beneficiary's bank. Rather, the originator's bank is liable for its own default as well as for the improper appointment or supervision of an intermediary bank not designated by the originator. For damages incurred due to the improper appointment or supervision of either an intermediary bank designated by the originator or the beneficiary's bank (the latter being universally designated by the originator), the originator's bank is liable only when the originator's bank has neglected to act on the basis of adverse knowledge at its disposal, namely where it failed to advise the originator of, or to act on, facts known to it relating to the unfitness or untrustworthiness of the intermediary or beneficiary's bank. In turn, an intermediary bank, whether designated by the originator or by a bank, as well as the beneficiary's bank, is in direct agency relationship with the originator. As such, this bank is directly liable to the originator for that bank's own default.

[7]   There is some case law which is consistent with this summary. One case involved the originator's action against the originator's bank for damages incurred due to the default of the beneficiary's bank. Another case was concerned with the originator's action against the originator's bank for damages incurred due to the default of an intermediary bank designated by the originator. Both actions were dismissed. Underlying each decision was the view that the role of the originator's bank under the mandate was limited to the transmission of a corresponding payment order and the making of further appropriate arrangements for the carrying out of the credit transfer. No duty was breached by the originator's bank in the course of this activity and hence no liability to the originator existed. In turn, one Court held that a direct agency relationship between the beneficiary's bank and the originator can be implied from art. 105(2) cc. Consequently, it was observed, the originator was entitled to recover from the breaching bank damages the latter had caused.

It is however also maintained that while the originator's bank is not vicariously liable for damages incurred due to the default of an intermediary or beneficiary's bank, the originator's bank remains under a duty to assist the originator to recover such damages. This duty on the part of the originator's bank compensates the originator, at least in part, for being deprived of a cause of action against his own bank, and instead, forced to deal with a bank with which he has no privity and that may be situated in a remote place or jurisdiction. The duty is derived from art. 654 cc. which upon the termination of the mandate, requires the mandatary, where 'circumstances of urgency exist', to 'take all necessary measures in respect of the affairs entrusted, until the mandator . . . is in a position to take over the management'.

According to one view, liability of an intermediary or the beneficiary's bank to the originator is not based on direct agency but rather on tort or restitution. Arguably, this is so since direct agency under art. 107(2) cc., affording a subagent 'the same rights and duties as the agent towards the principal . . .', would have entitled the intermediary or beneficiary's bank to obtain payment directly from the originator,[184] regardless of the solvency of the originator's bank, and even where the originator has already paid the originator's bank. However, this fear may reflect excessive formalism. In any event, the acceptance of this revision in the application of the mandate theory to the credit transfer, would not change the allocation of liability rules: each bank remains liable for its own default.

Nevertheless, there is an alternative view to the application of the man- **[8]** date theory to the credit transfer. This alternative view does lead to the liability of the originator's bank to the originator for the default of any bank. This includes liability by the originator's bank for loss incurred by the default of an intermediary or the beneficiary's bank. Thus, in one case, the Court viewed the task assigned by the mandate to the originator's bank as the transfer of funds to the beneficiary, to be carried jointly with, or with the assistance of the beneficiary's bank. Consequently, the erroneous misdirection of funds by the beneficiary's bank to an account other than the one of the beneficiary, could not be regarded as a satisfactory performance of the mandate of the originator's bank. Accordingly, inasmuch as in the facts of the case, the originator's bank failed 'to effect performance in accordance with the tenor and purport of [its own] obligation', it became liable to the originator (art. 415 cc.).

This precedent sticks to the traditional view that a payment order creates a mandate. At the same time, it is unique. While adhering to the mandate theory, the case fastens on the originator's bank vicarious liability. This liability is for the default of the beneficiary's bank, the latter being characterized as an assisting agent.

Under Japanese law, the obligation of the beneficiary's bank to a bene- **[9]** ficiary to carry out and complete an incoming credit transfer derives from their ordinary deposit account contract. Ordinarily, the standard contract terms provide that the sum of an incoming payment order is not withdrawable by the beneficiary until credit has been posted to the account. They further state that incoming credit transfers may be credited to the

---

[184] Under arts. 649–50 cc., discussed in s. 6, above.

account. However, the latter term is not taken to suggest that the beneficiary's bank has any discretion in crediting the sum of a payment order for which it has received cover. Rather, it is obliged to credit the account with that sum and may not reject the pertaining payment order.

Once the beneficiary's account has been credited, the underlying debt between the originator and beneficiary is discharged and the credit transfer becomes irrevocable.[185] The credit to the beneficiary's account cannot be reversed except for on the basis of the beneficiary's relationship with his bank.[186] Whether credit to the beneficiary's account may be reversed if cover has not been received by the beneficiary's bank, namely whether credit to the beneficiary's account must be final and cannot be provisional and conditional upon the receipt of cover by the beneficiary's bank, is unclear in Japan.

[10]   As between the originator and the beneficiary, the risk of delay and loss, occurring at a bank other than that of the beneficiary, falls on the originator. Usually however, the originator may pass the risk on to the defaulting bank. In the case of a defaulting intermediary bank, depending on the theory adhered to as to the nature of the contract under the payment order, the originator can pass the risk on to it either directly, or indirectly, first recovering from the originator's bank which may then proceed along the chain of participating banks.[187]

Where delay or loss occurs at a beneficiary's bank, that defaulting bank is liable to the beneficiary.[188] Damages may also be recovered by the originator, either directly from the defaulting beneficiary's bank, or from the originator's bank that will pass them on along the chain of participating banks, up to the defaulting beneficiary's bank.[189]

As between the originator and beneficiary, damages for delay or loss occurring at a beneficiary's bank are ordinarily allocated to the beneficiary. This is fair since, in the final analysis, it is the beneficiary and not the originator who has selected the beneficiary's bank. Presumably, this is true also when the underlying contract between the originator and beneficiary requires the former to deposit funds at the beneficiary's account by a specified deadline. Then too, the risk of missing this deadline, when due to the default of the beneficiary's bank, falls on the beneficiary and not the originator.

---

[185] See s. 2, above.

[186] But cf. Iwahara, above, n. 176 at 313, referring to cases allowing the invalidation of credit to the beneficiary's account on the basis of the lack of entitlement of the beneficiary to the funds (mistakenly wired by the originator). While the originator's right in restitution to recover an erroneous payment is subject to the rights of the beneficiary's creditors, the originator's right on the basis of the invalidation (or reversal) of credit is ahead of such competing rights.

[187] See ss. 5–8, above.   [188] See s. 9, above.

[189] Depending on the applicable theory, as discussed in ss. 5–8, above.

(VII) QUEBEC[190]

In Quebec, under art. 1564(2) cc., a monetary debt may be discharged where **[1]** the debtor remits the amount due by means of 'the transfer of funds to an account of the creditor in a financial institution', provided 'the creditor is in a position to accept it'. Quebec law treats the payment order initiating such a transfer of funds in the context of the mandate. Under art. 2130(1) cc., '[m]andate is a contract by which a person, the mandator, empowers another person, the mandatary, to represent him in the performance of a juridical act with a third person, and the mandatary, by his acceptance, binds himself to exercise the power'. Accordingly, in his payment order, the originator (being the mandator) empowers the originator's bank (that is, the mandatary) to represent him (i.e. the originator) in the performance of the payment obligation of the originator to the beneficiary (being a third person). A contract of mandate is created where the originator's bank accepts the payment order so as to bind itself to exercise the power it was given by the originator. In fact, under art. 2130(2) cc., the payment order, being the power given by the mandator-originator to the mandatary-originator's bank, is called 'power of attorney'.[191]

According to L'Heureux and Fortin, '[t]he payment order is given to **[2]** carry out payment. By itself it does not have any discharging or novating effect on the debt which it is designed to extinguish. Like the cheque, [the payment order] cannot be the equivalent of payment unless and until the credit transfer is carried out.'[192] However, in a previous edition,[193] L'Heureux expressed the view that by giving the order, the originator assumes an obligation towards the beneficiary under which he guarantees the ultimate receipt of funds by the beneficiary. This may suggest that the payment order accepted by the originator's bank serves to suspend or conditionally discharge the underlying debt between the originator and beneficiary. Furthermore, in a given case, depending on the interpretation of the applicable contract, towards the beneficiary, the originator may have not been in breach of the originator's contractual payment

---

[190] See in general, N. L'Heureux and È. Fortin, *Droit bancaire*, 3rd edn. (Cowansville, Que: Les Éditions Yvon Blais, 1999), primarily pp. 543–55. See also, M. Lemieux, 'La Responsabilité du banquier du donneur d'ordre dans les transferts électroniques de fonds', in Canadian Comparative Law Association & Association Québécoise de Droit Comparé (eds.), *Contemporary Law 1994 Droit Contemporain* (Cowansville, Que.: Les Éditions Yvon Blais Inc., 1994), 227.

[191] According to art. 2130(2) cc., '[t]he power and, where applicable, the writing evidencing it are called the power of attorney'. All cites are from a bilingual edition of the Quebec Civil Code, *Code Civil du Practicien* (Montreal: DACFO, 1995).

[192] See above, n. 190 at 547 (my translation).

[193] N. L' Heureux, *Le Droit bancaire* (Sherbrook: Les Èditions Revue de Droit Universitè de Sherbrooke, 1988), at 351.

obligation, when on due date, the originator merely sets the process in motion, by causing the originator's bank to dispatch or direct the funds towards the beneficiary, with funds actually reaching their destination at a later date.[194] In any event, in a credit transfer, absolute discharge of the originator's debt to the beneficiary occurs only where the beneficiary authorized the originator to pay into the beneficiary's account and upon payment by the beneficiary's bank to the beneficiary, usually by crediting his account.[195]

[3]   A mandate is terminated by virtue of the revocation by the mandator, renunciation of the mandatary, death of either party, or bankruptcy. Unilateral revocation or renunciation is subject to liability to pay damages to the injured party.[196] So far as revocation is concerned, it seems that the originator's power exists until the full completion of credit transfer, that is, until payment by the beneficiary's bank is made to the beneficiary, usually by crediting his or her account.

[4]   As a mandatary, the originator's bank is bound to fulfil the mandate and act 'with prudence and diligence in performing it.' It must further 'act honestly and faithfully in the best interests of the mandator [i.e. the originator]' (art. 2138 cc). Particularly, this requires timely and accurate execution and the selection of a competent correspondent, acting as an intermediary bank where necessary. In fact, according to L'Heureux and Fortin, the bank holding an account for a customer containing adequate cover, is under an obligation to that customer to carry out credit transfers according to authorized payment orders, even before assuming the position of a mandatary by virtue of the acceptance of the payment order which triggers the mandate.

In turn, as a mandator, the originator is bound to cooperate with the mandatary/originator's bank and cover its costs (arts. 2149–51 cc).

[5]   In principle, under art. 2140(1) cc., '[t]he mandatary is bound to fulfill the mandate in person unless he is authorized by the mandator to appoint another person to perform all or part of it in his place.' The appointment of a substitute by the mandatary is also permitted 'where unforeseen

---

[194] See e.g. *J. Raymond Dupuis Inc.* v. *Produits généraux de la construction (1980) Ltée* [1988] A.Q. No 1087 (Que. C.A.), on-line: QL (QJ), where the contract between the originator and the beneficiary required the originator to pay by having, by a certain date, a specified sum of money dispatched ('acheminée') to the beneficiary's account by means of a credit transfer. The originator instructed the originator's bank to make payment in the required sum, and the originator's bank acted on the instructions, by that date. It was held that the originator was not in breach of contract notwithstanding the arrival of funds to the beneficiary at a later date.

[195] See *Héli-Forex Inc.* v. *Nation Cri de Wemindji* [2000] J.Q. No. 478 (Que. C.A.) at paras. 24–5.

[196] For the first proposition, see art. 2175 cc. Both the mandator's right to revoke and the mandatary's right to renounce may be effectively renounced. See art. 2179 cc. For the second proposition, see arts. 2178 and 2181 cc.

circumstances prevent [the mandatary] from fulfilling the mandate and he is unable to inform the mandator thereof in due time' (art. 2140(2) cc.). Upon an unauthorized substitution, the mandatary remains liable to the mandator for any default by the substitute. At the same time, where substitution has been authorized, the mandatary 'is accountable only for the care with which he selected his substitute and gave him the instructions' but not for the default of a properly selected substitute. In any case, regardless as to whether his appointment has been authorized, the substitute is directly liable to the mandator for its own default (art. 2141 cc.).

Substitution of a mandatary ought to be distinguished from the [6] appointment of an assistant to whom powers are delegated by the mandatary. The latter is permissible in the performance of the mandate, 'unless prohibited by the mandator or usage'. The mandatary remains liable to the mandator for any default by such an assistant (art. 2142 cc.).

L'Heureux and Fortin do not characterize the intermediary bank as a [7] substitute. Rather, in their view, it is a mandatary of its sender. Stated otherwise, the first intermediary bank is a mandatary of the originator's bank. In effect, the intermediary bank thus acts as a subagent for the originator, so that there is no privity between the originator and an intermediary bank. Hence the intermediary bank is not to be held directly liable to the originator.[197] Effectively, the intermediary bank ought then to be regarded as the assistant of its sender[198] so as to trigger the liability of the originator's bank to the originator for that intermediary bank's default.[199]

Towards the beneficiary, the risk of delay or loss occurring at a bank, [8] other than that of the beneficiary, is thus borne by the originator. On his part, the latter may shift the risk on the defaulting bank by recovering first from the originator's bank which will ultimately reach the defaulting bank itself. There is no automatic 'money-back guarantee rule' and the originator will be able to recover only where delay or loss occurred due to a default, namely breach of duty, by a bank (other than that of the beneficiary). Deficient execution by the originator's bank may also trigger its direct liability to the beneficiary.

Under the law of mandate, the beneficiary's bank must act prudently.[200] The beneficiary's bank is responsible to both the beneficiary and its sender, namely, at least indirectly, to the originator. According to L'Heureux and Fortin, inasmuch as the beneficiary's bank has been chosen by the beneficiary, risks associated with the default by that bank are

---

[197] There is however a reference in L'Heureux and Fortin, above, n. 190 at 552, to a direct liability by the intermediary bank to the originator, though its grounds are not explained.

[198] While they do not state this explicitly it follows from the tenor of their discussion.

[199] In fact, L'Heureux and Fortin merely concede, above, n. 190 at 551, that this is the common law position.

[200] See e.g. *Pollack v. Canadian Imperial Bank of Commerce* [1981] C.A. 587 (Que.)

to be borne by the beneficiary. This does not preclude direct liability by
the beneficiary's bank to the originator. There is also authority for the liability of a negligent beneficiary's bank to a non-customer beneficiary, possibly on the basis of viewing the contract between the originator and the
originator's bank as containing stipulations for the benefit of the beneficiary who could thus sue the beneficiary's bank as the mandatary of its
sender.[201]

Under art. 1613 cc., the normal rule in contract is that 'the debtor is
liable only for damages that were foreseen or foreseeable at the time the
obligation was contracted,' provided the breach was neither intentional
nor due to gross fault. But even where the breach resulted from 'intentional or gross fault' of the breaching party, 'the damages will include
only what is an immediate and direct consequence of the nonperfor-
mance'. Damages caused due to the delayed execution, improper execution, or non-execution of a credit transfer are to be assessed according to
these rules.[202]

(VIII) THE COMMON LAW

[1]   The ensuing discussion focuses on the common law which governs credit
transfers in England. In principle, this law applies in Australia and the
nine common law provinces of Canada, as well as in the other
Commonwealth jurisdictions. Pre-Article 4A American law is dealt with
here only insofar as it highlights or specifically contradicts a point under
discussion.

(a) Characterization

[2]   It is universally accepted that 'there is no express or implied trust in
favour of the [beneficiary] resulting from the [originator's] bank accepting instructions to make a credit transfer'.[203] Whether there is a similar
consensus as to the creation of an assignment of funds by means of the
originator's payment order will be discussed next.

[3]   Being a mandate, the originator's payment order may be regarded to be
like a cheque, with respect to which, as to any other bill of exchange, the

---

[201] Ibid. The stipulation for the benefit of a third person (currently, under art. 1444 cc.) as
the basis for liability in the absence of direct privity, was advocated in the judgment of
L'Heureux-Dubé, ibid. at 589–92.

[202] Cf. *Pollack*, ibid. at 589 (*per* Kaufman JA), where liability for out-of-pocket expenses, 'as
well as [for] aggravation and lost time', was assessed 'in the most arbitrary manner' to be
in the sum of $1,000.

[203] R. R. Pennington, A. H. Hudson, and J. E. Mann, *Commercial Banking Law* (Estover, Ply-
mouth: MacDonald and Evans, 1978) at 285.

assignment theory is specifically rejected.[204] On the basis of this statutory position, Pennington, Hudson, and Mann maintain that 'it seems likely that by analogy the acceptance of the [payment order] by the [originator's] bank similarly does not constitute an assignment of funds'. Nonetheless, they further acknowledge that 'since the Bills of Exchange Act . . . only applies to bills and cheques, the argument is by no means conclusive and a deeper analysis is desirable'.[205]

English law distinguishes between legal and equitable assignment. The former must be absolute, under a written communication from the assignor, and perfected by notice to the debtor.[206] In a credit transfer, whether the assignee is the beneficiary or the beneficiary's bank, no direct communication is usually given to the assignee from the assignor (namely the originator), at least as part of the credit transfer process. Also, the originator (debtor)'s direction instructing the originator's bank to pay, can hardly be seen as a notice of an assignment which has not taken place yet, and in fact, may not even happen at all; for example, for the lack of funds in the originator's account to cover the originator's payment order. As well, a legal assignment must be for the entire debt.[206a] This undermines the possibility that the originator's payment order initiates legal assignment.

At the same time, an equitable assignment may be made more informally and may be for part of a debt. However, 'even so, not every mandate or authorization to pay money amounts to an equitable assignment'.[207]

Support to the application of the assignment theory comes from the American case of *Delbrueck* v. *Manufacturers Hanover Trust Co.*[208] It was stated in this case[209] that the originator's payment order to the originator's bank, ultimately followed by a payment order ('notice') given by the originator's bank to the beneficiary's bank, constitutes an assignment of funds held by the originator at the originator's bank either to the beneficiary's bank or to the beneficiary. It was held that while no assignment occurs in the absence of some form of communication to the assignee, such

---

[204] See s. 53(1) of the *Bills of Exchange Act* 1882 (UK), corresponding e.g. to s. 126 of the Canadian *Bills of Exchange Act*, R.S.C. 1985, C. B–4.; s. 53(a) of the Israeli *Bills of Exchange Ordinance* (Laws of the State of Israel New Version 1957, 12); s. 51 of the South African *Bills of Exchange Act* (No. 34 of 1964); and s. 88 of the Australian *Cheques and Payment Orders Act* 1986 (No. 145 of 1986), superseding (for cheques) s. 58 of the Australian *Bills of Exchange Act* 1909. See discussion in B(iii) s. 2 above.   [205] Above, n. 203 at 285.

[206] The standard provision is s. 136(1) of the *Law of Property Act*, 1925 (UK), c. 20, on which similar provisions are modelled throughout the Commonwealth. See e.g. s. 53(1) of the *Ontario Conveyancing and Law of Property Act*, R.S.O. 1990, c. C.34. But, notwithstanding Pennington, Hudson, and Mann, above, n. 203 at 285, the statutory language does not exclude the possibility that the notice to the debtor is to be given by someone other than the assignor, e.g. the assignee.

[206a] In *re Steel Wing Co. Ltd* [1921] 1 ch. 349

[207] Pennington, Hudson, and Mann, above, n. 203 at 286.

[208] 609F.2d 1047 (2nd Cir. 1979).   [209] Ibid., at 1051, alternative holding.

communication need not necessarily emanate from the assignor (origina-tor). Nor must it be directed to the assignee (where it is the beneficiary and not the beneficiary's bank). Suffice it for the communication to be given by the debtor (the originator's bank) to the assignee's agent (the beneficiary's bank). The Court thus bypassed the question as to whether the assignee is the beneficiary himself or the beneficiary's bank, the latter being treated either as the assignee or his agent.[210]

In effect, the Court treated the payment order issued to the beneficiary's bank, in the facts of the case, by the originator bank, as the 'notice' or com-munication completing the assignment of the debt owed by the origina-tor's bank to its customer, the originator, to the beneficiary or beneficiary's bank. Presumably, according to this reasoning, where the payment order of the originator's bank is issued to an intermediary bank, rather than to the beneficiary's bank, the assignment is completed only by the payment order sent to the beneficiary's bank by its own sending (intermediary) bank.

It seems that *Delbrueck* is premissed on viewing the originator's bank and each intermediary bank, respectively, as an agent and subagent act-ing for the originator (assignor) in advising the assignee or the assignee's agent (the beneficiary's bank) of the assignment, thereby completing it. Indeed, so far as equitable assignment is concerned, there is nothing to preclude the notice to the debtor (namely the originator's payment order to the originator's bank), which is not a required element of the assign-ment, from preceding the assignment itself, constituted by the advice given to the beneficiary's bank. Similarly, under that view, in an in-house transfer, the originator's payment order to the bank may be treated as serving both the assignment and the notice to the debtor.

Nevertheless, the assignment view of the credit transfer is fraught with difficulties. First, this view presupposes that a payment order is irrevoca-ble, so as to confer, from its inception, rights on the receiving bank. This is true for a CHIPS payment order, as the one sent to the beneficiary's bank in *Delbrueck*. As indicated in s. 14, below, this however, is not the case for payment orders in general. Second, a complex account transfer involving one or more intermediary's banks is not easily accommodated by the assignment view. Rather than one assignment from the originator to the beneficiary or the beneficiary's bank, such a transfer actually involves a series of assignments from each sender to the participant which is subsequent to the sender's own receiving bank. This introduces com-plications to the previous analysis and is in contradiction with the origi-nator's (and in fact each sender's) intention, who cannot be taken to

---

[210] For the beneficiary's bank as the beneficiary's agent see s 18, below.

intend to benefit any third party other than the beneficiary (or the beneficiary's bank).

Third, the debt owed by the beneficiary's bank to the beneficiary, at the conclusion of the credit transfer, is in fact viewed as distinct and original, rather than as derivative of the original debt owed at the initiation of the transaction by the originator's bank to the originator. Otherwise under the assignment theory, the beneficiary, as the assignee, if the beneficiary is to be so regarded, is to be owed directly by the originator's bank, as the debtor of the assigned debt. Furthermore under the assignment theory, the entitlement of the beneficiary or the beneficiary's bank would have been subject to defences which may be raised by the originator's bank against the originator, as is the universal rule governing the subjection of the assignee's claim against the debtor to the debtor's defences against the assignor.[211]

Fourth, an originator's bank may carry out a credit transfer even in the absence of funds in the originator's account, thereby creating a debt owed by the originator to the originator's bank, rather than transferring a debt owed by it to the originator. Fifth, a credit transfer may take place between two accounts belonging to the same person, in which case, no assignment can be said to occur.

Perhaps for all such reasons, in *Libyan Arab Foreign Bank* v. *Banker's Trust Co.*,[212] Staughton J. purported to reject the assignment view altogether. Accordingly, he stated that '[a]n [interbank] account transfer means the process by which some other . . . institution comes to owe money to the [beneficiary] . . ., and the obligation [of the originator's bank to the originator] is extinguished or reduced pro tanto'. Specifically rejecting 'dicta in one American case,' apparently referring to *Delbrueck*, he went on to note that in this context, '[t]ransfer may be a somewhat misleading word, since the original obligation is not assigned . . .; a new obligation by a new debtor is created'.[213]

Staughton J.'s view seems to be in line with the ultimate conclusion of Pennington, Hudson, and Mann. Having thoroughly reviewed pertinent case law, they stated that '[i]t is . . . generally accepted that a mere mandate to pay does not constitute an equitable assignment of funds, whether the payee is notified of the mandate or not.'[214]

Neither creating a trust nor initiating an assignment of funds, but **[4]** rather, being a mere mandate to pay, the originator's payment order generates 'a string of operations carried out by the different banks acting in a

---

[211] See, in general, ch. 3 of B. Geva, *Financing Consumer Sales and Product Defences* (Toronto: Carswell Legal Publications, 1984). [212] [1988] 1 Lloyd's L.R. 259 (Q.B.).
[213] Ibid., at 273. [214] Above, n. 203 at 288.

representative capacity'.[215] That is, the legal position of each participant is primarily determined under agency law. The leading case to that effect is *Royal Products Ltd.* v. *Midland Bank Ltd.*,[216] further discussed below in connection with the chain of liability of participating banks.[217]

(b) Completion, payment, and irrevocability

Introduction

[5]   The Jack Report[218] distinguished among the following four related concepts: discharge of the obligation paid by credit transfer, completion of payment, the countermand or revocability of the credit transfer, and the availability of funds. Cranston adds a fifth concept, that of bank reversal.[219] The occurrence of some may coincide at the same milestone; yet, each responds to a different legal issue and thus they are all conceptually distinct.

Among these concepts, discharge and revocability are self-explanatory. Completion concerns banks and not their customers. According to Cranston,[220] it refers to the point at the internal process of a bank where payment cannot unilaterally be reversed by it and in which the originator's bank has fulfilled its obligation. Funds availability, unlike completion, focuses on the beneficiary. It refers to the point of time where the beneficiary can use the funds deposited to his account. Finally, 'bank reversal' refers to the point beyond which a bank on its own volition cannot reverse a transfer.

[6]   I find this proliferation of concepts and terms to be unhelpful. To begin with, 'bank reversal' seems to be covered by 'completion'. On its part, insofar as it coincides with the accrual of rights to the beneficiary, 'completion' coincides with 'discharge'. As such it is the completion of payment between the originator and the beneficiary on their underlying transaction.

Alternatively, 'completion' may refer to the interbank payment for a payment order. In this sense, 'completion' should actually encompass the completion of payment, or its lack of reversibility (or revocability), for any payment order, including that of the originator. It is the equivalent of the

---

[215] E. P. Ellinger and E. L. Lomnicka, *Modern Banking Law*, 2nd edn. (Oxford: Clarendon Press, 1994) at 446.   [216] [1981] 2 Lloyd's L.R. 194 (Q.B.).

[217] See s. 15, below.

[218] R. B. Jack (chairman), *Banking Services: Law and Practice Report by the Review Committee* (London: Her Majesty's Stationery Office, 1989) at 107, around n. 6 and more in general, throughout ch. 12.

[219] R. Cranston, 'Law of International Transfers in England', in W. Hadding and U. H. Schneider (eds.), *Legal Issues in International Credit Transfers* (Berlin: Duncker & Hamblot, 1993), 223 at 223, 228, and 234.   [220] Ibid., at 228 and 231.

provision of cover for the payment order. In general, a payment order is paid by the sender in one of three ways. First, it can be paid by means of a debit to the sender's account with the receiving bank. Secondly, where the sender is a bank, the payment order can be paid by means of a credit to the receiving bank's account at the sending bank. Finally, an interbank payment order can be paid at a clearing or funds transfer system.

The time of payment at a clearing or funds transfer system is to be determined according to the funds transfer system rules. Payment by means of credit to an account is to be determined according to rules analogous to those determining when payment by credit to a beneficiary's account is made. This latter topic is discussed immediately below. Finally, payment by debit to the sender's account is determined by reference to the receiving bank's own procedures and practices.

Indeed, in this sense, the completion of payment is a distinct concept. Unlike the others, it relates to each individual payment order and not to the credit transfer as a whole.

Funds credited to the beneficiary's account may not become available [7] to the beneficiary's discretionary use due to priority accorded to claims against the beneficiary, whether by his bank or garnishing creditors. In principle, there is also the possibility of funds credited provisionally only so as not to confer on the beneficiary a right to use them.[221] Finally, a bank may be estopped from denying its customer access to funds on the basis of its representation as to their availability, even though in fact they are not.[222]

In all such cases 'funds availability' does not coincide with 'discharge'. Nevertheless, this may not generate a separate conceptual point of 'funds availability'. Thus, the first and third instances mentioned above, namely, creditors' priority and bank's estoppel, relate in general to the banker–customer relationship and are outside the mechanism of the credit transfer. The second instance, that of provisional credit, will be further discussed in connection with 'discharge'.

In fact, the Jack Report conceded that in practice, discharge 'will generally coincide with the point of funds availability'.[223] As an exception, however, it cited the situation involved in *The Chikuma*.[224] This case dealt with the Continental banking practice under which credit for a value-dated

---

[221] This is a standard practice (for example in Canada) in connection with the deposit of cheques by the payee/holder.

[222] Cranston, above, n. 219 at 234. But cf. *Astro Amo Compania Naviera S.A.* v. *Elf Union S.A. (The Zographia M)*, [1976] 2 Lloyd's L.R. 382 (Q.B.) at 393–5 (where notwithstanding the inaccurate information it provided, the bank did not remain responsible for *all* consequences).

[223] Above, n. 218 at 107, n. 6.

[224] *A/S Awilco* v. *Fulvia S.p.A. Di Navigazione, (The 'Chikuma')*, [1981] Lloyd's L.R. 371 (H.L.).

payment order (namely a payment order received prior to the indicated payment date) is posted promptly to the beneficiary's account upon the arrival of the payment order to the beneficiary's bank. Funds so posted to the account become available immediately to the beneficiary, subject to interest charges up to value date. If they remain in the account, they do not earn interest until value date. According to Lord Bridge, 'in the eyes of an English banker or lawyer' this practice 'has some strikingly unusual features' so as not to confer on the beneficiary '*unconditional* right to the immediate use of the funds transferred'.[225] For our purposes, this would mean that while funds became available at the time of crediting the account, no discharge has occurred yet, prior to the value date.

Nonetheless, such a scenario will not arise under the Anglo-North American banking practice, where until the payment due date the beneficiary's bank does not act on a value-dated payment order. Between receipt by the beneficiary's bank and the payment due date, the payment order is usually stored in that bank computer. No pre-due date advice is given to the beneficiary. Nor is the beneficiary's account forward valued. Credit is posted to the beneficiary's account and advice is given to him on the payment due date. 'Funds availability' thus coincides with 'discharge'.

Arguably, *The Chikuma* reflects a misunderstanding of the implications of the Continental banking practice. The better view would have been to regard 'discharge' as occurring upon 'funds availability' at the time the account was credited, though subject to interest charges. Regardless, as explained, this is an unusual situation which does not justify a conceptual separation between 'discharge' and 'funds availability'.

[8]   In the final analysis, 'completion' pertains to the payment of each individual payment order. As such, it is a distinct concept. However, as for the completion of the credit transfer as a whole, the two central concepts are 'discharge' and 'revocation'.[226]

Discharge: completion of payment between the originator and beneficiary[227]

[9]   It has long been established at common law that 'the relation between banker and customer, as far as the pecuniary dealings are concerned, [is] that of debtor and creditor'.[228] Money to the credit of the customer can be placed either by the customer himself or by a third party,[229] usually a debtor of the customer. Regardless from whom it is received, 'the money

---

[225] Ibid., at 374 and 375; emphasis added.

[226] Basically, this is Ellinger and Lomnicka's position. Above, n. 215 at 458–70.

[227] The ensuing discussion is an enhanced version of B. Geva, 'Payment into a Bank Account' [1990] 3 J. Int'l Bank. L. 108.

[228] *Foley* v. *Hill* (1848), 2 H.L.C. 28, at 45; 9 E.R. 1002, at 1009, *per* Lord Campbell.

[229] Ibid. 2 H.L.C. 28 at 43; 9 E.R. 1002 at 1008.

placed in the custody of a banker is . . . the money of the banker' who is obligated 'to repay to the [customer] when demanded, a sum equivalent to that paid into his hands'.[230]

It follows that payment by a third party into the customer's bank account is in effect a mode of discharging the payor's obligation to the customer by constituting the bank a debtor to the payee-customer,[231] in lieu of the payor, in respect of the sum payable.[232] True, in a given case, depending on the interpretation of the applicable contract, towards the beneficiary, the originator may have not been in breach of the originator's contractual payment obligation, when on due date, the originator merely sets the process in motion, by causing the originator's bank to dispatch or direct the funds towards the beneficiary, with funds actually reaching their destination at a later date.[233] However, even then, absolute discharge of the monetary debt occurs upon substitution. This substitution between the payor and the payee's bank as the payee's debtor is the equivalent of a payment in cash by the payor to the payee, whose effect is to discharge the underlying obligation between them. By the time this substitution occurs, the right to countermand payment has been lost to the payor, and funds have usually become available to the payee by his bank. In turn, this substitution must have occurred by the point in time when funds become available to the payee's bank.

The ensuing discussion aims at determining the point of time when the substitution between the payor and the payee's bank as the payee's debtor takes place so as to discharge the underlying obligation (and in this sense, complete payment) between the payor and the payee.

An obligation to make 'payment in cash' into a designated bank **[10]** account may be discharged by means of delivery of coins and bank notes to the bank. Alternatively, under 'modern commercial practice', as set out by Brandon J. in *The Brimnes*, such a payment may be carried out by 'any

---

[230] Ibid. 2 H.L.C. 28 at 36 to 37; 9 E.R. 1002 at 1005 to 1006, *per* Lord Cottenham LC.

[231] It must however be remembered that to discharge the debt, such method of payment must have been authorized by the payer and the payee. See R. M. Goode, *Payment Obligations in Commercial and Financial Transactions* (London: Sweet & Maxwell, 1983) at 109 and 111.

[232] R. King, 'The Receiving Bank's Role in Credit Transfer Transactions' (1982) 45 Mod. L. Rev. 369 at 381.

[233] For such determination under civil law, see e.g. *J. Raymond Dupuis Inc.* v. *Produits généraux de la construction (1980) Ltée* [1988] A.Q. No. 1087 (Que. C.A.), on-line: QL (OJ), discussed above, in (vii) s. 2, where the contract between the originator and the beneficiary required the originator to pay by having, by a certain date, a specified sum of money dispatched ('acheminée') to the beneficiary's account by means of a credit transfer. The originator instructed the originator's bank to make payment in the required sum, and the originator's bank acted on the instructions, by that date. It was held that the originator was not in breach of contract notwithstanding the arrival of funds to the beneficiary at a later date.

commercially recognized method of transferring funds, the result of which is to give the transferee the unconditional right to the immediate use of the funds transferred'.[234] In this context, 'unconditional' was broadly construed by the House of Lords in *The Chikuma* to mean 'unfettered and unrestricted' and not merely 'neither subject to the fulfilment of a condition precedent nor defeasible on failure to fulfil a condition subsequent.'[235] Accordingly, payment into a bank account is carried out by conferring on the payee an unfettered and unrestricted right against his own bank to the immediate use of the funds.

The 'modern commercial practice' referred to by Brandon J. in *The Brimnes*[236] is a credit transfer initiated by the originator-payor's instructions to his bank 'to transfer an amount standing to the credit of [the originator] . . . to the credit of [the beneficiary-payee's] account'.[237] Where the originator and beneficiary have their respective accounts at different banks, the instructions are communicated to the beneficiary's bank by means of one or a series of successive interbank payment messages. Irrespective of whether more than one bank is involved in the payment, the transfer results in the extinction of, or the reduction in, the debt owed to the originator by his bank, and the corresponding emergence of, or increase in, the debt owed to the beneficiary by his bank.[238]

In the course of the funds transfer from the originator's to the beneficiary's account, whether on the books of the same bank, or through other banks, there is uncertainty as to the precise point in time when an 'unfettered and unrestricted' right accrues to the payee so that payment is complete.[239] In *Rekstin* v. *Severo Sibirsko*, Talbot J. stated that payment from one account to another 'cannot be done by mere entries in the bank's books without communication with the transferee'.[240] However, *Rekstin* is not regarded as good authority for the proposition that notification to the beneficiary by his bank is required to complete payment into his account.[241] The facts were unusual. The case involved payment for no consideration to a beneficiary who did not expect to receive it, by an originator purporting solely to defeat a judgment creditor.[242] In addition, only the

---

[234] *The Brimnes, Tenax Steamship Co. Ltd* v. *The Brimnes (Owners)*, [1973] 1 All E.R. 769 at 782 *per* Brandon J.(Q.B.), aff'd [1974] 3 All E.R. 88 (C.A.).

[235] *The Chikuma*, above, n. 224 at 375.   [236] Above, n. 234 at 782.

[237] *Royal Products*, above, n. 216 at 198.

[238] See, in general, *Libyan Arab Foreign Bank*, above, n. 212 at 273.

[239] As required by Brandon J., see text at n. 235, above.

[240] [1933] 1 K.B. 47 (C.A.) at 57.

[241] The case is critically analysed in Pennington, Hudson, and Mann, above, n. 203 at 292 to 294.

[242] This was an attempt by a judgment debtor to transfer funds from his account to the account (in the books of the same bank) of a body enjoying diplomatic immunity, to whom it was not indebted, and for the sole purpose of defeating a judgment creditor. The bank

debit entry to the originator's account and the preparation of the transfer slip, but not the credit entry to the beneficiary's account, were completed by the bank prior to the service of the judgment creditor's garnishee order.[243] Thus, 'payment' may have not been completed prior to the service of the garnishee order for a reason other than absence of notification to the beneficiary. Finally, in normal commercial circumstances, the advice stage is not treated as part of the payment process.[244] A rule based on notification is thus quite impractical and strongly disfavoured.[245]

Attempts have been made to identify the emergence of the 'unconditional right to the immediate use of the funds'[246] in the course of the internal processing by the beneficiary's bank. In *The Brimnes*, Megaw J. was of the view that

[11]

> Whatever mode or process is used, 'payment' is not achieved until the process has reached the stage at which the creditor has received cash or that which he is prepared to treat as the equivalent of cash, or has a credit available on which, in the normal course of business or banking practice, he can draw, if he wishes in the form of cash.[247]

However, this is quite a flexible formulation which does not identify the precise point in the process where the equivalent to cash is received by the payee-creditor.

A convenient point of reference is the time when the designated account is credited.[248] Thus, Best CJ held in *Eyles* v. *Ellis* that payment was made when the '[transferred] sum was actually placed in the [benefi-

---

complied with the judgment debtor's instructions by debiting and closing the account and making out a transfer slip. A garnishee order nisi was served by the judgment creditor on the bank before notice had been given to the transferee.

[243] Above, n. 240 at 55, where the reference to the 'plaintiff's books' must have been meant to read as 'the bank's books'.

[244] Thus, even in an on-line payment, advice may be given off-line, and in theory only as part of the contents of a periodical statement.

[245] See, for example, *Momm* v. *Barclays Bank International Ltd.*, [1976] 3 All E.R. 588 (Q.B.) at 597, where the Court rejected counsel's submission 'that . . . Rekstin . . . decides that there could not have been any completed payment unless and until an advice note recording the credit to [the] account had been dispatched . . . or had been received'. See also *Royal Products*, above, n. 216 at 199.

[246] As required by Brandon J.; see text at n. 235, above.

[247] *The Brimnes, Tenax Steamship Co. Ltd.* v. *Owners of the motor vessel Brimnes*, [1974] 3 All E.R. 88 at 110 (C.A.), aff'g [1973] 1 All E.R. 769.

[248] An obligation to credit the beneficiary's account within specified time limits may be prescribed by a funds transfer system rule. For example, in Canada, under s. 43 of By-law No. 7 Respecting the Large Value Transfer System, passed by CPA Board of Directors in Nov. 1997 and approved by the Governor in Council on 2 Apr. 1998, PC 1998–568, and subject to specific exceptions (enumerated in ss. 43–7), a beneficiary's bank is required to credit the beneficiary's account no later than upon the completion of the pertaining settlement on the books of the Bank of Canada.

ciary's] account'.[249] A similar view was expressed in *The Laconia* by Donaldson J. at trial[250] and more strongly by Lord Fraser in the House of Lords.[251] Nonetheless, designating the posting of credit to the beneficiary's account as the point of 'payment' involves two uncertainties.

First, credit posted to a bank account may be provisional or conditional upon arrival of funds. This is a universal practice in connection with a cheque deposited to an account.[252] Arguably, in the absence of the receipt of adequate security, such as for example, a central bank's guarantee, the practice may also be exercised by a bank receiving an interbank message for which an interbank payment has yet to be received in cover. Needless to say, the posting of a provisional credit to a beneficiary's account cannot be viewed as conferring upon him an 'unfettered and unrestricted' right, as required.

Second, the precise point of finality or irreversibility in the internal process of posting a credit to an account may not be firmly established. The accounting process may be premissed on either manual or computer entries automatically posted throughout the day on the basis of incoming messages, subject to final judgment and discretionary decision-making at the end of the day. Alternatively, in both manual and computerized environments, account posting may be made by means of overnight batch processing. Either way, the actual point of crediting the account is hard to identify.

In fact, posting credit to a final funds balance ought to be regarded as the equivalent to giving cash to the beneficiary. Nonetheless, the question is whether an 'unconditional right to the immediate use of the funds' did not arise in the beneficiary's favour even earlier in the process.

These concerns gave rise to two responses which are set out in *Momm v. Barclays Bank International Ltd.*[253] The first response acknowledges the difficulty in ascertaining the moment of crediting the account. Consequently, it satisfies itself in ascertaining solely the day of posting the credit to the account. The second response substitutes the decision to credit the account for the actual posting of credit. In fact, the actual holding of *Momm* was premissed on the latter view. The former was regarded as setting the upper limit for 'payment' to occur.

In explaining the first view, Kerr J. purported to take into account views of lawyers and bankers who would be inclined to think that 'a payment

---

[249] (1827), 4 Bing. 112 at 113; 130 E.R. 710 at 711.

[250] *Mardorf Peach & Co. Ltd.* v. *Attica Sea Carriers Corp. of Liberia (The 'Laconia')*, [1975] 1 Lloyd's L.R. 634 at 640 (Q.B.).

[251] *Mardorf Peach & Co. Ltd.* v. *Attica Sea Carriers Corp. of Liberia, (The 'Laconia')*, [1977] 1 All E.R. 545 at 563 (H.L.).

[252] See, for example, *Bank of Nova Scottia* v. *Sharp*, [1975] 6 W.W.R. 97 (B.C. C.A.).

[253] Above, n. 245.

has been made if the payee's account is credited with the payment at the close of business on the value date, at any rate if it was credited intentionally and in good faith and not by error or fraud'.[254] Furthermore, lawyers and bankers would say that 'if a payment requires to be made on a certain day by debiting a pay[o]r customer's account and crediting a payee customer's account, then the position at the end of that day must be in fact and in law that this has either happened or not happened, but that the position cannot be left in the air'.[255] In Kerr J.'s opinion, 'both these propositions are correct in law'.[256] He considered the testimony of the bank's witnesses who had said that 'they acted on the basis that the following morning was to be treated as an extension of the value day, because the final balances for that day are not available from the computer until then, and because they always had in mind the possibility of being able to reverse the entries'.[257] This position was rejected altogether:

A day is a day. For banking purposes it ends at the close of working hours, and otherwise at midnight. Commerce requires that it should be clearly ascertainable by the end of a day whether a payment due to be made on that day has been made or not. Whether this has happened or not cannot be held in suspense until the following morning.[258]

It is nonetheless obvious that this response does not specifically address the possibility of posting to the account a mere provisional credit.[259] Furthermore, it fails to deal with situations where a more precise determination of the time of payment is required.[260] As indicated, it sets a deadline for 'payment' to have occurred but does not specify its actual occurrence.

Ultimately, Kerr J. preferred to be more specific and to formulate a response identifying the moment of decision and initiation of the internal process as the point of 'payment'. He thus noted that 'payment . . . was complete when [the bank] decided to accept [the] instructions to credit the [beneficiary's] account and the computer processes for doing so were set in motion'.[261] As the culmination of these processes, the posting of credit to the account was a non-discretionary ministerial act, a mere formality recording the earlier 'payment'.

This was well in line with the view expressed by Brandon J. in *The Brimnes*. Thereunder, payment occurs at 'the time when the order to transfer . . . is executed'. In an in-house transfer from the originator's account to that of the beneficiary, 'the effective time of execution . . . from the point

---

[254] Ibid., at 595.   [255] Ibid.   [256] Ibid.

[257] Ibid., at 598.   [258] Ibid.

[259] In the facts of the case this was not a realistic scenario. See text after n. 263, below.

[260] As where 'payment' competes with countermand of payment or a garnishment order as in *Rekstin*, discussed around nn. 240 to 242, above.

[261] See above, n. 245 at 598.

of view of availability of the funds to [the beneficiary] is the time of the decision to debit one account and credit the other'. Thus, 'the time of transfer or payment' is marked by 'decision'.[262]

Momm was criticized as containing ambiguities notwithstanding its 'appealing appearance of certainty'.[263] Indeed, like *The Brimnes*, it involved a transfer at a bank holding the payor's funds. Under such circumstances, the possibility of a decision to post a mere provisional credit to the payee's account was quite remote. The judgment may be less helpful where the possibility of a provisional credit is more likely to be present. Furthermore, in *Momm*, due to regulatory constraints, the execution of the payment instructions necessitated a decision by a supervisor. Usually however, there may be no more than 'the record of the various internal accounting processes . . .'.[264] Also, one decision may be overruled, or subject to be overruled, by a higher level. In sum, under normal circumstances, the precise moment of 'decision' may be quite illusive.[265]

Indeed, prior to computerization in the relevant bank in *Momm*, debits and credits were posted to respective accounts during the day as they arose. This afforded a final decision-making stage at the end of the day. With computerization, which was in place at the time the events giving rise to *Momm* took place, a customer's final balance became known only as it had been produced by computer during the night so as to be available on the following morning. In this context, there is no reference to the exercise of human judgment in normal circumstances.[266] Nevertheless, it does not follow that a 'decision' must be invented where it does not exist. By setting the end of the day as the upper limit for 'payment',[267] Kerr J. offered a fallback alternative to situations where no 'decision' is manifest. In practical terms then, the judgment sent a message to the banking community: set a 'decision' stage in the course of the day a message is processed or else 'payment' has been made at its end anyway, whether or not any 'decision' fell.[268]

The need to identify an obvious decision stage was bypassed in *Libyan Arab Foreign Bank v. Manufacturers Hanover Trust Co.*[269] In that case, the

---

[262] [1973] 1 All E.R. 769 at 784.

[263] B. Crawford, 'Credit Transfers of Funds in Canada: The Current Law' (1978–9) 3 Can. Bus. L.J. 119 at 142.   [264] Ibid.

[265] See also A. L. Tyree, 'Electronic Funds Transfer in New Zealand' (1978–9) 8 N.Z.U.L.R. 139, at 149 to 150.

[266] For the internal process, see above, n. 245 at 590 to 593.

[267] See discussion around nn. 261 to 266, above.

[268] This is contrary to *Houston Contracting Co.* v. *Chase Manhattan Bank* 539 F. Supp. 247 (S.D.N.Y., 1982) holding on technical grounds that under UCC Article 4 the receiver's failure to respond to a transfer order by midnight of the day of its issuance was not tantamount to an acceptance.

[269] [1989] 1 Lloyd's L.R. 608 (Q.B.).

receiving bank credited the beneficiary's account and debited its *nostro* account[270] with the sending bank where its funds had been held. It was held 'by parity of reasoning with Momm's case' that 'these actions within [the receiving bank] constituted a full completion of the payment . . .' as early as in the morning of the day.[271] Stated otherwise, the completion of the internal process in the course of the day within the receiving bank served as evidence that a 'decision' must have taken place. It is tempting to argue that had the internal process included an end of the day review stage, no 'decision' and hence no 'payment' would have been held to occur at an earlier point.[272]

As *The Brimnes* shows, a banking 'decision' may be involved also in normal circumstances. In that case, the internal processing at the beneficiary's bank was as follows: each telex transfer was received, verified, and tested, was given to the money transfer department to be logged in, and was taken to the bookkeeping department for determination as to whether sufficient funds were available in the remitting account to effect payment. Then, in each case, funds were withheld from the paying account, and the final decision to credit the payee's account was made. Subsequently, internal advices were posted in a journal. The journal was taken to the data-processing department where after business hours transaction information was transferred to a magnetic tape. Computer records were then updated by a night-work force between midnight and 5.00 a.m. the next morning. A print-out listing all transactions and final balance for the previous day was available between 4.00 and 8.00 a.m.[273] Under those circumstances, having carefully reviewed the process, Brandon J. could find that while 'the precise time of [the payment] decision cannot be fixed with certainty . . . its probable time can be established within certain limits'.[274] In the facts of the case, it occurred around noon on the day the telex was received and processed.[275]

It should be noted that while *Momm* was concerned with the 'completion' of payment by the beneficiary's bank, *The Brimnes* dealt with the originator's 'discharge' by payment to the beneficiary. Yet, each case focused on the same milestone, that of the 'decision' by the beneficiary's bank, as determining the occurrence of the event.

However, the uncertainty as to the universality of the 'decision' stage, **[12]** as well as banks' ability to manipulate their practices so as to time their

---

[270] In a correspondent bank relationship, the *nostro* ('our') account is an administrative or suspense account on the books of the depositor bank as the shadow of, and for reconciliation with, the *vostro* ('your') account on the books of the account holder bank.

[271] Above, n. 269 at 631. In the facts of the case 'notification to [the payee] confirmed the completion of the payment'. Ibid. at 632.

[272] But cf. text which follows n. 273, below.　　[273] See above, n. 262 at 779 to 780.

[274] Ibid., at 779.　　[275] See text at n. 310, below.

'decision' to coincide with any point in the course of the process, have prompted a search for alternatives. Attempts have thus been made to establish an earlier point in the process as 'payment'. The attempts have focused on the originator who cannot control the internal machinery at the beneficiary's bank as well as on an alleged mercantile custom. The attempts may be consistent with the view that 'payment' occurs simultaneously with the accrual in the beneficiary's hands of an unfettered and unrestricted right against his own bank,[276] only if the accrual of such right is quite an early point in the process.

In *The Brimnes*, Brandon J. referred to the possibility of regarding 'payment' as being made as early as when the payor sets the machinery in motion by requesting his bank to generate the funds transfer.[277] However, the point was not pursued in argument, and it may be universally agreed that this is too early a stage to be regarded as 'payment'.[278]

The earliest point seriously considered is that of communication to the payee's bank. In *The Georgios C*,[279] the payor's bank sent to the payee's bank 'a banker's payment slip'. According to Lord Denning, MR, 'such a slip is treated in commercial circles as cash'.[280] In fact, according to Phillimore LJ, 'it is agreed between the parties that this banker's payment slip was equivalent to cash'.[281] Hence, its delivery to the payee's bank was 'sufficient tender'.[282] An accepted tender is 'payment'.[283]

This view, based on mercantile custom, was further developed by Lord Denning in *The Laconia*[284] where he linked it to a policy reason focusing on the payor's lack of control over the internal process at the beneficiary's bank. Observing that the internal process at the beneficiary's bank, leading to the beneficiary's account being credited, may take up to twenty-four hours, Lord Denning stated:

. . . 'processing' was a piece of mechanism inside the [payee's bank] itself, which worked fast or slow according to the power put behind it. Its speed should not affect the legal position of the parties making or receiving payment . . . parties in business must know where they stand.[285]

---

[276] Notwithstanding text at nn. 239 and 252, above.   [277] See above, n. 262 at 783.

[278] But cf. *Delbrueck* above, n. 208 at 1051, regarding a bank-depositor's payment instructions as an assignment of funds.

[279] *Empresa Cubana de Fletes* v. *Lagonisi Shipping Co. Ltd. (The 'Georgios C')* [1971] 1 Lloyd's L.R. 7 (C.A.).

[280] Ibid., at 14.   [281] Ibid., at 15.

[282] Ibid., at 14, *per* Lord Denning MR. See also, at 16 *per* Cairns LJ.

[283] Tender denotes an attempted performance by the debtor that was not completed solely due to the creditor's refusal to receive it. *Dixon v. Clark* (1848), 5 C.B. 365 at 377; 136 E.R. 919 at 923 to 924 (Court of Common Pleas).

[284] *Mardorf Peach & Co.* v. *Attica Sea Carriers Corp. of Liberia, The Laconia*, [1976] 2 All E.R. 249 (C.A.) rvr'ng [1975] 1 Lloyd's L.R. 634 (Q.B.), rvr'd [1977] 1 All E.R. 545 (H.L.).

[285] [1976] 2 All E.R. 249 at 255.

Regarding the originator's bank as the originator's agent and the beneficiary's bank as the beneficiary's agent, and stressing that 'the banks themselves regard the "payment order"[286] as equivalent to cash' he continued:

If the paying bank had sent actual currency, the payment would be made when it was handed over the counter to the receiving bank, and accepted without objection. So also with the 'payment order'. It is equivalent to cash paid over to the receiving bank. If accepted without objection, it is the equivalent of its customer himself accepting cash without objection.[287]

On appeal to the House of Lords, Lord Russell was inclined to agree with Lord Denning as to the time of payment.[288] On his part, Lord Salmon was prepared to see 'no real difference between a payment in dollar bills and a payment by payment orders which in the banking world are generally regarded and accepted as cash'.[289] However, he stressed that when cash is delivered over the counter for deposit at a customer's account some time passes, and some internal processing is involved before credit is made available to the customer for withdrawal. Nevertheless, he said, delivery of cash just prior to bank closure on payment day is 'punctual payment'. He preferred 'to express no concluded view' as to whether the same is true for the delivery of a 'payment order' just prior to bank closure on payment day.[290] However, his language may well suggest that he in fact focused on 'funds availability' to the beneficiary, rather than on 'completion' of payment by the beneficiary's bank.

It is important to note that the interbank messages in *The Georgios C* and in *The Laconia* were embodied, respectively, in a 'banker's payment slip' and a 'payment order'. Each constitutes an obligation of the transmitting bank.[291] However, in *The Brimnes*, where the payment instructions had been telexed, Brandon J. declined to treat their receipt as 'conditional payment' in the same way the receipt of a cheque would be.[292] Likewise, in the Court of Appeal, Megaw LJ could not see any 'useful analogy between, on

---

[286] The nature of the payment order is further discussed in n. 291, below.
[287] Above, n. 285.   [288] [1977] 1 All E.R. 545 at 566 to 567.
[289] Ibid., 559.   [290] Ibid.
[291] According to Lord Wilberforce in *The Laconia*, 'A payment order is a document issued by one bank to another under the London Currency Settlement Scheme ('LCSS') by which banks maintain dollar suspense accounts in which they credit or debit each other with sums in dollars and make periodical settlements.' [1977] 1 All E.R. 545 at 551. The arbitrators in that case explained that the payment order is an advice having three characteristics: it is (1) 'an acknowledgement by the originating bank that it . . . credited the recipient' bank's suspense account with the dollar amount entered on the order, (2) 'a request by the originating bank to the recipient to inform' the payee of the payment, and (3) cash equivalent among banks. [1975] 1 Lloyd's L.R. 634 at 639. The LCSS is not a clearing system and no actual transfer of funds takes place thereunder. Accordingly, the recipient bank must be taken to receive on the payment order 'a promise of payment at their next settlement with the [originating bank].' [1977] 1 All E.R. 545 at 563 *per* Lord Fraser.
[292] Above, n. 262 at 782 to 784.

the one hand, a payment made by delivery of cash or of a cheque . . . and, on the other hand, telex instructions to pay'. Unlike the receipt of a cheque by a payee-creditor, 'the receipt [by the beneficiary's bank] of a telex containing instructions to transfer funds from one account into another account confers on the holder of the telex no [enforceable legal right to a sum of money]'. Hence, in the absence of evidence to the treatment of such telex instructions as irrevocable, he saw no ground for holding them to constitute 'payment by the mere receipt of the document containing the instructions'.[293]

No distinction between telex instructions and a 'payment order' was made by Lloyd LJ, the trial judge in the subsequent case of *The Afovos*.[294] He thought that the acceptance of the telex instructions constitute 'payment'. In his view, payment made by telex transfer from one bank to another, for the account of a customer, is complete 'when the telex is received and tested by the receiving bank'.[295] In *The Brimnes*, the telex message reached the bank at 4.53 a.m. The bank opened business at 9.00 a.m. Only then was the telex tested and verified. Subsequently, it was logged in the money transfer department. Around noon the telex was acted on at the bookkeeping department. Balances were updated overnight. Under those circumstances, 'receipt' appears to have occurred shortly after 9.00 a.m. and 'decision' to have fallen around noon.[296] It thus seems that Lloyd LJ would have held that 'payment' was made shortly after 9.00 a.m.[297]

Where unlike in *The Brimnes*, no cover is provided for the telex message, this result is quite startling. Surely it cannot mean that 'payment' is made upon the receipt and testing of a telex irrespective of the availability of funds. Perhaps anticipating this criticism in *The Afovos*, Lloyd LJ linked 'payment' also to the movement of funds. Thus, while stressing that 'it is unnecessary that the funds should have been credited to the [beneficiary's] account' as well as that 'the [beneficiary] should have been in position to transfer the funds out of the account', he nevertheless anticipated that 'the funds should have been received by the bank for the owner's account'.[298] Accordingly, under what may be characterized as a 'hypothetical positive response' test, payment occurs at the first point in time when an inquiry by the beneficiary-customer as to arrival of funds would be responded to by a positive answer from the bank.[299]

---

[293] [1974] 3 All E.R. 88 at 111 to 112.

[294] *Afovos Shipping Co. SA* v. *R. Pagnan and F. Lli*, (*The 'Afovos'*), [1980] 2 Lloyd's L.R. 469 (Q.B.), *rvs'd* [1982] 3 All E.R. 18 (C.A.), *aff'd* [1983] 1 All E.R. 449 (H.L.).

[295] [1980] 2 Lloyd's L.R. 469 at 473. In the House of Lords, as to 'what is to be regarded as the time of payment when effected by telex transfers', Lord Hailsham '[did] not feel that the present case [was] a suitable occasion to decide this question.' [1983] 1 All E.R. 449 at 454.

[296] Above, n. 262 at 779 to 780.   [297] See text at n. 295, above.

[298] [1980] 2 Lloyd's L.R. 469 at 473; emphasis in the original.

[299] Ibid.

Obviously, this may require the determination as to when cover was provided to the receiving bank. This is where the issue of the 'completeness of payment', inasmuch as it pertains to the individual payment order sent to the receiving bank, becomes relevant.[300]

The proposed distinction between *The Brimnes* and *The Afovos* is supported by *The Zographia M.*[301] In this judgment, Ackner J. specifically distinguished *The Afovos* from *The Brimnes* on the basis of the provision of cover to the receiving bank in conjunction with the dispatch of the telex instructions in the latter but not in the former case.[302]

In *Royal Products Ltd.* v. *Midland Bank Ltd.*[303] Webster J. held that:

[the originator's bank] had carried out [the originator's] instructions when it had enabled [the beneficiary] to draw on or otherwise use the amount of credit transferred, which [the beneficiary] would have been able to do once [the originator's bank] had, in one way or another and either directly or indirectly, *made funds available [to the beneficiary's bank]* . . . and had notified [it] that the sum was to be credited to the account of [the beneficiary].[304]

In that case, funds were made available to the beneficiary's bank by the transmitting bank which had opened a provisional account for the beneficiary's bank and credited it with the amount transferred.[305] 'Notice' given to the beneficiary's bank in effect marked 'payment' solely on the basis of funds availability, and irrespective of the absence of 'assent' given to the transfer by the beneficiary's bank.[306] Indeed, no 'hypothetical positive response' test was mentioned; however, inasmuch as funds availability and notice to the beneficiary's bank were held as sufficient to enable the payee to use the funds, such a test must have been implied in the judgment.

In fact, a 'hypothetical positive response' test goes back to *The Effy.*[307] In that case, Mocatta J. explained *The Georgios*[308] on the basis of such a test and implied that a receipt of communication by the beneficiary's bank in the case at bar would have been tender of payment.[309] It should however be noted that in *The Effy* the transmitting bank provided cover to its cable by crediting the account of the beneficiary's bank. Thus, 'receipt' of telex instructions by the beneficiary's bank can mark payment only where

---

[300] See s. 6, above.   [301] Above, n. 222.

[302] Ibid., at 390.   [303] Above, n. 216.

[304] Ibid., at 198 to 199. Emphasis added. In that case, the payor and payee were the same person. This is irrelevant for our purposes.

[305] This was in clear departure from the standard practice of a clearing house settlement between the two Maltese banks which usually took place on the books of the reserve bank. Ibid., at 200.   [306] Ibid., at 198 to 199.

[307] *Zim Israel Navigation Co. Ltd* v. *Effy Shipping Corp. (The 'Effy')*, [1972] 1 Lloyd's L.R. 18 (Q.B.).   [308] Discussed in text at n. 279–82, above.

[309] Above, n. 307 at 33.

funds are available. However, even then some judgment ought to be made at the receiving bank as to the actual availability of funds.

This analysis narrows the gap between the 'receipt' and 'decision' benchmarks. Certainly, 'hypothetical positive response' requires some measure of discretion and decision making. Furthermore, no 'hypothetical positive response' can be given prior to communication to the department in charge of the account. 'Receipt' thus implies that some internal process has been underway. In *The Brimnes* it must have occurred closer to noon than to 9.00 a.m.[310]

It follows that Lloyd LJ's straight 'receipt' test[311] should not be taken at face value. In fact, he himself had in mind a subsequent point, namely that of 'hypothetical positive response'.[312]

It is noteworthy that the 'hypothetical positive response' test may be supported also by *Momm*. Thus, according to Kerr J., following the 'decision' to credit their account.[313] the [beneficiaries] would have been allowed to draw against [the sum paid to their account] at once. If they had enquired whether the payment had been made, they would have been given an affirmative and not an equivocating answer . . .'[314]

In the final analysis, the 'hypothetical positive response' test is particularly useful in the absence of an early 'decision'. Provided the point of the 'hypothetical positive response' can be identified, the test seems to work better than the end of the day upper limit proposed by Kerr J. in *Momm*[315] as a fall-back benchmark. Accordingly, a bank which delays 'decision' to the end of the process may nevertheless be regarded as 'paying' earlier on. In other words, the 'hypothetical positive response' test narrows the area for manipulation, at least where funds are available. In the absence of available cover, lack of 'decision' may still defer 'payment' to the end of the day.

Indeed, the timing of a 'hypothetical positive response' is naturally linked to the internal procedures of the beneficiary's bank. This may not satisfy the originator's control rationale, so as to meet Lord Denning's wishes that the internal process at the beneficiary's bank should not affect the occurrence of 'payment'.[316] However, as demonstrated by *Momm*, banks are not given an open-ended power to devise internal practices and procedures aimed at postponing accountability to the beneficiary indefinitely,[317] it is reasonable to assume that the timing of a 'hypothetical positive response' within the internal processing procedures of a bank will be closely scrutinized. In any event, it must be recognized that even a

---

[310] See text at n. 296, above.   [311] See text at n. 295, above.
[312] See text at n. 299, above.   [313] As discussed around n. 262, above.
[314] [1976] 3 All E.R. 588 at 594.   [315] See discussion around nn. 266–8 and 272, above.
[316] See text following n. 285, above.
[317] Bank practice is relevant but not always decisive. See Tyree, above, n. 265 at 149 to 150.

straight 'receipt' test may not always satisfy the originator's concerns. Thus, the timely 'receipt' by the beneficiary's bank is anyway dependent on internal processing at the originator's bank and possibly at intermediary banks.[318] The originator himself has no more control on that than on the processing by the beneficiary's bank. Nevertheless, the 'hypothetical positive response' test is likely to establish 'payment' early on the process and thereby reduce uncertainty. Furthermore, in response to Megaw LJ's doubts as to the juridical nature of telex instructions,[319] the test implies the irrevocability of such instructions, at least once acted upon. It thus adds certainty to payment by wire transfer.

In fact, both 'hypothetical positive response' and 'decision' tests put the beneficiary's bank holding the transmitting bank's funds at some risk. Thus, an account having sufficient funds at the time of either the 'hypothetical positive response' or 'decision' may be subsequently depleted, prior to the pertaining debit firmly posted to it. This however ought to be regarded as a risk voluntarily assumed by a bank which does not act promptly on a funded interbank message. Stated otherwise, any rule other than that providing that 'payment' is made only at the closing of the banking day,[320] necessarily results in encouraging banks to continuously monitor incoming and outgoing payments and firmly post them to the pertaining account throughout the day.

So far, views applying a straight 'receipt' test to 'payment' by means of a 'banker's payment slip' or 'payment order'[321] have not been overruled. Nonetheless, judgments stating these views may be flawed in several respects. First, as clearly demonstrated in *The Laconia*, the rationalization of the 'receipt' test is strongly flavoured with agency terminology. It regards the payee's bank as acting as the beneficiary's agent in receiving payment.[322] This position however has not been universally accepted, and in fact was criticized as contrary to principle.[323] Indeed, coins and bank notes delivered by the payor to the payee's bank in payment to the payee's account do not belong to the payee as principal but rather to his bank which in turn becomes indebted to him.[324] The same applies to an

---

[318] For communications breakdown at an intermediate bank see *Evra Corp.* v. *Swiss Bank Corp.*, 673 F 2d 951 (7th. Cir., 1982), *rev'g* 522 F. Supp. 820 (ND Ill., 1981).

[319] See text following n. 292, above.   [320] Cf. discussion around n. 266–75, above.

[321] See text at n. 284–97, above.

[322] In the Court of Appeal, Lord Denning explicitly stated that 'the receiving bank is the agent of its customer to receive [payment].' [1976] 2 All E.R. 249 at 255. In the House of Lords, Lord Wilberforce spoke of the receiving bank as an agent of the owners with a limited authority. [1977] 1 All E.R. 545 at 551. The scope of the bank's authority to act for the payee is further discussed by Lord Salmon: [1977] 1 All E.R. 545 at 559.

[323] See King, n. 232, above.

[324] *Foley* v. *Hill*, n. 228, above, 2 H.L.C. 28 at 36 to 37; 9 E.R. 1002 at 1005 to 1006. See text at nn. 228–30, above.

instrument such as an 'interbank payment order' as well as to the cover for a telex message. However, in the final analysis, as explained in s. 18, below, this author supports the view that the beneficiary's bank is the beneficiary's agent, which undermines this aspect of the criticism on the 'receipt' test. But in any event, other flaws, outlined immediately below, are more obvious.

Thus, and notwithstanding Lord Salmon's queries in *The Laconia*,[325] internal processing should not have one effect on payment in cash and another on payment by means of an interbank 'payment order'. Both payment methods require an acceptance process by the bank before it becomes indebted to the payee. This is true even in the absence of a genuine credit risk, as is the case when payment to the payee's bank is made either in cash or by means of a funded telex message. Hence, as in the case of a funded telex message, in the absence of an early 'decision', the 'hypothetical positive response' test is quite appropriate to payment in cash as well.

Last but not least, the 'payment order' is not truly a cash equivalent. It is an item which has yet to be cleared and settled.[326] As such it is an irrevocable banker's obligation which is only as good as 'cash' as the creditworthiness of the particular obligor-banker. In principle, it should not be treated differently from any other interbank message binding the transmitting bank.[327]

Regardless, 'receipt of payment order as cash equivalent' may be tantamount to the receipt of cash when the beneficiary's bank is prepared to assume the credit risk associated with the bank liable on the payment order. In such a case a positive response will be given to the beneficiary upon the receipt of the payment order by the beneficiary's bank. It is only in this situation that a mere 'receipt' of the 'payment order' will confer on the beneficiary an unconditional right to the immediate use of the funds. That is, the crucial factor is not so much the nature of the 'payment order' as cash equivalent. Rather, it is the reliance of the beneficiary's bank on the creditworthiness of the sender which would generate a positive response to the sender's inquiry so as to confer on him the unconditional right to the immediate use of the funds.

In the final analysis, 'payment' ought to be identified with the credit risk decision, whether real or hypothetical, of the beneficiary's bank. Having received instructions to credit the beneficiary's account, is the bank satisfied with the cover provided so that no credit risk is present? Alter-

---

[325] See text at nn. 250–1, above.   [326] See n. 291, above.

[327] From this perspective, the interbank payment order is very much like a bank draft. For the distinction between 'irrevocable payment undertaking' and 'payment' see Goode, above, n. 231 at 17, 27, and 112.

natively, is the bank prepared to assume the credit risk pending the arrival of cover? If either question is answered affirmatively, a credit risk decision has been made, the bank became indebted to the beneficiary, and consequently, 'payment' occurred.

Ultimately, the need for an actual 'decision' after receipt of payment by the beneficiary's bank arises only where the beneficiary's bank acts partly as the originator's subagent, a point further discussed in s. 18, below. In such a case, the 'decision' by the beneficiary's bank is tantamount to the attornment by the beneficiary's bank to the beneficiary; that is, 'decision' marks the point from which the beneficiary's bank is said to act as an agent for the beneficiary. Otherwise, if the beneficiary's bank acts exclusively for the beneficiary, actual 'decision' is not required in order to give rise to the liability of the beneficiary's bank to the beneficiary upon the receipt of funds by the beneficiary's bank for the beneficiary. Stated otherwise, if acting for the beneficiary, the beneficiary's bank becomes obligated to the beneficiary upon merely receiving funds designed to be directed to the beneficiary.

In contrast to the actual 'decision', the 'hypothetical decision' leading to the 'hypothetical positive response' is consistent with the beneficiary's bank acting throughout as the beneficiary's agent. By marking the point in which the beneficiary's bank becomes aware of its obligation to the beneficiary, the 'hypothetical decision' merely provides the mental element required for that liability.

At the same time, 'decision', whether actual or hypothetical, is of tremendous importance, regardless of whose agent the beneficiary's bank is, where it is demonstrated to have occurred prior to the receipt of payment by the beneficiary bank. In such a case, 'decision' will mark the rise of liability by the beneficiary's bank to the beneficiary, coupled with the assumption of credit risk by the beneficiary's bank for non-payment by its sender.

The remaining question is then that of 'receiver finality'. In the absence **[13]** of the receipt of either sender's funds or adequate security, such as for example, a central bank's guarantee,[328] does the decision to post credit to the beneficiary's account necessarily imply a credit risk decision made by the beneficiary's bank, so as to shift to itself the risk of sender failure? Alternatively, is it within the powers of the beneficiary's bank to decide to post to the beneficiary's account provisional credit, pending the arrival of cover and even allow the payee to withdraw such credit with recourse? Would such provisional credit serve as 'conditional payment' of the orig-

---

[328] For 'finality' under such circumstances (namely, Bank of Canada's guarantee of settlement supported by fully collateralized clearing participant's obligations) see e.g. s. 45 of Canadian By-Law No. 7, above, n. 248.

inator to the beneficiary? In this context, where the receiving bank is not prepared to assume the credit risk of sender's failure, what are its rights where cover is to be provided after the close of the banking day of value date? Does it have the liberty to post a mere provisional credit or even delay acceptance, or must it reject the unfunded payment? What is the time frame for such a decision?

By holding that payment was completed when the beneficiary bank had credited the beneficiary's account and debited its own *nostro* account with the transmitting bank, *Libyan Arab Foreign Bank* v. *Manufacturers Hanover Trust Co*,[329] should not necessarily be taken to accommodate the possibility of a reversible provisional credit to the beneficiary's account. Indeed, the Court viewed the debit to the *nostro* account rather than the credit to the beneficiary's account as 'the critical fact'[330] leading to the completion of payment. However, in banking practice, this debit merely mirrors the credit posted to the beneficiary's account and does not indicate a separate discretionary step undertaken by the beneficiary bank, in the absence of which credit to the beneficiary's account is provisional. At the same time, the case is not an unequivocal authority for receiver finality either. In the circumstances, funds availability was not the issue; as in *The Effy*, cover was to be provided by the transmitting bank which held the receiving (beneficiary's) bank's funds.[331] The transmitting bank's creditworthiness could not have been questioned by the beneficiary's bank and was a risk it had voluntarily assumed anyway.[332] Accordingly, the weight given to the posting of credit in the beneficiary's account (and the accompanying debit to the *nostro* account) should not be taken as establishing receiver finality in circumstances where funds availability (namely, credit risk) is an issue. In the final analysis, the case can be explained as a straightforward application of the 'hypothetical positive response' test: having received a funded payment message, the beneficiary's bank was in no position to reject it. Hence, the absence of an explicit 'decision' stage could not be determinative to the issue of 'payment'. From this perspective, 'payment' was completed in the early morning even regardless of the credit and debit posted by the beneficiary's bank.[333]

The distinct nature of each stage at the beneficiary's bank, namely receiving the transmitting bank's payment message, crediting the beneficiary's account, and making the credit risk decision can be demonstrated in reference to the facts of the American case of *Delbruek Co.* v.

---

[329] Note 269, above.   [330] Ibid., at 631.   [331] See discussion following n. 309, above.

[332] Obviously this is not so in unusual circumstances, such as those dealt with in *Royal Products*, where the transmitting bank in effect unilaterally made itself the correspondent of the beneficiary's bank. See text at n. 305, above. However, that case involves failure of the beneficiary's bank and not the transmitting bank.

[333] Cf. text around nn. 307–10, above.

Manufacturers Hanover Trust Co.[334] The case involved a payment made through CHIPS, the New York based large-dollar payment network. The receipt of the message by the beneficiary's bank occurred around 11.30 a.m., the beneficiary's account was credited at 9.00 p.m.,[335] and the inter-bank settlement on the books of the Federal Reserve Bank of New York was struck in the course of the next business day.[336] The judgment turned on the irrevocability of payment under CHIPS rules on the dispatch of the message by the transmitting bank around 11.30 a.m. However, the facts of the case provide an ideal setting for further discussing completion of payment and receiver finality.

Thus, if payment depends either on credit to the account or on the decision to post it, 'payment' occurred either at 9.00 p.m. or, presumably, shortly before. At the same time, it seems that nothing could have happened between 11.30 a.m. and around 9.00 p.m. so that a 'hypothetical positive response' to the beneficiary's inquiry would have been given shortly after 11.30 a.m. Nonetheless, it was not until the next day that the credit risk was eliminated, and there is nothing in the reported judgment to suggest that a conscious credit risk decision had been made by the beneficiary's bank at any time between 11.30 a.m. and 9.00 p.m., or in fact at any time. In the absence of a 'receiver finality' rule it is impossible to suppose that the risk was voluntarily assumed by the beneficiary's bank. Indeed, the transmitting bank was a large New York bank; this could have assisted a fact finder searching for a credit risk decision. However, in the absence of a receiver finality rule, no such decision can be identified to exist as a matter of law. 'Payment' could thus not be completed until the arrival of funds on the next day.

In the absence of a receiver finality rule, credit posted to a final funds balance confers on the beneficiary an unconditional right to the immediate use of the funds, irrespective of the provision of cover to the beneficiary's bank. Otherwise, in the absence of receiver finality rule as well as of cover, provisional credit may provide no more than conditional discharge. In the absence of credit risk assumption, no unconditional right to the immediate use of the funds, and hence, no absolute discharge or payment is provided thereby.

Revocability

Compared to discharge, the common law analysis regarding revocability **[14]** appears to be much more straightforward. In principle, as the originator's

---

[334] Above, n. 208.

[335] The same internal procedure would have been applied to a cash payment or bank draft. Ibid., at 1051.

[336] Ibid., at 1049, n. 1. Since then CHIPS Rules have changed to provide for same-day settlement at the end of the business day.

agent, the originator's bank must comply with the originator's countermand of payment, which effectively terminates the mandate created by the (now countermanded) payment order. In an in-house credit transfer, the revocation instruction must reach the bank before it acted on the payment order, that is, prior to the payment into the beneficiary's account.[337] Otherwise, in an inter bank transfer, the originator's revocation right comes to an end when the beneficiary's bank has received the payment order instructing payment to the beneficiary as well as cover.[338] Neither payment nor advice to the beneficiary is required. Arguably, however, the revocation right comes to an end also where the beneficiary's bank binds itself to the beneficiary before receipt of cover.

It ought however to be recalled, *per* the discussion in s. 12 above, that other than by receipt of payment, the beneficiary's bank binds itself to the beneficiary by means of a 'decision', whether actual or hypothetical, which 'completes' the process of payment. This is the point of the 'discharge' of the originator's debt to the beneficiary. It thus appears that in the final analysis the 'completion' of payment, the 'discharge' of the debt, and the 'irrevocability' of the credit transfer coincide more than was thought at the beginning of the discussion. As will be seen further below, in (x) ss. 8–10, the point was not lost by the drafters of UCC Article 4A in the USA, who thus came up with the completion of the funds (namely, credit) transfer, as a milestone marking both discharge and loss of revocability. However, as will be seen in (x) s. 5 below, perhaps due to the uncertainty as to the occurrence of any 'decision', these drafters bypassed altogether the 'completion of payment' as a relevant concept.

Returning to 'irrevocability', an attempt will be made to address the mechanism to achieve it when other than in an in-house transfer, the originator's bank issued its payment order in execution of the originator's instructions. Presumably, in an interbank transfer, where the originator has no privity with any receiving bank other than his own, revocation instructions must be communicated by the originator to his bank. The originator's bank must then transmit the revocation instructions onward through the chain of participating banks, all the way up to the beneficiary's bank where they must reach prior to the above-mentioned cut-off point.

In connection with interbank payment orders transmitted over a funds transfer system, irrevocability may be forwarded by participating banks to the point of the release of the payment order by the sending bank. This

---

[337] *Gibson v. Minet* (1824), 2 Bing. 7, 130 E.R. 206. Payment into the beneficiary's account is discussed in ss. 9–13, above.

[338] See *Royal Products* above, n. 216 at 198–9. For the receipt of cover for a payment order, see s. 6, above.

may be established by a funds transfer system rule.[339] In the absence of such a rule, irrevocability upon release may be inferred on the basis of the nature of the system and pertinent banking practices.[340] Obviously, irrevocability upon release is tantamount to no revocability.

(c) Duties, chain of liability, and scope of damages

The classic common law position with regard to the legal nature of the **[15]** payment order and the resulting chain of liability among sending banks can be found in *Royal Products Ltd.* v. *Midland Bank Ltd.*[341] In the course of his judgment, Webster J. specifically declined to treat the originator's instructions in an interbank transfer as 'any separate or distinct contract of any kind'. Rather, he regarded such instructions as 'simply an authority and instruction, from a customer to its bank, to transfer an amount standing to the credit of that customer with that bank to the credit of [the beneficiary] with another bank'. As such, the originator's instructions give rise to 'an ordinary banking operation', namely 'of a kind which is often carried out internally'.[342]

Stated otherwise, the payment order is a mandate. In carrying it out, the originator's bank acts as the originator's agent.[343] As such, the originator's bank owes the originator 'a duty to use reasonable care and skill'. It is not absolutely responsible for completing the credit transfer. Rather, in case of non-completion, delayed completion or miscompletion, the originator's bank is liable to the originator for damages arising from the breach of the above-mentioned duty.

As the originator's agent, the originator's bank 'would be vicariously liable for the breach of that duty by any servant or agent to whom [it] delegated the carrying out of the instructions'.[344] Accordingly, the originator's bank is liable to the originator for the intermediary bank's negligence.[345] In that respect, there is no difference in the responsibility of the originator's bank for the negligence of a branch (that is, of the servants or employees of the originator's bank) on one hand, and for the negligence of a correspondent bank (namely, of its agent).

---

[339] In the UK this is so provided under the CHAPS Rules. According to Rule 2, a CHAPS payment order must command 'an *irrevocably* guaranteed unconditional sterling payment for same-day settlement'. Emphasis added.

[340] See e.g. *Delbrueck* above, n. 208 at 1051 (with respect to CHIPS before CHIPS Rules were revised to state irrevocability expressly in current Rule 2).

[341] Above, n. 216.   [342] Ibid., at 198.   [343] See s. 4, above.

[344] *Royal Products*, above, n. 216 at 198.

[345] Under agency law, this holds true even when the use of the subagent by the agent is contemplated by, and the particular subagent has specifically been nominated at, the suggestion of the principal. See *Calico Printers' Association, Ltd.* v. *Barclays Bank, Ltd.* (1930), 38 Lloyd's L.R. 105 at 108–11.

Webster J. specifically rejected the application of the strict compliance doctrine, emanating from the law of letters of credit, to the standard of compliance required from the originator's bank as agent. Rather, the required standard is that of a duty of care. This means that in complying with the originator's instructions the originator's bank '[is] required [possibly through the use of a correspondent bank, its agent] to make funds available to [the beneficiary's bank] *in one way or another* . . . and to notify [the beneficiary's bank] that the sum [is] to be credited to the account of [the beneficiary]'.[346] That is, the originator's instructions must be carried out 'with reasonable care and skill'.[347] It is however submitted that 'strict compliance' ought to be regarded as the required standard for the duty of the originator's bank to issue onwards a corresponding payment order matching that of the originator.[348]

[16]   In the USA, prior to Article 4A, *Walker* v. *Texas Commerce Bank*[349] stated that in receiving a payment order from a sender, a receiving bank is under a duty 'to implement commercially reasonable internal procedures designed to process [a payment order] in accordance with [the sender's] instructions, to verify the accuracy of, and compliance with, instructions, to detect and minimize inaccuracy, and to act diligently to remedy errors.'[350] This is quite in line with the receiving bank's 'duty to use reasonable care and skill' in carrying out a payment order set out in *Royal Products*.[351] More specifically, *Walker* provides a rationale underlying cases allocating the risk of erroneous execution of payment orders to the erring bank. This applies to the erroneous issue of a duplicate payment order,[352] a payment order containing a higher amount than instructed,[353] or a payment order designating an unintended beneficiary.[354] In such cases, the erring bank is left with an action in restitution against the overpaid or wrongly paid beneficiary or its bank.

Furthermore, *Walker*, as a derivative of *Royal Products*, also appears to underlie *Royal Bank of Canada* v. *Stangl*.[355] In the latter case, a beneficiary's bank was held liable to its sender (an intermediary bank) in negligence for the failure to clarify the contents of a payment order instructing payment to an account that did not belong to the named beneficiary.[356]

---

[346] *Royal Products*, above, n. 216 at 199, emphasis added.   [347] Ibid.

[348] See *Clansmen Resources Ltd.* v. *Toronto Dominion Bank* (19 Dec. 1986), 86/00047; [1987] B.C.J. No. 618 (B.C.S.C.), on-line: QL (BCJ), *aff'd* on other grounds (1990), 43 B.C.L.R. (2d) 273 (C.A.).   [349] 635 F. Supp. 678 (S.D. Tex. 1986)

[350] Ibid., at 682.   [351] Above, n. 216 at 198.

[352] *Morgan Guaranty Trust Co. of New York* v. *Outerbridge* (1990), 72 O.R. (2d) 161 (H.C.J.).

[353] *A.N.Z. Banking Group* v. *Westpac Banking Corporation* (1988), 78 A.L.R. 157 (Aust. H.C.).

[354] *Clansmen Resources Ltd.* v. *Toronto Dominion Bank* (1990), 43 B.C.L.R. (2d) 273 (C.A.).

[355] (1992), 32 A.C.W.S. (3d) 17 (Ont. Gen. Div.) [092/066/089–19]; [1992] O.J. No. 378, on-line: QL (OJ).

[356] For a critical case comment, see B. Geva, 'Ambiguous Wire Instructions: *Royal Bank of Canada* v. *Stangl*' (1995), 24 Can. Bus. L.J. 435. See also 4.E(i) s. 5, below.

On its part, the intermediary bank owes 'no duty of any kind direct to [the originator]'. While the originator's bank is entitled to carry out the originator's instructions by using the services of a correspondent bank, the originator typically gives the originator's bank 'no authority which would have . . . the effect of creating privity of contract between the [originator] and [the intermediary bank]'.[357] Stated otherwise, in the absence of privity of contract between the originator as principal and the intermediary bank as subagent, the latter owes no duty to the former and thus is not liable to it for damages generated by its negligence.[358] Rather, acting as an agent for the originator's bank, the intermediary bank's duty of care is owed to its principal, the originator's bank. In turn, as already indicated, the originator's bank is vicariously liable to the originator for damages arising from the intermediary bank's negligent acts or omissions.

Prior to Article 4A, American common law, contrary to the common law of England, allowed the originator to recover directly from a defaulting intermediary,[359] or beneficiary's bank.[360] Recovery was allowed on the basis of agency, negligence, or a third party beneficiary theory.

In the USA, prior to UCC Article 4A, in *Evra* v. *Swiss Bank*,[361] the originator sued a negligent intermediary bank for substantial consequential damages incurred due to a loss of a profitable contract. In this case, the underlying contract required the originator to make punctual payment to the beneficiary and further entitled the beneficiary to terminate the contract upon a breach by the originator of the punctual payment term. Due to its own negligence, the intermediary bank failed to issue its payment order to the beneficiary's bank. As a result, payment to the beneficiary was not timely made and the beneficiary terminated the contract. The consequential damages incurred by the failure to make a $27,000 transfer were in the sum of $2.1 million.

Ultimately, judgment was given against the originator on the basis of lack of foreseeability. Particular reliance was put on the rule in *Hadley* v. *Baxendale*,[362] an English precedent, holding 'that consequential damage, will not be awarded unless the defendant was put on notice of the special

---

[357] Above, n. 216 at 198.

[358] See e.g. *Balsamo* v. *Medici* [1984] 1 WLR 951, 958–62 (Ch.D). However, this view may not be universally shared. Thus, R. Powell, *The Law of Agency*, 2nd edn. (London: Sir Isacc Pitman & Sons, Ltd., 1961) at 309, concludes that '[i]n the present state of authorities it cannot be said with certainty that the sub-agent would never be liable to [the principal] for negligence'. It is possible that liability in negligence will be fastened 'where the sub-agent [is] a person who professe[s] a particular skill'.

[359] See e.g. *Evra Corp.* v. *Swiss Bank Corp.*, 522 F. Supp. 820 (N.D. Ill. 1981), rvs'd on other grounds, 673 F. 2d 951 (7th Cir. 1982).

[360] See e.g. *Securities Fund Ser. Inc.* v. *Am. Nat'l Bank & Trust Co. of Chicago*, 542 F. Supp. 323 (N.D. Ill., 1982). [361] Above, n. 318.

[362] (1854), 9 Ex. 341, 156 E.R. 145.

circumstances giving rise to them'.[363] In the facts of the case, no such notice was given by the originator to its own bank. Obviously, the negligent intermediary was without notice as to the special circumstances of the case.

It is very likely that, in an action of the originator against his bank, a similar result will be reached under English common law as well. That is, consequential damages are recoverable, provided they are foreseeable. Special circumstances, such as the potential loss of a profitable contract, must be advised by the originator to its bank (which in turn, must pass on the information). Otherwise, consequential damages are not recoverable.[364]

(d) Risk allocation: delay and loss

[17]   As between the originator and the beneficiary, the risk of a delay or loss occurring at a sending bank (namely, the originator's and an intermediary bank) falls on the originator. This is so since the originator's bank is an agent of the originator and each intermediary bank is an agent of its sending bank. The originator may then shift the loss created, due to the default of a sending bank, on to the originator's bank which is responsible for its own default as well as for default by an intermediary bank. Recovery is available to each sender from its receiving bank, until ultimately the loss falls on the defaulting intermediary bank.[365]

[18]   As for the risk of delay or loss occurring at the beneficiary's bank, the legal position is not as straightforward. According to *Chitty on Contracts*, it is indisputable that the beneficiary's bank is engaged as an agent. However, as between the originator and beneficiary, 'it is less certain who is to be regarded as [its] principal'.[366]

The prevailing view in England is that the beneficiary's bank acts as an agent for the beneficiary with a limited authority[367] to receive payment and credit it to the beneficiary's account.[368] Support to this view exists also

---

[363] Above, n. 318 at 955–6. *Evra* was rejected by UCC §4A–305. See (x) s. 12, below.

[364] This will be consistent with the rule requiring special notice to be given to a carrier of goods in order to charge him with liability for consequential damages for late (or non) delivery. See e.g. in Canada, *B.D.C. Ltd.* v. *Hofstrand Farms Ltd.* (1986), 26 D.L.R. (4th) 1 (S.C.C.), commented on by J. Blom (1986–87), 12 Can. Bus. L.J. 43.

[365] See s. 15, above.

[366] 26th edn. (London: Sweet & Maxwell, 1989), vol. ii *Specific Contracts*, ¶2956 (ch. 3: 'Bills of Exchange and Banking' by E. P. Ellinger).

[367] The authority is not to receive notices, as well as to make commercial decisions (such as to receive late payments), on the beneficiary's behalf. See e.g. *Midland Bank Ltd.* v. *Conway Corp.*, [1965] 1 W.L.R. 1165 and *The Laconia* above, n. 284, judgments of Lord Wilberforce (with whom Lord Simon agreed) and Lord Salmon.

[368] *The Laconia*, ibid. See also *Royal Products* above, n. 216 at 198–9 and 201–3, as well as *Chitty* above, n. 366 at ¶2956. For the same result in Australia, see *ANZ* v. *Westpac*, above, n.

in pre-UCC Article 4A American jurisprudence.[369] In this context, the authority given to the beneficiary's bank by the beneficiary may be actual or implied, on the basis of their account agreement. Alternatively, authority may be apparent, on the basis of the account information furnished by the beneficiary to the originator in connection with their agreement as to the mode of payment.[370]

To the extent that the beneficiary's bank is to be treated as the beneficiary's agent, the risk of delay or loss occurring at that bank is allocated to the beneficiary. In turn, the latter may shift it to its defaulting bank.

Nonetheless, it is not universally accepted that the beneficiary's bank acts as the beneficiary's agent. Richard King argued that 'in the same way that it is inappropriate to say that the bank receives money paid by the customer into his account as agent for the customer it is also inappropriate to say that the bank receives money paid by a third party for the account of the customer as agent for the customer'.[371] Rather, in a credit transfer, '[all] banks . . . *including the [beneficiary's] bank*, are the agents or sub-agents of the [originator]'.[372] Accordingly, in a credit transfer, 'the [beneficiary] agrees not that the [beneficiary's] bank should receive the payment as agent but that liability of the [originator] may be discharged by constituting the bank a debtor of the [beneficiary] in respect of the sum payable'.[373]

Indeed, the position of the beneficiary's bank as a subagent of the originator is supported by some *obiter* judicial statements.[374] It follows, under the foregoing view, that the risk of delay or loss occurring at the beneficiary's bank falls on the originator. Obviously, the originator may pursue his remedies indirectly against the defaulting beneficiary's bank, by recovering from the originator's bank, which will then pass the loss along the chain of participating banks, onwards to the beneficiary's bank, as its subagent.[375] It is nonetheless submitted, that having selected the beneficiary's bank, even under this analysis, the beneficiary (and not the

---

353. For the liability of the beneficiary's bank to the beneficiary who maintains an account with it, see also *Tafreschi* v. *Canadian Imperial Bank of Commerce* [1986] B.C.J.. No. 2096 (B.C. S.C).

[369] See e.g. *Delbrueck*, above, n. 208 at 1051–2.

[370] For this point, see *Chitty* above, n. 366 at ¶2956.

[371] King, above, n. 232 at 373.   [372] Ibid., at 379. Emphasis added.   [373] Ibid., at 381.

[374] See e.g. *Brimnes*, above, n. 247 at 99 and *Gilbey Distillers and Vintners* v. *ABSA Bank*, Case No. 12698/94 (High Court of South Africa, Cape of Good Hope Provincial Division), ¶60 (unreported 4 Dec. 1998), *per* Brand and Traverso JJ. I provided expert assistance to ABSA Bank in whose favour judgment was given. *Brimnes* might have been explained on the basis of the beneficiary's bank holding funds for the sender in an account the sender maintained with the beneficiary's bank. However, in *Gilby*, unlike in *Brimnes*, the beneficiary's bank neither had on its books an account maintained for the sender, nor did it hold otherwise funds for the sender.

[375] Cf. s. 15, above (indirect recovery from a defaulting intermediary bank).

originator) ought to bear the risk of loss incurred due to the insolvency of the beneficiary's bank.

In the final analysis, if payment to the beneficiary's bank discharges the originator towards the beneficiary, it must be that the beneficiary's bank is the beneficiary's agent. Notwithstanding King, in receiving 'money' for a beneficiary-customer, the beneficiary's bank receives something which discharges the originator's debt to the beneficiary. It is appropriate then to view the beneficiary's bank as acting as an agent for the beneficiary-customer. In fact, a contractual duty to pay into a bank account may be analogized to a contractual duty to deliver a package into a room in a secure office building. In the latter case, the delivery to an authorized person at the reception area will discharge the obligation. Similarly, payment to the bank maintaining the account, thereby constituting it a debtor to the payee, will discharge the payor's payment obligation. The bank is thus the payee's agent along the same lines under which the authorized person in the reception area is the agent for the person entitled to the delivery of the package.[376]

It is recognized that the beneficiary's bank has a contract with both its sender and the beneficiary. At first blush, it may appear that while in receiving the money the beneficiary's bank acts for the beneficiary, in carrying out the instructions contained in a payment order it nevertheless acts for the sender. It should however be pointed out that even in carrying out the instructions to pay a beneficiary-customer, the beneficiary's bank acts under its contract with the beneficiary. The payment order addressed to a beneficiary's bank instructing payment to the customer is more of an advice of forthcoming money or payment for the customer than an instruction to pay the customer.[377] The act of payment to the customer by the beneficiary's bank is thus under the contract with the customer, more than in the fulfilment of the sender's instructions, so that the beneficiary's bank ought to be regarded as acting throughout as an agent for the beneficiary.

---

[376] Perhaps the most articulate analysis of a view to the contrary appears in Switzerland, as set out in (iv) s. 3, above. It is noteworthy that the position of the beneficiary's bank as an agent for the beneficiary is consistent with the treatment of the discharge between the originator and the beneficiary as occurring on the receipt of funds by the beneficiary's bank, even before credit is posted to the beneficiary's account, as is the rule under the common law (see s. 12, above). By the same token, the position of the beneficiary's bank as an agent for the sender is consistent with the treatment of the discharge between the originator and the beneficiary as occurring only upon the posting of credit by the beneficiary's bank to the beneficiary's account, or otherwise actual payment to the beneficiary to the beneficiary's bank, as is the rule in Switzerland (see (iv) s. 5, above).

[377] In fact, this is supported by *Royal Products*, above, n. 216 at 198, where the communication from the intermediary to the beneficiary's bank is referred to as 'advice' of payment to the beneficiary, rather than as a payment order instructing payment to him.

Obviously, the beneficiary's bank is not an agent for a non-customer beneficiary to whom it is instructed to pay. Until it attorns and obligates itself to the beneficiary, it acts for its sender.[378] Also, as will be seen in 4.E s. 6, below, a beneficiary's bank acting for a beneficiary-customer may be regarded as acting also for the sender, insofar as the beneficiary's bank is either provided with specific instructions, as for example, to pay into a blocked account of the beneficiary, or is under a duty to ascertain the meaning of ambiguous instructions. For example, in the USA, prior to the adoption of UCC Article 4A, *Securities Funds Ser. Inc.* v. *Am. Nat'l Bank & Trust Co.*[379] held that the beneficiary's bank is to be treated as a subagent, directly liable to the originator[380] for the failure to notice in the text of the payment order it had received that the destination account did not belong to the named beneficiary.[381] This however is limited agency, restricted to the particular duties assigned to the beneficiary's bank. Otherwise, in discussing the allocation of the risk of delay or loss, the beneficiary's bank ought better to be regarded as acting exclusively as the beneficiary's, and not the sender's agent.

(IX) ISRAEL

Israel does not have a domestic large value credit transfer system. Credit transfers are nonetheless used in connection with domestic ACH transactions, such as payroll deposits, as well as part of international foreign currency payments. There is virtually no comprehensive legal discussion on the subject.[382]

A recent leading case[383] dealt with the nature of an irrevocable order given by an account holder advising its bank that a designated nominee

---

[378] For support, see discussion in *Royal Products* above, n. 216, at 209, of *Official Assignee of Madras* v. *D. Rajam Ayyar*, (1910) 33 I.L.R. (Madras Series), 299, and 36 I.L.R. (Madras Series) 499. [379] Above, n. 360.

[380] In English law, even if the beneficiary's bank is a subagent of the originator, in the absence of privity between them, no direct liability lies. See s. 15, above.

[381] Alternatively, the beneficiary's bank was held liable to the originator either in negligence or as a third party beneficiary of the undertaking of the beneficiary's bank to deliver funds as directed. In the facts of the case, a dishonest employee of the originator generated an authorized payment order naming a legitimate beneficiary and an account number belonging not to that named beneficiary but to the dishonest employee's innocent creditor. The dishonest employee counted on the automatic processing at the beneficiary's bank that would direct funds to the account without matching the number with the name. That is what in fact happened. *Securities* was rejected by UCC §4A–207(b) (1). See (x) s. 6, and 4.E(iv) s. 15, below.

[382] The exception is R. Ben-Oliel, *Banking Law—General Part* (Jerusalem: Sacher Institute, 1996) [in Hebrew], at 413–28.

[383] *Israel Union Bank* v. *Eran Tours Ltd. and Schiller*, C.A. 717/89, S.C., 27.2.95, unreported. The judgment of the Court was given by D. Levin, J.

is to exclusively act in the account up to a certain ceiling. Particularly rely-ing on the scholarly work of Lerner,[384] the Supreme Court (the highest court in the country) treated this order as the assignment of the account holder's right to the balance in the bank account in the beneficiary's favour.[385] The Court acknowledged that an assignment requires an agree-ment between the assignor and assignee, namely the account holder and the beneficiary, and is not created by the mere notice given by the assignor to the debtor, namely, by the account holder to the bank. Nevertheless, fol-lowing Lerner, the Court held, an order given by a creditor to his debtor, directing him to pay the debt to a third person, may constitute an assign-ment of the creditor's right to that third person, provided the third person (namely, the assignee) had been in the picture in advance and had been advised ahead of time. Inasmuch as it is envisaged that the third person beneficiary substitutes the account holder as the creditor of the bank, this transaction, in the Court's view, is not a contract for the benefit of the third person;[386] rather, it is an assignment of the bank's debt to him. The Court further treated the document as an authorization, which constitutes an agency, or mandate, securing the rights of a third person, namely, the bene-ficiary, and as such, is irrevocable.[387] The principal's duty to act for the third person was said to emerge from the assignment.

Under this reasoning, it is possible to treat every payment order, antic-ipated by the beneficiary, as an assignment of the account balance from the account holder-originator. This view renders the originator's payment order as irrevocable from its inception. It may not well accommodate interbank transfers, would expose the assignee-beneficiary to the debtor-bank's defences against the assignor-originator,[388] and would not cover credit transfers by the originator to himself or to a beneficiary who does not expect to receive the credit transfer. Similarly, the possibility of treat-ing the payment order as creating a trust for the beneficiary is highly disfavoured, if only because the originator's bank is not required to seg-regate funds earmarked for transfer.[389]

In principle, the contract between the originator and his bank could be governed by the Contract of Work and Service Law, 1974. The latter, may

---

[384] S. Lerner, 'Assignment of Obligations', in D. Friedman (ed.), *Law of Obligations—Gen-eral Part* (Tel Aviv: Aviram, 1994) [in Hebrew] 21, at 54–6.

[385] The Court considered the fact that the beneficiary was not identified in the order as irrelevant. In fact, pursuing the Court's analysis, the irrevocable order could have been seen as an assignment to the designated nominee as a trustee for the unidentified beneficiary.

[386] Under s. 34 to the Contracts Law (General Part), 1973, a right may be conferred by con-tract to a third person, if so intended by the contracting parties.

[387] Under s. 14 of the Agency Law.

[388] Under s. 7 to the Assignment of Obligations Law, 1969.

[389] See e.g. Ben-Oliel, above, n. 382 at 422. In Israel, the trust is governed by the Trust Law, 1979.

however be too laconic in establishing the parties' rights. Its principal provision, s. 2, simply states that '[t]he contractor's duty is to perform the work or provide the service, while the employer's duty is to pay the remuneration, all as agreed between the parties'. It therefore seems that agency is the most convenient point of reference.

Under s. 1(a) of the Israeli Agency Law, 1965, agency is defined as 'the authorization of an agent to do in the name or behalf of a principal a juridical action towards a third person'. A 'juridical action' refers to a lawful act or default, *designed* and *intended* to alter the principal's legal position, namely his rights, duties, or powers and immunities. A mere physical act, even achieving or resulting in a juridical result, will not suffice. Accordingly, representing someone in a public event is not agency. Similarly, building a house from materials belonging to another, is not a juridical action, even though it may confer on the builder ownership in the building. Conversely, abandoning a chattel, is a juridical action, since the intention to lose ownership is an essential element.[390] Arguably, payment in discharge of a debt, is a juridical, and not mere physical action, so as to be a proper subject for agency.[391]

Not viewed as intended to secure to the beneficiary an independent right, the payment order, as any authority, terminates upon its revocation, death, incapacity, or insolvency, by either the principal or the agent.[392] In this context, it has not yet been discussed in Israel whether revocability of a payment order is lost as early as upon the execution of the payment order by the originator's bank, as late as upon the completion of the credit transfer, or at any other time. Similarly, questions as to the time the credit transfer becomes completed, as well as to determining the time of the discharge of the underlying debt between the originator and the beneficiary, have not been touched upon.

Under the Agency Law, the agent must act faithfully, comply with the principal's instructions, account to the principal for profits and assets coming to his hands in the course of the agency, and is entitled to be indemnified for reasonable expenses.[393] Under general law, the agent owes the principal a duty of care.[394] Under s. 16 of the Agency Law, an agent

---

[390] See in general, A. Barak, *The Law of Agency*, vol. i (Tel -Aviv: Nevo, 1996) [in Hebrew] at §§211–23, particularly at §§214–15.

[391] Unfortunately, there is no consensus on this point. Barak regards the delivery of a book in fulfilment of a contractual duty as a mere physical act resulting in, but not intended to bring about, legal change. See ibid., at §214. Conversely, Tedeschi regards the delivery of the book as intended to alter the legal position, by conferring a discharge of the duty to deliver, and hence, as a juridical action. G. Tedeschi, 'On the Nature of the Fulfillment of an Obligation' (1985), 15 Mishpatim 21, at 23–4 at n. 15 [in Hebrew]. Qualified application of agency is advocated by Ben-Oliel, above, n. 382 at 422–6, if only for consistency with the law of cheques.   [392] Under s. 14 of the Agency Law.

[393] Ss. 8, 10 and 11.   [394] Barak, above, n. 390, vol. ii, at §§733 and 738.

may not appoint an agent, except for under implicit or explicit authority, or in an emergency.

Arguably, whenever the beneficiary's account is at a bank other than that of the originator, authority is given to the originator's bank to appoint an agent. Thus, in the context of the credit transfer, it would not matter whether s. 16 precludes the appointment of a substitute agent, subagent, or both. In principle, a substitute agent is liable directly to the principal, as his own original agent. Conversely, the subagent is the agent's agent, and there is no direct agency relationship, or in fact, any privity, between him and the principal. However, under s. 14 of the Torts Ordinance [New Version], as the principal of the subagent, the original agent is vicariously liable to his own (namely, the original) principal for the subagent's wrongs.[395]

Unlike a substitute agent, a subagent acts for or on behalf of the original agent. It seems that an intermediary bank is appointed to act for or on behalf of its own sender, and not the originator, and is thus a subagent and not a substitute. The risk of delay or loss occurring at any transmitting bank thus falls on the originator, who may pursue his remedies against the originator's bank, but only where the delay or loss occurred due to a breach of duty by a transmitting bank. Stated otherwise, there is no 'money-back guarantee rule'. Whether the beneficiary's bank is a subagent of the originator, agent for the beneficiary, or both, has not been explored yet under Israeli law. Ben-Oliel adheres to the view regarding the beneficiary's bank as the beneficiary's agent.[396] It should follow, that the risk of delay or loss, taking place at the beneficiary's bank, falls, according to Ben-Oliel, on the beneficiary.

The scope of damages allowed to an injured party is governed in Israel by s. 10 of the Contracts Law (Remedies for Breach of Contract), 1971. Under s. 10, the injured party is entitled to be compensated for foreseen and foreseeable damages, at the time the contract was entered to, as a likely result from the breach. Obviously, consequential damages are contemplated, provided they are foreseen or foreseeable. One can thus speculate that in appropriate situations, for example where special circumstances were advised to the originator's bank, upon default of a transmitting bank causing delay or loss, items such as exchange losses or the loss of a profitable contract, may be recovered from the originator's bank.

---

[395] This is similar to the employer's vicarious liability for the wrongs of his employee, but usually, not to that of his independent contractor. See ss. 13 and 15 of that Torts Ordinance.

[396] Above, n. 382, at 427.

(x) UNITED STATES[397]

(a) Introduction

In the United States, pre-Article 4A law governing credit transfers was **[1]**
described as 'a poorly developed framework of legal rules'.[398] In their
Prefatory Note, the drafters explained the need for Article 4A on the basis
of the absence of a 'comprehensive body of law that defines the rights and
obligations that arise from wire transfers'. Article 4A of the Uniform
Commercial Code was designed to meet this inadequacy and 'provide a
comprehensive body of law that we do not have today'. It is now in force
in all American states. It was specifically adopted by the two LVTSs in the
USA, Fedwire and CHIPS, as the law governing a credit transfer that
passes through each of these networks.

UCC Article 4A strongly influenced the Model Law on International
Credit Transfers, prepared by UNCITRAL for consideration for adoption
by UN member states as national legislation.[399] To avoid duplication, no
separate discussion on UNCITRAL Model Law will appear here. However, major departures from UCC Article 4A are noted below in footnotes
to outline the salient features of the Model Law.

The transaction covered by Article 4A is a non-consumer credit transfer, **[2]**
called a 'funds transfer'.[400] The typical transaction is high-speed (usually
same day) large value credit transfer between sophisticated business or
financial organizations. Another characteristic is low cost in relation to the
value of the payment.[401] Finally, high-speed automatic processing is usually assumed.[402]

A 'funds transfer' governed by UCC Article 4A consists of a series of
transactions, beginning with the originator's payment order, made for the
purpose of making payment to the beneficiary of the order.[403] A 'payment
order' means an instruction of a sender to a receiving bank, transmitted

[397] The ensuing discussion draws on B. Geva, *The Law of Electronic Funds Transfer* (New
York: Matthew Bender, 1992–2000) at ch. 2. See also e.g. C. Felsenfeld, 'Article 4A of the
United States Uniform Commercial Code', in W. Hadding and U. H. Schneider (eds.), *Legal
Issues in International Credit Transfers* (Berlin: Duncker & Humblot, 1993), 345.

[398] H. Scott, 'Corporate Wire Transfers and the Uniform New Payments Code' (1983), 83
Colum. L. Rev. 1664.

[399] See Resolution 47/34 (A/Res/47/34) adopted by the UN General Assembly on 25
Nov. 1992, encouraging UN member states to consider enacting the Model Law as national
legislation. The full text of the Model Law is annexed to the Report of the United Nations
Commission on International Trade Law, 25th Sess. UN Doc. A/47/17. For the recognizable
influence of UCC Article 4A on the Model Law, see B. Crawford, 'International Credit Transfers: The Influence of Article 4A on the Model Law' (1991), 19 Can. Bus. L. J. 166.

[400] UCC §4A-104 and 108. The Model Law calls the transaction (in Article 2(a)) 'credit
transfer'. [401] See Prefatory Note to Article 4A.

[402] See e.g. UCC §4A-207(b)(1) and Official Comment 2.

[403] UCC §4A-104(a). Pertinent terms are defined in §§4A 103 to 105.

orally in writing, or electronically (whether on-line or off-line), to pay, or cause another bank to pay, a fixed or determinable amount of money to a beneficiary.[404] Accordingly, for each payment order, the parties are the sender and the receiving bank. In connection with a complex account transfer, the parties to a funds transfer are the originator, the originator's bank, one or more intermediary banks, the beneficiary's bank and the beneficiary.

[3]   An interbank payment order may be transmitted over a 'funds transfer system', that is, a communication network of a clearing house or other association of banks.[405] The domestic LVTS for each country, such as CHIPS and Fedwire in the USA, as well as the international SWIFT network is such a 'funds transfer system'. To some extent, a rule adopted by a funds transfer system ('funds transfer system rule'), and to a lesser extent, even a bilateral agreement, may supersede the provisions of Article 4A.[406]

Unless displaced by a bilateral agreement or a funds transfer system rule, the law applicable to each payment order is that of the jurisdiction in which the receiving bank is located. Similarly, the law of the jurisdiction in which the beneficiary's bank is located governs the relationship between the beneficiary's bank and the beneficiary, as well as the discharge of the originator's debt to the beneficiary. A funds transfer system rule, displacing any of the above, binds *all* participants to a *funds transfer* having notice that the funds transfer system might be used in the funds transfer and of the choice of law made by the system. Both CHIPS and Fedwire effectively selected Article 4A as the governing law. However, as indicated, unless displaced by either a funds transfer system rule or bilateral agreement, applicable law is determined under Article 4A by reference to each individual bilateral relationship (that is, sender-receiving bank, beneficiary's bank-beneficiary, and originator-beneficiary) and not the funds transfer as a whole.[407]

(b) The payment order

[4]   A payment order is a request by the sender to the receiving bank which can be accepted or rejected. It does not create agency or mandate. Nor is it tantamount to the assignment of funds; rather, acceptance by a receiving bank of a sender's payment order generates a contract *sui generis* that does not fall into any established relationship. A receiving bank is neither

---

[404] UCC §4A-103(a)(1).   [405] UCC §4A-105(a)(5).
[406] UCC §4A-501. Federal Reserve regulation and operating circular supersede inconsistent provisions of Article 4A under UCC t4A-107.
[407] Choice of law is governed by UCC §4A-507. In the Model Law, the conflict of laws provision is optional. It does not deal with the effect of a funds transfer system rule.

an agent (of the sender, beneficiary, or of any other participant), nor an assignee (of the originator's funds at the originator's bank). Acceptance inures solely to the benefit of an immediate party in privity. Thus, acceptance by a receiving bank other than the beneficiary's bank inures to the benefit of the sender; acceptance by the beneficiary's bank inures to the benefit of the beneficiary.[408]

Acceptance of a payment order by the beneficiary's bank is either by paying (or advising) the beneficiary, or where the beneficiary has an account at the beneficiary's bank, also by obtaining cover for such a payment.[409] Acceptance by a receiving bank other than the beneficiary's bank is by the *execution* of the payment order, that is, by the issue of a corresponding payment order, intended to carry out the one received by the bank.[410] The executing bank must issue a payment order that strictly conforms to that received by it with respect to the amount, the ultimate destination of the funds, and the identity of any specifically designated intermediary bank. Otherwise, the executing bank's duties as to speed, the means of communication, the use of a funds transfer system, and the selection of an intermediary bank where none is designated by the sender, are to be carried out with reasonable care and skill.[411] Nothing short of 'execution' serves as acceptance by a receiving bank other than that of the beneficiary. Stated otherwise, giving notice of acceptance, obtaining cover for the payment order or incurring an obligation to accept, will not serve as acceptance by a non-beneficiary's bank.[412] An effective obligation to accept must be solely by express agreement but by itself is not acceptance.[413]

An unaccepted payment order expires after five days,[414] but may anyway be rejected, at the receiving bank's discretion, even earlier. Notice of rejection is required to avoid liability for interest. In one case, notice of rejection precludes acceptance by a beneficiary's bank holding adequate

---

[408] See, in general UCC §4A–212 (any official comment) as well as §4A–209, Official Comment 1.

[409] Under Article 9(1) of the Model Law, acceptance by the beneficiary's bank is constituted also (i) upon receipt of the payment order (but only if so agreed with the sender) or (ii) by giving notice to the sender.

[410] UCC §§4A–209 and 301.

[411] UCC §4A–302.

[412] In this respect, the Model Law is different. Under Article 7, acceptance by a receiving bank other than the beneficiary's bank may occur not only by execution, but also (i) upon receipt of the payment order by the receiving bank (but only if so agreed), (ii) by giving notice of acceptance to the sender, (iii) by debiting the sender's account, or (iv) automatically after the expiry of the rejection period, (usually on the second banking day following the receipt of the payment order) provided no notice of rejection had been given (but only where sender's funds are available and sender information in the payment order is adequate).   [413] UCC §4A–212.

[414] UCC §4A–211(d).

funds as cover.[415] Otherwise, there is no acceptance by inaction or mere passage of time. Suspension of payment by a receiving bank is tantamount to rejection by operation of law. In general, the occurrence of either acceptance or rejection is irreversible.[416] No duty is fastened on a bank that has neither accepted nor rejected a payment order.[417]

[5]   Acceptance of a payment order by a receiving bank obliges the sender to pay the amount of the order.[418] Sender's payment is carried out usually by means[419] of (i) an interbank final settlement over a funds transfer system; (ii) a credit by the sending bank to the receiving bank's account, in which case payment occurs at midnight of the day on which the credit is withdrawable and the receiving bank learns of this fact, unless credit was withdrawn earlier, in which case payment occurred at the time of withdrawal,[420] or (iii) a debit by the receiving bank to the sender's account, provided funds are actually available in the account. Where the receiving bank is that of the beneficiary, payment by means of a debit to the sender's account containing adequate cover, in fact, even by means of the availability of cover for a debit in such an account, will constitute acceptance only at the opening of the next funds transfer system day, provided the payment order was not rejected until one hour thereafter.[421]

Under what came to be known as the 'money-back guarantee' rule,[422] payment by the sender is excused, or can be refunded to him, where the funds transfer is not completed.[423] Nonetheless, an originator that selected a failed intermediary bank is responsible for the amount prepaid by the sender to that bank. Otherwise, where loss occurred at an intermediary bank, the effect of the money-back guarantee rule is to shift the risk of loss

---

[415] See text at n. 460, below.

[416] Rejection of payment order is governed by UCC §4A–211.

[417] Conversely, the Model Law imposes on a receiving bank that has not rejected a payment order, assistance, inquiry, and notice obligation, even in the absence of acceptance on its parts. See e.g. Articles 8, 10, and 13.

[418] UCC §4A–402.

[419] UCC §4A–403.

[420] Conversely, under Article 6(b) of the Model Law, sending bank's payment of a payment order by crediting the receiving bank's account occurs when this credit is used or, if not used, on the banking day *following* the day on which the credit is available for use to the knowledge of the receiving bank (rather than at midnight of the day on which the credit is withdrawable as under Article 4A).

[421] UCC §4A–209(b)(3). Conversely, under Article 9(1)(c) of the Model Law, acceptance of the beneficiary's bank by means of debiting the sender's account occurs when the beneficiary's bank actually debits the account. Under Article 9(1)(h), automatic acceptance by the mere availability of sender's funds (without actually debiting the sender's account) takes place on the second banking day following the receipt of the payment order (containing sufficient information to identify the sender) unless notice of rejection was given prior to that.

[422] See UCC §4A–402 Official Comment 2.

[423] For the completion of the funds transfer by the acceptance of the beneficiary's bank, see s. 8, below.

away from the originator, and to place it on the sender to the insolvent bank, regardless of whether loss was caused by a breach of duty.

A payment order must identify the beneficiary, as well as the benefi- [6] ciary's bank. It may further identify an intermediary bank. A beneficiary is typically identified by name or account number. A bank may be identified by name or identification number. Misdescription may lead to diversion of funds to an unintended beneficiary.

A payment order for non-existent or unidentifiable beneficiary cannot be accepted by the beneficiary's bank.[424] Where a payment order identifies the beneficiary by name and number, the beneficiary's bank acting without knowledge of any inconsistency between the name and number may rely on the number.

Where funds consequently reach an unintended beneficiary, the loss will fall on the originator (who remains liable to the intended beneficiary). A non-bank originator who was not advised of this risk may shift the loss to the originator's bank. Recovery from the person identified by number who was not entitled to receive payment from the originator is available, to the extent allowed by the law of mistake and restitution.[425]

Where a payment order identifies an intermediary or beneficiary's bank by number or name and number, the receiving bank acting without knowledge of any inconsistency may act either on the number or the name. The rules applicable to erroneous execution determine the allocation of loss.[426]

In an electronic environment, typical errors in payment order include [7] the transmittal of a duplicate payment order, an increase in the amount of a payment order (for example, by the addition of zeros to the sum), or the instruction of payment to an unintended beneficiary (usually by erring in the account or identification number of the intended beneficiary). Article 4A provides for the allocation of responsibility for such errors.

In principle, the sender is responsible for the contents of his own payment order. He is also responsible for a discrepancy arising in the course of the transmittal of a payment order through a third party communication system (e.g. SWIFT). This means that such an intermediary system is deemed to be an agent of the sender who is bound by the contents of the payment order as sent to the receiving bank by that communication system.[427]

A sender can nevertheless shift the loss arising from the transmittal of an erroneous payment order (whether by itself or by a communication system acting as its agent) where the receiving bank has failed to comply

---

[424] UCC §4A–207(a). [425] UCC §4A–207(b), (c), and (d).
[426] UCC §4A–208. For the rules applicable to erroneous execution, see s. 7, below.
[427] UCC t4A–206.

with an *agreed-upon* security procedure which would have detected the error. Such a procedure may require a unique code for each payment order (so as to alert the receiving bank in the case of a duplicate payment), different codes for different levels of amounts, or identify regular beneficiaries.[428] In order to benefit the sender, the security procedure, with which the receiving bank failed to comply, must have been agreed upon in advance.

The sender is not responsible for the erroneous execution of its payment order by the issue of a nonconforming payment order by the receiving bank. A receiving bank executing the sender's order is required to issue a conforming payment order of its own.[429] Effectively, this means that the risk of an erroneous execution is placed on the erring receiving bank.[430] For example, in case of overpayment resulting from the issue by the erring bank of a payment order in a larger amount than indicated in the one it received, the erring bank is required to pay the (larger) amount of its own payment order but is entitled to be paid only the (smaller) amount of the payment order it received.

Recovery of an erroneous payment, resulting either from an erroneous payment order[431] or from erroneous execution,[432] can be made, but only to the extent allowed under the law of mistake and restitution. Such recovery is available to the erring bank only directly from the actual beneficiary, irrespective whether the two are in privity.

A sender notified of his erroneous payment order who negligently failed to report the error cannot shift the loss to the receiving bank which did not comply with the agreed upon security procedures.[433] On his part, a sender notified of an erroneous execution of his payment order, and who was negligent in advising his bank of the error, is not entitled to interest on a refunded amount.[434]

(c) Completion, discharge, and revocation

[8]   A funds transfer is completed 'by acceptance by the beneficiary's bank of a payment order for the benefit of the beneficiary of the originator's payment order'.[435] Acceptance by the beneficiary's bank further constitutes payment by the originator to the beneficiary, namely a discharge of the

---

[428] UCC §4A–205.   [429] UCC §4A–302 discussed in s. 4, above.
[430] UCC §4A–303 dealing with erroneous execution leading to overpayment, underpayment, or payment to a wrong beneficiary. The receiving bank is effectively exonerated where its nonconformance is in the selection of an intermediary bank other than that selected by the sender but the funds transfer is nevertheless completed without exception (so that in fact no loss occurred).   [431] UCC §4A–205(a).
[432] UCC §4A–303.   [433] UCC §4A–205(b).   [434] UCC §4A–304.
[435] UCC §4A–104(a).

originator's obligation on the underlying transaction, that is, of the debt paid by means of the funds transfer.[436]

Finally, as indicated,[437] acceptance by the beneficiary's bank is by making payment to the beneficiary or by advising the beneficiary of the receipt of the payment order (or that the account of the beneficiary has been credited with respect to the order). For a beneficiary holding an account by a beneficiary's bank, which is obviously the usual case, acceptance by the beneficiary's bank is also by receiving payment from its sender.[438] Acceptance (in fact, otherwise than by payment to the beneficiary) generates an obligation by the beneficiary's bank to pay the beneficiary.[439]

A beneficiary's bank that accepted a payment order but failed to pay [9] the beneficiary may be held liable for consequential (but foreseeable) loss.[440] Payment by the beneficiary's bank to the beneficiary can be made by crediting the beneficiary's account or in any other manner. Payment by crediting the beneficiary's account occurs upon notification to the beneficiary of the right to withdraw the credit, the lawful application of the credit to a debt of the beneficiary (whether to the beneficiary's bank or a garnishing creditor), or the availability of funds to the beneficiary.[441] Presumably, a beneficiary's bank crediting a final funds balance is to be taken as making funds available to the beneficiary even in the absence of further advice to him.

In principle, payment by the beneficiary's bank to the beneficiary is 'final' and cannot be made provisional or conditional on the receipt of funds from the sender.[442]

Article 4A times the obligation of the beneficiary's bank to pay the beneficiary to coincide with the day of acceptance.[443] However, on this point, Article 4A is pre-empted by federal law. The latter effectively provides that the beneficiary's bank must make funds available to the beneficiary no later than at the start of the next business day after the banking day of acceptance by means of receiving a sender's payment.[444]

---

[436] UCC §4A–406.   [437] See s. 4, above.

[438] UCC §4A–209(b) and (c). For the Model Law variation, see n. 421, above.

[439] UCC §4A–404; corresponding rule is provided for the Model Law. UCC §4A–404 further requires the beneficiary's bank (at the risk of incurring liability for interest and possibly reasonable attorney's fees) to advise the beneficiary of a payment order instructing payment to the beneficiary's account before midnight of the next funds transfer business day following the payment date (the latter being usually the day the order is received by the beneficiary's bank).

[440] UCC §4A–404(a). The beneficiary's bank avoids liability for such damages where it 'proves that it did not pay because of a reasonable doubt concerning the right of the beneficiary of the payment'.   [441] UCC §4A–405.

[442] Ibid. No corresponding rule appears in the Model Law.

[443] UCC §4A–404(a).

[444] Reg. CC, Availability of Funds and Collection of Checks, 12 C.F.R. 229 (1988), section 229.10(b)(1).

[10]   A payment order is cancelled by operation of law if it remains unaccepted for five days, as well as where the receiving bank knows of the sender's death or legal incapacity before acceptance. Otherwise, a payment order can be cancelled or amended by means of a communication of the sender to his receiving bank. Cancellation or amendment can be made by the sender unilaterally up to the time of acceptance by that receiving bank. After acceptance, and in the absence of an agreement or a funds transfer system rule to the contrary, cancellation or amendment requires the agreement of the receiving bank. Where a receiving bank other than that of the beneficiary agrees to the cancellation or amendment, a conforming cancellation or amendment must be issued by it to its own receiving bank.[445] The funds transfer is thus effectively aborted if the last receiving bank to receive a payment order is advised by its sender of the cancellation or amendment prior to the acceptance of the payment order by that receiving bank.

Where the receiving bank is the beneficiary's bank, post-acceptance cancellation or amendment can be made only with respect to an unauthorized or mistaken funds transfer. As with respect to any post-acceptance cancellation or amendment, agreement of the receiving bank, in this case the beneficiary's bank, is required.

Unless otherwise provided by an agreement or funds transfer system rule, the sender is liable to a receiving bank for any loss incurred by that bank in a post-acceptance cancellation (or amendment) or attempted cancellation (or amendment).[446]

Injunction and creditor process by the originator's creditors can prevent the originator's bank from initiating a funds transfer. Likewise, an injunction and creditor process by the beneficiary's process can prevent the beneficiary from receiving the benefit of payment once the funds transfer has been completed. A funds transfer cannot, however, be intercepted by third parties between acceptance by the originator's bank and by the beneficiary's bank.[447]

(d) Scope of damages and risk allocation

[11]   The liability of a receiving bank for late or improper execution, as well as for non-execution in breach of contract, is limited to interest losses, expenses,[448] and in some circumstances, reasonable attorney fees. There is no liability for consequential loss, even foreseeable, including exchange losses, or loss of a profitable contract due to the failure to meet a contrac-

---

[445] UCC §4A–211.   [446] Ibid.   [447] UCC §§4A–502 and 503.
[448] Expenses may not be recovered in the case of mere delay. See UCC §4A–305(a).

tual payment deadline,[449] except by express written contract.[450] In the view of the drafters,[451] this rule is rationalized on the need 'to effect payment at low cost and great speed'.[452]

As between the originator and the beneficiary, the risk of delay or loss **[12]** occurring at a bank other than that of the beneficiary falls on the originator. This is so since until acceptance by the beneficiary's bank the underlying originator's debt to the beneficiary subsists.[453] When the transfer is not completed by the acceptance of the beneficiary's bank, namely, when loss occurs, the originator usually benefits from the money-back guarantee rule so that the ultimate party with a remedy against the bank where loss occurred is the immediate sender to that bank.[454] With respect to delay, the originator has a direct remedy against the defaulting bank, regardless of whether they are immediate parties in the transfer chain, though only for interest losses, expenses, and, in some circumstances, reasonable attorney's fees. Interest losses for late execution may be recovered from the defaulting bank directly by the beneficiary.[455] By allowing a direct remedy and bypassing the action against the originator who would then have a recourse from the defaulting bank, this rule avoids the circuitry of actions.

As indicated, there is no recovery for consequential loss.[456] On the other hand, liability for loss, under the money-back guarantee rule, is absolute and not dependent on the breach of any particular duty by the receiving bank. Likewise, when delay occurs due to the failure to act timely, liability is absolute. Obviously, however, breach by the receiving bank of its obligations in executing the payment order,[457] causing loss or delay, gives rise to recovery (of interest, expenses, and attorney's fees, as applicable).

Vis-à-vis the originator, an event causing delay or loss occurring after the acceptance by the beneficiary's bank is at the beneficiary's risk. This is so since acceptance by the beneficiary's bank discharges the originator's debt to the beneficiary and makes the beneficiary's bank accountable to the beneficiary.[458] Consequential foreseeable damages may be recovered by the beneficiary from the beneficiary's bank.[459]

---

[449] This is an obvious departure from the common law rule of *Evra Corp.* v. *Swiss Bank Corp.* 673 F.2d 951 (7th Cir. 1982), discussed in (viii) s. 16, above.

[450] UCC §4A–305.   [451] Official Comment 2 to UCC §4A–305.

[452] In general, the Model Law followed suit, but with more moderation. Thus, Article 18 specifically does not exclude 'any remedy that may exist when a bank has improperly executed, or failed to execute, a payment order (a) *with specific intent to cause loss*, or (b) *recklessly and with actual knowledge that loss would be likely to result*' [emphasis added]. Mere negligence, and even gross negligence, will not suffice.

[453] See s. 8, above.   [454] See s. 5, above.

[455] UCC §4A–305 (discussed in s. 11, above).

[456] Ibid.   [457] Under UCC §4A–302. See s. 4, above.   [458] See s. 8, above.

[459] See s. 9, above.

In principle, the risk of delay or loss occurring at the beneficiary's bank prior to acceptance by that bank falls on the originator. Where the beneficiary has an account with the beneficiary's bank, this risk is of an extremely short duration since sender's payment would constitute the acceptance of the beneficiary's bank.[460] In any event, where loss occurs at the beneficiary's bank prior to its acceptance, the originator benefits from the money-back guarantee rule. There seems to be no remedy available to the originator in the case of a pre-acceptance delay at the beneficiary's bank.

(XI) SOUTH AFRICA

[1]   Credit transfers may be processed in South Africa either individually or in bulk.[461] On the basis of the conclusive academic position to that end,[462] it was held with respect to credit transfers, that 'the relationship between [an originator] and [the originator's bank] which result[s] from the transfer instruction to the latter [is] one of mandate'.[463] Mandate is governed in South Africa by Roman-Dutch law.[464] At the same time, it was recognized, in the context of the law governing the payment order, that 'the South African banking law—most notably in regard to the relationship between banker and customer—is largely derived from English law'.[465] It however appears that insofar as questions relating to privity and liability are concerned, there may be a large degree of consensus between the two legal systems, and that at least with regard to most fundamental issues there may not be a pressing practical need to determine what law applies.

[2]   As indicated, an intermediary bank is treated at common law as a subagent of the originator, rather than as a substitute agent, with which the

---

[460] See s. 4, above.

[461] See e.g. South African Reserve Bank Payment System Division, *South African National Payment System Framework and Strategy* (Pretoria: SA Reserve Bank, 1995), at 42–3. A real-time South African Multiple Option Settlement (SAMOS) system for high-value interbank payments has been operational since 1998.

[462] See e.g. F. R. Malan and J. T. Pretorius, *Malan on Bills of Exchange, Cheques and Promissory Notes in South African Law*, 3rd edn. (Durban: Butterworths, 1997) at 330. See also I. Meiring, 'The South African Payment System' ABLU'96 at p. 4 of her paper.

[463] *Gilbey Distillers and Vintners* v. *ABSA Bank*, Case No. 12698/94 (High Court of South providAfrica, Cape Good Hope Provincial Division) ¶58, 4 Dec. 1998, *per* Brand and Traverso JJ. I ed expert assistance to ABSA Bank in whose favour judgment was given.

[464] See in general, D. J. Joubert and D. H. Van Zyl, 'Mandate and Negotiorum Gestio', in W. A. Joubert (ed.), *The Law of South Africa*, vol. xvii (Durban: Butterworths, 1983), 1.

[465] *Gilbey*, above, n. 463 at ¶59. For the broader proposition as to the application of English law to the relationship between banker and customer in South Africa, the Court cited *Rosen* v. *Barclays National Bank, Ltd.* 1984 (3) S. A. 974 (W) *in fine*; and *Standard Bank of SA* v. *Onenate Investments (Pty) Ltd.* 1995 (4) S. A. 510 (C) at 566, paras. A–D. *Gilbey*, ibid. at ¶59, n. 31.

originator has no privity, but for whose negligence the originator's bank is vicariously liable to the originator.[466] To a similar end, under the law mandate in South Africa,[467] a sub-mandatary is responsible to the mandatary and must account to him in terms of their contract, while the mandatary is responsible to the mandator for the sub-mandatary's actions in respect of any breach involved. Conversely, with respect to a substitute mandatary, a new and direct contract of mandate, superseding the original one between the mandator and the original mandatary, is concluded between the mandator and the substitute mandatary. It was held that a bank acting in a credit transfer for the originator's bank is a sub-mandatary, and that in the footsteps of English law, there is no direct privity between a participating bank, other than the originator's bank, and the originator.[468]

In this context, and in the absence of a direct contract of mandate **[3]** between them, no contract whatsoever exists between the originator and the beneficiary's bank, even if the beneficiary's bank is to be regarded as a sub-mandatary of the originator's bank.[469] Certainly, no contract of deposit can be said to exist between the originator and the beneficiary's bank by virtue of 'written offers' made to the beneficiary's bank by the originator through the agency of the originator's bank.[470] This is so even without the participation of any intermediary bank in the credit transfer, so that the originator's 'written offers' are to be passed on by the originator's bank directly to the beneficiary bank. Also, particularly in the absence of 'some relationship of proximity between the parties', the beneficiary's bank is not liable to the originator in delict (that is, torts).[471]

It was not expressly stated that the beneficiary's bank acts as a mandatary for the beneficiary. It was, however, specifically recognized, on the basis of the undertaking by a bank to receive money and to collect bills for the customer's account, as pronounced in the common law,[472] that 'where [a] bank receives funds by transfer, which are identified as being for a credit of a customer's account, it has a contractual duty to that customer [namely, to the beneficiary] to credit that account accordingly'.[473] Stated otherwise, a direct contractual relationship exists between the beneficiary and the beneficiary's bank.

---

[466] See (viii) s. 15.   [467] See Joubert and Van Zyl, above, n. 464 at ¶¶9, 10.
[468] *Gilbey*, above, n. 463 at ¶59.   [469] Ibid., at ¶60.
[470] As was contended in *Gilbey* by the originator, ibid. at ¶23.
[471] *Gilbey*, ibid. at ¶78, and in general, ¶¶66–86. The tort liability for economic loss of a collecting bank to the true owner of a stolen cheque, discussed in 4.D (iv)(d) (South Africa) above, was specifically and correctly distinguished in *Gilbey*, ibid. at ¶81. Indeed, in a credit transfer but not in the stolen cheque situation, all parties are situated in a chain of contractual relationships so that remedies are adequately provided in contract.
[472] To that end, the Court cited, in *Gilbey*, ibid. at ¶57, n. 28, the leading English case of *Joachimson v. Swiss Bank Corporation* [1921] 3 K.B. 110 (C.A.) at 127.
[473] *Gilbey*, ibid. at ¶57.

[4]   In principle under South African law, the mandate is revocable by the mandator's unilateral act.[474] No special rules have been developed with regard to the revocation of the payment order, the completion of the transaction, as well as to the discharge of the debt paid by the credit transfer.

(XII) THE EUROPEAN UNION: TRANSPARENCY AND MINIMUM STANDARDS FOR CROSS-BORDER RETAIL CREDIT TRANSFERS

[1]   Directive 97/5/EC of the European Parliament and of the Council of 27 January 1997 on cross-border credit transfers (the 'Transparency Directive')[475] deals with the transparency and minimum standards for the performance of Pan European cross-border credit transfers of no more than 50,000 euro. The Transparency Directive falls short of providing a comprehensive body of law for credit transfers in the European Union. It does not deal with systemic risk and settlement finality. Nor does it cover domestic transfers. Moreover, aspects of cross-border credit transfers not specifically governed by the Transparency Directive will remain to be governed by national laws, as determined in each case by the applicable choice-of-law rules.[476] This includes all aspects of cross-border transfers above the 50,000 euro ceiling. Also, this includes transfers of sums of 50,000 euro or less, where standards of performance higher than those provided by the Transparency Directive, or remedies not envisaged by it, exist under the applicable national law. Regrettably, the Transparency Directive does not provide for uniform conflict of laws rules to secure an easy and smooth identification of the applicable domestic law to a given type of dispute.

As a rationale, the Transparency Directive cites in the Preamble, among other reasons: the increasing volume of cross-border payments; the need of individuals and businesses, 'especially small and medium-sized enterprises', to be able to make credit transfers rapidly, reliably, and cheaply from one part of the Community to another; the reduction of completion time for cross-border credit transfers; as well as the need of furthering the goal of implementing the economic and monetary union and, particularly, assisting the EMI in its task of promoting the efficiency of cross-border

---

[474] See Joubert and Van Zyl, above, n. 464 at ¶16, p. 19.

[475] 1997 OJ L 43, p. 0025.

[476] On this aspect, from the perspective of the domestic laws of Belgium and France, see X. Thunis, 'La Responsabilité du banquier dans les virements transfrontiers: le droit commun du virement face à la Directive Europèene du 27 Janvier 1997', 2 *Mélanges Christian Mouly* 417 (Paris: Litec, 1998).

payments 'with the view to the preparation of the third stage of economic and monetary union'.

The Transparency Directive consists of four sections, containing altogether thirteen Articles. Section I (Articles 1–2) deals with scope and definitions. Section II (Articles 3–4) provides for transparency of conditions for cross-border credit transfers. Section III (Articles 5–10) provides for minimum obligations of institutions in respect of such transfers. Section IV (Articles 11–13) contains the final provisions.

According to Article 1, the Transparency Directive applies to 'cross-border credit transfers in the currencies of the Member States' up to the equivalent of 50,000 euro ordered by a person other than a credit or financial institution. Under Article 2(f), 'cross-border credit transfer means a transaction carried out on the initiative of an originator via an institution or its branch in one Member State, with the view to making available an amount of money to a beneficiary at an institution or its branch in another Member State . . .'.[477] The originator and the beneficiary may be the same person. [2]

Section II, dealing with transparency of terms, contains two Articles. Article 3 covers pre-transaction disclosure. Article 4 provides for post-transaction information. In each case, the information ought to be given by each institution, namely, the bank of the originator and that of the beneficiary, as fit. The information must be given 'in writing, including where appropriate by electronic means, and in a readily comprehensible form'. [3]

Article 3 provides for the institutions' duty to make available to their actual and prospective customers 'information on conditions for cross-border credit transfers'. The information shall be given in advance and include at least:

- an indication by the originator's institution of the time needed for carrying out the transfer to the account of the destination institution;
- an indication by the beneficiary's institution receiving a cross-border credit transfer of the time for crediting the received funds to the beneficiary's account;

---

[477] Under art. 2, 'originator means a natural or legal person that orders the making of a cross-border credit transfer to a beneficiary'. 'Beneficiary' is 'the final recipient of a cross-border credit transfer for whom the corresponding funds are made available in an account to which he has access'. 'Institution' means 'a credit institution or other institution'. 'Other institution' corresponds to anyone 'that by way of business executes cross-border credit transfers'. A 'credit institution' is defined in art. 1 of First Council Directive 77/780/EEC of 12 Dec. 1977 on the co-ordination of laws, regulations, and administrative provisions relating to the taking up and pursuit of the business of credit institutions (the 'First Banking Directive'), 1977 OJ L 322, p. 0031, as 'an undertaking whose business is to receive deposits or other repayable funds from the public and to grant credits for its own account'. The term corresponds to 'depository institution' or 'bank', but purports not to be limited to any technical definition, particularly of the latter.

- the manner of calculation of any commission fees and charges, 'including where appropriate the rates' payable by the institutions' respective customer, namely, the originator or the beneficiary;
- 'the value date, if any, applied by the institution'; and
- an 'indication of the reference exchange rates used'.

Article 4 provides for 'clear information' to be furnished to customers subsequent to the execution or receipt of the transfer, 'unless the latter expressly forgo this'. This information shall include at least:

- 'a reference enabling the customer to identify the . . . transfer';
- 'the original amount of the . . . transfer';
- 'the amount of all charges and commission fees payable by the customer'; and
- 'the value date, if any, applied by the institution'.

Furthermore, where the originator has specified that the charges for the transfer are to be borne, in whole or in part, by the beneficiary, 'the latter shall be informed thereof by his own institution'. Finally, where any amount has been converted to another currency, the converting institution 'shall inform its customer of the exchange rate used'.

[4]   Section III, containing Articles 5 to 10, sets out institutions' minimum obligations. Such obligations relate to the time needed for carrying out the transfer, the charges involved, compliance with the instructions, refund upon the non-execution, and the settlement of disputes. However, these obligations are not absolute. Under Article 9, 'institutions participating in the execution of a cross-border credit transfer order shall be released from the obligations laid down in this Directive where they can adduce reasons of *force majeure*'. This is stated to mean 'abnormal and unforeseeable circumstances beyond the control of the person pleading *force majeure*, the consequences of which would have been unavoidable despite all efforts to the contrary'.

Article 5 requires the institution, '[u]nless it does not wish to do business with that customer', at the customer's request, to 'give an undertaking concerning the time needed for execution', as well as 'the commission fees and charges payable, apart from those relating to the exchange rate used'.

Under Article 6(1), the originator's institution is required to execute the transfer 'within the time limit agreed with the originator'. Where arrival of funds to the beneficiary's institution is delayed beyond this time limit or, in its absence, beyond the fifth banking business day following the acceptance of the payment order by the originator's institution,[478] the latter is required to compensate the customer for loss of interest.[479] Other types of loss are not mentioned; nor are they specifically excluded. Article 6(2) requires the beneficiary's institution to make the funds available to the beneficiary 'within the time limit agreed with the beneficiary'. Where completion is delayed beyond this time limit or, in its absence, beyond the end of the banking business day following the day on which the beneficiary's institution received the funds, the beneficiary's institution is required to compensate the beneficiary for loss of interest. Under Article 6(3), no compensation under these provisions is payable to a customer to whom the delay is attributable. The burden of proof as to the customer's fault is on the institution.

Article 7 provides for an institution's obligation to follow the instructions contained in the payment order. In fact it deals with only one aspect of this duty, namely, the duty to carry out the transfer in the amount instructed by the originator. Article 7(1) requires the originator's institution, any intermediary institution, and the beneficiary's institution, which has accepted a cross-border credit transfer order, 'to execute that credit transfer for the full amount thereof unless the originator has specified that the costs of the cross-border credit transfer are to be borne wholly or partly by the beneficiary'. This does not prejudice the right of the beneficiary's institution to levy a charge on the beneficiary relating to the administration of the beneficiary's account. Under Article 7(2), '[w]ithout prejudice to any other claim which may be made', the originator's institution is to transmit to the beneficiary any amount deducted by the originator's or an intermediary institution in breach of paragraph (1). On its part, the breaching intermediary is accountable to the originator's institution. Under paragraph (3), a breaching beneficiary's institution is obligated to credit the beneficiary's account with the amount wrongly deducted.

Article 8 deals with the institution's obligation to refund in the event of non-execution of transfers. Effectively, it provides for a partial, and actually qualified, 'money-back guarantee rule'.[480] Article 8(1) deals with the case where the amount of a cross-border credit transfer that had been

---

[478] Under paragraph 10 of the Preamble, the Commission, in the report that it must submit to the European Parliament and the Council within two years from the implementation of the Directive, 'should particularly examine the time-limit to be applied in the absence of a time-limit agreed between the originator and his institution, taking into account both technical developments and the situation existing in each Member State'.

[479] Also, where the delay is attributable to an intermediary institution, 'that institution shall be required to compensate the originator's institution'.

[480] The term, referred to in Official Comment 2 to UCC §4A–402, highlights the originator's right to obtain refund where the credit transfer has not been completed. See Geva, *The Law of Electronic Funds Transfers*, above, n. 1, §2.04[2].

accepted by the originator's institution was not credited to the beneficiary's account with the beneficiary's institution. Under such circumstances, 'and without prejudice to any other claim which may be made',[481] the originator's institution is obliged to refund the originator with the amount of the cross-border transfer, but only up to a ceiling of 12,500 euro,[482] plus applicable interest and charges. The refund obligation arises upon the originator's request, to be made after the expiry of either the time agreed for execution or, in the absence of such an agreement, at the expiry of the five-day statutory limit for execution under Article 6(1). The originator's institution has fourteen banking business days to comply with the originator's refund request, and is excused where the funds have in the meantime reached the beneficiary's institution.

Paragraphs (2) and (3) of Article 8 provide for situations where the refund obligation under paragraph (1) does not apply in full or in part. There are three such situations, consisting of the non-completion of the transfer due to (i) the 'non-execution by an intermediary institution chosen by the beneficiary's institution', (ii) 'an error or omission in the instructions given by the originator to [the originator's] institution', or (iii) 'the non-execution of the . . . transfer by an intermediary institution expressly chosen by the originator'.

Article 8(2) deals with the first situation. It provides that in such a case, presumably because the beneficiary's institution bears at least some responsibility for the loss, paragraph (1) does not apply. Instead of the originator's institution refunding the originator, it is then the duty of the beneficiary's institution, which has chosen the defaulting intermediary, 'to make the funds available to the beneficiary up to 12,500 [euro]'.

Article 8(3) deals with the second and third situations, where loss is attributed, at least to some extent, to the originator. In such cases, the refund obligation of the originator's institution under paragraph (1) does not apply. Nevertheless, 'the originator's institution and the other institutions involved shall endeavour as fast as possible to refund the amount of the transfer'. An originator's institution that has recovered the amount is obliged to credit it to the originator. However, '[t]he institutions, including the originator's institution, are not obliged in this case to refund the charges and interest accruing, and can deduct the costs arising from the recovery if specified'.

---

[481] As explained in recital 12 of the Preamble, 'Article 8 does not affect the general provisions of national law whereby an institution has responsibility towards the originator when a cross-border credit transfer has not been completed because of an error committed by that institution'.

[482] Recital 11 of the Preamble explains that this ceiling was set since 'the obligation to refund imposes a contingent liability on institutions which might, in the absence of any limit, have a prejudicial effect on solvency requirements'.

Article 10 deals with the settlement of disputes. In fact, it does not properly belong to section III, providing for obligations fastened on institutions. Rather, it imposes an obligation on member states to 'ensure that there are adequate and effective complaints and redress procedures for the settlement of disputes' between an institution and its customer, whether the originator or the beneficiary of a cross-border retail credit transfer. Perhaps, the inclusion of this provision in section III amounts to the imposition of a duty on each institution to resort to such mechanisms to resolve disputes with its customers.

The final provisions of the Transparency Directive are contained in section [5] IV, consisting of Articles 11–13. Article 11 requires each member state to implement the Directive by passing the necessary laws into its own legal system. Article 12 requires the Commission to submit a report to the European Parliament and Council on the application of the Directive. Finally, Article 13 provides for the national implementation of the Transparency Directive by the member states within thirty months from the date of its publication in the *Official Journal of the European Communities*, that is, 14 February 1997.

D. The Disposition of Funds Held in Non-depository Account-Holding Institutions

(1) INTRODUCTION

[1] The cashless payment system provides the facility for non-cash payments by allowing payers and payees access to funds held in the financial system. A cashless payment transaction consists of the following elements:

1. The pre-existing account relationships of customers with account- (or value-) holding institutions. Account-holding institutions may be depository or non-depository institutions that may provide asset, investment, and credit accounts that can be used for payments;

2. The communication of payment instructions by customers;

3. Clearing of payment instructions (namely, the processing and exchange mechanism that enables participants to determine their debit and credit positions towards others);

4. Settlement (namely, the process of payment for positions established in the clearing).

[2] Generally speaking, in each domestic payment system, access to clearing and settlement facilities linking customer accounts throughout the country is effectively limited, either by law or by practice, to supervised regulated depository institutions, such as, though no longer exclusively, banks.[1] Yet, funds may be held by the public in non-depository financial institutions, such as securities dealers or insurance companies. In recent years, pressure has been mounted for expanding direct access to non-depository account-holding financial institutions. To that end, specific recommendations were made in Australia[2] and Canada.[3] Particular

---

[1] In this section, reference is made to a 'depository institution' which is not only a 'bank', in order to highlight the distinction between all types of 'depository institutions' (and not only 'banks') and non-depository institutions. Reference to a 'bank' in this section usually relates to a depository institution specifically regulated as 'bank'.

[2] See *Financial System Inquiry Final Report* (Canberra, Mar. 1997) ('The Wallis Report' after the committee chairman) at 382–414.

[3] Task Force on the Future of the Canadian Financial Services Sector, *Change, Challenge and Opportunity* (Sept. 1998) ('The MacKay Report' after the Task Force chairman) at 92–4, and Recommendation 13 at 196. See also Bill C-8, An Act to Establish the Financial Consumer Agency of Canada and to Amend Certain Acts in Relation to Financial Institutions, 1st Sess., 37th Parl., 2000 (28 February 2001 (Commons)) which, among other things, provides for reform of access to the payments system in Canada.

attention was given in Canada to life insurance companies, securities dealers, and money market mutual funds.[4]

The present discussion examines mechanisms available for providing **[3]** customers of non-depository account-holding financial institutions access to the payment system through the intermediation of deposit-taking institutions directly linked to the country-wide clearing and settlement system. Such intermediation is required in an environment which restricts clearing and settlement access to depository institutions. Also, for business reasons, such intermediation ought not to be excluded even where direct access to the country-wide clearing and settlement system by non-depository institutions is not precluded. The mechanisms to be examined are designed to ensure that cashless payments could be carried out on a nationwide basis from and into accounts held in non-depository institutions, to and from accounts held anywhere else, particularly in depository institutions participating in the domestic clearing and settlement system.

Payment out of funds held at non-depository financial institutions can **[4]** be initiated by either electronic or paper-based instructions. They could be either credit transfers, 'pushing' funds out of the account held with the non-depository financial institution, or debit transfers, collecting or 'pulling' funds out of such account.[5] Typically, electronic payment instructions to non-depository institutions are not governed by any specific statute, as is the case with written instruction initiating a credit transfer.[6]

Conversely, in all jurisdictions, the drawer's written unconditional order instructing a non-depository financial institution to make payment to the holder presenting it falls within the definition of a bill of exchange or draft, and is thus governed by legislation covering bills of exchange.[7]

---

[4] The access issue surfaced in Canada in proceedings before the Competition Tribunal. For an overview preceding the MacKay Report, see S. Chinoy and B. Geva, 'Access to the Canadian Payments System', in *The Regulation of Financial Institutions—Issues and Perspectives*, being the 1996 Queen's Annual Business Law Symposium (Toronto: Carswell, 1997), 411. For a discussion following the MacKay Report, see D. A. Chamberland, 'Access to the Payments System—The Task Force on the Future of the Canadian Financial Sector' (1999), 14 B.F.L.R. 555.

[5] For the distinction between credit and debit transfer see 3.A, above.

[6] For example, in the USA, Article 4A of the Uniform Commercial Code (UCC), governing wire transfers, is limited to non-consumer transfers carried out by the banking system. Similarly in the USA, EFTA and Reg. E implementing it are limited to transfers initiated out of consumer accounts in depository institutions. For the latter point see B. Geva, *The Law of Electronic Funds Transfers* (New York: Matthew Bender, 1992–2000), at §6.04[2][b] [iii]. For the scope of UCC Article 4A see *id*. at §2.02[3].

[7] For complete global definitions, see UCC §3–104 (a) and (e) (US); The Uniform Law on Bills of Exchange and Promissory Notes (UBL) (under the Geneva Convention of 1932) art. 1 (the basis of legislation in France, Germany, Italy, Japan, and Switzerland); Bills of Exchange Act 1909 s. 8(1) (Australia); Bills of Exchange Act 1882 s. 3 (UK); Bills of Exchange

Such a draft 'pulls' funds from the drawer's account and carries out a debit transfer. It is either payable to the holder over the counter, or collected by the holder into his or her account. The American Uniform Commercial Code (UCC) specifically provides for drafts which may be drawn on non-depository institutions but are payable either through or at depository institutions.[8]

[5]		In all jurisdictions, a cheque must be drawn on a depository institution. It carries out a debit transfer from funds kept at a depository institution, and as such is outside the present inquiry.[9] However, a positive balance in an account kept at a depository institution may be funded by a transfer from an account held at a non-depository institution. A cheque drawn on the account held at the depository institution may thus effectively carry out payment from funds held at the non-depository institution, and is thus of interest in the present context.

Furthermore, a cheque drawn on the account of a non-depository institution kept at a depository institution may carry out payment of a customer of the non-depository institution, and thus falls within the ambit of this discussion. To a similar end, Australian law provides for the agency cheque, which can broadly be described as a cheque drawn on the account of a financial institution, typically non-bank,[10] held in a depository institution, typically a bank,[11] and carrying out payment by a customer of the financial institution. The financial institution, on whose account the agency cheque is drawn, is typically either a credit union or building society, namely, a non-bank depository institution.[12] However, the financial institution, on whose account the agency cheque is drawn, could also be a special services provider[13] or a registered corporation within the meaning of

Act R.S.C. 1985, c.B-4 s. 16 (Canada); Bills of Exchange Act No. 34 of 1964 s. 2 (South Africa); and Bills of Exchange Ordinance [New Version] s. 3 (Israel).

[8] See UCC §§4–106(a) and (b) discussed below, in (ii) and (iii). (See also (iv).)

[9] For cheques and cheques legislation in the various jurisdictions see 3.B, above.

[10] Under s. 100 of the Australian Cheques Act 1986, Act 145 as am. (most recently by Act No. 77 of 1998) an agency cheque is to be drawn either by an FIC institution or an FCA institution. According to definitions in s. 3, and as explained below, such an institution is a building society, credit union, special services provider, or registered corporation under the Financial Corporations Act 1974.

[11] Under s. 10 of the Australian Cheques Act a cheque must be drawn on a financial institution, the latter being broadly defined in s. 3 to cover domestic as well as foreign banks, the Reserve Bank of Australia, building societies, credit unions, and special services providers.

[12] Until the end of 1998, an instrument drawn on a credit union or building society and payable on demand was not a 'cheque'; rather, it was called 'payment order'. In comparison to the cheque, the payment order was less familiar and less popular. In response, building societies and credit unions facilitated the use of agency cheques by their customers.

[13] In Australia, a special services provider (SSP) provides to member institutions settlement services, treasury management services, loans or other financial accommodation facilities, and investment facilities for deposits. In practice, members institutions are non-bank depository financial institutions, namely, credit unions and building societies. The term is not defined, but is specifically referred to, in the Cheques Act.

the Financial Corporations Act 1974 (FCA),[14] as may be prescribed. In addition to credit unions and building societies which are depository institutions, the FCA covers financial intermediaries, which borrow from and lend to the public. However, borrowing need not necessarily be made by taking deposits. Issuing long-term debt instruments such as debentures will also qualify. At the same time, the FCA does not cover insurance companies or securities firms. Regardless, to date, no non-depository financial institution falling within the FCA has been prescribed, so that in practice, the agency cheque is one drawn on the account of a non-bank depository institution kept at a bank.

Agency cheques come in Australia in two forms. First, at the request of a customer, a credit union or building society may issue its own cheque, drawn on its own account with a correspondent bank, to the order of the payee and for a sum as instructed by the customer. Second, under a more sophisticated variation, the customer receives a chequebook with blank cheque forms of the credit union or building society, drawn (once filled in and signed) on its account at the correspondent bank. The customer is given authority to draw such cheques, which are presented for payment at the drawee bank. However, payment of such cheques by the drawee bank requires referral to and receipt of confirmation from the credit union or building society. Technically, such an agency cheque is the cheque of the credit union or building society, drawn on the bank, by the customer as an agent for the credit union or building society. The Cheques Act, however, expressly releases the credit union or building society from any liability for a dishonoured agency cheque signed by the customer. Such agency cheques are visibly distinguishable from cheques actually drawn by the credit union or building society which constitute an obligation of that institution rather than of its customer.[15] In principle, the agency cheque models may become available for the transmission of funds held in non-depository institutions which are precluded from providing chequing services.

It should be pointed out that legislation in all jurisdictions contains pro- **[6]** visions applicable exclusively either to cheques or to the bank and customer relationship.[16] Such provisions are stated to apply neither to drafts drawn on non-depository institutions nor to the relationship between such institutions and their customers. For example, in the UK, the Bills of Exchange Act (BEA) provides for special rules governing the extent of

---

[14] Financial Corporations Act 1974, ch. 2, as am.

[15] Agency cheques are governed by s. 100 of the Australian Cheques Act.

[16] Cheque provisions in the various jurisdictions, including those dealing with the bank and customer relationship, particularly in relation to cheques, are extensively examined above, in 3.C and below, in 4.B and D. The differences between statutory provisions relating to cheques and bills of exchange, however, are not specifically reviewed.

drawer's discharge upon the delayed presentment of a cheque, the revocation of the drawee's authority to pay a cheque upon the countermand of payment or the receipt of notice of the customer's death, and cheque crossing (ss. 74–81). Similar provisions, with some modifications which may vary from one jurisdiction to another, exist in Israel (BEO ss. 75–82), South Africa (BEA ss. 72–82), and Australia (Cheques Act ss. 53–57 and Part VI). They also exist in Canada (BEA ss. 166–75), where cheque crossing is nonetheless not practised. Also, specific protections are given in the UK, under the Cheques Act 1957, to banks collecting or paying cheques or other instruments drawn on banks or government. In Canada, there is also a special provision governing the position of a bank, in which a cheque is deposited, as a holder in due course of that cheque (s. 165(3)). Legislation in the UK (BEA ss. 74A–74C) and Australia (Cheques Act s. 62) provides for cheque truncation.

Similarly, for civil law jurisdictions, the Geneva Uniform Law on Cheques provides for special cheque rules. For example, it provides for crossed cheques and cheques payable in account (arts. 37–9). It further precludes the acceptance of a cheque (art. 4), and states that neither death nor incapacity of the drawer-customer affects the cheque (art. 33). Further, the presentment of a cheque at a clearing house is stated to be the equivalent to presentment for payment (art. 31).

In the USA, under the UCC, a conspicuous statement contained in an instrument under which the instrument is not negotiable excludes it from the scope of Article 3 only if it is not a cheque (UCC §3–104(d)). Regardless, 'Item' is defined in UCC §4–104(9) to cover an 'order to pay money handled by a bank for collection or payment' which may be broad enough to encompass not only the cheque, but also a draft drawn on a non-depository institution, as long as it is handled by a bank. Nevertheless, provisions relating to payment (UCC §§4–301 to 303) and customer's rights (UCC §§4–401 to 407) are stated to be limited to the context of a payor bank so as not to cover the payment by, and position of, a non-depository institution. The latter provisions, relating to customers' rights, cover matters such as the bank's authority to debit the account, liability for wrongful dishonour, the customer's right to stop payment, stale cheques, the customer's duty to discover and report unauthorized signature or alteration, and the effect of improper payment. Under UCC §4–105(1), 'bank' is defined as 'any person engaged in the business of banking, including a saving bank, saving and loan association, credit union, or trust company'. This effectively covers any type of a depository institution, but arguably, not a non-depository one.

For all jurisdictions, the above list may not be exhaustive. Also, the possibility of the application by analogy of any of the above-mentioned provisions to either the draft payable on demand or to the relationship between the customer and the account-holding non-depository institution will not be explored here. Space limitations also require that the ensuing discussion not explore the legal framework governing the activity of non-depository institutions as either collecting or paying institutions. Discussion, rather, is limited to (i) the nature of the instruments and facilities available for the payment out of funds kept in accounts held in non-depository institutions, and (ii) the responsibility attached to the depository institution providing access to such mechanisms into the interbank payment system.

(II) MECHANISMS AND RISKS

In an environment where entities other than depository institutions ('entities') participate neither in clearing nor in settlement, access to an entity's customer ('customer') to the payment system can be provided through a depository institution (DI). Several options could be considered: [7]

1. The customer may instruct the entity to make payment into a designated account at a designated DI (or for that matter, even at an entity);

2. The customer may instruct the entity to issue its own cheque (or draft) on the entity's account with its own DI;

3. The customer may draw his own cheque, as if in the name of the entity, on the entity's account with its DI;

4. The customer may draw his own draft on the entity, the draft being 'payable through' the entity's DI;

5. The customer may draw his own draft on the entity, the draft being 'payable at' the entity's DI; or

6. The customer may draw a cheque on, or otherwise instruct payment from, his account with the entity's DI, with that account being funded by the customer's funds transferred from the entity.

The following is an analysis of each of these mechanisms, and its incumbent risks: [8]

1. The first scenario is the one actually occurring in the Netherlands for customers of mortgage banks or security credit institutions, which do not provide direct payment services to their customers. However, these institutions are quasi-commercial banks, and hence DIs. In our context, the customer will instruct the entity to make the payment. The entity will debit the customer's account, and will instruct its own DI to carry out the payment to the designated account elsewhere. The entity's DI will then

debit the entity's account and will carry out an ordinary credit transfer accordingly. In this setting, no unusual risk is involved.

Alternatively, as we shall see below, the customer may instruct payment to a merchant, by means of a payment card issued to the customer by the entity, inserted and authenticated at a POS terminal on the merchant's premises ("off-line debit card"). In such a case, a procedure must exist for confirming the authenticity of these instructions, as well as of the availability of funds or credit. In this scenario, the entity's DI is likely to incur liability to the merchant's DI, before obtaining reimbursement from the entity. The DI may thus face the risk of failure by the entity.

2. The second scenario is actually that of the less sophisticated Australian agency cheque. In this context, having received the customer's instructions, the entity will debit the customer's account and issue its own cheque to the payee, on the entity's account with the DI, as per the customer's instructions. The customer will deliver the cheque to the payee. The payee (or a subsequent indorsee) will have the cheque presented at the entity's DI. Assuming the availability of funds in the entity's account, the entity's DI will honour the entity's cheque. No unusual risk is presented in the course of this process.

3. The third scenario is that of the more sophisticated Australian agency cheque. In our context, the customer is to be provided with blank cheque forms of the entity on its account with the DI. The customer then draws a cheque on that account and delivers it to the payee. The payee (or a subsequent indorsee) will have the cheque presented for payment at the entity's DI. The DI will pay the cheque only if there are available funds at the customer's account with the entity, and will be reimbursed by the entity.

This process gives rise to the following risks: (i) the instrument might erroneously be taken as that of the entity, on which it is liable, regardless of the availability of funds in the customer's account with it. Accordingly, the cheque form must be drafted so as to distinguish between it and the usual cheque of the entity itself. Also, the law must specifically provide for such agency cheques, since the usual agency rules provide that a principal (here, the entity) may be bound by an agent (here, the overdrawing customer) acting outside his *actual* authority, but within his *apparent* authority. Both conditions are satisfied under Australian law and practice,[17] but not elsewhere; (ii) there has to be a mechanism allowing the DI to find out expeditiously, within the time permitted to return dishonoured items through the clearing or under the clearing rules, whether funds are available in the customer's account with the entity; and (iii) there must be a reliable arrangement for the reimbursement of the DI by the entity.

---

[17] See above, in (i), text in paragraph containing n. 15.

4. The fourth scenario, that of the 'payable through' draft, exists in the USA and is provided for under UCC Article 4. It involves a draft of the customer on his account with the entity which is 'payable through' the entity's DI. Under §4–106(a):

If an item states that it is 'payable through' a [DI] identified in the item, (i) the item designates the [DI] as a collecting bank and does not by itself authorize the [DI] to pay the item, and (ii) the item may be presented for payment only by or through the [DI].

As explained by the Official Comment,

An item identifying a 'payable through' [DI] can be presented for payment to the drawee [entity] only by the 'payable through' [DI]. The item cannot be presented to the drawee [entity] over the counter for immediate payment or by a collecting bank other than the 'payable through' [DI].

The mechanism actually operates similarly to that in the third scenario, except that the legal presentment is not at the DI; rather, it is by the DI at the entity. Stated otherwise, the interbank collection process will direct the instrument to the entity's DI, which will then refer it to the entity.

Compared to the third scenario, the first risk only is not involved; that is, a 'payable through' instrument is unlikely to give rise to any apparent liability on the part of the entity itself. Indeed, in the UK, and the numerous jurisdictions which followed its model,[18] the Bills of Exchange Act does not provide for the 'payable through' instrument; arguably, however, this does not preclude its use.[19] The two issues to be resolved in the course of the operation of the 'payable through' mechanism are thus, (i) the confirmation of availability of funds at the customer's account with the entity, or the obtainment by the DI of authorization from the entity (so as to overcome the risk of miscommunication), and (ii) the securing of a reliable and smooth mechanism for the reimbursement of the DI that paid the draft, from the entity (so as to overcome the risk of default by the entity).

5. The fifth scenario is that of the instrument 'payable at' the entity's DI. The customer draws a draft on the entity instructing it to pay a third party at the DI. Under the UCC, an instrument payable at a bank in the United States must be presented for payment 'at the place of payment'.[20] Similarly, in Bills of Exchange Act jurisdictions, where a bill designates a

---

[18] For these jurisdictions see 2.B(iii).

[19] It may however be questioned whether an 'order' to pay only through a particular institution does not render the order 'conditional' so as to undermine its negotiability and thereby exclude it from the coverage of the Bills of Exchange Act. At the same time it is hard to distinguish between such a 'condition' and a designation of a place of payment which is undoubtedly permissible.   [20] UCC §3–501(b)(1).

place for payment, presentment must be made at the designated place.[21] This identifies the DI as the proper place for presentment, though under the Bills of Exchange Act, only where its address is given on the draft. This is nevertheless inconclusive as to who, as between the entity and the DI, is to make the payment decision at the DI. Typically, in connection with an instrument drawn on an entity and payable at a DI, the DI will run the customer's account with the entity on the entity's behalf, and will maintain its records. In practice, it is thus envisaged that presentment will take place at the DI that will be able to make a payment decision on the basis of the information in its hands. There is, however, a controversy as to the exact legal effect of such an instrument. Some American states view the 'payable at' DI as a co-drawee, who can thus make a payment decision. Others view the 'payable at' DI as a collecting bank, with no power to make a payment decision, which must be made by the entity.[22] However, even the latter view does not necessitate actual referral by the DI to the entity for payment decision and does not preclude a decision by the DI on the entity's behalf. Accordingly, under a separate agreement between the entity and the DI, the entity may authorize the DI to make the payment decision on the entity's behalf. In the absence of such an agreement, the 'payable at' draft is regarded, by those viewing the DI as a collecting bank, as an equivalent of a 'payable through' draft.

In any event, where the payment decision falls at the DI, there is no risk attributed to the failure of communication between the DI and the entity. There is also no reasonable risk of someone being misled to think that the instrument embodies an engagement of the entity rather than of its customer. However, also here, the DI incurs the risk of failure by the entity, namely, that the entity will not reimburse it.

The 'payable at' draft is used in Canada as an instrument instructing payment out of funds held in an account kept at a non-bank subsidiary of a bank, and payable at a designated branch of the parent bank itself. Presumably, the practice is designed to save on reserve costs and, possibly, to localize in the subsidiary the costs of raising retail deposits. The legal ramifications of the instrument have neither specifically been set out in legislation nor judicially or scholarly discussed.[23] Pursuant to BEA s. 87(a),

---

[21] See Bills of Exchange Act s. 50 (d)(I) (Australia); s. 87(a) (Canada); s. 44(d)(1) (of the Bills of Exchange Ordinance) (Israel); s 43(4)(a) (South Africa); and s. 45(4)(a) (UK).

[22] UCC §4–106(b) does not settle the controversy. Rather, it provides two alternatives for the meaning of 'payable at' instruments. (See Official Comment 2.) 'Collecting bank' is defined in §4–105(5) as a bank handling an item for collection except the payor (drawee) bank.

[23] Note, however, that where the bank subsidiary is a member of a Canadian Payments Association (CPA), the instrument is a straightforward 'cheque', as defined in BEA s. 165(1).

such a draft is likely to require presentment at the designated branch, the latter being the specified place of payment, which may hinder its truncation.

6. The sixth scenario contemplates that the entity's customer will maintain a zero balance account at the DI. In making payments to third parties the customer will draw cheques on the DI. The amount of each withdrawal will be debited to the customer's account with the DI and either create or increase an overdraft. Ultimately, at the conclusion of each banking day, the total overdraft will be covered by 'sweeping' its amount from the customer's account with the entity into the customer's account with the DI.

This facility involves a simple banking arrangement between the customer and the DI, dovetailed to the relationship between the customer and the entity. No risk of misleading the public as to the liability of the entity on the instrument is involved; the entity is even not identified on the customer's cheque. At the same time, the risk of miscommunication between the DI and the entity, where the latter seeks information as to the availability of funds in order to authorize payment, is present. Likewise, there is the risk incurred by the DI that the entity will fail to reimburse it, namely to sweep funds for customers' cheques that were paid throughout the day. In Canada this 'sweep account' mechanism is favoured by the Canadian Payments Association (CPA).[24] The CPA specifically prefers the 'sweep account' mechanism over the 'payable through' draft facility, set out above as the fourth scenario, on the grounds of the predominant role of the depository institution in making the payment decision in the 'sweep' but not 'payable through' model.[25]

It thus appears that altogether, in connection with access to funds held **[9]** in accounts held at non-depository institutions, three types of risks ought to be considered. The first is the legal risk, namely, the risk that the

---

This is so since under BEA s. 164, a 'bank', on which a cheque must be drawn under s. 165(1), is defined in terms of CPA membership. Generally speaking, CPA membership is accorded to regulated depository financial institutions, such as banks, trust companies, and credit unions. However, also a non-bank subsidiary of a bank, which is a 'loan company . . . that accepts deposits transferable by order to a third party' and which meets prescribed statutory requirements as to statutory stability, such as in relation to deposit insurance and supervision, qualifies for a CPA membership. (See CPA Act, R.S.C. 1985, c. C-21, ss. 3 and 30.) It is thus the draft payable at a bank, but drawn on a bank subsidiary that is not a CPA member, which falls into the scope of the present discussion.

[24] Under the CPA Act (ibid.) s. 5, the CPA's statutory mandate is 'to establish and operate a national clearings and settlements system and to plan the evolution of the national payments system'.

[25] See CPA, 'Sweep Accounts and Payable-through Arrangements – Risk-Related Issues and Possible Mechanisms to Address Them' (Aug. 1997). For an earlier Working Paper, see CPA, 'Sweep Account Arrangements—Policy Issues and Possible Action to Deal with Them', 4 May 1995.

payment instrument may mislead the public to think that it bears the entity's engagement. This risk may be minimized by careful drafting. In some cases, however, legislative intervention may be warranted. The second risk is that of communication failure between the entity and the DI. Enhanced technology may minimalize this risk. Alternatively, if the account is not to be run by the DI, individual credit lines for customers may be given and updated periodically. Unequivocally, all this presupposes reliability of equipment and human resources. Where the entity is a regulated financial institution, the risk of equipment failure and human error may diminish, but still exists.

[10]   The third and most serious risk is that of the failure to reimburse, namely that of the entity's default. No such risk exists in the first two scenarios, that of the credit transfer through the entity's account with the DI (unless an off-line debit card is involved), and that of the entity's own agency cheque on its account with the DI. However, both are 'credit push' devices which require initiation at the entity (or the DI) and are hence cumbersome. Otherwise, in the first scenario where an off-line debit card is involved, as well as in the fourth remaining models (namely, that of an agency cheque by the customer, 'payable through' instruments, 'payable at' instruments, and 'sweeping funds' to a 'zero balance' account), the failure to reimburse risk, that is, the risk of entity's default, is present.

In a sense, this is a normal risk a DI incurs in conjunction with the extension of credit to customers. The risk is minimal where the DI's customer, namely the entity, is a regulated financial institution, whose customers' payment activity is not expected to be substantial. It is up to the DI to assess the risk and protect itself, for example, by taking collateral or a cash deposit. Arguably, the failure to take proper safety measures, where they are warranted, justify regulatory intervention, as in the case of any other unsafe conduct by a regulated and supervised DI.

It should be noted that under normal circumstances, default by the entity may occur prior to the expiry of the period for the return of the cheques by the DI; in such a case, loss will be shifted to a third party other than the DI. This option is, however, unavailable for off-line debit card access, where the engagement to pay becomes irrevocable as soon as authorization is given.

[11]   Commonly, entities are either asset management or life insurance companies. The ensuing analysis discusses concrete situations.

(III) FUNDS HELD IN ACCOUNTS OPERATED BY ASSET
MANAGEMENT COMPANIES[26]

Chequing access to mutual funds (or cash management trusts in the   **[12]**
Australian terminology) held at deposit-taking institutions is available,
for example, in Australia. Such a scheme envisages the sweeping of funds
out of the trust to cover the amount of a cheque drawn on an ordinary
chequing account kept for the customer at the same institution managing
the trust. While the Wallis Report contemplates the situation under which
'[i]nstitutions can offer transaction facilities in conjunction with a bank[,]
e.g. cash management trusts with linkages to DTI accounts',[27] inter-
institutional linkages do not exist except for, as discussed in the following
section, in connection with life insurance companies. Nor were they
specifically recommended. Conversely, in the USA, access to the payment
system is available out of investment funds held at non-depository
institutions.

In the USA, asset management companies, such as brokerage firms   **[13]**
(hereafter referred to as 'firms') have provided their customers with
chequing as well as debit card facilities since the late 1970s. These two
services are provided in conjunction with money market accounts. Limited chequing facilities (primarily, in terms of number of cheques to be
used within a given time period) may be offered also in connection with
mutual funds. An investment account managed by an asset management
company to which access to the payment system is attached is often
referred to as an asset management account. Both the chequing and the
debit card facilities are offered directly by the firm to the customer, but in
conjunction with an overall bilateral arrangement of the firm with a sponsoring depository institution. This provides both (i) access to the clearing
and settlement system as well as (ii) processing services. Usually such
depository institutions specialize in offering such services to firms, rather
than themselves giving retail services to their own customers. Hence, no
conflict is likely to arise between the firm and the depository institution
as to diversion of customers. The accounts offered by the firms usually
operate like ordinary bank accounts, and typically also allow the customer to deposit third party cheques and other payments. Obviously,
funds managed in conjunction with these accounts purport to give a
higher yield than funds held in a bank account, but are not

---

[26] See affidavit dated 27 Mar. 1996 by Liam J. Carmody before the Canadian Competition
Tribunal in the matter of the *Director of Investigations and Research* v. *Bank of Montreal et al*,
CT-95/2.   [27] The Wallis Report above, n. 2 at 412.

FDIC-insured.[28] They typically require a high minimum balance (usually no less than $10,000 US) and hence are available only to investors. Technically, the customer is a 'shareholder' of the relevant fund.

Such facilities are not specifically authorized by law. Rather, they exist, mainly because they are not precluded. Also, they are limited in practice almost exclusively to money market accounts (or to fixed income/bond funds) not due to any legal limitation. Instead, it is the nature of the money market (or fixed income) fund, which is designed to maintain a stable net asset value, in contrast to other mutual funds which seek to build long-term profit, and hence is less liquid, which produces this restriction. Finally, the involvement of the sponsoring depository institution, effectively acting as gatekeeper, intermediating between the firm and the clearing and settlement system, precludes payment system risks and hence any major concern coming from the Federal Reserve. A firm seeking to provide its customers with access to the payment system must thus establish a bilateral relationship with a sponsoring depository institution, providing access and processing services, as well as incurring liability in the course of the clearing of the firm's outgoing payments.

[14]   Asset management accounts do not contain federally insured funds. However, in contrast to the bank account, the investment account to which these chequing or card facilities are attached does not constitute a mere debt of the firm. Rather, this is a securities account backed by financial assets, namely the securities of which the fund consists. The assets of each fund are segregated and are neither mingled with the assets of the firm, nor are they available to the firm's general creditors. A federal insurance scheme protects shareholders from misappropriation by brokerage firms. By law, each fund is managed by a third party custodian, which is a regulated financial institution. Money market funds are required by law to invest in high-quality securities to ensure the maintenance of steady value. A money market fund is specifically required[29] 'to maintain a stable net asset value per share' and to 'limit its portfolio investments to those United States Dollar-Denominated securities that the fund's board of directors determines present minimal credit risks'.[30] Generally speaking, government and high-quality corporate paper satisfy this standard. It is this liquid, stable, and secure nature of the fund, usually precluding instant fall in value, to which the sponsoring depository institution looks in pursuing its reimbursement upon making payments.

---

[28] Insurance for deposits in federal banks is provided in the USA by the Federal Deposit Insurance Corporation (FDIC) under the Federal Deposit Insurance Corporation Act (12 U.S.C. §1813).

[29] See *Rules and Regulations, Investment Company Act of 1940*, 17 C.F.R. §270.2a-7 (1998).

[30] Ibid.

Nonetheless, alone, and notwithstanding any perception to the contrary, the proprietary nature of the fund may not protect the DI, which appears to have a bare reimbursement right against the firm, unsecured by the fund itself. Namely, the payment instructions of the customer are in fact instructions to the firm to redeem fund shares in the requested sum. The firm thus redeems the shares, and uses the proceeds in payment to the DI. As long as the firm is solvent, the DI may effectively count on the fund as a solid source of liquidity. However, if the firm becomes insolvent, proceeds realized from the redemption of the shares may not be beyond the reach of the firm's other creditors, at least in the absence of a mechanism transferring the benefit of the proprietary right to the DI. One such a possible device is to structure each redemption of customer's shares to pass through the DI, so that the DI's reimbursement claim would be for the price of the shares 'bought' from the customer before their redemption. To date, there is no indication that this practice is utilized.

In practice, the sponsoring DI usually does not take any security; **[15]** instead, it counts on its ability to unwind settlement for the instruments and recover their value once no refund has been advanced by the sponsored firm. Thus, under §4–214 of the American Uniform Commercial Code, a collecting bank (such as the sponsoring DI)[31] may revoke settlement given for instruments that have been ultimately dishonoured and recover their value from the depository institution that forwarded them to it in the collection process. The collecting bank must return the dishonoured instrument or send notification before its midnight deadline. This midnight deadline is the next banking day following the banking day on which it learnt of the dishonour, or within a longer reasonable time thereafter. Accordingly, settlement revocation by the sponsoring DI applies to instruments drawn on funds held at a sponsored drawee firm and presented to that firm for payment by its sponsoring DI on day 1. For such instruments subject to revocation the sponsored firm had been called to transmit funds on day 1 and failed to do so, so as to have them dishonoured. The sponsoring DI may revoke settlement and obtain refund from the depository institution that forwarded them to it for collection, at least as long as the sponsoring DI acts before midnight of day 2. Ultimately, upon the revocation of settlement, the depository institution of deposit can go after the payee/holder of the instrument, who will then pursue his remedies against the drawer, that is, the customer of the firm. Where shares have already been redeemed, but the proceeds failed to reach the bank prior to the insolvency of the firm, the drawer/customer may be

---

[31] 'Collecting bank' is defined in UCC §4–105(5) as 'a bank handling an item for collection except the payor [drawee] bank'.

covered by federal insurance applicable to assets held by financial firms; this aspect is, however, outside the scope of the present inquiry.

[16]   Thus, upon the timely dishonour of the instruments, the sponsoring DI does not incur any risk. Rather, the risk is shifted away from the payment system. This does not, however, apply to debit card payments out of assets held by a sponsored firm. In such a case, as set out below, the sponsoring DI incurs liability to the acquiring depository institution upon the authorization of the transactions. The subsequent failure of the firm, namely between authorization and payment to the sponsoring DI, will not excuse the DI. However, particularly due to the existence of individual credit limits on customers, this risk is considered to be quite low.

[17]   The chequing facility out of an asset management account operates as follows—each instrument drawn by the customer on the fund is presented for payment through the sponsoring depository institution, to which it is directed in the clearing on the basis of the identification number of the depository institution which it bears. There is usually a daily (or even more frequent) electronic file transmission from the sponsoring depository institution to the firm with details of all customers' instruments as well as a gross amount of all outgoing payments. For each instrument, the payment decision is typically made by the firm, where individual account records are kept. Alternatively, the sponsoring depository institution may be provided by the firm, on a frequent (usually daily) basis, with information as to a credit line for each individual customer, so as to be able to reach the pay or no pay decision without further communication to the firm. Either way, posting to the customer's account is usually done by the firm; only the firm, and not the sponsoring depository institution maintains the account records for individual customers/shareholders. The obligation incurred in the course of the clearing, by virtue of the presentment of the instrument through the sponsoring depository institution, is solely of that institution, and not that of the firm. Payment by the firm to the sponsoring depository institution of the gross amount of all outgoing individual customers' payments is usually made daily, either at an account the firm holds at the depository institution, or by wiring the funds.

[18]   Under the Uniform Commercial Code, a cheque must be drawn on a depository institution.[32] Technically speaking, an instrument drawn on a firm is thus not a 'cheque' but rather a 'draft'. It may however name the depository institution. UCC §4–106 covers three situations of a draft drawn on a non-depository institution but which nevertheless names a depository institution:[33]

---

[32] UCC §3–104(f) in conjunction with the definition of 'bank' in §4–105(1) (by reference from §3–103(c)).

[33] See (ii) above, text around n. 19 (fourth and fifth scenarios).

(a) Where a draft states that it is 'payable through' a depository institution, the draft designates the depository institution as a 'collecting bank' and does not by itself authorize the depository institution
to pay the draft. The draft must however be presented for payment
only by or through the named depository institution;

(b) Where a draft states that it is 'payable at' a named depository
institution two alternatives are presented. Some states view such a
draft as drawn on that institution, while others view the draft as
'payable through' that institution;

(c) Where a draft is drawn on someone other than a depository institution and it is not clear whether a depository institution named in the
draft is a co-drawee or a collecting bank, the depository institution
is a collecting bank. Namely, the draft is to be regarded as 'payable
through' the named depository institution.

In principle, drafts drawn by the customer could be marked 'payable **[19]**
through' the DI. Besides the miscommunication concern, this would have
given rise to the risk of entity's default. In practice however, firms market
the instruments as 'cheques', indicating the firm's and DI's names, and
possibly also the name of the fund. This could still be viewed as a
'payable through' draft, under UCC §4–106(c) discussed above. Alternatively, perhaps from a strictly legal point of view, the instrument may be
viewed as a true 'cheque', drawn on the DI, and indicating the firm/fund
name as a mere source of reimbursement. This does not change the mechanism for reimbursement. Nevertheless, payment system risks may actually change if the instructions to pay and reimburse from the fund are
viewed as addressed by the customer directly to the depository institution (as a drawee). This may give the latter direct access to the fund, not
intermediated by the firm, and hence, insulated from any intervention by
the firm's creditors.

Debit cards issued by firms are either Visa or Mastercard cards. In POS **[20]**
terminals they operate as off-line debit cards, namely as credit card transactions, where following the usual on-line authorization, charges are
posted directly to the cardholder's money market account, rather than to
a credit account, to be settled periodically by a separate payment. The
cards can also be used for on-line cash withdrawals from the money market account at ATM terminals. At POS terminals, transactions are authenticated by means of a manual signature on a sales draft, as is the universal
practice with credit cards. At ATM terminals transactions are authenticated by means of a PIN, as in the case of usual on-line debit card ATM
withdrawals.

Firms are not members of the card organizations. As far as Mastercard
or Visa organizations are concerned, the member issuing the card is not

the firm but rather a sponsoring depository institution providing the firm with access to the clearing and settlement system and with processing services. While, typically, the name of the sponsoring deposit institution does not appear on such a card, its sorting code does appear. The authorization request is thus directed from the terminal to the sponsoring depository institution. Customer's accounts are not maintained at the sponsoring depository institution, which either directs the request to the firm or provides authorization on the basis of individual credit lines for customers. The credit lines are advised and updated by the firm daily, and bulk information of the daily charges is transmitted from the sponsoring depository institution to the firm. In any event, the actual posting to the customer's account at the firm is carried out by the firm. Under the clearing rules, the authorization binds the sponsoring depository institution towards the acquiring depository institution and the other clearing participants, as if this is an authorization for its own (rather than the firm's) customer. At the end of the daily cycle it is the sponsoring depository institution which must settle with the other clearing participants. The firm reimburses it either at an internal account or by wiring the funds.

The involvement of the sponsoring depository institution in the card operation is quite crucial. Yet this involvement is invisible to the firm's customer. From a legal point of view, in issuing the card to its customer, the firm acts as an agent for an undisclosed principal.

[21]   Asset management accounts facilitate ACH[34] direct debit and credit entries as well as deposits. Deposits are made at the firm and not at the sponsoring bank.

(IV) FUNDS HELD WITH LIFE INSURANCE COMPANIES[35]

[22] Life insurance companies would like to afford to beneficiaries of death claims the option of keeping the payouts with the insurer, at least temporarily, while having access to the payment system. They may further be interested in providing customers with payment system access to investment products they sell. Such options are not available in the UK, where it is, however, common for a life insurance company to utilize a bank subsidiary to meet the objective. In Australia, a customer of a life insurance company may open a bank account with a designated depository institution. The customer may either instruct the insurer to

---

[34] ACH is the abbreviation for the Automated Clearing House and denotes the nationwide bulk electronic clearing system in the USA.

[35] For background information, see J. E. Lauria, 'Many Default to the Retained Asset Account', National Underwriter, 22 Sept. 1997; and T. Attrino, 'P-C Agents Issue Checkbook Claims', National Underwriter, 20 July 1998.

pay into that account, usually small amounts from time to time, as the customer requires, or arrange for funds to be swept to the account from the life insurance company to cover cheques as they are presented. The customer may then withdraw funds or make payments to third parties, as needed, by means of cheques drawn on the bank. Linkages between cash management trusts managed by an institution other than a deposit-taking one, and an account held at a depository institution, were specifically recognized in Australia by the Wallis Report.[36]

In fact, among the scenarios set out above in section (2), this corresponds to the sixth generic model for accessing funds at a non-depository institution through the banking system. Under such an arrangement, the banking relationship is exclusively between the beneficiary/customer and the depository institution. An arrangement of sweeping funds from the life insurance company to the customer's account at the depository institution is conceptually distinct, though obviously connected.

A more sophisticated scheme is that of the retained asset account in the [23] USA. The scheme was introduced in the 1980s and exists in conjunction with group as well as individual life insurance contracts. Instead of sending the death benefit disbursement to the beneficiary in the form of a lump sum cheque, the insurer advises the beneficiary of the availability of the benefit in the insurer's hands at the beneficiary's disposal, either for withdrawal in full or for partial withdrawals, by means of draft forms supplied to the beneficiary by the insurer. In the hands of the insurer, the funds earn interest for the beneficiary from the moment of the death. In contrast, between the time of sending of a benefit cheque and its subsequent collection by the beneficiary, the beneficiary earns no interest. This is a relatively long period, particularly when taking into account that the cheque is reaching a mourning beneficiary, usually a widow, who may be unsophisticated in financial matters. For example, a 10–14-day delay in collection, which is quite typical, may cost the beneficiary a few hundred dollars in lost interest, depending on the size of the benefit.

Typically, the interest payable on funds held in a retained asset account is governed by some index, such as government bond index, and is set weekly. Sometimes, a minimum interest rate (around 3 per cent) is guaranteed by the insurer. The amount in the account, principal and interest, is guaranteed by the insurer. Very often a draft drawn on the account must be above a certain floor, usually between $100 and $250, and the account may remain open only until some floor, in the neighbourhood of between $1,000 and $3,000, is reached as to the balance, at which point the insurer is entitled to close the account and remit the balance to the bene-

---

[36] Above, n. 2 at 412.

fiary. Such account is held for the beneficiary for no charge, other than for NSF and cheque certification. No deposit can be made to such an account, and currently, there is access to it by draft only; no debit card access is available, at least for the time being.

In the view of insurers, this retained asset account scheme responds to the need of beneficiaries for safety, immediate and quick and efficient access, as well as a reasonably competitive rate of interest during the transitional period between payout and long-term investment. Obviously, the programme slows down the rate of departure of funds from the life insurance companies. In practice, a retained asset account is closed within a year to eighteen months after its opening.

[24]   Similarly as in connection with the asset management account discussed above, access to the payment system and draft-processing facilities are provided to the life insurer by a sponsoring depository institution, with which the insurer reaches a bilateral agreement. The draft is effectively presented at the depository institution, on the basis of the identification number marked on it. Towards clearing participants, it is the responsibility of the sponsoring depository institution to handle the draft as well as to pay it. However, in contrast with asset management accounts, retained asset accounts are actually managed by the sponsoring depository institution, as a third party administrator, which makes the decision regarding payment, and posts debits to the customer's account. Information is, however, usually passed on to the insurer daily, so that a customer's inquiry relating to the account may be directed to and accommodated by both institutions. Payment for the gross debit amount for all drafts is usually made by the insurer to the sponsoring depository institution daily, either by the wiring of funds or by having its account at the depository institution debited.

[25]   Drafts drawn by a beneficiary on a retained asset account may be marked as 'payable through' drafts. However, in the context of the preliminary analysis in (II) above, they are in fact 'payable at' instruments. Perhaps the reason for the form drafters' preference to 'the payable through' language is the lack of uniformity in the USA as to the legal position of the 'payable at' depository institution as a co-drawee or collecting bank. Wishing to designate it as a collecting bank nationwide, the form drafters preferred the 'payable through' language. Yet, as a 'payable at' mechanism, at least in substance, it does not raise risks associated with either potential legal liability or miscommunication. It does raise the risk of failure to reimburse. Nevertheless, in connection with each account, the exposure is coextensive with the life insurance company's payment obligation under the insurance policy, a risk which is looked after in the context of the regulation of the insurance company by its state regulator. Stated otherwise, the retained asset programme does not create a new

liability of the insurance company, beyond and above the one to pay the death benefit; it simply breaks down an existing liability into small payment obligations as instructed by the beneficiary. In fact, from the sponsoring depository institution's point of view, the risk in connection with such a programme is no different from the one which exists in connection with the payment of the insurance company's lump-sum liability cheques. In the latter case, the insurance company's account is not prefunded. Its cheques are paid by the depository institution as they are presented, to a zero-balance account; reimbursement is promptly made by the insurance company throughout the day.

In fact, similarly to DIs sponsoring asset management firms, DIs sponsoring insurance companies also tend to rely on their ability to unwind settlement for drafts for which cover was not timely provided by sponsored insurers. They specifically rely on the temporal gap between arrival of drafts to the sponsoring DI, and the next-day midnight deadline for returning unpaid drafts to the depository institution of deposit in order to obtain refund. Payment from the sponsored drawee insurer to the sponsoring DI is already due the first day, that of the arrival of the drafts at the sponsoring DI. Whenever payment is not made by the insurer, so that the drafts are dishonoured, there is thus ample time to return them. In such a case, the depository institution of deposit may go after the payee/holder, who will then pursue his or her remedies against the insurance beneficiary/drawer. In any event, for small insurers, as well as for those known to be in financial difficulties, a sponsoring DI may require a minimum balance or prefunded account to be kept from which reimbursement is to originate.

Due to this lack of any new exposure, as well as due to the responsibil- **[26]** ities incurred by the sponsoring depository institution in the payment process, the scheme has not raised serious concerns by the Federal Reserve. State insurance supervisory authorities have viewed the programmes as providing an alternative method of availability of funds to beneficiaries, and consequently, as wholly legitimate in the context of the insurance business. Benefit claims against insurance companies are state insured or guaranteed, so that no safety issue appears to be involved. Insofar as this state insurance or guaranty is concerned, upon the failure of an insurance company, claims of retained asset account holders to principal plus interest rank equally with claims of policy holders; both categories are regarded as benefit claims against the failed insurance company. However, state insurance supervisory authorities have been concerned with disclosure issues, namely, whether beneficiaries offered retained asset accounts are always well informed and fully cognizant of their rights. As a result, disclosure guidelines have been published. They have been adopted formally by ten states, but are in fact followed in the USA nationwide.

[27]   As indicated, money held in retained asset accounts is not invested in money market or mutual funds. Some insurers may encourage beneficiaries to move the money to such facilities, managed by asset management companies which may belong to the same corporate family of the insurer. Where this happens, the arrangement falls into the category of assets management accounts discussed in the previous section.

[28]   Three recent developments should be mentioned. First, plans to introduce access to retained asset accounts by off-line debit cards are well under way. Secondly, retained asset programmes have been extended in the USA to property and casualty insurance. Overall, this is a straightforward application of the same principles applicable to life insurance, except that (i) increased attention is given to providing the insured with immediate access to the funds, and (ii) the amount placed in such an account may be increased by the insurance company in the course of processing the claim, though absolutely not by the customer himself. Third, an American bank has recently established retained asset programmes in Australia. This operation has been premissed on a sponsorship between an Australian insurer and its Australian bank, with the American bank providing the administrative assistance and account management. Drafts are presented at the sponsoring local bank that transmits information both to the sponsored insurer for reimbursement, and to a local office of the American bank, for further transmission to the USA for processing and payment decision. Account management facilitating customer service is primarily provided by the American bank, relying on its infrastructure, which thereby releases the sponsoring local Australian bank from dealing with a financial product for which it may lack adequate expertise.

(v) Conclusion

[29]   As demonstrated above, mechanisms facilitating access to the domestic payment system for funds held in non-depository institutions are available in practice, and are sound in principle. Yet the current situation may not be satisfactory to non-depository institutions holding funds with respect to which access depends, in each case, on some kind of a relationship between the non-depository financial institution holding the funds and a depository institution which may be a potential competitor. The ultimate objective of non-depository account-holding financial institutions is direct access to clearing and settlement facilities. This raises public policy issues which are currently addressed by regulators in several

countries, and are beyond the scope of the present discussion.[37] Regardless, even in the context of mechanisms outlined in this section, legislation in all jurisdictions is needed to accommodate their coverage by cheque and credit transfer legislation.

Summary Table
ACCESS TO VALUE STORED IN ACCOUNTS HELD AT NON-DEPOSITORY INSTITUTIONS: COMPARATIVE FEATURES

	Risk of misleading legal effect of instrument	Risk of DI-NDI mis-communication	Risk of default by NDI after payment by DI
Credit transfer through the NDI's account with the DI	No	Yes	No (unless off-line) (debit card)
Agency cheque by NDI on its account with DI	No	No	No
Agency cheque by customer (on NDI's account with DI)	Yes	Yes	Yes
'Payable through' DI draft on customer's account with NDI	No	Yes	Yes
'Payable at' DI draft on customer's account with NDI	No	No	Yes
'Sweeping' funds from customer's account at NDI into a 'zero balance' account of customer at DI	No	Yes	Yes

DI: Depository Institution
NDI: Non-Depository Institution

---

[37] For these issues in Australia and Canada, see sources cited in n. 2 and 3, above.

PART 4

Third party's fraud: breach of the Mandate and misdelivery of funds

A. Introduction

Generally speaking, as discussed in 2.C, in carrying out payment instruc- [1]
tions, as a mandatary, a bank is required to act as instructed by its customer, the mandator. However, either error or third party's fraud may
lead a bank to act otherwise than as instructed by the customer. This part
of the book is concerned with the allocation of losses resulting from a
third party's fraud leading to a payment which was either not instructed
at all or made to a person other than originally instructed.

Third party's fraud may lead to the issue of forged or unauthorized
payment instructions, appearing to emanate from the customer or under
the customer's authority, but in fact, originating from a defraudster. Alternatively, due to an intervention of a defraudster, funds may be misdirected to an unintended recipient even under genuine payment
instructions, properly issued by a customer or under the customer's
authority. The first situation is dealt with in 4.B and C, below. 4.B covers
forged or unauthorized written payment instructions, primarily cheques.
4.C deals with unauthorized payment instructions issued electronically.

The second situation, that of misdirection of payment under payment
instructions originating from the customer or under the customer's
authority, is dealt with in 4.D and E. 4.D discusses the forged indorsement of a properly issued cheque. 4.E covers the issue of ambiguous payment instructions initiating a credit transfer, usually under some
inducement and misrepresentation of a defraudster, who counts on either
automated processing by the beneficiary's bank, or further misrepresentation to that bank, to emanate from the defraudster, as to the meaning of
the ambiguous payment instructions, in a way that will carry out the
fraudulent design.

Under all such circumstances, the liability of the defraudster is a given [2]
in all jurisdictions. Nevertheless, quite universally, the defraudster is not
a promising defendant. It is usually the case that the defraudster has
absconded, is insolvent or otherwise impecunious, or is even in jail, with
the proceeds of the fraud spent long ago. Recovery from the defraudster
is likely to prove impractical and will thus not be the focus here. Rather,
the issue to be dealt with in the ensuing discussion is the allocation of
losses among innocent parties.

Once payment has been made, in such a way so as to inadvertently
carry out the defraudster's design, the initial question is whether recourse
is available to the paying bank from either the customer, from whom the
original instructions either emanated or appeared to have emanated, or

from another innocent participant in the payment process. This in fact is the principal theme of the ensuing discussion.

[3]   Also, a question arises as to recovery from an innocent recipient of payment, who might have been equally victimized by the defraudster. In common law jurisdictions, including in the United States, recovery is under the law governing mistake and restitution. In civil law jurisdictions, the question is determined in the context of the provisions governing unjust enrichment.[1]

In the United States, the UCC nevertheless provides for a limitation, specifically applicable to the recovery from an innocent recipient of payment of a forged cheque. Thus, under UCC §3–418(c), remedies for the recovery of payment made under the mistaken belief that the cheque has been genuine and dully authorized may not be asserted 'against a person who took the instrument in good faith and for value or who in good faith changed position in reliance of the payment . . .'.

This language purported to codify the 'finality of payment' rule[2] of the eighteenth-century English case *Price* v. *Neal*.[3] However, in England, the jurisdiction of its inception, and consequently, possibly throughout the common law world, the authority of *Price* v. *Neal* has been seriously curtailed. Under *National Westminster Bank* v. *Barclays Bank International Ltd.*,[4] 'finality of payment', namely, preclusion from recovery by the drawee bank, is applicable solely against an indorsee other than a collect-

---

[1] Obligations resulting from unjust enrichment, or quasi-contract, are governed in Switzerland by CO arts. 62–7, in France by CC arts. 1371–81, in Germany by BGB §§812–22, in Japan by CC arts. 703–8, in Italy by CC arts. 2041–2, and in Quebec by CC arts. 1491–1496 (see also arts. 1699–1707). For texts in English see *The French Civil Code Revised Edition* (as amended to 1 July 1994), trans. J. H. Crabb (Littleton, Colo.: Fred B. Rothman & Co., 1995); *The German Civil Code* (as am. to 1 January 1975) trans. I. S. Forrester, S. L. Goren, and H. M. Ilgen (South Hackensack, NJ: Fred B. Rothman & Co., 1975) (with 1981 Supp. trans. S. L. Goren); *The Civil Code of Japan* (translation) (Tokyo: Ministry of Justice, 1972); *The Italian Civil Code*, trans. M. Beltramo, G. E. Longo, and J. H. Merryman (Dobbs Ferry, NY: Oceana, 1969); *Swiss Contract Law, English Translation of Selected Official Texts—Swiss Code of Obligations* (Zurich: Swiss-American Chamber of Commerce, 1997); and the bilingual edition of the Quebec Civil Code, *Code civil du practicien* (Montreal: DACFO, 1995).

[2] The title of the pre-1989 Code provision (§3–418) was 'Finality of Payment or Acceptance'.

[3] (1762), 3 Burr. 1354, 97 E.R. 871. See J. B. Ames, 'The Doctrine of Price v. Neal', in *Lectures on Legal History and Miscellaneous Legal Essays* (Cambridge, Mass.: Harvard University Press, 1913) at 270, as well as S. B. Dow, 'The Doctrine of *Price* v. *Neal* in English and American Forgery Law: A Comparative Analysis' (1998), 6 Tulane J. Of Int'l Comp. Law 113.

[4] [1975] Q.B. 654, by Kerr J.

ing bank,[5] and not against the original payee of the cheque.[6] This was rationalized on the release of the indorser to whom it becomes too late to give a notice of dishonour.[7] Elsewhere,[8] I have questioned these premisses.[9] First, change of position is an established defence to an action in restitution.[10] The singling out of the loss of recourse against an indorser, as the only relevant change of position on the basis of payment which precludes restitution seems to me unjustified. Second, arguably, no loss of recourse against an indorser is even involved in the case of payment of a forged cheque to an indorsee.[11] Regardless, this rational is inapplicable to Australia, where an indorser remains liable on a dishonoured cheque,[12] whether or not the indorser received a notice of dishonour, so that no loss of recourse results from the failure to give a timely notice of dishonour.

The doctrine of *Price* v. *Neal* does not appear to be acknowledged in

---

[5] No 'finality of payment' appeared to be argued in *Banque Nationale du Canada* v. *Caisse Centrale Desjardins du Québec*, [1997] A. Q. no 3783, No. 500–05–003771–951, (Que. S.C. C. C.), 4 Nov. 1997, where as between the drawee and depositary banks forged cheque loss was allocated to the depositary bank. In that case, the drawee bank returned the cheque to the depositary bank through the clearing seventeen days after its presentment for payment. Arguably, at the point of time, the forged cheque was already 'paid'. See above 3.B(iii) s. 8, particularly at n. 129.

[6] This was recognized as good law in *Barclays Bank* v. *WJ Simms Son & Cooke (Southern) Ltd.*, [1980] Q.B. 677 at 700–1, by Goff J.

[7] Upon the dishonour of a cheque, an indorser is entitled to receive from the holder a prompt notice of dishonour. Otherwise, the indorser is released from liability on the cheque. See ss. 48–9 (UK), ss. 95–7 (Can.), ss. 47–8 (Israel), and ss. 46–7 (South Africa). Consequently, the indorsee/holder is entitled to know immediately whether the cheque has been dishonoured, so as to be able to give the required statutory notice in a timely fashion. Conversely, the payee, who had no recourse on the cheque against a prior indorser anyway, has not lost any recourse by virtue of not being promptly advised of the dishonour. Consequently, recovery by the drawee bank of the mistaken payment against the payee is not precluded. References are to the Bills of Exchange Act in the UK: 1882, 45 & 46 Vict., c. 61; Canada: R.S.C. 1985, c. B-4; and South Africa: No. 34 of 1964; as well as the Bills of Exchange Ordinance [New Version] Laws of the State of Israel No. 2 p. 12, as am.

[8] B. Geva, 'Reflections on the Need to Revise the Bills of Exchange Act: Some Doctrinal Aspects' (1981–2), 6 Can. Bus. L.J. 269 at 308–13.

[9] In connection with both points, I share the view of Stephen A. Scott, p. 129 of his (unpublished) 'Law of Banking and Negotiable Instruments Course Notes and Syllabus' (1977).

[10] As specifically acknowledged in *Barclays Bank* v. *WJ Simms Son & Cooke (Southern)*, above, n. 6 at 703.

[11] Arguably, the delay by the indorsee, who was mistakenly paid on the forged cheque, in giving the notice of dishonour, is excused, since it was 'caused by circumstances beyond [the indorsee's] control', within the meaning of s. 50(1) (UK); s. 104(1) (Can.).

[12] S. 70 of the Cheques Act 1986 (No. 45 of 1986).

civil law jurisdictions[13] and is quite controversial in South Africa.[14] On the other hand, Ames rationalized it on the drawee bank's negligence, on the existence of an irrebuttable presumption as to the drawee bank's knowledge of its customer's signature, but primarily, on the finality of payment in favour of an innocent recipient.[15] Ultimately, it is this latter rational, pertaining to the finality of payment, which the present author finds to be the most convincing.

---

[13] Notwithstanding Ames, above, n. 3 at 271.

[14] For a comprehensive, learned discussion see F. R. Malan and J. T. Pretorius, *Malan on Bills of Exchange, Cheques and Promissory Notes in South Africa*, 3rd edn. (Durban: Butterworths, 1997) at ¶210 pp. 358–71. Outspoken critics are D. V. Cowen and L. Gering, *Cowen on the Law of Negotiable Instruments in South Africa*, 4th edn. (Cape Town: Juta & Co. Ltd., 1966) at 393, according to whom '[i]t would certainly be unfortunate if an English rule whose rational has never been clear, which has been condemned as harsh, and which moreover involves illogical distinctions, should be incorporated as part of South African law . . .'. However, I submit, as the facts of *National Westminster Bank* v. *Barclays Bank International Ltd.* above, n. 4, demonstrate, it is actually the (unjustified) inapplicability of the rule which was unfair and produced harsh results. In the facts of that case, a payee of a forged cheque did not depart from the consideration in the underlying transaction until payment was confirmed by the drawee bank, which subsequently was nevertheless allowed to recover from the payee, upon the discovery that the cheque had been forged.

[15] Ames, above, n. 3 at 271–2.

B. Allocation of Forged Cheques Losses

(I) INTRODUCTION

The present discussion is on the allocation of losses incurred in connec- [1]
tion with the unauthorized payment by a bank of forged cheques. Forged
cheques are broadly defined to cover cheques bearing a forged drawer's
signature as well as cheques bearing a genuine drawer's signature, but
which have been completed or altered fraudulently, or at least, contrary,
or not according to the drawer/customer's authority. In fact, forged
drawer's signature cheques include cheques bearing an unauthorized
drawer's signature, no drawer's signature, or even a missing drawer's
signature on a cheque requiring more than one such signature. Upon the
payment of a forged cheque by the bank, who bears the loss?

This text discusses the allocation of risk between the paying bank and
its customer. The position of the innocent payee or holder who obtained
payment is not dealt with. Also, forged indorsements fall outside the
scope of this discussion. These matters are dealt with in 4.A and D. The
following discussion covers (i) jurisdictions that have adopted a statute
modelled on the English Bills of Exchange Act (BEA, or 'the Act'),[1] conveniently, though not always accurately, referred to below as common law
jurisdictions,[2] (ii) the United States where the Uniform Commercial Code
(UCC) Articles 3 and 4 apply to cheques,[3] and (iii) several civil law

---

[1] 1882, 45 & 46 Vic., c. 61.

[2] Such jurisdictions include Canada (R.S.C. 1985, c. B-4); Israel (Laws of the State of Israel
New Version 1957, 12); South Africa (No. 34 of 1964); and in fact also Australia, where
cheques were excluded from the coverage of BEA 1909 and are currently governed by the
Cheques Act 1986 (No. 145 of 1986). Strictly speaking, Israel, South Africa, and the Province
of Quebec in Canada are not common law jurisdictions. Nevertheless, though the allocation
of forgery losses is not necessarily a matter relating to the law of bills and notes in the strict
sense, all such jurisdictions followed in principle the English scheme, and are thus treated,
for our purposes, as common law jurisdictions (in the sense that on this point, they followed
the common law). For the 'common law' treatment of the subject in these jurisdictions, see
F. R. Malan and J. T. Pretorious, *Malan on Bills of Exchange, Cheques, and Promissory Notes
in South Africa*, 3rd edn. (Durban: Butterworth, 1997) ¶208 pp. 350–5; D. V. Cowen and
L. Gering, *Cowen on the Law of Negotiable Instruments in South Africa*, 4th edn. (Cape Town:
Juta, 1966) at 386; N. L'Heureux & É. Fortin, *Droit bancaire*, 3rd edn. (Cowansville, Quebec:
Éditions Yvon Blais, 1999) at 59–61, 145–50; and R. Ben-Oliel, *Banking Law—General Part*
(Jerusalem: Institute for Legislative Research, 1996) at 303–20 [in Hebrew]. For the recent
'civilian' oriented change in South Africa, see s 27, below.

[3] UCC Article 3—Negotiable Instruments, and Article 4—Bank Deposits and Collections.
The current text of Article 3 is from 1990. Its passage was accompanied by the passage of
conforming and miscellaneous amendments to Article 4.

jurisdictions,[4] where cheques are governed by a statute modelled on the Geneva Uniform Law on Cheques.[5]

In the United States, the question of forged cheque losses is dealt with by specific provisions of the UCC. No specific provisions exist in common law jurisdictions, as well as in most civil law countries.[6] In common law jurisdictions, the question is mainly determined according to diverse, and often complex general principles of law.[6a] In civil law countries, governing principles are derived mainly from civil codes, primarily as applied to the mandate. Particularly in civil law countries, to some extent in common law jurisdictions, but much less under the UCC, contract also plays a role in the loss allocation scheme. In all jurisdictions and subject to specific statutory provisions, as may be applicable, governing principles are not limited to cheques and apply to any forged written payment instructions. Unauthorized electronic payment instructions are discussed below, in 4.C.

The ensuing discussion critically examines governing principles and doctrine in light of pertinent policies. It further examines specific proposals for law reform. Ultimately, the text proposes a desired rule, to be adopted by statute, that purports to implement the desired policies better than the current schemes.

It will be seen that the American UCC provides for predominantly fault principles, thus purporting to implement a loss reduction policy. Conversely, in the common law jurisdictions, the objective mostly implemented by the loss allocation scheme is that of loss distribution. On their part, civil law jurisdictions are the least favourable to customers. They impose on the customer heavy diligence duties and in some cases allocate

---

[4] Jurisdictions covered are Switzerland, France, Germany, Italy, and Japan. The provisions of the Quebec Civil Code will also be referred to. In Switzerland, relevant provisions are in the Code of Obligations (CO) rather than in the Civil Code (CC), as in the other civil law jurisdictions under discussion. For texts in English see *The French Civil Code*, rev. edn. (as am. to 1 July 1994), trans. John H. Crabb (Littleton, Colo.: Rothman and Deventer, 1995); *The German Civil Code* (as am. to 1 January 1975) trans. I. S. Forrester, S. L. Goren, and H. M. Ilgen (South Hackensack, NJ: Fred, B. Rothman, 1975) (with 1981 Supp. trans. S. L. Goren); *The Civil Code of Japan* (translation) (Tokyo Ministry of Justice, 1972); *The Italian Civil Code*, trans. M. Beltramo, G. E. Longo, and J. H. Merryman (Dobbs Ferry, NY: Oceana, (1969)); *Swiss Contract Law, English Translation of Selected Official Texts—Swiss Code of Obligations* (Zurich: Swiss-American Chamber of Commerce, 1997); and the bilingual edition of the Quebec Civil Code, *Code civil du practicien* (Montreal: DACFO, 1995).

[5] *Convention Providing a Uniform Law for Cheques*, with Annexes and Protocol, 19 Mar. 1931, 143 L.N.T.S. 355, adopted by the Second Geneva Convention, as part of an international effort which further generated the Geneva Uniform Law on Bills of Exchange and Promissory Notes (agreed upon in 1930).

[6] A notable exception is art. 1132 of the Code of Obligations of Switzerland, further discussed in text around n. 37 below, under which the drawee bank bears the loss of a forged or fraudulently altered cheque where the customer acted without fault. The customer's fault notably consists in not taking good care in the custody of the customer's chequebook.

[6a] A very recent notable exception, discussed in s. 27 below, is South Africa.

the loss to the customer even in the absence of negligence by him. Loss allocation on a non-negligent customer is repugnant in the common law as well as under the UCC. My own proposed model for reform purports to implement loss reduction in a broader context of loss distribution.

(II) THE CHEQUE AS A MANDATE: CIVIL LAW JURISDICTIONS AND BACKGROUND TO THE COMMON LAW SCHEME

In both common law[7] and civil law[8] jurisdictions, the cheque is discussed   **[2]** in terms of a mandate, given by the drawer as a mandator to the drawee bank as mandatary. Furthermore, under the civil law, the entire relationship between a customer and a drawee bank, under which the latter is to carry out the former's payment instructions, may be regarded as a mandate.[9] One can therefore anticipate the law of mandate to play a major role in the allocation of forged cheque losses in both the common and civil law.

Indeed, according to Pothier,[10] the underlying contract between a   **[3]** drawer and drawee of a bill of exchange[11] is that of a mandate. Such a contract is implicitly made by a banker upon receiving funds from the drawer for paying the latter's bills. A distinction is drawn between the specific mandate relating to each bill of exchange, and the general mandate governing the overall agreement under which the banker is to pay the drawer's bills drawn on that banker.

In Pothier's opinion, the risk of unauthorized material alteration and forged drawer's signature with respect to a bill of exchange is allocated according to the principles that govern the mandate contract. They can be enumerated as follows:

1. Where the instrument has been materially altered without the drawer's authority, for example, by having its amount raised, the drawee bank is responsible for the resulting overpayment, but only where the alteration could have been perceived by the exercise of due care. This is

---

[7] See e.g. *London Joint Stock Bank* v. *Macmillan*, [1918] A.C. 777 at 789 (H.L.), and in general, H. Luntz, 'Cheques as Mandates and as Bills' (1997), 12 B.F.L.R. 189.

[8] See e.g. J. L. Rives-Lange and M. Contamine-Raynaud, *Droit bancaire*, 6th edn. (Paris: Dalloz, 1995) at 287 ¶300.

[9] See e.g. in Switzerland, D. Guggenheim, *Les Contrats de la pratique bancaire suisse*, 2nd edn. (Geneva: Georg Éditeur, 1989) at 256.

[10] R.-J. Pothier, *Traité du contrat de change*, new edn. (ed. J.-B. Hutteau) (Paris: Letellier, Garnery, 1809) at 55–68.

[11] Cheques are effectively bills of exchange drawn on a bank and payable on demand. In BEA jurisdictions (other than in Australia) and under the UCC, the cheque is specifically defined to be species of a bill of exchange (or draft, which is the bill of exchange equivalent in the USA). See e.g. s. 73 in the UK, s. 165(1) in Canada, s. 1 in South Africa, and s. 73 in Israel, as well as UCC §3–104(f) in the United States. See 3.B(iii) s. 1 n. 29 and (iv) s. 1 n. 139.

so regardless of any fault by the drawer who might have drawn the bill carelessly so as to facilitate the alteration.

2. However, where no fault can be attributed to the drawee bank, the loss falls on a drawer whose fault caused the bank's error. Specifically, the drawer's fault could be in writing the bill in a manner that facilitated the alteration, such as by leaving unnecessary spaces or writing the sum in figures only.

3. The more difficult case is that of material alteration where neither the drawer nor the drawee bank were negligent. On one hand, Pothier brings forward the opinion of Scaccia, under which loss is to be sustained by the drawer, since the drawee bank, as a mandatary, is entitled to be reimbursed by the drawer, as a mandator, for all expenses for which the carrying out of the mandate has given rise. From this perspective, the drawer's liability as a mandator to reimburse the non-negligent drawee as a mandatary is absolute and arises irrespective of the former's lack of fault. On the other hand, and this is the view that Pothier ultimately seems to support, in connection with the reimbursement right of a non-negligent drawee-mandatary, a distinction could be drawn between two types of losses. First, for losses incurred by the non-negligent mandatary by virtue of the mandate (namely, *ex causa mandati*), the drawer-mandator is responsible, irrespective of lack of negligence on his part. At the same time, for losses incurred by the non-negligent mandatary on the occasion of the mandate (namely, *à l'occasion du mandat*), the drawer-mandator is not responsible, as long as he was not negligent.[12] Payment according to authentic drawer's instructions falls into the former category, while payment according to the drawer's altered instructions falls into the latter. Under that view, where neither the drawee bank not the drawer are at fault, the loss incurred by the unauthorized material alteration of the bill of exchange falls on the drawee bank.

4. Payment of a bill of exchange bearing a forged drawer's signature is outside the general mandate given by the purported drawer to the drawee bank, to pay solely the former's bills of exchange, and hence, is at the latter's risk. In Pothier's view, forgery of a signature cannot be caused by the fault of the person whose signature has been forged. The purported drawer's liability is thus excluded on the basis of the drawee's action outside the mandate, as well, presumably, on the basis of an irrebuttable presumption of remoteness between the purported drawer's conduct and the

---

[12] In support of this distinction, Pothier, above, n. 10 at 60–1, provides an example. Suppose a slave you had bought for me at my instructions stole from you before the delivery of the slave to me. Since there was no fault on my part, such as in not warning you on the basis of information I had as to the possibility of that slave being a potential thief, and as the loss occurred on the occasion and not because of the mandate, I am under no duty to indemnify you.

forgery. Unfortunately, the relative weight of each rationale is not specifically spelled out by Pothier.

In any event, 'mandate' does not necessarily mean the same thing in **[4]** both common and civil law. In Roman law, the mandate was broadly defined as 'a contract whereby one person (mandator) gives another [mandatary] a commission to do something for him . . .'.[13] In principle, this definition was adopted by the various civil codes.[14] Conversely, in the common law, the scope of the mandate is substantially narrower; it merely denotes 'a direction or request',[15] or an instruction.[16] Accordingly, in English law, the mandate[17] did not attract such vast scholarship, doctrine, and jurisprudence as in the civil law.

However, as will be seen below, even in the common law, Pothier's text was the *locus classicus* of the statement of principle governing the allocation of forgery losses.[18] Furthermore, in its reluctance to impose duties on the customer to prevent or detect signature forgery,[19] the common law appears to have been influenced by the reservations of Pothier[20] more than civil law. Contrary to Pothier, in dealing with the customer's duties to his bank, civil law has not hesitated to fasten on the customer a broad responsibility to prevent and detect the forgery of his signature.[21]

All this does not deny the centrality of mandate doctrine in the alloca- **[5]** tion of forgery losses in the various civil law jurisdictions. However, unlike in common law cases, mandate analysis in the civil law has not

---

[13] See e.g. R. W. Lee, *The Elements of Roman Law*, 4th edn. (London: Sweet & Maxwell, 1956) at 334.

[14] See e.g. Swiss CO art. 394(1), French CC art. 1984 (where the mandatary's action must be in the mandator's name), Italian CC art. 1703, Japanese CC art. 643 (in conjunction with art. 656), Quebec CC art. 2130 and BGB §662 (in conjunction with §675) in Germany. In Italy and Quebec the mandate is limited to the accomplishment of a legal transaction or the performance of a juridical act. Arguably, the payment of the drawer's debt falls into this category.

[15] J. Burke, *Jowitt's Dictionary of English Law*, 2nd edn. (London: Sweet & Maxwell, 1977) at 1140.

[16] See e.g. *National Westminster Bank* v. *Barclays Bank International*, [1975] Q.B. 654 at 666; and *Barclays Bank* v. *W. J. Simms Son & Cooke (Southern)*, [1980] 1 Q.B. 677 at 699.

[17] 'We are apt to think of [mandate] in terms of agency . . . But this is incorrect. In the law of contract agency implies a contractual relationship established between one person . . . and a third party by another person . . . who acts as an intermediary . . . But mandate is essentially a contract of employment and its rules are concerned only with the reciprocal rights and duties of the mandator . . . and the [mandatary] . . .': Lee, above, n. 13 at 336. Indeed, there is some English case law characterizing the banker and customer relationship 'in respect of the payment of the customer's cheques' as that of an agent and principal. See e.g. *Selangor United Rubber Estates* v. *Cradock No. 3*, [1968] 1 W.L.R. 1555 at 1594 (Ch. D). Nevertheless, it has not been attempted in English law to explain the reciprocal duties between a banker and customer in terms of the relationship between an agent and principal.

[18] This will be set out in text to nn. 76–85, below.   [19] As will be seen in (iii), below.

[20] See his fourth principles, text subsequent to n. 12, above.

[21] See text to n. 35, below.

been confined to Pothier. Rather, it expressed a broader range of views relating to the mandate in general.

Mandate doctrine has not fastened on the parties reciprocal duties of care. In the classical law, the mandatary was liable only for *dolus*,[22] namely, an intentional wrongful act.[23] In the course of the years, the mandatary's liability had been expanded[24]; in the current civil codes, the mandatary is held to a duty of care.[25] As for the mandator's liability, at present, other than in Switzerland,[26] the prevailing view is that it is not limited to negligence; rather, it extends to all losses and damages incurred by the mandatary in connection with the execution of the mandate,[27] and arises even in the absence of any negligence on the part of the mandator.[28]

This would have meant that as between the bank and the customer, each bears the loss attributed to that party's fault. Where none was at fault, other than in Switzerland, losses would have been borne by the mandator. Nonetheless, two factors, operating in opposite directions, have interfered with the application of this scheme to the banking relationship and have introduced greater complexity:

1. Indeed, pursuant to a minority civilian view, the bank's obligation towards the customer under their general mandate agreement is to carry out payment instructions whose authenticity is not suspect.[29] Accordingly, when the bank is not negligent in paying forged cheques, it has not broken its contract with the customer, and may debit the customer's account even where the customer has not been negligent. It is, however, generally recognized that in fact, the converse is true. Under the prevailing view, a bank not paying according to its customer's instructions, acts outside the

---

[22] Lee, above, n. 13 at 335.   [23] Ibid. at 287.

[24] See discussion by R. Zimmermann, *The Law of Obligations: Roman Foundations of the Civilian Tradition* (Cape Town: Juta, 1990) at 426–30.

[25] See Swiss CO art. 398 (with references to arts. 321a(1) and 321e(1)); French CC art. 1992; Japanese CC art. 644; Italian CC art. 1710; BGB §276 in Germany (for any debtor in general); and Quebec CC art. 2138.   [26] CO art. 402(2).

[27] See French CC art. 2000; Italian CC art. 1720; Japanese CC art. 650 and Quebec CC art. 2154. Some of these provisions are drafted so as not to distinguish between damages suffered 'because' of the mandate and those incurred 'on the occasion' of the mandate. For this distinction by Pothier, see his third principle, text to n. 12, above. In Germany BGB §670 reads to entitle the mandatary to claim from the mandator only expenses or outlays (and not losses or damages) incurred by the mandatary in the course of carrying out the mandate. However, '[these] narrow confines . . . were soon left behind by courts and legal writers. The principle of a liability (not based on fault) for risks arising from and connected with activities undertaken by another person in the debtor's interest, is widely acknowledged today'. See Zimmermann, above, n. 24 at 432.

[28] For this development see Zimmermann, ibid. at 430–2. In fact, both the narrow scope of the *original* mandatary's liability and the *modern* broad scope of the mandator's liability are reminiscent of the original gratuitous nature of the mandatary's undertaking.

[29] See e.g. R. von Buren, *La Responsabilité du banquier pour le paiement des chèques faux ou falsifiés* (Lausanne: Imprimerie Centrale, 1939) at 83. See also at 48, where the author discusses a (minority) proposal to that effect submitted in an international conference.

mandate. Whether losses thereby caused ought to be considered as aris-ing even 'on the occasion of the mandate', so as nevertheless to fall on the mandator/customer, is disputed. Statutory provisions requiring a dis-charging payment to be made to the true creditor may be invoked in order to shift forged cheque losses away from the non-negligent customer to the non-negligent bank.[30] This is particularly true other than in Switzerland, namely in those countries where under mandate principles, a non-negligent bank could have debited the account of a non-negligent cus-tomer with the amount of a forged cheque.

2. Express terms in the banking contract may purport to shift forgery losses away from the bank and allocate them to the customer. As long as the bank did not act intentionally or with gross negligence, such terms are usually effective, though to a degree which varies from one civil law jurisdiction to another.

The following is an outline of the resulting scheme of allocating cheque [6] forgery losses in civil law jurisdictions.[31] The scheme draws on mandate principles, as modified by the above-mentioned considerations.

Material alteration losses fall on the customer, except when the bank was grossly negligent.[32] The rules governing the allocation of forged sig-nature losses are set out as follows:

1. As between a negligent customer and a non-negligent bank, the loss falls on the customer.[33] Customer's negligence may specifically apply to the safekeeping of blank cheque forms and to the supervision of employ-ees. Fraud committed by an employee of the customer in the course of the customer's employment is at the customer's responsibility.[34] In Germany,

---

[30] See e.g. French CC arts. 1239 and 1937, requiring, respectively, the extinction of a debt by payment to the creditor or the creditor's nominee, as well the discharge of the deposi-tary's obligation by delivery to the depositor or to the depositor's nominee. See J.-L. Guil-lot, 'Chèque, fausse signature du tireur, faute de la banque, responsabilité de la banque', *Banque*, No. 536—Mar.–Apr. 1993, at 88, commenting on Cass. com., 9 Feb. 1993.

[31] See e.g. *Encyclopédie juridique Dalloz: Répertoire de droit commercial*, 2nd edn., 'Chèques', by M. Cabrillac, ¶¶385–400, Rives-Lange, above, n. 8 at 306–7 ¶313 (both on France); A. Petitpierre-Sauvain 'Le Chèque I—Caractéristiques—Validité—Mentions essentielles', in *Fiche juridique suisse* No. 721 (Mise au point 1er février 1993) at 9–11 (in Switzerland). For some discussion see *Jura Europae—Droit bancaire et boursier* (Munich: Verlag C. H. Beck; Paris: Editions Techniques Juris-Classeurs, 1974) at 10.31.9 (Germany) and 40.31.9 (Italy).

[32] Cf. in France, M. Cabrillac, R.T.D. com. 49(1), Jan–Mar. 1996 at 92, commenting on Com. 17 Oct. 1995, *Sté Bordelaise c/SNC Diparco*, where a collecting bank that received a cheque containing the sum in figures only was found to be grossly negligent, so as to release the drawer who had facilitated the material alteration by writing the sum in figures only.

[33] See e.g. in France, J. L. Rives-Lange, *Revue banque* No. 503—Mar. 1990, at 310, com-menting on Cass. com., 5 Dec. 1989.

[34] See e.g. Swiss CO art. 101, covering liability for damage caused by household members as well as employees carrying out tasks entrusted to them; French CC art. 1384(5); Italian CC art. 2049; Japanese CC art. 715 (further providing that due care in the appointment of the employee and in the supervision of the task, as well as circumstances where damage

this is under the 'theory of spheres' which allocates losses falling within a person's 'sphere of influence' or 'field of control' to that person.

2. As between a negligent bank and a non-negligent customer, the loss falls on the bank. The bank's responsibilities primarily relate to the verification of the drawer's signature. It is however recognized that the process of verification is fast and in comparing between a signature on a cheque and that kept on a signature card, the bank is not required to meet such a high standard as would be required from a graphology expert.

3. As between negligent bank and negligent customer, loss is apportioned according to the degree of each's respective fault.[35]

4. No consensus exists where neither the bank nor the customer was negligent. As we saw, under mandate principles, loss may be allocated to the customer. However, this rule is not universally adhered to. For example, in Switzerland, a general statutory provision applicable to the mandate,[36] as well as a specific one applicable to cheques,[37] allocate the loss to the bank. In France, the same result is achieved, though it is not dictated by any statutory provision applicable either to the mandate or the cheque. This is also the situation in Germany.

5. In any event, to a large extent, the above-listed rules 2 to 4 are usually superseded by contract.[38] Generally speaking, banks are able to effectively exonerate themselves from liability, other than for intentional wrongful act or gross negligence.[39] In France and Germany, such exemp-

---

would have ensued even if due care had been exercised, release the employer); Quebec CC art. 1463; BGB §278 in Germany.

[35] For the reciprocal duties between a bank and customer, as well as for the standard of care that a bank must meet in verifying its customer's signature, see M. Cabrillac, R.T.D. com. 49(4), Oct.–Dec. 1996, at 696, commenting on Com. 9 July 1996, *BNP c/Amsellem*.

[36] Under Swiss CO art. 402(2), the mandator is liable to the mandatory 'for any and all damages sustained by the [mandatary] in the course of the performance of the mandate, *to the extent that the [mandator] is unable to prove that the damage was caused without his fault.*' (emphasis added).

[37] Swiss CO art. 1132 provides that in the absence of fault by the customer, the damage resulting from a forged cheque is at the drawee's responsibility. Careless safekeeping of blank cheque forms is particularly singled out as such possible fault (which would preclude the application of the provision).

[38] See e.g. Article 16 of the Current Account Regulations in Japan and para. 3 of the Special Conditions for Cheque Transactions in Germany.

[39] See e.g. J. Hamel, G. Lagarde, and A. Jauffret, *Traité de droit commercial* (Paris: Librairie Dalloz, 1966) at 773; R. Ben-Oliel, 'Banker's Liability in the Bank Deposit Relationship' (1979), 14 Israel L. Rev. 164 at 174–6. In Switzerland, under CO 100(2), at the discretion of a court, a disclaimer clause purporting to exonerate banks from liability even for slight negligence by their *organs*, may be considered void. However, liability for slight negligence for acts or omissions by bank *employees* may contractually be excluded under CO art. 101(3). In general, an exemption clause purporting to disclaim liability for an intentional wrong or gross negligence is rendered void under CO art. 100(1). For the application of CO arts. 100(2) and 101(3) to banks, as carrying on 'an occupation for which a public licence is necessary' or 'an officially licensed trade' (that is, in both cases, 'une industrie concédée par l'autorité' in the French original), see a 1986 decision of a Federal Court, ATF 112 II 450.

tion clauses are limited to situations where blank cheques were lost by or stolen from the customer (even without the customer's negligence) and not timely countermanded. In Germany, this applies only to blank cheques lost by or stolen from business or public law entities.

In sum, in Italy, Switzerland, and Japan, forged drawer signature losses **[7]** are allocated to a customer, even where the customer was not negligent, provided the bank neither acted intentionally nor was grossly negligent. In these three countries, a bank which either acted intentionally or was grossly negligent bears the loss, but is nevertheless able to apportion some of it to a negligent customer, though only to the extent of the latter's negligence. Customers fare better in France and Germany, where in principle, each party is liable according to that party's fault, and where both acted without fault, the loss falls on the bank. However, in these two countries, a bank which neither acted intentionally nor was grossly negligent, may nevertheless allocate to a non-negligent customer some losses caused by cheque forgery. This is so only with regard to forgery losses that follow the loss by or theft from the customer, of a blank cheque form, where the loss or theft has not been timely advised to the bank. In Germany, such an exemption clause works only against a customer who is a business or public law entity.

(iii) COMMON LAW JURISDICTIONS

The starting point in the common law is that as 'custodians of the cus- **[8]** tomer's money' providing for 'a safe place of deposit',[40] '[b]ankers can only charge their customers with sums of money paid pursuant to order'.[41] They 'are bound to know the hand-writing of their customers',[42] and must abide by any forgery loss, even where the cheque 'was altered in such a manner that no one in the ordinary course of business could observe it'.[43] In *Hall* v. *Fuller* the position was well put by Bayley J. as follows:

The banker, as the depositary of the customer's money, is bound to pay from time to time such sums as the latter may order. If, unfortunately, he pays money belonging to the customer upon an order which is not genuine, he must suffer,

---

Specifically for the parties' ability to contract out of the scheme of CO art. 1132 in Switzerland, see SJ 1977 at 44.

[40] *National Bank of Virginia* v. *Nolting* 26 S.E. 826 at 828 (Va. S.C. 1897), *per* Harrison J.
[41] *Hall* v. *Fuller* (1825), 5 B.C. 750 at 757;108 E.R. 279 at 282, *per* Abbott CJ.
[42] *Smith* v. *Mercer* (1815), 6 Taunt 76 at 86; 128 E.R. 961 at 965, *per* Heath J.
[43] *Hall* v. *Fuller*, above, n. 41 at 756 (B.C.), 282 (E.R.), in argument.

and to justify the payment, he must show that the order is genuine, not in signature only, but in every respect . . .[44]

Stated otherwise, the bank's liability for unauthorized payment is
absolute. Moreover, whenever the customer contests the propriety of payment, it is incumbent on the bank to prove that payment has been authorized.

[9]   The Bills of Exchange Act does not preclude the ratification of an unauthorized signature 'not amounting to a forgery'.[45] This seems to preclude
the ratification of forgery, presumably, with the view of preserving the
civil as well as criminal liability of the forger.[46] It was, however, held in
Canada that the provision is limited to the unilateral act of *ratification*, and
thus, does not preclude the *adoption* of a forged cheque, against valuable
consideration, provided the consideration is not illegal.[47] With respect to
the liability of the customer, who has chosen to be bound by an unauthorized, including forged, cheque, from whom it appeared to emanate, all
such distinctions are not persuasive,[48] and were specifically rejected in
Australia, where ratification is not precluded under s. 32(1)(b) for any
type of an unauthorized signature on a cheque.

Whatever their effect, ratification and adoption purport to nullify the
lack of authority after the event, with full knowledge of it. As such, they
are premissed on the informed waiver of rights, and do not represent a
true exception to the principle under which a customer is not bound by
the forgery of that customer's signature. It was however recognized in
Young v. *Grote*, as a true exception to the non-binding effect of lack of
authority, that this principle did not apply where the customer was at
fault[49] or 'guilty of negligence'.[50] What legal basis underlies this exception,
what amounts to fault or negligence, and finally, what proximity ought to
exist between the customer's fault or negligence and the loss sustained by
virtue of the forgery, have been elaborated in subsequent case law.

[10]   As for the basis for the exception, estoppel, torts, and contract have primarily been considered. In fact, it is not contested that a party may be

---

[44] Ibid, at 757 (B.C.), 282 (E.R.).

[45] See s. 24(2) in the UK, s. 23(b) in Israel, s. 22 in South Africa, and s. 48(2) in Canada. For
a pre-UCC American analysis of grounds for liability on a forged cheque, along similar,
though not identical, lines of the position under English law, see H. W. Arant, 'Forged
Checks—The Duty of the Depositor to His Bank' (1921), 31 Yale L.J. 598.

[46] See *Brook* v. *Hook* (1871), L.R. 6 Ex. 89.

[47] *Newell* v. *Royal Bank of Canada* (1997), 147 D.L.R. (4th) 268 (N.S. C.A.), where the bank's
forbearance to prosecute the forger was regarded as such illegal consideration, precluding
the bank from recovering the customer.

[48] For advocating, in Israel, a narrow construction for 'forgery' that cannot be ratified see
S. Lerner, *The Law of Bills and Notes* 452–3 (Tel-Aviv: Israeli Bar, 1999) [in Hebrew].

[49] (1827), 4 Bing 253 at 258; 130 E.R. 764 at 766, *per* Best CJ.

[50] Ibid., at 260 (Bing), 767 (E.R.), *per* Park J. See also, judgments of Burrough J., who spoke
of the customer's 'blame', and of Gaselee J. who spoke of the customer's 'great negligence'.

estopped from raising the defence of forgery or lack of authority. In fact, this is provided for in the Act itself: 'the forged or unauthorized signature is wholly inoperative . . . unless the party against whom it is sought to retain or enforce payment . . . is precluded from setting up the forgery or want of authority.'[51] Technically, this statutory estoppel is only vis-à-vis parties claiming on the instrument, rather than towards the drawee bank, whose relationship with the customer is, generally speaking, outside the Act. However, estoppel has been used widely to shift forgery losses from drawee banks to their customers. Estoppel could be by representation or conduct, by negligence, or by contract.[52]

Another device used to shift forgery losses to customers has been a duty of care, deriving either from contract or torts. Since estoppel by negligence also presupposes a duty of care, there is a substantial overlap, if not confusion, in the employment of all these tools. However, as a matter of legal doctrine, the amount of loss to which the customer is held responsible may depend on the particular ground under which loss has been allocated to him in the first place.

Thus, once the bank suffered any loss or detriment, an estopped customer is responsible for the entire amount of the forged cheques.[53] Conversely, the customer's liability in tort is up to the amount of the bank's actual loss. In principle, the latter is true also in contract, except that the measure of damages may be agreed upon in advance. There will be a difference between the amount of the forged cheques, for which the estopped customer is fully responsible, and the detriment suffered by the bank, for which the customer is liable in damages, whether in tort or in contract, where the bank can recover some loss from the forger. Unless the measure of damages was agreed upon by contract, loss recoverable from the forger ought to be deducted from the amount of the forged cheque(s) in order to establish actual damages for which the breaching customer is liable to the bank. Further, as discussed below,[54] the effect of the bank's own negligence on the existence or scope of the customer's liability may also depend on the rationale selected for finding the customer responsible.

Estoppel by representation or conduct consists of the failure to advise

[51] Section 24(1) in the UK, s. 22 in South Africa, s. 23(a) in Israel, and s. 48(1) in Canada. See also s. 32(1)(a) in Australia (*semble*).

[52] Strictly speaking, other than in the context of BEA s. 24(1) (UK), and its corresponding provisions elsewhere, ibid., estoppel by contract is a misnomer, since the existence of 'contract' bypasses the need to resort to estoppel. Cf. the extensive discussion on the promissory estoppel in M. P. Furmston, *Cheshire, Fifoot and Furmston's Law of Contract*, 13th edn. (London: Butterworths, 1996) at 100–9.

[53] See e.g. *Greenwood* v. *Martins Bank Ltd.*, [1932] 1 K.B. 371 at 383–4 (C.A.), Scrutton LJ.

[54] See text following n. 149, below.

the drawee bank or the holder of a known[55] or suspected forgery.[56] The essential elements of such an estoppel are: (1) a representation (or conduct amounting to a representation) intended to induce a course of conduct by the person to whom the representation is made, (2) an act or omission, by that person, resulting from the representation, and (3) a detriment to that person as a consequence to such act or omission.[57]

Unlike estoppel by representation or conduct, estoppel by negligence consists of a representation of facts that though are unknown to the representor, they ought to have been known to him, had he acted with care. Estoppel by negligence presupposes the existence of a duty of care.[58] Obviously, a duty of care is also required to establish liability in the tort of negligence. As will be seen below, the scope of a duty of care on the part of a bank customer, other than by express contract, was held to be quite narrow.

[11]   The authority of a drawee bank to debit the account of a drawer for the full amount of a cheque that was negligently drawn, so as to permit its subsequent alteration by the insertion of words and figures without erasures, was established in England in 1827 in *Young* v. *Grote*.[59] For some time, the real meaning,[60] and even the authority,[61] of the case were doubted, until fully re-established by the House of Lords in *London Joint Stock Bank* v. *Macmillan*, where it was stated that the 'sole ground upon which *Young* v. *Grote* was decided . . . was that Young was a customer of the bank owing to the bank the duty of drawing his cheque with reasonable care . . .'.[62] It does not matter whether the customer's negligence in breaking this duty creates estoppel or gives ground to liability in negligence,[63] its legal foundations appear to be an incident or an implied term

---

[55] Means of knowledge may be equated with knowledge, where the customer is specifically alerted to suspicious circumstances, as in *Brown* v. *Westminster Bank Ltd.*, [1964] 2 Lloyd's L.R. 187 (Q.B. (Com.)), as well as where one 'knows so much that it is a policy of an ostrich to know no more'. See e.g. *Morison* v. *London County and Westminster Bank*, [1914] 3 K.B. 356 at 385.

[56] See e.g. *Greenwood* v. *Martins Bank Ltd.*, [1933] A.C. 51 (H.L.); *Ewing* v. *Dominion Bank* (1905), 35 S.C.R. 133; and *Ontario Woodsworth Memorial Foundation* v. *Grozbord* (1966), 58 D.L.R. (2d) 21 (Ont. C.A.), *aff'd.* [1969] S.C.R. 622.

[57] *Greenwood*, ibid. at 57.

[58] *Swan* v. *North British Australasian Co.* (1863), 2 H. & C. 175, 182–3; 159 E.R. 73, 76 (Exch. Chamber), *per* Blackburn J.   [59] Above, n. 49.

[60] It had been questioned whether the case stood for apparent authority, duty of care in favour of all takers of a negotiable instrument, or a contractual duty to take care owed by a customer/depositor to his bank with respect to cheques. See 'Careless Spaces on Negotiable Instruments' (1918), 31 Harv. L. Rev. 779, and further below, n. 63.

[61] It was treated as no longer good law by the Privy Council in *Colonial Bank of Australasia* v. *Marshall*, [1906] A.C. 559 (P.C.), as well as by the House of Lords in *Scholfield* v. *Earl of Londesborough* [1896] A.C. 514.   [62] Above, n. 7 at 793 by Lord Finlay LC.

[63] Ibid. at 793–4.

of the mandate contract, created by the cheque, between the bank and customer.[64]

Merely signing a blank form cheque,[65] and even entrusting it either for safekeeping, or with authority to complete and issue it, does not fasten liability on the signer for the amount of the cheque, as subsequently completed and issued without or contrary to the signer's authority.[66] This is so, even when the cheque was so issued and completed by the signer's own agent who had been in lawful possession of the cheque.[67] A signatory to a blank form cheque is liable only where he delivered it 'in order that it may be converted into a bill', namely, with power to issue it as a complete cheque (and not merely for safekeeping), and where the cheque, completed contrary to the signer's authority, has been negotiated to a holder in due course.[68] Furthermore, a signer pleading against a holder in due course *non est factum*, namely, that he intended to sign a radically or fundamentally different document from the instrument actually signed

[64] Ibid. at 789: see also at 804. Doubts as to the existence of such a duty in Israeli law, at least on the basis of an implied contract, were raised by G. Tedeski, 'On the Nature of the Bank Deposit', in *Zusmann Book* (Jerusalem: Daf-Chen, 1984) 209 at 239 [in Hebrew]. According to H. Luntz, 'Banker and Customer: Reciprocal Absence of a Duty of Care?' (1996), 4 Torts L.J. 99 at 102, following *Macmillan*, '[t]he predominant view seems to have been that the liability of the customer is based on estoppel by negligence'. Acknowledging that negligence requires a duty of care, he goes on to state that '[t]he duty was found in an implied contractual term . . .'. In my view however, once a contractual duty is recognized, the estoppel by negligence explanation becomes redundant.

[65] See *Baxendale* v. *Bennet* (1878), 3 Q.B.D. 525 (C.A.), where a bank form signed instrument, that had been stolen and completed without authority, reached the hands of a bona fide endorsee for value, who was nevertheless not allowed to recover on it from the signer. The same result was recently reached in Canada with respect to a stolen unissued *complete* cheque in *National Bank of Canada* v. *Tardivel Associates* (1993), 15 O.R. (3d) 188 (Ont. Gen. Div.), *aff'd* 17 O.R. (3d) 61 (Div. Ct.). Arguably, the latter case was wrongly decided as a matter of doctrine and statutory interpretation, as well as policies. See strong criticism by this author in 'Negotiable Instruments and Banking: Review of Some Canadian Case Law' (1993–4), 9 B.F.L.R. 197 at 203–5, and in greater detail by B. Crawford, 'Is This a Cheque I See Before Me? National Bank v. Tardivel and the Scope of Defence of Non-Delivery' (1995), 24 Can. Bus. L.J. 1.

[66] At some point, *Young* v. *Grote*, above, n. 49, was understood to establish such liability. See e.g. *Robarts* v. *Tucker* (1851), 16 Q.B. 560 at 579–80; 117 E.R. 994 at 1001–2 *per* Parke B. In *Young* v. *Grote*, the customer delivered a blank signed cheque to an inexperienced person who subsequently filled it in negligently, thereby facilitating the ultimate unauthorized alteration. For a while, it was not certain whether the customer's operative negligence was in the delivery of the incomplete signed form to the inexperienced person or in the careless completion of the cheque by the latter. In adhering to the second alternative, as discussed in the preceding paragraph, *Macmillan* conclusively settled this issue.

[67] See e.g. *Herdman* v. *Wheeler* [1902] 1 K.B. 361.

[68] See s. 20 in the UK or ss. 30–1 in Canada and *Smith* v. *Prosser*, [1907] 2 K.B. 735 (C.A.), and discussion by I. Ackermann, 'Signature and Liability in the Law of Bills and Notes' (1993), 8 B.F.L.R. 295. Prior to the BEA, in *Foster* v. *Mackinnon* (1869), L.R. 4 C.P. 704 at 712, Byles J. thought that the signer of a blank bill who 'parts with it . . . is liable' to a holder in due course 'to the extent of any sum' that it was improperly filled up, and regardless of the purpose for which the signer had parted with the instrument.

by him, may be met by a counterplea as to the signer's own negligence in signing the paper.[69] This seems to be the extent of the signer's duty of care in executing his signature.[70]

[12]   In restoring the authority of *Young* v. *Grote*,[71] the House of Lords in *Macmillan* has nevertheless established that the drawer's (contractually implied) duty of care in drawing his cheques is confined to the customer-drawee bank relationship.[72] As a result, the duty cannot be invoked in favour of a subsequent holder including a collecting bank. Furthermore, the duty of care has also been confined to acts or omissions relating exclusively to the drawing and signing of cheques: 'the negligence must be in the transaction itself, that is, in the manner in which the cheque is drawn.'[73] Consequently, no duty was recognized in English case law, even towards the drawee bank, to exercise reasonable care, (a) in the safekeeping of chequebooks or corporate seals, (b) in the general course of carrying business, including in the selection of employees, so as to detect or prevent forgeries, as well as (c) in relation to the examination of periodical bank statements, so as to discover and report forgeries and prevent their repetition. Hence, a customer who was negligent in such matters was found neither liable in negligence nor estopped by his negligence from asserting the forgeries.[74]

The position was well summarized in the South African case *Big Dutchman (South Africa)* v. *Barclays National Bank*, where Philips J. stated:

'A customer's duty to his banker is a limited one. Save in respect of drawing documents to be presented to the bank and in warning of known or suspected for-

---

[69] See *Saunders* v. *Anglia B.S.*, [1971] A.C. 1004 (H.L.), *aff'ng* [1969] 2 Ch. 17, followed by *United Dominions Trust* v. *Western Ltd.*, [1976] 1 Q.B. 513 (C.A.). In any event, a signer on a blank cheque form who delivered it 'in order that it may be converted into a bill' may be unable to plead *non est factum* (and hence, is liable) in the first place. For a successful negligence counterplea against a signer of a complete note pleading *non est factum*, see *Crédit Lyonnais* v. *Barnard*, [1976] 1 Lloyd's Rep. 557 (Q.B. (Com.)).

[70] It has been argued that to be successful in his counterplea, the party asserting the signer's negligence must himself not be negligent, or at least, that his negligence ought to be taken in account in apportioning the loss. See R. Nobles, 'Marvco Color Research Ltd. v. Harris' (1985), 10 Can. Bus. L.J. 377.

[71] See discussion in paragraph containing nn. 49–50, above.

[72] *Macmillan*, above, n. 7 at 803–10, *per* Lord Finlay LC, where *Scholfield*, above, n. 61, as well as the subsequent case of *Colonial Bank of Australasia* v. *Marshall*, above, n. 61, rejecting the existence of a duty of care owed by the acceptor to a subsequent holder, are approved, and distinguished.

[73] *Macmillan*, ibid. at 795. An earlier authority holding that negligence must be 'in or immediately connected with the transfer itself' is *Bank of Ireland* v. *Trustees of Evans' Charities* (1855), 5 H.L.C. 389, 410; 10 E.R. 950, 959, *per* Parke B.

[74] See e.g. *Bank of Ireland* v. *Trustees of Evans' Charities*, ibid. at 409–10 (H.L.C.), 959 (E.R.) *per* Parke B.; *Lewes Sanitary Steam* v. *Barclay* (1906), 95 L.T. 444 *per* Kennedy J; and *Kepitigalla Rubber Estates* v. *National Bank of India*, [1909] 2 K.B. 1010, esp. at 1020–6, *per* Bray J. See also *Scholfield*, above, n. 61 at 531; *Arnold* v. *Cheque Bank* (1876) 1 C.P.D. 578 at 586–90; *Macmillan*, above, n. 7 at 799–800.

geries he has no duty to the bank to supervise his employees, to run his business carefully, or to detect frauds.'[75]

The role of the law governing the mandate relationship, as set out by [13] Pothier,[76] in reaching this legal position, should now be highlighted. First, *Hall* v. *Fuller*[77] will be considered. This was an action by a customer against his banker who paid, without negligence on his part, a cheque signed by the customer, whose amount had been fraudulently raised by the holder. Having paid the raised amount, the banker debited accordingly the customer's account. The customer sued the banker for wrongful debit. Counsel for plaintiff cited Pothier for the proposition that the mandatary is entitled to be reimbursed by the mandator only for expenses incurred *ex causa mandati*, and not for other expenses incurred on the occasion of the mandate.[78] Judgment was given for plaintiff, but without any reference to either the mandate relationship or to Pothier.[79] To this day, this case is the authority for the proposition that under no circumstances a bank may debit a non-negligent customer with any forged cheque amount.

In *Young* v. *Grote*,[80] an extract from Pothier served the explicit basis for dismissing a negligent customer's action against a non-negligent bank that paid the fraudulently raised amount of a cheque drawn by the customer.[81] Not surprisingly, in rejecting altogether the authority of that judgment, *Scholfield* v. *Earl of Londesborough* entirely dismissed the notion that the law of mandate, together with any principle laid down by Pothier, 'forms any part of the mercantile law of England'.[82] Ultimately however, the re-establishment of the authority of *Young* v. *Grote* in *London Joint Stock Bank* v. *Macmillan*, was accompanied by the reapplication of the mandate relationship as well as the reinstatement of the authority of Pothier.[83] In fact, as already indicated,[84] the common law's reluctance to recognize a broad customer's duty to prevent and detect forgeries, before and after *Macmillan*, is quite consistent with the negative view of Pothier on this point.[85]

However, without being repudiated, Pothier's text has ceased to play

---

[75] 1979 (3) S.A. 267 (W.L.D.) at 283, cited with approval in *Holzman* v. *Standard Bank* 1985 (1) S.A. 360 (W.L.D.) at 363. Effectively to the same end in Australia, see *National Australia Bank Ltd.* v. *Hokit Pty. Ltd.* (1995–6) 39 N.S.W.L.R. 377 (C.A.). See s. 27 below for the recent departure by statute from this position in South Africa.

[76] See text following nn. 10–11, above.   [77] Above, n. 41.

[78] See principle 2, text following nn. 10–11, above.

[79] See e.g. the extract quoted from Bayley J.'s judgment, text to n. 44, above.

[80] Above, n. 49.

[81] This is according to principle 2, text following nn. 10–11, above.

[82] Above, n. 61 at 524. See also at 531 and 532, *per* Lord Halsbury LC.

[83] Above, n. 7 at 792 and 799, *per* Lord Finlay LC.

[84] See text around nn. 19–20, above.

[85] As reflected in the fourth principle, text which follows n. 12, above.

an explicit role in subsequent case law. Also, continuous reference to the mandate relationship has not been linked to the application of any general mandate doctrine or principles. In the common law, *Macmillan* has become an authority in banking law, namely, as the foundation of the bank–customer contract, rather than an application of principles governing the mandate relationship to the banking contract.

[14]   According to *Macmillan*, unauthorized alteration for which the customer is responsible must be 'a natural and direct consequence of the customer's negligence . . .'.[86] Leaving a blank space after the payee's name on the cheque is not unusual, and hence, is not such negligence, notwithstanding the unauthorized alteration it facilitated.[87] In any event, even conceding, at least for the sake of argument, the existence of both a duty of care and its breach, namely negligence by the customer, a proximity has been required to lie between such negligence and the loss caused by the forgery it led to. Such proximity is said to exist in connection with the customer's negligence facilitating the material alteration of a properly signed cheque, since the bank is unlikely to detect the forgery: '[n]either any rule of law nor the ordinary course of business renders it a matter of suspicion that the body of the [cheque] . . . is not written in the handwriting of the . . . drawer.'[88] Conversely, so far as the customer's signature is concerned,[89] the drawee bank is 'bound to know the [customer's] hand-writing';[90] in verifying its customer's signature, the drawee bank has thus been held to a very high standard, to a point of strict liability. While under a modern trend, the rule providing that 'a banker is under a duty to know his customer's signature' is regarded as incorrect and a mere aphorism, it is still recognized that '[t]he principle is simply that a banker cannot debit his customer's account on the basis of a forged signature, since he has . . . no mandate from the customer for doing so'.[91] Consequently, the customer's negligence facilitating the forged signature is not the proximate cause for the damage suffered by the bank's payment over that signature.[92] Pay-

---

[86] Above, n. 7, at 789, *per* Lord Finlay LC.
[87] *Slingsby* v. *District Bank*, [1931] 2 K.B. 588.
[88] *Nolting*, above, n. 40 at 827, quoting with agreement Morse, *Banks*, s. 480.
[89] Ibid.   [90] *Smith* v. *Mercer*, above, n. 42 at 86 (Taunt); 965 (E.R.).
[91] *National Westminster Bank* v. *Barclays Bank International*, above, n. 16 at 666, *per* Kerr J.
[92] In *Bank of Ireland* v. *Evans' Trustees* above, n. 73 at 410–11 (H.L.C.), 959 (E.R.), Parke B. commented on the lack of causal link as follows: 'If a man should lose his cheque-book or neglect to lock the desk in which it is kept, and a stranger should take it up, it is impossible . . . to contend that a banker paying his forged cheque would be entitled to charge his customer with that payment. Would it be contended that if he kept his goods so negligently that a servant took them and sold them, he must be considered as having concurred in the sale, and so be disentitled to sue for their conversion . . .? It is clear . . . that the negligence . . . is much too remote . . .'. See also *Baxendale* v. *Bennet*, above, n. 65 at 533, as well as *Scholfield*, above, n. 61 at 522, where Lord Halsbury LC purported even to reject *Young* v. *Grote* (drawer's duty to prevent alteration), stating: 'A man . . . does not lose his right to his

ment of the cheque bearing the forged drawer's signature is thus not 'a very natural consequence' of the customer's negligence. While the customer's negligence in facilitating the forgery 'gave occasion' to the bank's payment over the forged cheque, it was not 'immediately connected' to the transaction itself[93] so as to *cause* the payment, and possibly, even the forgery itself. Similarly, the loss sustained by the forgery of cheques included in a first statement to which the customer did not respond was not caused by the customer's failure to notify the bank of the forged cheques. True, had the customer promptly detected the forgeries upon receiving the first statement, subsequent forgeries would not have taken place. Yet, the customer's failure to do so 'was not in law the cause' of these subsequent forgeries; 'at the most it was the *causa sine qua non*', that is, a necessary or inevitable cause, without which the subsequent forgeries could not have happened, 'but that would not do'.[94]

This reasoning restricting the customer's liability to proximate loss caused by negligence in the transaction did not appear to prevail in *Greenwood* v. *Martins Bank*.[95] Holding that a customer is estopped from asserting forgeries known to him but which he failed to disclose to the bank, Scrutton LJ declined to see the specific cheque transaction as the only context where the customer's duty of care arises: **[15]**

'Now *Macmillan* has laid stress on the relations of banker and customer as giver and executor of a mandate, and the duties which are . . . mutual, to use reasonable care in the execution of the mandate. . . . But the relation does not merely refer to one cheque; it is a continuing relation in which the customer may draw cheques from time to time, and the banker is under a continuing duty to honour mandates. This . . . involves a continuing duty on either side to act with reasonable care to ensure the proper working of the account.'[96]

In the facts of the case, cheques had been forged and paid before the customer became aware of it. Accordingly, the customer's 'silence could not be the proximate cause of the Bank's mistake' in paying the forged cheques. Nevertheless, 'the silence or failure to disclose prevented the Bank from suing the forger, for when the truth was disclosed the forger was dead'. Consequently, inasmuch as 'the silence of the customer has

---

property if he has unnecessarily exposed his goods, or allowed his pocket-handkerchief to hang out of his pocket, but could recover against a bona fide purchaser of any article so lost, notwithstanding the fact that his conduct had to some extent assisted the thief'.

[93] *Lewes Sanitary Steam*, above, n. 74 at 447.

[94] *Walker* v. *Manchester and Liverpool District Banking Co.* (1913), 29 T.L.R. 492 at 493, *per* Channell J. (K.B.).   [95] Above, note 53, *aff'd* above, n. 56.

[96] Ibid. at 380–1 (C.A.).

caused the Bank to lose its right of action, the customer is estopped from alleging the fact . . . that the cheques were forged'.[97]

It is noteworthy that *Greenwood* did not overrule the 'immediate proximity' requirement. In the Court of Appeal, Scrutton LJ spoke of customer duties relating to the account. Following earlier jurisprudence,[98] he specifically pointed out the remoteness of the loss occurring by virtue of the customer's failure to keep chequebooks safely, and did not go as far as to fasten a duty of care in carrying on business. Rather, instead of linking the 'immediate proximity' to the specific *cheque transaction*, as in *Macmillan*, he was prepared to go further and find the customer liable for loss 'immediately proximate' to a breach of a duty arising from the entire *account relationship*.

In the course of his judgment, Scrutton LJ discussed mutual duties of a banker and customer designed 'to ensure the proper working of the account'. He confined his discussion to situations where forgeries were actually discovered by either the bank or the customer. No more was required in the facts of that case. Unfortunately, so far as the customer's negligence is concerned, as distinguished from the customer's silence, Scrutton LJ specifically affirmed the rule under which 'the neglect must be in the transaction itself . . .'.[99] Thereby, he created an untenable distinction between the duty to disclose, which extends to the entire account relationship, and the duty to prevent and detect forgeries, which is limited to a cheque transaction itself. Consequently, his reasoning, given in the context of the customer's duty to disclose, has not been extended to the customer's duty to prevent or detect forgeries.

[16]   Under English law, the customer does not acquire knowledge of the forgery merely by possessing a periodic statement containing a forged cheque.[100] Thus, where the forger is an employee in the customer's accounting department to whom the periodic bank statements are sent,

---

[97] Ibid. at 382–3 (C.A.). This is a complete answer to *Walker*, under which the failure of the customer to advise the bank of forgeries contained in cheques covered by the first statement caused no loss. See text preceding n. 94, above.

[98] At 381–2 he cited and quoted from *Bank of Ireland*, above, n. 73. Other earlier leading cases include *Baxendale* v. *Bennett*, above, n. 65 at 533, *Lewes Sanitary Steam*, above, n. 74 at 447, and *Walker*, above, n. 94 at 493.

[99] Above, n. 53 at 381.

[100] Conversely, in the United States, even prior to the UCC, the prevailing view has been that 'a depositor must be held chargeable with knowledge of all the facts that a reasonable and prudent examination of the returned bank statements . . . would have disclosed had it been made by a person on the depositor's behalf who had not participated in the forgeries'. See *Screenland Magazine* v. *National City Bank of New York* 42 N.Y.S. 2d 286 at 289 (S.C. 1943) and subsequent cases cited by J. J. White and R. S. Summers, *Uniform Commercial Code*, 3rd edn. (St. Paul, Minn.: West Publishing Co., 1988) at 696, n. 5. No parallel discussion exists in the current 4th edition (1995).

his knowledge of the forgery is not that of the customer.[101] Hence, no duty to disclose the forgery arises. Alternatively, the silence generating estoppel must be deliberate or intentional,[102] so that actual knowledge either by an individual employer or an organ of a corporate employer is required. It is along these lines that English law has kept apart the duty to disclose under *Greenwood* and has not allowed it to bypass the absence of a broader duty to prevent or detect forgeries.

The logic underlying these distinctions, namely between the duty to disclose and that to prevent, and to a lesser extent, between the knowledge of the customer and that of his wrongdoing employee, leading to the exoneration from liability of a bank customer for forgery losses facilitated by that customer's own negligence, is not infallible. It has thus not remained unchallenged. In Israel, a duty is fastened by law, irrespective of contract, on a bank customer to review periodic bank statements, so as to discover and promptly report any forgery, or unauthorized payment. Having broken this duty, the customer becomes estopped from raising the forgery and contesting the debit(s) to his bank account.[103] In effect, this amounts to a customer's duty of care. The existence of such a duty was rationalized on the customer's superior position to prevent the occurrence of forgery, and thereby to reduce loss.

It seems however, that in fastening such a duty on a bank customer, the **[17]** majority of the Supreme Court of Israel departed from the conventional understanding of *Brown* v. *Westminster Bank Ltd.*[104] Thereunder, closing the eyes to the means of knowledge, and not merely the availability of such means, is equated to actual knowledge of the forgery, which estopped the customer from raising it.[105] Unfortunately, in declining to explicitly recognize its departure from the current (though in my view, unjustified) distinction between the consequences of the failure to disclose forgeries known to the customer himself (but not to his wrongdoing employee)

---

[101] See *Columbia Graphophone Co.* v. *Union Bank of Canada* (1916), 34 D.L.R. 743 at 745 (Ont. S.C.).

[102] See speech of Lord Tomlin in *Greenwood* (in the House of Lords), above, n. 56 at 57 and 58.

[103] The leading case is *A. Shtauber* v. *Mizrahi Bank.* C/A 550/66, 22 (1) P.D. 240 (1968). It was followed by *Tanenbaum (Estate)* v. *Bank Leumi Le'Israel*, C/A 618/75, 31(3) P.D. 141 (1977).

[104] Above, n. 55, heavily relied on by Vitkon J. in delivering the majority opinion in *Shtauber*.

[105] See above, n. 55 and text. For this conventional understanding of *Brown*, see e.g. E. P. Ellinger and E. Lomnicka, *Modern Banking Law*, 2nd edn. (Oxford: Clarendon Press, 1994) at 178. Furthermore, in *Brown*, the customer made an active representation to the bank manager, in the form of an express statement in response to his questions, acknowledging that the cheques were genuine: see p. 202. It is noteworthy that in his dissent in *Shtaub*, Cohen J. understood *Brown* to be premised on actual knowledge of the forgery, and would not follow this judgment beyond it.

and those of the failure to prevent and detect forgeries, the Israeli Supreme Court undermined the emergence of a credible breakthrough.

[18]   In Canada, in *Arrow Transfer* v. *Royal Bank of Canada*, Laskin J. (as he was then) found the customer to be negligent, in employing an untrustworthy employee in a sensitive position, as well as in utilizing inadequate procedures for discovering fraud. In his majority judgment, purporting to break new grounds, he did 'not think it [was] too late to fasten upon bank customers . . . a duty to examine bank statements with reasonable care and to report account discrepancies within a reasonable time'.[106] The invitation was taken up by Montgomery J. in *Canadian Pacific Hotels* v. *Bank of Montreal*,[107] who recognized that 'while the relationship between a banker and its customer is contractual[,] the written contract or banking agreement does not necessarily govern the whole relationship'.[108] He then held, on the basis of 'commercial custom',[109] that 'a sophisticated commercial customer . . . owes a duty to the bank to operate an acceptable internal control system so that both the bank and its customer are engaged in prevention and minimization of losses occurring through forgeries'.[110]

Similarly, in *Tai Hing Cotton Mill Ltd.* v. *Liu Chong Hing Bank Ltd.*, Cons J. of the Hong Kong Court of Appeal was cognizant of the current reality, under which it is not anymore economically feasible for a bank 'to subject the signature on each and every cheque . . . to a thorough examination or comparison with the specimen signature card'. He was thus of the opinion that 'in the world in which we live today, it is a necessary condition of the relation of banker and customer that the customer should take reasonable care to see that in the operation of the account the bank is not injured'.[111]

[19]   Ultimately, both *CP Hotels* and *Tai Hing* were reversed. They thus failed to make a breakthrough and were forced into conformity with orthodoxy. First, *Tai Hing* was disposed of. In its decision,[112] the Privy Council rejected the argument that due to recent developments in the law of contract and tort, a customer owes his banker a general duty to take reasonable precautions in the management of the customer's business to prevent forged cheques from being presented for payment. Recognizing, on the basis of

---

[106] (1972), 27 D.L.R. (3d) 81 at 101 (S.C.C.). See also *Number 10 Management* v. *Royal Bank of Canada* (1976), 69 D.L.R. (3d) 99 (Man. C.A.) where Monnin JA spoke (at 103–4) of 'a duty on a bank's customer to examine bank documents regularly and to report discrepancies in such documents within a reasonable time of any discovery of error or forgeries'.
[107] (1981), 32 O.R. (2d) 560 (Ont. H.C.)   [108] Ibid. at 571.   [109] Ibid. at 573.
[110] Ibid. at 574. A majority of the Ontario Court of Appeal affirmed the decision with no written opinion: (1983), 139 D.L.R. (3d) 575. Lacourcière JA dissented. He was inclined to support the majority holding, but thought that such an innovation should be done only by statute of Parliament or by decision of the Supreme Court of Canada.
[111] [1984] 1 Lloyd's Rep. 555 at 560 (H.K. C.A.).   [112] [1986] A.C. 80.

Liverpool City Council v. *Irwin*,[113] that the test of implication is necessity, Lord Scarman nevertheless held that *Macmillan* 'decisively illustrates that it is not a *necessary* incident of the banker–customer relationship that the customer should owe his banker the wider duty of care'.[114] Accordingly, Lord Scarman could not find an implied term.[115] Nor did he believe, 'particularly ... in a commercial relationship', 'that there is anything to the advantage of the law's development in searching for a liability in tort where the parties are in a contractual relationship'.[116] The Privy Council thus rejected the existence of a specific duty on the customer to examine periodic bank statements to discover unauthorized debits and to notify the bank of them. Ultimately, the Privy Council reaffirmed the authority of *Macmillan* and *Greenwood*, and regarded them as providing for the high water mark of a customer's duty to his banker. As recalled, this duty is first, to refrain from drawing a cheque in such a manner as to facilitate unauthorized alteration, fraud, or forgery, and second, to inform the bank of any known forgery.[117] Such duties were thus treated as 'plainly necessary incidents of the relationship' between a bank and its customer.[118]

In the course of his judgment, while adhering to a quite limited customer's liability, Lord Scarman nevertheless repudiated its 'proximate cause' rationale. Thus, an argument was made that *Macmillan* 'proceeded on a now outmoded and rejected view of the nature of causal link which the law requires to be proved between breach of duty and damage' recoverable in an action on the tort of negligence.[119] In responding to this argument, while considering it to be the 'least plausible attack' on the authority of *Macmillan*, Lord Scarman acknowledged that *Macmillan* 'was decided before the Board in *The Wagon Mound*[120] ... substituted "foreseeability" for "direct cause" as the test for liability ...', However, in his view, 'it is travesty ... to suggest' that under *Macmillan*, 'causation in the law of tort had anything to do with ... limiting the duty of care of the transaction of drawing the cheque'. Rather, *Macmillan*, and hence the narrow duty of care, are premissed on the fact that 'the relationship between banker and customer is contractual and that its incidents, in the absence of express agreement, are such as must be implied into the contract because they can be seen to be obviously necessary'.[121]

It is submitted that Lord Scarman overstated the contractual basis of both *Macmillan* and *Greenwood*. In the former, Lord Finlay specifically defined the controversy as whether loss was 'a natural and direct

---

[113] [1977] A.C. 239, 254.   [114] Above, n. 112 at 105, emphasis in the original.
[115] An earlier case (preceding both *Macmillan* and *Tai Hing*, as well as *Irwin*) reaching the same conclusion on the basis of the same reasoning is *Kepitigalla*, above, n. 74 at 1025.
[116] Above, n. 112 at 107.   [117] See text to n. 75, above.   [118] Above, n. 112 at 106.
[119] Ibid. at 104.   [120] [1961] A.C. 388.   [121] Above, n. 112 at 104.

consequence of the customer's negligence in drawing the cheque'.[122] In *Greenwood*, the House of Lords downplayed the role of contract; Lord Tomlin's judgment evolved around estoppel by representation.[123] Nevertheless, in reinterpreting both decisions, *Tai Hing* re-established and strengthened their authority, at least from a doctrinal viewpoint.

[20]   In *CP Hotels*, the principal judgment of the Supreme Court of Canada[124] was given by Le Dain J. Thoroughly surveying authorities in various common law jurisdictions, including the Privy Council's advice in *Tai Hing*, he declined to extend *Macmillan* formulation as to the foundations and limits of the customer's duty of care. He thus concluded that a bank customer does not owe a duty to the bank to examine his bank statements and vouchers with reasonable care and to report any discrepancies within a reasonable time. Nor does a customer owe a duty to his bank to maintain an adequate system of internal accounting controls for the prevention or minimization of forgery losses. Le Dain J. declined to draw any distinction between a 'sophisticated commercial customer' and other customers and further rejected the existence of any implied term, whether or not based on commercial custom or usage, regarding a duty to examine a bank statement and report discrepancies. For a commercial custom or usage to apply, evidence must have been brought 'such as to support an inference of an understanding between the bank and the customer that the customer would examine his bank statements with reasonable care and report any discrepancies within a reasonable time, failing of which he would be precluded from setting up the discrepancies against the bank'.[125] No such evidence was brought forward. In the final analysis, the revolt of the lower courts in both *CP Hotels* and *Tai Hing* was thus suppressed. *Macmillan*, side by side with *Greenwood*, thus remained the governing law.

[21]   Both the Privy Council in *Tai Hing* and the Supreme Court of Canada in *CP Hotels* recognized however the potential of increasing the customer's liability by express contract, or a 'verification agreement' or 'verification clause'. In fact, in *Arrow Transfer*, the account agreement contained an express term which placed on the bank's customer a duty to examine bank statements and report any discrepancy within a prescribed time limit, failing of which the customer becomes bound by, or estopped from challenging, the correctness of, the account as kept by the bank. This term was given effect by the Supreme Court of Canada. The majority of the court read such a contract clause as estopping the customer from raising forgeries of cheques included in periodic statements for which timely

---

[122] Above, n. 7 at 789.
[123] See also *Ewing* v. *Dominion Bank*, above, n. 56, dealing with estoppel to the holder by the failure to disclose a known forgery.   [124] (1987), 40 D.L.R. (4th) 385 (S.C.C.).
[125] Ibid. at 430.

objection was not made.[126] This aspect of *Arrow Transfer* was approved in *CP Hotels.*[127]

In his minority opinion in *Arrow Transfer*, Laskin J. appears to have recognized that the mere failure by the customer to respond to a bank statement is not tantamount to the adoption of the balance and each of its items.[128] Discussing earlier Canadian precedents,[129] he specifically highlighted a distinction between 'a mere signed acknowledgment of the correctness of the account as a periodic settlement' on one hand, and 'a specific undertaking by the customer to examine the statement and vouchers and to make timely objection'.[130] He had no difficulty in agreeing that the former, being a 'mere acknowledgment of the correctness of the balance',[131] is not specific enough to preclude the customer from subsequently asserting forgeries of individual items included in the account so stated. Nonetheless, he continued, even a specific undertaking to verify each item and make timely objection, will not suffice, notwithstanding the clear contractual preclusion to raise objections later, without a specific reference in the contract, drafted by the bank, to the risk of forgery. 'There is every reason to construe [the verification agreement] *contra proferentem*, and . . . its words do not provide protection against the forgery of the drawer's signature.'[132] As already indicated, he thus preferred to find against the customer, irrespective of contract, on the basis of its negligence in employing an untrustworthy employee in a sensitive position as well as in utilizing inadequate procedures for discovering fraud.

On his part, speaking for the majority, Martland J. gave a different interpretation to the earlier authorities. In his view, what is needed to exonerate the bank is a 'contract on the part of the customer . . . to verify the statement of the account, and accept it as conclusive unless any errors were notified to the bank within a stipulated period'.[133] In the absence of

---

[126] The failure to make the timely objections was attributed to the fact, which is quite typical in such cases, that the forgery was committed by an insider in the customer organization, to whose sole attention and examination the periodic statements were subsequently brought.

[127] Above, n. 124 at 419–21, though in *obiter dictum*, since in the facts of the case, there was no verification agreement.

[128] A leading authority in this regard, is *Kepitigalla*, above, n. 74, at 1027–9, where it was held that the taking out of a passbook by the customer, and its subsequent return to the bank, does not constitute a settled account.

[129] Leading cases, in his view, were *Bank of Montreal* v. *The King* (1906), 38 S.C.R. 258 on one hand, and *Columbia Graphophone Co.* v. *Union Bank of Canada*, above, n. 101 on the other hand.   [130] Above, n. 106 at 96.

[131] Ibid.   [132] Ibid at 98.

[133] Ibid. at 87. *Arrow Transfer* was followed in Quebec. See e.g. *Les Productions Mark Blandford Inc.* v. *Caisse Populaire St-Louis de France*, [1997] R.J.Q. 1779 at 1783 (C.S.) where verification clause was nevertheless narrowly construed. See M. Lemieux, 'L'Affaire *Produc-*

such contract, even a signed acknowledgement given by the customer to the bank as to the correctness of the balance will not suffice to charge the customer.[134] At the same time, where such contract exists, it is broad enough 'to apply in respect of forged cheques'.[135]

[22]   *Tai Hing* involved three account agreements with three separate banks. The first two agreements purported to bind the customer to the balance of each periodic statement unless the customer has advised the bank of any error within a prescribed period of time.[136] The third agreement required the customer to examine all entries in each statement, advise the bank promptly of any error, and return the confirmation slip duly signed. The third agreement further provided that in the absence of any objection to the statement within a specified time limit 'the account shall be deemed to have been confirmed'.

    The first two agreements failed to require the customer to verify the account statements. They would thus have failed to meet even the standard put forward in Canada by Martland J., speaking for the majority in *Arrow Transfer*, not to mention that of Laskin J. in that case. The third agreement would have satisfied Martland J. but not Laskin J. Echoing the latter, the Privy Council held that all these clauses were not specific or 'rigorous' enough: '[i]f banks wish to impose upon their customers an express obligation to examine their monthly statements and to make those statements, in the absence of query, unchallengeable by the customer after expiry of a time limit, the burden of the objection and of the sanction imposed must be brought home to the customer'.[137] Thus, both the Supreme Court of Canada and the Privy Council accept in principle the binding effect of a verification clause, and even its ability to shift the forgery risk to the customer. Nevertheless, compared to the Canadian position, the Privy Council would require a much more specific language to that effect. In general, banks in the United Kingdom are reluctant to use such a language in their standard form account agreements.

[23]   Some uncertainty still exists where a customer actually signs a confirmation or acknowledgement as to the statement balance, containing, not to the customer's knowledge, forged cheques. In England, Bray J. appears to suggest in *Kepitigalla Rubber Estates* v. *National Bank of India*[138] that such

---

tions Mark Blandford Inc. v. *Caisse Populaire de St-Louis de France* et les accords de vérification en droit québécois' (1977) 76 *Can. B. Rev.* 478.

[134] This was his interpretation of *Bank of Montreal* v. *The King*, above, n. 129.

[135] Above, n. 106 at 87. This was the interpretation of *Columbia Graphophone* v. *Union Bank of Canada*, above, n. 101.

[136] In fact, the second agreement was poorly drafted to state that the customer is bound by the statement balance in the absence of confirmation, rather than in the absence of advice of error.   [137] Above, n. 112 at 110, *per* Lord Scarman.

[138] Above, n. 74 at 1028.

a signed document binds the customer to the entire balance, including the amount of the forged cheques. This was how Bray J. was understood in Canada in *Columbia Graphophone Co.* v. *Union Bank of Canada*.[139] In the latter, *Kepitigalla* was considered to be good law, notwithstanding the contrary authority of *Bank of Montreal* v. *The King*,[140] which was decided before *Kepitigalla* and was not even mentioned in *Columbia Graphophone*. Subsequently in Canada, Martland J. purported to reconcile the conflicting authorities, by holding in *Arrow Transfer* that a signed acknowledgement is binding upon the customer only where verification is required from the customer by contract.[141] In England, the question has not been revisited in recent years, and has not been dealt with by the Privy Council in *Tai Hing*.

In England, the need for a specific contractual clause to fasten liability **[24]** on a negligent customer is also reflected in case law concerning traveller's cheques. Both *Braithwaite* v. *Thomas Cook Travellers Cheques Ltd.*[142] and *El Awadi* v. *Bank of Credit and Commerce International SA Ltd.*[143] dealt with the issuer's duty to refund the value of traveller's cheques lost by or stolen from the purchaser before they were 'countersigned'. In *Braithwaite*, a plastic bag containing a large quantity of traveller's cheques was stolen from the purchaser in the course of a London underground ride. The ride took place late at night, when the purchaser was asleep with the bag on his lap, after an extremely long day, concluded with heavy drinking at various pubs. The stolen bag also visibly contained a carton of cigarettes. In *El Awadi*, a plastic bag containing a large quantity of traveller's cheques was stolen from the purchaser's car where it had been left unattended. The car itself was parked unattended for significant time stretches during less than a twenty-four-hour period.

In *Braithwaite*, the purchaser's contract required the issuer to replace or refund the value of lost or stolen traveller's cheques, provided the purchaser complied with certain conditions. Under one of these conditions, the purchaser was obliged to safeguard each instrument against loss or theft. The court declined to read this clause literally and held that mere momentary inadvertence resulting in theft would not have disentitled the purchaser to a refund. Furthermore, the Court required the issuer to prove negligence, as well as a causal link between the purchaser's failure to safeguard the instruments and the ultimate loss. Nevertheless, in the facts of the case, both negligence beyond momentary inadvertence and causal link were proved, and the purchaser's action was consequently dismissed.

---

[139] Above, n. 101 at 745.
[141] See text around nn. 133–5, above.
[142] [1989] Q.B. 553.
[140] Above, n. 129.
[143] [1990] 1 Q.B. 606.

Conversely, no corresponding contractual term existed in *El Awadi*. Finding the purchaser 'guilty of the most serious negligence',[144] the court nevertheless declined to read any implied qualification to the issuer's refund obligation and held for the purchaser.

Both *Braithwaite* and *El Awadi* are consistent with the earlier authority of *Fellus* v. *National Westminster Bank*.[145] In the latter case, the contract stipulated that a refund by the issuer for lost or stolen traveller's cheques is precluded in the case of 'undue negligence'. However, in the facts of the case, the issuer failed to prove any 'undue negligence' of the purchaser leading to the loss; the instruments fell, or were stolen, from the purchaser's overcoat pocket while he carried it on his arm due to the heat.

According to a summary of this jurisprudence, 'even in the absence of an express contractual provision an issuer of travellers' cheques will be regarded as legally bound to refund the value of lost or stolen [such] cheques'. Furthermore, 'the law will not readily imply a term protecting issuers against the recklessness or negligence of their customers, although [courts] will of course give effect to express contractual provisions precluding the right of a negligent purchaser to reimbursement'. Accordingly, 'banks can and should readily protect themselves by carefully drawn contracts'.[146] It can plausibly be argued that this jurisprudence may hint as to the possible construction of a clause that would require a customer to safeguard his chequebooks.[147]

[25]　　　The duty of a bank to its customer to exercise 'reasonable care and skill' in the performance of its banking services is well established.[148] In fact, this duty was characterized as '[t]he most significant implied term' in the banking contract.[149] There is however no uniform rule as to whether a bank customer to whom forgery loss is allocated may nevertheless exonerate himself, in full or in part, on the basis of the bank's negligence that has contributed to the loss. In principle, in the context of the tort of negligence, contributory or comparative negligence is available to apportion

---

[144] Ibid at 615.　　　[145] (1983), 133 N.L.J. 766 (Q.B.).

[146] A. Pugh-Thomas, 'Travellers' Cheques—Who Carries the Loss?' [1989] 4 J.I.B.L. 75, 80–1.

[147] A duty to take care of chequebooks is fastened in the UK on personal customers pursuant to ¶14.1 of the Banking Code (January 2001) discussed in 2.A(v) s. 28 above. Such a duty may also appear in a standard form account agreement in Israel. See R. Ben-Oliel, *Banking Law—General Part* (Jerusalem: Sacher Institute, 1996), 72–3 [in Hebrew]. *Quaere*, whether such a provision is to be viewed as an onerous term or disclaimer clause. For onerous terms and disclaimer clauses in accounts agreements, under the laws of the various jurisdictions, see 2.A(iv) and 2.C(iii) and (iv) above.

[148] *Hilton* v. *Westminster Bank Ltd.* (1926), 135 L.T. 358 at 362 (C.A.), where the duty was stated by Atkin LJ to exist in relation to 'communications which the customer sends', is a leading authority.

[149] B. Crawford, *Crawford and Falconbridge, Banking and Bills of Exchange*, 8th edn. vol. i (Toronto: Canada Law Book, 1986) at 746.

the loss according to the degree of fault. In the context of estoppel, it was held in *Greenwood* v. *Martins Bank Ltd.*, that a negligent bank may nevertheless invoke its customer's estoppel, where available, and shift the entire loss to the estopped customer. This was decided by Scrutton LJ with respect to cheques whose forgery was not caused by the customer's negligence; namely, where loss occurred due to the customer's failure to advise the bank of the forgeries, a failure which precluded effective recourse from the forger, and only in connection with such forgeries. As was explained by Scrutton LJ, 'while the carelessness of the Bank was a proximate cause of the Bank's loss in paying [such] forged cheques, it was not the proximate cause of the Bank's losing its right of action against the forger'.[150] This reasoning may not be applicable where each party's negligence was a proximate cause,[151] and is anyway of doubtful validity today, in light of the repudiation of the proximity rationale in *Tai Hing*.[152] Nevertheless, the position overlooking the bank's negligence was followed in Israel, also with respect to cheques forged after the customer failed to advise the bank of earlier forgeries, specifically where the customer's fault was judged to be more instrumental in causing the loss.[153]

In the context of contract, in the absence of an express provision dealing with the bank's negligence, the position may depend on the judicial interpretation of the contractual term. But even in the context of a reciprocal contractually implied duty of care owed by a bank to its customer,[154] the question is whether its breach is taken into account either as contributory negligence or as grounds for exonerating the customer altogether from responsibility for his own negligence. Alternatively, there may be circumstances where the breach of the bank's duty may not be taken into account in assessing the negligent customer's responsibility for the loss. So far, we derive only limited and inconclusive guidance from case law with respect to the impact of the bank's negligence upon the customer's breach of a contractually implied or express duty of care.

It is noteworthy that a typical verification clause does not refer to negligence. In Canada, there is no agreement as to whether a negligent bank may rely on a verification clause and fasten the entire liability on a breaching customer. In *Le Cercle Universitaire d'Ottawa* v. *National Bank*,[155] the verification clause was found to protect the bank from liability for its own

---

[150] Above, n. 53 at 384 (C.A.), *aff'd*, on this point, above, n. 56 at 58–9 (H.L.).

[151] For this interpretation of Scrutton LJ's position see, e.g. A. Barak, 'Forgery in Cheque Drawing: Goal and Means in Risk Allocation Between Bank and Customer' (1967–8), 1 *Mishpatim* 134, 142 and n. 49 [in Hebrew].

[152] See discussion at text around nn. 120–1, above.

[153] See cases cited in n. 103, above. For the scope and a critique of this aspect of *Greenwood*, as well as of its application in Israel, see Barak, above, n. 151 at 141–5.

[154] For the mutuality of the contractual duties of a banker and customer, see *Greenwood*, above, n. 53 at 380–1.   [155] (1987), 61 O.R. (2d) 456 (H.C.).

negligence in allowing an employee of its customer to deposit a cheque into the employee's own account. The cheque was payable to the employer and endorsed restrictively for deposit to the employer's account only. Similarly, in *Don Bodkin Leasing* v. *Toronto Dominion Bank*,[156] a verification clause was found to protect a bank that negligently acted on an oral direction of a non-signing officer in procuring a series of bank drafts payable to himself and an accomplice. Both judges found support for their interpretation of the verification clauses from the majority judgment in *Arrow Transfer*.[157] However, such interpretation of the verification clause, effectively turns it, at least in part, into an implied disclaimer, of the bank's duty of care.[158] Accordingly, other cases declined to extend the coverage of verification clauses to protect a negligent payor bank and in interpreting such agreements, have instead, followed the principle of strict construction, advocated by Laskin J.'s separate judgment in *Arrow Transfer*.[159]

[26]   Dissatisfaction with *Tai Hing*, namely with the need for an express contractual term to shift forgery losses to a negligent customer, led the Banking Review Committee in the United Kingdom to propose statutory law reform. The committee thus endorsed the passing of 'a statutory provision whereby, in an action against a bank ... arising from an unauthorized payment, contributory negligence may be raised as a defence, but only if the court is satisfied that the degree of negligence shown by the plaintiff is sufficiently serious'.[160] This would impose on the customer a broad duty of care to prevent as well as to detect forgeries. Presumably, in the case of mutual breaches by the parties, namely negligence by both the customer and the bank, loss is to be apportioned according to the degree of fault. So far, however, no action was taken on this recommendation.

[27]   Law reform efforts in the area have proved to be more effective in South Africa. A proposal to amend the South African Bills of Exchange Act

---

[156] (1993), 14 O.R. (3d) 571 (Gen. Div.); *aff'd*, (1998) 40 O.R. (3d) 262.

[157] See also *Kelly Funeral Home* v. *CIBC* (1990), 72 D.L.R. (4th) 276 (Ont. H.C.).

[158] A disclaimer clause purporting to exclude bank liability notwithstanding the bank's fault was narrowly construed and could not be invoked by a negligent bank in *CIBC* v. *Haley* (1979), 100 D.L.R. (3d) 470 (N.B. C.A.). See discussion on that case (as well as on *CIBC* v. *Schweitzer* [1976] W.W.D. 9 (Alta. Dist. Ct.)) by M. H. Ogilvie, *Canadian Banking Law* (Toronto: Carswell, 1991) at 424. Crawford is less enthusiastic: above, n. 149 at 748–9.

[159] See e.g. *Cavell Developments* v. *Royal Bank of Canada* (1991), 54 B.C.L.R. (2d) 1 (B.C. C.A.); *239199 Alberta* v. *Patel* (1992), 1 Alta. L.R. (3d) 215 (Q.B.), and *Armstrong Baum Plumbing & Heating* v. *Toronto-Dominion Bank* (18 Feb. 1994), Toronto 91-CQ-6231 (Ont. Ct. Gen. Div.). See also *Action Petroleum Services Ltd.* v. *Prince Albert Credit Union Ltd.* [1999] S.J. No. 767 (Sask. Q.B.), on-line: QL (SJ). The apportionment of loss according to the degree of fault, rather than 'an all or nothing solution', is advocated by N. Rafferty, 'Account Verification Agreements: When Can a Bank Protect Itself against Its Own Negligence?' (1993), 8 B.F.L.R. 403.

[160] R. B. Jack (chairman), *Banking Services: Law and Practice—Report by the Review Committee* (London: Her Majesty's Stationery Office, 1989) at 43.

included a new provision, above section 73, entitled 'Prevention of Fraud'. The accompanying memorandum on objectives (April 1996) rationalized the proposal by explaining that

Banks have historically been liable in circumstances in which a customer's negligence has enabled the customer's agent or a third party to forge and receive payment on a cheque. Banks are unable either to prevent or to detect such frauds and there is presently no incentive for customers to take the necessary precautions. The new section will ensure that those most able to prevent and detect fraud are obliged to do so.

The original language fastened reciprocal duties on the drawee and every drawer of a cheque. The drawee was required to 'exercise reasonable care in the payment of cheques', while the drawer[161] was to 'exercise reasonable care in the custody of cheque forms and the drawing of cheques'. A further duty was fastened only on a bank customer required by law to have his financial statements audited. Such a person was required to 'exercise reasonable care in operating his account'. In a case where both the customer and the drawee bank broke their respective duties, damages were to be apportioned according to the degree of each party's fault.

A subsequent Bill[162] kept the distinction between the financially auditable customer and any other customer, but applied it differently, and abandoned the explicit reference to the apportionment of losses. Proposed s. 72B had two principal elements. First, it compelled a bank customer required by law to have his financial statements audited, and not every customer as in the proposal, to 'exercise reasonable care in the custody of cheque forms, the drawing of cheques and the operating of his account'. Second, a bank that paid a forged cheque 'in good faith and without negligence' was entitled to recover from the customer on whose account the forged cheque was drawn, loss caused by the customer's negligence.[163]

---

[161] The duty was stated to apply to 'the drawer', which appears to exclude a bank customer whose drawer's signature has been forged on a blank cheque form stolen from, or lost by, him due to his failure to exercise reasonable care in the custody thereof. This must have been an oversight; the provision must have been taken as intending to apply also to the 'purported drawer', namely the bank customer whose drawer's signature has been forged. In any event, an earlier version specifically referred to the 'customer' rather than to the 'drawer'. It imposed on every bank customer a duty to 'exercise reasonable care towards the drawee in the drawing and custody of cheques and in the operation of his account.' See J. T. Pretorius, 'The Forgery of a Drawer's Signature on a Cheque: Proposals for Reform of the Southern African Law', in Visser (ed.), *Essays in Memory of Ellison Kahn* (Cape Town: Juta, 1989), 271 at 288.

[162] Bills of Exchange Amendment Bill 1998, Republic of South Africa Government Gazette, Vol. 397, No. 19075, 21 July 1998.

[163] A third element would have allowed a depositary bank to put a hold on funds represented by a cheque deposited by 'a depositor who is—on the face of it—not a holder of the cheque', for a period of up to one day, 'as may be required to obtain urgent relief from a court'.

This applied to any customer, not necessarily the financially auditable one; arguably, however, there was nothing to preclude from treating such negligence as covering also the custody of cheque forms, a duty explicitly stated to be confined to the sophisticated customer.[164]

As finally adopted, s. 72B (proclaimed 1 March 2001) abandoned the duty of care in the drawing of cheques, as well as the express right of the drawee bank to recover from a negligent customer. It further substituted a duty 'in the reconciliation of . . . bank statements' for a duty 'in . . . operating [the] account'.[164a] It thus requires a financially auditable or accountable person, namely, a sophisticated business customer, to 'exercise reasonable care in the custody of cheque forms and in the reconciliation of . . . bank statements'. While the recourse of a bank against a person in breach of such provision can easily be implied, no similar implication can be made with regard to an unsophisticated customer; it now abundantly clear that the latter is not affected at all by the new provision, which, however, remains silent on loss apportionment where both the bank and the customer are negligent.

The duty to examine bank statements so as to discover and promptly report any forgery must be taken as included in the duty to exercise reasonable care in the reconciliation of bank statements. In turn, the duty to reconcile bank statements, is not only with respect to forged cheques charged to the account; rather it, it is in connection with any contested item. In fastening on a sophisticated bank customer both such duty, and the duty of care in the custody of cheque forms, the effect of s. 72B is to render South African law that governs the allocation of forged cheque losses closer the law on the subject applicable in civil law jurisdictions.

(IV) AMERICAN LAW

[28] Similarly to English law, the starting point under the UCC is that a customer is not liable with respect to a forged cheque[165] or unauthorized alteration fraudulently made.[166] However, the Code departed from the complex position of English law in several major respects.

First, in an apparent clear departure from the Bills of Exchange Act,

---

[164] To borrow the language of Montgomery J. in *CP Hotels*, above, text around nn. 107–10.
[164a] Bills of Exchange Amendment Act 2000, (Act No. 56 of 2000) Govt Gazette 21846, 6 December 2000. As passed, s. 72B also abandoned the third element, relating to one-day funds holding by a depositary bank, as set out in n. 163, above.
[165] UCC §3–403(a).   [166] UCC §3–407(b).

UCC §3–403(a) provides that '[a]n unauthorized signature may be rati-fied'.[167] Official Comment 3 explains that

Ratification is a retroactive adoption of the unauthorized signature by the person whose name is signed and may be found from conduct as well as from express statements. For example, it may be found from the retention of benefits received in the transaction with knowledge of the unauthorized signature. Although the forger is not an agent, ratification is governed by the rules and principles applica-ble to ratification of unauthorized acts of an agent.

The exclusion of ratification under the Bills of Exchange Act is designed to prevent any implication as to the possible effect of ratification to release the forger from civil or criminal liability, a possibility which is specifically eliminated for ratification under UCC §3–403(c). Article 3 improves on the BEA position in effectively eliminating the consideration requirement from adoption, allowing it to be a unilateral act, and not using the forger's liability as grounds for exonerating a customer who has chosen to be bound by a forged cheque which appears to have emanated from that customer.[168]

A second point of departure from English law is more fundamental. **[29]** Thus, under UCC §3–407(c), vis-à-vis an innocent party, a signer of an incomplete instrument completed subsequent to signature by someone other than the signer and without the signer's authority, is bound accord-ing to the terms of the instrument as completed. An incomplete instru-ment is defined to mean 'a signed writing, whether or not issued by the signer, the contents of which show at the time of signing that it is incom-plete but that the signer intended it to be completed by the addition of words or numbers'.[169] Similarly, and on this point, in line with English law, one who pleads the defence of *non est factum*, may be met by a plea based on his negligence in signing the document.[170]

Third, and perhaps most significantly, the UCC provides for broad **[30]** duties of care on the part of bank customers and establishes a compre-hensive scheme for the allocation of forgery losses attributed to fault. This

---

[167] Conversely, BEA s. 24(2) in the UK, s. 23(b) in Israel, s. 22 in South Africa, and s.48(2) in Canada appear not to preclude only 'the ratification of an unauthorized signature not amounting to a forgery'.

[168] For the comparable BEA position, see s. 9, above.

[169] UCC §3–115(a). For the comparable English position, requiring both delivery of the incomplete instrument with an authority to issue, and the subsequent negotiation of the complete instrument to a holder in due course, see text around nn. 65–70, above.

[170] See UCC §3–305(a)(1)(iii) providing for the defence (available against a holder in due course under UCC §3–305(b)) of 'fraud that induced the obligor to sign the instrument with neither knowledge nor reasonable opportunity to learn of its character or its essential terms'. Accordingly, the defence is unavailable to one who negligently signed a document, notwithstanding the existence of a 'reasonable opportunity to learn of its character or its essential terms'. For the comparable English position, see text and nn. 69–70, above.

is done in two provisions. While §3–406 deals generally with negligence contributing to forged signature or alteration of instrument, §4–406 provides for a customer's specific duty to discover and report unauthorized signature or alteration.

The general principle is provided for in UCC §3–406(a):

> A person whose failure to exercise ordinary care substantially contributes to an alteration of an instrument or to the making of a forged signature on an instrument is precluded from asserting the alteration or the forgery against a person who, in good faith, pays the instrument or takes it for value or for collection.

The scope of the customer's duty under §3–406(a) is quite broad. It applies to the unauthorized alteration of the instrument, as well as the forgery of a signature, not necessarily that of the negligent party, and is not restricted to the bank and customer relationship; rather, it provides for a comprehensive duty of care, also specifically benefiting a subsequent innocent holder.

[31]   In the Official Comment, the drafters specifically acknowledged that '[w]ith respect to alteration, §3–406 adopts the doctrine of *Young* v. *Grote*, . . . which held that a drawer who so negligently draws an instrument as to facilitate its material alteration is liable to a drawee who pays the altered instrument in good faith'. They further explained that '[b]y issuing the instrument and 'setting it afloat upon a sea of strangers' the . . . drawer voluntarily enters into a relation with later holders which justifies imposition of a duty of care. In this respect an instrument so negligently drawn as to facilitate alteration does not differ in principle from an instrument containing blanks which may be filled . . .' They thus chose to significantly expand the customer's duty of care beyond its narrow grounds in English law.[171]

Several specific points are highlighted by the Official Comments as follows:

1. No attempt is made to define particular conduct that will constitute 'failure to exercise ordinary care' that 'substantially contributes to an alteration of an instrument or to the making of a forged signature on an instrument' so as to give rise to the preclusion under §3–406(a).[172] Under UCC §3–103(a)(7), ' "Ordinary" care in the case of a person engaged in business means observance of reasonable commercial standards, prevailing in the area in which the person is located, with respect to the business in which the person is engaged.' One of the examples given by the Official

---

[171] For *Young* v. *Grote* in English law, see text around nn. 49–50 and 56–64, above.

[172] For the view that the issue of negligence is thus left strictly to the fact finder on a case-by-case basis, see, e.g. *Chicago Heights Currency Exchange* v. *Par Steel Products & Service Co.* 463 N.E. 2d 829 at 830 (Ill. App. 1st Cir. 1984). See also *Curtis* v. *Hibernia National Bank* 522 So. 2d 705 at 708 (La. App. 5th Cir. 1988).

Comment to the 'failure to exercise ordinary care' is that of an employer leaving blank cheque forms and the rubber stamp of his signature in an unlocked desk drawer.[173]

2. Under §3–406(a), the negligent party, in our case, the bank customer, becomes estopped from asserting the alteration or forgery. He does not become liable in tort for damages. Stated otherwise, the principle underlying the provision is not tort. Nor is it implied contract. Rather, it is estoppel, based on a duty of care addressed to the drawee as well as to a subsequent holder. As long as the party asserting the estoppel was not negligent, a point to be addressed shortly, the effect of the provision is to render the estopped negligent customer liable for the full amount of the cheque, regardless of the actual loss sustained by the party asserting the estoppel.

3. The party estopped from asserting the alteration or forgery must have 'substantially contribut[ed]' to the alteration or forgery. This 'substantially contributes' test was specifically preferred to the 'direct and proximate cause test' which might have required a more strict and direct causal link between the customer's negligence and the loss caused by the alteration or forgery.[174]

Cases considering whether particular conduct constituted 'failure to exercise ordinary care' which 'substantially contribut[ed]' to forgery cover instances such as involving (i) the hiring, supervising, or vouching for an employee, (ii) reviewing bank statements, and (iii) the safekeeping of blank cheques or authenticating devices.[175]

Finally, §3–406 adopts a concept of comparative negligence.[176] Thus, **[32]** §3–406(b), deals with the case where the person asserting the preclusion under subsection (a), namely either the drawee bank or a subsequent holder, 'fails to exercise ordinary care in paying or taking the instrument'. As recalled,[177] the standard of 'ordinary care' in the case of a person engaged in business is stated in UCC §3–103(a)(7) to be the 'observance of reasonable commercial standards'. Where the failure 'to exercise

---

[173] Case No. 1 in Official Comment 3 to UCC §3–406.

[174] Undoubtedly, this conclusion is confirmed by the English experience, discussed in text around nn. 92–4, above. The reference to the 'proximate cause' in *Commercial Credit Equipment Corp.* v. *First Alabama Bank of Montgomery* 636 F.2d 1051 at 1055 (5th Cir. 1981) is thus unfortunate.

[175] For a not so up-to-date account, see G. D. Spivey, 'Commercial Paper: What Amounts to "Negligence Contributing to Alteration or Unauthorized Signature" under UCC §3–406' (1975), 67 A.L.R. 3d 144, particularly at 169–74.

[176] This is in departure from the previous provision of the pre-1990 Official Text, under which the preclusion of the negligent party was effective 'against a holder in due course or . . . a drawee . . . who pays the instrument in good faith and in accordance with . . . reasonable commercial standards'. Stated otherwise, a negligent drawee could not assert the preclusion of the negligent customer, regardless of the degree of fault or causation.

[177] See text following n. 172, above.

ordinary care' of the person asserting the preclusion 'substantially contributes to loss', the loss is apportioned between the precluded person, in
our case the bank customer, and the person asserting the preclusion,
namely, either the bank or the subsequent holder, 'according to the extent
to which the failure of each to exercise ordinary care contributes to the
loss'. For the person asserting the preclusion, as for the precluded person,[178] neither 'ordinary care' in general, nor the 'observance of reasonable
commercial standards' in particular,[179] is defined. However, under UCC
§3–103(a)(7),

In the case of a bank that takes an instrument for processing for collection or payment by automated means, *reasonable commercial standards do not require the bank to
examine the instrument* if the failure to examine does not violate the bank's prescribed procedures and the bank's procedures do not vary unreasonably from
general banking usage not disapproved by this Article or Article 4. [emphasis
added]

Elsewhere, this rule is rationalized on the encouragement of banks to
adopt 'an automated collection or payment procedure in order to deal
with the great volume of items at a lower cost to all customers'[180] This rule
effectively means, that by itself, the drawee bank's failure to examine
individually a forged cheque, which is the only means to disclose unskilful forgery, may not constitute a failure to exercise ordinary care, and
hence, would not justify the shifting of loss away from a negligent
customer.

[33]   The reciprocal standard of both the precluded party, in our case the customer under §3–406(a), and the person asserting the preclusion, namely,
either the drawee bank or a subsequent holder under §3–406(b), is that of
'ordinary care'.[181] Under UCC §1–102(3), 'the obligations of good faith,
diligence, reasonableness and care . . . may not be disclaimed by agreement but the parties may by agreement determine the standards
by which the performance of such obligations is to be measured if such
standards are not manifestly unreasonable'. Under UCC §3–406(c), the
burden of proving failure to exercise ordinary care by the precluded person, in our case the bank customer, is on the person asserting the preclu-

---

[178] See above, n. 172 and text around it.

[179] It was held in connection with a drawee bank that what constitutes 'reasonable commercial standards' is a mixed question of fact and law. See *Valley Bank* v. *Niebaur* 819 P. 2d
1133 at 1141 (Idaho 1991).

[180] Comment 4 to UCC §4–406. No corresponding rule existed in the pre-1990 Official
Text. See e.g. *Herzog, Engstrom and Koplovitz, PC* v. *Union National Bank* 640 N.Y.S. 2d 703
(A.D. 3 Dept. 1996).

[181] In fact, notwithstanding cases cited in nn. 172 and 179, above, there is no justification
for a different standard to determine what constitutes failure 'to exercise ordinary care' in
the case of a customer (question of fact) and the drawee bank (mixed question of fact and
law). Arguably, no distinction was intended.

sion, namely, either the drawee bank, or a subsequent holder. Conversely, the burden of proving failure to exercise ordinary care by the person asserting the preclusion is on the precluded person.

As indicated, on the top of the general duty of care under UCC §3–406, **[34]** a bank customer has, under UCC §4–406, a specific duty to discover and report unauthorized signature or alteration.[182] This provision is restricted to the bank and customer relationship. It arises where the bank provides the customer with a statement of account or cancelled cheques. Thus, under §4–406(c),

If a bank sends or makes available a statement of account or items[183] . . . the customer must exercise reasonable promptness in examining the statement or the items to determine whether any payment was not authorized because of an alteration of an item or because a purported signature by or on behalf of the customer was not authorized. If, based on the statement or items provided, the customer should reasonably have discovered the unauthorized payment, the customer must promptly notify the bank of the relevant facts.

Where with respect to an item, the bank proves that the customer failed to comply with these duties, the customer becomes precluded, under subsection (d), from asserting against the bank,

(1) the customer's unauthorized signature or any alternation on the item, if the bank also proves that it suffered a loss by reason of the failure; and

(2) the customer's unauthorized signature or alteration by the same wrongdoer on any other item paid in good faith by the bank if the payment was made before the bank received notice from the customer of the unauthorized signature or alteration and after the customer had been afforded a reasonable period of time, not

---

[182] In a clear departure from English law, such a duty has existed in American common law, and thus preceded the introduction of the UCC. An early leading authority is *Leather Manufacturers' National Bank* v. *Morgan* (1886), 117 U.S. 96, 29 Law. Ed. 811 (mentioned by Le Dain J in *CP Hotels*, above, n. 124 at 392). See also *First National Bank* v. *Allen* 14 So. 335 (Ala. 1893).

[183] The bank's duties in sending or making available to the customer a statement of account or items are provided for in subsections (a) and (b). While historically the customer's duty of care to discover and report forged cheques included in a periodic bank statement was linked to the practice of returning to the customers the cheques themselves, the duty is stated to exist today regardless of the practice. In departure from the previous Official Text (old UCC §4–406(1)), the physical return of the items themselves is accordingly no longer absolutely required. Instead, the statement of account may provide sufficient information 'to allow the customer reasonably to identify the items paid'. Each item must thus be described 'by item number, amount, and date of payment'. Payee name and date of issue need not be included. Items not physically returned, or their copies, must be retained and made available to the customer upon request, until the expiration of seven years.

exceeding 30 days,[184] in which to examine the item or statement of account and notify the bank.

[35]   The first clause of this subsection (d) covers loss created by the delay in advising the bank of the forgery. The scenario contemplated is that where during the delay the forger either absconded or became impecunious. Actual loss must thus be proved by the bank. However, recovery by the bank that proved actual loss, is in the full amount of the cheque. The second clause contemplates loss occurring by the repetition of the forgery by the same wrongdoer that could have been prevented had the customer discovered the earlier one in a timely manner. In this context, the customer's failure to discover and advise the bank caused the loss created by the subsequent forgeries. Loss is thus irrebuttably presumed to be in the amount of the subsequent forged items,[185] and so is the amount to be recovered from the estopped customer.

It is noteworthy that the customer's duty under subsection (c) is to 'exercise reasonable promptness in examining the statement or the items' and promptly notify the bank of facts 'the customer should reasonably have discovered' on the basis of 'the statement or items provided'. The previous Official Text of the provision[186] was more definite in imposing on the customer a duty of care. It required the customer to 'exercise reasonable care and promptness to examine the statement and items . . .' with the view of discovering 'his unauthorized signature or any alteration on an item', and to 'notify the bank promptly after discovery thereof'.[187] Nevertheless, even the current language ought better to be understood in terms of the customer's duty of care, rather than as attributing to the customer knowledge of forged items contained in a statement sent to the customer.[188] It may accordingly be plausibly argued that no breach of present subsection (c), and hence, no preclusion under subsection (d), arise where the delay was justified, as for example, due to illness or temporary absence of the customer. Presumably, even an occasional or otherwise explicable office oversight not amounting to negligence could be

---

[184] Under the previous Official Text, the period was fourteen days only. In the drafters' view, '[a]lthough the 14-day period may have been sufficient when the original version of Article 4 was drafted in the 1950s, given the much greater volume of checks at the time of the revision, a longer period was viewed as more appropriate'. See Comment 2 to §4–406.

[185] Consider the following numerical example: the value of the forged cheques included in the first statement was 3. The customer did not discover the forgeries which enabled the forger to keep forging. When the forgeries were discovered, the value of those committed subsequent to the first statement was 30. At that point the forger absconded. Under para. (d)(2), the customer is precluded from asserting the forgeries of those subsequent cheques totalling 30. To assert preclusion as to the first cheques totalling 3, the bank must prove, under para. (d)(1), that shortly after the first statement, recovery from the forger would have been feasible, at least in part.   [186] Pre-1990 UCC §4–406(1).

[187] For a discussion, see e.g. *Key Bank of Florida* v. *First United Land Title Co.* 502 So. 2d 1280 at 1283 (Fla. App. 2 Dist. 1987).   [188] Compare text and n. 100, above.

excused.[189] The thirty-day limit under para. (d)(2) is not absolute; rather, it is triggered only upon the breach of the principal duty under subsection (c), as proved by the bank. Unfortunately, however, in situations where the forger was an employee of the customer, by attributing to the customer the forger's knowledge,[190] courts may have effectively replaced the customer's duty of care to discover and report forgery, mandated by UCC §4–406, by a customer's absolute responsibility to wrongs carried out in the customer's own organization or sphere.

As under UCC §3–406, the customer's responsibility under UCC §4–406 is premised on preclusion, and neither on contract nor on torts. Similarly, in the footsteps of §3–406, UCC §4–406 adopts the concept of comparative negligence.[191] According to UCC §4–406(e), **[36]**

> If subsection (d) applies and the customer proves that the bank failed to exercise ordinary care in paying the item and that the failure substantially contributed to loss, the loss is allocated between the customer precluded and the bank asserting the preclusion according to the extent to which the failure of the customer to comply with subsection (c) and the failure of the bank to exercise ordinary care contributed to the loss.

Conversely, subsection (e) continues, '[i]f the customer proves that the bank did not pay the item in good faith, the preclusion under subsection (d) does not apply'.

As in connection with UCC §3–406, the bank's 'ordinary care' is defined to provide that sight examination of individual cheques is not required, provided the drawee bank's procedure is reasonable and is commonly followed by other comparable banks in the area.[192] This is in recognition of the effects of current practices of high-volume automated cheque processing and the desirability of keeping cheque-processing costs low to customers.[193] Under UCC §4–103(a), contracting parties 'cannot disclaim a bank's responsibility for its lack of good faith or failure to exercise ordinary care or limit the measure of damages for the lack or failure'. They may, however, 'determine by agreement the standards by which the bank's responsibility is to be measured', but only 'if those standards are not manifestly unreasonable'.[194]

---

[189] This is a plausible interpretation of *Jackson* v. *First National Bank of Memphis* 403 S.W. 2d 109 (Tenn. C.A. 1966).

[190] For relevant case law see White and Summers, 3rd edn., above, n. 100 at 696 and n. 5.

[191] As in connection with §3–406, this is an innovation of the 1990 Official Text. Under previous UCC §4–406(3), '[t]he [customer's] preclusion ... does not apply if the customer establishes lack of ordinary care on the part of the bank in paying the item(s)'.

[192] See UCC §3–103(a)(7), applicable to Article 4 by UCC §4–104(c).

[193] See Comment 4 to UCC§ t4–406.

[194] Similarly, so far as the customer's duties are concerned, under UCC §1–102(3), 'the obligations of good faith, diligence, reasonableness and care ... may not be disclaimed by

[37]   In sum, UCC §4–406 fastens on the customer and bank reciprocal duties. The customer is required to exercise reasonable promptness in examining bank statements or cheques and discovering and reporting forgeries. The bank is required to exercise ordinary care and good faith in paying cheques. The breach of the customer's duty entitles the bank to raise preclusion. However, where the breaching customer is able to prove the bank's failure to exercise ordinary care, loss is allocated according to the degree of fault. Conversely, where the defaulting customer is able to prove the bank's breach of the good faith duty, no preclusion can be asserted against the customer and loss is allocated to the bank.

Finally, subsection (f) is a 'statute of repose'. It effectively superimposes a year limit to the customer's right to contest forged cheques, irrespective of compliance with, or breach of, the customer's and bank's reciprocal duties of care.[195] Thereunder,

> Without regard to care or lack of care either of the customer or the bank, a customer who does not within one year after the statement or items are made available to the customer … discover and report the customer's unauthorized signature on or any alteration on the item is precluded from asserting against the bank the unauthorized signature or alteration.

(v) Reflections on the Desired Rule

[38]   Around thirty years ago, in an important article dealing with the allocation of forged cheque losses between the bank and its customer,[196] Barak indicated the existence of two tests for the desired rule: risk distribution and fault. Obviously, compared to the customer, the bank is the better risk bearer, who is able to distribute losses among all customers, whether in the form of bank charges, or through the availability of insurance. Conversely, a customer on whom forgery loss is allocated is unable to distribute losses. Quite the contrary, the customer may be forced to insolvency, which may cause a chain reaction further affecting the economic stability of trade counterparties.

Prima facie, the better test is then risk distribution, which would allocate the loss initially onto the bank. This test actually enjoys some judicial

agreement but the parties may by agreement determine the standards by which the performance of such obligations is to be measured if such standards are not manifestly unreasonable'.

[195] Interestingly, breach of the bank's good faith obligation is not mentioned. Presumably, this means that the customer is entitled to contest forged cheques paid in bad faith even beyond the year limit.   [196] Above, n. 151.

endorsement in England[197] as well as in Canada.[198] However, its adoption overlooks the importance of fault in loss reduction, minimization, or even prevention. Allocating losses to the party at fault would encourage diligence and the maintenance of sound practices to detect and eliminate forgery losses.[199]

However, beside loss distribution, the allocation of forgery losses to banks will encourage forgery detection as well as promote higher investment in technologies directed to that end.[200] This provides further support to the rule, existing in the common law,[201] under the UCC,[202] as well as in some but not all civil law jurisdictions,[203] under which forgery losses are not allocated to a non-negligent customer. From this perspective, in the absence of fault, loss allocation to the bank is consistent with loss reduction and prevention.

As indicated, under UCC Article 3, the 'substantially contributes' test **[39]** was specifically preferred to the 'direct and proximate cause test', which might have required a more strict and direct causal link between the customer's negligence and the loss caused by the alteration or forgery. As well, the customer's general duty of care is not only towards the bank but is also owed to subsequent holders. Furthermore, in conformity with a logical application of the fault test, the principle of comparative or contributory negligence is fully recognized in both Articles 3 and 4. The fault test is thus well implemented by the UCC preclusion scheme relating to cheques, as well as in principle, reciprocal common law duties of care in torts.

The same can also be said on the allocation of forgery losses according to fault principles under the various civil codes. This is correct for the common law only in relation to material alteration as well as to loss allocation under an effective verification agreement. In general, however, in the absence of either knowledge or an effective verification agreement, the common law allocates forged drawer's signature losses to the bank. This does not recognize fault as the determinant test. Similarly, estoppel in English law, as well as the Canadian interpretation of verification clauses, do not incorporate comparative negligence principles and require

---

[197] See e.g. *Kepitigalla*, above, n. 74 at 1026.

[198] See e.g. concurring judgment of La Forest J. in *CP Hotels*, above, n. 124 at 434, which specifically follows *Kepitigalla*.

[199] The allocation of forgery losses to a negligent customer was criticized by E. Rubin, 'Efficiency, Equity, and the Proposed Revision of Articles 3 and 4' (1991), 42 Ala. L.R. 551, 564–70, as well as by Luntz, above, n. 64 at 109. As will be seen below, I accept this criticism only so far as it pertains to the elevation of the customer's fault to the prevailing principle in the loss allocation scheme.

[200] A point stressed e.g. by both Rubin, ibid. at 568–9, as well as Luntz, ibid.

[201] Above, text around nn. 40–50.   [202] Above, text around nn. 165–6.

[203] Above, text around nn. 29–30.

strict bank and customer privity. As such, they are not effective tools to fully implement the fault test. Between the UCC preclusion scheme and reciprocal duties of care in torts, the former seems to be more efficient, as recovery bypasses the further complexity of considering the chance of collecting from the forger.

[40]   It seems to me that contract is a poor vehicle for implementing the fault test. While the existence of an implied term is unclear,[204] the scope of an express term may depend on the way it is drafted, invariably by the bank, as well as by the interpretation given to it by courts,[205] not to mention the general law of the jurisdictions applicable to standard form contracts and exemption clauses. In fact, in some civil law jurisdictions, contract was used to allocate forgery losses on diligent customers as well. Contract is thus a hopeless facility for achieving certainty, fairness, and full implementation of risk reduction through the fault test. Indeed, the discrepancy between the reading of the verification clause by the Supreme Court of Canada and the Privy Council[206] is a case to the point.

Against the restrictive customer's obligations in connection with the prevention and detection of forgeries, the use of verification clauses may nevertheless be on rise in Australia, though it is recognized that current trends in the interpretation of such clauses may not be all that favourable to banks.[207] In response to the inadequacy of verification clauses, Canadian banks increasingly impose on their corporate customers, in respective account agreements, detailed positive obligations to supervise employees and prevent cheque forgeries.[208] At the same time, broadly drafted exemption clauses may not have lost all their utility; there is a Canadian authority allowing a bank to rely on a clause in a customer agreement authorizing the bank to 'act on instructions . . . from or purporting to be' from the customer, 'even if they did not come from' the customer, as long as the bank was not grossly negligent or 'engaged in wilful misconduct'.[209]

At the same time, there are strong views in the professional literature in

---

[204] As a matter of the law of contract, neither *Macmillan*, above, n. 7, nor its limits, above, text around nn. 86–94, are all that self-explanatory. Tedeski's criticism in Israel, above, n. 64, may well apply to English law itself.

[205] For two non-exhaustive examples (not involving current account agreements) where the *contra proferentem* rule led to results which absolutely did not conform to the intention of the drafter of a standard form agreement, see *Tilden Rent-A-Car* v. *Clendenning* (1978), 18 O.R. 601; 83 D.L.R. (3d) 400 (Ont. CA), and *Manulife Bank of Canada* v. *Conlin* (1997) 139 D.L.R. (4th) 426 (S.C.C.).   [206] Above, text around nn. 129–37.

[207] See T. Damain, 'The Customer is Nearly Always Right: Banks and Unauthorized Cheque Payments' (Dec. 1996), 7: 4 J.B.F.L.P. 277.

[208] See K. W. Perret, 'Account Verification Clauses: Should Bank Customers be Forced to Mind Their Own Business?' (1998–9), 14 B.F.L.R. 245, particularly at 257–69.

[209] *Stan-Ka Auto Corp. Ltd* v. *Blinkova*, [1998] O.J. No. 1047, on-line: QL (OJ), Court File No. 95-CQ-64407A, Ont. Court of Justice (Gen. Div.), 12 Mar. 1998, Spence J. (unreported).

the USA, to the effect that, primarily by reference to the good faith requirement, and as against a non-negligent customer; a bank may not disclaim liability for paying a forged cheque. Conversely, according to the proponents of these views, a bank may set by contract reasonable time and format requirements for communications from its customer.[210] Along these lines, and in fact, in both in Canada and the USA, many banks enter into positive pay service agreements with their corporate customers, requiring the latter, upon presentment, either to affirmatively approve the payment of a particular cheque or object to its payment.[211] But overall, contract has failed to properly regulate forged cheque losses.

As indicated by me elsewhere,[212] even assuming the exclusive fault of   **[41]** the customer, the estoppel by contract theory (on the basis of the verification clause), as implemented by the Supreme Court of Canada, is less responsive to the fault test than the estoppel by negligence (or to that end, also the tort duty of care) theory. Thus, suppose unauthorized payments have been included in a long series of bank statements sent to a customer and not responded by him. Under the verification clause, a customer who finally detects the fraud and informs the bank of unauthorized cheques included in the most recent bank statement will not be responsible for such amounts included in that most recent statement. The reason for this is that with respect to that statement, the customer has complied with the verification agreement and contested to the unauthorized payments made by the bank in a timely fashion. This is so, even though the customer's failure to detect the previous unauthorized payments, included in the earlier statements, substantially contributed to this most recent loss. By the same token, the effect of the verification agreement is to charge the customer with liability with respect to unauthorized payments included in the very first statement, as the customer did not contest to them in a timely fashion. This is so, even though the customer's fault has not contributed at all to that loss, except that attributed to the subsequent impecuosity of the wrongdoer.

Where the customer's negligence is in not detecting the unauthorized payments so as to prevent their repeated occurrences, the opposite result is accomplished under the estoppel by negligence (also, in fact, under the

---

[210] See e.g. J. J. White and R. S. Summers, *Uniform Commercial Code*, 4th edn. (St. Paul Minn: West Publishing Co., 1995) at 652–9 and B. Clark, *The Law of Bank Deposits, Collections and Credit Cards*, rev. edn. Boston: Warren, Gorham & Lamont: 1970–95) at ¶3.01 [3][b]. See 2.C (iv) s. 14, above.

[211] See e.g. Subcommittee on Payments—Uniform Commercial Code Committee, *Model Positive Pay Services Agreement and Commentary* (Section of Business Law—American Bar Association, 1999), and the Subcommittee on Payments, 'Deterring Check Fraud: The Model Positive Pay Services Agreement and Commentary' (1999), 54 Bus. Law. 637.

[212] B. Geva, 'Reflections on the Need to Revise the Bills of Exchange Act—Some Doctrinal Aspects' (1982), 6 Can. Bus. L.J. 269 at 323–4.

duty of care in torts) theory. The customer will not be responsible for unauthorized payments included in the first statement since his negligence in failing to detect the unauthorized payments did not cause the loss. With respect to that statement, he may only be responsible for losses attributed to the subsequent impecuniosity of the wrongdoer. The customer will, nevertheless, be answerable to unauthorized payments included in the last statement, notwithstanding the timely notification by the customer; the loss in connection with this statement was caused by his failure to prevent the repetition of the wrongdoer by declining to detect unauthorized payments in previous statements. The customer's prompt notification after the last statement prevents further loss, but is not an answer to a claim based on the customer's failure to detect.

Typically, the amount of unauthorized payments included in the last statement will be substantially larger than of those included in the first statement. This is caused by the fact that since a wrongdoer, typically an employee in the customer's organization, is likely to commence unauthorized withdrawals cautiously, and increase the stakes as he keeps succeeding in being undetected. Thus, the parties' exposure differs under the contract and negligence theories. Compared to contract, negligence allocates the loss in greater conformity with the fault test.

[42]   Nevertheless, the fault test, even when it is fully implemented as under Articles 3 and 4 of the UCC, is not always defensible or flawless. First, quite frequently, the determination of customer's fault could involve a lengthy and complex litigation, of which the result may not always be predictable. Indeed, English cases dealing with the duty to safeguard traveller's cheques are to the point.[213] They do not promise an easy resolution to questions of negligence in cheque forms custody.[214] Second, within the fault test, apportioning liability under a comparative negligence analysis may equally prove not to be a straightforward task. Furthermore, a comparative negligence test overlooks the bank's primary responsibility in detecting forgeries and unauthorized payment orders. Third, an overemphasis on the fault test overlooks the fact that from a practical point of view, bank deposits are the customer's property, for which the customer seeks theft insurance, as with respect to any other type of property. Presumably, not infrequently, the cheapest insurance may be provided for in the form of bank liability, with the bank reinsuring itself, where necessary.

In connection with the first point, and perhaps the first aspect of the second, Hal Scott spoke of 'a trade-off between costly litigation and

---

[213] See above, text and nn. 142–6.
[214] As recently adopted in South Africa. See text around nn. 161–4a, above.

unforseeability of all questions of negligence'.[215] Consider the following: does leaving a chequebook in a hotel room, rather than in a safe deposit box, constitute negligence? Alternatively, does taking a chequebook (and not leaving it at the hotel) into an unsafe part of a foreign city constitute negligence? Acknowledging that 'defining such situations is a costly matter of litigation',[216] Hal Scott proposed that '[w]ith respect to an unauthorized order or series of related unauthorized orders which aggregate less than $500, drawn on a consumer account, the person against whose account the order or orders are drawn is liable, to the extent of any loss sustained by the payor account institution to a maximum of $50'.[217] Otherwise, he would keep the fault system for cheques and further apply it to electronic funds transfers, including those initiated by consumers.

In support of Scott's proposal, one may add that in dealing with small [43] amounts, customers may invariably find themselves disadvantaged vis-à-vis the bank. the latter may routinely assert negligence on the customer's part, and count on customer's understandable reluctance to be engaged in a lengthy protracted and thus at least relatively expensive litigation. In my view, however, Scott's proposal did not go far enough. Joining the call for a statutory intervention,[218] my own proposal for a regulatory model, responding to the desired policies, would contain the following elements:

(a) In principle, to implement effectively the policy of loss or risk distribution, as well as in order to encourage forgery detection and promote the development of pertinent technologies, forgery losses are to be allocated to the bank. Undoubtedly, the bank is the better risk bearer or insurer, as well as the superior prepayment detector. Presumably, the current English experience (no customer's duty of care to prevent or detect forged drawer's signature'[219]) supports the viability of such a scheme without the imposition of additional cost. In any event, charging costs to customers, either in the form of insurance premiums or reduced return for bank deposits is quite consistent with this general principle.

(b) Exceptions to this general principle could exist, and some loss may be allocated to the customer, provided two conditions have been met:

(i) The customer has not advised the bank of the loss or theft of cheque forms. Stated otherwise, customer's notification, perhaps followed by a reasonable 'response' time required to block the cheque automated processing system, is the cut-off point for *any* customer's liability. In other words, the notice serves as an effective countermand or stop payment.

---

[215] H. S. Scott, *New Payment Systems: A Report to the 3–4–8 Committee of the Uniform Commercial Code* (Philadelphia, Pa: Permanent Editorial Board for the Uniform Commercial Code, 8 Feb. 1978) at 151.   [216] Ibid.

[217] New Payment Code, §200 (3), P.E.B. (as revised), 25 May 1982.

[218] In line with Damain, above, n. 207 at 293–4.   [219] See (iii), above.

(ii) The bank itself has not acted negligently. Thus, in departure from a strict fault or comparative negligence approach, I believe that having been entrusted with the primary responsibility for the safe operation of the payment system, banks should not be allowed to escape the consequences of their own negligence. Compared to the customer's negligence, the bank's negligence is a relatively easy question for determination. The bank must devise a system for individual examination of each cheque in order to detect any *unskilful* forgery. I reject the UCC position excusing the bank from individual examination of each cheque with the view of accommodating cheque-processing technology enhancements.[220] Technological enhancements should not be used as an excuse to neglect basic responsibilities. Rather, they should be made to accommodate them.[221]

(c) Where these two conditions have been met, (i) to accommodate the policy of loss reduction while avoiding complex and wasteful litigation, as well as (ii) in order not to undermine the effective and inexpensive insurance for bank customers, while not allowing the abuse of the scheme, the general principle, that of bank responsibility, is compromised as follows:

(i) Following the UCC position,[222] vis-à-vis an innocent party, a signer of an incomplete instrument, including an instrument containing any blank space in a material part, which subsequent to signature is completed by someone other than the signer, and either without or contrary to the signer's authority, is bound on the instrument according to its terms as so completed.

(ii) Repeated occurrences of forgery cases in an account of the same customer may be responded by increased insurance premiums, withdrawal of payment services facilities, or perhaps, due to the rarity of such cases, by the imposition of a duty of care on 'recidivist' grossly negligent customers.

(iii) For each case of forgery loss, the customer would be charged with a relatively small deductible sum. In fact, this is a system of coinsurance, encouraging diligence of the customer. The deductible may be fixed, dependent on the size and activity volume in the account, or linked to past experience with the same customer.

---

[220] See above, text around n. 180. For the rejection of a similar position in France, see e.g. source cited at n. 35, above.

[221] For example, cheque truncation could be accompanied by a cheque image transmission to the drawee bank. See e.g. 7:4 *Canadian Payments Association Forum* (Dec. 1991).

[222] See text and n. 169, above.

(iv) A duty of care to examine periodic bank statements, and detect and report forgeries within a prescribed time limit, ought to be fastened on all bank customers.[223] I prefer a duty of care to an absolute duty to detect and report, since in a given case, a court may be able to find alleviating circumstances.[224] I do not believe that in this context, there is a real danger of wasteful and extensive litigation on the breach of the duty of care.

(v) Finally, following the reversed judgment in *CP Hotels*,[225] and the recent statutory amendment in South Africa,[226] a sophisticated business bank customer ought to be charged with a duty of care to prevent forgeries. Alternatively perhaps, forgery losses above a specified high ceiling, reflecting a high volume of monetary activity, would be allocated to a negligent customer.[227] However, with the view of eliminating wasteful and lengthy litigation, I would disfavour a broad open ended duty of care. Rather, I would propose to substitute it by a code of conduct consisting of a series of standards for appropriate office procedures, designed to prevent as well as detect forgeries. Such a code ought to be negotiated between associations of banks and large corporate users of bank payment services.[228]

I believe that such a model properly reconciles between the loss reduction **[44]** and distribution policies. It thus appears to be superior to the current schemes in the various legal systems.

---

[223] This is in line with Ellinger and Lomnicka, above, n. 105 at 172–3, criticizing the Privy Council in *Tai Hing*, above, n. 112, for failing to give consideration to the argument that 'both common sense and good business practice require the bank's customer to verify the entries made in his account'. [224] See above, text and nn. 188–90.
[225] See above, text and nn. 107–10. [226] See above, text around nn. 161–4a.
[227] A high-amount cheque ought to give rise to a greater than usual diligence by the bank. At the same time, a high-amount forged cheque is bound to be spotted more quickly by the customer in fulfilment of the customer's proposed duty to detect and report forgeries.
[228] The contract-making process could be in line with a proposal for a publicly supervised negotiated statutory standard form contract for car rental, put forward by R. Hasson, 'The Unconscionability Business—A Comment on *Tilden-Rent-a-Car* v. *Clendenning*' (1979), 3 Can. Bus. L.J. 193 at 196–8. In fact, current code of conducts in the banking sector effectively implement such a proposal.

C. Unauthorized Electronic Funds Transfers

[1] Generally speaking, an electronic funds transfer is initiated when a bank customer, acting as a sender, transmits payment instructions to the sending bank's computer[1] from a terminal.[2] Such communication from the customer to the computer of the customer's bank can take place from:

(1) a public access terminal, usually either an automated teller machine (ATM) or an automated banking machine (ABM);

(2) a point-of-sale (POS) terminal at a retail establishment; or

(3) an exclusive-access terminal used solely by one sender and located at the sender's place of business or home, which could be the sender's own computer or, at the other extreme, a simple telephone or television set.

In fact, the first two types of terminals are both publicly accessed. In practice, they are used for such transactions as cash withdrawals, bill payments, same person inter-account transfers, and retail purchases. Terminals falling into the third category may be used for inter-account transfers, whether belonging to the same person, or from an account of one person to an account of another. Usually, the first two categories are associated with consumer card funds transfers. The third category is associated with both consumer home banking and business-to-business payments.

In each case, the sender's instructions are usually authenticated by means of an access device, in the form of a secret code,[3] either alone, or in conjunction with a physical device, such as a card, to be inserted at the terminal. Cards are primarily used, though not necessarily exclusively, in publicly accessed terminals. In each case, authentication is immediately followed by verification by the bank according to its security procedure.

---

[1] Throughout the ensuing discussion, 'bank' denotes any depository financial institution, and 'customer' means an account holder in such an institution.

[2] The customer may also deliver instructions to the bank in writing or in diskettes, in which case input to the computer system may be carried out by the bank itself. The present discussion is however limited to electronic transmission from a terminal, purportedly by the customer or on the customer's behalf. For more on the communication flow in an electronic funds transfer see B. Geva, *The Law of Electronic Funds Transfers* §1.03[5] (New York: Matthew Bender, 1992–9).

[3] Instances of unauthenticated electronic instructions are outside the scope of the present discussion.

Thereafter, the bank proceeds to execute the instructions and carry out the funds transfer.

The present discussion concerns the initiation of an electronic funds **[2]** transfer authenticated without the authority of the sending bank's customer, but which is nevertheless carried out. The focus is on a card payment transaction, as well as on a home banking or business-to-business credit transfer from a sending payor to a receiving payee or beneficiary.[4] The issue to be considered here is the loss allocation between the sending bank and the customer on whose behalf the transfer purported to be initiated.[5] This issue will be explored here under (i) the common law, applicable in England, Canada,[6] and other jurisdictions with current or historical connection to the Commonwealth, or its predecessor, the British Empire, such as Australia, (ii) American law, and (iii) Swiss law, with reference to other civil law jurisdictions.[7]

In the common law, the issue is to be determined under general principles of law, many of which may be derived by analogy to the law governing loss allocation in the case of a forged cheque. Voluntary codes of practice may supplement or supersede such rules in consumer card transactions. In Switzerland the issue is governed by the general provisions of the Code of Obligations. Conversely, in the United States, specific legislation applies to the question. Thus, in the various states, UCC Article 4A[8] governs business-to-business credit transfers. In turn, the federal Electronic Fund Transfer Act,[9] and Regulation E[10] that implements it, govern the issue in consumer transfers.

Five important preliminary observations ought to be noted. The first **[3]** relates to the definition of an 'unauthorized funds transfer'. Thus,

---

[4] In a credit transfer, the paying party's instructions are transmitted directly to that party's bank so that funds are then 'pushed' to the account of the payee or beneficiary. Conversely, in a debit transfer, it is the beneficiary or payee who transmits the message to the beneficiary's or payee's bank, so as to collect or 'pull' funds from the payor's account. For more on the distinction, see 3.A s. 1, above.

[5] The additional issue, that of recovery from the payee or beneficiary, will not be dealt with here.

[6] However, this is not a matter of 'banking', nor is it covered by the federal Bills of Exchange Act. Consequently, it is subject to provincial jurisdiction in Canada, so that in the Province of Quebec, civil law, rather than principles of common law, may determine the issue.

[7] Swiss law is not necessarily identical to that of other civil law countries, such as Germany, France, Italy, and Japan. However, in all such legal systems, the customer–bank relationship is analysed from the common perspective of the mandate. This ensures substantial degree of similarity of general applicable principles. See, further, (iv) below.

[8] UCC Article 4A was approved in 1989 by the ALI and the NCCUSL. As of March 1996 it was adopted by all fifty states and the District of Columbia, as well as CHIPS, Fedwire, and NACHA. The UNCITRAL Model Law on International Credit Transfers usually follows UCC Article 4A. [9] 15 U.S.C.S. §1693, enacted in 1978.

[10] 12 C.F.R. Part 205, originally passed in 1981, as am.

circumstances where a transfer is initiated by an agent or third person entrusted by the customer with an access device do not give rise to 'unauthorized funds transfers'. Rather, they may involve an agent exceeding his actual authority, a case which falls outside our enquiry, and which usually entails the customer's responsibility for the entire amount of the transfers. It is also my view that the same rule ought to apply whenever the customer voluntarily entrusts a third person with the access device, for whatever purpose, and not necessarily with the authority to use it.[11] It follows that an unauthorized transfer must emanate from someone who either assumed control of the access device unlawfully, or bypassed the access device altogether. Such a person may be a member of the customer's household, the customer's employee or associate, or a total stranger.

The second observation relates to the possibility that the customer's fault or negligence may or may not have contributed to an unauthorized funds transfer. That is, a person may unlawfully assume control of the access device, or bypass its use altogether, and initiate an unauthorized transfer, either or not due to the customer's fault, and even in the absence of any fault. For example, the customer might not have properly secured the safekeeping of the access device or any pertinent information. Or again, the customer may have been negligent in the choice of the secret access code, where such choice was available to the customer. Thus, the customer could have selected obvious numbers or letters, such as those consisting of the customer's car licence plate, birthday, or name. Or else the customer might have failed to advise the bank properly and promptly of the loss or theft of the access device. Also, upon receiving notification from the bank of a transfer, the customer may have failed to act diligently and promptly in discovering the lack of authority. The customer may have thereby precluded prompt recourse by the bank against the wrongdoer, prior to the latter's disappearance or insolvency, and further enabled that wrongdoer to continue drawing on the account without the customer's authority. An alternative scenario is one where the customer has been quite diligent in the safekeeping, as well as in giving required notice to the bank.

[4]   The third preliminary point concerns the nature of the electronic authentication and the ensuing process of bank verification. A handwritten or manual signature is individual to the signer; as such, it *identifies* the

---

[11] For cheques, a contrary rule exists in English law under *Smith* v. *Prosser* [1907] 2 K.B. 735 (C.A.). Thereunder, a distinction is drawn between the consequences of an unauthorized completion and issue of a blank signed cheque delivered by the signer (i) with authority to issue it, and (ii) for a mere safekeeping. This, however, is an aberration (see e.g. I. Ackermann, 'Signature and Liability in the Law of Bills and Notes' (1993), 8 B.F.L.R. 295), derived from a particular strict interpretation of a provision in the Bills of Exchange Act, which needs not to be extended to the area of electronic funds transfer.

signer. Any signature, other than that of the authorized signer, is by definition unauthorized, and may not serve as a valid authentication on the purported signer's behalf. Prima facie, the bank thus would not be justified in debiting the purported signer's account. Conversely, electronic authentication is carried out by means of an access device, which can be entered into a terminal by anyone to whom the device, together with access to a terminal, becomes available. Electronic authentication is a means of *legitimizing* the action of that person, but not of identifying him. It is very much like a door key facilitating entry to the system, or better, a seal affixed to an instrument, authenticating it, but not identifying the one who actually placed it. Consequently, any technologically effective entry of the access code, even when it is carried out by an unauthorized person to whom it may have become available unlawfully, appears to the bank as a valid authentication. Prima facie, the electronic authentication would thus justify the bank in debiting the customer's account. In this sense, the authentication by means of an access code is not an 'electronic signature'; rather, it is more analogous to the placement of an 'electronic seal'.[12]

This distinguishing feature of the electronic authentication is of tremendous consequence in ascertaining the bank's duties in preventing and detecting unauthorized transfer losses. Indeed, in the case of a manual signature, the bank's obligation is in detecting the forgery on each instrument, individually. At the same time, in the case of the electronic authentication, the bank is bound to implement a safe system for the distribution of access devices, a safe security procedure for the authentication of payment instructions, as well as an effective system of blocking access upon being advised of loss or theft of the access device.[13] At least historically in English law, banks' liability for payment of forged cheques has been premissed on banks being 'bound to know the hand-writing of their customers',[14] rather than on a duty of care to detect forgeries. In contrast, in an electronic environment, the banks' duty ought to be premissed on negligence. Typically, such negligence is not individual to a bank employee, as where the latter failed to detect the forgery of a manual signature; rather, in the electronic context, we are concerned with 'systemic negligence', by the bank organization as a whole, and on the level of implementing satisfactory computer as well as office procedures.[15] Breach

---

[12] See I. Billotte-Tongue, *Aspects juridiques du virement bancaire*, 174–5 (Zurich: Schulthess, 1992).

[13] The bank may also be charged with a duty to ensure the safety and security of public-access terminals.

[14] *Smith* v. *Mercer* (1815), 6 Taunt 76 at 86, 128 E.R. 961 at 965, *per* Heath J.

[15] A point well taken by L. Thévenoz, 'Le Banquier, son client et l'ordinateur-Réflections sur la prestation de services en masse', 1993 Le Semaine judiciaire, 17, particularly at 22–3, 42, and 44–5.

of required standards by the bank, while not necessarily attributable to any individual employee, is nonetheless negligence.

[5]   The fourth preliminary observation stems from the third. In their customer agreements, it is common for banks to link their right to debit the customer account to the verification of the proper authentication, purportedly on the customer's behalf, rather than on the instructions being actually authorized by the customer. In light of banks' inability to differentiate between an authorized and unauthorized authentication, this is quite understandable.

Finally, the fifth point is that 'unauthorized transfers' ought to be distinguished from properly authenticated instructions containing unauthorized or unintended contents. In principle, discrepancies in the contents of properly authenticated payment instructions are at the customer's risk and responsibility. However, subject to some restrictions, UCC Article 4A allows the parties to shift the risk to the bank. Pertinent scenarios can be associated with those of unauthorized transfers; the UCC treatment will thus be analysed below, as part of the discussion on American law.

(ii) COMMON LAW JURISDICTIONS

[6]   American authorities dealing with negotiable instruments have given full effect to corporate resolutions authorizing the use of facsimile signatures to bind corporate entities.[16] This must be correct in English law as well.[17] Case law requiring that the 'engraved representation of [a] signature' must be placed on a document 'by means of a rubber stamp' by the signatory himself,[18] rather than by somebody acting on his behalf, ought to be narrowly read and is inapplicable. Such case law is limited to situations where a signature requirement is linked by statute to a decision which the signer must have made personally. Accordingly, the agreement to be bound by the electronic authentication must be taken to recognize its sufficiency to establish liability.

[7]   There is no case law dealing directly with the bank's responsibilities in carrying out the verification of instructions transmitted to it from a terminal. However, in the USA, prior to UCC Article 4A, *Walker* v. *Texas Commerce Bank*[19] stated that, in receiving a payment order from a sender, a

---

[16] See e.g. *Perini Corp.* v. *First National Bank of Habersham Cty.* 553 F. 2d 398 (5th Cir. Ga. 1977).

[17] D. A. L. Smout, *Chalmers on Bills of Exchange*, 13th edn. (London: Stevens & Sons, 1964) at 285.

[18] *Goodman* v. *J. Eban Ld.* [1954] 1 Q.B. 550 at 557 (C.A.), *per* Evershed, MR. See also *Lazarus Estates Ltd.* v. *Beasely* [1956] 1 Q.B. 702 at 710 (C.A.).

[19] 635 F. Supp. 678 (S.D. Tex. 1986).

receiving bank is under a duty 'to implement commercially reasonable internal procedures designed to process [a payment order] in accordance with [the sender's] instructions, to verify the accuracy of, and compliance with, instructions, to detect and minimize inaccuracy, and to act diligently to remedy errors'.[20] This is quite in line with the receiving bank's broad 'duty to use reasonable care and skill' in carrying out a payment order, set out in England in *Royal Products Ltd.* v. *Midland Bank Ltd.*[21] In fact, the bank's duty to 'use reasonable care and diligence in the discharge of its instructions and the performance of all its banking functions' was characterized as '[t]he most significant implied term' in the banking contract.[22] Accordingly, a bank establishing a reasonable security procedure for verifying electronic authentication has discharged its contractual obligation to the customer and may be justified in debiting the customer's account once the procedure has been performed.

In practice, a terminal may be accessed either publicly, or in the exclusive possession of the customer. The access device usually consists of a secret code, which must be entered into the terminal with or without a physical device, such as a card. A short secret code, such as one consisting of no more than four digits, may be guessed by an unauthorized user. Particularly in connection with publicly accessed terminals, and even where a physical device is required, a question may then arise as to the reasonableness of this aspect of the bank's security procedure. Indeed, the physical device may be lost, stolen, or even imitated by a technologically sophisticated defrauder. In fact, a sophisticated dishonest observer may also be successful in 'spying' on the customer to discover the secret code itself. Furthermore, a sophisticated 'electronic thief' or 'pirate' may figure out how to bypass the authorized electronic access facility and obtain access without it. This latter case raises the question as to whether a bank will be required to implement a foolproof security procedure, rather than a mere *commercially reasonable* one. [8]

Where the security procedure is held to be inadequate, and the customer has not been negligent, unauthorized transfer loss ought to be allocated to the bank. The question is more complex whenever neither the bank nor the customer was negligent, as well as where the customer was negligent, either alone or together with the bank. An analysis focusing on causality or degree of fault may be hopelessly unpredictable and unsatisfying. The distinct nature of electronic authentication, as described above, makes the case law dealing with handwritten signature authentication not particularly helpful. Nonetheless, the following rules may emerge:

---

[20] Ibid., at 682.   [21] [1981] 2 Lloyd's L.R. 194 at 198 (Q.B.).
[22] B. Crawford, *Crawford and Falconbridge Banking and Bills of Exchange*, 8th edn., vol. i, 746 (Toronto: Canada Law Book, 1986).

(1) In principle, a customer is not liable in the absence of a proper authentication according to the security procedure agreed upon with the bank.

(2) The customer may nevertheless be liable even in the absence of such proper authentication where the customer's negligence enabled a sophisticated 'electronic thief' or 'pirate' to obtain information that facilitated the bypassing of the security procedure in the initiation of the unauthorized payment order.

(3) Where the unauthorized payment order has been properly authenticated, in the absence of fault by the bank, there may be no common law grounds to fasten liability on the bank; the customer is bound by the properly authenticated payment order regardless of whether on not he has been negligent.

(4) Nevertheless, the customer's negligence may become relevant in situations where the bank has been negligent as well. In fact, in addition to the degree of adequacy or reasonableness of the security procedure implemented by the bank (that is, the standard of care the bank is required to meet), the question of the customer's negligence, but only in a situation where the bank was negligent as well, remains uncertain. Thus, even where the unauthorized payment order has been properly authenticated, where both the customer and the bank were at fault, a question arises as to how the loss is to be apportioned. The question is whether loss is to be apportioned between the bank and the customer according to their respective degree of fault, whether the loss is nevertheless allocated to one of the parties, or whether an elusive search for the party primarily responsible, that is, for the proximate or immediate cause to the loss, should be launched. So far, no definite answer has been provided.

The second and fourth rules presuppose the existence of a duty of care owed by the customer to the bank. However, apart from where provided by express contract, the existence of such a duty, so as to give rise to estoppel, liability in tort, or liability for breach of an implied contract, is far from certain. In turn, where such a duty exists, its theoretical foundation may resolve, at least on a doctrinal level, the uncertainty involved in the fourth rule. Thus, in the context of the tort of negligence, contributory or comparative negligence is available to apportion the loss according to the degree of fault. In the context of estoppel with respect to forged cheques known to the customer as such, it was held in *Greenwood* v. *Martins Bank Ltd.*[23] that a negligent bank may nevertheless invoke its customer's estop-

---

[23] [1933] A.C. 51 at 58–9 (H.L.), *aff'g* [1932] 1 K.B. 371 at 383–4 (C.A.).

pel, where available,[24] and shift the entire loss to the estopped customer.[25] In the context of contract, the position may depend on the judicial interpretation of the contractual term.

Nevertheless, in connection with forged cheques, English law provides **[9]** for a quite narrow duty of the customer to his bank.[26] Indeed, *Young* v. *Grote* dealt with a customer who was 'guilty of negligence'[27] by drawing a cheque so as to permit its subsequent unauthorized alteration by the insertion of words and figures without erasures. The Court held that under such circumstances, the customer's account may be debited by the bank, for the entire raised amount had been paid in good faith by the bank. Subsequently, in *London Joint Stock Bank Ltd.* v. *Macmillan*,[28] the House of Lords held that the drawer's duty of care is confined to acts or omissions relating exclusively to the drawing and signing of cheques: 'the negligence must be in the transaction itself, that is, in the manner in which the cheque is drawn'.[29] Consequently, while a customer is liable for material alteration caused by careless drawing of a cheque, no duty is recognized in English case law, even towards the drawee bank, to exercise reasonable care (a) in the safekeeping of chequebooks or corporate seals, (b) in the general course of carrying on business, including the selection of employees, so as to detect or prevent forgeries, as well as (c) in relation to the examination of periodic bank statements, so as to discover and report forgeries and prevent their repetition. In all such cases, a customer who was negligent is neither liable in negligence nor estopped by his negligence from asserting the forgeries.[30] Stated otherwise, there is no duty to prevent or detect forgery of one's own signature. There is, however, estoppel by

---

[24] See text at n. 31, below.

[25] This may, however, only be true in connection with cheques whose forgery was not caused by the customer's negligence; namely, where loss occurred due to the customer's failure to advise the bank of the forgeries, a failure which precluded effective recourse from the forger: 'while the carelessness of the Bank was a proximate cause of the Bank's loss in paying [such] forged cheques, it was not the proximate cause of the Bank's losing its right of action against the forger' [1932] 1 K.B. 371 at 384, *per* Scrutton LJ. For this interpretation of this aspect of the judgment, and its misapplication in Israel, see A. Barak, 'Forgery in Cheque Drawing: Goal and Means in Risk Allocation between Bank and Customer' (1967–8), 1 Mishpatim 134 at 142 & n. 49 [in Hebrew].

[26] See B(iii), particularly ss. 11–12, above.

[27] (1827), 4 Bing. 253 at 258; 130 E.R. 764 at 766, *per* Best CJ.

[28] [1918] A.C. 777 at 789 (H.L.).

[29] Ibid., at 795. An earlier authority holding that negligence must be 'in or immediately connected with the transfer itself' is *Bank of Ireland* v. *The Trustees of Evans' Charities* (1855), 5 H.L.C. 389 at 410; 10 E.R. 950 at 959, *per* Mr Baron Parke.

[30] See e.g. *Bank of Ireland* v. *The Trustees of Evans' Charities*, ibid., at 409–10 (H.L.C.), 959 (E.R.) by Mr Baron Parke; *Lewis Sanitary Steam Laundry Co.* v. *Barclay and Co. Ltd.* (1906), 95 L.T. 444 by Kennedy J.; and *Kepitigalla Rubber Estates, Ltd.* v. *National Bank of India, Ltd.* [1909] 2 K.B. 1010, particularly at 1020–4, by Bray J. See also *Scholfield* v. *Earl of Londesborough* [1896] A.C. 514 at 531. *Arnold* v. *Cheque Bank* (1876), 1 C.P.D. 578; and *Macmillan*, above, n. 28 at 800.

representation or conduct where the customer fails to advise the bank of an actually known or suspected forgery.[31]

The position was well summarized in the South African case *Big Dutchman (South Africa)* v. *Barclays National Bank*, where Philips J. stated:

A customer's duty to his banker is a limited one. Save in respect of drawing documents to be presented to the bank and in warning of known or suspected forgeries he has no duty to the bank to supervise his employees, to run his business carefully, or to detect frauds.[32]

The position was recently rationalized by Lord Scarman in *Tai Hing Cotton Mill, Ltd.* v. *Liu Chong Hing Bank, Ltd.* on the fact that 'the relationship between banker and customer is contractual and that its incidents, in the absence of express agreement, are such as must be implied into the contract because they can be seen to be *obviously necessary*'.[33] Accordingly, while the duty to draw cheques carefully, as well as the duty to inform the bank of any known forgery, are 'plainly necessary incidents of the relationship' between a bank and its customer,[34] the duty to prevent signature forgery is not, and hence requires express contract.

[10]   Arguably, however, a stronger case can be made for an implied customer's duty to exercise reasonable care and diligence to prevent unauthorized electronic funds transfers. First, as indicated, the bank is incapable of detecting unauthorized but properly authenticated electronic instructions. Second, it was correctly observed that 'the traditional duties which the common law has imposed on both banker and customer in relation to one another are essentially reciprocal and mutual in nature'.[35] It may thus follow that inasmuch as the banker owes the customer a duty of care in maintaining the security of the system, the customer may be charged with a corresponding duty of care to prevent unauthorized initiation of electronic funds transfers. Yet, the point is uncertain, and it may well be that in English law there is no customer's duty to prevent unauthorized electronic funds transfers, just as there is no customer's duty to prevent the forgery of his signature.

[11]   In principle, the sender of a payment order ought to be held responsible for the contents of all properly authenticated payment orders, regardless of unauthorized alterations occurring either in the customer's own organization or in a third party communication system employed by the customer. This conclusion is supported by the general law of agency.

---

[31] The leading case on this point, is *Greenwood* v. *Martins Bank*, above, n. 23.

[32] 1979 (3) SA 267 (W), at 283, cited with approval in *Holzman v. Standard Bank* 1985 (1) SA 360 (WLD) at 363.

[33] [1985] 3 W.L.R. 317 at 327 (P.C.). Emphasis added.

[34] Ibid., at 329.

[35] M. H. Ogilvie, *Canadian Banking Law*, 2nd edn. (Toronto: Carswell, 1998) at 445. On that point, see Scrutton LJ's judgment in the Court of Appeal in *Greenwood*, above, n. 31 at 381–2.

Obviously, the customer and the bank may agree on a different loss allocation formula. For example, they may agree on identifying codes to indicate varying amounts or specific beneficiaries on a payment order, and may allocate to the bank risks stemming from its overlooking such codes.[36]

It seems quite obvious that apart from express contract, there is no common law duty to examine periodic bank statements in order to discover and promptly report unauthorized electronic funds transfers. No such duty exists with respect to forged cheques,[37] and on that point, there are no compelling distinguishing features that could be used as grounds for a separate and broader liability rule for electronic transfers.[38] In connection with cheques, and by parity of reasoning, this also applies to electronic funds transfers; there is, however, disagreement as to the required language in a verification clause which is necessary in order to bind the customer. In Canada, the leading case is *Arrow Transfer Co. Ltd.* v. *Royal Bank of Canada*.[39] Speaking for the majority, Martland J. thought that what is needed to exonerate the bank and to bind the customer is an express undertaking by the latter 'to verify the statement of [the] account, and to accept it as conclusive unless any errors were notified to the bank within a stipulated period'.[40] However, such language did not satisfy the Privy Council in *Tai Hing Cotton Mill* v. *Liu Chong Hing Bank*.[41] Echoing the dissenting opinion of Laskin J. in *Arrow Transfer*, Lord Scarman required more specific or 'rigorous' language: '[i]f banks wish to impose on their customers an express obligation to examine their monthly statements and make those statements, in the absence of a query, unchallengeable by the customer after the expiry of a time limit, the burden of the objection and of the sanction imposed must be brought home to the customer . . .'.[42] A clearer language as to the responsibility for unauthorized payments is thus required.

With respect to forged cheques, there is also no consensus on the ability of a negligent bank to rely on an effective verification clause and allocate the loss to the customer.[43] In principle, this uncertainty ought to be carried

---

[36] As recognized in the American Uniform Commercial Code, and discussed below, in text around n. 63.

[37] Leading cases are *Tai Hing Cotton Mill* v. *Liu Chong Hing Bank*, above, n. 33, and *Canadian Pacific Hotels* v. *Bank of Montreal* (1987), 40 D.L.R. (4th) 385 (S.C.C.). See B(iii) ss. 16–22.

[38] Conversely, for the case for a narrower liability rule in electronic funds transfers under the American Uniform Commercial Code, see (iii), text around nn. 64–5 below.

[39] (1972), 27 D.L.R. (3d) 81 (S.C.C.).   [40] Ibid., at 87.   [41] Above, n. 33.

[42] Ibid., at 332.

[43] For example, a negligent bank was allowed to invoke the verification clause against the customer in *Le Cercle Universitaire d'Ottawa* v. *National Bank* (1987), 61 O.R. (2d) 456 (H.C.J.), as well as in *Don Bodkin Leasing* v. *Toronto-Dominion Bank* (1993), 14 O.R. (3d) 571 (Gen. Div.). See also *Kelly Funeral Homes Ltd.* v. *CIBC* (1990), 72 D.L.R. (4th) 276 (Ont. H.C.J.). Cases that went the other way, namely, refused to extend the coverage of verification clauses to protect

over to unauthorized funds transfers as well. In fact, there is a Canadian authority allowing a bank to rely on a clause in a customer agreement authorizing the bank to 'act on instructions ... from or purporting to be' from the customer, 'even if they did not come from' the customer, as long as the bank was not grossly negligent or 'engaged in wilful misconduct'.[44]

[12] Some uncertainty also exists where a customer actually signs a confirmation or acknowledgement as to the statement balance, containing, not to the customer's knowledge, unauthorized electronic funds transfers. In England, Bray J. appeared to suggest in *Kepitigalla Rubber Estates* v. *National Bank of India*[45] that such a signed document binds the customer to the entire balance, including the amount of forged cheques included in the statement.[46] This was how Bray J. was understood in Canada in *Columbia Graphophone Co.* v. *Union Bank of Canada*.[47] In the latter case, *Kepitigalla* was considered to be good law, notwithstanding the contrary authority of *Bank of Montreal* v. *The King*,[48] that was decided earlier, and was not even mentioned in *Columbia Graphophone*. Subsequently in Canada, Martland J. purported to reconcile the conflicting authorities, by holding in *Arrow Transfer* that a signed acknowledgement is binding upon the customer only where verification is required from the customer by contract.[49] In England, the question has not been revisited in recent years, and was not dealt with by the Privy Council in *Tai Hing*. In the absence of any compelling distinguishing feature, this uncertainty is thus imported from forged cheques into unauthorized electronic funds transfers.

[13] Voluntary codes of practice (or conduct) in Australia, Canada, and the United Kingdom are unanimous in fastening the entire amount of unauthorized use losses on a negligent consumer debit card holder. These codes provide so, regardless of the fault of the bank, except for the fact that arguably, in some circumstances, the adequacy of its security procedure may be an important element for the bank's case that the payment order was indeed initiated pursuant to that procedure. However, the codes exempt the customer from any substantial responsibility in the absence of fault on his part. Thus, under ¶14.8 of the UK Banking Code,[50] irrespective of fault, customers' liability for transactions not authorized

---

a negligent payor bank, include *Cavell Developments Ltd.* v. *Royal Bank of Canada* (1991), 54 B.C.L.R. (2d) 1 (C.A.), *239199 Alberta Ltd.* v. *Patel* (1992), 1 Alta. L.R. (3d) 215 (Q.B.), and *Armstrong Baum Plumbing & Heating* v. *Toronto-Dominion Bank* [1994] O.J. No. 331 (Ont. Ct. Gen. Div.), on-line: QL(OJ). The apportionment of loss according to the degree of fault, rather than 'an all or nothing solution', is advocated by N. Rafferty, (1993), 8 B.F.L.R. 403.

[44] *Stan-Ka Auto Corp. Ltd.* v. *Blinkova*, Court File No. 95-CQ-64407A, [1998] O.J. No. 1047 (Ont. C.J. Gen. Div.), on-line: QL(OJ), Spence J.   [45] Above, n. 30 at 1028.
[46] See B(iii) s. 23.   [47] (1916), 34 D.L.R. 743 at 745 (Ont. S.C.).
[48] (1906), 38 S.C.R. 258.   [49] Above, n. 39 at 87.   [50] January 2001.

by them, and carried out before the card issuer has been notified of the loss or theft of the card, will be limited to a maximum of £50. Evidently, this no-fault limited exposure is designed to encourage customers to be diligent in safekeeping the card and access code. There is no liability for an unauthorized use of card details where the card had not been lost. In any event, the £50 ceiling does not apply where the customer acted fraudulently or without reasonable care, in which case he will be liable for all losses. Taking care of a card and code may consist of the failure to observe any of the following safeguards, set out in ¶14.1: (a) not to keep the chequebook together with the card, (b) not to permit anyone else to use the card and code, (c) to learn the code and destroy the notification promptly upon receipt, (d) never to write down the code, and (e) to take reasonable steps to keep the card safe and the code secret.

Similarly, s. 5.6 of the Australian Electronic Funds Transfer (EFT) Code of Conduct of 1989 deals with such situations as '[w]here the cardholder has contributed to losses resulting from unauthorized transactions by voluntarily disclosing the [code], indicating the [code] on the card, or keeping a record of the [code] (without making any reasonable attempt to disguise the [code]) with any article carried with the card or liable to loss or theft simultaneously with the card'. In such cases, the customer's liability is for the entire actual losses, up to the time of notification to the issuer. Unlike under its UK counterpart, a $50 no-fault liability is imposed on the customer under s. 5.5 only where it is unclear whether the customer has contributed to losses resulting from unauthorized transactions. No such liability is fastened on a customer where it is evidently clear that he has not contributed to the loss.

No-fault liability does not exist under the Canadian Code of Practice for Consumer Debit Card Services of 1992 (rev. February 1996). However, under s. 5, a customer is liable for losses incurred 'when a [customer] contributes to unauthorized use'. Such would be the case where the customer voluntarily discloses the code, writes it on the card, or keeps a poorly disguised record of it in proximity with the card, as well as upon the customer's failure to promptly advise the issuer of the loss, theft, or misuse of the card, or the loss of confidentiality as to the code.[51]

In connection with all these voluntary codes, difficulties arise in the interpretation of some of the specific requirements giving rise to

---

[51] Two recent cases which strictly enforced the contract obligations against the customer with regard to the confidentiality of the code and the duty to advise the bank of loss of the card are *Couture* v. *Caisse populaire de Bathhurst Ltée.* (1997) 185 N.B.R. (2d) 386 (N.B. C.A.) and *Royal Bank of Canada* v. *Devarenne* (1998) 2os N.B.R. (2d) 250 (N.B. Q.B.).

unlimited customer's liability. For example, under the Australian provision, the circumstances under which a customer will 'keep . . . a record of the [code] (without making any reasonable attempt to disguise [it]) with any article carried with the card or liable to a loss or theft simultaneously with the card', are not all that self-evident.[52] Also, difficulties may arise in gathering the evidence establishing the specific requirements. Presumably, the onus is on the bank that purports to prove the customer's fault.

[14]   Regardless of these codes of conduct, a most difficult question is that concerning the onus of proof. Generally speaking, in a civil case, the onus is that of a fair preponderance of credible evidence. The question is who, as between the bank and the customer, has to prove what. Presumably, where a customer challenges a debit to his account pleading an unauthorized payment order, a three-stage process may exist:

(1) It is adequate for the bank to initially prove a proper authentication of the payment order by means of the agreed-upon security procedure. As part of its case, the bank must prima facie prove that the security commercial procedure is adequate. Whether 'adequacy' ought to be determined according to 'commercial reasonableness', or by reference to a stricter standard, has yet to be determined.[53]

(2) At this point, a customer who objects to the debit, must (at least) *plead* that the payment order was unauthorized, and *prove* that the security procedure for the authentication of the payment order was not adequate. Alternatively, under codes of conduct, and only where they are applicable, the customer objecting to the debit, may prove that the payment order, even though properly authenticated, was not authorized. For example, a customer cardholder may prove that he had lost the card prior to the payment. In the absence of an allegation as to the loss or theft of the card, where the customer simply denied the initiation of the payment instruction and alleged full continuous possession of the card, one American judge was 'not prepared to go so far as to rule that where a credible witness is faced

[52] See e.g. M. Sneddon, 'A Review of the Electronic Funds Transfer Code of Conduct' (1995), 6 J. Bank. & Fin.—Law & Prac. 29 at 40–1.

[53] A recent worldwide development is the adoption by many jurisdictions of a statute modelled on a Uniform Electronic Evidence Act ('UEE') (available online at http:www.law.ualberta.ca/alri/ulc/current/eeeact.htm) which may have clarified some aspects relating to the onus of proof. For example, under section 5 of the UEE in Canada, 'In the absence of evidence to the contrary, the integrity of the electronic records system in which an electronic record is recorded or stored is presumed . . . by evidence that supports a finding that at all material times the computer system . . . was operating properly or, if it was not, the fact of its not operating properly did not affect the integrity of the electronic record, and there are no other reasonable grounds to doubt the integrity of the electronic records system . . .' Such evidence may be introduced by an affidavit given to the best of the deponent's knowledge or belief, on which the deponent may be cross-examined.

with the adverse "testimony" of a machine, he is as a matter of law faced also with an un-meetable burden of proof'.[54] Obviously, it does not follow that the customer's testimony will always be preferred. Furthermore, in accepting the customer's testimony in that case, that judge specifically took into account the fact that the bank's 'own witness testified to physical malfunctions of the very system in issue,'[55] though not in connection with the specific transaction.

(3) Where the customer met the burden of proof, the onus shifts back to the bank. Where the customer was successful in discrediting the bank's security procedure, the bank may nevertheless be successful in maintaining the debit in the customer's account where it proves that this was in fact a properly authenticated or authorized payment order. Alternatively, where the bank is unsuccessful in proving this, as well as in a transaction governed by a code of conduct where the customer successfully proved an unauthorized payment order, it is open to the bank to prove that the customer's fault has caused or contributed to the unauthorized payment order.[56] Where the bank is able to establish it, in the case of a payment order subject to a code of conduct, the customer becomes fully responsible for the entire loss. As indicated, otherwise, that is, in the case of a payment order not subject to a code of conduct, the effect of the customer's negligence, as proven by the bank, is not entirely clear.

A bank may be able to prove that the customer's negligence enabled a sophisticated 'electronic thief' or 'pirate' to obtain information that facilitated the bypassing of the security procedure in the initiation of the unauthorized payment order. Arguably, this would shift the loss to the customer, regardless of the applicability of a code of conduct. Other than under a code, the effect of the inadequacy of the security procedure, as proved by the customer, is again unclear. As indicated, the bank's fault is usually irrelevant under a code of conduct.

(III) AMERICAN LAW[57]

In the United States, non-consumer (that is, business-to-business) funds **[15]** transfers initiated from exclusive access terminals are governed by a

---

[54] *Judd* v. *Citibank*, 435 NYS 2d 210 at 212 (City Civ. Ct. 1980).   [55] Ibid.
[56] Under ¶14.8 of the UK Banking Code, above, n. 50, for a disputed transaction, the onus of proving that the customer has acted "fraudulently or without reasonable care" is on the banks.
[57] For unauthorized electronic funds transfers under American law, see Geva, above, n. 2 at §§2.05, 2.06, 6.05.

different body of law from that governing consumer transfers initiated from either public access (that is, ATM as well as POS) terminals or exclusive access terminals (namely, home banking). The former is Article 4A of the Uniform Commercial Code, adopted by the various individual states and jurisdictions. The latter is the federal Electronic Fund Transfer Act[58] and Regulation E[59] implementing it.

[16]   UCC Article 4A deals with three separate situations involving an unauthorized funds transfer. First, a payment order initiating a funds transfer that reached a receiving bank might not have been sent by the purported sender, namely, the bank customer, or on his behalf. Second, a payment order may be issued by the sending customer, containing different instructions from those intended. Finally, before its arrival to the receiving bank, the text of a payment order may be altered in the course of its transmission over a communication system. While the first case is one of an unauthorized authentication, the two others are of unauthorized or unintended content.

In principle, a person is responsible for an authorized, and in fact authenticated, payment order sent by himself or on his behalf. The starting point is that one is not responsible without either proper authorization or authentication, but is fully responsible for any mistake or discrepancy in the content of a properly authorized or authenticated payment order. This broad principle is further refined and occasionally defied by the provisions of UCC Article 4A.

First, as to authorization or authentication, the starting point of Article 4A is that the customer is liable to his bank for the amount of any authorized payment order[60] for which the customer is bound under the law of agency. Authority may be express, implied, or apparent.[61] The customer is also liable for the amount of any payment order, including an unauthorized one, accepted by the bank in good faith, whose authenticity was verified by the bank pursuant to a commercially reasonable security procedure agreed upon between the customer and the bank[62]. A security

---

[58] Above, n. 9.   [59] Above, n. 10, as amended effective 1 May 1996.

[60] Jurisprudentially, in honoring an unauthorized (and unauthenticated) payment order, the receiving bank is in breach of contract with the customer. However, the bank is in breach of neither a duty of good faith and fair dealing nor of a fiduciary duty. See *Fernandes* v. *First Bank & Trust Co.* 1993 WL 339286 (N.D. Ill.).

[61] *Quaere* as to whether estoppel, by negligence or conduct, from denying authority, is also included.

[62] According to UCC §4A-202(c): 'Commercial reasonableness of a security procedure is a question of law to be determined by considering the wishes of the customer expressed to the bank, the circumstances of the customer known to the bank, including the size, type, and frequency of payment orders normally issued by the customer to the bank, alternative security procedures offered to the customer, and security procedures in general use by customers and receiving banks similarly situated. A security procedure is deemed to be com-

procedure may require the use of algorithms or other codes, identifying words or numbers, encryptions, or call-back procedures. It may not be constituted by a mere comparison between a manual signature and an authorized specimen signature. A verified payment order may not be beyond the scope of any written agreement between the bank and the customer or instruction of the customer, restricting the acceptance of payment orders to be issued in the customer's name. However, in two situations, an unauthorized order does not bind the customer notwithstanding its proper verification. First, where the customer and the bank agreed to allocate the loss, in whole or in part, to the bank. Second, where the customer proves that the order was not caused by a person other than an interloper,[63] namely, where the customer in fact puts forward evidence leading to the conclusion that the order was initiated by an interloper. In effect, under UCC §4A-203(2), such an interloper is an outsider to the customer's organization, or more specifically, a person other than one

(i) entrusted at any time with duties to act for the customer with respect to payment orders or the security procedure, or (ii) who obtained access to transmitting facilities of the customer or who obtained, from a source controlled by the customer and without authority of the receiving bank, information facilitating breach of the security procedure, regardless of how the information was obtained or whether the customer was at fault. Information includes any access device, computer software, and the like.

The entire scheme can be described as follows: the risk of a payment [17] order, purporting to emanate from the customer but not authenticated with the customer's authority, initially falls on the bank. The risk shifts to the customer if the bank proves its own compliance with an agreed-upon commercially reasonable security procedure. The risk shifts back to the bank where the loss is proved by the customer to be caused by an interloper, or is allocated to the bank by agreement. Fault, by itself, other than as part of what constitutes an interloper, is not a factor in the loss

mercially reasonable if (i) the security procedure was chosen by the customer after the bank offered and the customer refused, a security procedure that was commercially reasonable for the customer, and (ii) the customer expressly agreed in writing to be bound by any payment order, whether or not authorized, issued in its name and accepted by the bank in compliance with the security procedure chosen by the customer.'

[63] UCC §§4A-201 to 203. Suggestion for revisions are explored by P. S. Turner, 'The UCC Drafting Process and Six Questions about Article 4A: Is There a Need for Revisions to the Uniform Funds Transfer Law?' (1994), 28 Loy. L.A. L. Rev. 351. His four out of six questions relate to the unauthorized payment order provisions: (i) Can the 4A-505 statute of repose (discussed below) be shortened by agreement? (ii) May a customer who chooses a security procedure that may not be commercially reasonable waive his right to shift liability to the bank when the customer can prove that fraud was perpetrated by an interloper? (iii) What does the bank have to show in order to prove that it accepted an authorized payment order in good faith? and (iv) Are the rules on unauthorized funds transfers unfair to customers?

allocation. On the other hand, the scope of the customer's liability to transfers initiated by an unauthorized insider is quite broad and is not even stated to be linked to the proximity between access given to the transmitting facilities and the actual misuse of that access. For example, the customer may be held responsible for an unauthorized transfer by a cleaner who was permitted access to the facilities in the course of his employment and who managed to initiate the transfer by means of an access device and code illegally obtained.

Under UCC §4A-204, a receiving bank that paid a payment order for which the customer is not responsible is liable for interest, subject to the customer's duty to notify the bank 'within a reasonable time not exceeding 90 days' after being advised of the transfer.

[18]   The second and third types of unauthorized payment orders are those with unauthorized or unintended contents. Typical cases of unauthorized or unintended content, irrespective of proper authentication, include the transmittal of a duplicate payment order, an increase in the amount of a payment order (for example, by the addition of zeroes to the sum), or the instruction of payment to an unintended beneficiary (for example, by erring in the account or identification number of the intended beneficiary). In an electronic environment, such deviations from the intended text may result from either error or fraudulent design. UCC §§4A-205 and 206 provide for the customer's responsibility towards his bank under such circumstances.

In principle, a sending customer is responsible for the contents of his own payment order. He is also responsible for a discrepancy arising in the course of the transmittal of a payment order through a third party communication system. This means that such an intermediary system is deemed to be an agent of the sender. The sender is then bound by the contents of the payment order as sent to the receiving bank by that communication system.[64]

[19]   A sender can nevertheless shift the loss arising from the transmittal (whether by himself or by a third party communication system acting as his agent) of a payment order with unauthorized contents where the receiving bank has failed to comply with an *agreed-upon* security procedure which would have detected the discrepancy. Such a procedure may require a unique code for each payment order (so as to alert the receiving bank in case of a duplicate payment), different codes for different levels of amounts, or identify regular beneficiaries.[65] In order to benefit the sending customer, the security procedure with which the receiving bank failed

---

[64] UCC §4A-206.
[65] UCC §4A-205. While the provision is stated to deal with 'erroneous' payment orders, it must be read as covering also 'errors' fraudulently precipitated.

to comply must have been agreed upon between the customer and the bank in advance.

A customer notified of a payment order with unauthorized contents, **[20]** who negligently failed to report the discrepancy 'within a reasonable time, not exceeding 90 days' of being advised, cannot shift the loss to the receiving bank which did not comply with the agreed-upon security procedure.[66]

Having reimbursed the bank for a payment order, the customer is precluded under UCC §4A-505 from asserting lack of authority or lack of verification, unless he notifies the bank of any objection within one year from being advised by the bank of the payment order. This is true for a payment order not authenticated with the sending customer's authority, as well as for a payment order with unauthorized or unintended contents.

In connection with forged cheques, UCC §4–406(c) fastens on a bank **[21]** customer a specific duty to

exercise reasonable promptness in examining [a periodic] statement [of account] or [cancelled cheques] to determine whether any payment was not authorized because of an alternation of [a cheque] or because a purported signature by or on behalf of the customer was not authorized . . . [and] promptly notify the bank of the relevant facts.

This indeed, is quite similar to the customer's duty under UCC §4A-204(a) to 'exercise ordinary care to determine' that a payment order with which his account was debited 'was not authorized' and 'notify the bank of the relevant facts within a reasonable time not exceeding 90 days after the date the customer received notification from the bank' of the payment order or the corresponding debit to his account. It is equally similar to the customer's duty under UCC §4A-205(b) to 'exercise ordinary care' and discover a payment order with unauthorized contents 'within a reasonable time, not exceeding 90 days' of being advised. However, in connection with cheques, upon breach of the duty, the customer becomes precluded, under UCC §4–406(d), 'from asserting against the bank: (1) the customer's unauthorized signature or any alteration on the [cheque]', provided, the bank proves either a resulting loss, or recurring forgery by the same wrongdoer. Similarly, under UCC §4A-205(b), '[i] the bank proves that the [customer] failed to perform [the] duty' to discover and report a payment order with unauthorized contents, 'the [customer] is liable to the bank for the loss the bank proves it incurred as a result of the failure . . .', up to the amount of the customer's order.

---

[66] UCC §4A-205(b). Liability may however be varied 'as provided in an agreement of the bank and the customer'. See Official Comment 3 to UCC §4A-205.

[22]   Conversely, however, under UCC §4A-204(a), the bank is required to
refund the customer with the amount of the unauthorized payment
order, even when the customer was in breach of the prompt notification
requirement. Under that provision, breach of the customer's prompt
notification duty results in loss of interest, but not principal. This is so,
notwithstanding the Official Comment's own admission that 'in some
cases prompt notification [by the customer] may make it easier for the
bank to recover some part of its loss from the culprit'.[67] Principal will
nevertheless be lost to a breaching customer under UCC §4A-505, but
solely upon the failure to object to the unauthorized debit 'within one
year after the notification . . .'.

In fact, the treatment of the consequences of the customer's failure to
discover and report unauthorized funds transfers under UCC §4A-204 is
not all that fundamentally different from the treatment relating to the consequences of the customer's failure to discover and report forged cheques
under UCC §4A-406, as might appear at first blush. Thus, preclusion for
the full amount of forged or altered cheques by a customer under UCC
§4A-406, requires lack of negligence by the bank.[68] In turn, with respect to
unauthenticated payment orders, the bank's duty to refund under UCC
§4A-204, is premissed on the bank's own breach of duty to the customer.
Presumably, however, the bank's duties under UCC §4A-205 with respect
to payment orders with unauthorized contents are less tightly scrutinized, so that their breach by the bank does not preclude recovery from a
breaching customer.

[23]   The approach for regulating unauthorized consumer transfers under
Reg. E is entirely different. The underlying principle is that a consumer is
liable for authorized transfers as well as for a limited amount of unauthorized transfers, up to the time of notification to the bank. Where such
a notification is not given, the customer is liable for the entire amount
after the expiry of the notification period. The consumer's negligence contributing to an unauthorized transaction is not a factor in determining the
consumer's exposure.

Reg. E §205.2(m) defines '[u]nauthorized electronic fund transfer' to
mean:

an electronic fund transfer from a consumer's account initiated by a person other
than the consumer without actual authority to initiate the transfer and from which
the consumer receives no benefit. The term does not include an electronic fund
transfer initiated:

---

[67] Official Comment 2 to UCC §4A-204.
[68] UCC §4-406(e), providing for comparative negligence. This obviously differs from
UCC §4A-204 (as well as, in fact, from the pre-1989 Official Text of UCC §4-406 itself) which
effectively precludes the breaching bank from reversing the debit for the unauthorized payment, and does not entail the apportionment of the loss between the two breaching parties.

(1) by a person who was furnished the access device[69] to the consumer's account by the consumer,[70] unless the consumer has notified the financial institution that transfers by that person are no longer authorized;

(2) with fraudulent intent by the consumer or any person acting in concert with the consumer; or

(3) by the financial institution or its employee.

Transfers thus excluded are evidently deemed authorized to which the consumer is fully responsible.

It was held that '[i]n an action involving a consumer's liability for an **[24]** electronic fund transfer . . . the burden of going forward to show an "unauthorized" transfer . . . is on the consumer'. However, '[t]o establish full liability on the part of the consumer, the bank must prove that the transfer was authorized'.[71] This can be reconciled as follows: to succeed in its action, the bank must initially make a prima facie case that the transfer was authorized. To that end, it is adequate for the bank to prove that the transfer was initiated by means of the access device it had issued to the consumer. At that point, the burden of proof shifts to the consumer alleging an unauthorized transfer. Proof of loss or theft of the access device, put forward by the consumer, is adequate to meet this burden. Obviously, notice of loss or theft given by the consumer to the bank is no more than prima facie evidence of loss or theft.

Ultimately, however, where loss or theft of the access device is not claimed, in determining the question of 'authorized' or 'unauthorized' transfer, the court may be forced to choose between the consumer's testimony and the bank's computer printout, often backed by some evidence as to the reliability of its security procedure. A review of case law reveals that a credible witness, usually where his testimony is corroborated, typically by some system malfunction, has consistently overcome the

---

[69] Defined in Reg. E §205.2(a)(1) to mean 'a card, code, or other means of access to a consumer's account, or any combination thereof, that may be used by the consumer to initiate electronic fund transfer'.

[70] In 'furnishing' the access device, the consumer must have acted voluntarily. Accordingly, where control of the access device is surrendered by the consumer as a result of robbery or fraud, the fund transfer initiated by the robber or the defrauding person is 'unauthorized'. In contrast, the exception applies so that the transfer is not 'unauthorized' where 'a consumer furnishes an access device and grants authority to make transfers to a person (such as a family member or co-worker) who exceeds the authority given'. Official Staff Commentary to §205.2(m), as am. effective 2 May 1996. Prior to this interpretation by the Federal Reserve Board, there was some judicial disagreement on the first point (that of *voluntarily* furnishing the access device). See e.g. *Feldman* v. *Citibank*, 443 N.Y.S. 2d 43 (Civ. Ct. 1981); *Ognibene* v. *Citibank*, 446 N.Y.S. 2d 845 at 847 (Civ. Ct. 1981); and *State* v. *Citibank*, 537 F. Supp. 1192 at 1194 (S.D.N.Y. 1982).   [71]*Ognibene*, ibid., at 847.

machine.[72] Nevertheless, witness credibility may differ from one case to another. Furthermore, relevant case law is from the first half of the 1980s; it is quite possible that with time, confidence in the reliability of computer systems increase, so that greater weight may be given to evidence generated by them.

[25]   The extent of consumer liability for unauthorized transfers is governed by Reg. E §205.6.[73] Thereunder, and subject to specified ceilings, liability is limited to unauthorized transfers occurring before the consumer advises the bank either of the loss or theft of the access device or of an unauthorized transfer that appears on a periodic statement. Where the consumer is not aware of the loss or theft of the access device, for unauthorized transactions occurring up to sixty days after the transmittal of a periodic statement containing an unauthorized transfer, the consumer is not liable. However, for such transfers, the consumer is liable up to a $50 ceiling where the consumer learns of the loss or theft of the access device and advises the bank of it within two business days. The $50 ceiling does not apply where the consumer learns before the expiration of that sixty-day period of the loss or theft of the access device but fails to advise the bank of the loss or theft within two business days. In such a case, the $50 ceiling applies only until the close of two business days after learning of the loss or theft, and the overall liability for the period ending at the close of the sixty-day period will not exceed $500. Liability beyond the sixty-day period is unlimited, until notice is given to the bank. To be entitled to the $500 as well as the unlimited ceilings, the bank must establish that the consumer's timely notification would have prevented the loss.

Under Reg. E §205.6(4), time periods for notification may be extended 'to a reasonable period' where the consumer delayed notifying the bank 'due to extenuating circumstances'. However, in *Kruser* v. *Bank of America NT&SA*,[74] this provision did not assist a consumer who admitted that 'she received . . . bank statements during her recuperation'.[75] In one such a statement, she failed to notice and advise the bank of a $20 unauthorized ATM withdrawal. Almost a year later, the consumer received statements

---

[72] See e.g. *Judd* v. *Citibank*, above, n. 54; *Feldman* v. *Citibank*, above, n. 70; and *Porter* v. *Citibank*, 472 N.Y.S. 2d 582 (Civ. Ct. 1984).

[73] To be entitled to the amounts specified in the provision, the bank must have provided the consumer with certain disclosures as to the extent of the liability, the telephone number and address for providing notices to the bank, and the bank's business days. Also, '[i]f the unauthorized transfer involved an access device, it must be an accepted access device and the financial institution must have provided a means to identify the consumer to whom it was issued'. Reg. E §205.6(a). An 'accepted access device' is generally defined (in §205.2(a)(2)) as an access device requested and received or used by the consumer. In order to be entitled to *any* amount of unauthorized transfers, the bank must establish the existence of these conditions. See *Ognibene* v. *Citibank*, above, n. 70 at 847.

[74] 281 Cal. Rptr. 463 (Cal. App. 5th Dist. 1991).   [75] Ibid., at 467.

containing close to $10,000 unauthorized ATM withdrawals. The consumer then promptly advised the bank of all unauthorized withdrawals, including the one that was almost a year old. In the Court's view, the consumer failed to show the required 'extenuating circumstances'. Having delayed the notice for the first $20 unauthorized transaction, the consumer was thus held liable for the entire amount of the unauthorized transfers.

(IV) SWITZERLAND AND OTHER CIVIL LAW JURISDICTIONS[76]

Under the Swiss Code of Obligations (CO), in carrying out a funds transfer, the bank performs its obligation under a mandate.[77] Accordingly, the bank, as a mandatary, incurs liability to the customer, as a mandator, for the damage it causes in breach of its obligations, under CO art. 398, to carry out the mandate faithfully and diligently.[78] Under CO art. 400(1), the mandatary/bank is further 'liable to submit upon demand at any time a proper accounting of the performance of [its obligations], and to deliver

[26]

[76] This part heavily draws from Billotte-Tongue, above, n. 12 at 129–210, to which the reader is referred for further detail. See also Thévenoz, above, n. 15 at 36–48. An earlier comprehensive discussion is by H. Schönle, 'La Responsabilité des banques et leurs clients en cas d'utilisation abusive et frauduleuse des moyens électroniques de paiement et de mauvais fonctionnement du système automatisé d'opérations bancaires', in B. Stauder (ed.), *Les Nouvaux Moyens électroniques de paiements* (Payot Lausanne: 1986) at 105.

[77] The subject-matter of a mandate is effectively defined in CO art. 394 (1), as 'the contractually agreed business transactions or services with which [the mandatary] has been entrusted'. Similar definitions appear in the civil codes of France (CC art. 1984), Italy (CC art. 1703), Japan (CC art. 643 in conjunction with art. 656), Quebec (CC art. 2130), and Germany (BGB §662 in conjunction with §675). For texts in English see: *The French Civil Code Revised Edition* (as amended to 1 July 1994), trans. J. H. Crabb (Littleton, Colo.: Fred B. Rothman & Co., 1995); *The German Civil Code* (as am. to 1 January 1975) trans. I. S. Forrester, S. L. Goren, and H. M. Ilgen (South Hackensack, NJ: Fred B. Rothman & Co., 1975) (with 1981 Supp. trans. S. L. Goren); *The Civil Code of Japan* (translation) (Tokyo: Ministry of Justice, 1972); *The Italian Civil Code*, trans. M. Beltramo, G. E. Longo, and J. H. Merryman (Dobbs Ferry, NY: Oceana, 1969); *Swiss Contract Law, English Translation of Selected Official Texts—Swiss Code of Obligations* (Zurich: Swiss-American Chamber of Commerce, 1997); and the bilingual edition of the Quebec Civil Code, *Code civil du practicien* (Montreal: DACFO, 1995). For the Swiss Code of Obligations I used the French language 1993 Official Text but quoted from the above-mentioned English translation. Words in square brackets may reflect disagreement with this translation. Particularly, inasmuch as the civil law 'mandate' is not identical with the common law 'agency', I prefer the 'mandator-mandatary' terminology to that of 'principal-agent'.

[78] CO art. 398(1) provides that '[t]he [mandatary] is obligated, in general, to use the same care as the employee under the employment contract'. The 'faithful and careful' (or in French, 'la bonne et fidèle') performance of the mandate is required by the mandatary under CO art. 398(2). An employee is required to perform with care, and is liable to his employer for damage he causes intentionally or by negligence. See CO arts. 321a(1) and 321e(1), applicable to the mandate on the basis of the referral from CO art. 398(1).

everything which has come into [its] possession in the course of the performance of [its] mandate . . .'. In turn, so far as the customer's duties are
concerned, under CO art. 402, as a mandator,

(1) [he] is obligated to reimburse the [mandatary] for costs and expenses . . .
incurred by him in the proper performance of his mandate . . . [and]

(2) . . . is also liable to the [mandatary] for any and all damages sustained by the
[mandatary] in the course of the performance of the mandate, to the extent
that the [mandator] is unable to prove that the damage was caused without his
fault . . .

[27]   Where the bank carries out authorized payment instructions, it incurs
'costs and expenses . . . in the proper performance of [its] mandate', so as
to fall squarely within CO art. 402(1), and thus to be entitled to a reimbursement from the customer. Conversely, in connection with unauthorized payment instructions, as long as the bank acted without fault, there
is a difference of opinion as to the applicability of the provision. According to a minority view, whether a transfer is carried out in 'the proper performance of [the] mandate', is determined subjectively, solely from the
mandatary-bank's point of view. Hence, where it acted without fault, the
bank is entitled to be reimbursed by the customer under CO art. 402(1).

The majority view, however, is that the requirement of CO art. 402(1) is
not satisfied merely by the absence of fault by the bank. Whether a transfer is carried out in 'the proper performance of [the] mandate' is thus
determined objectively, so that an unauthorized transfer is excluded. The
bank is thus not entitled to be reimbursed by the customer under CO art.
402(1); a wrongful debit entitles the customer to have the account re-
credited on the basis of CO art. 400(1).

[28]   Nevertheless, a faultless bank may recover from a negligent customer
under CO art. 402(2). Indeed, CO art. 402(1) provides for the manda-
tor/customer's obligation to reimburse 'costs and expenses . . . incurred
by [the mandatary/bank] in the proper performance of [the] mandate'. At
the same time, CO art. 402(2) sets out the mandator/customer's liability
for 'all damages sustained by the [mandatary/bank] in the course of the
performance of the mandate'. '[T]he course of the performance of the
mandate' under subsection (2), is thus broader than 'the proper performance of [the] mandate' under subsection (1), and may thus also cover
unauthorized transfers that are subjectively (and erroneously) determined by the bank, acting diligently, to be authorized. Furthermore, while
the purpose of subsection (1) is to compensate the mandatary/bank for a
service properly given, subsection (2) is designed to provide the man-
datary/bank with a remedy so as to preclude injury to it.

[29]   It is however important to stress that by its own terms, CO art. 402(2)

limits recovery by the recovering mandatary/bank to circumstances where the mandator/customer 'is unable to prove that the damage was caused without his fault'. Namely, recovery can be made only from a negligent customer.[79] Accordingly, where the only party at fault is the mandatary/bank, neither the mandator/customer's reimbursement obligation under CO art. 402(1) nor the mandator/customer's liability or damages under CO art. 402(2) arises. Subsection (1) is inapplicable since, as before, carrying out the unauthorized transfer is not a 'proper performance of [the] mandate'. At the same time, subsection (2) does not apply since the mandator/customer was not at fault. Furthermore, the mandatary/bank is in breach of its diligence obligation under CO art. 398 and is thus liable for damages caused by its negligence to the mandator/customer. In sum, a negligent bank is liable to a faultless customer for damage caused by carrying out an unauthorized transfer.

In connection with an unauthorized transfer, in circumstances where **[30]** neither the mandator/customer nor the mandatary/bank was negligent, neither CO art. 402, nor CO art. 398 provides for a remedy. The former does not apply for the reasons discussed above. The latter is not helpful in the absence of the mandatary/bank's negligence. Nonetheless, in any event, the mandator/customer retains his action under CO art. 400(1), to have his account re-credited with the amount of the unauthorized transfer erroneously debited to the account. It thus follows that the loss falls on the bank. However, according to one view, where the wrongdoer is an insider in the customer's organization or household, the German 'theory of spheres' ought to apply. Under this theory, each party is absolutely, namely, irrespective of the lack of his own negligence, responsible to wrongs committed out of his 'field of control' or 'sphere of influence'. This would have placed the loss even on a faultless customer, but only where the wrong emanated from the customer's sphere or 'field of control'. Overall, however, as applied in this context, this theory is disfavoured in Switzerland, partly because the injury, that is, the unauthorized payment, actually occurred in the sphere of influence of the bank. The prevailing view is thus that where neither the customer nor the bank is negligent, the loss falls on the bank.

Where the mandator/customer and the mandatary/bank were both negligent, both parties have reciprocal claims. The mandator/customer has a claim, under CO art. 400(1), in restitution for the sum erroneously debited to his account, as well as an action for damages, based on the mandatary/bank's negligence, under CO art. 398. In turn, the mandatary/bank has a claim for damages against the negligent

---

[79] To simplify matters, I thus assume that inability to prove lack of fault means fault or negligence on the mandator/customer's part.

mandator/customer under CO art. 402(2). It has been argued that where each party's fault is of equal degree or severity, both reciprocal actions for damages extinguish each other, so that only the customer's contract claim survives. The better view, however, is that where both parties are at fault, the loss is to be apportioned between them according to the degree of fault attributed to each in causing the loss. Doctrinally, this opinion is premissed on the view that the customer's negligence claim under CO art. 398 is superseded by his contract claim for reimbursement under CO art. 400(1).

In the final analysis, the loss resulting from an unauthorized transfer is not allocated to a non-negligent customer. In fact, this is consistent with the result under CO art. 1132 providing that in connection with a forged cheque, in the absence of the customer's fault, the loss falls on the drawee bank. Where both the customer and the bank were negligent, unauthorized transfer loss is allocated according to comparative negligence principles. Otherwise, either where only the bank (but not the customer) was negligent, or where neither the customer nor the bank was negligent, loss falls on the bank.

[31]   It seems, so far as the onus of proof is concerned, that in order to trigger the customer's reimbursement obligation under CO art. 402(1), the bank must prove that in carrying out a funds transfer, it acted 'in the proper performance of [its] mandate'. To that end, it is arguably enough for the bank to prove proper legitimation, namely, an authentication pursuant to the agreed-upon security procedure.[80] At that point, it is up to the customer to prove that the transfer was unauthorized, thereby taking the case out of CO art. 402(1), and bringing it into the ambit of CO art. 402(2). This however, will not suffice, to preclude the bank from recovering damages under CO art. 402(2); the customer must also prove that 'the damage was caused without his fault', namely, that he was not negligent. Stated otherwise, to allocate the loss to the bank, the customer has the formidable task of proving both lack of authority and the absence of negligence.

Where the customer proves that the transfer was not authorized, but fails to prove that he was not negligent, he may still go ahead and prove negligence by the bank, which gives rise to the bank's liability under CO art. 398. In such circumstances, as discussed, loss is shared between the bank and the customer according to the degree of each party's fault. At the same time, where the customer is successful in proving both unauthorized transfer, as well as the absence of negligence on his part, he needs not prove that the bank was negligent; in the absence of negligence

---

[80] Obviously, part of the bank's case is that the pertinent security procedure meets the required standard, e.g. 'commercial reasonableness'.

on the part of the customer, the entire loss is allocated to the bank anyways, even without any fault on its part.

In their customer contracts, Swiss banks purport to disclaim liability for [32] unauthorized transfers and pass the loss on to their customers. However, under CO art. 100(1), '[a]ny agreement in advance purporting to exclude liability for intentional illegality or gross negligence is void'. Furthermore, under CO art. 100(2), at the discretion of the court, a disclaimer clause purporting to exonerate banks from liability even for slight negligence by their *organs*, may be considered void. At the same time, liability for slight negligence for acts or omissions by bank *employees* may contractually be excluded under CO art. 101(3).[81] As previously indicated,[82] inasmuch as in electronic funds transfers, bank negligence is typically linked to the overall operation of the computer or office systems, negligence by an organ, rather than that of an employee, facilitating the non-detection of an unauthorized transfer, is not all that a remote possibility. Liability for bank organ's negligence may thus not be effectively disclaimed altogether; liability for slight, though not gross, negligence by an employee, is however, disclaimable.

It follows that under an effective disclaimer clause, a customer who proves lack of negligence on his part, may nevertheless be liable, unless he proves either gross negligence (or intentional illegality) by bank employees or even slight negligence by bank organs. That is, where both parties were not negligent, as well as where the customer was not negligent but the bank was only slightly at fault, as long as the slight negligence was attributed to employees and not bank organs, the loss falls on the customer. There are, however, consumer contractual arrangements that allow a non-negligent customer to have recourse from a designated reimbursement fund set by banks, usually subject to a deductible.

Notwithstanding an effective disclaimer clause, and due to its limited [33] reach, the loss falls on the bank exclusively where the customer was not at all at fault, and either bank employees were grossly negligent (or

---

[81] This is the rule under CO art. 101(3) with respect to 'liability [that] arises from carrying on an officially licensed trade', which is the same as 'liability [that] arises from the exercise of an occupation for which a public licence is necessary' under CO art. 100(2) (that is, both translate the same phrase in the French Official Text, namely, the case where *la responsabilité resulte de l'exercice d'une industrie concédée par l'autorité*. While the same phrase was translated differently in both provisions, it should be taken to mean the same thing.). Personal negligence, including that of corporate organs (other than employees), even slight, may not be disclaimed at all in respect of such liability. See CO art. 100(2). Otherwise, namely, not in connection with 'liability [that] arises from the exercise of an occupation for which a public licence is necessary', even personal slight negligence, including that of corporate organs, as well as negligence by employees, may be disclaimed altogether. See CO arts. 100(2) and 101(3). Since 1986 it is conceded that 'banking' is 'an officially licensed trade' or 'an occupation for which a public licence is necessary', as decided by a Federal Court in ATF 112 II, 450. See Thévenoz, above, n. 15 at 39.　　　　[82] See text at n. 15, above.

committed intentional illegality), or bank organs were even slightly negligent. At the same time, where the customer and the bank were both negligent, the better view seems to be that loss is not shouldered by the bank
alone. Rather, where the situation involved either gross negligence (or
intentional illegality) by bank employees or even slight negligence by
bank organs, loss is to be apportioned between the bank and its customer
according to the degree of their respective fault. Otherwise, as indicated,
the bank is released from liability, so that the customer bears the loss in
full. Obviously, where the customer alone was negligent, whether grossly
or slightly, the entire loss falls on him.

[34]   Swiss standard form bank agreements invariably require the customer
to advise his bank promptly of any complaint he has with respect to a
statement or contested transfer for which he was advised. Upon failing to
do so within the time period set by the bank, the customer is deemed to
have approved all dispositions.[83] This seems to be broad enough to cover
unauthorized transfers, advised to the customer, and which he failed to
notice and promptly report. Regardless, losses occurring due to unauthorized transfers may have been prevented had the customer not
failed to exercise due diligence in discovering and reporting earlier
unauthorized transfers by the same wrongdoer. Also, losses from such
earlier unauthorized transfers might have been precluded, or at least
reduced, upon prompt discovery and disclosure by the customer. This is
so where prompt discovery and disclosure could have facilitated timely
recourse by the bank against the wrongdoer, who in the meantime might
have disappeared or become impecunious. Such losses, from the earlier as
well as latter undiscovered and hence unreported unauthorized transfers,
are then 'damages sustained by the [bank as a mandatary] in the course
of the performance of the mandate'. For such losses, the customer, as a
mandator, is liable under CO art. 402(2), 'to the extent that [he] is unable
to prove that the damage was caused without his fault'. There is thus a
duty on the bank customer to discover and promptly report unauthorized
transfers. The customer's duty may be absolute under the banking contract and is based on fault under the Code of Obligations. Where the bank
effectively disclaims liability for unauthorized transfers, other than for
the gross negligence (or intentional illegality) of its employees or even the
slight negligence of its organs, this customer's duty is relevant only in
assigning the customer's share in the loss, as against the bank's share,
attributed to the bank's own negligence, as such bank's negligence is
found to exist in that case.

---

[83] See e.g. D. Guggenheim, *Les Contrats de la pratique bancaire suisse*, 2nd edn. (Geneva:
Librairie de l'Université George et Cie, 1981) at 72.

In fastening on the mandatary a duty of care in CO art. 398,[84] the Swiss **[35]** position follows the current prevailing civilian views,[85] as provided in contemporary civil codes in various jurisdictions.[86] However, as for the mandator's liability, at present, contrary to Swiss CO art. 402(2), the prevailing view is that such liability is not limited to negligence; rather, the mandator's liability extends to all losses and damages incurred by the mandatary in connection with the execution of the mandate,[87] and arises even in the absence of any negligence on the part of the mandator.[88] Nonetheless, in some countries such as France and Germany, notwithstanding the absence of a corresponding provision to Swiss CO art. 402(2), no liability for unauthorized transfers is fastened on a non-negligent customer under general law.[89]

However, the prevailing civilian view is, as in Switzerland, that an effective exemption clause may exonerate the bank from any liability, unless the bank either committed an intentional wrongful act, or acted with gross negligence.[90] Thus, in civil law jurisdictions, under an appropriate exemption clause, a bank, other than one that acted wrongfully (either intentionally or gross negligently) is able to fasten unauthorized transfer losses on a customer, even when the latter was not negligent at all.

(V) CONCLUSION: OBSERVATIONS AS TO THE DESIRED RULE

Fault plays a significant role in the allocation of losses under the common **[36]** law as well as in Switzerland and other civil law jurisdictions. In contrast,

---

[84] See n. 77 and text, above.

[85] See discussion by R. Zimmermann, *The Law of Obligations—Roman Foundations of the Civilian Tradition* (Cape Town: Juta, 1990) at 426–30.

[86] See CC art. 1992 in France; CC art. 644 in Japan; CC art. 1710 in Italy; BGB §276 in Germany (for any debtor in general); and CC art. 2138 in Quebec.

[87] See CC art. 2000 in France; CC art. 1720 in Italy; and CC art. 2154 in Quebec. In Germany and Japan, the statutory provisions (BGB §670 and CC art. 650 respectively) read to entitle the mandatary to claim from the mandator only expenses or outlays (and not losses or damages) incurred by the mandatary in the course of carrying out the mandate. However, at least in Germany, '[these] narrow confines . . . were soon left behind by courts and legal writers. The principle of a liability (not based on fault) for risks arising from and connected with activities undertaken by another person in the debtor's interest, is widely acknowledged today.' See Zimmermann above, n. 85 at 432.

[88] For this development see Zimmermann, ibid. at 430–2.

[89] This can be justified either by viewing the unauthorized payment as occurring outside the mandate, even the general mandate generated under the account agreement, or by reference to statutory provisions, such as CC arts. 1239 and 1937 in France, requiring payment to the true creditor in order to discharge a debt.

[90] See e.g. R. Ben-Oliel, 'Banker's Liability in the Bank Deposit Relationship' (1979), 14 Israel L. Rev. 164, 174–6.

fault concepts are downplayed in the American statutory schemes. Among the three systems, uncertainty as to existing rules exists, particularly under the common law, mainly with regard to business-to-business transfers. To a large extent, this uncertainty is attributed to the uneasy importation of rules developed in cheque law.

In assessing the current schemes, and determining what ought to be the desired rule, the following observations are noteworthy. First, a rule based on fault is hopelessly complicated, particularly in determining the customer's negligence, its degree, as well as the causal link between it and the actual loss. Second, a rule which allocates unlimited loss to the customer, even where he was not at all at fault, is unfair. It overlooks the role of the bank as a depositary for the customer's funds, responsible for their safekeeping. Further, it does not provide banks with adequate incentives to keep investing in the enhancement of their security systems so as to further reduce losses. It thus follows, that both the common law and the Swiss legal system (as other civil law jurisdictions) provide unsatisfactory solutions.

However, the desired rule ought not to exonerate the customer altogether. Indeed, a scheme allocating the entire loss to the bank may be effective in redistributing losses among all bank customers, as well as in encouraging banks to enhance security measures. However, it fails to encourage customers to take even minimum precautions. An effective rule should provide incentives to the customer to eliminate, or at least reduce, losses. This can be done either by taking fault into account, at least to a specified extent and in relation to well-defined and easily provable events, or by providing for the limited participation of the customer in the amount of the loss, regardless of fault, as if under an insurance scheme providing for a deductible or coinsurance. At the same time, such a rule ought to avoid resorting to complex factual determinations as to the degree of fault and its causal link with the actual loss. The rule should also not ignore the bank's capacity as the best loss absorber and redistributor.

[37]   As pointed out by Thévenoz, an optimal system may not be produced by mere market forces.[91] Speaking of Switzerland, he refers to the oligopolistic nature of the payment services market, dominated by large players, as well as to the inherent underestimation of losses by customers. For example, while the loss of a wallet is limited to the value of the money it contains, the potential loss stemming from the theft of an access device may not be so ascertainable. In general, these observations hold true elsewhere. Here lies the rationale for the need for a specific statutory rule.

From the three systems reviewed, American law seems to be the most

---

[91] Thévenoz, above, n. 15 at 51.

effective in meeting the desired standard. It provides incentives to eliminate or reduce loss, while at the same time avoiding the preoccupation with customer's fault. Thus, for business-to-business transfers, by fastening liability on the customer for unauthorized transfers initiated by an insider, UCC Article 4A effectively implements a 'sphere of influence' theory. This rule may be too harsh for consumer unauthorized transfers. Accordingly, for the latter, the Electronic Fund Transfer Act and Regulation E implementing it provide for a deductible, which keeps increasing as the delay in informing the bank of an unauthorized transfer of the delay grows. Both schemes thus avoid the need to determine customer's fault, its degree, and causation.[92] In the final analysis, regardless of detail, the American model is worth considering elsewhere.

[92] The absence of a duty under Article 4A to promptly disclose and report unauthorized transfers, as noted in (iii) above, is however, quite enigmatic.

D. Forged Indorsements

[1]   This chapter discusses the allocation of losses incurred in connection with the collection and payment of cheques bearing forged or unauthorized indorsements. The discussion covers (i) jurisdictions that have adopted a statute modelled on the English Bills of Exchange Act (BEA, or 'the Act'),[1] conveniently, though not always accurately, sometimes referred to below as common law jurisdictions,[2] (ii) the United States where the Uniform Commercial Code (UCC) Articles 3 and 4 apply to cheques,[3] and (iii) several civil law jurisdictions[4] where cheques are governed by a statute modelled on the Geneva Uniform Law on Cheques (UCL).[5]

(II) AN OVERVIEW: MAJOR LEGAL SYSTEMS, POLICIES, AND HISTORICAL EVOLUTION

[2]   Negotiable cheques[6] are either payable to bearer or to order.[7] The former

---

[1] 1882, 45 & 46 Vic., c. 61.

[2] Jurisdictions covered are Canada (Bills of Exchange Act, R.S.C. 1985, c. B-4), Israel (Bill of Exchange Ordinance [New Version] 1957, Laws of the State of Israel No. 2 p. 12, as am.); South Africa (Bills of Exchange Act, No. 34 of 1964); and Australia, where cheques were excluded from the coverage of BEA 1909 and are currently governed by the Cheques Act 1986 (No. 145 of 1986). Strictly speaking, Israel, South Africa, and the Province of Quebec in Canada are not common law jurisdictions.

[3] UCC Article 3—Negotiable Instruments, and Article 4—Bank Deposits and Collections. The current text of Article 3 is from 1990. Its passage was accompanied by the passage of conforming and miscellaneous amendments to Article 4.

[4] Jurisdictions covered are Switzerland, France, Germany, Italy, and Japan.

[5] *Convention Providing a Uniform Law for Cheques*, with Annexes and Protocol, 19 Mar. 1931, 143 L.N.T.S. 355, adopted by the Second Geneva Convention, as part of an international effort which further generated the Geneva Uniform Law on Bills of Exchange and Promissory Notes (agreed upon in 1930).

[6] The term 'negotiable cheques' is used here to distinguish them from cheques not transferred by 'negotiation', namely (i) cheques payable to a specified person marked 'not to order' under UCL art. 14(2), (ii) cheques containing words prohibiting transfer or indicating an intention that it should be transferable under the UK BEA s. 8(1) (as well as s. 7(1) in Israel, s. 6(5) in South Africa and s. 20(1) in Canada), and (iii) non-transferable cheques under art. 43(1) of the Italian Cheques Law and the UK BEA s. 81 and s. 75A (proclaimed 1 March 2001) in South Africa, added under the Bills of Exchange Amendment Act 2000, (Act No. 56 of 2000) Govy. Gazette 21846, 6 December 2000 (hereafter the SA Bill). All cheques are negotiable under the Australian Cheques Act and the American UCC. See in general, 3.B(iii)(7), (iv)(1), and (vi)(4) and (12), above.

[7] Under each relevant piece of legislation, a 'negotiable' cheque payable to order is effectively interchangeable with a cheque payable to a specified person. See 3.B(iii)(7), (iv)(1), and (vi)(4), above.

are transferred by delivery. The latter are transferred by delivery accompanied by signature, called an 'indorsement'.[8] Under the BEA, UCL, and UCC, a bona fide purchaser of a cheque payable to bearer acquires a good title to the instrument, defeating thereby any adverse claim of ownership that might have been good against his predecessor.[9] Accordingly, payment by the drawee bank to that acquirer discharges the cheque as well as the drawer's engagement thereon, so as to allow the drawee bank to debit the drawer's account.[10] No such uniformity of view and consistent simplicity of rules apply to cheques payable to order. With respect to such cheques, the discussion focuses on the effect of an unauthorized or forged indorsement or an absence of indorsement. All these cases, involving a transfer by delivery of a cheque payable to order, other than by or under the authority of the designated holder, are collectively referred to below as concerning 'forged indorsements'.[10a]

According to Cockburn CJ in *Goodwin* v. *Robarts*, '[a]bout . . . the close   **[3]** of the sixteenth or the commencement of the seventeenth century, the practice of making bills payable to order, and transferring them by indorsement, took its rise'.[11] Holden points out that, in fact, the earliest indorsed bill was drawn in Naples on Florence in 1519.[12] Yet, it is universally recognized that the wide use of indorsements goes back to no earlier than around the middle of the seventeenth century. Thus, in his famous book *Lex Mercatoria*, published in 1622, Malynes did not mention indorsements.[13] Conversely, in a subsequent renowned work, *Advice Concerning Bills of Exchange*, which originally appeared in 1651, Marius dealt with indorsements extensively.[14]

Indorsements are thus of Continental origin. They became widespread in both Continental Europe and England around the same time. At present, however there is a fundamental difference between Anglo-American (common law) and Continental (civil law) jurisdictions in their basic attitude on the effect of forged indorsements on negotiable instruments including cheques. In the Anglo-American legal systems, the starting point is that subject to specified exceptions which are not uniform

---

[8] See 3.B(iii)(7), (iv)(1), and (vi)(4), above.   [9] Ibid.   [10] Ibid.

[10a] I submit, notwithstanding *Smith v Lloyds TSB Bank plc* [2000] E.W.J. no. 4361 [No. 1999/0975/B2] (CA) to the contrary, that this is broad enough to cover the case where a forger skilfully altered the payee's name to correspond to that of the forger who then indorsed it. However, the UK Court of Appeal was of a different view and treated the situation as that of material alteration of a cheque.

[11] (1875), L.R. 10 Ex. 337, 347–348 *aff'd.* (1876), L.R. 1 App. Cas. 476 (HL).

[12] J. M. Holden, *The History of Negotiable Instruments in English Law* (London: Athlone Press, 1955; repr. 1993, Wm. W. Gaunt & Sons, Holmes Beach, Fla.) at 44–5 and n. 8.

[13] G. Malynes, *Lex Mercatoria* (1622).

[14] See e.g. J. Marius, *Advice Concerning Bills of Exchange* (London: Printed 1684) at 9, 11, and 30.

throughout the various jurisdictions, a forged indorsement is wholly inoperative and may not pass title to an instrument even to a bona fide purchaser. Conversely, in the Continental legal systems, a forged indorsement may pass title to an instrument, so that a holder acquiring an instrument in good faith and without gross negligence through an uninterrupted series of indorsements has good title even where the instrument was lost or stolen and one indorsement it bears is forged.

Consequently, unless a recognized exception is involved, a drawee bank in an Anglo-American jurisdiction is not discharged if it pays someone claiming the cheque through a forged indorsement, and may not effectively debit the drawer customer account with the amount of a cheque bearing such a forged indorsement. Conversely, in civil law jurisdictions, a drawee bank is discharged if it pays in good faith to a holder who can establish his title through an uninterrupted series of indorsements, even where one is forged; the drawee bank may then lawfully debit the account of the drawer customer with the amount of the cheque.

[4]   The Anglo-American basic rule favours the purported indorser, whose signature has been forged, or more generally, the true owner of the instrument from whom it was stolen, at the expense of the bona fide purchaser of the instrument bearing the forged indorsement. This promotes a policy of property protection: a thief may neither forfeit nor pass title, or more in general, no one can pass property to something, including to a negotiable instrument, not owned by that person. The 'true owner', who lost the instrument or from whom the instrument was stolen, retains his ownership in the instrument, to the exclusion of anyone else, including a bona fide purchaser, and remains the only one entitled to both sue and give discharge on it. Among innocent parties, loss ultimately falls on the taker from the forger. The recognition that this principle may not always be benevolent has led to specified though varied exceptions but did not undermine the principle itself.

[5]   At the same time, the Continental rule favours the bona fide purchaser of the instrument bearing a forged indorsement, at the expense of the purported indorser or true owner, on whom the loss ultimately falls. This promotes negotiability or currency, namely, the smooth transferability of instruments from hand to hand, free from adverse claims of ownership, as if negotiable instruments are money. With respect to stolen instruments, Anglo-American law effectively preserves this policy only as to instruments payable to bearer whose transferability does not require an indorsement.

[6]   In providing discharge to a drawee who in good faith paid an indorsee claiming under a forged indorsement, Continental systems promote finality of payment. To some extent, they encourage creditors, as potential indorsees, to accept indorsed bills in payment of debts due to them. True,

for a creditor holder of the cheque, the loss of the instrument may be tantamount to the loss of actual money. Yet, once a bill bearing a forged indorsement has been paid, neither the drawee nor the bona fide indorsee is exposed to any action. Conversely, in denying discharge from a drawee who paid over a forged indorsement, Anglo-American law does not shield the indorsee from the drawee's subsequent restitutionary claim, thereby undermining finality, and leading to a multiplicity of remedies: the drawee must re-credit the drawer's account and sue the recipient, who has recourse from each prior indorser subsequent to the forgery. Yet, the Anglo-American scheme encourages debtors to draw and issue bills in payment of debts, since the debtor is protected in case of the theft of the bill on its way from the drawer to the payee. Finally, arguably, the taker from the forger is typically a more appropriate loss bearer than the innocent owner from whom the bill has been stolen, as the taker from the forger needs to be vigilant in scrutinizing the identity of his own indorser. Consequently, in imposing the risk of loss on the taker from the forger, compared to its Continental counterpart, Anglo-American law is more consistent with the policy of risk reduction.[15] Also, insofar as the taker from the forger is not infrequently a bank, the Anglo-American system implements a risk distribution policy: a bank can pass onto customers, and distribute among them in the form of charges, the cost of both risk reduction measures and insurance against remaining losses.

These fundamental distinctions between the two major systems have [7] evolved over the years.[16] The original position in both Continental Europe and England was uniformly along the lines of the basic present Anglo-American approach. Thereunder, a forged indorsement passed no title; the true owner's property was thus protected at the expense of the bona fide indorsee, so that the currency of instruments payable to order was not promoted. In the course of the eighteenth century this position was reinforced in England and commenced to disintegrate in Continental Europe.

The English leading case, decided in 1790, is that of *Mead* v. *Young*.[17] It [8] concerned a bona fide indorsee of a bill who acquired it through a forged indorsement. His action against the drawee/acceptor of the bill was dismissed. According to Kessler, '[t]he most interesting aspect of the case is that the judges did not confine themselves to the conventional legal

---

[15] A. Barak, *The Nature of the Negotiable Instrument* (Jerusalem: Academic Press, 1972) at 153 [in Hebrew]; as well as A. Barak, 'Forgery in the Indorsement of a Bill or Note' (1971), 3 Mishpatim 451, 457–61 [in Hebrew]. Hereafter, respectively, 'Barak (Nature)' and 'Barak (Forgery)'.

[16] For an excellent discussion, on which the ensuing analysis draws, see F. Kessler, 'Forged Indorsements' (1938), 47 Yale L.J. 863 at 863–71.

[17] (1790), 4 T.R. 28; 100 E.R. 876.

arguments, but talked for the first time in practical terms and weighed the interests of an indorsee against those of the other parties'.[18] Speaking for the majority, Buller J. rationalized the protection of the true owner's property on the basis of promoting loss prevention or at least minimization:[19]

. . . if the [bona fide indorsee] cannot recover on this bill, he will be induced to prosecute the forger; and that would be the case even if it had been passed through several hands, because each indorser would trace it up to the person from whom he received it, and at last it would come to him who had been guilty of the forgery; whereas if [the bona fide indorsee] succeed in this action, he will have no inducement to prosecute for the forgery; the drawer, on whom the loss would in that case fall, might have no means of discovering the person who committed the forgery, and thus he would probably escape punishment.

Lord Kenyon CJ did not agree. In his dissent, he could not 'distinguish this case from that of *Miller* v. *Race*[20] where the innocent holder of a note [payable to bearer], which had been taken when the mail was robbed, was held entitled to recover'. In his view, 'if the [bona fide indorsee] cannot recover, it will put an insuperable clog on this species of property'; 'it would throw too great a burden on persons taking bills of exchange to require proof of an indorsee that the person from whom he received the bill was the real payee.'[21]

Effectively concurring with Buller J., Ashhurst J. thus pronounced the ultimate rule: 'no title can be derived through the medium of fraud or forgery' so that '[i]n order to derive a legal title to a bill of exchange, it is necessary to prove the handwriting of the payee'.[22] The underlying prevailing policy is thus that by inquiring into the indorser's title the indorsee will be able to eliminate or reduce fraud and resulting losses.

[9]   In the same period that the old doctrine was rationalized and solidified in England, doubts and challenge were steadily gaining a foothold in Continental Europe, ultimately leading to reversal. First, a more limited line of attack emerged in France in the middle of the eighteenth century. This attack did not challenge the ineffectiveness of the forged indorsement to pass title; rather, it sought to protect the drawee who paid in good faith to one claiming over a forged indorsement. It was pointed out that a rule requiring the drawee to satisfy himself with the validity of each indorsement puts a heavy burden on a conscientious drawee and enables a recalcitrant one to gain time. 'It was felt that this result would paralyze completely the use of bills of exchange, the utility of which depended upon their prompt liquidation at maturity.'[23] A specific law was thus passed in France in 1787, three years before *Mead* v. *Young*, providing dis-

---

[18] Above, n. 16 at 867.

[20] (1758), 1 Burr. 452; 97 E.R. 398.

[22] Above, n. 17 at T.R. 30, E.R. 878.

[19] Above, n. 17 at T.R. 31–2, ER 878.

[21] Above, n. 17 at T.R. 30, E.R. 877.

[23] Kessler, above, n. 16 at 868–9.

charge to a drawee who paid in good faith to an indorsee claiming under a forged indorsement. In the 1930s France adopted the Geneva Uniform Laws, thereby expanding protection to the bona fide indorsee as well.

A limited application of the French rule protecting the drawee who **[10]** paid in good faith over a forged indorsement, applicable to cheques only, crossed the Channel and was incorporated into the English Stamp Act of 1853.[24] It has remained a feature of English law to this very day as the most prominent exception to the dogma under which the forged indorsement does not pass title. While spreading to other BEA jurisdictions, at least in the Anglo-American context, this rule never crossed the Atlantic, and did not find its way to North America. It is not law in either the United States or Canada. The latter may in fact be the only BEA jurisdiction not to have any variation of such a rule.

Accordingly, in connection with a cheque paid over a forged indorse- **[11]** ment, so far as the protection of the drawee is concerned, the Anglo-American system may be divided into the English and American variants or subsystems, with Canada being the only BEA jurisdiction to adhere to the American subsystem. Between the two, it is thus the American subsystem which faithfully follows the Anglo-American orthodox approach by not providing for any protection to a drawee that paid over a forged indorsement.

Like the American or the Anglo-American orthodox approach, the English variant allocates the loss to the taker from the forger. Notwithstanding the discharge of the cheque by the drawee's payment over the forged indorsement, the taker from the forger remains liable to the true owner.[25] However, in departure from the American variant, the English model does not shield the drawer against the paying drawee's action or debit to the drawer's account. Consistently, and thus unlike the American variant, the English model provides for the discharge of the cheque by the drawee's payment, so as to release the drawer from his engagement on both the cheque and the contract for which it was given. As under the Continental scheme, following the payment of the cheque, the drawer under the English variant is not exposed to an action by a subsequent party.

Arguably, where the cheque was stolen from the drawer, the drawer may, under the English variant, pursue his recourse against the taker from the forger.[26] Regardless, where the taker from the forger was the drawee

---

[24] 16 and 17 Vic. C. 59, s. 19. See in detail, Holden, above, n. 12 at 222–9.

[25] Obviously, the true owner may recover from the person who was paid by the drawee bank, and in fact, from any prior indorsee, up to the taker from the forger, against whom each such indorsee has recourse. As to who is the true owner, see below, (iv)(a) and (iv)(c).

[26] Presumably, this would be the bank's action for payment made under a mistake of fact to which the drawer is subrogated. For more details, see (iv)(c).

bank, loss may fall under the English variant, as in the Continent, on the person from whom the cheque was stolen. Since the cheque was discharged by the drawee's payment to the thief, the theft victim remains with no cause of action on the cheque. Where the theft victim was the drawer, loss thus falls on him.

Compared to the current Continental scheme, the English variant provides only a limited encouragement to creditors to accept indorsed cheques in payment of debts due to them. Under the English variant, as under the Anglo-American orthodox position, an indorsee through a forged indorsement is not protected from the true owner's action. Nor does the indorsee through a forged indorsement have a cause of action against parties who signed the bill prior to the forgery. Indeed, unlike the American variant, the English one bypasses the drawer's action to have his account re-credited, as well as the drawee's ensuing restitution claim against the recipient. However, compared to Continental law, the English variant does not eliminate the true owner's action. The principal benefit accorded by the English variant is the encouragement accorded to the drawee to pay, since as under present Continental law, having paid a cheque bearing a forged indorsement, the drawee is shielded from both the drawer's and true owner's actions.[27]

[12]   The second challenge to the traditional doctrine as to the ineffectiveness of forged indorsements developed in Germany, as of the beginning of the eighteenth century. It was broader in its scope and proved to be more formidable. It was argued that a transferee of a bill of exchange could only be expected to examine the external regularity of the chain of indorsement, and not to go beyond investigating the title of his own transferor. To enhance their role as instruments of commerce, bills of exchange ought thus to circulate like money. This currency theory is in fact no different from the dissenting view of Lord Kenyon in *Mead* v. *Young*, except that in Germany it fared better, and became law by the middle of the nineteenth century. According to Kessler,[28]

Under the new theory the title of a bona fide indorsee is not in the least derivative, that is dependent upon the previous indorser's title, but is completely independent. If the indorsee is bona fide, i.e., not grossly negligent, he always acquired title even if his predecessor had none, provided there is an indorsement to him plus delivery. With title he acquires the rights incorporated in the instrument against all prior parties whose promises are binding, irrespective of whether there are non-binding promises in between, because the individual promises are independent of each other.

---

[27] Barak (Nature), above, n. 15 at 154.   [28] Above, n. 16, at 870.

This currency theory took over and became part of the Geneva Uniform Law regime. It was thus adopted in Continental Europe, including in France, and worldwide, other than in the United States and BEA jurisdictions.

As indicated, the Anglo-American position has not remained static. Over the years, the dogmatic property approach, not recognizing any effectiveness to forged indorsements, has been compromised through the introduction of specific exceptions. Such exceptions vary from place to place but may be divided into the following categories:

(1) Protections afforded to drawee and collecting banks that pay or collect cheques in good faith and without fault over forged indorsements. As indicated, such exceptions are prevalent in BEA jurisdictions other than Canada, but not in the United States. The few BEA provisions in Canada are effectively bypassed so that in that regard Canadian law and practice follow the United States;

(2) Protections afforded to both bona fide drawee and indorsee in the case of an indorsed instrument payable to a fictitious or non-existing person. Such protection is available throughout all Anglo-American jurisdictions, and;

(3) Protections afforded to both bona fide drawee and indorsee in the case of negligence substantially contributing to the forgery of an indorsement. Broad rules to that effect exist only in the United States, where further specific provisions validate, on the basis of presumed or *per se* negligence, indorsements made, under specified circumstances, by employees or impostors. Indorsements on instruments payable to fictitious or non-existent payees fall into this group but were categorized separately here in order to highlight that that particular exception is not limited to the United States.

An interesting compromise position, purporting to bridge the gap [13] between the basic Anglo-American and Continental approaches, was advanced by the UN Convention on International Bills and Notes prepared by the United Nations Commission on International Trade Law (UNCITRAL) and adopted by the UN General Assembly.[29] Strictly speaking, the Convention does not apply to cheques; its scope is rather confined to international promissory notes and bills of exchange other than cheques. Nevertheless, insofar as it purported to accommodate policies underlying the laws of both major systems, the particular forged indorse-

---

[29] Annex to the Report of the Sixth Committee to the Fortythird session of the General Assembly of the United Nations (A/43/820, 21 Nov. 1988), adopted by the UN General Assembly on 9 Dec. 1988.

ment rule is of interest to us.[30] The Convention adopted the Geneva Uniform Law rule but added a cause of action in favour of the 'true owner' against the taker from the forger. By protecting the bona fide purchaser, the Convention follows the Continental rule, thereby enhancing the free circulation and finality policies. At the same time, the true owner's cause of action against the taker from the forger secures the policy of loss reduction, as pronounced by Buller J. in *Mead* v. *Young*, and adopted in Anglo-American law. The scheme undermines finality only insofar as it allows the true owner to recover from the taker from the forger. It encourages creditors to accept bills in payment of debts due to them, as well as encouraging drawees to pay such bills, since both good faith indorsees and drawees are protected. Compared to the Continental system, some protection is also accorded to a debtor/drawer, who, when the instrument was stolen in transit to the payee, may sue the taker from the thief.[31]

[14]   In the final analysis it seems to me that compared to its Continental counterpart or even to the UNCITRAL compromise it is the Anglo-American system which implements the more desired policies. This is so since, in practice, cheques seldom circulate or are negotiated other than to a depository bank.[32] Hence, the protection of free circulation and finality of payment to an indorsee neither outweighs nor ought to be reconciled with the policies of risk prevention or reduction and loss distribution, which underlie the basic scheme of the Anglo-American system.

[15]   The use of either crossed cheques or cheques payable in account may contribute to the reduction of stolen cheques or forged indorsement losses. Cheque crossing is provided for by both the BEA and the UCL but not under the UCC. 'Payable in account' cheques are provided for only by the UCL. Neither practice exists in the United States and Canada. Each

---

[30] For the position under the Convention, in comparison with both Anglo-American and Continental laws, see e.g. W. C. Vis, 'Forged Indorsements', (1979), 27 Am. J. Comp. L. 547; and C. Felsenfeld, 'Forged Endorsements under the United Nations Negotiable Instruments Convention: A Compromise between Common and Civil Law' (1989), 45 Bus. Law 397. See also D. V. Cowen and L. Gering, *Cowen The Law of Negotiable Instruments in South Africa*, 5th edn. vol. i *General Principles* (Cape Town: Juta, 1985) at 126–7.

[31] Evidently, the origin of the scheme, and the basis of the discussion here, is Barak (Nature), above, n. 15 at 154–5, and Barak (Forgery) ibid. 461–5. Barak co-authored the Draft of the UNCITRAL Convention and advised the Commission in the ensuing drafting process.

[32] A payee who does not deposit the cheque to a bank account typically obtains payment through a cheque-cashing facility not operated by a bank. But even this is not a case of indorsing a cheque in payment of a debt owed by the payee to the indorsee. For a defence of each of the UCC and Continental Systems, in its own context, see E. Wallenbrock, 'Forged Indorsements under French Negotiable Instrument Law and the U.S. Uniform Commercial Code: A Comparative Study' (1996), 28 U.C.C. L.J. 393.

practice prohibits payment over the counter[33] and requires collection through a bank account.[34] It thus makes it more difficult for the thief to obtain payment, and furthermore, lengthens the payment process, thereby enabling the dispossessed owner to prevent payment. Where this fails and payment is nevertheless carried out, the practice provides a record of payment through the banking system, thereby making it easier to trace the one who collected payment, usually the thief. Nevertheless, the practice does not preclude the thief from passing on the cheque to an innocent subsequent purchaser.[35] In fact however, for lack or inadequacy of other channels, thieves overwhelmingly resort to the banking system for collecting stolen cheques.[36]

In any event, by itself, the payment of cheques into bank accounts, as required for crossed cheques as well as cheques payable in account, does not reallocate cheque theft losses. Inasmuch as it reduces loss, the use of crossed cheques or cheques payable in account thus primarily benefits the party on whom the loss falls. Under both the UCL and BEA, losses stemming from the theft or loss of cheques payable to bearer[37] fall on the dispossessed owner,[38] who therefore becomes the beneficiary of crossing. Under the BEA, some reallocation of loss away from the dispossessed owner may nevertheless occur in connection with crossed cheques payable to bearer due to the increase in the standard for bank responsibility for crossed cheques. Thus, in BEA jurisdictions, having taken an open cheque payable to bearer, a bank is protected if it has acted in good faith. At the same time, having dealt with a crossed cheque and seeking to be protected, a bank must have acted in good faith and without negligence. No such differentiation exists under the UCL where the

---

[33] Nevertheless, the drawee bank incurs no liability to its customer for negligently paying the crossed cheque over the counter, as long as payment has been made to the true owner of the crossed cheque, since the customer has suffered no loss caused by such payment contrary to the crossing. See the Israeli judgment of *Kupat Aliya* v. *Kirstein*, C.A 144/62, (1963). 17 PD 2282 (SC).

[34] For cheque crossing in BEA jurisdictions see above, 3.B(iii)(8). For crossed cheques under the UCL and the various civil law jurisdictions see above, 3.B(vi)(4) and (12).

[35] See e.g. Y. Susmann, *The Law of Bills of Exchange* 3rd edn. (Tel Aviv: Avuka, 1965) at 353–4; B. Russell, *A Commentary on the Bills of Exchange Act* (Calgary: Burroughs, 1921) at 456–63; and J. M. Holden, 'Suggested Reform of the Law Relating to Cheques', (1951) 14 Mod. L. Rev. 33 at 38–9.

[36] More specifically, compared to banks, non-banking channels, such as cheque-cashing services, may be as rigorous in verifying and recording the identity of the person submitting a cheque to be collected, more expensive in providing their services, and less generous in providing prompt funds availability. Simply put, cheques do not freely circulate in money markets.

[37] For example, the use of cheques payable to bearer is widespread in Australia.

[38] Throughout the ensuing discussion, 'dispossessed owner' denotes the dispossessed owner of either an issued or unissued cheque. In the former case, the dispossessed owner is usually the holder and 'true owner'. In the latter, it is the drawer. For these two categories, see below, (iv)(a) and (iv)(c).

statutory standard for protection is that of good faith and absence of gross negligence.

[16]   However, as indicated, on the whole, for cheques payable to bearer, crossing has a similar effect under the BEA and UCL. Under both schemes crossing reduces bearer cheque losses allocated to the dispossessed owner. No similar consistency in results exists for cheques payable to order. For such cheques, under the UCL, forged indorsement losses fall on the dispossessed owner. Consequently, loss reduction, achieved through the use of crossed cheques or cheques payable in account, consistently favours him. This, however, is not so under the BEA, where forged indorsement losses fall on the taker from the forger who is typically a bank. For cheques payable to order under the BEA, loss reduction thus appears to be primarily beneficial to the collecting bank.

Moreover, banks collecting crossed cheques over forged indorsements have been provided with protection under the BEA, as long they acted in good faith and without negligence. Where the drawee bank is similarly protected, as is the case under the BEA, this results in the reallocation of forged indorsement losses to the first innocent party prior to the collecting bank. Where the one who collected payment through a bank account was the thief, such innocent party is the dispossessed owner. Crossing has thus reallocated the loss to the dispossessed owner, away from the collecting bank that took the cheque from the thief.

Nonetheless, in the UK and Australia, protection to collecting banks is no longer restricted to crossed cheques. The reallocation of losses away from banks paying or collecting cheques in good faith and without negligence has thus become a permanent feature of their laws, irrespective of crossing. Where either an open or crossed stolen cheque has been collected by or paid to the thief, loss is allocated to the dispossessed owner. From the dispossessed owner's point of view, as under the UCL, this makes crossing quite attractive, due to its loss reduction feature, from which it is he who primarily benefits.

[17]   In all BEA jurisdictions, including Australia and the UK, where a cheque payable to order is collected or paid over a forged indorsement for or to a non-bank situated in the chain of title subsequent to the thief, loss is allocated to the non-bank taker from the thief. This is so regardless of whether the cheque was collected for or paid to the innocent taker from the thief or someone deriving title from him. This is true irrespective of crossing. Arguably, however, where the cheque is paid into a bank account, it will be easier for the dispossessed owner to trace that person and shift the loss to him. In this scenario, by forcing collection through a bank account, crossing may become somewhat beneficial to the true owner. This is, however, at the expense of the innocent indorsee. Benefit is not in the reallocation of losses. Rather, it is in the enhancement of

enforcement. Otherwise, under the BEA, outside the UK and Australia, with regard to cheques payable to order, other than in reducing losses,[39] crossing is not beneficial to the dispossessed owner, as well as more generally, to bank customers.[40]

Finally, the effect of restricting negotiability[41] will be dealt with. Both the UCL[42] and the BEA,[43] but not the UCC[44] and the Australian Cheques Act,[45] recognize the effectiveness of limits imposed on the indorsability of, namely the ability to negotiate, cheques payable to a specified person. There is, however, no uniformity as to the impact on and treatment of the curtailment of transferability or assignability of cheques under general principles of law. Further variations exist as to the effect on the allocation of fraud losses. **[18]**

Among UCL jurisdictions, Italy provides for a cheque payable to a specified person and marked 'non-transferable'. Such a cheque is neither indorsable nor assignable.[46] Otherwise, under the UCL, a cheque payable to a specified person, in which the words 'not to order' or any equivalent expression have been inserted, is not indorsable but is nevertheless assignable according to general law.[47] On its part, the BEA has a provision dealing with a bill containing words prohibiting transfer or indicating an intention that it should not be transferable. Such an instrument is stated to be 'not negotiable'. Accordingly, such an instrument cannot be negotiated by the payee to another holder. There appear, however, to be local variations as to the ultimate reach of that provision. Thus, the assignability of unindorsable instruments governed by that provision was recognized in Canada but not in Israel. Among the BEA jurisdictions, only the UK, and more recently, South Africa (in a provision proclaimed 1 March 2001), specifically preclude by statute the transferability, namely the assignability, and not only the indorsability, of certain cheques. In the UK, it is a crossed cheque bearing across its face the words 'account payee', or

---

[39] This is not to suggest that loss reduction is by itself not beneficial to customers who thereby minimize friction and disputes with their banks.

[40] For the inadvisability of cheque crossing in Canada from a customer's point of view, on the basis of lack of a statutory protection on banks in Canada other than in connection with crossed cheques, see e.g. B. Crawford, *Crawford and Falconbridge Banking and Bills of Exchange*, 8th edn. vol ii (Toronto: Canada Law Book, 1986) at 1805. However, statements to that effect should not be read as suggesting that crossing is necessarily beneficial to bank customers in other BEA jurisdictions.

[41] I speak here on 'negotiability' in the sense of transferability by negotiation, that is, with respect to cheques payable to order, transferability by endorsement and delivery. 'Negotiability' in its other sense, namely insofar as it denotes the ability to confer or acquire a better title to an instrument, can be curtailed under the BEA with respect to crossed cheques. See 3.B(iii)(7), above. Since a forged indorsement does not pass title anyway, this, however, will not impact forged indorsement losses. See Holden, above, n. 12 at 40–1.

[42] See 3.B(vi)(4), above.   [43] See 3.B(iii)(7), above.   [44] See 3.B(iv)(1), above.
[45] See 3.B(iii)(7), above.   [46] See 3.B(vi)(12), above.   [47] See 3.B(vi)(4), above.

'a/c payee', with or without the word 'only'. In South Africa, it is a cheque marked 'non transferable' or 'not transferable', either with or without the word 'only' after the payer's name.[48]

It seems that the true owner of a non-assignable and non-indorsable cheque payable to a specified person is protected against the risk of loss.[49] The drawee bank that pays such a cheque other than to the specified payee, as well as anyone taking it by whatever means of transfer, does so at his own risk. Conversely, where restrictions do not affect assignability under general law the picture is more complex. Under the UCL, an assignee of a cheque payable to a specified person does not enjoy any of the presumptions that benefit a holder. Consequently, an unauthorized or forged assignment cannot pass title and loss is allocated as under the basic Anglo-American scheme for forged indorsement losses. Under the BEA, the effect of an unauthorized or forged assignment is identical to that of a forged indorsement; both do not pass title. However, under the English variant, there may be an increase in the standard of care to be expected from banks seeking statutory protection in verifying the chain of title of the purported assignee.

In the final analysis, limits on the assignability of cheques payable to a specified person minimize losses and are quite useful, particularly in light of the fact that cheques normally do not circulate, and may only be transferred for collection through the banking system.[50] In fact, there seems to be no justification for allowing cheques payable to a specified person to be assignable, or transferable other than by negotiation, that is, by indorsement. Indeed, the right of an assignee to bring an action to enforce payment on a dishonoured[51] cheque need not be precluded. At the same time, in a mass processing environment, a bank ought to be required to deal only with cheques presented for payment by respective holders, namely, in connection with a cheque payable to a specified person, the payee or an indorsee, or by someone acting on the holder's behalf.

---

[48] See 3.B(iii)(7), above.

[49] *Quaere* whether this applies also to the risk of someone either impersonating the payee or acting under a forged authorization from him.

[50] For a judicial recognition of the protection afforded by the non-transferable cheque (preceding the most recent amendment in South Africa, expected to be proclaimed 1 March 2001) see e.g. *Kwamashu Bakery Ltd.* v. *Standard Bank of South Africa Ltd.* 1995 (1) S.A. 377 at 393.

[51] 'Dishonour' ought then to be redefined by reference to refusal to pay to the purported owner or someone acting on his behalf, rather than merely to the 'holder'.

(III) CIVIL LAW JURISDICTIONS: THE GENEVA UNIFORM LAW ON
CHEQUES (UCL)

Under UCL art. 19, '[t]he possessor of an endorsable cheque is deemed to **[19]**
be the lawful holder if he establishes his title to the cheque through an
uninterrupted series of endorsements'. Nonetheless, under UCL art. 21,
where a person has been dispossessed of a cheque, notwithstanding the
lack of an uninterrupted series of indorsements on the cheque, 'the holder
in whose possession the cheque has come is not bound to give up the
cheque unless he has acquired it in bad faith or unless in acquiring it he
has been guilty of gross negligence'. Such holder defeats the title of the
previous 'lawful holder' who has been dispossessed of the cheque, and
effectively becomes its new lawful holder. As such he is entitled to enforce
payment on the cheque against all parties who became liable on it,
whether before or after the forgery, so that the loss falls on the dispossessed previous lawful holder or dispossessed owner.

Consistently with art. 21, UCL art. 35 provides that '[t]he drawee who **[20]**
pays an endorsable cheque is bound to verify the regularity of the series
of endorsements, but not the signature of the endorsers'. Stated otherwise, a drawee bank is released vis-à-vis the drawer, where it pays to the
holder claiming under what appears to be an uninterrupted series of
indorsements, even where in fact it is interrupted. Effectively, then, the
combined effect of UCL arts. 21 and 35 is to put a bona fide purchaser of
an indorsable cheque on similar footing with a bona fide purchaser of a
cheque payable to bearer. Surprisingly, however, unlike art. 40(3) of the
Geneva Uniform Law on Bills of Exchange and Promissory Notes (UBL),
UCL art. 35 does not require the drawee of the cheque, as a condition for
its discharge, not to be 'guilty of fraud or gross negligence'.

In fact, under the UCL, a drawee bank which pays a holder who **[21]**
acquired title under art. 21 is discharged vis-à-vis the drawer, even where
the bank was fully aware of the previous owner's adverse claim. Similarly, a collecting bank that collects for a holder who acquired title under
art. 21 is not liable to the previous owner regardless of the collecting
bank's knowledge of the previous owner's title. This is so, in both cases,
because the previous owner's title has been expunged by the operation of
art. 21, so that each bank acted for the current lawful holder and owner. A
bank's knowledge or fault becomes relevant when interacting with a
holder who failed to satisfy the conditions of UCL art. 21, namely a holder
acting either with gross negligence or in bad faith, as for example, the
thief/forger himself.

At first blush, a drawee bank seems to be immune from liability, even **[22]**
when it has acted either negligently or with knowledge of the fraud. As
indicated, departing from its counterpart under the UBL, UCL art. 35

does not require the drawee bank to act in good faith and without negligence as a condition precedent for its discharge. Conversely, a collecting bank acting either with gross negligence or in bad faith is not protected under UCL art. 21. By itself, however, this does not provide the dispossessed owner with a cause of action against a collecting bank out of possession of the cheque.

[23] Civil law jurisdictions may have specific provisions protecting a debtor paying in good faith to an apparent creditor.[52] However, in the absence of a direct liability from the drawee to the holder, it is far from certain if the drawee could properly be viewed as a debtor of the holder of a cheque, within the meaning of such provisions. Furthermore, such general provisions are likely to be superseded by UCL art. 35, as adopted by the various jurisdictions, the latter being a specific law applicable to cheques. Regardless, courts in civil law jurisdictions held drawee and collecting banks, acting with negligence or bad faith, delictually liable to the dispossessed owner whose title to the cheque had not been forfeited under UCL art. 21.[53] As applied to the drawee bank, this liability was rationalized either on an analogy with UBL art. 40(3),[54] or on a strict interpretation of UCL art. 35. It was argued that while UCL art. 35 dispenses with the drawee bank's duty to verify indorsement signature, it does not dispense with that bank's duty to verify the identity of the holder.[55]

[24] Either way, these are incomplete explanations. Both fail altogether to clarify the collecting bank's liability. Likewise, the one based on the strict interpretation of UCL art. 35 fails to illuminate the drawee bank's liability, which is typically not for the failure to verify the presenter's identity, but rather, in the failure to detect a patent irregularity in the chain of indorsements.

[25] To a large extent, the difficulty concerning the availability of exceptions to the drawee bank's discharge under UCL art. 35 may have been bypassed due to the nature of the drawee bank's duty under that provision. It is only the failure to discover the existence of a patent irregularity

---

[52] See e.g. CC art. 1240 in France, CC art. 478 in Japan, and CC art. 1189 in Italy.

[53] F. R. Malan, 'Professional Responsibility and the Payment and Collection of Cheques', 1978 De Jure 326 at 332–3, 338–45; *Jura Europae—Droit bancaire et boursier* (Munich: Verlag CH Beck & Paris: Éditions Techniques Juris Classeurs, 1974) at 40.31.9; G. Ripert and R. Roblot, *Droit commercial*, vol. ii, 13th edn. (Paris: LGDJ, 1992) at 289–91; J. L. Rives-Lange and M. Contamine Raynaud, *Droit bancaire*, 6th edn. (Paris: Dalloz, 1995) at 307 ¶313. In principle, the dispossessed owner's fault that contributed to the loss will reduce or extinguish altogether the damages caused by the bank's fault and for which the bank is responsible.

[54] See e.g. R. Hoerni, 'Le Cheque II endossement paiement recours faute de paiement conflits de lois' p. 4, *Fiche juridique suisse* No. 722 (Mise au point 1 janvier 1943). In Switzerland, UCL art. 35 is CO art. 1121. This is also the prevailing view in Japan.

[55] See e.g. A. Petitpierre Sauvain, 'Le Cheque II circulation paiement garantie conflits de lois' p. 7, *Fiche juridique suisse* No. 722 (Mise au Point 1 fevrier 1993), replacing Hoerni, ibid.

in the series of indorsements which will deny discharge to the drawee bank. Typically, a patent irregularity is easily discoverable, and hence, its mere undiscovery by the drawee bank may be taken to be in violation of the provision. Under this interpretation, neither good faith nor lack of gross negligence by the drawee bank will excuse the breach of the verification duty under UCL art. 35.

A cheque paid by a drawee bank in breach of the verification duty **[26]** under UCL art. 35 is not discharged. Its drawer remains liable to the true owner, though he is entitled to reimbursement from the drawee bank.[56] Is the drawee bank also liable to the true owner?

Both the drawee and collecting banks' liability may be conceptualized in tort. Not arising in a direct contractual relationship, such tort liability may not be disclaimed by means of a disclaimer clause in the banking contract.[57]

In France, such tort liability may be invoked on the basis of the general provision of CC art. 1382.[58] This provision fastens on each person a duty to compensate another for injury caused to the latter due to the former's fault. Similarly in Switzerland, CO art. 41 imposes on anyone causing damage to another in an unlawful manner, whether intentionally or negligently, a duty to pay him damages. This provision was invoked to charge the drawee with liability to the dispossessed lawful owner.[59] Furthermore in Switzerland, doctrine as well as an industry-wide interbank agreement fasten responsibility on the collecting bank by analogy to CO art. 1121 which corresponds to UCL art. 35.[60]

A duty to pay damages for '[a]ny fraudulent, malicious, or negligent act that causes an unjustified damage to another', or for the intentional or negligent violation of the right of another, respectively exists in both Italy and Japan.[61] However, in Japan, no delictual liability is fastened on either the collecting or the drawee bank in the dispossessed owner's favour.

In Germany, a similar provision, BGB art. 823, provides for general delictual liability of a person, 'who, wilfully or negligently, unlawfully injures ... another'. In appropriate circumstances, this provision may,

---

[56] *Quaere* as to the possible effect of the drawer's contributory negligence on this rule. For example, the drawer may be negligent in misspelling the payee's name or sending the cheque to the wrong address.

[57] In general, in civil law jurisdictions, banks are able, by contract, to effectively exonerate themselves from liability, other than intentional wrongful acts or gross negligence. See above, 4.B(ii).

[58] Cf. e.g. CA Paris, 3e ch, 14 Apr. 1995, D. 1996. Somm. 35 dealing with bank's responsibility in collecting a materially altered cheque.

[59] But according to Hoerni, such liability is only for gross negligence. Above, n. 54 at 4.

[60] See Association suisse des banquiers, Convention XIII simplifiant l'encaissement des effects de change et des cheques, art. 4 (1 July 1984).

[61] See CC art. 2043 in Italy and CC art. 709 in Japan.

however, be superseded by the more specific BGB art. 989. The latter provides for the remedy of an owner of property against an unlawful possessor. The possessor is liable to the owner 'for damage which occurs because in consequence of his fault the thing becomes deteriorated or cannot for any other reason be surrendered by him'. However, under art. 990, the possessor's liability to the owner 'from the time of acquisition' exists only where 'the possessor was not in good faith when he acquired the possession'; otherwise, liability is for damage incurred solely from the date the action was filed.[62]

[27]   Finally, the delictual nature of banks' liability to the dispossessed owner leads to two observations. First, the latter's fault that contributed to the loss will reduce, or extinguish altogether, the damage caused by the bank's fault, and for which the bank is responsible. In civil law, this conforms to the general rule in modern delicts law.[63] Second, in principle, liability is not solely restricted to gross negligence or intentional wrongs, but is, rather, for ordinary fault as well.[64] Paradoxically, then, compared to UBL art. 40(3), which excuses the drawee for light negligence, so far as the drawee bank is concerned, the omission of the good faith and lack of gross negligence standard from UCL art. 35, appears to have resulted in increasing rather than reducing its responsibility. This, however, is consistent with one of the interpretations previously offered for UCL art. 35 itself, under which irrespective of any delictual responsibility, and regardless of the lack of fraud or gross negligence, any failure by the drawee bank to verify the regularity of the chain of indorsements is a breach of the provision.

[28]   In sum, where a stolen cheque payable to order is collected through a collecting bank over a forged indorsement, and is ultimately paid by the drawee bank, the allocation of loss among innocent parties may be outlined as follows:

    (A) Where the cheque was stolen from the true owner/holder, and col-

---

[62] See also the heading of BGB art. 989. Note that under art. 992, as for 'the possessor [who] has taken possession by an unlawful interference or by criminal offence', namely, the thief, liability to the owner is 'pursuant to the provisions concerning damages for delicts', which in our context may be taken to refer back to the above-mentioned art. 823.

[63] See e.g. CO art. 44 in Switzerland and BGB art. 254 in Germany. For an outline of the various stages of the civil law evolution on the subject, see e.g. R. Zimmermann, *The Law of Obligations: Roman Foundations of the Civilian Tradition* (Cape Town: Juta, 1990; repr. 1992, Deventer: Kluwer) at 1010–13, 1030, and 1047–9.

[64] See e.g. J. Percerou and J. Bouteron, *La Nouvelle Législation française et internationale de la lettre de change, du billet a ordre et du cheque*, II Cheque (Paris: Librairie du Recueil Sirey, 1951) at 88–9. Note however that this view is not unanimous. See for example Hoerni's position, referred to in n. 59, above.

lected through the collecting bank by the thief,[65] the following rules apply:

(1) Where neither drawee nor collecting bank broke a duty, drawee may debit drawer's account. Drawer is then discharged towards true owner (dispossessed holder) on whom the loss falls.

(2) The analysis does not change where collecting bank (but not drawee) broke a duty, except that true owner may have a remedy against collecting bank.

(3) Where drawee broke a duty, it may not debit drawer's account. Whether it may recover from a non-negligent bona fide collecting bank may depend on the law of restitution. In principle, drawee bank may be held liable to the true owner, except that in the absence of discharge given to the drawer (due to the inapplicability of UCL art. 35 by reason of the drawee's breach), the true owner has typically suffered no loss.

(4) The analysis does not change where both drawee and collecting bank are in breach except for the possible liability of the collecting bank. A remedy against the latter may be available to the drawee bank. In principle, it may also be available to the true owner, except that, as above, in the absence of discharge given to the drawer (due to the inapplicability of UCL art. 35 by reason of the drawee's breach), the true owner has typically suffered no loss.

(5) In each case, particularly where it is in tort, liability may be reduced or extinguished by the party liable successfully invoking plaintiff's contributory negligence.

(B) Where a signed and complete cheque was stolen from the drawer before its delivery to the payee, and was collected through the collecting bank by the thief,[66] the following rules apply:

(1) Where neither drawee nor collecting bank broke a duty, drawee may debit drawer's account. Loss thus falls on the drawer (who remains liable to the payee for the payment for which the cheque had been made out).

---

[65] Or someone who derives title from the thief and for some reason has not acquired title to the cheque under UCL art. 21. Such will be the case (i) where that person did not acquire the cheque in good faith and without gross negligence, or (ii) where that person derived title from someone who following the theft and forgery did not acquire the cheque in good faith and without gross negligence.   [66] Ibid.

(2) The analysis does not change where the collecting bank (but not drawee) broke a duty, except that the drawer may have a remedy against the collecting bank.

(3) Where drawee broke a duty, it may not debit drawer's account. Whether it may recover from a non-negligent bona fide collecting bank may depend on the law of restitution.

(4) The analysis does not change where both drawee and collecting bank are in breach except that the drawee has a cause of action against the collecting bank in either tort or contract.

(5) In each case, particularly where it is in tort, liability may be reduced or extinguished by the party liable successfully invoking plaintiff's contributory negligence.

(C) Where the cheque was stolen either from the drawer or from the true owner/holder, but was collected for and paid to a person who, notwithstanding the forged indorsement and the title derived from the thief, acquired a good title to it under UCL art. 21,[67] loss falls on the dispossessed owner. This rule applies irrespective of any knowledge or negligence by either the drawee or the collecting bank.

(IV) THE ANGLO-AMERICAN SYSTEM: THE BASIC SCHEME IN BEA JURISDICTIONS[68]

(a) The dispossessed 'true owner' (purported indorser)'s remedy

[29] In BEA jurisdictions, a forged indorsement constitutes a breach in the chain of title to the cheque: 'no right to retain the bill.[69] or give a discharge therefor or to enforce payment thereof against any party thereto can be acquired through or under [a forged] signature'.[70] A forged indorsement passes neither title nor lawful possession.[71] Title and the right to posses-

---

[67] Namely, where such a person acquired the cheque in good faith and without gross negligence.

[68] For a previous discussion, solely from a Canadian perspective, on which the current text draws and which it purports to improve, see B. Geva, 'Reflections on the Need to Revise the Bills of Exchange Act: Some Doctrinal Aspects' (1981–2), 6 Can. Bus. L.J. 269 at 314–31.

[69] Other than in Australia, a cheque is a species of a bill of exchange. See 3(iii)(1).

[70] See s. 24 in the UK, s. 48(1) in Canada, s. 23(a) in Israel, and s. 22 in South Africa. In Australia, an indorsement of a cheque is not effective unless it is signed by the indorser. See s. 41(1)(a). Unless otherwise indicated, all statutory references are to the BEA in the UK, South Africa and Canada, to the BEO in Israel and the Cheques Act in Australia.

[71] This is true also for a collecting bank in Canada, notwithstanding BEA s. 165(3) providing that '[w]here a cheque is delivered to a bank for deposit to the credit of a person and the bank credits him with the amount of the cheque, the bank acquires all the rights and

sion remain with the original (ex-)holder whose signature has been forged.

A transferee who derives title, directly or indirectly, through a forged indorsement is not a 'holder' in relation to parties whose signatures on the cheque preceded the forgery. This is so since no transferee can become a 'holder' without the 'negotiation' of the cheque to him,[72] and the negotiation of a cheque payable to order is by 'the indorsement of the holder'.[73] While being in possession of the cheque, the forger is neither its named payee nor indorsee, and thus is not a 'holder'.[74] Consequently, the taking from the forger, even by indorsement, is not 'negotiation'; hence, while being an indorsee in possession of the cheque, neither the taker from the forger, nor, consequently, any transferee deriving title from him, is a 'holder'.[75]

By definition, a 'holder in due course' must be a 'holder'.[76] Since the acquirer of a cheque payable to order through a forged indorsement is not a holder, no one who takes a cheque subsequent to a forged indorsement can be a holder in due course in relation to parties whose signatures preceded the forgery.[77] A holder in due course obtains a clear title to the

---

powers of a holder in due course of the cheque'. In *Boma Manufacturing* v. *Canadian Imperial Bank of Commerce* (1996), 140 D.L.R. (4th) 463 (S.C.C.), *rvs'g* 120 D.L.R. (4th) 250 (B.C. C.A.), *partially rvs'g* [1993] 7 W.W.R. 368 (B.C. S.C.), noting the broad language of the provision, but recognizing its underlying purpose, and speaking on that point for a unanimous court, Iacobucci J. held that 'the "person" in s. 165(3) must mean a person who is entitled to the cheque', such as 'the payee or the legitimate endorsee'. See paras. 74 and 76, and in general, paras. 69–85. La Forest J. ultimately agreed. See paras. 107–9. For an earlier authority in the same direction, see *Morguard Trust Co.* v. *Bank of Nova Scotia* (1982), 40 O.R. (2d) 211 (H.C.J.), *aff'd* (1983), 44 O.R. (2d) 384 (C.A.), where Maloney J. rationalized this rule (at 217), stating that '[s]ection 165(3) refers to the "delivery" of a cheque. Section [39] of the Act states that delivery "in order to be effectual must be made either by or under the authority of the party drawing, accepting or endorsing . . .". In this case there was no delivery within the meaning of this section and therefore there was no delivery of the cheque within the meaning of s. 165(3) . . .'. A proponent of the contrary view on the effect of s. 165(3) is I. Baxter, 'A Non Negotiable Crossing' (1982–3), 7 Can. Bus. L.J. 141. Note that strictly as a matter of technical statutory interpretation, Maloney J.'s explanation is not convincing since the quoted provision requires 'delivery' to be authorized by the 'endorser' and not the last 'endorsee'. Iacobucci J.'s policy oriented explanation in *Boma* is thus far more convincing.

[72] 'Negotiation' is the mode of transfer constituting the transferee 'the holder' of the instrument. See s. 31(1) in the UK, s. 59(1) in Canada, s. 30(a) in Israel, s. 29(1) in South Africa, and s. 40(1) in Australia.

[73] See s. 31(3) in the UK, s. 59(3) in Canada (where 'endorsement' substitutes 'indorsement'), s. 30(c) in Israel, and s. 29(3) in South Africa. See also s. 40 (2) in Australia.

[74] A holder of a cheque payable to order is defined as the payee or indorsee in possession of the cheque. See s. 1 in Israel and South Africa, s. 2 in the UK and Canada, and s. 3 in Australia.

[75] Notwithstanding the statutory definition, ibid.

[76] See s. 29 (1) in the UK, s. 55(1) in Canada, s. 28(a) in Israel, s. 27(1) in South Africa and s. 50(1) in Australia, each requiring a holder in due course to be a 'holder'.

[77] Consequently, the preclusions of a party from raising forgery against a holder in due course, discussed in (iv)(e) below, do not benefit a claimant through a forged indorsement.

cheque, free from 'any defect of title',[78] including all adverse claims,[79] which would have covered the claim of ownership of the person from whom the cheque has been stolen, and whose signature has been forged. But as indicated, a forged indorsement precludes holding in due course, without which forgery could not have overcome.

[30]   In the common law, the 'true owner', namely the one from whom the cheque has been stolen and whose indorsement has been forged,[80] may sue either in conversion or in money had and received any person through whose hands the cheque passed subsequent to the forgery. Each post-forgery indorsee, and possibly, as discussed further below, the drawee who paid the bill, fall into this category. In both actions, the defendant need not necessarily be the one in possession of the cheque at the time of the action. Also, having provided an indemnity against any possible adverse claim, the true owner may sue, on the lost cheque, prior parties liable thereon.[81]

[31]   Conversion is a tort of strict liability 'in which the moral concept of fault . . . plays no part'.[82] It has been defined as an act of wilful exercise of

---

[78] See s. 38(2) in the UK, s. 73(b) in Canada, s. 37(2) in Israel, s. 36(b) in South Africa and s. 49(2) in Australia.

[79] 'Defect of title' is the statutory equivalent of the common law 'equity attaching to the bill'. See *Alcock* v. *Smith* [1892] 1 Ch. 238, 263. Corresponding to the duplex nature of the negotiable instrument as both a chattel and a chose in action, such an 'equity' is either as to liability on the instrument, or as to its ownership. Equity as to ownership is an adverse claim. See Z. Chafee, 'Rights in Overdue Paper' (1917–18), 31 Harvard L. Rev. 1104 at 1109.

[80] Ownership of an instrument (other than that of a holder in due course) is established under general principles governing ownership in chattels. See e.g. in South Africa *First National Bank of SA* v. *Quality Tyres (1970) (Pty) Ltd.* 1995 (3) S.A. 556, particularly 567–70 (AD); and in Israel, *Kirstein*, above, n. 33 at 2286. *Kirstein* thus correctly held that a voidable title to an instrument acquired under a rescindable contract that has not yet been rescinded is nevertheless ownership. At the same time, *Quality Tyres* should not be taken to suggest that in the common law the transfer of ownership of a chattel requires the transfer of possession. Anyway, in the facts of that case, and notwithstanding the Court's view to the contrary, it is hard to see why there was not a constructive delivery of the instrument.

[81] In BEA jurisdictions, in connection with a lost or stolen cheque, both actions in conversion and money had and received are not statute based. Conversely, the action to enforce liability on a lost instrument is governed by ss. 69–70 in the UK, ss. 155–6 in Canada, ss. 69–70 in Israel, ss. 67–8 in South Africa, and s. 116 in Australia.

[82] *Marfani & Co.* v. *Midland Bank* [1968] 2 All E.R. 573 (C.A.) at 578, Diplock LJ, further defining fault, which is irrelevant in conversion, 'in the sense of either knowledge by the doer of an act that is likely to cause injury, loss or damage to another, or lack of reasonable care to avoid causing injury, loss or damage to another'. Ibid. Accordingly, and 'as a matter of principle', to a defendant sued in conversion, 'contributory negligence would not be available in the context of strict liability in tort'. *Boma*, above, n. 71 at 477, Iacobucci J. But cf. the case where a collecting bank loses its statutory protection (where available) from a conversion action due to its own negligence, in which case, it may arguably invoke the negligence of the plaintiff in reduction (or extinction) of its own liability. See v(b) s. 63, below. Cf. also *Nesbitt Burns Inc.* v. *Canada Trust & Mortgage*, Docket C32077, 22 Mar. 2000 [unreported] where the Ontario Court of Appeal (Feldman JA) distinguished between 'negligence' and 'preclusion' under s. 48(1) (Can.) (to which correspond s. 24 in the UK, s. 23(a) in Israel, s. 22 in South Africa, and s. 32(1)(e) in Australia (*semble*) and was prepared to

control over a chattel, without lawful justification, in a manner inconsistent with the right of the person entitled to it, and irrespective of the defendant's innocence or lack of knowledge as to any adverse entitlement.[83] It is an action for damages for the misappropriation of property[84] by the person entitled to the possession of the misappropriated chattel. Liability is restricted neither to the thief nor to one in possession of the converted chattel. Rather, '[a]ny person who, however innocently, obtains possession of the goods of a person who has been fraudulently deprived of them, and disposes of them whether for his own benefit or that of any other person, is guilty of conversion'.[85]

In the case of the conversion of a cheque, the remedy is available to the one entitled to the paper, and thus to the debt or claim embodied in it. It is the claim to the cheque, as a valuable chattel representing a monetary debt or claim, rather than the mere claim to the intangible debt itself, which provides the basis for the action for damages for the conversion of the cheque. Damages are however measured by the face value of the converted cheque,[86] namely, by the debt embodied therein; this is so notwithstanding the true owner's surviving remedy against parties that became liable on the instrument prior to its theft and the forgery of the indorsement, which has not been forfeited by the theft and forgery.[87]

In connection with the theft of a chattel and the conversion of its pro- **[32]** ceeds to the defendant's use, and as an alternative to conversion (or more precisely, to its predecessor trover), the action for money had and received

---

accept it as a defence to an action in conversion, even when in the particular facts of the case preclusion was by negligence.

[83] For a general discussion in the context of cheques, see e.g. Crawford, above, n. 40 at 1386; and A.G. Guest, *Chalmers and Guest on Bills of Exchange, Cheques and Promissory Notes*, 15th edn. (London: Sweet & Maxwell, 1998) at 167.

[84] 'For conversion there must be some conduct, however innocent in its intent, which amounted in effect to a denial of the plaintiff's rights in the goods . . . [T]he claim [is] for damages only.' See C. H. S. Fifoot, *History and Sources of the Common Law: Tort and Contract* (London: Stevens & Sons, 1949; rep. 1970, New York: Greenwood) at 109, and for the entire development, 102–25.

[85] *Hollins* v. *Fowler* (1875) L.R. 7 H.L. 575 at 797, Lord Chelmsford.

[86] *International Factors* v. *Rodriguez*, [1979] Q.B. 351 at 358, Sir David Cairns.

[87] In fact, unlike under the common law (see Crawford above, n. 40 at 1702–3), under BEA ss. 155–6 in Canada (as well as parallel provisions cited in n. 81 above), dealing with the action on a lost instrument, the claim on the instrument is not forfeited with the loss of the physical possession of the paper. However, an action on a lost instrument may be costly and cumbersome, and in any event, loss of tangibility leads to the impairment of the marketability of the claim embodied in the (now out of possession) paper. In fact, loss of possession may lead to the loss of the total value of an instrument payable to bearer (which may ultimately reach the hands of a holder in due course), but usually, not one payable to order. Nevertheless, the law has overlooked this distinction (as well as the change introduced by allowing an action on a lost instrument) and accorded damages to the extent of the full value of a converted instrument, even where payable to order, as if the loss of possession is tantamount to the loss of the entire claim embodied in it.

was introduced in the late seventeenth or early eighteenth century. This is a specie of *indebitatus assumpsit*, that can be brought instead of conversion on the basis of 'waiver of tort': 'the plaintiff may dispense with the wrong and suppose [the disposition of the valuable chattel by the defendant] made by his consent, and bring an action for . . . money received to his use', as if the defendant has always acted in the disposition of the chattel on the plaintiff's behalf, as his agent.[88] The conversion could thus have been waived, but the plaintiff, that is, the dispossessed owner, could 'sue for the same amount as money had and received to his use'.[89] No action based on the waiver of tort lies where the true owner has no tort to waive; hence, such an action is a mere alternative to conversion, and cannot be brought in the absence of its availability.

Historically, compared to trover (or conversion), '[t]he advantages of the new [money had and received] remedy were considerable; the pleadings were simpler, the action was not extinguished by death, and the plaintiff need not . . . declare and prove the precise value of the goods which the defendant had converted to his use'.[90] Over the years, the advantages have faded away. In principle, as applied to the misappropriation of cheques, the two alternative actions are quite indistinguishable today.[91]

(b) May the dispossessed 'true owner' (purported indorser) sue the drawee?

[33]　Under the BEA, in the absence of acceptance, the drawee 'is not liable on the instrument'.[92] This, however, does not seem to preclude liability in tort or money had and received, provided the elements of such liability are present.[93] According to Crawford, '[i]t has been repeatedly held that a

---

[88] See *Lamine* v. *Dorrell* (1705), 2 Ld. Raymond 1215; 92 E.R. 303, Powell J. For a comprehensive account, see J. Beatson, 'The Nature of Waiver of Tort' (1979) 17 U.W.O.L. Rev. 1.

[89] *Morrison* v. *London County and Westminster Bank* [1914] 3 K.B. 356 at 365, Lord Reading CJ. See also *United Australia* v. *Barclays Bank* [1941] A.C. 1 (H.L.) at 19, Lord Atkin.

[90] Fifoot, above, n. 84 at 365.

[91] Except that the defence of change in position may be invoked by a defendant sued in money had and received but not in conversion. See e.g. E. P. Ellinger and E. Lomnicka, *Modern Banking Law*, 2nd edn. (Oxford: Clarendon Press, 1994) at 503.

[92] See s. 53(1) in the UK, s. 126 in Canada, s. 53(a) in Israel, s. 51 in South Africa, and (almost verbatim) s. 88 in Australia.

[93] Admittedly, as a matter of statutory interpretation, the question was more difficult in the USA, where prior to the UCC, the corresponding provision to the Uniform Negotiable Instruments Law, NIL s. 189, provided that 'the bank is not liable to the holder, unless and until it accepts or certifies the check'. While the BEA provision speaks solely of the exclusion of the drawee's liability 'on the instrument', the old American statute read more broadly to exclude liability 'to the holder', which might have included liability in tort. Yet, the prevailing view was, on the basis of its context, that this NIL provision did not prevent the drawee from being liable other than either as assignee of the funds providing cover for

bank converts an instrument by dealing with it under the direction of one not authorized, either by collecting it or, *semble* (although this has not yet actually been decided) by paying it and in either case, making the proceeds available to someone other than the person entitled to possession'.[94] Indeed, obtaining payment for the thief or someone deriving title through the thief's indorsement, a collecting bank undoubtedly commits conversion. At the same time, there is some uncertainty as to the availability to the dispossessed true owner of a remedy against the payor bank, or in fact, more generally, against the drawee of a bill that was paid to one claiming through a forged indorsement.[95]

As indicated by Ellinger and Lomnicka, '[t]he paying bank . . . does not appropriate the chattel either in its own name or on behalf of a principal. It simply purports to obey an instruction for payment embodied in the cheque and issued by the customer'. At the same time, they continue, '[i]t is . . . arguable that the payment of the cheque discharges the instrument and hence has the effect of destroying the value of the cheque as a negotiable instrument. The purported conversion is, thus, the destruction of the instrument as an item of property'.[96] Recognizing that at least one dictum supports this view,[97] they nevertheless ultimately observe that a cheque is not discharged by payment other than to a holder and that the claimant under a forged indorsement is not a holder.[98] It follows, then, that 'payment to such a person does not discharge the cheque or destroy its negotiability' so that in conclusion, '[t]he paying bank is . . . not subject to an action in conversion by the true owner'.[99]

the cheque or as party to the instrument (which is the same situation as under the BEA). See R. W. Aigler, 'Rights of Holder of Bills of Exchange Against the Drawee' (1925), 38 Harvard L. Rev. 857 at 883–4.

[94] Crawford, above, n. 40 at 1386. See also Guest, above, n. 83 at 167–8, and F. R. Malan, 'Professional Responsibility and the Payment and Collection of Cheques', 1978 De Jure 326 at 331.

[95] I disagree with Aigler's statement that '[i]f the intermeddling by [a collecting] bank . . . amounts to a conversion, on principle there ought not to be any reason to doubt that the subsequent payment by the drawee should make it too a converter'. Aigler, above, n. 93 at 882–3. No conversion by the drawee bank takes place if the required elements do not exist, even if they do exist in the case of the collecting bank.

[96] Ellinger and Lomnicka, above, n. 91 at 362.

[97] *Smith* v. *Union Bank of London* (1875) L.R. 10; Q.B. 291 at 295 Blackburn J., *aff'd* (1875) 1 Q.B.D. 31. Doubts expressed in *Charles* v. *Blackwell* (1877) 2 C.P.D. 151 at 162–3 by Cockburn CJ are criticized by Ellinger and Lomnicka, ibid. at 363–4. Inconclusive support to the availability of conversion appears also in a dictum in *El Awadi* v. *Bank of Credit and Commerce Int'l* [1990] 1 Q.B. 606 at 627, Hutchison J.   [98] See (iv)(a), above.

[99] Above, n. 91 at 362–3. Obviously, in the absence of tort, no action on the waiver of tort is available to the dispossessed true owner against the paying bank. Ibid., at 363–4. The authors further conclude (at 364) that in the absence of privity between them, no alternative action for money had and received based on either payment made under mistake of fact or the total failure of consideration can be brought by the dispossessed true owner against the paying bank.

The point thus remains unsettled. From a doctrinal perspective, I find Ellinger's and Lomnicka's doubts to be quite persuasive. Also, there are no compelling policy grounds supporting the true owner's action against the drawee. Being entitled to sue the drawer as well as any subsequent indorsee, including a collecting bank, the true owner is adequately protected. There are thus no valid reasons for fastening strict liability on the drawee in favour of the true owner. Whether a case could be made for the drawee's liability to be based on fault, is a different question, to be subsequently discussed.[100]

(c) The drawer's remedy[101]

[34] The drawer of a cheque payable to order which was paid by the drawee bank over a forged indorsement may sue that bank for breach of contract for paying the cheque contrary to the drawer's instructions. Such instructions, embodied in the drawer's/customer's order which constitutes the cheque, were to pay the cheque to the payee or someone deriving title from the payee. Payment to one claiming through a forged indorsement, that is, to someone other than one who derives title from the payee, is wrongful. Being contrary to the drawer's instructions, such payment constitutes a breach of the banking contract between the drawer/customer and his bank.

Under s. 48(3) of the Canadian Act, the drawer's action against the drawee is barred 'unless [the drawer] gives notice in writing of the forgery to the drawee within one year after he has acquired notice of the forgery'. This is an extremely long period and hence no meaningful protection to the drawee is provided thereby. According to Crawford and Falconbridge, 'the one year . . . probably ought to be regarded as a maximum . . . rather than a period that may be allowed to elapse with impunity'.[102] No corresponding provision exists elsewhere. There is however case law requiring a person, particularly a customer, to advise the drawee (or any other payor) promptly of any known forgery relating to that person's own signature.[103] In principle, this ought to be applicable to any known forgery, where the late notification to the drawee caused loss to the drawee, either by making payment, or by missing the opportunity to have an effective recourse against the forger or a party subsequent to him, who in the

---

[100] See (v)(b), below.

[101] Insofar as it concerns the drawer's remedy against the collecting bank, the ensuing discussion reproduces, with minor modifications, B. Geva, 'Conversion of Unissued Cheques and the Fictitious or Non Existing Payee: Boma v. CIBC' (1997), 28 Can. Bus. L.J. 177 at 186–92 (hereafter: Geva, 'Boma').   [102] Above, n. 40 at 1392.

[103] See e.g. *Greenwood* v. *Martin Bank Ltd*. [1933] A.C. 51 and *Ewing* v. *Dominion Bank* (1904), 35 S.C.R. 133, extensively discussed in 4.B(iii).

meantime has either become insolvent or absconded. Accordingly, a drawer with knowledge of a forged indorsement, who failed to advise the drawee promptly of the forgery, ought to be estopped from challenging the effectiveness of the drawee's payment, and hence, is bound by the corresponding debit to his account. Conversely, when timely notice has been given by the drawer to the drawee, the drawer's remedy against the drawee who paid on a forged indorsement is on contract, and arises regardless of any particular provision of the BEA.

Whether the drawer of an unissued cheque payable to order, from **[35]** whom the cheque was stolen, may sue in conversion a collecting bank, that is, a post-forged indorsement indorsee, who obtained payment from the drawee bank, was extensively dealt with by the Supreme Court of Canada in *Boma Manufacturing* v. *Canadian Imperial Bank of Commerce*.[104] Judgment was given for the drawer. Speaking for a unanimous court, and treating the drawer as the true owner of the cheque, Iacobucci J. followed the conventional wisdom.[105] The leading authority in Canada is *Jervis Webb Co.* v. *Bank of Nova Scotia*,[106] which followed a line of English authorities.[107]

Nevertheless, in my view, such a remedy in the drawer's hands is contrary to principle. As discussed,[108] conversion is an action for damages for the misappropriation of property. An action for the conversion of a cheque is available to the one entitled to the paper, and thus to the debt or claim embodied in it. Inasmuch as a forged indorsement does not pass title to the cheque, its true owner, such as the dispossessed holder whose indorsement signature has been forged, may sue in conversion, or in money had and received, any person through whose hands the cheque passed subsequent to the forgery. It is the claim to the cheque, as a valuable chattel representing a monetary debt or claim, which provides the basis for the action for the conversion of the cheque.

On his part, the drawer of an unissued cheque does not own a claim on **[36]** the instrument. In his hands, the cheque represents neither a claim against, nor a debt owed by, the bank, or for that matter, anyone else. In the drawer's hands, the unissued cheque is a mere piece of paper, whose

---

[104] Above, n. 71.

[105] See N. Rafferty, 'Forged Cheques: A Consideration of the Rights and Obligations of Banks and Their Customers' (1979–80), 4 Can. Bus. L.J. 208 at 228–9. Rafferty correctly points out (ibid. at 228), and Iacobucci J. agreed (above, n. 71 par. 37), that upon the issue of the cheque, namely, its delivery to the first holder, the right to sue in conversion is conferred on the first holder, so that from that point, all agree that no conversion remedy is available to the drawer.   [106] (1965), 49 D.L.R. (2d) 692 (Ont. H.C.J.).

[107] Ibid., 699–702. These authorities are discussed below. I thus overstated the case by saying in 'Reflections', above, n. 68 at 330, that '[n]one of the authorities ... compelled the result'. I should have said that none of the authorities is convincing, as further discussed below.   [108] See (iv)(a), above.

destruction, loss, or misappropriation, will not deprive him of any valuable asset. While he is the owner of the paper, the drawer is nevertheless not the owner of the cheque.[109] No foundation to an action of conversion thus exists.

Indeed, to avoid double liability, a party who discharged his obligation on an instrument is entitled to its surrender. Yet, he is not entitled to damages for the misappropriation of his property. In fact, the cancellation or destruction of the instrument is a complete defence to the discharged party's action.[110] Obviously, the wilful destruction of a chattel is not a good defence to a conversion action. This demonstrates that the discharged party's action to the surrender of the instrument is not in conversion.[111] Rather, it is an action on the discharge agreement. Similarly, a drawer who has defences to his liability, such as the absence of issue of the instrument,[112] is thereby discharged, and is entitled to the surrender (or destruction) of the instrument, as a piece of paper, on the basis of the discharge, and not because of its value as property incorporating a debt.

Stated otherwise, conversion is available to an adverse claimant, asserting an equity of ownership to the instrument. It is not available to one pleading an equity of liability or defence to an action on the instrument.[113] The adverse claimant must own the claim *on* the instrument through the claim *to* the instrument. Typically, he is a dispossessed holder.[114] On his

---

[109] A position to the contrary, emerging in South Africa, should not be welcome. See *obiter* in *Quality Tyres*, above, n. 80 at 567 followed in *African Life Assurance Co. Ltd.* v. *NBS Bank Ltd.* [2000], 1 All S.A. 545, 550 (Local Div.) and *Columbus Joint Venture* v. *ABSA Bank*, s. 2 Case No. 98/24221, 17 Dec. 1999 (H.C. Wit. Local Div.) [unreported].

[110] In early common law, it was the cancellation or destruction of a sealed document, rather than its mere surrender which secured the paying party's discharge. See e.g. F. Pollock, *Principles of Contract at Law and in Equity*, 3rd American edn., from 7th English edn. by G. I. Wald and S. Williston (Littleton, Colo.: Fred B. Rothman & Co. 1988), 843.

[111] Indeed, not every claim to the surrender of the instrument is tantamount to a claim of ownership or right to possession, so as to give rise to an action in conversion. Suppose A drew on B a bill payable to C. B's acceptance was procured by A's fraud. C negotiated the bill to D who took it with knowledge of the fraud so that D cannot be a holder in due course. Under such circumstances, B has an equity of liability or defence, but is not an adverse claimant to the instrument. At most, B is entitled to receive the instrument temporarily in order to cancel his signature. See Barak (Nature), above, n. 15 at 67–8.

[112] 'Issue' is defined in BEA s. 1 in South Africa and Israel, s. 2 in the UK and Canada, and s. 3 in Australia as 'the first delivery of [an instrument], complete in form, to a person who takes it as holder'. Under ss. 38–40 in Canada, s. 21 in the UK, s. 20 in Israel, s. 19 in South Africa, and ss. 25–9 in Australia, except as against a holder in due course, the absence of delivery is a defence to liability on an instrument. Holding in due course status cannot be acquired through a forged indorsement.

[113] For the fundamental distinction between these two types of equities affecting an instrument, namely, claims and defences, see Chafee, above, n. 79 at 1109.

[114] He could however be a dispossessed non-holder owner, as for example, a transferee of an unindorsed bill under s. 31(4) in the UK, s. 60(1) in Canada, s. 30 (d) in Israel, s. 29(4) in South Africa, and s. 42(1) in Australia.

part, the drawer may not recover on the instrument,[115] rather, he is the party liable on it, who may nevertheless have a defence to his liability. This does not provide standing to sue in conversion.

The point is well stated by an Official Comment to Article 3 of the Uniform Commercial Code.[116]

There is no reason why a drawer should have an action in conversion. The [cheque] represents an obligation of the drawer rather than a property of the drawer. The drawer has an adequate remedy against the [drawee] bank for re-credit of the drawer's account for unauthorized payment of the [cheque].

Indeed, as indicated, the drawer of an unissued cheque which was paid by the drawee bank over a forged indorsement may sue that bank for the breach of contract, namely for paying the cheque contrary to the drawer's instructions. In turn, as will be discussed below, the drawee bank may pass on the loss to the collecting bank. No direct remedy is, however, available to the drawer against the collecting bank. Circuity of action is thus not avoided, but for a good reason: the drawee bank, with whom the drawer is in an ongoing relationship, may be in a better position than the collecting bank, which may be a total stranger to the drawer, to raise defences to the drawer's action, such as estoppel, or under provisions dealing with the fictitious or non-existing payee.[117]

Precedents upholding the conversion action of a drawer of an unis-   **[37]** sued cheque are unconvincing. *Jervis B. Webb Co.*,[118] followed by Iacobucci J., does not have an analysis of its own, but is rather based on several English authorities, which will now be considered.

The first case is *Ogden* v. *Benas*.[119] This however was 'an action upon *concessit solvere* in the Lord Mayor's Court, London'.[120] Such an action was stated to be 'a form of action of debt on simple contract which lay by custom . . . [and] is said to have had the advantage of being more comprehensive count than almost any other . . .'.[121] This seems to be a poor

---

[115] Except for in unusual circumstances, such as under s. 59(2)(a) in the UK, (correspon-ding to s. 139(a) in Canada, s. 60(b)(1) in Israel, and s. 57(3) in South Africa, see also s. 87 in Australia) providing that 'where a bill payable to . . . a third party is paid by the drawer, the drawer may enforce payment thereof against the acceptor . . .'. Barak (Nature), above, n. 15 at 93–5 explains this result on the property acquired by the drawer in such circumstances. In such a case, then, there is no preclusion against a conversion action by a dispossessed drawer owner.

[116] Official Comment 1 to UCC §3–420, as revised in 1990.

[117] From an American perspective, the point is well presented in J. J. White and R. S. Summers, *Uniform Commercial Code*, 4th edn. (St Paul, Minn.: West, 1995) at §16–4. In the various American jurisdictions, under the UCC, where a duty of care is owed by the cus-tomer to his bank (see UCC §§3–406 and 4–406, as revised in 1990), the range of defences available to the drawee bank against its customer is likely to be broader than in BEA juris-dictions. See (vii), below. Yet, the policy argument is valid in BEA jurisdictions as well.

[118] Above, n. 106.   [119] (1874), L.R. 9; C.P. 513.   [120] Ibid.

[121] J. Burke, *Jowitt's Dictionary of English Law*, 2nd edn. (London: Sweet & Maxwell, 1977) at 408.

authority for the availability of the common law conversion action. More-over, in the course of his judgment, Keating J. spoke of 'the drawer's right to get back his money from one who has obtained it by means of the forged indorsement'. He further spoke of the wrongful payment by the drawee 'of the money of the [drawer]'.[122] This language strongly suggests a cause of action for the misappropriation or conversion of funds, a cause of action which is unknown to the common law, and is quite distinguish-able from the conversion of the cheque itself.

Arnold v. *Cheque Bank*[123] dealt with the action of the purchaser, and not the drawer, of a bank draft payable to the purchaser's creditor.[124] As such it is completely distinguishable. The next two English cases[125] were *Vinden* v. *Hughes*[126] and *Macbeth* v. *North & South Wales Bank*.[127] The former did not discuss any theory underlying the drawer's action. In the latter,[128] Bray J. thought that both *Ogden* v. *Benas* and *Arnold* v. *Cheque Bank* provided a basis for both conversion and money had an received. Both *Vinden* and *Macbeth* are thus poor authority for establishing the drawer's conversion action.

Finally, *Morison* v. *London County & Westminster Bank*[129] was relied upon. Indeed, in the course of his judgment, Lord Reading CJ stated that the drawer of an unissued cheque 'is entitled, prima facie, to recover . . . either . . . damages for conversion or [in] money had and received'.[130] Yet this statement was not supported by any rigorous analysis; rather, as its basis, he cited cases dealing with the *holder*'s conversion action,[131] clearly a very different situation.

In my opinion, therefore, the issue of the drawer's conversion action should have been reopened in *Boma*. For reasons explained above, the better view is the one expressed in the United States, in *Stone & Webster Engineering Corp.* v. *First National Bank & Trust Co.*,[132] under which neither doctrine nor policy justify the drawer's conversion action.

---

[122] Above, n. 119 at 516.   [123] (1876), 1 C.P.D. 578.

[124] For the purchaser of a bank draft payable to his creditor, known as 'remitter', as the first owner (though not holder) of the instrument, with the power to recover on it as well as to transfer it, see B. Geva, 'The Autonomy of the Banker's Obligation on Bank Drafts and Certified Cheques' (1994), 73 Can. Bar. Rev. 21 at 30–1. The remitter standing to sue in con-version is thus consistent with the property foundations of the conversion action.

[125] In both, as well as in *Morison*, n. 129 below, the drawer lost, though on grounds other than the unavailability of the drawer's action, which in fact was upheld.

[126] [1905] 1 K.B. 795.

[127] [1906] 2 K.B. 718, *aff'd* [1908] 1 K.B. 13 (C.A.), [1908] A.C. 137 (H.L.).

[128] [1906] 2 K.B. 718 at 721.   [129] [1914] 3 K.B. 356.   [130] Ibid., at 364.

[131] Ibid., These cases were *Gordon* v. *London City and Midland Bank* [1902] 1 K.B. 242, 246, and *Fine Art Society* v. *Union Bank of London* (1886–7) 17 Q.B.D. 705.

[132] (1962), 345 Mass. 1, 184 N.E. 2d 358, decided under the pre-1990 UCC Article 3, which did not specifically exclude the drawer's conversion action. In explaining the present statu-tory preclusion of the drawer's action, Official Comment 1 to current UCC §3–420 specifi-cally approves of this judgment.

In fact, a step in the right direction was already made in *Arrow Transfer Co. v. Royal Bank of Canada*.[133] There, the British Columbia Court of Appeal first dismissed a conversion action against a collecting bank by a plaintiff whose signature was forged on a blank cheque stolen from him. In the course of his judgment, Robertson JA stated that in order to succeed in conversion for the value represented by a bill of exchange, 'the plaintiff must be the true owner of the piece of paper *qua* cheque and not simply the owner of the piece of paper *qua* piece of paper'.[134] At the Supreme Court of Canada, both Martland[135] and Laskin[136] JJ approved of this statement.[137] In *Boma*, the trial judge purported to distinguish the cases on the basis that in *Boma* the cheques had been signed by authorized signing officers so that the signed cheques 'were not "worthless paper" '.[138] Nevertheless, he overlooked the fact that in *Arrow Transfer*, plaintiff was held to be estopped from asserting the forgery of his signature, so as ultimately, to be liable for the amount of the cheques.[139] Hence, the cases are not really distinguishable.

(d) The 'true owner''s remedy in BEA civil law jurisdictions

Neither the conversion nor the money had and received remedies are **[38]** specified by the BEA. Arguably, being common law remedies for the misappropriation of property in chattels generally, rather than providing specific recourse to the true owner of misappropriated cheques,[140] they do not form part of the law of bills and notes in the strict sense.[141] As such they

---

[133] (1972), 27 D.L.R. (3d) 81 (S.C.C.). See also *Number 10 Management* v. *Royal Bank of Canada* (1976), 69 D.L.R. (3d) 99 (Man. C.A.).

[134] (1971), 19 D.L.R. (3d) 420 (B.C. C.A.).   [135] Above, n. 63 at 87–8.

[136] Ibid., at 103–5.

[137] This aspect of *Arrow Transfer* was followed in Australia in *Koster's Premier Pty* v. *The Bank of Adelaide* (1981), 28 S.A.S.R. 355, critically commented on by A. Tyree, 'The Liability of Banks Collecting Forged Cheques' (1983), 11 Aust. Bus. L. Rev. 236.

[138] Above, n. 71 at 377.

[139] In fact, I agree with Tyree, above, n. 137, that to the extent that it is founded on the forged drawer's signature, the 'worthless paper' argument cannot be taken at face value. However, in my view, it is the unissued cheque which constitutes 'worthless paper', regardless of whether it was signed by the purported drawer. It is on this point that I part with Tyree, who relies on the English authorities discussed above, which permit the conversion action by the drawer of an unissued cheque signed by him, and then concludes that a same rule ought to apply where the drawer's signature has been forged.

[140] But see Crawford's opinion (above, n. 40 at 1368–9) to the contrary, discussed below.

[141] For the broad/strict sense distinction as to the law of negotiable instruments, and its relevance to the application of the common law to a case not covered by the express provisions of the BEA, see e.g. B. Geva, *Financing Consumer Sales and Product Defences* (Toronto: Carswell, 1984) at 255–61.

do not exist in those civil law jurisdictions where the BEA applies, such as South Africa and the Province of Quebec.[142]

In both jurisdictions, the discussion focuses on the position of a collecting bank that collected a cheque for a customer over a forged indorsement and handed over the proceeds to the customer, namely, to the depositor of the cheque. As in the common law, the position of an indorsee such as a collecting bank is equated to that of a purchaser of a stolen property who parted with it. However, unlike the common law, civil law does not fasten liability on such a person for the mere misappropriation of property, at least as long as he acted innocently.

South Africa[143]

[39]   In South Africa, the starting point is *Leal & Co.* v. *Williams*.[144] Dealing under Roman Dutch law with the true owner's right to recover the value of a stolen bank draft, Innes CJ recognized the right of a true owner of stolen property 'to follow his property and vindicate it anywhere' against the person actually in its possession, as well as to 'bring an action *ad exhibendum* to recover the property or its value (should it be consumed) against the thief or his heirs, or against any person who has received it with knowledge of the tainted title'. However, he conceded, unlike the common law doctrine of conversion, Roman Dutch law does not permit an action by the true owner against 'a bona fide intermediary, who obtained the stolen property and parted with it again'.[145]

Subsequently, this point was restated in *Yorkshire Insurance Co.* v. *Standard Bank*.[146] In the course of his judgment, Tindall J. specifically pointed out the departure from English law,[147] and recognized the application of 'the Roman Dutch authorities'. Thereunder, no parallel to the English tort of conversion exists, and 'the person who innocently received stolen property and has parted with it innocently . . . is not liable to the true owner for the value of the property'.[148] Furthermore, the statutory

---

[142] In Israel, the true owner may sue the collecting bank either in conversion as codified by s. 52 of the Torts Ordinance [New Version], 1968, Laws of State of Israel, No. 10, p. 266, or in restitution. R. Ben-Oliel, *Banking Law General Part* (Jerusalem: Institute, 1996) at 383.

[143] See C. Hugo, 'The Negligent Collecting Bank: Recent Decisions Introduce a New Era' (1992), 3 Stellenbosch L.R. 115, and South African Law Commission, *Report on the Investigation into the Payments System in South African Law* (Project 50, Aug. 1994) at 435–58 (hereafter 'SALC Report'). See also D. V. Cowen and L. Gering, *Cowen on the Law of Negotiable Instruments in South Africa*, 4th edn. (Cape Town: Juta, 1966) at 426–40; F. R. Malan and J. T. Pretorius, *Malan on Bills of Exchange, Cheques and Promissory Notes*, 3rd edn. (Durban: Butterworths, 1997) at 422–46; and L. Gering, *Handbook on the Law of Negotiable Instruments*, 2nd edn. (Cape Town: Juta, 1997) at 286–97.   [144] 1906 T.S. 554.

[145] Ibid., 558–9.   [146] 1928 W.L.D. 251.   [147] Ibid., at 278.

[148] Ibid., at 281–2. Roman Dutch law permits the owner to pursue his property into the hands of strangers, even those who came to it honestly, but only as long as they did not part with it honestly. See SALC Report, above, n. 143 at 438. For the fact that Roman Dutch law

protection of a collecting bank acting without negligence[149] was not read to suggest liability for negligence, but rather, to negate liability that might have existed otherwise.[150] Accordingly, under the law of delict, and in the absence of any rule fastening liability in negligence in such a case, only a collecting bank acting in bad faith was to be held liable to the true owner.[151]

This state of law was modified in 1943. The Bills of Exchange Amendment Act of that year adopted the common law action of conversion, though only for crossed cheques marked 'not negotiable'. It thus permitted the true owner 'to recover from any person who was possessor . . . after the theft or loss, [who] either gave consideration . . . or took it as a donee'. However, a collecting bank is not regarded as having given consideration for the cheque 'merely because it has in its own books credited its customer's account with the amount of the cheque before receiving payment thereof, or because any such payment is applied towards the reduction or settlement of any debt owed by the customer to the bank'.[152] In all such circumstances, inasmuch as it gave no consideration, a collecting bank is exonerated from liability under the statute. However, according to Hugo,[153]

A bank which allows its client to draw against a cheque deposited by him for collection before having received the proceeds of the cheque from the drawee, has . . . given consideration for the cheque, and is not protected . . . The same probably holds true where the bank, as consideration for the specific cheque, agrees to allow its client to draw against such cheque. A general agreement in terms of which the client is allowed to draw against deposited cheques, is more problematic . . . In terms of [the statute] consideration must be given 'therefore', that is for the specific cheque in question. The wording . . . suggests reciprocity, a true *quid pro quo*. Such a general agreement [while constituting 'value'] . . . will not suffice.

For a collecting bank handling a crossed cheque marked 'not negotiable' prior to its collection, a distinction was thus drawn between, on

---

does not recognize the English tort of conversion, see e.g. *Zimbabwe Banking Corp.* v. *Pyramid Motor Corp.* 1985 4 S.A. 553 (Z.S.C.) at 555.

[149] S. 80 of the Transvaal Bills of Exchange Proclamation, 'taken verbatim from section 82 of the English Bills of Exchange Act. Section 82 was designed to protect the bank . . . against its common law conversion liability'. Hugo, above, n. 143 at 117.

[150] For the English provision and its rationale, see (v)(b), below.

[151] In the technical jargon of South African Roman Dutch law, '[t]he *actio ad exhibendum* is clearly available to the true owner in the event of the collecting bank having collected in bad faith'. Conversely, in the absence of a legal duty imposed on the collecting towards the true owner not to cause him economic loss, 'there is no room for liability under the *lex Aquilia*'. See Hugo, above, n. 143 at 120 and 117.

[152] Currently, this is s. 81(1) and (5) of the South African Bills of Exchange Act No. 34 of 1964, as amended by a few grammatical and non-substantive changes, made by the SA Bill, above, n. 6, proclaimed 1 March 2001.

[153] Above, n. 143 at 119.

one hand, merely crediting the account with the amount of the cheque, and on the other hand, in addition, either allowing its customer to draw against the uncleared cheque, or agreeing to allow him to draw against it. Mere crediting is not considered as the giving of consideration. Thus, where the cheque bears a forged indorsement, mere crediting its amount to the account does not give rise to statutory conversion. Conversely, allowing the customer to draw or agreeing to allow him to draw against a specific uncleared cheque, involves the giving of consideration, so as to charge the collecting bank with statutory liability of the conversion of a cheque bearing a forged indorsement.

In the absence of any mention of good faith or lack of negligence, the prevailing view is that under the statute, a collecting bank that gave consideration or quid pro quo to a customer over a forged indorsement, is not protected from the statutory conversion action, regardless of its good faith and lack of negligence. Nor do negligence or bad faith fasten statutory liability on a collecting bank that merely credited the customer's account, namely, gave no consideration or quid pro quo. In short, under the statutory amendment, pre-1943 jurisprudence remained fully in force; a bank that collected for a customer over a forged indorsement any type of cheque, whether or not crossed and marked 'not negotiable', and whether the bank gave or did not give consideration for the cheque, was not liable in negligence.

As a matter of policy, the exoneration of the negligent collecting bank was rationalized on two grounds. The first was the alleged great burden to be placed on collecting banks. The second addressed alleged complications to be introduced by issues of causation and contributory negligence.[154]

Indac Electronics (Pty) v. Volkskas Bank[155] marked the turning point in dealing with the liability of the negligent collecting bank. Vivier JA pointed out that insofar as 'Aquilian liability for pure economic loss . . . was . . . recognised . . . in 1979', relieving the negligent collecting bank from liability to the true owner is out of line with developments in tort law, so that there is 'no reason in principle why a collecting banker should not be held liable under the extended *lex Aquila* for negligence to the true owner of a cheque . . .'.[156]

---

[154] See *Worcester Advice Office* v. *First National Bank* 1990 4 S.A. 811(C)

[155] 1992 1 S.A. 783 (A).

[156] Ibid. at 796–7. In the Roman Dutch terminology, Aquilian liability is tort (or delictual) liability. In the old Roman law, *lex Aquila*, attributed to the third century BCE, established general delictual liability. *Inter alia*, it stated that 'if any one shall have caused damage to another by wrongful burning, breaking, or spoiling, be he condemned to pay to the owner the value which the thing has had in the last thirty days'. See R. W. Lee, *The Elements of Roman Law* (London: Sweet & Maxwell, 1962) at 394. 'The lex Aquila was undoubtedly the most important statutory enactment on Roman private law subsequent to the XII Tables . . .

In the course of his judgment, Vivier JA founded the required unlawfulness of the collecting bank's conduct, without which Aquilian liability cannot arise, on the breach of a duty by the collecting bank. That duty was to avoid causing pure economic loss to the true owner of a lost or stolen cheque by negligently dealing with it.[157] As the basis for such duty, Vivier JA cited the resulting limited potential for liability in terms of claimants and amounts, the need to protect the true owner, and the position of the collecting bank as a provider of professional services in the collection of cheques who alone can ensure that a cheque is collected for the true owner and who has the most effective recourse against the typical wrongdoer, namely, its customer. He thus stated that a delictual action for damages is available to the owner of a stolen or lost cheque, where he can establish that (a) the collecting bank received payment of the cheque on behalf of someone who was not entitled to payment, that (b) in receiving such payment the collecting bank acted unlawfully and negligently, that (c) the conduct of the collecting bank caused the true owner to sustain loss, and that (d) the damages claimed represent proper compensation for such loss.[158]

Currently then, in connection with a lost or stolen cheque, case law in South Africa fastens on the collecting bank liability to the true owner in negligence.[159] This is apart from the statutory conversion liability to the true owner of any indorsee, whether a donee or one who gave quid pro quo, including a collecting bank, of a crossed cheque marked 'not negotiable'. A proposed Cheques Act would have deleted the statutory conversion provision and codified, in s. 59, the negligence rule.[160] In what is apparently consistent with the present law, the proposed legislation would have specifically recognized the availability to a negligent collecting bank of a contributory negligence plea. Finally, proposed s. 59 would

---

[T]he most important change brought about by [it] was the transition from a system of fixed penalties to a more flexible assessment of damage suffered by the victim of the wrong.' Zimmermann, above, n. 63 at 953, 961.

[157] Above, n. 155, at 801. See SALC Report, above, n. 143 at 445.

[158] Ibid., at 797. See SALC Report, above, n. 143 at 441. Technically, this was obiter. However, the view that such a collecting bank's duty is too onerous and that, therefore, in the interest of banking public, a collecting bank should not be liable to the true owner for negligence, was subsequently specifically rejected in *Kwamashu Bakery* v. *Standard Bank*, above, n. 50, thereby confirming the authority of *Indac Electronics*.

[159] The onus of proof as to the defendant collecting bank's negligence rests on the plaintiff true owner. See *Fedgen Insurance Ltd.* v. *Bankorp* Ltd. 1994 (2) S.A. 399 (W). In *Columbus Joint Venture*, above, n. 109, the court (Malan J.) considered the content of the duty to cover the account opening, but did not find a breach of such a duty in the facts of the case. See extensive analysis in s. 4.

[160] The proposed provision specifically provides for the liability to the true owner of 'any bank, whether or not it is also the paying bank, whose negligence in collecting payment of the cheque contributed to . . . loss'. See s. 59(1). This proposed Cheques Act appeared as Annexture B to the SALC Report, above, n. 143 at 524.

have partially defined the collecting bank's negligence in terms of (i) opening an account for a customer without taking reasonable steps to verify the identity, address, and standing of the customer, or (ii) collecting payment for a customer who, on the face value of the information on the cheque, does not appear to be entitled to payment.[161]   These proposals have not been acted on.

Quebec

[40]   In Quebec, the collecting bank may become liable to the true owner under CcQ art. 1457, which provides that '[e]very person has a duty to abide by the rules of conduct which lie upon him, according to the circumstances, usage or law, so as not to cause injury to another'. Having failed in this duty, this person 'is responsible for any injury he causes [by this fault][162] to another . . . and is liable to reparation for the injury'. Where a cheque is collected over a forged indorsement, the true owner's recourse is based on the collecting bank's fault[163] in failing to verify the indorser's identity or authority.[164] However, in connection with the collection of a cheque bearing a forged indorsement, some controversy exists as to the existence of loss, as well as to whether common law conversion has been entirely superseded.

The leading case is *Norwich Union Fire Insurance Society* v. *Banque Canadienne Nationale*.[165] In that case, an intermediary obtained from an insured, cheques payable to an insurance company, before the premiums for which they were given were due. The cheques were indorsed by the intermediary and deposited to his own account. The majority held that the intermediary was the insurance company's agent but that he had no authority to indorse the cheques. Nonetheless, the action of the insurance company, the true owner of the cheques, against the collecting bank was dismissed.[166]

---

[161] Conversely, under proposed s. 59(3)(b), 'a bank shall not be negligent in collecting payment of a cheque by reason only of the fact that the payee or indorsee of a cheque is wrongly designated or that his name is misspelt or by reason only that of any indorsement of the cheque, or the absence of the indorsement of the payee, or an irregularity in any indorsement in the cheque'.

[162] Surprisingly, the bracketed words, crucial as they are to the application of the provision (see immediately below), and which are part of the French text, do not appear in the corresponding English text.

[163] Accordingly, a non-negligent collecting bank was exonerated in *Rainville* v. *Banque Canadienne Nationale* [1972] C.S. 849.

[164] N. L'Heureux and É. Fortin, *Droit bancaire*, 3rd edn. (Cowansville, Que.: Yvon Blais, 1999) at 377–8.   [165] [1934] 4 D.L.R. 223 (S.C.C.).

[166] Dismissal was unanimous, as the third judge, Cannon J. thought that the intermediary's indorsement was authorized so that the insurance company's action could have been based solely on the bank's knowledge of the intermediary's breach of trust. In the facts of the case, neither knowledge nor bad faith were proven.

Forming the majority, both Duff CJC and Rinfret J. agreed that 'actions in conversion are unknown to the law of Quebec'.[167] Duff CJC specifically held that the predecessor of CcQ art. 1457 applies.[168] Both judges thought, however, that no damage was sustained by the insurance company.[169] Duff CJC suggested that in the common law, under conversion, the insurance company could have recovered the face value of the cheques. He recognized the collecting bank's potential liability under the predecessor of CcQ art. 1457 but went on to point out, in the facts of the case, that the insurance company had valueless rights against the insured, presumably, since premiums were not due yet. Duff CJC thus held that no damages were incurred by the insurance company, so that its action could not succeed.[170]

Rinfret J. concurred. Observing that 'the cheques never reached the insurance company itself' he stated that the insurance company 'still retains its full recourse for the premiums ... against [the insured]', so that the insured's underlying debt is still subsisting.[171] Accordingly, in his view, since it incurred no loss, '[t]he [insurance company's] action as brought could not be maintained'.[172]

Some aspects of the majority analysis are troublesome. It is hard to see how the original debt subsisted and had not been suspended upon the delivery of the cheque by the insured/drawer to the insurance company/true owner's agent,[173] even in prepayment of the premiums. In fact, and notwithstanding what seems to follow from Rinfret J.'s reasoning, there ought to be no difference between the facts in *Norwich Union* and the case where the drawer delivered to the payee a cheque payable to the payee, which was subsequently stolen by the payee's own employee or agent, who collected it for his own benefit over a forged indorsement. Stated otherwise, the cheque delivered to its agent was a valuable asset in the insurance company's hands.

Equally valuable was the insurance company/true owner's claim to the cheque following its misappropriation. True, under the BEA, the loss of a cheque does not forfeit the action on it,[174] whether in the context of the common law or the Quebec civil code, the true owner would have recourse against the drawer on the basis of the cheque ownership.

---

[167] Above, n. 165 at 230, Rinfret J. See also at 228–9, Duff CJC.
[168] Above, n. 165 at 229. That provision was CcBC art. 1053.
[169] This argument is supported by M. Deschamps in (1973), 33 Rev. du B 171.
[170] Above, n. 165 at 229.   [171] Above, n. 165 at 231.
[172] Above, n. 165 at 232. Rinfret J. further noted there that 'the real debate is between the bank and its customer', presumably the insured, who may be precluded from disputing the intermediary's authority to indorse the cheques. But surely this confuses the roles of the collecting and payor (drawee) banks.
[173] For the conditional payment principle see e.g. *Re Charge Card Services* [1988] 3 All E.R. 702 (C.A.) at 707.   [174] Ss. 155–6 in Canada.

However, as indicated, the availability to the dispossessed owner of a recourse against the drawer on the basis of the ownership of the lost or stolen cheque is no bar in the common law to the true owner's action in conversion.[175] Nor did this mere availability of recourse by the true owner against the drawer appear to trouble Duff CJC. It is submitted that both judges erred in holding that in the facts of the case, even prior to appropriation, the true owner had no recourse against the drawer on the cheque, so that his rights in the cheque had always been valueless. It is thus unclear to me why damages were not awarded against the collecting bank whose fault led to the loss.

Nonetheless, this criticism is directed at the application of both the law of negotiable instruments and the Quebec civil code to the facts of the case. The analysis does not affect the conclusion that common law conversion cannot be invoked in Quebec where it is superseded by a statutory provision fastening liability on a collecting bank only on the basis of fault. At the same time, the discussion points out that in principle, where the collecting bank was at fault, no difference arises between the scope of liability fastened on it under Quebec civil code and under common law conversion. This is true not only where the lost or stolen cheque was a valuable asset. Also, where a lost or stolen cheque has no value, as for example where liability on it is subject to defences, damages ought not to be awarded to the true owner under both the Quebec civil code and common law conversion.

The issue of the collecting bank's liability to the true owner under Quebec law was revisited by the Supreme Court of Canada in *Bank Canadian National* v. *Gingras*.[176] Concluding his judgment, Pigeon J. noted that he was 'not completely sure that it was correct to state in *Norwich Union* that the common law rules of conversion could not be applied in Quebec', particularly, since 'not a word was said [there] of s. 10 [now 9] of the Bills of Exchange Act . . .'.[177] This however, was obiter, since he actually resolved the question of the collecting bank's liability to the true owner under the Quebec civil code.

In allowing the true owner's action, Pigeon J. purported to distinguish rather than overrule *Norwich Union*. In *Gingras*, the cheques were issued

---

[175] See (iv)(a), above.   [176] [1977] 2 S.C.R. 554.

[177] Ibid. at 564. The provision, to which there is no counterpart in South Africa, states that '[t]he rules of the common law of England, including the law merchant, save in so far as they are inconsistent with the express provisions of [the BEA] apply to bills, notes and cheques'. It was however held that the provision exclusively applies to the law of bills and notes in the strict sense, and not to general principles of law of contract and property as applied to bills, notes, and cheques. See above. For a detailed discussion, bringing in a constitutional dimension, see J. Leclair, 'L'Interaction entre le droit privé fédéral et le droit civil québécois en matière d'effects de commerce: perspective constitutionnelle' (1995), 40 McGill L.J. 691.

in discharge of valid and subsisting debts owed to the true owner, so that in his hands, they 'were worth the full amount for which they were issued'.[178] Their misappropriation did not entitle the true owner to any remedy in delict against the drawer,[179] evidently because the drawer was faultless, and the cheques were actually paid out of the drawer's funds.[180] In any event, the true owner had recourse against the drawer, presumably on the cheque. Under the predecessor of CcQ art. 1457, this would trigger an action by the drawer against the collecting bank, whose fault led to the loss. In turn, and in order to avoid circuity of action, this justified a direct remedy by the true owner against the collecting bank.[181]

In the final analysis, the view under which the true owner's remedy **[41]** against the drawer in Quebec does not preclude the true owner's action in tort against the collecting bank appears to prevail.[182] At the same time, Pigeon J.'s doubts as to the inapplicability of the common law conversion in Quebec remains a lonely voice in the wilderness, at least so far as Quebec case law is concerned. These doubts, however, were embraced with enthusiasm by Crawford to whom it appears that the remedy of conversion is part of the law of bills and notes 'in the strict sense', so as to apply throughout Canada by virtue of BEA s. 9, the predecessor of old s. 10 referred to by Pigeon J. 'Although a remedy of a general application, [conversion] has been specifically adapted in its application to negotiable instruments . . . [I]t would be undesirable in an Act of national importance to have rights determined upon fault in one province and strict liability in all of the other'.[183]

Surely, Crawford is right from the point of view of uniformity. Yet, the operation of BEA s. 9 is premised on some measure of local autonomy. Taking into account the strong common law background of conversion, and the complete silence of the Act on the point, the path taken by Quebec jurisprudence is quite defensible. As the South African experience demonstrates, the injection of civil law concepts into a statute built on common law foundations need not be untenable.

(e) The ultimate loss allocation

As discussed,[184] under the BEA, a forged indorsement passes no title. Con- **[42]** sequently, one who derives title to a cheque through a forged indorsement may not enforce payment against a party prior to the forgery. Nor is

---

[178] As indicated, above, I dispute the validity of this distinction.
[179] Above, n. 176 at 563.
[180] For this explanation, see case note by G. Mure, (1978), 38 Rev. du B. 357 at 358.
[181] Above, n. 176 at 564.
[182] See e.g. *Robidoux v. Caisse Populaire Villeray* [1991] R.R.A. 9 (Superior Court).
[183] Above, n. 40, at 1388–9.   [184] See (iv)(a), above.

payment to him made in due course so as to discharge the cheque and hence to release the drawee against the drawer. The true owner, from whom the cheque was stolen and whose indorsement signature was forged, retains his rights to and on the cheque, and has given causes of action for the wrongful interference with his rights.

At the same time, one who derives title through a forged indorsement is entitled to sue on the cheque any prior indorser who took the cheque subsequent to the forgery. This is so since under the BEA an indorser of a cheque is precluded from denying (i) 'the genuineness and regularity . . . of . . . all previous indorsements' as well as (ii) that 'at the time of his indorsement . . . he had a good title'.[185] The former preclusion runs in favour of a 'holder in due course'. The latter runs in favour of an 'immediate and subsequent indorsee'. In relation to prior parties who indorsed the cheque subsequent to the forged indorsement, the possessor of the cheque is an 'immediate or . . . subsequent indorsee' as well as, depending on his compliance with required statutory conditions of good faith and taking the cheque for value,[186] a 'holder in due course'. Effectively then, the two enumerated statutory preclusions run in favour of all transferees subsequent to the taker from the forger. On the strength of these preclusions, 'the person in possession of a bill bearing a forged indorsement is considered a holder against every party who signed the bill after the forgery of the indorsement'.[187] Being precluded from asserting the forgery, a post-forgery party is thus liable on the cheque to a subsequent indorsee, as if the indorsee claims through a flawless chain of title to an impeccable instrument, bearing only genuine signatures. Consequently, where the thief/forger is unavailable or impecunious, the loss ultimately falls on the taker from him, as the taker from the forger is liable on his signature to subsequent parties. Other than in Quebec and South Africa, he is also always liable to the true owner in conversion or money had and received. No cause of action runs in his favour.

These two statutory preclusions do not run in favour of the drawee bank that paid a cheque to one claiming through a forged indorsement. Such a drawee may however be called to re-credit the drawer's account for making the non-discharging payment over the forged indorsement. Also, other than in Quebec and South Africa,[188] the paying drawee is possibly subject to a conversion action of the true owner. Accordingly, under s. 49 (1) of the Canadian BEA, where a bill bearing a forged indorsement

---

[185] Ss. 55(2)(b) and (c) in the UK, ss. 132 (b) and (c) in Canada, ss. 55(b)(2) and (3) in Israel, ss. 53(2)(b) and (c) in South Africa, and similarly, s. 74(1)(b) in Australia.

[186] The precise conditions to be complied with are set out in s. 29(1) in the UK, s. 55(1) in Canada, s. 28(a) in Israel, s. 27(1) in South Africa, and s. 50(1) in Australia.

[187] A. Barak, 'The Uniform Commercial Code Commercial Paper, An Outsider's View, Part II' (1968), 3 Israel L Rev. 184 at 186.　　　　　　[188] See (iv)(d), above.

has erroneously been paid 'in good faith and in the ordinary course of business', the paying drawee may recover the amount paid from 'the person to whom it was paid' or from 'any subsequent endorsee . . . subsequent to the forged . . . endorsement'.[189] Elsewhere in BEA jurisdictions, the recourse of the drawee bank for payment made over a forged indorsement is governed by the law governing mistake and restitution.[190] Regardless, where a cheque is paid over a forged indorsement and the thief/forger is unavailable or impecunious, the loss ultimately falls on the taker from him; recourse up to the taker from the forger is available to the drawee and parties subsequent to the taker from the forger, but not to the taker himself.

The position of a taker of a stolen cheque payable to bearer is funda- **[43]** mentally different from that a taker of a stolen cheque payable to order. The transfer of a cheque payable to bearer requires no indorsement,[191] so that any possessor, including a taker from a thief and its successor in title, is a 'holder',[192] who, depending on his compliance with statutory good faith purchase for value requirements,[193] may qualify as a holder in due course, so as to defeat the true owner's adverse claim to the instrument.[194] Effectively then, holding in due course of a bearer cheque forfeits the true owner's title to the instrument.[195] While the transferee of the bearer cheque may benefit solely from his own immediate predecessor's war-

---

[189] Similarly, and to the same effect as under the statutory preclusions discussed above, under s. 49 (2) of the Canadian BEA, a person from whom such amount has been recovered, 'has the like right of recovery against any endorser subsequent to the forged . . . endorsement'. To recover from such an indorser, the claimant, whether the drawee under s. 49(1) or an intermediate indorser under s. 49(2), must have given to him notice of the indorsement being forged. Under s. 49(3), such notice 'shall be given within a reasonable time after the person seeking to recover . . . has acquired notice that the endorsement is forged . . . and may be given in the same manner . . . as notice of protest or dishonour . . .'.

[190] As such, the drawee's claim is subject to defences available under restitution law. For example, the claim must be brought within a reasonable time after payment, since during the interim, the recipient's position may have been altered. A leading case is *London and River Plate Bank* v. *Bank of Liverpool* [1896] 1 Q.B. 7, particularly at 11. See in general e.g. Guest, above, n. 83 at 185, 496, and 509; Malan and Pretorius, above, n. 143 at 358; and H. Luntz, 'The Bank's Right to Recovery on Cheques Paid by Mistake', (1968), 6 Melbourne Uni. L. Rev. 308.

[191] S. 31 in the UK, s. 59 in Canada, s. 30 in Israel, s. 29 in South Africa, and s. 40 in Australia.

[192] For the 'bearer' as the holder of an instrument payable to bearer see definition of 'bearer' and 'holder' in s. 2 the UK and Canada, s. 1 in Israel and South Africa, and s. 3 in Australia.

[193] The precise conditions to be complied with are set out in s. 29(1) in the UK, s. 55(1) in Canada, s. 28(a) in Israel, s. 27(1) in South Africa, and s. 50(1) in Australia.

[194] Rights of a holder in due course are set out in s. 38(2) in the UK, s. 73(b) in Canada, s. 37(2) in Israel, s. 36(b) in South Africa, and s. 49(2) in Australia.

[195] As demonstrated in the classic case of *Miller* v. *Race*, above, n. 20.

ranty of title,[196] as a holder in due course he may recover from the drawer at the exclusion of anyone else. Loss is thus borne by the true owner.

[44]   The operation of these rules, in conjunction with the true owner's remedies, could be demonstrated in the following scenarios:

(1) As indicated, where the loss or theft of a cheque payable to order is discovered before payment and in time to prevent it, other than in Quebec and South Africa, the true owner may sue in conversion or money had and received any person who took the instrument subsequent to the loss or theft. In Quebec and South Africa the true owner's remedy is more restricted. Other than from the forger, the true owner may recover from the person who is currently in possession of the cheque, from anyone who took the cheque in bad faith subsequent to the forgery, and from a negligent collecting bank.[197] In South Africa the true owner may also invoke statutory conversion against 'any person who was possessor . . . after the theft or loss, [who] either gave consideration . . . or took it as a donee', but only in connection with a crossed cheque marked 'not negotiable'.[198] Regardless, in all BEA jurisdictions, the possessor at the time forgery is discovered may recover from any prior transferee deriving title through the forged indorsement. Such recourse is available to each transferee from whom recovery is made, so that the loss ultimately falls on the taker from the forger. On his part, the one who pays the true owner acquires thereby ownership in the cheque[199] and effectively, stepping into the latter's shoes, may recover on the cheque from the drawer or any indorser prior to the forgery.

(2) In all BEA jurisdictions, where the loss or theft of a cheque payable to order is discovered before payment and in time to prevent it, the true owner may choose not to bring an action against a post-forgery taker. Rather, he may choose to sue, on the lost cheque, the drawer or any indorser prior to the true owner.[200] On his part, the one in possession of the cheque at the time forgery is discovered, may go after any prior transferee who derives title to the cheque through the forged indorsement. The same applies to any post-forgery transferee from whom recovery is made. Ultimately, how-

---

[196] Under s. 58(3) in the UK, s. 137 in Canada, s. 59(c) in Israel, s. 56(3) in South Africa, and s. 77(3) in Australia.

[197] See generally (iv)(a) and (d), above.   [198] S. 81 of the South African BEA.

[199] This stems from the nature of the conversion action as well as the basis of the waiver of tort underlying the true owner's action for money had and received. It is more difficult to reach this result on the basis of an action in negligence.

[200] The action to enforce liability on a lost instrument is governed by ss. 69–70 in the UK, ss. 155–6 in Canada, ss. 69–70 in Israel, ss. 67–8 in South Africa, and s. 116 in Australia.

ever, no recourse (other than against the forger) is available to the one who took the cheque from the forger.

(3) Where payment to one deriving title to a cheque payable to order through a forged indorsement took place, and the drawee debited the drawer's account, the true owner has two options. First, he may sue, on the lost cheque, the drawer or any indorser prior to the true owner. Alternatively, other than in Quebec and South Africa, the true owner may bring an action, in conversion or money had and received, against a transferee subsequent to the forgery. In the latter case, the post-forgery defendant acquires title by payment and thus may sue on the cheque the drawer or any indorser prior to the true owner. Either way, this would lead to a double payment by the drawer. First, his account was debited upon the original payment of the cheque. Second, the drawer was called to pay the true owner, the post-forgery transferee who paid the true owner, or a pre-forgery indorser who has a recourse against him on the cheque. The drawer may then require the drawee to credit his account. Alternatively, other than in South Africa and Quebec, there is the possibility of an action by the true owner against the drawee.[201] Having either credited the drawer's account or paid the true owner, the drawee may recover from the one to whom it originally paid the cheque, who in turn, could recover from a prior transferee, all the way down to the taker from the forger, who is left with no recourse (other than against the forger).

(4) As discussed,[202] the better view is that a drawer from whom a cheque payable to order is stolen is not its true owner. He may thus not recover its face value in an action in conversion or money had and received. The drawer, who did not issue the cheque, is not liable thereon. Where the loss or theft is discovered before payment and in time to prevent it, the drawer faces no loss. The one is possession of the cheque at the time the forgery is discovered, and anyone sued by him, may go after a prior transferee who took the cheque subsequent to the forgery. However, no recourse (other than against the forger) is available to the one who took the cheque from the forger. Where payment occurred, the drawee bank must re-credit the drawer's account and may pursue its remedy against the one who was paid. The latter may go after any predecessor in title, up to the taker from the forger, who remains to bear the loss.

(5) A possessor of a stolen cheque payable to bearer, who took it for value and in good faith, is a holder in due course, who defeats the

---

[201] See (iv)(b).   [202] See (iv)(c).

true owner's previous title. Consequently, the former can enforce payment against the drawer. Payment to him is payment in due course which discharges the cheque and releases the drawer. Loss thus falls on the true owner. Having normally given value for the cheque, he can neither enforce payment nor recover damages.

(6) It should be pointed out that the ultimate loss allocation does not change in Quebec as well as in South Africa, not only for cheques payable to bearer (scenario no. 5), but also for those payable to order. Thus, where the loss or theft of a cheque payable to order is discovered before payment, scenario no. 2 applies. Alternatively, the true owner may sue the possessor, a negligent collecting bank, or in South Africa, but only in connection with a crossed cheque marked 'not negotiable', under the limited statutory conversion action, 'any person who was possessor . . . after the theft or loss, [who] either gave consideration . . . or took it as a donee'.[203] This case was already covered in the context of scenario no. 1. Where loss is discovered after payment, scenario no. 4 is slightly adapted. As in all other BEA jurisdictions, the true owner may recover, on the lost cheque, from any party prior to the forgery, up to the drawer. Alternatively, and instead of the common law remedies in conversion or money had and received, the true owner may have recourse against the possessor, a negligent collecting bank, as well as under a statutory limited conversion action in South Africa.[204] The post-forgery defendant who thus paid the true owner may sue any party prior to the forgery, up to the drawer. The drawer may then recover, on contract, from the drawee bank, which becomes entitled to recover from any party subsequent to the forgery, up to the taker from the forger, who is left with no recourse, other than against the forger himself. Where the cheque was stolen from the drawer scenario no. 4 applies.

[45]   The foregoing scenarios could be condensed into the following example. A drew on PB a cheque payable to C's order. The cheque was stolen, and transferred by the thief, forging C's indorsement, to E, who took it in good faith and for value. E indorsed the cheque to collecting bank DB with the view of collecting its proceeds from PB. Assuming the theft occurred after delivery to C, C is the true owner. Other than in Quebec and South Africa, C may recover from either E or DB in conversion or money had and received. DB may go after E. Whoever paid C, namely either E or DB, may sue A on the cheque. Alternatively, C could have sued A on the cheque and DB could have recovered from E (but not from A).

---

[203] S. 81 of the South African BEA.   [204] Ibid.

Had the cheque already been paid by PB to E (through DB), C would have sued either A (on the cheque) or, other than in Quebec and South Africa, DB or E (in conversion or money had and received). Between DB and E, whoever paid C may sue A on the cheque. Either way, A would have recovered from PB. PB could then have recovered from DB or E. If sued by PB, DB could have recovered from E.

Had the cheque been stolen from A, A would not have been liable on it, and DB could have recovered from E, with A remaining indebted to C. Had the cheque (that had been stolen from A) been paid, A could have his account with PB re-credited. PB could have pursued his remedies against DB or E, and if sued by PB, DB could have recovered from E.

Finally, in the case of a cheque payable to bearer drawn by A on PB, purchased in good faith and for value by E after its theft from C (to whom it was originally issued by A), loss falls on C, whose title has been expunged. DB may enforce payment and payment to it is a good discharge. This is in contrast to the case of the cheque payable to order where loss universally falls on E, the taker from the thief.

(V) THE ANGLO-AMERICAN SYSTEM: EXCEPTIONS TO THE BASIC SCHEME IN BEA JURISDICTIONS

Exceptions are introduced by the fictitious payee provision as well as [46] special statutory defences which may be available to paying and collecting banks.

(a) Cheques payable to fictitious or non-existing payees[205]

Legislation in most BEA jurisdictions contains a provision stating that [47] '[w]here the payee is a fictitious or non-existing person, the [instrument] may be treated as payable to bearer' (hereafter: 'the fictitious payee provision').[206] In the allocation of forgery losses, the fictitious payee provision operates to disregard the forgery of the payee's indorsement, on the basis that such indorsement was not required in the first place. Where the pro-

---

[205] For previous discussions on which the present text builds, see B. Geva, 'The Fictitious Payee and Payroll Padding: Royal Bank of Canada v. Concrete Column Clamps (1961) Ltd.' (1977–8), 2 Can. Bus. L.J. 418; and Geva, 'Boma', above, n. 101.

[206] See BEA s. 7(3) in the UK, s. 20(5) in Canada, and s. 6(c) in Israel. The Cheques Act s. 19(1)(b) in Australia similarly speaks of a cheque specifying as payee or indorsee 'a fictitious or non-existing person', thereby extending the provision to apply also to the fictitious indorsee. In South Africa, BEA s. 5(3) substituted 'a person not having capacity to contract' for a 'non-existing person'. However, under the SA Bill, above, n. 6 (proclaimed 1 March 2001), s.5(3) was amended to refer to a payee who is a 'fictitious or non-existing person, or a person not having capacity to contract'.

vision applies, its effect is twofold. First, a bona fide taker for value of the instrument, including a collecting bank that dealt with the thief, acquires good title. Second, payment in good faith, even to the thief, is payment in due course which discharges the drawee bank, so as to entitle it to credit the drawer's account. As in the case of theft of an instrument payable to bearer, and unlike in the usual situation of a theft of an instrument payable to order, loss thus falls on the person from whom the instrument was stolen.[207] The provision is of particular importance in Canada, where in effect, no specific broad protections against forged indorsements are given to banks collecting and paying cheques.[208]

The fictitious payee provision was passed against the background of pre-Act case law dealing with fraudulent bills of exchange. The rationale pronounced in pre-Act leading judgments was estoppel against a party with knowledge of the fraud.[209] Namely, a drawer or acceptor who knew that the bill did not reflect a real transaction, was estopped, usually as against a discounting bank, from raising a defence based on the forged indorsement of the payee, whose name was inserted by the creator of the instrument by way of pretence only, in order to create a misleading semblance of real transactions between the drawer and acceptor, as well as between the drawer and the payee.[210]

The fictitious payee provision does not specify that the knowledge of the party who challenges the validity of the payee's indorsement is a condition for the application of this provision. Accordingly, in *Bank of England* v. *Vagliano*,[211] shortly after the BEA was enacted in England, the House of Lords understood the fictitious payee provision as rejecting this rationale.[212] Declining to read into the provision the pre-Act limitation, Lord Herschell held that '[w]henever the name inserted as that of the payee is inserted by way of pretence merely, without any intention that payment shall only be made in conformity therewith, the payee is a fictitious person within the meaning of the statute'.[213]

---

[207] See (iv)(e), above.   [208] See (v)(b), below.

[209] A summary of the pre-Act authorities and rationale appears in the judgment of Bowen LJ in *Vagliano* v. *The Bank of England* (1889), 23 Q.B.D. 243 (CA), *rvs'd*, [1891] A.C. 107 (H.L.).

[210] For an excellent account, not limited to doctrinal aspects, explaining the historic and socio-economic background, see J.S. Rogers, *The Early History of the Law of Bills and Notes* (Cambridge: Cambridge University Press, 1995) at 223–49.   [211] Above, n. 209.

[212] In the words of Lord Herschell, 'the proper way to deal with such a statute as the Bills of Exchange Act, which was intended to be a code of the law relating to negotiable instruments . . . is in the first instance to examine the language of the statute and to ask what is its natural meaning, uninfluenced by any considerations derived from the previous state of the law . . .' Above, n. 209 at 144.

[213] Ibid. at 153. According to Chalmers, '[d]uring the controversy the draftsman of the [fictitious payee provision] must have felt much like the professor of Divinity who was asked by a student to explain some passage he had written in a theological tractate. "My dear friend", said the professor, "when I wrote that passage, only God and I knew what I

[48]

The objective of the provision has thus become the protection of banks from fraud exercised on the drawer by a third party, particularly, internal fraud within the drawer organization. Indeed, the general rule under the BEA is that a forged signature is not operative, so that the drawer does not usually bear the risk incurred by a forged indorsement.²¹⁴ Conversely, where the fictitious payee provision applies, namely where an insider in the drawer organization defrauds the drawer by generating instruments intended to be misappropriated, loss falls on the drawer, who is in a better position to minimize losses and obtain insurance. It is with the view of implementing this rationale that the fictitious payee provision ought to be construed.

However, the technical rules generated in the course of the judicial interpretation of the fictitious payee provision do not always meet this challenge successfully. In interpreting the provision, courts focused on the meaning of 'fictitious' and 'non-existing'. In this context, particular attention was given to the relevance of intention for the application of the provision. More specifically, while the definition of 'fictitious' in *Vagliano* has remained good law, courts have been seeking to define 'non-existing', as well as ascertain whose intention determines whether the payee is a 'fictitious or non-existing person'. In thus focusing their attention on the language of the provision, and thereby overlooking the basic policy behind it, courts failed to see the forest for the trees.

According to a classic statement of Falconbridge,²¹⁵

Whether a named payee is non-existing is a simple question of fact, not depending on anyone's intention. The question whether the payee is fictitious depends upon the intention of the creator of the instrument, that is, the drawer of a bill or cheque or the maker of a note.

In connection with this statement, a payee who is either a creature of imagination or a dead person is 'non-existing'.²¹⁶ A payee who is a real person, namely, who is neither imaginary nor dead, is 'existing'. Where the latter's name is inserted by the drawer by way of pretence, with no intention that he will receive payment, such a person, though 'existing', is nonetheless 'fictitious',²¹⁷ so as to still fall within the ambit of the

---

meant, and now only God knows".' Yet, Chalmers continued, 'I venture to think that Lord Herschell's judgment . . . puts the matter on a sound and intelligible basis'. Chalmers, 'Vagliano's Case' (1891), 7 L.Q.R. 216 at 218.   ²¹⁴ See (iv)(c), above.

²¹⁵ Above, n. 40, at 1259. The statement originally appeared in 1956 in the 6th edition.

²¹⁶ Obviously, this is broader than 'a person not having capacity to contract' as the South African fictitious provision stated. Hence the impetus for the amendment, set out in n. 206, above (proclaimed 1 March 2001). In any event, a cheque payable to the estate of a deceased person ought not to fall under the fictitious payee provision, regardless of its particular language. See Cowen and Gering, above, n. 143 at 70.

²¹⁷ For the exclusive relevance of the drawer's intention see *Vinden* v. *Hughes*, above, n. 126.

provision. However, a payee who is a real, that is, 'existing', person, who is intended by the drawer to receive payment, but who is made payee because of a third person's fraud, who falsely represents to the drawer that the drawer is indebted to such payee, is neither 'fictitious' nor 'non-existing', and thus falls outside the provision. The intention of the drawer determines whether the payee is 'fictitious', but not whether he is 'non-existing'.[218] In the quoted language from Falconbridge, while fictitiousness 'depends upon the intention of the . . . drawer', existence or non-existence 'is a simple question of fact, not depending on anyone's intention'. The two categories are thus mutually exclusive.[219] First, the 'non-existence' of the payee is determined objectively. Next, and upon failing to find the payee to be 'non-existing', the 'fictitiousness' of the 'existing' payee is settled subjectively, from the point of view of, and as intended by, the drawer. Otherwise, the provision does not apply.

[49]   In some situations, this interpretation leads to results which are consistent with the underlying policies of the provision. Thus, the fictitious payee provision applies where a signing officer defrauds its corporate employer and draws a cheque payable to a real creditor of the company, intending to misappropriate the cheque and its proceeds.[220] The result will not change where the payee's name was the product of the signing officer's imagination. The result is however less straightforward where the fraud perpetrator was an employee of the drawer company, who did not sign the cheque, as for example, in 'payroll padding'.

A leading case in Canada[221] is *Royal Bank of Canada* v. *Concrete Column Clamps*.[222] In their judgments members of the Supreme Court dealt with the situation of a fraudulent insider who was not the signer, but rather the one who either supplied the payees' names to, or prepared the cheques

---

[218] For the objective nature of 'non-existence', the leading authority is *Clutton* v. *Attenborough & Son* [1897] A.C. 90 (H.L.).

[219] This is true only because the provision expressly specifies these two categories. In South Africa, where the 'non-existing' category was not provided for, and notwithstanding a South African authority to the contrary (*Nedbank* v. *Window Press*, 1987 (3) S.A. 761 (SE)), I am attracted by the argument put forward by Gering, above, n. 143 at 329, according to which there was nothing to preclude 'fictitious' to be broad enough to include 'non-existing'. Undoubtedly, apart from language, there was no policy ground to support the exclusion of the cheque payable to a 'non-existing' person from the coverage of the South African provision. Undoubtedly, apart from language, there was no policy ground to support the exclusion of the cheque payable to a 'non-existing' person from the coverage of the South African provision, even in its original language. For the statutory amendment (proclaimed 1 March 2001) in South Africa, see n. 206, above.

[220] see e.g. *Fok Cheong Shing Investments* v. *Bank of Nova Scotia* (1981), 123 D.L.R. (3d) 416 (Ont. C.A.), *aff'd* (1982), 146 D.L.R. (3d) 617 (S.C.C.).

[221] In the absence of special protection in Canada to a collecting or drawee bank, as discussed in detail in (v)(b) below, the only defence available to banks is that of the fictitious payee provision. Perhaps this explains the proliferation of Canadian jurisprudence on the point.   [222] (1976), 74 D.L.R. (3d) 26 (S.C.C.).

for signature by, the authorized signing officer. The majority held that in such circumstances, the fictitious payee provision did not apply to cheques made out to 'existing' past employees. The ensuing loss thus did not fall on the drawer. While the fraudulent clerk was truly not 'the creator of the instrument' within Falconbridge's summary, inasmuch as the fraud was internal to the drawer organization, this interpretation is a clear victory of form over substance, which fails to bring the interpretation of the provision in line with its rationale. This becomes particularly obvious in light of the fact that in the facts of the case, cheques payable to 'non-existing' persons, whose names were equally supplied to the signer by the fraudulent clerk, were held to fall within the ambit of the provision, since 'existence' is an objective fact, determined irrespective of anyone's intention.[223]

Conversely, in *Fok Cheong Shing Investments* v. *Bank of Nova Scotia*,[224] the fraud was committed by the president, an authorized signing officer of the drawer company, who made out a cheque payable to an existing person, intending to misappropriate it. The fictitious payee provision was thus held to be applicable and the loss was correctly allocated to the drawer. Nonetheless, had the president signed the cheque fully intending to make payment to the payee, but changed his mind subsequently, deciding not to mail the cheque but rather to misappropriate it, the provision would not have been applied. What counts is the instrument creator's intention at the time of the creation; subsequent change of intention is irrelevant.

It is clear, then, that the current interpretation of the fictitious payee [50] provision, as correctly reflected in Falconbridge's summary, is less than a perfect tool in allocating internal fraud losses on the drawer. Efforts ought to be made for judicial improvement,[225] if not for a legislative

---

[223] Ibid. In the facts of the case, the distinction between 'non-existing' and 'fictitious' became even somewhat surrealistic as some of the 'non-existing' persons were names taken from the telephone book. It is hard to see why such names are of 'non-existing' persons while names of past employees were of 'existing' persons, who failed to be 'fictitious' only due to the absence of fraudulent intent by the signer. Unless, of course, 'existence' requires some actual dealings with the defrauded company, so that names randomly picked from the telephone book, and belonging to persons with no past or present contact with the company, cannot be of 'existing' persons.   [224] Above, n. 220.

[225] In this context, note Laskin CJ's dissent in *Concrete Column Clamps*, concluding that the named former employees were 'fictitious', since due to the purely mechanical role of the authorized signer, it is the intention of the dishonest clerk, and not the authorized signer, that should be attributed to the drawer company. Above, n. 222 at 38–43. Supporting the result, Spence J. added, in his dissent (at 46), that in the facts of the case, the bank was not 'guilty of any negligence whatsoever', while for the drawer, 'it would have been quite easy in proper office management to have designed sufficient methods of checking and verifying to have defeated [the dishonest clerk's] scheme'. See also P. E. Salvatori, 'Vagliano's Case Revisited' (1978–9), 3 Can. Bus. L.J. 296, arguing for the application of the provision in connection with 'fictitious' transactions, that is where the corporate customer has not intended

amendment.[226] Regrettably, at present courts focus their attention to the language of the fictitious payee provision rather than on its underlying policies.

[51]   A further unjustified departure not only from policy, but unfortunately also from jurisprudence, took place in *Boma Manufacturing* v. *Canadian Imperial Bank of Commerce*.[227] In that case, a bookkeeper/payroll clerk with a signing authority for two associated companies fraudulently prepared cheques, ostensibly on behalf of her corporate employers, intending to misappropriate their proceeds. She made out some cheques payable to existing employees and some payable to an imaginary person. She signed some cheques herself, but procured on others the signature of an innocent unsuspecting shareholder/officer who had signing authority. She collected all such cheques for her own use.

It seems that inasmuch loss was caused by fraud internal to the drawer's organization, it should have entirely been borne by the companies. Speaking for the majority of the Supreme Court of Canada, Iacobucci J. nevertheless thought that the fictitious payee provision did not apply to any of the cheques and shifted away the entire loss from the companies.[228] In the course of his judgment, he distinguished between cheques payable to existing employees and those payable to the imaginary person. He did not draw any distinction between cheques signed by the bookkeeper/payroll clerk and those signed by the shareholder/officer. In his view, cheques payable to existing employees, were intended by the shareholder/officer, as the guiding mind of the company and not as a mere signatory, to be actually paid to such real people. Because '[the bookkeeper/payroll clerk] was not the drawer, but was simply the signatory',[229] her intention was not determinative. As for the cheques payable to the imaginary person, Iacobucci J. appears first to concede that 'such a person would be categorized as "non-existing" and hence, fictitious'. Nevertheless, he continued, the shareholder/officer, effectively acting as the guiding mind of the company, 'was reasonably mistaken in thinking that [the imaginary person] was an individual associated with [the] companies' and 'honestly believed that the cheques were being made for an existing obligation to a real person known to the companies'.[230] Accordingly, in his view, these cheques ought to be regarded as payable to a real person, intended by the shareholder/officer to receive payment, who is

---

any valid business transaction. For an economic analysis supporting such 'no real transaction test', see M. Y. Haron, 'Revisiting s. 7(3) of the Bills of Exchange Act 1882: an Economic Analysis' (1998), Cambrian Law Review 53.

[226] For example, in line with pre-1990 UCC §3–405, set forth in Laskin CJ's judgment in *Concrete Column Clamps*, ibid. The current UCC provision is §3–404.

[227] Above, n. 71.   [228] Above, n. 71, paras. 42–67.   [229] Above, n. 71, para. 55.

[230] Above, n. 71, para. 60.

neither fictitious nor non-existing. This is so notwithstanding the book-keeper/payroll clerk's fraud who falsely represented to the share-holder/officer that there is money owed by the companies to that person.

It seems that in applying Falconbridge's summary, explicitly adopted by him,[231] to the facts of the case, Iacobucci J. overlooked two principles. First, in dealing with the cheques payable to the imaginary person, he did not recognize the basic distinction between a 'fictitious' and 'non-existing payee'. While 'fictitiousness' is a subjective matter, determined from the point of view of 'the creator of the instrument', 'non-existence' is an objective fact, 'not depending on anyone's intention'. Hence, the intent of neither the bookkeeper/payroll clerk nor the shareholder/officer should have counted in dealing with cheques payable to the imaginary person. A payee who is either a dead person or a creature of imagination is, by definition, 'non-existing', so as to fall within the ambit of the ficti-tious payee provision. Consequently, all the cheques payable to the imag-inary person, whether signed by the bookkeeper/payroll clerk or by the shareholder/officer, were payable to a 'non-existing' person, so that the loss with respect to them should have been allocated to the companies.

'Fictitiousness' and hence 'the intention of the creator of the instrument' matter only with respect to cheques payable to *existing* persons, or in the facts of *Boma*, with respect to cheques payable to existing employees. In identifying 'the creator of the instrument', the drawer of the cheques, Iacobucci J. departed from current authority, thereby overlooking a sec-ond principle.

Indeed, Iacobucci J. was correct in observing that in *Fok Cheong Shing Investment* v. *Bank of Nova Scotia*,[232] the signing officer, whose intention was held to determine the fictitiousness of the payee, was the president of the drawer company, namely, its guiding mind.[233] It is equally correct that *Royal Bank of Canada* v. *Concrete Column Clamps*[234] did not purport to deter-mine whether the signing officer actually *was* 'the creator of the instru-ment'. Rather, it held that the person who supplied a signing officer with the name of a payee with the intention of subsequently misappropriating the cheque *was not* 'the creator of the instrument'. Nevertheless, it was never held that 'the creator of the instrument' was anyone other than its actual signer. The distinction proposed by Iacobucci J. 'between the sig-natory and the drawer', the latter being the company through its guiding mind rather than a mere authorized signatory,[235] is unsupported in case law. In fact, in the leading case of *Bank of England* v. *Vagliano*,[236] 'the creator of the instrument', whose intention determined the fictitiousness of the payee, was neither a guiding mind nor even an authorized signatory of

[231] Above, n. 71, para. 46.   [232] Above, n. 220.   [233] Above, n. 220, paras. 50 and 56.
[234] Above, n. 222.   [235] Above, n. 71, para. 55.   [236] Above, n. 209.

the drawer; rather, it was a fraudulent employee of the acceptor, with respect to whose drawer's signature the acceptor was estopped from pleading forgery against its banker.[237]

Contrary to the desirable policies underlying the provision, Iacobucci J.'s interpretation shifts losses caused by internal fraud at the customer's organization from the customer to a bank. Nor is it likely that the interpretation will bring certainty; unlike in *Boma*, and particularly in connection with a large organization, it will not be always easy to establish what rank within the organization a signing officer must have to be considered a 'guiding mind' for the organization.

It appears that the dissenting judgment in *Boma*, given by La Forest J., better reflects the present jurisprudence. Thereunder, while all cheques payable to the imaginary person would have been payable to a 'non-existing' person, only cheques payable to existing employees and signed by the bookkeeper/payroll clerk would have been payable to 'fictitious' persons. Only cheques payable to existing employees and signed by the shareholder/officer would thus have fallen outside the fictitious payee provision, so that only their loss would have been shifted away from the drawer companies.

[52]   Neither jurisprudence nor the policy rationale takes into account the effect of negligence by the collecting bank.[238] Such negligence could be in allowing the fraudster to collect a cheque ostensibly payable to another.[239] However, even the drawer's conversion action against the collecting bank, disputed by me but recognized by case law, including a unanimous court in *Boma*,[240] does not allow for contributory negligence,[241] and hence,

---

[237] The case involved bills of exchange payable at a bank out of the acceptor's account. The fraudulent employee of the acceptor, purporting to act as a creditor of his employer, forged bills drawn on the employer payable to an existing firm, intending to forge the firm's indorsement and discount the bills. Unaware of the scheme, the employer accepted the bills, believing they represented genuine debts owed by it to the firm. The bills were subsequently presented for payment at the bank, over the indorsements forged by the fraudulent employee. The acceptor was precluded from asserting the forged drawing and thus the sole issue was whether the bills were payable to a fictitious person, so as to relieve the bank from responsibility for paying them over forged indorsements.

[238] But see Malan and Pretorius, above, n. 143 at 61, citing with approval Zimbabwean jurisprudence under which the permissive language of the fictitious payee provision, under which the instrument payable to a fictitious or non-existing person 'may' be treated as payable to bearer, authorizes courts to apply it only in favour of 'parties acting in good faith and without negligence or without notice of any irregularity', and not to apply it, for example, in favour of a negligent collecting bank.

[239] For example, in *Boma*, most cheques were deposited by the bookkeeper/payroll clerk to her bank account unindorsed. In his dissent at the BC Court of Appeal, Hutchison JA, thought loss for those cheques ought therefore to be borne by the collecting bank. Yet he rationalized this result on an erroneous interpretation of the fictitious payee provision. In any event, in the facts of the case there was an explanation for the departure of the collecting bank from its usual procedure. See Geva, 'Boma', above, n. 101 at 179.

[240] See discussion in (iv)(c), above.   [241] See discussion above, in (iv)(a).

does not remedy the situation. Nonetheless, I believe that in the footsteps of the civil law,[242] the common law ought to recognize an action by the drawer against the collecting bank for negligence.[243] In such an action, the relative fault of the drawer and the collecting bank may be assessed and weighed.

Fraud inducing a drawer to issue a cheque to either a 'fictitious' or [53] 'non-existing' person could be perpetrated not only within the drawer organization but also outside it. Such is the case, for example, where a fraudster impersonates a genuine creditor and induces the drawer to write a cheque to that creditor and deliver it to the fraudster. Alternatively, the fraudster may induce the drawer to issue a cheque to an imaginary charity. In both cases, the fraudster carries on his intention and cashes the cheques. In principle, such cases ought to be considered under the fictitious payee provision. Under Falconbridge's summary, the second case would be that of a 'non-existing' payee, while the first case will not be that of a 'fictitious' payee. Again, the drawer's intention determines fictitiousness but not non-existence. However, as before, policy considerations support the inclusion of both situations within the ambit of the provision.

In the final analysis, by allocating forgery losses to the organization from which they emanated, the fictitious payee provision is designed to promote loss prevention or reduction. It is however its interpretation, side by side with the absence of any complementary provision allocating losses to a negligent party, which has effectively undermined, or at least failed to fully implement, loss prevention or reduction policies.

(b) Defences available to paying and collecting banks

Overview

Other than in Canada, special protection is given under the BEA to a [54] drawee bank which paid a cheque over a forged indorsement in good faith and in the ordinary course of business. As discussed,[244] where the cheque is paid to an innocent indorsee from the thief, this protection does not impact the ultimate loss allocation to the taker from the forger. Its effect is to exonerate the drawee from litigation. Nonetheless, where the thief dealt directly with the drawee bank, loss may be reallocated to the

---

[242] For the collecting bank's negligence liability in BEA civil law jurisdictions, see (iv)(d), above.
[243] Notwithstanding some persistent judicial pronouncements specifically limiting any bank liability, other than expressly provided for by statute, to contract. See e.g. *Aucheteroni v. Midland Bank* [1928] 2 K.B. 294 at 298–9; *Lloyds Bank v. Savory* [1932] 2 K.B. 122 at 148, Greer LJ, *aff'd* [1933] A.C. 201 (H.L.) at 221, Lord Buckmaster; and in Israel, *Kirstein*, above, n. 33 at 2288.   [244] See (ii), above.

dispossessed owner, that is, the person from whom the cheque was stolen. Statutory protection is further given to a collecting bank collecting in good faith and without negligence a cheque bearing a forged indorsement. In Israel and Canada such protection is limited to crossed cheques; however cheque crossing is not practised in Canada. Where the forger deposits the cheque for collection the effect of this statutory protection is to shift away forged indorsement losses from the collecting bank to the dispossessed owner of the cheque. Finally, as will be indicated, doubts exist as to the applicability of statutory defences to a bank holding both the drawer's and depositor's accounts.

The paying bank[245]

[55] In general, a cheque is discharged by payment in due course. 'Payment in due course' must be made by the drawee to the holder, 'in good faith and without notice that [the holder's] title . . . is defective'.[246] Such payment releases the drawer,[247] and being in conformity with the drawer's instructions, authorizes the drawee bank to debit the drawer's account. Payment over a forged indorsement is, however, not payment to the holder; it is thus not a payment in due course. It does not discharge the cheque; it neither releases the drawer nor authorizes the drawee bank to debit the drawer's account.

Nonetheless, other than in Canada, special protection is given by the BEA to a bank drawee of a demand draft. In the UK, under BEA s. 60,

When a bill payable to order on demand is drawn on a banker, and the banker on whom it is drawn pays the bill in good faith and in the ordinary course of business, it is not incumbent on the banker to show that the indorsement of the payee or any subsequent indorsement was made by or under the authority of the person whose indorsement it purports to be, and the banker is deemed to have paid the bill in due course, although such indorsement has been forged or made without authority.

This provision succeeded, and so far as cheques are concerned, superseded,[248] s. 19 of the Stamp Act 1853.[249] Effectively, BEA s. 60 turns payment

---

[245] See, in general, M. Gottesman, 'Forged Indorsements and Bankers' Liability' (1972), 7 Israel L. Rev. 65; Ellinger and Lomnicka, above, n. 91 at 376–84; and from a historical perspective (until 1955), Holden, above, n. 12 at 222–9.

[246] BEA s. 59 in the UK, BEO s. 60(a) in Israel, and BEA s. 138 in Canada. See also Cheques Act ss. 78–9 in Australia and BEA ss. 57 and 1 in South Africa.

[247] As well as all other parties liable on the cheques, namely, each indorser. For the fundamental distinction between a discharge of a party, and the discharge of the instrument, which is the equivalent of the discharge of all parties, see e.g. Crawford and Falconbridge, above, n. 40 at 1667.

[248] *Carpenters' Co. v. British Mutual Banking Co.* [1938] 1 K.B. 511

[249] Above, n. 24. Thereunder, 'any draft or order drawn upon a banker for a sum of money payable to order on demand which shall, when presented for payment, purport to be

of a cheque made by the drawee bank over a forged indorsement, 'in good faith and in the ordinary course of business', into 'payment in due course'. Such payment releases the drawer from his engagement on the cheque and the debt paid by it.[250] Accordingly, it authorizes the drawee to debit the drawer's account, irrespective of the fact that payment was not made to the holder, but rather, contrary to the drawer's instructions, to someone claiming under a forged indorsement. As discussed,[251] the true owner's remedy against any party subsequent to the forged indorsement, and hence, the ultimate loss allocation to the taker from the forger, where such person exists, are not affected by this provision.[252] Its effect is merely to insulate the drawee bank from any involvement in the dispute concerning the forged indorsement. At the same time, in the absence of an innocent indorsee from the forger, the provision may shift away losses from the drawee bank, as the person who dealt with the forger, to the dispossessed owner. Due to the discharge of the cheque under the provision, the dispossessed owner is left with no cause of action.

BEA s. 60 does not specifically require the drawee bank to act without **[56]** negligence. It is however disputed whether the bank's 'ordinary course of business' does not require it anyway to act without negligence.[253]

Some controversy also exists as to the meaning of 'indorsement', whose forgery nonetheless does not preclude the drawee bank from paying in due course. It was held in South Africa[254] that the corresponding provision in its legislation is limited to payment to one claiming through the forged

---

endorsed by the person to whom the same shall be drawn payable, shall be sufficient authority to such banker to pay the amount of such draft to the bearer thereof; and it shall not be incumbent on such banker to prove that such endorsement, or any subsequent endorsement, was made by or under the direction or authority of the person to whom the said draft or order was or is payable either by the drawer or any endorser thereof'. Unlike that of its successor BEA s. 60, the quoted language does not appear to require the bank claiming the protection to have acted in good faith and in the ordinary course of business.

[250] *Charles* v. *Blackwell* (1877) 2 C.P.D. 151. See Kessler, above, n. 16 at 879.

[251] See (ii), above.

[252] *Ogden* v. *Benas*, above, n. 119; *Arnold* v. *Cheque Bank*, above, n. 123. See Barak (Nature), above, n. 15 at 120. Consider the following example: a cheque payable to order is stolen from the payee and ultimately paid to thief's indorsee. As the true owner of the cheque, the payee may recover from the thief's indorsee, regardless of whether s. 60 exits. Alternatively, in the absence of s. 60, the payee may sue the drawer, who will then be able to resist the debit to his account, in which case, the drawee will recover from the thief's indorsee. Either way, the loss falls on the thief's indorsee.

[253] See discussion by Holden, above, n. 12 at 227–9 and by Ellinger and Lomnicka, above, n. 91 at 378–9. Both disapprove of Slesser LJ's dicta in *Carpenters*, above, n. 248 at 534 under which '[n]egligence does not necessarily preclude the protection of Section 60 . . .' But see Gottesman, above, n. 245 at 92–6, in whose view, ordinary course of business and lack of negligence are '[c]learly . . . two concepts which can each be given independent content'. Ibid. at 93. For the 'ordinary course of business' requirement see M. Hapgood, *Paget's Law of Banking*, 11th edn. (London: Butterworths, 1996) at 383–4.

[254] *National Bank [of South Africa]* v. *Paterson* [1909] T.S. 322.

indorsement. It does not protect the drawee bank where it paid directly to the thief, against the thief's signature made at the bank, where the thief represented himself as the payee (or indorsee) from whom he stole the cheque. According to Innes CJ,[255]

> As applied to negotiable instruments [indorsement] is capable of three meanings. [1] In a general sense every signature written on the back of such an instrument is an indorsement, even if only placed there for the purpose of identification, or a receipt; that is the literal sense of the word. [2] Its ordinary legal meaning is the signing of a name on the back of an instrument *animo indorsandi* . . ., that is with the intention of undertaking the well understood liabilities of an indorser. And [3] there is a third meaning, which limits the term to an indorsement in the last named sense followed by the delivery of the document.

Taking into account the statutory definition of 'indorsement' as 'indorsement completed by delivery',[256] as well as a classic pre-Act English authority dictum on the meaning of 'indorsement' as distinguished from a mere 'receipt' signed on the back of an instrument,[257] Innes CJ concluded that the forged 'indorsement' against which the drawee bank is protected is in the third sense. In Gottesman's language, '[p]rotection thus extends as long as the indorsed signature is made to transfer the right of ownership in the instrument'.[258] Conversely, the thief's forged signature on the back of the cheque, inserted over the counter at the drawee bank, is not an indorsement to which the provision applies. Rather, it is a mere receipt, acknowledging the receipt of funds.[259] By no stretch of imagination can it be viewed as an indorsement, purporting to transfer the cheque as well as to charge the signer with the statutory liability of an indorser.

This position was followed in Australia,[260] and the prevailing view is that it holds true for all jurisdictions including the UK.[261] It was however pointed out that in fact 'delivery' occurs also where a recipient hands a cheque to the drawee for payment, so that where the recipient signs the back, there is an 'indorsement completed by delivery', which, by statute, constitutes 'indorsement'. Regardless, the thief may indorse the cheque in blank prior to presenting it to the drawee for payment, with the view of

---

[255] Ibid. at 326–7.

[256] Currently s. 1 in South Africa, and *semble*, s. 2 in Canada and the UK, and s. 1 in Israel.

[257] *Keene* v. *Beard* (1860), 8 C.B. (N.S.) 372 at 381–2; 141 E.R. 1210 at 1214 Byles J. followed in another context in *Gerald Mcdonald & Co.* v. *Nash & Co.* [1924] A.C. 625 (H.L.) at 633–4, Viscount Haldane LC.

[258] Gottesman, above, n. 245 at 85.

[259] For the distinction between a signature in the context of negotiation and that of surrender for payment, see also W. E. Britton, *Handbook of the Law of Bills and Notes*, 2nd edn. (St Paul, Minn.: West, 1961) at 422.

[260] *Smith* v. *Commercial Banking Co. of Sydney*, (1910) 11 C.L.R. 667 (H.C.) at 672–3, 677–8.

[261] See e.g. Ellinger and Lomnicka, above, n. 91 at 379, and Ben-Oliel, above, n. 142 at 322 (Israel).

converting the cheque to a bearer instrument. Technically, this could constitute adequate 'indorsement'.[262] Furthermore, the thief may present the cheque for payment purporting to hold it through the prior (forged) indorsement of the payee, rather than purporting to sign as the payee or someone collecting in the payee's behalf. It was thus argued that the distinctions drawn by Innes CJ are artificial, and that protection ought to be given whenever a drawee bank pays directly to the thief, and not only to someone claiming through him.[263] Indeed, even under Innes CJ's analysis, in the latter case, that of a thief purporting to present the cheque through a prior (forged) indorsement, the bank seems to be protected, since the indorsement purported to transfer ownership to the thief.

Also, it seems that under Innes CJ's analysis, the drawee bank is protected where it pays the cheque into the thief's account with that bank, even where the thief represented himself as the payee (or subsequent indorsee) from whom he stole the cheque. This is so since the indorsement and delivery of the cheque for deposit, rather than for cash payment over the counter, may be viewed as 'negotiation',[264] so as to allow the signature to be an 'indorsement'. However, there is a controversy whether a bank which pays a cheque into another account with itself[265] is protected by the provision. Undoubtedly, even in such a case, 'the banker on whom it is drawn pays the bill', as required by the provision;[266] yet it has been contended that the bank's action in collecting the cheque for the depositor falls outside the provision, so that the bank is not immune from liability.[267]

In Australia, BEA s. 65(1) corresponds to BEA s. 60 in the UK. For [57] cheques, it is, however, superseded by Cheques Act s. 94(1) which substitutes 'without negligence' for 'in the ordinary course of business'. In South Africa it is BEA s. 58 which corresponds to BEA s. 60. However, the South African provision adds a qualification: no protection is given to a drawee bank that paid over a forged indorsement that purports to be

---

[262] As was actually held in another South African case. See Cowen and Gering, above, n. 143 at 378. The case is *Stapleberg, N.O. v. Barclays Bank D.C. & O.* [1963](3) S.A.L.R. 120, reported in Afrikaans.

[263] See particularly, Gottesman above, n. 245 at 86. For an inconclusive criticism see also Ryder and Bueno, below, n. 274 at 300–1 & n. 18.

[264] For the negotiation of a bill of exchange, prior to its maturity, to the acceptor, see *Attenborough v. Mackenzie* (1856), 25 L.J. Ex. 244. Similarly, prior to payment, the drawee of a cheque to whom it was indorsed for deposit may have taken it as 'indorsee' so that the subsequent payment is over a forged indorsement.

[265] Strictly speaking, the controversy concerns a cheque deposited into a branch other than that of the drawer. In my view, a similar analysis applies where the both accounts are maintained at the same branch.

[266] See *Gordon v. London City and Midland Bank Ltd.*, above, n. 131 at 274–5, 281. See also the minority view in *Carpenters*, above, n. 248 at 538–9.

[267] See *Carpenters*, above, n. 248 at 529 and 532. Whether the bank will then be protected as a collecting bank is discussed below.

that of a customer at the branch on which the bill of exchange is drawn. That is, a banker is conclusively presumed to know the signature of his customer, not only as a drawer of a cheque drawn on an account held with the banker, but also as an indorser on someone else's cheque. It has been proposed to delete this proviso. Finally, in Israel, BEO s. 23(c) which corresponds to English BEA s. 60 is not limited to a bill payable to order on demand drawn on a banker. Rather, it applies to any type of bill of exchange, whether or not drawn on a bank, and whether payable on demand or at a fixed or determinable future time.

[58]   For crossed cheques,[268] banks in BEA jurisdictions enjoy additional protection. In the UK, BEA s. 80[269] states that,

> Where the banker, on whom a crossed cheque . . . is drawn, in good faith and without negligence pays it, if crossed generally, to a banker, and if crossed specially, to the banker to whom it is crossed, or his agent for collection being a banker, the banker paying the cheque, and if the cheque has come into the hands of the payee, the drawer, shall respectively be entitled to the same rights and be placed in the same position as if payment of the cheque had been made to the true owner[270] thereof.

The provision substitutes 'without negligence' for 'in the ordinary course of business'. As indicated, the latter may include the former, so that for crossed cheques, the defences may overlap. There is however an Australian authority[271] suggesting that there may be circumstances where a bank acts without negligence outside the ordinary course of its business. For crossed cheques, the defence of BEA s. 80 may be thus broader than that of BEA s. 60.[272]

In any event, payment against an absent or irregular indorsement is arguably both outside the ordinary course of business as well as negligent, so as to provide no protection to the drawee bank under either s. 60 or s. 80. Complementary protection, covering cases of irregularity in or

---

[268] For cheque crossing in BEA jurisdictions see 3.B(iii)(8), above. See also (ii), above.

[269] To whom correspond BEO s. 80 in Israel and BEA s. 79 in South Africa. In Australia Cheques Act s. 92 is to substantially the same effect. In Canada, English BEA s. 80 is reproduced almost verbatim as BEA s. 173. This may be one reason why cheque crossing is uncommon in Canada where in the absence of a counterpart to English BEA s. 60, crossing will give the drawee bank protection to which it is not entitled otherwise.

[270] For the view that in connection with crossing 'the expression ["true owner"] bears a specialized meaning derived from the context of the legislative enactment in which it occurs and its historical origin' see *Quality Tyres*, above, n. 33 at 567–9. Nonetheless, in my view, the better position is the one stated in *Kirstein*, above, n. 33 at 2286, under which also in this context the term 'true owner' ought to be defined by reference to general property law.

[271] *Australian Mutual Provident Society v. Derham* (1979), 39 F.L.R. 165.

[272] Note however, that while the drawer is explicitly protected only under BEA s. 80, it is effectively equally protected under BEA s. 60 as well.

absence of indorsement, was thus added in the UK by s. 1(1) of the Cheques Act 1957,[273] providing that,

Where a banker in good faith and in the ordinary course of business pays a cheque drawn on him which is not indorsed or is irregularly indorsed, he does not, in doing so, incur any liability by reason only of the absence of, or irregularity in, indorsement, and he is deemed to have paid it in due course.

'Irregularity' is not defined to exclude a forged indorsement. On the other hand, it was questioned whether protection is not limited only to situations where indorsement is not asked for, as permitted by the Act in connection with the deposit of cheques, but nevertheless appears.[274]

The UK Review Committee on Banking Services Law and Practice con-   **[59]**
sidered all these provisions, namely, BEA ss. 60 and 80, and s. 1 of the Cheques Act 1957.[275] It recommended that they should be combined into a single enactment, under which statutory protection will be available to a paying bank acting 'in good faith and without negligence'.[276] Indeed, multiplicity has been the outcome of historical development and does not serve a useful purpose.[277]

The collecting bank[278]

As discussed, the Anglo-American system allocates forged indorsement   **[60]**
losses to the taker from the forger. This is so whether or not protection is accorded to the drawee as under the English variant.[279] Infrequently, the taker from the forger is a collecting bank. Its position under the laws of Quebec and South Africa was already discussed.[280] Elsewhere in BEA jurisdictions, statutory protection is given to collecting banks so as to eliminate liability incurred in the collection of cheques over forged indorsements. Originally this protection was limited to crossed cheques. It expanded in the UK and Australia to apply to all cheques but remained limited to crossed cheques in Israel and Canada. In Canada, however, crossing is not practised, and consequently, this protection does not mate-

---

[273] To whom correspond Cheques Act s. 94(2) in Australia and BEA s. 83 in South Africa. No corresponding provision exists in either Israel or Canada.

[274] For both points see F. R. Ryder and A. Bueno, *Byles on Bills of Exchange*, 26th edn. (London: Sweet & Maxwell, 1988) at 301–3.

[275] Cm. 622, RB (Chair), *Banking Services: Law and Practice Report by the Review Committee* (London: Her Majesty's Stationery Office, 1989) at 53–4.

[276] Rec. 7(5).

[277] In reviewing the law and making its proposals, the Review Committee specifically endorsed (above, n. 275 at 53) Professor Goode's criticism, which now can be found in R. M. Goode, *Commercial Law*, 2nd edn. (London: Penguin Books, 1995) at 611.

[278] See in general, Ellinger and Lomnicka above, n. 91 at 512–36; Ryder and Bueno, above, n. 274 at 313–30; A. Tyree, *Australian Law of Cheques and Payment Orders* (Sydney: Butterworth, 1985) at 155–85; and Ben-Oliel, above, n. 142 at 380–92.

[279] See (ii), above.   [280] See (iv)(d), above.

rialize. Nor is a collecting bank protected in Canada under BEA s. 165(3).[281]

Prior to 1957, the central provision in the UK was BEA s. 82, providing that, 'where a banker in good faith and without negligence receives payment for a customer of a cheque crossed generally or specially to himself, and the customer has no title or defective title thereto, the banker shall not incur any liability to the true owner of the cheque by reason only of having received such payment'. It was originally held that a bank that has credited its customer's account prior to the collection of a cheque, received payment for itself, and not the customer. Accordingly, in receiving under such circumstances payment for a crossed cheque deposited by a customer to an account, the bank falls outside the statutory protection given under s. 82 to 'a banker . . . [who] receives payment for a customer'.[282] In response, s. 1 of the Bills of Exchange (Crossed Cheques) Act 1906 was enacted to clarify that, 'A banker receives payment of a crossed cheque for a customer within the meaning of section 82 of the Bills of Exchange Act 1882, notwithstanding that he credits his account with the amount of the cheque before receiving payment thereof.' In Israel, BEO s. 82 is modelled on both provisions. In Canada, BEA s. 175 reproduces UK BEA s. 82. Since crossed cheques are anyway not used in Canada, no statutory clarification was ever added as to the meaning of receiving payment for a customer.

In the UK, both BEA s. 82 and s. 1 of the Bills of Exchange (Crossed Cheques) Act were repealed by the Cheques Act 1957 which specifically expanded the protection to open cheques and other payment documents. Its s. 4 provides, in its pertinent part, as follows:

> (1) Where a banker, in good faith and without negligence (a) receives payment for a customer of [a cheque]; or (b) having credited a customer's account with the amount of [a cheque], receives payment thereof for himself; and the customer has no title, or defective title, to the [cheque], the banker does not incur any liability to the true owner of the [cheque] by reason only of receiving payment thereof.

> . . .

> (3) A banker is not to be treated . . . as having been negligent by reason only of his failure to concern himself with absence of, or irregularity in, indorsement of [a cheque].

---

[281] The latter provides that '[w]here a cheque is delivered to a bank for deposit to the credit of a person and the bank credits him with the amount of the cheque, the bank acquires all the rights and powers of a holder in due course of the cheque'. It was held that this provision deals only with a collecting bank handling a cheque for the true owner. See (v)(b)(iii), below.

[282] *Capital and Counties Bank* v. *Gordon* [1903] A.C. 240.

In Australia, Cheques Act s. 95(1) corresponds to UK Cheques Act s. 4(1). **[61]** However, unlike UK Cheques Act s. 4(3), other than in connection with the collection of a cheque for another financial institution,[283] the Australian statute does not provide a blank exemption to the bank for its failure to concern itself with absence of, or irregularity in, an indorsement. Rather, under Cheques Act s. 95(2), it is only in a prescribed narrow set of circumstances that 'the [bank] shall not be treated . . . as having been negligent by reason only of its failure to concern itself with the absence of, or irregularity in, an indorsement of the cheque'. Such is the case of a cheque payable to order deposited by the customer, as the purported payee of the cheque,[284] in which the name specified as that of the payee,

(i)   is the same as the name of the customer;

(ii) is the same as a business name or trade name of the customer; or

(iii) is so similar to the name of the customer, or a business name of the customer, that it is reasonable in all the circumstances for the [bank] to have assumed that the customer was the person intended by the drawer to be the payee. [·]

In all jurisdictions, protection is thus given to a bank collecting a cheque **[62]** 'in good faith and without negligence' for a 'customer'. Protection is provided to the collecting bank as early as of the time the cheque was given to it for collection,[285] rather than only as of the time of receiving payment for it, as literal reading might have suggested.[286]

'Customer' means any person in whose name the bank opened or agreed to open an account.[287] 'Good faith' is established by the collecting

---

[283] The position of a financial institution which either receives payment of a cheque for another financial institution, or receives payment of a cheque and, before or after receiving payment, pays another financial institution the sum ordered to be paid by the cheque, is governed by Cheques Act s. 95(3) and (4). Such a financial institution 'does not incur any liability to the true owner by reason only of having received payment [in good faith and without negligence] of the cheque'. It 'shall not be treated . . . as having been negligent by reason only of its failure to concern itself with the absence of, or irregularity in, an indorsement of the cheque'.

[284] Or in the language of Cheques Act s. 95(2)(b), 'the cheque is a cheque drawn payable to order that has not been transferred by negotiation'. Obviously, the provision would have been clearer had it specified that the collecting bank's customer is the purported payee. Nevertheless, it would not make sense to construe it as precluding negotiation or indorsement to the collecting bank rather than to the customer.

[285] See *Lloyds Bank Ltd.* v. *Savory*, above, n. 243, dealing with the question under the pre-1957 legislation in the UK.

[286] For raising this possible interpretation, see *Capital and Counties Bank*, above, n. 282 at 244 and *Morison* v. *London County and Westminster Bank* [1914] 3 K.B. 356, Lord Reading.

[287] See e.g. *Commissioners of Taxation* v. *English, Scottish and Australian Bank* [1920] A.C. 683 (P.C.). The converse nineteenth-century view, according to which a customer was defined by reference to habitual services already performed by the bank (see e.g. *Matthews* v. *William Brown & Co.* (1894), 10 T.L.R. 386), was questioned in *Lacave* v. *Credit Lyonnais* [1897] 1 Q.B. 148 at 154 and subsequently discarded in *Ladbroker* v. *Todd* (1914), 30 T.L.R. 433. See Ellinger and Lomnicka, above, n. 91 at 102–7.

bank by the denial of actual knowledge and of any suspicion of the existence of a defect in the customer's title.[288] Whether the bank has acted 'without negligence' ought to be determined by reference to prevailing banking practice at the relevant time and place.[289] The collecting bank's negligence may relate to diverse aspects, such as in opening an account for an individual or entity without carrying out sufficient identification or investigation, in connection with cheques payable to employers or beneficiaries and deposited to employees or trustees' personal accounts, in paying inadequate attention to specific details of the cheque such as crossing, or in relation to the examination of indorsements.

Statutory defence is given to a bank that collected a cheque for a customer's account 'in good faith and without negligence' regardless of whether the bank's conduct actually caused the true owner's loss.[290] Finally, a question may arise as to whether a bank collecting a cheque from another account held with itself actually 'receives payment' so as to be protected. It may however be unreasonable to argue that since a bank both collects and pays a cheque it may not raise any defence that would be available to it for each of these actions done separately.

Effect on the ultimate loss allocation

[63] As discussed,[291] where statutory protection is available to the drawee bank, the true owner is nevertheless left with a remedy against any party subsequent to the forged indorsement. Hence, where the cheque is paid to an innocent indorsee from the thief, the drawee bank's protection does not impact the ultimate loss allocation to the taker from the forger. Conversely, where the thief dealt directly with the drawee bank, loss may be reallocated to the dispossessed owner, that is, the person from whom the cheque was stolen. Arguably, this is so other than when payment was made over the counter to the thief impersonating himself as the payee (or indorsee) from whom he stole the cheque. The latter case may not be a payment over a forged indorsement and thus may fall outside the statutory protection, in which case loss falls on the drawee bank, as the one who dealt with the forger.

As further indicated,[292] where the forger deposits the cheque bearing the forged indorsement for collection to his account, the effect of the statutory protection accorded to the collecting bank is to shift away forged indorse-

---

[288] According to Ellinger and Lomnicka, above, n. 91 at 515 & n. 56, '[t]here is only one reported case in which the collecting bank's good faith was questioned and even in this instance the bank was successful'. See *Lawrie* v. *Commonwealth Trading Bank of Australia* [1970] Qd. R 373.

[289] See e.g. *Marfani* v. *Midland Bank*, above, n. 82 at 973.

[290] *Savory* v. *Lloyds Bank*, above, n. 243 at 216.   [291] See (ii), above.

[292] See (ii), above.

ment losses from the collecting bank to the dispossessed owner of the cheque. Conversely, where the cheque bearing the forged indorsement is deposited for collection by a bona fide indorsee claiming the cheque through the forged indorsement, the loss allocation to the taker from the forger is not affected by the statutory defence available to the collecting bank.

In general, only a bank that has acted in good faith and either without negligence or in the ordinary course of business may successfully raise a statutory defence. The defence is unavailable where the bank fails to meet the required test. The effect of the unavailability of the defence on the loss allocation scheme will now tentatively be considered. In this context, two questions arise: (a) May the bank that acted negligently[293] be able to raise a plea based on the dispossessed owner's contributory negligence? (b) In the pursuit of recourse by the negligent bank against parties subsequent to the forgery, does negligence, whether of the bank or of any of the defendants, play any role?

In answering the first question, a distinction will be drawn between the **[64]** true owner's action against the collecting bank and the dispossessed drawer's action against the drawee. The former is an action in conversion. The latter is in breach of contract.[294] Whether a collecting bank which did not act 'in good faith and without negligence' may invoke the true owner's contributory negligence so as to reduce or eliminate its own liability has not been settled yet. According to Ellinger and Lomnicka, in this context, 'the plea of contributory negligence provides an equitable solution'.[295] Indeed, while the plaintiff's negligence is usually not a good defence to a conversion action,[296] it ought to be recalled that had the collecting bank not been negligent, it would not have been held liable in the first place, as it could have raised the statutory protection. It is its negligence which precludes the collecting bank from raising the defence, and hence triggers its liability in conversion. Arguably, once the collecting bank's negligence becomes relevant in charging it with liability, it is hard to justify the elimination of the true owner's own negligence in assessing responsibility.

Whether the dispossessed drawer's negligence is available as a defence to the negligent drawee bank is a matter of the construction of their contract on which the drawer's action is brought. An implied term to that effect may well be inferred in the banking contract.

---

[293] Or for that matter, in bad faith or, depending on the specific statutory defence, outside the ordinary course of business. In the ensuing text, 'negligence' of a bank refers to all such breaches as applicable.   [294] See (iv)(c), above.

[295] See Ellinger and Lomnicka, above, n. 91 at 529, and in general, at 528–30. For similar views (and some jurisprudence) see also Ben-Oliel, above, n. 142 at 385–6, and Tyree, above, n. 137 at 180–3.   [296] See (iv)(a), above.

[65]   In answering the second question, relating to the effect of negligence on the recovery from a post-forgery defendant, a distinction is drawn between the collecting bank's recourse and the drawee bank's action. The former is an action on the cheque against a post-forgery indorsee. Arguably, in such an action, the collecting bank is entitled to recover the full amount of the cheque regardless of either its own or the defendant's negligence. The latter is the drawee bank's action to recover its mistaken payment. Arguably, also in this action, negligence is irrelevant.

It may thus follow that a negligent drawee bank would be able to recover from a non-negligent collecting bank. Indeed, the statutory defence is available to the latter against the true owner, but not against the drawee bank. Nonetheless, this is a startling result that should be avoided. It is quite unreasonable to fasten liability on a collecting bank that was exonerated due to its lack of negligence, only because the drawee bank was negligent! In any event, it is the collecting and not drawee bank that was likely to deal with the forger. The scenario of a negligent drawee and a non-negligent collecting bank is thus hardly feasible.

[66]   In the final analysis, the special protection accorded to bona fide non-negligent drawee and collecting banks has raised complex questions of statutory interpretation. In a given case, it is likely to precipitate extensive and costly litigation over the existence or absence of negligence or good faith. Regardless, such protection can hardly be justified on policy grounds. Where its effect is simply to insulate banks from litigation it may not be cost effective, taking into account what is required to be determined in order to have the protection apply. Indeed, protections given to paying and collecting banks undermine the policies of loss prevention or reduction and loss distribution in several ways:

(1) As indicated, it is not settled whether in order to benefit from the statutory protection, a drawee bank in the UK need have acted without negligence. Protection afforded to a negligent bank undoubtedly undermines the policy of loss prevention or reduction.

(2) Fastening liability on banks regardless of their lack of negligence is likely to produce more stringent loss prevention policies than where liability is based on negligence alone.

(3) The combined effect of protecting both collecting and drawee banks is to shift losses away from banks to customers. Where the forger dealt directly with the depositary bank loss is shifted to the dispossessed owner. Regardless, loss distribution is seriously undermined by reallocating losses away from banks. Furthermore, assuming both the dispossessed owner and the bank which dealt with the forger were not negligent, it is the bank which is capable

of maintaining more rigorous loss prevention policies. Accordingly, to say the least, no gain in loss prevention or reduction is realized so as possibly to offset the erosion in the loss distribution policy occurring upon shifting losses away from banks.

Where the effect of the statutory protection is to shift away losses from a bona fide non-negligent bank into the bona fide non-negligent dispossessed owner, it can be rationalized on neither loss prevention (or minimization) nor loss distribution grounds.

The specific case of Canada

As indicated, standard BEA provisions affording protection to banks collecting or paying crossed cheques are reproduced in full in Canada.[297] Cheque crossing is, however, not practised in Canada so that these provisions are a dead letter. No protection is usually provided in Canada to a bank collecting or paying over a forged indorsement an open cheque payable to order. Nor is a collecting bank protected in Canada under BEA s. 165(3). The latter provides that '[w]here a cheque is delivered to a bank for deposit to the credit of a person and the bank credits him with the amount of the cheque, the bank acquires all the rights and powers of a holder in due course of the cheque'. It was held that this provision deals only with a collecting bank handling a cheque for the true owner.[298]

[67]

Protection is nevertheless accorded in Canada to a drawee bank where the drawer failed to advise it of the forgery within one year of acquiring notice. In such a case, the drawee bank which paid a cheque over a forged indorsement need not reverse the debit to the drawer's account and the cheque is to be considered as paid in due course. The governing provisions are ss. 48(3) and (4).[299] These subsections have no parallel in the other

---

[297] See ss. 173 and 175, corresponding to s. 80 and (now repealed) s. 82 in the UK, respectively providing protection to the paying and collecting bank.

[298] In *Boma Manufacturing* v. *Canadian Imperial Bank of Commerce*, above, n. 71, noting the broad language of the provision, but recognizing its underlying purpose, and speaking on that point for a unanimous court, Iacobucci J. held that 'the "person" in s. 165(3) must mean a person who is entitled to the cheque', such as 'the payee or the legitimate endorsee'. See paras. 74 and 76, and in general, paras. 69–85. La Forest J. ultimately agreed. See paras. 107–9. For an earlier authority in the same direction, see *Morguard Trust Co.* v. *Bank of Nova Scotia*, above, n. 71, where Maloney J. rationalized this rule (at 217), stating that '[s]ection 165(3) refers to the "delivery" of a cheque. Section [39] of the Act states that delivery "in order to be effectual must be made either by or under the authority of the party drawing, accepting or endorsing . . .". In this case there was no delivery within the meaning of this section and therefore there was no delivery of the cheque within the meaning of s. 165(3) . . .'. A proponent of the contrary view on the effect of s. 165(3) is Baxter, above, n. 71.

[299] For a comprehensive analysis, N. Rafferty and J. Watson-Hamilton, 'Forged Payees' Endorsements: Liability of Collecting Banks to Drawers and the Effect of Section 48(4) of the Bills of Exchange Act' (1998), 13 B.F.L.R. 271.

BEA jurisdictions.[300] They were added to the Canadian BEA to offset the consequences of the deletion of a counterpart to the UK s. 60, providing protection to a drawee bank paying a cheque over a forged indorsement. In Canada, BEA s. 48 thus provides,

(3) Where a cheque payable to order is paid by the drawee on a forged[301] endorsement out of the funds of the drawer, or is so paid and charged to his account, the drawer has no right of action against the drawee for the recovery of the amount so paid,[302] nor any defence to any claim made by the drawee for the amount so paid, as the case may be, unless he gives notice in writing[303] of the forgery to the drawee within one year[304] after he has acquired notice of the forgery.

(4) In case of failure by the drawer to give notice of the forgery within the period referred to in subsection (3), the cheque shall be held to have been paid in due course with respect to every other party thereto or named therein, who has not previously instituted proceedings for the protection of his rights.

Under subsection (3), where timely notice has not been given by the drawer to the drawee, the drawee is protected from liability to the drawer and need not reverse the debit to the drawer's account in the amount of the cheque paid over the forged indorsement. In such circumstances, under subsection (4), payment over the forged indorsement discharges parties liable on the cheque, such as the drawer and indorser. Nevertheless, as under BEA s. 60 in the UK,[305] the true owner is left with a remedy against any party subsequent to the forged indorsement. Hence, where the cheque is paid to an innocent indorsee from the thief, the protection under BEA s. 48 in Canada ought not to impact the ultimate loss allocation to the taker from the forger. Its effect is to exonerate the drawee from litigation. Conversely, where the thief dealt directly with the drawee bank, loss may be reallocated to the dispossessed owner, that is, the per-

[300] The lack of any UK equivalent was noted by Crawford and Falconbridge, above, n. 40 at 1385.

[301] Strangely, the subsection, in departure from e.g. ss. 48(1) and 49(1), is specifically restricted to 'forged' indorsements and thus appears to exclude 'unauthorized' ones.

[302] The subsection was held to impose a notice requirement as a condition for recovery, implicitly contained in all banking contracts, rather than a mere limitation period for bringing an action. See *Bank of Montreal v. Attorney General of Quebec* (1979), 96 D.L.R. (3d) 586 (S.C.C.), Pratte J.

[303] *Quaere* as to the consequences of notification in any other medium, e.g. orally. While the writing requirement is categoric, I doubt that courts will so take it.

[304] It may, nonetheless, be too late then for the drawee bank to effectively pursue its remedies under s. 40(1). According to Crawford and Falconbridge, above, n. 40 at 1392, 'the one year . . . probably ought to be regarded as a maximum . . . rather than a period that may be allowed to elapse with impunity'. Stated otherwise, the restitutionary defence of change of position may be accorded to the bank also within the year. See discussion in (iv)(c), above.

[305] See (ii) and (v)(b), above.

son from whom the cheque was stolen. Arguably, this is so other than when payment was made over the counter to the thief impersonating himself as the payee (or indorsee) from whom he stole the cheque. The latter case may not be a payment 'on a forged endorsement' and thus may fall outside the subsection, in which case loss falls on the drawee bank. Where an unissued cheque was stolen from the drawer and paid over a forged indorsement, the drawer may pursue his recourse against anyone deriving title from the forger, such as the collecting bank, by bringing an action in conversion or money had and received. Alternatively, if such an action is unavailable, as I argues;[306] the drawer could be subrogated to the bank's action for payment made under mistake of fact.

It was nonetheless held that s. 48(4) exonerates the collecting bank from liability.[307] It was explained that the collecting bank is a 'party thereto or named therein . . .' with respect to whom 'the cheque shall be held to have been paid in due course' under the subsection, so that no action could be brought by the drawer against it. In my view, however, this is an erroneous interpretation. Indeed, it is unfortunate that s. 48(4) does not stop after 'paid in due course'; the ensuing 'with respect' clause is simply redundant. The subsection ought nevertheless to be construed as providing discharge to all parties liable on the cheque, which is the normal effect of 'payment in due course'.[308] The collecting bank which presents the cheque for payment is not such a party. Moreover, while discharge on the cheque ought to lead to a discharge on the underlying transaction,[309] it need not affect other actions, such as conversion or restitution. In the final analysis, in the narrow circumstances ss. 48(3) and (4) operate, there are no compelling reasons why they should depart from s. 60 of the UK BEA and reverse the ultimate forged indorsement loss allocation scheme.

(VI) THE ANGLO-AMERICAN SYSTEM: THE BASIC SCHEME UNDER THE UCC

(a) Introduction

Cheque fraud losses are dealt with in the various American states in both **[68]**

---

[306] See (iv)(c), above.

[307] *Enoch Band of Stony Plain Reserve No. 135* v. *Morin* (1995), 128 D.L.R. (4th) 754 (Alta.Q.B.), aff'd (1997), 152 D.L.R. (4th) 383 (Alta. C.A.). Application for leave to appeal denied [1997] S.C.C.A. No. 230.

[308] For the effect of 'payment in due course' to discharge the instrument see s. 59 in the UK, s. 78 (in conjunction with s. 79) in Australia, s. 138 in Canada, s. 60 in Israel, and s. 57 (in conjunction with s. 1) in South Africa. For the discharge of an instrument as the equivalent of the discharge off all parties liable on it see e.g. Crawford and Falconbridge, above, n. 40 at 1667.   [309] See (iv)(d) and (v)(b), above.

Articles 3 and 4 of the Uniform Commercial Code (UCC or 'Code').[310] The basic scheme under the UCC is the same as under the BEA.[311] The fundamental distinction is between cheques payable to bearer and those payable to order. In connection with the former, theft losses fall on the person from whom the instrument has been stolen. In connection with the later, theft losses are allocated to the taker from the forger.

Thus, the transfer of a cheque payable to the bearer requires no indorsement,[312] so that any possessor, including a taker from a thief and its successor in title, is a 'holder',[313] who, depending on his compliance with statutory good faith purchase for value requirements,[314] may qualify as a holder in due course, so as to defeat any adverse claim to the instrument.[315] Effectively then, holding in due course of a bearer cheque forfeits any prior title and right to possess the instrument,[316] and hence the right to enforce it.[317] As a holder in due course the transferee of the bearer cheque may recover from the drawer at the exclusion of anyone else. Loss is thus borne by the ex-holder who lost possession.

Conversely, as will be seen below, the transfer of a cheque payable to order requires an authorized indorsement so that a transferee deriving title through a forged indorsement[318] lacks title and is a wrongful possessor. He is not a 'holder' and hence cannot be a holder in due course. Title and the right to possession remain in the hands of the dispossessed[319] holder. Notwithstanding loss of possession, he may be entitled to enforce the instrument against prior parties and could also sue in conversion anyone deriving title through the forged indorsement and the drawee. Payment over the forged indorsement is in breach of the account agreement so that the drawee must recredit the drawer's account. Anyone who derives title through the forged indorsement may be sued by a subse-

---

[310] UCC Article 3 deals with negotiable instruments. UCC Article 4 governs bank collections and deposits. The current text is of 1990 when a new text for Article 3 was issued and Article 4 was revised. 'If there is a conflict, . . . Article [4] governs Article 3 . . .'. See UCC §4–102 (a).   [311] As discussed in (iv), above.

[312] See UCC §3–201.

[313] For the 'bearer' as the holder of an instrument payable to bearer see definition of 'bearer' and 'holder' in UCC §1–201(5) and (20).

[314] The precise conditions to be complied with are set out in UCC §3–302(a).

[315] See UCC §3–306.

[316] This goes back to the classic English case of *Miller* v. *Race*, above, n. 20.

[317] Under §§3–301 and 309.

[318] 'Forged indorsement' is used here broadly, and unless otherwise indicated, covers all cases where an authorized indorsement is missing, and thus includes unauthorized indorsement as well as the lack of any required indorsement. Similarly, a thief and any other unauthorized transferor is loosely referred below, as 'the forger'. Unless specifically indicated otherwise, the ensuing discussion will accordingly treat forgery and lack of authority indistinguishingly. The distinction between 'forged' and 'unauthorized' indorsement is relevant, however, in the discussion in (vii), below.

[319] Again, 'dispossessed' and 'dispossession' are loosely used here to cover also the case of loss of possession, followed by finding leading to wrongful detention of the cheque.

quent transferee as well as the drawee who has paid the cheque. Ultimately, the loss falls on the taker from the forger.

As will be seen below, in reaching a substantially identical loss allocation scheme, there are however a few variations between the routes selected by the UCC and the BEA. In turn, the choice of different means to the same end resulted in some not fundamental differences. Three points should be highlighted. First, compared to the BEA, under the UCC, the dispossessed ex-holder's action on the cheque against prior parties is available in more limited circumstances. Second, under the UCC, the conversion remedy is provided by statute. Effectively, this has left no room for the corresponding action of money had and received. Also, it makes conversion applicable also in the civil law jurisdiction of Louisiana. Finally, the express UCC statutory provision governing conversion denies the remedy to the drawer and makes it available against the drawee. Thereby the provision settles two controversies existing in BEA jurisdictions as to the reach of common law conversion. Third, under the UCC, among post-forgery parties, loss is allocated to the taker from the forger on the basis of statutory transfer and presentment warranties, rather than, as under the BEA, under statutory preclusions and the law of mistake and restitution.

An analysis of the Code's basic scheme is fully set out immediately below.

(b) The dispossessed ex-holder (purported indorser)'s remedy

Introduction

The starting point of UCC §3–403 (a) is that 'an unauthorized signature is **[69]** ineffective'.[320] 'Unauthorized' signature is defined in UCC §1–201 (43) as 'one made without actual, implied or apparent authority and includes a forgery'. Since under §3–204, '[i]ndorsement' requires 'a signature', it follows, that as in BEA jurisdictions,[321] a forged indorsement constitutes a breach in the chain of title to the cheque; it passes neither title nor lawful possession. Title and the right to possession remain with the original (ex-)holder whose signature has been forged.

A transferee who derives title, directly or indirectly, through a forged indorsement is not a 'holder' in relation to parties whose signatures on the cheque preceded the forgery. This is so since no transferee can become

---

[320] This rule is stated to be subject to two enumerated exceptions and to exist '[u]nless otherwise provided in this Article or Article 4'. The enumerated exceptions pertain to ratification and the effectiveness of the unauthorized signature to bind the signer. The other exceptions are discussed in (vii), below.   [321] See (iv)(a), above.

a 'holder' without the 'negotiation' of the cheque to him,[322] and the negotiation of a cheque payable to order is by 'its indorsement by the
holder'.[323] While being in possession of the cheque, the forger is neither its
named payee nor indorsee, and thus is not a 'holder'.[324] Consequently, the
taking from the forger, even by indorsement, is not 'negotiation'; hence,
while being an indorsee in possession of the cheque identifying him, neither the taker from the forger, nor, consequently, any transferee deriving
title from him, is a 'holder'.[325]

By definition, a 'holder in due course' must be a 'holder'.[326] Since the
acquirer of a cheque payable to order through a forged indorsement is not
a holder, no one who takes a cheque subsequent to a forged indorsement
can be a holder in due course in relation to parties whose signatures preceded the forgery. A holder in due course obtains a clear title to the
cheque, free from claims to it, such as 'a claim of a property or possessory
right in the instrument or its proceeds';[327] this would have covered the
claim of ownership of the person from whom the cheque has been stolen,
and whose signature has been forged. But as indicated, a forged indorsement precludes holding in due course, without which forgery could not
have been overcome.

Under the UCC, as in BEA jurisdictions,[328] two options are available to
the dispossessed owner ex-holder of the cheque. First, he may call on
prior parties liable on the cheque. Alternatively, he may sue subsequent
parties on the basis of their unlawful interference with his possession or
property right. The former action is governed by UCC §3–309. The latter
is governed by §3–420.

Action on the cheque

[70]   The enforcement of lost, destroyed or stolen instruments is provided for
by UCC §3–309. Under §3–309(a), a person out of possession is given the
right to enforce the instrument upon satisfying certain conditions. First,

---

[322] 'Negotiation' is the mode of transfer constituting the transferee 'the holder' of the
instrument. See UCC §3–201(a).
[323] See UCC §3–201(b). Strictly speaking, the provision speaks of 'an instrument payable
to an identified person' rather than to order. However, under §3–109(b), a promise or order
payable to order 'is payable to the identified person'. Identification of the person to whom
the cheque is payable is determined by the signer's intention. See UCC §3–110. Where a
cheque is made payable to a person identified by name and account number, it 'is payable
to the named person, whether or not that person is the owner of the account identified by
number'. See UCC §3–110(c) (i) which is consistent with *Continental Airlines Inc.* v. *Boatman
Nat'l Bank* 13 F.3d 1254 (8th cir. 1994) decided under the pre-1990 code.
[324] A holder of a cheque payable to order is defined as the identified person in possession
of the cheque. See UCC §1–201 (20).
[325] Notwithstanding the statutory definition, ibid.
[326] See UCC §3–302 requiring a holder in due course to be a 'holder'.
[327] UCC §3–306.   [328] See above, (iv)(a).

the person must have been in possession of the instrument and entitled to enforce it when loss of possession occurred. Second, the loss of possession must not have been the result of a transfer by the person or a lawful seizure. Stated otherwise, loss of possession was neither voluntary nor the result of a lawful act. Third, 'the person cannot reasonably obtain possession of the instrument because the instrument was destroyed, its whereabouts cannot be determined, or it is in the possession of unknown person or a person that cannot be found or is not to service or process'.

Pre-1990 Article 3 restricted the claim on a lost, destroyed, or stolen instrument solely to its 'owner'.[329] While in my view, 'owner' could have been broadly interpreted to include the rightful possessor, the first condition of present §3–309 eliminates this ambiguity; it confers the right on the one who 'was in possession of the instrument and entitled to enforce it when loss of possession occurred'. Under §3–301, a '[p]erson entitled to enforce' an instrument is its holder or non-holder in possession who has the rights of the holder.[330] This is broader from the corresponding BEA provision which confers the right only on the holder at the time loss occurred.[331] It is however obvious that an ex-holder, who either lost possession of a cheque, or from whom the cheque was stolen, satisfies the first two conditions of the present §3–309.

Conversely, the third condition, which is without precedent in the corresponding provisions of both the BEA and pre-1990 Article 3, will not be always satisfied in the case of loss or theft. For example, once the cheque is paid, though to a wrongful claimant, possession can usually be easily obtained by the ex-holder. Equally, prior to payment, the third condition is not satisfied, where the unlawful possessor is known or can be found, and is amenable to service of process.[332] The third condition will however be satisfied where the cheque has been destroyed, its whereabouts cannot be determined, or is in the wrongful possession of an unknown person or a person who cannot be found or is not amenable to service of process. This is more likely to happen when the loss or theft is discovered prior to payment.[333]

---

[329] Pre-1990 UCC §3–804.

[330] According to the Official Comment, a non-holder in possession includes a subrogee, transferee without negotiation, or successor to the holder under any applicable law. A third category of a 'person entitled to enforce' enumerated in UCC §3–301 includes a claimant under §3–309. In general, 'Person entitled to enforce' an instrument corresponds to the 'true owner' in BEA jurisdictions.

[331] See e.g. ss. 155–6 of the BEA in Canada.

[332] Practically speaking, this means that where feasible, the ex-holder is required first to recover possession, before taking any action against a party liable on the instrument.

[333] But cf. e.g. *Chase Manhattan Bank* v. *Concord Utilities Corp.* 7 UCC Rep. Serv. 52 (N.Y. City Ct. 1969), dealing with the loss of a cheque in the course of its collection. While this was a pre-payment loss, it demonstrates that banks are not immune from the risk of loss, which may occur even after payment.

Under §3–309 (b), upon proving compliance with the three conditions specified in subsection (a), the claimant 'must prove the terms of the instrument', in which case, the action proceeds as if it is on the instrument. However, no judgment will be given against the party liable, unless he 'is adequately protected against loss that might occur by reason of a claim by another person to enforce the instrument'.[334] In departure from both its predecessors in the BEA and the pre-1990 Article 3, 'adequate protection' is not stated to be limited to an indemnity; rather, under UCC §3–309(b), '[a]dequate protection may be provided by any reasonable means'. According to the Official Comment, 'adequate protection is a flexible concept'; it is hinted that it may not be required 'if the instrument was payable to the person who lost the instrument and that person did not indorse the instrument', in which case, 'no other person could be a holder of the instrument'.[335] A party liable on a cheque who paid to one not entitled to enforce it, such as one who claims on the instrument through a forged indorsement, is not discharged,[336] and remains liable to the ex-holder who has satisfied the conditions set out in §3–309(a); he is not protected by whatever 'adequate protection' is provided by the ex-holder.

Action for the conversion of the cheque

[71] Alternatively, and in fact, concurrently, the ex-holder may sue parties who handled the cheque after the loss or theft. This action is in conversion. Unlike under the BEA, the conversion cause of action is provided in Article 3 itself. No comparable statutory basis is accorded to the alternative action for money had and received, which in this context, seems to be overlooked in the USA.[337]

The applicable statutory provision is UCC §3–420. It first states in subsection (a) that '[t]he law applicable to conversion of personal property applies to instruments'. As explained in the Official Comment to the pre-1990 corresponding provision, '[a] negotiable instrument is the property of the holder. It is a mercantile specialty which embodies rights against other parties, and a thing of value.'[338] The starting point is thus that an instrument, including a cheque, is a chattel, and the general law applica-

---

[334] Arguably, 'adequate protection' is required also to cover against legal fees and costs incurred in defending a possible action by an adverse claimant. See e.g. *Chase Manhattan Bank* v. *Concord Utilities Corp*, ibid.

[335] Yet, even in such a case 'adequate protection' may be required, first against the possibility of mistaken or fraudulent negotiation by the claimant, and second, against the risk that another court will later hold the effectiveness of the thief's indorsement, for example, on the basis of the ex-holder's negligence.   [336] UCC §3–602.

[337] For both conversion and money had and received in common law BEA jurisdictions see (iv)(a), above.

[338] Official Comment 2 to pre-1990 UCC §3–419.

ble to the conversion of chattels applies.[339] This puts the matter, though by statute, on equal footing with its treatment in common law BEA jurisdictions.[340] Yet, the ensuing text of the provision elaborates on as well as possibly modifies the application of the general law of conversion to instruments.

The second sentence of §3–420(a) provides that '[a]n instrument is also converted if it is taken by transfer, other than a negotiation, from a person not entitled to enforce the instrument or a bank makes or obtains payment with respect to the instrument for a person not entitled to enforce the instrument or to receive payment.' This is both a partial or incomplete definition as well as a possible addition to the common law definition. Thus, it does not cover the actual dispossession of the ex-holder; this remains covered by the first sentence of §3–420(a). In this sense the second sentence is only an incomplete or partial definition of conversion. At the same time, the second sentence covers anyone who dealt with the thief after the theft; neither the thief nor a transferee deriving title for the thief is a person entitled to enforce the instrument, and the transfer from either one is not 'negotiation'. As stated by the Official Comment, the second sentence of subsection (a) 'covers cases in which a depositary or payor bank takes an instrument bearing a forged indorsement'. As applied to a depositary bank, this is indeed a restatement of the common law. But so far as the application to the drawee or payor bank, this takes a position and settles a controversy in the common law as to the application of conversion in such a case.[341]

It seems to me that payment or giving value to an authorized indorser will not constitute conversion[342] regardless of whether the indorser was in breach of a fiduciary duty or otherwise an embezzler. In such a case, depending on the required degree of knowledge,[343] a bank or anyone else paying or giving value may be found liable in knowing receipt of trust

---

[339] See Official Comment 1 to UCC §3–420. This opening sentence of §3–420(a) has no counterpart in the pre-1990 Code. Since conversion is a common law tort, this sentence was deleted in Louisiana, which is a civil law jurisdiction. Instead, Louisiana retained the first two subsections of the pre-1990 provision, under which conversion is constituted also by the drawee's refusal to return or pay upon the delivery of an instrument for acceptance or payment. In principle, however, Louisiana retained the balance of §3–420, so that like Israel, but unlike Quebec and South Africa (see (iv)(d) above), Louisiana incorporated the common law conversion into its cheque law.

[340] But not necessarily with the treatment in BEA civil law jurisdictions. See (iv)(d), above.

[341] See (iv)(b), above.

[342] However, handling cheques contrary to restrictive indorsements requiring payment to banks may constitute conversion under UCC §3–206(c). This case of conversion of cheques bearing authorized indorsements is outside the scope of the present discussion.

[343] Notice of breach of fiduciary duty is governed by UCC §3–307

funds or knowing assistance in the breach of trust; yet, no conversion has been committed.[344]

The third sentence of §3–420(a) deals with standing to sue in conversion. The underlying assumption is that standing is reserved for the one entitled to enforce the instrument[345] prior to the loss or theft, typically the ex-holder who has the right to immediate possession. Accordingly, the third sentence of subsection (a) points out who is *not* entitled to sue in conversion. Thereunder, 'an action for conversion of an instrument may not be brought by (i) the issuer or acceptor of the instrument or (ii) a payee or indorsee who did not receive delivery of the instrument either directly or through delivery to an agent or a co-payee'. Both clauses of the third sentence settle controversies under the pre–1990 Article 3 in a way consistent with doctrine as well as policy, though in one situation departing from the prevailing, albeit in my view unjustified, position in BEA jurisdictions.

As applied to cheques, clause (i) of the third sentence of subsection (a) effectively provides that the drawer, being the issuer of the cheque,[346] lacks standing to bring an action in conversion. This is so regardless of whether theft or loss occurred prior or subsequent to the issue of the cheque, namely, irrespective of whether theft or loss occurred while the cheque had been in the possession of the drawer or subsequent holder. In explicitly following the leading case of *Stone & Webster Engineering Corp.* v. *First National Bank & Trust Co.*,[347] the Official Comment explains that '[t]here is no reason why a drawer should have an action in conversion'. As a matter of doctrine, '[t]he check represents an obligation of the drawer rather than property of the drawer'. To the same end, as a matter of policy, '[t]he drawer has an adequate remedy against the payor bank for recredit of the drawer's account for unauthorized payment of the check'.[348] This double rationale is quite convincing; on this point the departure from the dubious contrary prevailing view in common law BEA jurisdictions, facilitating a conversion action by the drawer,[349] is fully justified.

Clause (ii) of the third sentence of subsection (a) responds to the 'split of authority under former Article 3 on the issue of whether a payee who never received the instrument is a proper plaintiff in a conversion action'.[350] Again, in denying standing to the payee or indorsee who never received possession, the provision is consistent with both doctrine and policy, and in this case, is not in disagreement with the state of law in

---

[344] For a view to the contrary see White and Summers, above, n. 117 at 553–5.
[345] As defined in t3–301.   [346] See UCC §3–105(c).   [347] Above, n. 132.
[348] For the drawer's remedy against the drawee (payor bank) see (vi)(c), below.
[349] For an analysis as well as a critique, see (iv)(c), above.
[350] Official Comment 1 to UCC §3–420.

common law BEA jurisdictions. As explained by the Official Comment, as a matter of doctrine, '[u]ntil delivery, the payee does not have any interest in the check. The payee never became the holder of the check nor a person entitled to enforce the check'. And as a matter of both doctrine and policy, '[n]or is the payee injured by the fraud . . . [I]f the check is never delivered to the payee, the obligation owed to the payee is not affected . . . Since the payee's right to enforce the underlying obligation is unaffected by the fraud of the thief, there is no reason to give any additional remedy to the payee.'[351] Obviously, as recognized by clause (ii) itself, delivery to the payee need not necessarily be in person; the delivery to the payee's agent will suffice to give the payee a standing to sue in conversion on the subsequent loss of the cheque by or its theft from the agent. Also, '[i]f the check is payable to more than one payee, delivery to one of the payees is deemed to be delivery to all the payees'.[352]

UCC §3–420(b) deals with the measure of liability in an action under subsection (a). It states that 'the measure of liability is presumed to be the amount payable on the instrument, but recovery may not exceed the amount of plaintiff's interest in the instrument'. The 'amount payable' is not limited to the principal or face value; rather, it includes the interest that would have been recovered by the holder had he not lost possession. At the same time, the limit to 'plaintiff's interest' addresses multiple payee checks; it prevents a payee with a limited interest from receiving a windfall.[353]

Finally, UCC §3–420(c) limits the liability in conversion of '[a] representative, other than a depositary bank, who has in good faith dealt with the instrument or its proceeds on behalf of one who was not the person entitled to enforce the instrument'. The liability of such a representative is limited to the amount of proceeds remaining in its hands; the representative 'is not liable in conversion to that person beyond the amount of any proceeds that it has not paid out'.[354] This defence or limitation to exposure is not available to a depositary bank, whose measure of liability is, as provided generally in subsection (b), up to the amount payable on the cheque. According to the Official Comment, 'the defense provided by §3–420(c) is limited to collecting banks other than the depositary bank', namely, the 'representative' of which the subsection speaks is an

---

[351] An instrument, including a cheque, affects the underlying obligation only when it is 'taken' by, namely, delivered to, the holder or any other person entitled to enforce it. See UCC §3–310.

[352] Official Comment 1 to UCC §3–420.   [353] Official Comment 2 to UCC §3–420.

[354] In the pre-1990 Article 3, the limitation benefited the depositary bank as well. This only precipitated multiple actions, aimed at fastening full liability on the depositary bank on the basis of breach of warranty (discussed below, in (iv)(d)), and could thus hardly be justified; in fact, several courts managed to circumvent this limitation altogether. See Official Comment 3 to §3–420.

intermediary bank acting as a collecting agent on behalf of the depositary bank.[355] To invoke the defence, the 'representative' must have acted 'in good faith'.[356]

(c) The drawer's remedy

[72]   As a matter of general legal principles, the drawer of a cheque payable to order which was paid by the drawee bank over a forged indorsement may sue that bank for breach of contract for paying the cheque contrary to the drawer's instructions. Such instructions, embodied in the drawer/customer's order which constitutes the cheque, were to pay the cheque to the payee or someone deriving title from the payee. Payment to one claiming through a forged indorsement, that is, to someone other than one who derives title from the payee, is wrongful; it does not discharge the drawer from liability on the instrument.[357] Being contrary to the drawer's instructions, such payment constitutes a breach of the banking contract between the drawer/customer and his bank.

In this respect, there is no difference between the US and BEA jurisdictions.[358] However, to some extent, UCC Article 4 codified the point in §4–401(a), permitting a bank to 'charge against the account of a customer an item which is properly payable from the account . . .', thereby implicitly indicating that a bank may not charge to the account an item which is not 'properly payable'.[359] The provision goes on to state that '[a]n item is properly payable if it is authorized by the customer and is in accordance with any agreement between the customer and bank'. Official Comment 1 clarifies that '[a]n item containing a forged drawer's signature or forged indorsement is not properly payable'. Accordingly, a drawee bank which pays a cheque over a forged indorsement is in breach of duty. Whether this is a breach of contract, subject to the general limitation period in each enacting state, or a breach of a 'duty . . . arising under . . . [Article] 4', so

---

[355] But see White and Summers, above, n. 117 at 560 stating that a liquor store that cashed a stolen cheque is such a representative, whose exposure is unjustifiably limited by §3–420(c). However, this expanded definition of 'representative' is contrary to the language of the Official Comment. Also, in this scenario, in my view, the liquor store is better viewed as a purchaser of the cheque rather than as an agent for collection, and thus is not a 'representative'. Accordingly, it is liable for the full amount of the cheque regardless of the amount of the proceeds remaining in its hands.

[356] 'Good faith' is defined in UCC §3–103(a)(4) as 'honesty in fact and the observance of reasonable commercial standards of fair dealing'.

[357] Under UCC §3–602(a). Discharge by payment requires payment 'to a person entitled to enforce the instrument'. One claiming through a forged indorsement is thus excluded.

[358] For this position in BEA jurisdictions, see (iv)(c), above.

[359] For support to this interpretation, see White and Summers, above, n. 117 at 551.

as to be subject to three-year statute of limitations under §4–111, is not entirely clear.[360]

The Code is silent as to the effect of the customer's knowledge of the forged indorsement or negligent failure to discover it, as well as of the ability to contractually redefine 'properly payable' so as to include a cheque bearing a forged indorsement. Presumably, lack of disclosure may constitute negligence contributing to a subsequent forgery, for which the customer is answerable under UCC §3–406.[361] This however does not fasten responsibility on the customer for the un-disclosed original forgery. In the absence of a specific disclosure duty or general preclusion language, as under the BEA,[362] responsibility may perhaps be fastened on the non-disclosing customer in the context of a general good faith obligation.[363] Presumably, it is in connection with a corresponding good faith obligation fastened on a bank that an expansive definition of 'properly payable' purporting to cover a cheque bearing a forged indorsement will be resisted by courts. Perhaps even more promising in this context are unconscionability and other doctrines governing standard form or adhesion contracts and unequal bargaining power.

As indicated, in connection with a cheque paid over a forged indorsement, the drawer's remedy under the Code is only against the drawee bank. §3–420 specifically settles a pre-1990 Article 3 as well as BEA controversy and denies the drawer a conversion action against parties who handled the lost or stolen cheque, such as the depositary bank or anyone else deriving title through the forged indorsement.[364]

(d) Transfer and presentment warranties

Transfer warranties

As discussed,[365] under the BEA, one who derives title through a forged indorsement is entitled to sue on the cheque any prior indorser who took the cheque subsequent to the forgery. This is so since under the BEA an indorser of a cheque is precluded from denying (i) 'the genuineness and regularity ... of ... all previous indorsements' as well as (ii) that 'at the time of his indorsement ... he had a good title'.[366] The former preclusion runs in favour of a 'holder in due course'. The latter runs in favour of an

[73]

---

[360] For this point, see White and Summers, above, n. 117 at 551.

[361] Discussed further below, in (vii)(b).

[362] For the position in BEA jurisdictions, see (iv)(c), above.

[363] An obligation of good faith in the performance or enforcement of '[e]very contract or duty within [the UCC]' is imposed by §1–203.

[364] See (vi)(b), above.   [365] See (iv)(e), above.

[366] S. 55(2) (b) and (c) in the UK, ss. 132 (b) and (c) in Canada, ss. 55(b)(2) and (3) in Israel, ss. 53(2)(b) and (c) in South Africa, and similarly, s. 74(1)(b) in Australia.

'immediate and subsequent indorsee'. In relation to prior parties who indorsed the cheque subsequent to the forged indorsement, the possessor of the cheque is an 'immediate or . . . subsequent indorsee' as well as, depending on his compliance with required statutory conditions of good faith taking of the cheque for value,[367] a 'holder in due course'. Effectively then, the two enumerated statutory preclusions run in favour of all transferees subsequent to the taker from the forger. On the strength of these preclusions, 'the person in possession of a bill bearing a forged indorsement is considered a holder against party who signed the bill after the forgery of the indorsement'.[368] Being precluded from asserting the forgery, a post-forgery party is thus liable on the cheque to a subsequent indorsee, as if the endorsee claims through a flawless chain of title to an impeccable instrument, bearing only genuine signatures.

No similar provisions exist in the UCC. Nevertheless, a similar result, namely liability of a post-forged indorsement party to any subsequent transferee is achieved by means of an altogether different technique, that is, 'vendor's warranty'.[369] The theory is that a cheque is a chattel whose vendor warrants title, uninterrupted by any forged indorsement. Unlike under the BEA, a post-forged indorsement transferor is not liable to a subsequent transferee on the cheque; the transferor is however liable to a subsequent transferee on the breach of warranty.[370]

Among other matters,[371] the transferor warrants that '[he] is a person entitled to enforce the [cheque]', that 'all signatures on the [cheque] are authentic and authorized', and that 'the [cheque] has not been altered'. This covers the authenticity and validity of each indorsement and the title to the cheque. Under UCC §3–416, this warranty is made by any 'person who transfers an instrument for consideration . . . to the transferee and if the transfer is by indorsement, to any subsequent transferee'. Under UCC §4–207 this warranty is made by any 'customer or collecting bank that transfers an item and receives settlement or other consideration . . . to a transferee and to any subsequent collecting bank'.[372] Indeed, this is a vendor's warranty of title, given by each transferor of value, not only to the

---

[367] The precise conditions to be complied with are set out in s. 29(1) in the UK, s. 55(1) in Canada, s. 28(a) in Israel, s. 27(1) in South Africa, and s. 50(1) in Australia.

[368] See Barak, above, n. 187 at 184, 186.

[369] The technique is available under the BEA for an instrument payable to bearer, on which the transferor is not liable. See e.g. s. 137 in Canada and discussion in (iv)(e), above.

[370] See Barak, above, n. 187 at 185, and 180–90.

[371] The other enumerated warranties relate to the freedom of the warrantor's entitlement from any adverse claim or defence and to the warrantor's lack of knowledge of insolvency proceedings against the drawer.

[372] Both provisions are substantially identical. While §3–416 applies to 'instruments', §4–207 applies to 'items'. A cheque is both an 'instrument' under Article 3 (see §3–104) and an 'item' (defined in §4–104(a)(9)) under Article 4.

immediate transferee, but also to any subsequent indorsee or collecting bank, up to the last indorsee or collecting bank in the chain,[373] and regardless of whether the claiming beneficiary gave value for the cheque.[374] With respect to cheques, these warranties cannot be disclaimed.[375]

A beneficiary of these warranties, who took the cheque in good faith, may recover damages from the warrantor for the breach of the warranty. Damages are stated to be in 'an amount equal to the loss suffered as a result of the breach, but not more than the amount of the [cheque][376] plus expenses[377] and loss of interest incurred as a result of the breach'.[378] However, '[u]nless notice of a claim for breach of warranty is given to the warrantor within 30 days after the claimant has reason to know of the breach and the identity of the warrantor, the liability of the warrantor is discharged to the extent of any loss caused by the delay in giving notice of the claim'.[379]

Subsection 4–207(b) provides that a customer or collecting bank that transfers a cheque, whether or not by indorsement, undertakes to pay it if it is dishonoured. This obligation runs in favour of the transferee and any subsequent collecting bank that takes the cheque in good faith. It cannot be disclaimed. To the extent that this subsection (b) applies to a cheque bearing a forged indorsement, it overlaps with the transferor's warranty, and arguably fastens on the transferor liability on the instrument itself. However, this subsection (b) applies only when the cheque has not been paid and returned dishonoured.

Presentment warranties

Transfer warranties under the Code do not benefit the drawee of the **[74]** cheque, who is neither a transferee nor a collecting bank, targeted under §§3–416 and 4–207. This is quite similar to the position under the BEA, where the statutory preclusions do not run in favour of the drawee. However, in BEA jurisdictions other than in Canada, the remedy of the drawee bank which paid to one claiming the cheque through a forged indorse-

---

[373] In theory, this warranty is also given to the ultimate transferee by a pre-forged indorsement party, except that the latter is not in breach and thus not liable to the former. As under the BEA, a forged indorsement does not trigger any liability by a pre-forgery party to a post-forgery one.

[374] This is fair, since a transferee by way of gift (donee) is able to sue on an instrument.

[375] UCC §§4–207(d) and 3–416(c). Transfer warranties may be disclaimed with respect to any instrument except a cheque. See Official Comment 5 to §3–416.

[376] Where the claimant had not been a holder in due course even if claiming through an effective indorsement, liability on the instrument, and hence the amount of damages for breach of warranty, would have been accordingly reduced.

[377] 'Expenses' may include attorney's fees, as determined by state law. See Official Comment 6 to §3–416.

[378] UCC §4–207(c) as well as §3–416(b).

[379] UCC §4–207(d) and almost verbatim, UCC §3–416(c).

ment is governed by the general law of mistake and restitution. In Canada recovery is provided by the BEA.[380] At first blush, the UCC combines these two approaches. First, it provides in UCC §3–418(b) for the recovery of a mistaken payment made over a forged indorsement. Second, such recovery is stated in UCC §3–418(c) to be subject to defences based on either taking the cheque in good faith and for value or good faith change of position in reliance of payment. However, regardless, irrespective of such defences, and in departure from the position in all BEA jurisdictions, the drawee or payor bank benefits under the Code from specific presentment warranties running in its favour and facilitating recovery on a strict liability basis.

The relevant provisions are UCC §§3–417 and 4–208.[381] Thereunder, where a cheque is presented for payment, the presenter and any prior transferor warrants to the drawee[382] that 'the warrantor is, or was, at the time the warrantor transferred the [cheque], a person entitled to enforce the [cheque] or authorized to obtain payment . . . of the [cheque] on behalf of a person entitled to enforce the [cheque]'.[383] This amounts to a warranty of good title by virtue of lack of any forged indorsement. The warranty is stated to be triggered not solely by the mere presentment of the cheque but also by the ensuing payment (or acceptance) by the drawee. At first blush, this may appear to confuse the loss (upon payment) and the warranty itself (upon presentment) under which damages for the loss may be recovered. This however seems to be an oversight from which nothing significant emerges. Alternatively, by analogy to the vendor's or transferor's warranty, given only in connection with a sale or transfer for consideration, the presentment warranty may be stated to be given only in connection with the receipt of money by the presenter.

To assert the warranty, the drawee must have paid in good faith,[384] though not necessarily without negligence. Recoverable damages are stated in subsection (b) to be 'equal to the amount paid by the drawee' plus 'compensation for expenses[385] and loss of interest resulting from the breach'. Recovery under the presentment warranty is available to the drawee bank from the presenter as well as any transferee who derives

---

[380] See (iv)(e), above.

[381] For cheques, both provisions overlap. Effectively, remedies under §3–417 supersede those for mistaken payment under §3–418(b). See §3–418(c).

[382] 'There is no warranty made to the drawer under subsection (a) when presentment is made to the drawee'. See Official Comment 2 to §3–417.

[383] Subsection (a)(1) of both provisions. Other presentation warranties enumerated in subsection (a) pertain to the fact that the cheque has not been altered and to the lack of knowledge as to the fact that the drawer's signature is unauthorized.

[384] Subsection (a) in both provisions.

[385] 'Expenses' may include attorney's fees, as determined by state law. See Official Comment 5 to §3–417.

title through the forged indorsement.[386] A defendant against whom recovery is made may invoke the transfer warranties all the way back to the taker from the forger on whom the loss ultimately falls.

(VII) THE ANGLO-AMERICAN SYSTEM: EXCEPTIONS TO THE BASIC SCHEME UNDER THE UCC

(a) Introduction: the role of negligence

As under the BEA, the basic scheme is subject to exceptions. It is however **[75]** in relation to the scope of such exceptions that major differences between the two subsystems lie. First, unlike in BEA jurisdictions other than Canada, no special protections to collecting and drawee banks are provided for in the Code. Second, to a large extent, the UCC loss allocation scheme is superseded by fault principles, fastening responsibility on negligent parties. A general provision to that effect is accompanied by a series of provisions, applicable in prescribed circumstances, and allocating losses to parties in whose sphere of control or influence fraud, which generated the losses, was precipitated. No similar provisions exist under the BEA, other than the one dealing with the fictitious payee. Otherwise, while under the BEA a party may be precluded from asserting forgery, such preclusion has not given basis to either a general or even more specific duty of care.

Statutory exceptions to the general scheme, premised on fault or negligence, are enumerated in §§3–404 to 406. All these exceptions apply exclusively to 'forged' rather than unauthorized indorsements. This is specifically stated in both §§3–406 and 3–405 and is implicit in §3–404.[387] As explained in Official Comment 2 to §3–406, '[u]nauthorized signature is a broader concept that includes not only forgery but also the signature of an agent which does not bind the principal under the law of agency'. In the view of the drafters, '[t]he agency cases are resolved independently under agency law', irrespective of either §3–406 or any of the other exceptions to the general scheme. Nonetheless, I see no reason why 'forgery' will not be understood to include any fraudulent unauthorized signature which does not bind the purported principal under agency or any other

---

[386] Technically, the warranty to the drawee is also made by any pre-forged indorsement transferor, except that the latter is not in breach of that warranty and hence no damages are recoverable from him.

[387] See §§3–406(a) and 3–405(a)(2). As will emerge from the ensuing discussion of both subsections (a) and (b) of §3–404, by its nature, the fraud covered by that section will invariably, if not exclusively, lead to a forged indorsement.

law,[388] including a signature fraudulently made by an agent exceeding his authority.

All exceptions may be invoked only by 'a person who, in good faith, pays the instrument or takes it for value or for collection'.[389] Stated otherwise, 'good faith' is an indispensable prerequisite for any variation in the basic scheme. 'Good faith' is defined in §3–103(a)(4) as 'honesty in fact and the observance of reasonable commercial standards of fair dealing'. While this includes an objective component of 'observance of reasonable commercial standards' the latter are stated to relate only to 'fair dealing' and not the conduct of business in general.[390]

This is not to say, however, that the negligence of one who invokes a statutory exception premised on the negligence of another is not pertinent. In each of the three provisions such negligence is relevant, though in a different way from the breach of the good faith requirement; it is relevant not as a complete bar to relying on the exception, but rather, merely for the purpose of ascertaining the amount of the loss to be allocated to each party. Accordingly, having failed 'to exercise ordinary care in paying or taking the instrument' so as to substantially contribute[391] to loss, a person who, in good faith, paid or took the cheque for value or for collection, becomes liable to the person bearing the loss to the extent that the failure to exercise ordinary care contributed to the loss.[392] The principle is then of comparative negligence, under which loss is apportioned according to the degree of fault in substantially contributing to the loss.

Typically, the person who dealt with the forger was a depositary bank or a cheque-cashing facility. A failure to exercise ordinary care occurs, for example, where a cheque payable to a corporation is indorsed and/or deposited to an account of an individual, where the identity of an indorsee or account holder is not adequately scrutinized, and where suspicious account operation is overlooked. In such cases, compliance with reasonable commercial standards could have facilitated the detection of the forgery and hence the prevention of the loss.[393]

White and Summers correctly point out that negligence rules play a role only in connection with a forged indorsement; such rules do not apply to an unauthorized as well as fraudulent but authorized indorsement.[394]

---

[388] In this respect, it is quite unfortunate that §3–405(a)(2) reads as if 'fraudulent indorsement' is a species of a 'forged indorsement' rather than the other way around.

[389] See UCC §§3–404(a), 404(b)(2), 405(b), and 406(a).

[390] A point well made by White and Summers, above, n. 117 at 572–3.

[391] Both 'ordinary care' and 'substantially contributed' are discussed below, in (b) in connection with discussion on §3–406.

[392] See UCC §§3–404(d), 405(b), and 406(b).

[393] For some case law see e.g. J. M. Norwood, 'Bank Negligence and the Forgery Doctrine' (1998), 115 Banking L.J. 254 at 262–9.

[394] White and Summers, above, n. 117 at 569–70.

While I agree that this distinction is unjustified, its impact may be reduced if, along lines suggested above, a forged indorsement is taken to encompass any fraudulent unauthorized indorsement, including one fraudulently made by an agent exceeding his authority. Yet, I agree that a statutory revision eliminating the distinction and equating the role of negligence in all cases of absence and misuse of authority would be an improvement.

A forged indorsement that becomes effective under UCC §§3–404 to 406 is a complete defence to a drawee's action for the breach of presentment warranties under §§3–417 and 4–208.[395] This is logical; the statutory language could however be improved by protecting the one invoking any of the former three provisions only to the extent he did not substantially contribute to the forgery, namely, only beyond his share in the loss under the comparative negligence rules provided by the applicable provision.[396]

(b) The statutory exceptions: UCC §3–406 and an overview of UCC §§3–404 and 405

The general fault or negligence principle is pronounced in UCC **[76]** §3–406(a):

A person whose failure to exercise ordinary care substantially contributes to an alteration of an instrument or to the making of a forged signature on an instrument is precluded from asserting the alteration or the forgery against a person who, in good faith, pays the instrument or takes it for value or for collection.

For a person engaged in business, 'ordinary care' is defined in terms of the 'observance of reasonable commercial standards, prevailing in the area in which the person is located, with respect to the business in which the person is engaged'.[397] The 'substantially contributes' language is designed to preclude the application of strict proximation requirements between the negligent conduct and the causation of the loss. Negligent conduct substantially contributing to a forged indorsement could be the

---

[395] UCC §§3–417(c) and 4–208(c).

[396] On this point see White and Summers, above, n. 117 at 605–11. They correctly point out, for example, that where the drawee shared 10% of the responsibility and the depositary bank was responsible for 50% of the loss (with the remaining 40% being allocated to the customer of the depositary bank with whom the drawee bank settled), literal reading of §4–208(c) (and hence §3–417 as well) results in the depositary bank being fully protected against the drawee's breach of presentment warranty claim so that it could avoid paying its share.

[397] UCC §3–103(a)(7). For a bank, in connection with the automated collection and payment of cheques, reasonable commercial standards may not require a physical examination of each cheque. This however is inapplicable to a depositary bank. Support for the latter proposition is implied in Official Comment 5 to §3–103. See White and Summers, above, n. 117 at 578.

mailing of a cheque to an address other than that of the intended payee which is the address of another person with an identical or similar name,[398] handling incoming as well as outgoing cheques so as to facilitate unauthorized access and theft either by outsiders or unauthorized personnel,[399] and hiring for sensitive positions inappropriate staff with inadequate scrutiny. Negligence could lead to the forgery of either one's own or of another's signature.[400]

Provisions providing for specific exceptions to the general scheme are UCC §§3–404 and 405, respectively dealing with cheques[401] issued to impostors and to unintended or fictitious payees, and cheques fraudulently indorsed by employees entrusted with responsibilities. In each such a case, the Code provides for the effectiveness of the fraudulent indorsement in favour of a person who, in good faith, pays the instrument or takes it for value or for collection. Thereby the Code validates both title derived through the fraudulent indorsement and payment made over it. For §§3–404 and 405 to apply, the fraudulent indorsement of the cheque, rendered effective by these provisions, ought to have been made in the name of the person to whom the cheque is payable. However, under both provisions, such indorsement includes (i) an indorsement in a substantially similar name and (ii) the deposit of the cheque, whether indorsed or not, in a depositary bank, to an account in a name substantially similar to that of that person.[402]

Loss is thus allocated under both UCC §§3–404 and 405 to the best loss avoider within whose sphere of influence forgery was precipitated, so that it was either caused or not prevented due to the fault of that person.[403] The principle underlying both provisions is that of fault or negligence substantially contributing to the forged indorsement and the resulting loss. In fact, both provisions state an irrebuttable presumption of such fault or negligence in each specific situation they delineate.

The following is a detailed discussion of UCC §§3–404 and 405. As indi-

---

[398] See Case No. 2 in Official Comment 3 to UCC §3–406 as well as facts of *Park State Bank* v. *Arena Auto Auction* 207 N.E. (2d) 158 (Ill. App. 1965). For the incorrect designation by the drawer of the payee's name as negligence contributing to forged indorsement, see also *Dominion Construction, Inc.* v. *First National Bank of Maryland* 271 Md. 154; 315 A. 2d 69 (Md. App. 1974).

[399] See Case No. 1 in Official comment 3 to UCC §3–405.

[400] For case law under the pre-1990 UCC, wherein courts considered whether particular acts constituted negligence substantially contributing to forgery, see annotation by G. D. Spivey, 'Commercial Paper: What Amounts to "Negligence Contributing to Alteration or Unauthorized Signature" under UCC §3–406' (1975), 67 A.L.R. 3d 144.

[401] By their terms, both provisions apply to all types of instruments. The Official Comments recognize however that they are primarily important with respect to cheques.

[402] See UCC §§3–404(c) and 405(c).

[403] For this rationale see in general Official Comment 2 to §3–404 and Official Comment 1 to §3–405.

cated, as under §3–406, the party on whom loss is fastened under each of these provisions has at his disposal an action against the person invoking it so as to have the loss apportioned according to the degree of fault that substantially contributed to the loss.[404]

(c) UCC §3–404(a): cheque issued to impostor

UCC §3–404(a) deals with a case where a fraudster either impersonates or poses as an agent for a legitimate payee and induces the issue of a cheque payable to the legitimate payee, either to the fraudster in person or to a person acting in concert with him. The inducement may take place 'by use of the mails or otherwise'; actual face-to-face impersonation is not required.[405] Where the provision applies, 'an indorsement of the instrument by any person in the name of the payee is effective as the indorsement of the payee in favor of a person who, in good faith, pays the instrument or takes it for value or for collection'. Effectively then, loss generated by the forgery of the payee's signature is allocated to the issuer of the cheque, rather than to the taker from the forger, as if the cheque has originally been issued payable to the bearer and not to the payee's order.

Several points are noteworthy:

(1) The fraudster is described in the provision as an 'impostor', which is not defined in the Code. Yet, the meaning of the term is clarified by the description of the fraud committed; the 'impostor's' fraudulent act is stated to be carried out 'by impersonating the payee . . . or a person authorized to act for the payee'. This is quite consistent with the dictionary definition of 'impostor', according to which he is 'one that assumes an identity or title not his own for the purpose of deception'.[406] One ambiguity may however remain. It is not entirely clear whether the subsection applies where the fraudster properly identifies himself, but cheats as to his status as an agent for the legitimate payee. True, in such a case the fraudster 'assumes . . . title not [of] his own for the purpose of deception', so as to be an 'impostor' within the dictionary definition. Nevertheless, may the fraudster be said then to 'impersonate . . . a person authorized

[77]

---

[404] See UCC §§3–404(d), 405(b), and 406(b). On this point, present 1990 Article 3 deviated from its predecessor in two respects. In the pre-1990 Article 3, the counterpart of present §3–406 regarded the contributory negligence of the person relying on the provision as a complete bar to invoking it, while under the counterpart of present §3–404 the negligence of the person relying on the provision was immaterial. There was no corresponding provision to present §3–405.

[405] A point elaborated on in Official Comment 1 to pre-1990 UCC §3–405, the predecessor of present §3–404.

[406] *Webster's Ninth New Collegiate Dictionary* (Markham, Ont: Thomas Allen, 1984).

to act for the payee' as required by the subsection? Probably yes; the essence of 'impersonating' is not necessarily acting as someone else, but rather, assuming or acting in 'the character of' someone else.[407] Arguably then, 'impersonating' is broad enough to cover the assumption of the character as an agent, even where the actor himself does not pretend to be another person, in which case, the ambiguity disappears.

(2) The fraud dealt with by the provision is impersonating, which induces the defrauded person to believe he is dealing with, and thus making payment to, the legitimate payee. As indicated, the provision extends also to the case where the impostor impersonates an agent of the legitimate payee, which is an expansion of the former Code corresponding provision.[408] The provision thus applies whenever the impostor impersonates a real creditor of the drawer, as well as where he impersonates an agent for such a creditor or for a charity to which the drawer wishes to pay. The former Code corresponding provision covered only the impersonation of the creditor himself. It excluded a drawer, who having dealt with one impersonating an agent, nevertheless took 'the precaution of making the instrument payable to the principal', thereby becoming 'entitled to have [the principal]'s indorsement.'[409] This shifted the loss resulting from the forged indorsement away from the defrauded drawer onto the taker from the forger. Present §3–404(a) specifically rejects this limitation and its underlying rationale.[410] The provision will thus apply whenever the drawer was defrauded to write a cheque to a payee and deliver it to an impostor impersonating either the payee or the payee's agent. Other fraud in inducement, as for example, where the drawer is induced to issue a cheque for consideration that the payee does not intend to provide, does not fall within the ambit of the provision.

(3) The provision applies solely to the case where the impostor induces the issue of an instrument rather than the indorsement or negotiation of an existing one. For a cheque, 'issue' is the first delivery of the cheque by the drawer, for the purpose of giving rights on it.[411]

(4) As indicated, for a cheque whose issue was induced by an impostor, §3–404(a) provides for the effectiveness of the 'indorsement of

---

[407] 'Impersonate' is defined as 'to assume or act in the character of'. Ibid.
[408] The former provision was pre-1990 UCC §3–405(1)(a).
[409] Official Comment 2 to pre-1990 UCC §3–405.
[410] Official Comment 1 to present (1990) UCC §3–404.
[411] 'Issue' is defined in §3–105(a).

the instrument by any person in the name of the payee'. That is, for the provision to apply, the fraudulent indorsement or forgery need not necessarily be made by the impostor or his accomplice. Moreover, as indicated, under UCC §3–404(c), 'an indorsement is made in the name of the payee if (i) it is made in a name substantially similar to that of the payee or (ii) the instrument, whether or not indorsed, is deposited in a depositary bank to an account in a name substantially similar to that of the payee'. Stated otherwise, subsection (a) of §3–404 will apply regardless of (i) who indorsed, (ii) whether there was an indorsement to a depositary bank, and (iii) whether the indorsement or deposit was in the exact name of the payee, as long as it was in a substantially similar name.

(5) The rationale for UCC §3–404(a) is the presumed negligence of the defrauded person, who is deemed to be fully responsible within his sphere of control. Underlying the rule is thus a 'know with whom you are dealing' rationale.

(6) No parallel to UCC §3–404(a) exists in the BEA. Thereunder, the closet provision is that dealing with the fictitious payee. For example, a cheque whose issue was induced by an imposter which is payable to an imaginary charity can be said to be payable to a 'non-existing' person within the meaning of the BEA fictitious payee provision. However, usually the payee dealt with in UCC §3–404(a) cannot be described as 'non-existing', and is undoubtedly not 'fictitious' from the point of view of the drawer, regardless of whether he is required to be the 'guiding mind' of the drawer corporation.[412]

(d) UCC §3–404(b): cheque issued to unintended or fictitious payee

UCC §3–404(b) deals with a cheque issued to an unintended or fictitious **[78]** payee. It covers two situations. First, subsection (b)(i) applies to the case where 'a person whose intent determines to whom an instrument is payable . . . does not intend the person identified as payee to have any interest in the instrument'. Second, subsection (b)(ii) applies where 'the person identified as payee of an instrument is a fictitious person'. In either case, anyone in possession of the instrument is its holder and any indorsement in the payee's name is effective as the payee's indorsement 'in favor of a person who, in good faith, pays the instrument or takes it for value or for collection'. Effectively then, loss generated by the forgery of the payee's signature is allocated to the issuer of the cheque, rather

---

[412] For the 'fictitious payee' provision under the BEA see above, (v)(a).

than to the taker from the forger, as if the cheque has originally been issued payable to the bearer and not to the payee's order.

Undoubtedly, UCC §3–404(b) traces its roots to the fictitious payee provision of the BEA.[413] While there is difference in language, in the final analysis, as discussed below, the impact of each provision is not necessarily substantially different:

(1) In the BEA the provision applies to the case where the payee is 'a fictitious or non-existing person'. Conversely, under the Code, the designated payee is either unintended or fictitious. Obviously, as a counterpart for 'fictitious', 'unintended' differs from 'non-existing'; but furthermore, as will shortly be shown, the meaning given in the USA to 'unintended' necessitates a meaning for 'fictitious' which differs from that under the BEA. Between the UCC and the BEA, not only does the scope of the provision not appear to be identical, but the meaning of a key term also appears to differ.

(2) The BEA is silent as to whose intention determines whether a cheque is payable to a fictitious or non-existing person. Conversely, whether a person identified as payee is not intended to have any interest in the instrument so as to bring it into subsection (b)(i) is determined under §3–110(a) or (b), to which UCC §3–404(b)(i) specifically refers. Under §3–110(a), it is the signer's intention which is usually determinative.[414] A narrow exception is provided for under §3–110(b): 'If the signature ... is made by automated means, such as a check-writing machine, the payee of the instrument is determined by the intent of the person who supplied the name or identification of the payee'. Either way, the crucial moment for determining the intention of the relevant person is that of the signature under subsection (a) and that of the supply of the name under subsection (b).[415] A transformation of an honest intent into a dishonest one, occurring after the signature or the supply of the name to the signing machine, will not bring the case into UCC §3–404(b); but as will be seen below, the case may anyway be covered by UCC §3–405. A classic example for the application of UCC §3–404(b)(i) is the case where either the signer or the name supplier to an automated signing machine causes a cheque to be made out to an existing individual or entity, who may or may not be

---

[413] See discussion in (v)(a), above. The original language was much more apparent in section 9(3) of the Uniform Negotiable Instruments Law (NIL) which was the predecessor of UCC Article 3.

[414] Where more than one signs on an issuer's behalf, 'the instrument is payable to any person intended by one or more of the signers'. *Id*.

[415] See e.g. Case No. 2 in Official Comment 2 to UCC §3–404.

owed by the issuer, without intending the cheque to be delivered to that payee.

(3) In BEA jurisdictions, case law has defined 'fictitious' in terms of being inserted as payee by way of pretence, without any intention that payment will be made to him.[416] This however strongly matches the 'unintended' category of §3–404(b)(ii). It follows that the meaning of 'fictitious' under UCC §3–404(b)(ii) cannot be the same as under the BEA. Indeed, examples given in the Official Comment to §3–404 demonstrate that 'fictitious' under the Code means 'imaginary'[417]; 'fictitious' under the Code is basically the parallel of the BEA 'non-existing' as determined objectively irrespective of anyone's intention.[418] Accordingly, what is 'unintended or fictitious' in the USA is 'fictitious or non-existing' under the BEA. For example, a cheque payable to 'Mickey Mouse' will be payable to a non-existing payee under the BEA and to a fictitious payee under the UCC. Either way, it will fall within the provision.

(4) As indicated, in specifically providing whose intent determines the application of §3–404(b)(i), the Code provision is clearer than that of the BEA. Yet, other than in relation to a name supplier to an automated signing machine under §3–110(b), the UCC test for determining whose intention determines whether the payee is unintended, is along similar lines to the classic pre-*Boma*[419] test for determining whether payee is 'fictitious' under the BEA.[420] For example, as under the BEA, but in departure from the Code's pre–1990 position,[421] so far as a 'real' payee is concerned, payroll padding, that is, the supply of a name to a real person who will consequently sign a cheque payable to that name, thereby unknowingly executing the name supplier's fraudulent design, falls outside the provision. Yet, as will be seen below, the case falls into the ambit of UCC §3–405 anyway, to which the BEA has no counterpart.

(5) Both UCC §3–404(b) and the BEA fictitious payee provision do not cover a cheque payable to an intended real payee. Such a cheque is payable neither to an unintended nor fictitious payee under the Code as well as neither to a fictitious nor non-existing payee under the BEA. Accordingly and as indicated, theft followed by the forgery of the indorsement of the cheque originally made out payable to an intended real payee falls outside the provision both under the UCC and the BEA, so that so far as that provision is concerned, loss

---

[416] This is on the basis the classic definition of Lord Herschell in *Bank of England* v. *Vagliano*, above, n. 209 at 153. See (v)(a), above.

[417] See Cases Nos. 1 and 2 in Official Comment 2.   [418] See (v)(a), above.

[419] Above, n. 71.   [420] See (v)(a), above.   [421] See pre-1990 UCC §3–405(1)(c).

does not fall on the drawer. The provision will not apply also where the real intended payee is either an accomplice of or a phony corporation set by the defrauder whose intention determines to whom the instrument is payable; however, in such a case, the fraudulent payee's indorsement is effective and payment over it is a valid discharge, so that loss will fall on the drawer[422] anyway. On this point, there is no difference between the UCC and the BEA.

(6) Both subsections (a) and (b) of §3–110 specifically state that the person whose intent determines to whom an instrument is payable may be either an unauthorized signer or name supplier to an automated writing machine. That is, §3–404(b) may apply also with respect to cheques drawn without authority. Yet, as recognized in the Official Comment, this will allocate fraud losses to the apparent drawer only where he is liable for the drawer's signature under some other rule, as for example, under an agreement allowing the bank to debit drawer's account for payment of cheques produced by a cheque-writing machine whether or not authorized,[423] or where the purported drawer is precluded from asserting the forgery of his drawer's signature under §3–406. Otherwise, the rules applying to a forged drawer's signature apply.[424] In principle, on this point, the Code position does not differ from that of the BEA, except that in the latter this point is not provided for by statute. Also, as between the UCC and the BEA, the rules governing liability for a forged drawer's signature vary.[425]

(7) As indicated, for a cheque issued to an unintended or fictitious payee, §3–404(b) provides for the effectiveness of the 'indorsement by any person in the name of the payee'. That is, for the provision to apply, the fraudulent indorsement or forgery need not necessarily be made by the perpetrator of the fraud or his accomplice. Moreover, as indicated, under UCC §3–404(c), 'an indorsement is made in the name of the payee if (i) it is made in a name substantially similar to that of the payee or (ii) the instrument, whether or not indorsed, is deposited in a depositary bank to an account in a name substantially similar to that of the payee'. Stated otherwise, subsection (b) of §3–404 will apply regardless of (i) who indorsed,

---

[422] This may very well be the answer to the query raised by White and Summers, above, n. 117 at 583 as to the inapplicability of the provision to such a case. The same result applies to a cheque issued by the person with the determinative intent to himself, as in the scenario set out in Case No. 2 of Official Comment 1 to UCC §3–405.

[423] See Case Nos. 4 and 5 in Official Comment 2 to UCC §3–404.

[424] As in fact was held, even without the benefit of a specific provision, under the pre-1990 Article 3, in the landmark case of *Perini Corp. v. First National Bank of Habersham*, 553 F. 2d 398 (5th. Cir. 1977)   [425] See (c), above.

(ii) whether there was an indorsement to a depositary bank, and (iii) whether the indorsement or deposit was in the exact name of the payee, as long as it was in a substantially similar name. Indeed, this is quite broad, but not as broad as under the BEA, where an instrument falling under the fictitious payee provision is deemed to be payable to bearer, regardless of the existence or absence of any indorsement, and where it exists, irrespective of its proximity to that of the payee's name. This difference stems from the theoretical underpinning of each provision in relation to the fraudulent indorsement; while the BEA provision applies on the basis of bypassing the indorsement, the application of the UCC counterpart is premissed on its effectiveness.

(8) Finally, in the footsteps of subsection (a), subsection (b) of §3–404 is stated to apply solely to the case of the original issue of the cheque rather than the indorsement or negotiation of an existing one. For a cheque, 'issue' is the first delivery of the cheque by the drawer, for the purpose of giving rights on it.[426] This is also the case under the BEA; other than for cheques in Australia, the provision applies only to a fictitious or non-existing payee and not indorsee.

(e) UCC §3–405: cheques fraudulently indorsed by employees entrusted with responsibilities

UCC §3–405 allocates to an employer losses caused in connection with [79] cheques fraudulently indorsed by employees entrusted with responsibilities with respect to cheques. In the footsteps of §3–404, it implements its objective by providing for the effectiveness of the fraudulent indorsement in favour of a bona fide payor or taker for value or collection.

Unlike §3–404, UCC §3–405 applies not only to cheques issued by the employer but also to cheques payable to him. It further differs from §3–404 in having neither a predecessor in the pre-1990 Code nor a counterpart anywhere else. A third difference is that §3–405 does not cover an indorsement made by anyone. Rather, it covers only an indorsement made by an employee entrusted by the employer with responsibility with respect to the cheque or a person acting in concert with the employee. At first blush, there is a fourth difference. While both subsections of §3–404 appear to apply to any 'indorsement . . . in the name of the payee', §3–405 is stated to be limited to a 'fraudulent indorsement', which under subsection (a)(2) must be 'a forged indorsement'. However, the fraud covered by §3–404 will invariably, if not exclusively, lead to a fraudulent or forged

---

[426] 'Issue' is defined in §3–105(a).

indorsement, so that in this respect, no real distinction exists between the two provisions.

As under §3–404, §3–405 applies only where the indorsement is made in the name of the person to whom the cheque is payable. Where the cheque is payable to the employer such a person is the employer. For a cheque made out by the employer it is the payee. Also, along similar lines to both subsections of §3–404, UCC §3–405(c) provides that 'an indorsement is made in the name of the person to whom an instrument is payable if (i) it is made in a name substantially similar to the name of that person or (ii) the instrument, whether or not indorsed, is deposited in a depositary bank to an account in a name substantially similar to the name of that person'. Stated otherwise, like §3–404, §3–405 will apply regardless of (i) whether there was an indorsement to a depositary bank, and (ii) whether the indorsement or deposit was in the exact name. However, as indicated, unlike in the context of §3–404, the position held by the actual indorser is crucial under §3–405. Indeed, as indicated, a fraudulent indorsement is effectively required for the application of both §§3–404 and 405. Yet, while both subsections of §3–404 look to the circumstances of the issue of the cheque that was subsequently fraudulently indorsed, §3–405 focuses on the circumstances underlying the fraudulent indorsement itself.

The scope of §3–405, particularly in relation to identifying the employees and their responsibilities caught within the ambit of the provision, as well as in relation to other Code provisions, can be further elaborated as follows:

(1) 'Employee' is broadly defined in subsection (a)(1) to include 'an independent contractor and employee of independent contractor retained by the employer'. Presumably corporate officers are covered as well.

(2) For §3–405 to apply to a fraudulent indorsement on a cheque made out by the employer to a third party, the forger/defrauding employee must have had authority to sign or indorse, prepare or process instruments for issue, supply information determining the names or addresses of payees, or control the disposition of such instruments. For example, an employee authorized to supply information determining the payee's address could intentionally replace data and divert a cheque payable to a real creditor of the employer to the employee's own address. Upon the cheque arrival, the employee could obtain or collect payment cover the payee's fraudulent indorsement made by that employee.[427]

---

[427] See Case No. 5 in Official Comment 3 to §3–405. See also Case No. 6 dealing with embezzlement by an employee charged with authority or control over the disposition of outgoing cheques.

(3) For §3–405 to apply to a fraudulent indorsement on a cheque payable to and received by the employer, the forger/defrauding employee must have had authority to sign or process incoming instruments for any purpose, including bookkeeping or deposit to an account. A theft of an incoming cheque and its fraudulent indorsement by a bookkeeper who has the authority to post incoming payments to debtors' accounts with the employer will be covered.[428] Conversely, the indorsement by an employee who has the authority to indorse is valid, irrespective and outside UCC §3–405, even when inserted with the view of stealing the incoming cheque and diverting its proceeds. Loss will anyway fall on the employer unless the depositary bank had notice of a breach of a fiduciary duty by the employee as determined under §3–307.[429]

(4) In any event, with regard to both outgoing and incoming cheques, the authority to sign, process instruments or information, and control disposition do not exhaust all cases of 'responsibility' entrusted to an employee whose fraudulent indorsement is validated by UCC §3–405. Subsection (a)(3)(vi) explicitly states that in addition to all tasks described above, 'responsibility' with respect to instruments includes the authority 'to act otherwise with respect to instruments in a responsible capacity'. This open-ended category may not be all that helpful, except for signalling the broad scope of the provision; any narrow interpretation of the particular duties will be overshadowed by the breadth of this residual category. Some assistance is nevertheless provided by subsection (a)(3) further providing that ' "[r]esponsibility" does not include authority that merely allows an employee to have access to instruments or blank or incomplete instrument forms that are being stored or transported or part of incoming or outgoing mail, or similar access'. Notwithstanding access to storing facility, a janitor will thus not be an employee entrusted with responsibility with respect to instruments so that the janitor's fraudulent indorsement falls outside §3–405. In any event, the janitor's employer, whose negligence might have substantially contributed to the loss, may nevertheless be held responsible under §3–406.[430]

(5) Effectively providing for the allocation of forged indorsement losses to an organization whose insider precipitated the fraud resulting in the losses, UCC §§3–404(b) and 405 partly overlap and partly

---

[428] See Case No. 3 in Official Comment 3 to §3–405.
[429] See Case No. 4 in Official Comment 3 to §3–405.
[430] For the inapplicability of UCC §3–405 to the janitor's case, and the possible application of §3–406, see Case No. 4 in Official Comment 3 to §3–405.

complement each other. Thus, where an employee entrusted with responsibility causes the employer to generate a cheque payable to a fictitious, namely imaginary, person, and then indorses the cheque in the name of the payee and collects its proceeds, both provisions validate the indorsement so as to allocate the loss on the employer. Similarly, both provisions apply where such an employee is the person whose intent determines to whom the cheque is payable, who causes the employer to generate a cheque payable to a real person on whom the employee does not intend to confer any interest in the cheque. The overlap is however not total. For example, only §3–404(b) will apply in each of the above-mentioned cases if the fraudulent indorsement is not made by the defrauding employee but rather by a third party acting independently, as where the latter frustrated the perpetrator's design by stealing the cheque, either from the employer or the employee, and collecting its proceeds for his own benefit. Conversely, only §3–405, and not §3–404(b), applies (i) to a fraudulent indorsement, made by an employee entrusted with responsibility, on an incoming cheque payable to and received by the employer, (ii) where the forged indorsement is made by an employee entrusted with responsibility who supplies the name of a real person to an honest co-employee who signs a cheque payable to that person,[431] as well as (iii) where an employee whose intent determines to whom a cheque is payable, having caused the employer to generate a cheque payable to a real person, fully intending him to have an interest in the cheque, changes his mind, and collects the proceeds of the cheque over his fraudulent indorsement.[432]

(VIII) THE ANGLO-AMERICAN SYSTEM: CONCLUDING REMARKS ON NEGLIGENCE AND CONVERSION

[80]   In the Anglo-American system, where an indorsement on a cheque has been forged, the true owner may sue prior parties on the instrument and subsequent parties in conversion (as well as money had and received under the BEA). The drawer is entitled to have his account credited (or not debited in the first place) with the amount of the cheque. Loss falls on the one who dealt with the forger. Where an exception to this scheme applies, the taker from the forger obtains title and payment to him is a

---

[431] See Case No. 7 in Official Comment 3 to §3–405.
[432] See Case No. 6 in Official Comment 3 to §3–405.

good discharge. Loss falls on the one from whom the cheque was stolen or misappropriated.

The principal features distinguishing the UCC from the BEA are the extent of the exceptions and the operation, within their framework, of the comparative negligence rules.[433] UCC exceptions are based on fault, whether presumed or proved, ability to prevent loss, and responsibility within one's sphere of influence. The exceptions thus contribute to loss prevention or reduction and constitute an improvement in relation to the BEA under which the exceptions actually undermine both loss prevention or reduction and loss distribution. At the same time, the UCC comparative negligence rules do not appear to me to be appropriate. First, they may prolong litigation. Second, comparative negligence rules are likely to require close analysis of degree of causation, which is precisely the task sought to be avoided by substituting a 'substantially contributed' test for any proximity requirement. Third, in many fact situations, the task of apportioning fault may be impossible.

Also, a general duty to exercise ordinary care may be too open ended. As such, it is likely to unnecessarily prolong litigation and bolster the position of the stronger party, not infrequently a bank. This is an important consideration, particularly in connection with cases involving consumers and small businesses. Thus, while the UCC exceptions rest on sound policies, their proper implementation requires further refinement.

I accordingly propose three modifications to the American scheme. First, 'ordinary care' or reasonable commercial standards ought to be prescribed in codes of conduct agreed between bank and customer organizations,[434] in a process that may be facilitated by government. Such codes of conduct may be national, regional, or even limited to specific sectors.[435]

Second, I propose to eliminate the application of comparative negligence rules. In this respect I am inspired by the pre-1990 principle of absolute preclusion, but the scheme I have in mind is not necessarily identical to that of the old Code. My proposal is that the failure by the person who dealt with the forger to comply with reasonable commercial standards will nullify an otherwise applicable exception and restore the ineffectiveness of the indorsement, provided such compliance could have

---

[433] As discussed in (ii) above, the other major difference, that of the specific statutory protections accorded to paying and collecting banks in BEA jurisdictions other than in Canada, does not affect the ultimate loss allocation.

[434] Rules prescribed in such codes will fulfil the same function of UCC §§3–404 and 405.

[435] For example, there may be different standards for large businesses, small businesses, and non-profit organizations. At the same time, some common elements, for example in scrutinizing employees, may exist across the board. For a proposal for publicly supervised negotiated statutory standard form contracts see R. Hasson, 'The Unconsionability Business—A Comment on Tilden-Rent-a-Car v. Clendenning' (1979), 3 Can. Bus. L.J. 193, at 196–8.

detected the forgery and prevented the loss. Under such circumstances, the failure by the taker from the forger to comply will serve as a basis for preclusion for anyone to rely on the exception. Furthermore, a drawer against whom an exception could have been raised will have a direct cause of action against the taker from the forger, based on the negligence or failure to comply of the taker from the forger, to restore the effectiveness of the indorsement. Usually, the one who dealt with the forger is either a bank or a cheque-cashing facility, whose compliance with reasonable commercial standards will not be hard to determine, particularly in the context of a code of conduct along the lines set out above. The negligence of any party other than the one who has dealt with the forger will be considered as too remote to be a relevant factor.[436]

Third, I propose to eliminate all exceptions in connection with consumer cheques, or at least, for most of their categories. Alternatively, some rules which are to be retained are to be modified in the consumer context.[437] Regardless, under my proposal, anyone who fails to disclose a forged indorsement known to him will be unable to shift the loss onto another.

Finally in connection with the allocation of forged indorsement losses in the Anglo-American system and apart from the application of negligence principles, an issue arises as to the remedy of the true owner, that is, the person entitled to enforce the cheque, against post-forgery parties. Under both the BEA and UCC I re-examine the role of conversion, side by side with the action for money had and received in BEA jurisdictions, in implementing the Anglo-American basic scheme. In my view, the true owner's action on the lost instrument provides him with an adequate remedy. Any action against post-forgery parties unnecessarily adds lawsuits. In providing for additional defendant(s), the availability of such an action improves the true owner's position compared to that which would exist in the absence of forgery. In any event, there seems to be no difference in the true owner's burden in proving his entitlement whether he sues prior parties on the cheque or subsequent ones in conversion (or money had and received); hence, no extra hardship is involved in limiting his remedy to prior parties. Also, in most cases, the true owner cannot be said to suffer loss due to the disappearance of the benefit of negotiability,

---

[436] Notwithstanding *Trust Co. of Georgia Bank of Savannah, N.A.* v. *Port Terminal & Warehousing Co.* 266 SE 2d 254 (Ga Ct. of App., 1980), where the court was less categorical on this point.

[437] For example, even if the impostor rule under §3–404(a) is retained with respect to consumers, I propose to exclude from its operation a consumer who took the precaution of writing the cheque to the alleged principal of the impostor (as in effect was the general rule under the Pre-1990 Code). See point 2 in (c), above.

since regardless of negotiation, he remains responsible for any defect in his own title.[438]

It thus seems that the true owner's remedy from a post-forged indorsement party ought to be limited to the physical return of the instrument. There appears to be no justified grounds for any monetary claim. The availability of conversion (or money had and received) under present law can thus be viewed as an obsolete remnant from the archaic rule conferring on an instrument all attributes of a chattel. It would have followed from such a rule that the physical loss of the instrument necessarily entails the forfeiture of its entire economic value in the form of the loss of the right to recover on it. This, however, is not the law, at least anymore, so that the conversion (or money had and received) action of the true owner against a post-forged indorsement party does not appear to be justified and seems unnecessary in the implementation of the Anglo-American scheme.

However, upon further reflection, this is true only with respect to the pre-payment situation, which could arise, for example, in connection with the theft of post-dated cheques, whose payment is thus delayed. After payment, for example in the case of embezzlement by an employee of the true owner of several cheques payable to the true owner by the true owner's debtors, it may be more efficient for the true owner to bypass the action against the various drawers, whose accounts have been already debited, and sue directly the taker from the forger, usually the forger's bank acting as a depositary bank, thereby avoiding circuity of action. Indeed, there is no policy ground to support the involvement in the litigation of the drawer of a cheque stolen from the payee, whose account has been already debited; in this sense, the true owner's direct remedy against the taker from the forger eliminates wasteful litigation. I am inclined to propose that conversion (and money had and received) be limited to post-payment situations, and be available only against the actual taker from the forger, and not against anyone deriving title from him. On the other hand, a true owner to whom conversion (as well as money had and received) is so available, ought to be required to invoke this remedy first, before becoming able to pursue any remedy against any prior party.

Ironically then, in a post-payment situation, my proposal to require the true owner to sue first the taker from the forger, prior to pursuing his

---

[438] True, when the true owner is an indorsee not a holder in due course who would have managed to transfer the instrument to a holder in due course, upon the recovery by the latter from the drawer, the true owner is not exposed to any liability. Yet, this is not the typical situation; usually the true owner is the payee. Second, to use such a scenario as a basis for an action in conversion (or money had and received) is tantamount to recognizing a right of a holder not in due course to the full value of the cheque. Such a right, however, does not exist.

recourse from any pre-forgery party liable on the instrument, and to eliminate any other remedy in conversion or money had and received, though
motivated by the avoidance of circuity of action, and not by the reconciliation between the competing policies underlying the Anglo-American
and Continental systems, appears to produce a substantially similar result
as that under the UNCITRAL proposal.[439] Indeed, the latter accords title to
one claiming under a forged indorsement, while making the taker from
the forger liable to the true owner. Conversely, my own proposal does not
accord title to one claiming under the forged indorsement; yet, once the
cheque is paid, my proposal requires the true owner to bypass prior parties, who have already paid, and pursue recovery directly from the taker
from the forger, as under the UNCITRAL proposal. Regardless, following
the American subsystem as modified in my proposal, exceptions based on
negligence and the ability to eliminate, reduce, or at least distribute losses,
should be an integral part of any sound scheme for the allocation of
forged cheque indorsement losses.

---

[439] For this proposal see (ii), above.

E. Misdirected Credit Transfers

(I) THE SETTING AND GOVERNING PRINCIPLES IN GENERAL LAW
JURISDICTIONS

To accord discharge to the originator's debt to the beneficiary, a credit [1]
transfer must be completed by payment to the specific beneficiary as designated by the originator.[1] Misdirection of funds is the payment other
than, or not as, intended by the originator, as can be determined from the
originator's payment order.[2] The ensuing discussion deals with the misdirection of funds other than solely by means of an unauthorized or
unverified payment order which does not bind the originator.[3] The issue
to be considered is the allocation of loss among the various participants in
the payment transaction.

Misdirection of funds may occur due to any of several deficiencies in
the credit transfer process. Such deficiencies can broadly be classified into
four categories. First, a perfectly non-defective originator's payment
order may nevertheless be unintended, namely issued either contrary to
or not according to the originator's intention. Second, the originator's
payment order may be defective. It may thus be incomplete, ambiguous,
or incapable of being carried out. Third, misdirection of funds may be
brought about by the deficient execution of the originator's, or any subsequent, payment order, purporting to implement the originator's
instructions. Such a deficient execution occurs when the receiving bank
issues a payment order which does not conform to that received by it.

Generally, in each of these three cases, misdirection of funds to a beneficiary not intended by the originator occurs because the beneficiary's

---

[1] Discharge occurs and no liability is incurred by a bank directing payment to an account
at a bank other than designated by the originator, provided payment was made to the
intended beneficiary. I am advised that a case to the point in Italy is Cassazione 2 agosto
1991, n. 8517, reviewed in *Foro Italiano* 1992, 1, col. 336, as well as in *Giurisprudenza bancaria*
11/12, p. 120.

[2] Accordingly, and notwithstanding n. 1 ibid., the indication of a specific account of the
beneficiary may be material, and a beneficiary's bank overlooking it may do so at its own
peril. In Germany, a contractual term authorizing the bank to overlook any such indication
was invalidated. See H. Schimansky et. al. *Bankrechts-Handbuch* (Munich: C. H. Beck, 1997)
at 882 [in German. I relied on an unofficial translation]. See in Switzerland ATF 121 III 310
(1996), where the beneficiary's bank was held to be negligent in overlooking the specific
sender's instructions to deposit the funds to a designated blocked account of the beneficiary rather than pay the funds into the regular beneficiary's account. See also in Canada:
Clansmen Resources Ltd. v. *Toronto-Dominion Bank* [1990] 4 W.W.R. 73 (B.C. C.A.), where the
originator's instructions to pay jointly to itself and its creditor were erroneously overlooked
and payment was made to the creditor's own account.

[3] For unauthorized electronic credit transfers see 4.C, above.

bank receives a payment order which contains an ambiguity or misdescription, commonly with regards to the beneficiary. Possibly, however, the ambiguity or misdescription could be as to the beneficiary's bank, and in fact, a prior payment order could have misidentified an intermediary bank, so that if acted upon, the payment order received by the last bank in the chain is likely to divert funds away from the beneficiary actually intended by the originator.

Fourth, even when the payment order received by the beneficiary's bank properly identifies the beneficiary, misdirection may be caused by the deficient completion of the funds transfer by the beneficiary's bank by means of a non-conforming payment, namely, payment made not in accordance with the payment order the beneficiary's bank received.

[2]   An unintended or defective originator's payment order may be precipitated either by innocent error or fraud. Fraud may be either internal or external to the originator's organization. Internal fraud may be that of an authorized officer of the originator or of an employee fraudulently inducing the authorized officer to issue the payment order. External fraud occurs with the inducement of an authorized officer of the originator to issue the payment order by an outsider to the originator's organization. Fraud is particularly relevant in connection with the originator's payment order. Both deficient execution and completion are likely to be caused by an internal (honest, rather than fraudulent) error of the receiving bank.

Typically, fraud losses are likely to be more extensive, and less recoverable, particularly in connection with a continuous scheme. However, whether an error has been fraudulently or innocently precipitated, and whether fraud has been external or internal, does not affect the loss allocation. Between an erring sender and its receiving bank, responsibility may be allocated to the receiving bank by contract. Such is the case where the receiving bank is contractually bound to scrutinize incoming payment orders transmitted pursuant to a security procedure for the detection of error.[4] Otherwise, the starting point is universally that loss initially falls on the erring party.[5]

Granted, such an erring party may be accorded an action in restitution or under any similar doctrine against the unintended recipient of the funds.[6] The issue to be discussed here is whether such loss may be reallo-

---

[4] See e.g. §4A–205 of the American Uniform Commercial Code (UCC).

[5] This includes losses caused by an error of a communication system employed by the sender. In the USA, see UCC §4A–206.

[6] In the USA, see UCC §4A–303(c). For a cause of action under common law against the beneficiary's bank, namely, the bank of the unintended beneficiary, as long as that bank is left with the funds at its disposal, see *ANZ Banking Group* v. *Westpac Banking Corp.* (1988), 78 A.L.R. 157 (Aust. H.C.), commented on by H. Luntz, 'Mistaken Payments: *Australia & New Zealand Banking Group* v. *Westpac Banking Corp.*' (1988–9), 3 B.F.L.R. 363.

cated away from the original erring party, other than by contract. The real-location may occur directly or indirectly, either to the receiving bank or to the beneficiary's bank (which could have spotted the error); in the latter case, the bank is then left with an action against the wrongful funds recipient. More specifically, the issue here is whether misdirection of funds, precipitated by a defect in a payment order, usually of the originator, could have been prevented by the compliance of the beneficiary's bank with a duty, breach of which could thus be considered as the real cause for the loss. This effectively limits the discussion to loss allocation in connection with the second category enumerated above: that of a defective payment order, typically issued by the originator, namely, a payment order which is incomplete, ambiguous, or incapable of being carried out. In determining responsibility in such a case, particular attention will be given to the electronic environment in which credit transfers predominantly take place.

In allocating liability for misdirected credit transfers in general law [3] jurisdictions,[7] the starting point is the obligation of a bank participating in the payment transaction as a mandatary or agent.[8] In the case of ambiguity, in connection with the identification of the intended beneficiary, the role of the beneficiary's bank as a mandatary is supported by the Quebec judgment of *Pollack* v. *Canadian Imperial Bank of Commerce*.[9] The case was concerned with a credit transfer originated by an originator in Israel through a Swiss bank, directed to the Montreal branch of the beneficiary's bank via an intermediary bank in New York and the international department of the beneficiary's bank in Toronto. Payment was to be made to a non-customer of the beneficiary's bank. The payment order received by the Toronto international department of the beneficiary's bank, which was passed on to its Montreal branch, instructed payment to one Pollak, whose address was noted as '1466 Duscharme Avenue, Autrement.' In fact, the intended beneficiary's name was Pollack (rather than Pollak), who lived at 1466 Ducharme (not Duscharme) Avenue in Outremont (and not Autrement). The beneficiary's bank was further specifically instructed, in the payment order addressed to it, to advise the beneficiary 'by mail or otherwise'.[10]

Having failed to find the named beneficiary in the telephone directory,

---

[7] For the distinction between general law and special statute jurisdictions in relation to credit transfers, see 3.C(i)(k), above.

[8] For the application of the law of mandate or agency, see 3.C(i)(k) s. 9, above. For a direct authority, in connection with the position of a beneficiary's bank that received a payment order containing an inconsistency between the beneficiary's name and account number, see e.g. in Switzerland, BGE/ATF 126 III 20 (1999), unofficial translation to French [2000] *La Semaine judiciaire* at 251 (Swiss Federal Court 17 Dec. 1999). The case is further discussed in (iv) s. 19, as well as in (i) s. 6, below   [9] [1981] C.A. 587 (Que.).

[10] Ibid. at 588.

the beneficiary's bank advised the sender of its inability to locate the beneficiary. In turn, the sender passed on this information to its 'principals'.[11]
Three weeks later, the beneficiary learnt of the arrival of the funds to the
beneficiary's bank and received payment, from the beneficiary's bank, on
the following day.[12]

In dealing with the liability of the beneficiary's bank for the delay in
making payment to the beneficiary, in light of the fact that the beneficiary's bank did not reject the payment order or the mandate,[13] the Court
did not accept the position that in the facts of the case, 'a bank [has] no
greater duty . . . than to look for a name in the local telephone directory,
and upon not finding it to ask the sender for more detailed instructions'.[14]
Rather, taking into account standard knowledge of local geography, the
intended beneficiary could have been located. Furthermore, 'elementary
prudence would have required that a *written* communication be sent' to
the address noted in the payment order, and only '[h]ad such a letter or
telegram been returned, the Bank would have had no alternative but to
ask further instructions'. Accordingly, 'failure to do so amounted to negligence on the part of the bank'. In the Court's view, the alternative is that,
in addition to a name and address, 'future banking practice would com-
pel a transferor of funds to furnish a telephone number' for the beneficiary. This, however, the Court added, is quite unacceptable.[15]

Underlying this judgment is the assumption that the beneficiary's bank
may reject an unclear or ambiguous payment order. Having chosen not to
reject such a payment order,[16] the bank is nevertheless bound to exercise
due diligence in identifying and locating the beneficiary. Yet, no general
principles underlying the required standard of care, as applied to different situations, emanated from this decision.

[4]   In the absence in any particular jurisdiction of any comprehensive body

---

[11] Ibid. It is not clear how far back all this was communicated, namely whether communication reached all the way to the originator, or whether it stopped earlier at the originator's bank. The point is of no importance for the Court's analysis.

[12] Presumably, this was done on the basis of amended instructions the beneficiary's bank
received from its sender, in pursuance to the clarifications the beneficiary's bank had
sought. The point is not clear from the report.

[13] A point noted by Laflamme JA, ibid. at 592.

[14] Ibid. at 589, *per* Kaufman JA, who gave the principal judgment on this point.

[15] Ibid. Emphasis in the original.

[16] Note, however, that in the eyes of the Court, a request for sender's clarifications was
not taken to satisfy the due diligence requirement. Further note that in the USA, under UCC
§4A–211(d), automatic cancellation of an unaccepted payment order occurs five days (usually) after receipt of the payment order by the receiving bank, in which case, no further act
of rejection is required to terminate the effectiveness of the payment order. Presumably, pursuant to UCC §4A–212, there is no duty on a beneficiary's bank, even towards a customer
who is the intended but unidentifiable beneficiary, to promptly reject a payment order containing irreconcilable ambiguity, rather than allow it to expire after five days. See (iv) s. 25,
below.

of law elaborating on bank's duties in relation to incomplete or erroneous payment orders, an attempt will be made here to explore generalities applicable to all jurisdictions, focusing on principles developed, albeit in the context of Belgian law, by two Belgian authors. The starting point under classic doctrine, as stated by Thunis, is that a receiving bank carrying out a payment order must assure itself that the order is clear, free of anomalies, and that it contains all relevant information.[17] According to Bruyneel,[18] a bank does not commit a breach of duty in rejecting a payment order containing inexact or incomplete information relating to the beneficiary. At the same time, a bank may not rely on an internal practice which precludes the examination of a payment order for internal consistency and preformability. Having found incomplete or erroneous information on the payment order, the bank is not, however, prevented from attempting to rectify it rather than to reject the payment order; the former course, that of rectification, may in fact be dictated by customer and hence, commercial, pressures. Nonetheless, in purporting to carry out the presumed intention expressed in an incomplete or erroneous payment order, the bank acts at its own risk—if the reasonableness of its action does not pass judicial scrutiny.

Regardless, no duty to detect 'implausibility' is fastened on an originator's bank that is expected to execute the originator's payment order. This is so unless participating banks operate in the context of a clearing house requiring a standardized format, whose breach is patent. Any duty to detect an error is fastened on the bank required to act on that erroneous information. Thus, an obligation to detect an error with respect to the identity of the beneficiary rests on the beneficiary's bank. Logically, and to a similar end, an error with respect to the identity of an intermediary or beneficiary's bank must be allocated to the sender of that bank. Nonetheless, other than under Article 4A of the American Uniform Commercial Code, there is no discussion relating to a duty for such a sender.

Two cases, one from Canada and the other from Belgium, demonstrate [5] the peril which a beneficiary's bank brings upon itself in purporting to rectify an error in a payment order. First, in the Canadian case *Royal Bank of Canada* v. *Stangl*,[19] the beneficiary's bank received a payment order directing payment at a designated branch to *Lynwil* International Trading

---

[17] X. Thunis, *Responsabilité du banquier et automitisation des paiements* (Namur: Presses universitaires de Namur, 1996) at 141–7, particularly 142.

[18] A. Bruyneel, 'Le Virement', in C. G. Winandy et als. (eds.), *La Banque dans la vie quotidienne* (Brussels: Éditions du jeune barreau, 1986), 345 at 430–42, particularly 439–40.

[19] [1992] O.J. No. 378; on-line: QL(OJ); No. 29464/88 (Gen. Div.), unreported. Judgment is reproduced in B. Geva, *Negotiable Instruments and Banking*, being vol. ii of J. S. Ziegel, B. Geva, and R. C. C. Cuming, *Commercial and Consumer Transactions Cases, Text and Materials*, 3rd. edn. (Toronto: Emond Montgomery Publications Ltd., 1995) at 621.

Inc., account no. 916327. This account, however, belonged to an entity, which had several accounts at that branch, one of which was in the name of *Linwell* International. Having consulted that entity, the branch of the beneficiary's bank deposited the funds into one of that entity's accounts. In fact, the intended beneficiary, as indicated in the payment order, was *Lynwil*, a different entity, that had no account at that branch. Both Lynwil and Linwell were involved in mining operations in Guyana. This may explain both the originator's error, in allocating to one the account number of the other, as well as of the beneficiary's bank, that was unaware of the existence of Lynwil and did not see anything unusual in the transfer to Linwell's account. Judgment was, however, given in favour of the intermediary bank against the beneficiary's bank, on the basis of its alleged negligence. Elsewhere, I have argued that inasmuch as it was plausible for the beneficiary's bank to believe that the beneficiary's name was misspelled and not that it referred to someone other than the account holder, this aspect of the decision is not defensible.[20]

Second, in the Belgian case *Frablemar*,[21] the originator's payment order identified the beneficiary as 'Debor Décoration' as well by an account number. However, the account number was short of one figure and thus incomplete. The beneficiary's bank took the initiative and added a figure completing the number to an account belonging to 'Decor Integration', a name with 'adequate phonetic resemblance' with that of the named beneficiary; funds were thus deposited to that account. Decor Integration, which was not the intended beneficiary, became insolvent, and the originator, who remained owing to Debor Décoration, sued the bank. The court declined to see the conduct of the beneficiary's bank as reasonable. Recognizing the fact that both the originator and the beneficiary's bank were at fault, the court was nevertheless of the view that the fault of the beneficiary's bank was more serious, and allocated to it 80 per cent of the responsibility.

Unlike *Stangl*, the result of *Frablemar* is quite defensible. In *Stangl*, the beneficiary's bank acted on the basis of the number as was given, and purported to rectify what it perceived to be a spelling error in the beneficiary's name. On the other hand, in *Frablemar*, the bank purported to rectify both name and number, without having any real foundation to base its conclusion as to the possible error in the name. The bank thus became involved in a much more speculative endeavour, which ought to have dictated a straightforward rejection of the erroneous payment order.

---

[20] B. Geva, 'Ambiguous Wire Instructions: *Royal Bank of Canada* v. *Stangl*' (1995), 24 Can. Bus. L.J. 435.

[21] Mons, 13 février 1984, Rev. Banque 1984, p. 49, as outlined by Bruyneel, above, n. 18 at 439, and Thunis, above, n. 17 at 142 and n. 55.

Regardless, in a given case, there may be more than one reasonable **[6]**
interpretation to an ambiguous payment order. In such a case, in purporting to implement the originator's presumed intention, the beneficiary's bank ought to be protected as long as it has taken what is a
'reasonable' course of action, even when in hindsight it does not implement the originator's own intention.[22] At the same time, the beneficiary's
bank is not considered to be acting diligently when it decides to adopt one
course of action, to the exclusion of all other plausible avenues: both those
actually known and possibly those that ought to have been known to it.
Rather, in such a case, when there are serious doubts as to whether the
particular course taken actually implemented the originator's instructions, the beneficiary's bank ought to reject the payment order, not act on
it where no acceptance by passage of time could occur, or, where feasible,
seek its sender's instructions. The beneficiary's bank may not, however,
rely on the beneficiary's instructions. Conversely, once a course of action
selected by the originator's bank has been brought to the attention of the
originator, possibly in the form of an item included in an account statement, and the originator has not objected to it, the beneficiary's bank may
be protected in taking the same action with regard to any similar payment
order in the future. Indeed, strictly speaking, any understanding on the
basis of a bank statement is a matter between the originator and the originator's bank. At the same time, the beneficiary's bank may rightfully
count on an advice being sent by the originator's bank to the originator,
at a time mandated either by law or banking practice, as well as on the
lack of protest by the originator relating to the debit in question, and rely
on it as providing legitimacy to the course of action taken. This is so
regardless of the reasonableness of the interpretation leading to the initial
course of action.

It must however be recognized that for a beneficiary's bank, there is a
danger inherent in acting other than on the basis of the sender's explicit
and unequivocal advice in connection with an ambiguous payment order
susceptible of more than one plausible interpretation and, hence, amenable
to alternative courses of action. This is demonstrated by a Swiss judgment decided in 1964.[23] In that case, the beneficiary's bank received a
payment order instructing payment to 'maison Inro'. Rather than seek
clarifications from its sender, the beneficiary's bank credited the account
of 'S.à.r.l. Inro' and not that of 'Inro Corserty Ltd', which had an account

---

[22] For the protection accorded in the common law to an agent acting on a reasonable
(though erroneous) interpretation of the principal's instructions, see *Ireland* v. *Livingston*
(1872) L.R. 5 H.L. 395 at 416 (commercial agency); *Midland Bank* v. *Seymour* [1955] 2 Lloyd's
Rep. 147 (Q.B.) at 153 (letter of credit); and *Commercial Bank Co. of Sydney* v. *Jalasard Pty. Ltd.*
[1973] A.C. 279 (P.C.) at 285–6 (letter of credit).
[23] ATF 18 II 239 (1964).

at the beneficiary's bank, and to whom the originator actually intended to make payment. It was found that the beneficiary's bank had not acted diligently.[24]

For the beneficiary's bank, reliance on the beneficiary is permissible only when the beneficiary's identity unequivocally emanates from the payment order and the ambiguity relates to the manner of making the funds available to the beneficiary. Accordingly, in another Swiss case,[25] a beneficiary's bank received a payment order identifying the beneficiary by both name and account number. In fact, the account did not belong to the named beneficiary. The beneficiary's bank complied with the account holder's instructions and directed the funds to the specified account. Judgment was given against the beneficiary's bank that wrongfully relied on information emanating not from its sender, but rather, from a customer claiming to be the beneficiary, who in fact, was not intended by the originator to receive funds.

Conversely, in a Japanese case,[26] the originator's payment order instructed payment to a beneficiary identified by name only. Unknown to the beneficiary's bank, the beneficiary undertook towards the originator to open an account at the beneficiary's bank, in the beneficiary's own name, but under actual exclusive control of the originator, to which the funds ought to have been directed. The beneficiary broke this contract, did not open the account, and instructed the beneficiary's bank to deposit the funds in the account of a third party. It was held that in complying with these instructions, the beneficiary's bank was not in breach of any duty. Indeed, there was no ambiguity in the description of the beneficiary, so that the beneficiary's bank, having accepted the payment order addressed to it, and being unaware of the originator-beneficiary contract, was actually bound to comply with the beneficiary's instructions.

[7]   As indicated, upon the misdirection of funds, the unintended recipient of the funds is responsible for their return under the laws of mistake and restitution. Also, when misdirection has occurred as a result of an ambiguity or any other defect in the last payment order in the credit transfer, depending on the circumstances and legal system, a breach of duty may have been committed by the beneficiary's bank.[27] In the USA, under the 'money-back guarantee' rule of §4A–402(c) and (d), such a breach negates the acceptance

---

[24] However, in the facts of the case, there was more to undermine the reasonableness of the beneficiary's bank. Thus, in 1959, before the issue of the payment order dealt with by the Court, the originator advised the beneficiary's bank that 'S.à.r.l. Inro' stopped its activity. Yet, the payment order in the case at bar contained information according to which the credit transfer was designed to pay 1960 bills, namely, bills arising after the demise of 'S.à.r.l. Inro'.

[25] BGE/ATF 126 III 20 (1999), n. 8, above. The case is further discussed in (iv) s. 19, below.

[26] *Lyo Bank* v. *Yamaguchi*, 1383 Kinyuhoumujilyou 37 (1994) [in Japanese. I relied on an unofficial translation].   [27] See s. 2, above.

by the beneficiary's bank, and either discharges the originator of the credit transfer from the obligation to the originator's bank, or entitles the originator to a refund of the amount already paid to the originator's bank.[28]

In some general law jurisdictions, the beneficiary's bank acts for a sender in the credit transfer, namely as an agent, substitute agent, or sub-agent for the originator. In those jurisdictions, recourse to the originator for the breach committed by the beneficiary's bank is available either directly from the breaching beneficiary's bank, or from the originator's bank, which is vicariously liable for breach by the beneficiary's bank. At the same time, in other general law jurisdictions, where the breaching beneficiary's bank is regarded as agent for the beneficiary, the question of the originator's recourse for the breach by the beneficiary's bank is more complex. This is particularly true in circumstances where no real intended beneficiary can be detected, such as where the originator was defrauded into issuing a payment order to an unidentifiable beneficiary.[29]

Indeed, in the absence of a 'money-back guarantee rule' accruing to the benefit of the originator, one may speculate that in those general law jurisdictions, where the beneficiary's bank is treated as the beneficiary's agent, recourse by the originator for the breach committed by the beneficiary's bank ought to be linked to the fact that the payment order sent to and acted upon by the beneficiary's bank is a contract between that bank and its sender. This is so at least to the extent that such payment order requires more than payment to an existing and well-identified customer's account. Accordingly, breach of duty by the beneficiary's bank may be regarded as breach of this contract.[30] Whether recourse is then available to the originator directly from the breaching beneficiary's bank, or through the originator's bank, and on what theory, still has to be worked out in each such general law jurisdiction.

Regardless, it should be recognized in general law jurisdictions that while due diligence by the beneficiary's bank could have prevented the misdirection of funds, the initial identification error leading to the misdirection was nevertheless committed by the originator. Accordingly, in allocating the loss, there is also the possibility of shared responsibility between the two mistaken parties, namely, the originator and beneficiary's bank.[31]

---

[28] See 3.C (x) s. 5, above.

[29] In principle, direct recourse from the beneficiary's bank is available to the originator in Switzerland, Japan, Quebec, and France but not in Germany, UK, common law Canada, Australia, Israel, and South Africa. See summary in 3.C(i) s. 10, above, and for each jurisdiction, a more detailed discussion as applicable in each of 3.C(ii)–(xi), above.

[30] In Canada, this is supported by *Stangl*, above, n. 19, which involved an action by the intermediary bank against, *inter alia*, the beneficiary's bank.

[31] I. Billotte-Tongue, *Aspects juridiques du virement bancaire* (Zurich: Schulthess Polygraphischer Verlag, 1992) at 266–7.

(II) SPECIFIC SITUATIONS AND UCC ARTICLE 4A

[8]   In the USA, Article 4A of the Uniform Commercial Code does not analyse the duties of the beneficiary's bank in terms of agency or mandate. Further, to an extent, Article 4A disfavours open-end obligations and purports to define funds transfer participants' obligations in specific and concrete terms.[32] Accordingly, the issue of misdirection of funds by virtue of misdescription of a beneficiary is dealt with in the context of two concrete situations, that of non-existent or unidentifiable beneficiary, and a beneficiary identified by means of a name and number which do not match. The ensuing discussion deals with the provisions governing these two situations. It demonstrates that even under the UCC, the broader issue of the due diligence obligation of a beneficiary's bank cannot be avoided altogether. Accordingly, particularly in relation to the specific question of the duty to match a name and number and spot any discrepancy, the analysis of the UCC provision is carried out in a broader comparative context.

Under Article 4A, a payment order must identify the beneficiary, as well as the beneficiary's bank.[33] It may further identify an intermediary bank.[34] A beneficiary may be identified by 'name, bank account number, or other identification'.[35] A bank may be identified by name or by an identifying number.[36] Misdescription may lead to diversion of funds, so that the originator's debt to the beneficiary is not discharged.

Article 4A anticipates a clear and unambiguous description of the beneficiary so as to facilitate timely and satisfactory completion of the transfer. At the same time, Article 4A does not require that both alternate descriptions, that is name and number, be present in any given case, as either one is a valid description.[37] A receiving bank, in carrying out instructions given to it, is generally bound by the description as commu-

---

[32] For UCC Article 4A, see 3.C(x), above.

[33] This emerges from the definition of 'payment order' in UCC §4A–103(a)(1). Briefly stated, because a payment order directs payment to a beneficiary by a bank, the payment order must identify a beneficiary and a beneficiary's bank.

[34] UCC §4A–302.   [35] UCC §4A–207(a).   [36] UCC §4A–208.

[37] But *cf* in the US federal 'travel rule' issued by the Treasury Department, namely, 31 CFR 103, 60 Fed. Reg. 230, as am., Financial Recordkeeping and Reporting of Currency and Foreign Transactions, Title 31—Money and Finance: Treasury, §103.33(g), Information financial institutions must include in transmittal orders: For the transmittal of funds in the amount of $3,000 or more, the transmitter's financial institution is required to include in the transmittal order information pertaining to '[a]s many of the following items as are received with the transmittal order: . . . [t]he name and address of the recipient; . . . [t]he account number of the recipient; . . . [and] [a]ny other specific identifier of the recipient; . . .'. But even this does not amount to an unequivocal requirement to describe beneficiary by both name and number.

nicated to it, no matter how erroneous it is.[38] The two situations dealt with in §§4A–207 and 4A–208 are where:

(1) the beneficiary, as described in the payment order, is non-existent or unidentifiable; and

(2) where the description, as given in the payment order, is ambiguous so as to require two inconsistent courses of action.

A discussion of each provision immediately follows.

(III) NON-EXISTENT OR UNIDENTIFIABLE BENEFICIARY

§4A–207(a) deals with a payment order received by the beneficiary's bank [9]
containing 'the name, bank account number, or other identification of the
beneficiary' which 'refers to a nonexistent or unidentifiable person or
account'. In such a case, 'no person has rights as a beneficiary of the
order,' so that the funds transfer cannot be completed. Since the completion of a funds transfer is marked by the acceptance by the beneficiary's
bank,[39] §4A–207(a) recognizes that 'acceptance of the order cannot occur'.
Consequently, since the transfer is not completed by acceptance by the
beneficiary's bank, each sender is excused from its obligation to pay the
payment order under §4A–402(c).[40]

§4A–207(a) applies when 'the name, bank account number, or other
identification of the beneficiary' appears in a payment order which 'refers
to a nonexistent or unidentifiable person or account'. Under the language
of §4A–207(a), 'nonexistent' may mean an objective fact, though presumably a payment order in favour of a beneficiary who has died will not fall
into §4A–207(a), notwithstanding the 'nonexistence' of the beneficiary.[41]
'Unidentifiable' arguably refers to the standard of normal banking practices as maintained by a reasonable banker of the type of the beneficiary's
bank. In the simplest case, an instruction which does not direct payment
to any person or account 'refers to [an] ... unidentifiable person or
account' within the meaning of §4A–207(a).

For §4A–207(a) to apply, the beneficiary must be either non-existent or

---

[38] The receiving bank's obligation to execute pursuant to the sender's instructions (no matter how erroneous such instructions might be) is tempered by an agreement to use a security procedure for error detection. See UCC §4A–205.
[39] UCC §4A–104(a).   [40] See Official Comment 1 to UCC §4A–207.
[41] The effect of the sender's death is governed by UCC §4A–211(g). Where the beneficiary dies before the issuance of the payment order and acceptance by payment into that beneficiary's account, UCC §4A–207(a) may apply. This seems to be the assumption made in dictum in *The Department of Retirement Systems* v. *Kralman*, 867 P.2d 643 (Wash. App. 1994) at 648.

unidentifiable. Technically, a non-legal entity can be identifiable, though it is legally non-existent. It is, however, questionable whether subsection (a) is meant to apply to such a case. It is also uncertain whether subsection (a) purports to apply to a situation where the beneficiary is identified by name only and there are at least two persons meeting the description.[42] Technically, this is a case of an existent but unidentifiable beneficiary. It is arguable, however, that subsection (a) only covers the case where, from the 'four corners' of the instruction, the beneficiary's bank, acting as a reasonable banker, cannot find any identifiable and existing person or account to whom payment would carry out the sender's intention as expressed in the payment order.

[10]   Literally read, particularly due to its disjunctive language, §4A–207(a) appears to apply whenever any identification of the beneficiary, whether by name, account number or otherwise, refers to either a non-existent or unidentifiable beneficiary, in terms of either name or number. This is so since the disjunctive language pertains to both the method of identification of the beneficiary (whether by name or number) and its being non-existent or unidentifiable. Stated otherwise, a literal reading leads to the conclusion that the provision applies when the named beneficiary is non-existent, the named beneficiary is unidentifiable, the number is non-existent, as well as where the number is unidentifiable. Each such fact, by itself, and regardless of any sense which could otherwise be made out of the payment order, will bring the case into the ambit of the provision.

As discussed below, this reading appears to defeat the purpose of §4A–207(a) and thus, ought to have been rejected. Unfortunately, however, it has received judicial support. The ensuing discussion will propose an interpretation consistent with the policies underlying the provision and will examine the current position of case law.

In general, whether 'the name, bank account number, or other identification of the beneficiary' in a payment order refers to 'a nonexistent or unidentifiable person or account' should be examined as a whole and not by breaking down the phrases into their various components. Thus, if the name is unidentifiable but the account number is identifiable or vice versa, §4A–207(a) should not apply. For example, a payment order instructing payment into an existing and identifiable account of a non-existent or unidentifiable person ought not to fall within the scope of §4A–207(a)[43] and may be accepted by the beneficiary's bank. Such would be the case where an account is opened (either mistakenly or fraudulently) in the name of a non-existent entity. In this case, subsection (a)

---

[42] See *Nicoletti* v. *Bank of Los Banos*, 214 P.51 (S.C. Cal. 1923).
[43] But see *Corfan Banco Asunción Paraguay* v. *Ocean Bank*, 715 So. 2d 967 (Fla. Dist. Ct. App. 1998), discussed in s. 13, below.

should not bar the bona fide acceptance by the beneficiary's bank solely on the basis of the account number. This is confirmed by §4A–207(b), dealing with the case of a conflicting name and account number, which supersedes §4A–207(a).[44] However, the proposed interpretation of subsection (a) also follows from the objective underlying it. The provision does not amount to a licence given to a beneficiary's bank that has not rejected a payment order not to exercise due diligence in identifying the beneficiary. Rather, it is a shield in situations where, from the information contained in the payment order, the beneficiary is truly unidentifiable. Where the beneficiary is existent and identifiable, 'acceptance' by the beneficiary's bank may occur, notwithstanding lack of correct identification.[45]

It was held in *Donmar Enterprises, Inc.* v. *Southern National Bank of North*   **[11]** *Carolina*[46] that §4A–207(a) requires a beneficiary's bank to reject a payment order when it does not specify 'at least one identifiable beneficiary'. Identification can be made 'in any number of ways including the plain wording of the [payment] order or the circumstances of the transfer'. In *Donmar*, the beneficiary's bank received two payment orders from the originator's bank, specifying the sum and stating 'ATT INTL DIV RE STC DONMAR TRANS CODE 102–1011'. The beneficiary's bank directed the funds to the account of its customer Stephen's Trading Co. (STC), at least in the second funds transfer, on the basis of that customer's directions. Donmar was not a customer of the beneficiary's bank. The court found that 'the STC/Donmar language' in the payment orders identified these two as the parties to the transaction and made clear 'within the context of the transaction that STC was the beneficiary of the money and that Donmar was the payor'. Even assuming that both parties were named as beneficiaries, 'Stephen's Trading Co. was clearly an identifiable beneficiary whether measured objectively or subjectively'. In the final analysis, 'there was admittedly at least one identifiable beneficiary, and since §4A–207 requires no more, the [beneficiary's bank] was not required to refuse the transfer . . .'.

The payment orders could have easily been construed as designating STC and Donmar as joint beneficiaries,[47] as argued by the originator Donmar. However, taking into account the ambiguity or insufficiency of the language of the payment orders, the course of action taken by the beneficiary's bank was adequately reasonable to afford it full protection.

---

[44] See UCC §4A–207(a), (b). On its own terms, subsection (a) is stated to be subject to subsection (b).

[45] See Official Comment 6 to UCC §4A–209.

[46] 828 F. Supp. 1230 (W.D.N.C. 1993) at 1239–40, *aff'd*, 64 F.3d 944 (4th Cir. N.C. 1995).

[47] In which case, inasmuch as Donmar had no account with the beneficiary's bank, no acceptance could have occurred by payment to the beneficiary's bank under §4A–209(b) and (c), discussed above, in 3.C(x) ss. 4 and 8.

Nonetheless, as a matter of statutory interpretation, by themselves, ambiguous instructions should not be assumed sufficient to render the beneficiary 'unidentifiable' under §4A–207(a). For the provision to apply, no identification could have been made even under any reasonable interpretation of the ambiguous instructions. Unfortunately, while reaching the correct result, the court did not elaborate on this point.

[12]   In *United States* v. *BCCI Holdings (Luxemburg), S.A.*,[48] UBAF Bank in London purported to wire payment into BCC (E)'s account with Bank America in New York. Due to a clerical error at UBAF, the beneficiary was identified in the payment order as 'Bk. Credit & Commerce (GC) Abu Dh.' No account under this or a closely similar name existed at BankAmerica. Since the payment order[49] did not specify a bank account or other numerical identifier, BankAmerica had to process it manually. It ultimately credited the money into account no. 86052 of BCCI S.A., as a 'beneficiary's bank', noting BCC (GC) as the beneficiary, and advising BCCI S.A. accordingly.[50]

The court conceded that the association between the BCCI S.A. Abu Dhabi account and a payment order referencing GC, for Grand Cayman, 'was not taken out of the air'. BCCI S.A. had a treasury (or cash management) division which managed the surplus funds of the various BCCI entities and branches. Account 86052 was used by that division to receive and transfer funds owned by the Grand Cayman Treasury, to which the surplus liquidity of the BCCI entities worldwide was transferred daily.

---

[48] Criminal No. 91–0665 (JHG), US District of Columbia (Aug 22, 1995), unreported. This was a petition of UBAF for recovery of funds forfeited by the US government in connection with criminal charges brought against various BCCI entities. UBAF's petition challenged the legal title to the funds of BCCI S.A., arguing lack of acceptance by Bank America of a payment order, allegedly issued to a 'nonexistent or unidentifiable' beneficiary. I acted as an expert witness for the United States, against whom judgment was given.

[49] In fact, the payment order received by BankAmerica was a CHIPS payment order, issued by UBAF's New York correspondent, Bankers Trust, acting in the funds transfer as an intermediary bank. The content of Bankers Trust's payment order fully conformed to that issued to it by UBAF.

[50] Judgment was, however, premissed on BankAmerica acting throughout as a beneficiary's bank, according to the payment order it received. That is, BankAmerica must have treated account no. 86052 as belonging, at least beneficially, to the designated beneficiary. Alternatively, having identified the Grand Cayman Treasury as the beneficiary, for whom it held no account, BankAmerica might be regarded as having proceeded to pay it by issuing a payment order to BCCI S.A., where to its knowledge, the Grand Cayman Treasury had an account. Under this alternative, BCCI S.A. might not have been in a position to accept BankAmerica's payment order, due to the closure of its New York operations. See UCC §4A–210(c) under which suspension of payments by a receiving bank is tantamount to the rejection of all unaccepted payment orders issued to it. Inasmuch as the court found that no acceptance occurred under the first alternative, it did not pursue the second, noting only that '[b]ecause Article 4A treats separate branches of banks as distinct banks and the Abu Dhabi branch of BCCI S.A. was not shutdown until [several days later], it is unclear whether BCCI S.A. Abu Dhabi had suspend[ed] payments' [on the day BankAmerica credited its account]'.

Nevertheless, the Court concluded that the beneficiary in the payment order received by BankAmerica was both 'nonexistent' and 'unidentifiable' so that under UCC §4A–207(a), no acceptance occurred. 'Nonexistence' was rationalized on the absence in BankAmerica of any BCC account including 'GC' or 'Grand Cayman'.[51]

There are several difficulties with the construction and application of §4A–207(a) by the Court. First, there is no reason why 'nonexistence' ought to be defined solely by reference to the list of account holders at the beneficiary's bank. A non-account holder, non-customer, may well be 'existent'. In the facts of the case, there was an 'existent' Grand Cayman BCC unit, whose funds were received and transferred through account 86052. Moreover, the name 'Bk Credit & Commerce (GC) Abu Dh' was selected at UBAF from a particular beneficiary data base. True, in the facts of the case, the particular selection was mistaken; but, this does not render the selected beneficiary non-existent. There is no indication, indeed, that UBAF's database was so unreliable, as to include non-existent persons.

Second, too much emphasis was put on the disjunctive language of §4A–207(a). As already suggested, to avoid arbitrary results whether 'the name, bank account number, or other identification of the beneficiary' in a payment order refers to a 'nonexistent or unidentifiable person or account' should be examined as a whole and not by breaking down the phrases into their various components. Accordingly, in my view, 'non-existence' comes into play only for an 'identifiable' beneficiary, in situations where notwithstanding proper identification, no reasonable course of action can be taken by the bank. Such is the case for a payment order directing payment to a historical figure, such as Napoleon Bonaparte. Obviously, he is 'identifiable'; nonetheless, inasmuch as the beneficiary's bank is unable to carry payment to him, no acceptance could occur due to his 'non-existence'. However, the provision ought not to apply to a 'non-

---

[51] This view was restated, *albeit* by the same court, without additional reasoning, and only as an alternative holding, in *United States* v. *BCCI Holding (Luxembourg), S.A.* 980 F. Supp. 21 (D.D.C. 1997). Specifically, the court explained that due to the disjunctive wording of UCC §4A–207(a), namely, due to the reference to 'a nonexistent *or* unidentifiable person or account' (emphasis added) in the provision, 'non-existence' could not be saved by 'identifiability,' or the belief thereof by the beneficiary's bank. In any event, the court went on to conclude that in the facts of the case, the beneficiary was also 'unidentifiable,' since BankAmerica did not take reasonable steps to identify the intended beneficiary. The unreasonableness of BankAmerica's conduct was predicated, according to the court, on the unusual situation on the day the payment order was received by BankAmerica, resulting from the earlier seizure of account no. 86052, as part of BCCI's shutdown by the regulators on that day. According to the court, '[t]his need for special treatment was exacerbated by the history of confusion between the BCCI S.A. and BCC(E) accounts at BankAmerica, and the fact that BankAmerica could have placed the money in a virtually risk-free suspense account pending a determination of the beneficiary of the payment order'.

existent' but 'identifiable' beneficiary, where a reasonable course of action to carry the originator's intent, as expressed in the payment order issued to the beneficiary's bank, is available to the latter. For example, such could be the case where the named beneficiary just died or is an unincorporated organization. In sum, 'identifiability' may or may not save 'non-existence', and the disjunctive language of §4A–207(a) ought not to be determinative. As applied to the facts of our case, even if the named beneficiary was 'non-existent,' in the technical sense, surely its identification as the Grand Cayman Treasury, coupled with BankAmerica's ability to carry out payment to it, ought to have excluded the case from the coverage of the provision.

This brings us to the issue of 'identifiability' in §4A–207(a). I am in full agreement with the court that for an 'ambiguous' beneficiary, reasonable identification is required. However, I have difficulties in sharing the court's conclusion that BankAmerica did not take reasonable steps to identify the intended beneficiary. As the Court stated, manual processing of payment orders not including a numerical identifier was a common occurrence at BankAmerica, in which case, while no written guidelines existed, 'several steps were commonly taken ... BankAmerica personnel could rely on directories, lists of account holders, BankAmerica policies and experience'. There was no indication that these steps were not pursued. Neither that day closure of BCCI S.A.,[52] nor the past confusion between BCCI S.A. and BCC(E)[53] rendered the beneficiary on the payment order issued to BankAmerica less 'identifiable' and its identification process less reasonable.

[13]   Criticism on the judgment thus relates to both the interpretation of 'nonexistent or unidentifiable' and the weight put on the disjunctive language of §4A–207(a). Yet the centrality of the disjunctive language of the provision, to the exclusion of any other consideration in its proper interpretation, was subsequently reinforced in *Corfan Banco Asunción Paraguay v. Ocean Bank*.[54] In that case, the originator's bank erred as to the beneficiary's account number, so that the payment order instructed payment to a non-existent account of an existing and identifiable customer of the beneficiary's bank, intended to be the beneficiary of the payment order. The

---

[52] Even if crediting payment to a frozen account of an insolvent bank may be wrongful (as in *Sheerbonnet, Ltd.* v. *American Express Bank, Ltd.*, 905 F. Supp. 127 (S.D.N.Y. 1995)), rep. 951 F. Supp. 403, corrected and superseded by 1996 WL 221829 (1 May 1996), the identification of that account by the beneficiary's bank (as opposed to its crediting) does not become thereby more unreasonable.

[53] After all, there was nothing in the payment order to alert BankAmerica to the possibility that BCC(E) might have been involved. As for the court's suggestion to put the money into a suspense account at BankAmerica, this might not have precluded acceptance by receipt of payment under UCC §4A–209(b)(2) which would have triggered an obligation to pay the beneficiary under UCC §4A–404.   [54] Above, n. 43.

beneficiary's bank credited the named beneficiary's account. The originator's bank discovered its error and sent a second payment order, correctly identifying the beneficiary by name and number, but failing to note that it was in replacement of (that is, an amendment to) the previous payment order. The amount was thus credited twice to the account of the named beneficiary who withdrew the funds and failed to reimburse the originator's bank.[55] The originator's bank sued the beneficiary's bank, challenging the effectiveness of the acceptance of the first payment order on the basis of §4A–207(a). The majority held, on the basis of the 'plain wording' of the provision, namely, its disjunctive language, that it applied, so that no acceptance by the beneficiary's bank could have occurred. The majority was prepared to carry its conclusion to its full logic and cited with approval the view[56] that apparently, under §4A–207, even 'if the payment order name and account number provide an identifiable or known person but 'other identification of the beneficiary' refers to a non-existing or unidentifiable person or account, subsection 4A–207 (a) is literally applicable'[57] In contrast, the dissent thought that the provision 'should neither be construed in the disjunctive or the conjunctive,' but rather should be construed to promote behaviour designed 'to better comport with the overall statutory scheme relating to funds transfers'. The dissent further thought that imposing the responsibility for the error on the originator's bank, which would result from §4A–207 being inapplicable, would enhance the 'longstanding equitable tenet' under which 'as between two innocent parties, the best suited to prevent the loss caused by a third party wrongdoer must bear the loss'.[58]

In the final analysis, the purpose of §4A–207(a) is to protect a sender, **[14]** usually the originator, from an unwarranted or unreasonable identification by a beneficiary's bank handling an ambiguous payment order. The purpose is not to protect the originator from the consequences of an internal mistake at the originator's end in the selection of the beneficiary, as seems to be done in both *United States* v. *BCCI Holdings (Luxemburg), S.A.* and

---

[55] In contrast to the first payment order that had been processed manually (due to the absence of the numbered account), the second payment order (containing a correct account number) was processed automatically.

[56] W. D. Hawkland and R. Monero, *Uniform Commercial Code Series* (Wilmette, Ill.: Callaghan, 1993) §4A–207: 01—published in looseleaf form from 1982 onwards.

[57] See *Corfan Banco*, above, n. 43 at 969 n. 4. Compare with *Tafreschi* v. *Canadian Imperial Bank of Commerce* [1986] B.C.J. No. 2096 (B.C. S.C.), where a payment order properly identified the beneficiary by name, but misidentified the beneficiary's account by omitting one digit from the account number. It was held that the beneficiary's bank was negligent in confusing the beneficiary's middle name with his family name and consequently in declining to accept the payment order and credit the beneficiary's correct account. This seems to me more appropriate than to treat the beneficiary of the payment order as 'non-existent or unidentifiable' and condone the conduct of the beneficiary's bank under UCC §4A–207(a).

[58] See *Corfan Banco*, ibid. at 971 and 972.

Corfan. In any event, it should be stressed that an action in restitution is available to a mistaken sender, whether against the beneficiary's bank, where §4A–207(a) applies, or against the unintended beneficiary, as in the case of any other erroneous payment order.[59]

(IV) MISDESCRIPTION OF BENEFICIARY: CONFLICTING NUMBER AND NAME

[15]   A beneficiary may be identified erroneously in a payment order by a name and/or account number which does not belong to that named beneficiary. The ambiguity in the instructions may have been generated either by mistake or by fraudulent design.[60]

An example of a fraudulent design is a situation where a dishonest insider in the originator's organization manages to generate a payment order from the originator which appears to instruct payment to a genuine creditor of the originator, or even to the originator itself, at the beneficiary's bank. The payment order identifies the beneficiary by name and account number. In effect, the named beneficiary is not the account holder[61] and the dishonest insider uses, as a destination account at the beneficiary's bank, the bank account of the insider, of an accomplice of the insider,[62] or even of a genuine but unsuspecting bona fide creditor of the insider.[63] Through the use of either the originator itself or of one of its creditors as named beneficiary, the payment order does not raise any suspicion in the originator's organization. The dishonest insider counts on automatic processing at the beneficiary's bank, which would overlook the named beneficiary and misdirect the funds into the target destination account.[64]

In such a case, remedies are available against both the perpetrator and

---

[59] In the facts of the case, the latter action (under UCC §4A–205) would have been inadequate in the context of the forfeiture proceedings, where UBAF's recovery must have been premissed on its legal interest in the funds, and its absence in the hands of BCCI S.A.

[60] See Official Comment 2 to UCC §4A–207.

[61] An example is where the payment order instructs payment to account no. 12345 of X. In fact, the account holder of account no. 12345 is Y and not X.

[62] *Cf.* (Dec. 1987) Int'l Fin. L. Rev. 24, where the thief gave the originator's bank an account number at the beneficiary's bank and a budget number. In fact, the account was held by a correspondent bank and the budget number identified the account of the thief's accomplice.

[63] See e.g. *Securities Fund Services, Inc.* v. *American National Bank & Trust Co. of Chicago*, 542 F. Supp. 323 (N.D. Ill. 1982).

[64] Where the thief is not an insider but, rather, an outsider who forges the originator's payment order, the case involves an unauthorized payment order, dealt with in UCC §4A–202 and discussed in 4.C(iii), above, so as to fall outside UCC §4A–207. For such a pre-Article 4A case, see *Bradford Trust Co. of Boston* v. *Texas American Bank*, 790 F.2d 407 (5th Cir. 1986).

the unintended recipient, in either fraud or restitution. Only too often, however, absconding perpetrators and innocent recipients are not promising defendants; the former is likely to be too far away or too insolvent, while the latter may successfully raise a defence under the law governing mistake and restitution, such as change of position and discharge for value.[65] Hence, the loss may be allocated to an innocent participant in the credit transfer that breached a duty.

Needless to say, the beneficiary's bank cannot strictly comply with instructions to pay a named person into an account other than of that person: it can pay either the named person or the numbered person or account, but not both. The issue to be discussed here is whether the beneficiary's bank is required to spot the inconsistency and either reject the payment order or seek sender's clarifications or whether it is protected when acting on either the name or number.

A duty to determine the consistency between the name and account **[16]** number of the beneficiary can be rationalized easily in general law jurisdictions, due to the nature of the beneficiary's bank as a mandatary or agent.[66] At first blush, automatic processing appears to be inconsistent with the duty of the beneficiary's bank to carry out the originator's presumed intention. The latter is likely to be better reflected in the name rather than in the number which is prone to be designed only to assist the direction of the funds to the intended beneficiary identified by name. This is particularly true for an originator's payment order given in writing. In Germany, the prevailing view is that by executing the originator's written payment order by issuing its own electronic payment order, a bank may not alter the originator's fundamental expectations that the credit transfer be carried out as manifested by the originator's intention, so that the beneficiary's bank does not become free from its duty to reconcile name and number.

At the same time in Germany, the issuance of the originator's payment order in electronic format is taken to demonstrate the originator's agreement as to the impact of automated processing. Only under such circumstances is the originator seen as relinquishing any reliance on the reconciliation by the beneficiary's bank between name and number so as to constitute a valid waiver.[67]

Clearing rules and interbank agreements may, however, release a receiving bank from any duty to find errors and inconsistencies, in which

---

[65] A leading authority in the USA for the discharge for value defence, dispensing with the good faith change of position, and being satisfied with the good faith application of the payment to the discharge of a debt owed to the recipient, see *Banque Worms* v. *Bank America International*, 77 N.Y. 2d 362, 568 N.Y.S. 2d 541 (N.Y. C.A. 1991), applied 928 F. 2d 538 (2d Cir. N.Y. 1991).   [66] See (i) s. 3, n. 8, and text above.

[67] See Schimansky, above, n. 2 at 882–5.

case, loss is to be allocated to the sending bank. Such arrangements exist in Germany,[68] Belgium,[69] as well as under the CHAPS Rules in the UK,[70] and the LVTS By-law in Canada.[71] In Holland, for large value domestic transfers, matching is undertaken by the clearing house.[72] There is, however, no consensus as to the impact of such arrangements on the originator, who is not a party to any such interbank agreement, and whether loss may be allocated to the originator by contract.[73]

All this is premissed on the existence of a duty by the beneficiary's bank to match name and number, so that the debate focuses on whether such a duty may be contracted out of. At the same time, the very existence of such a duty may nevertheless be put to question in an electronic environment of which participants are cognizant. Indeed, much can be said in the electronic age in favour of automatic processing, and the resulting efficiency gains in automated systems, of which participants in a credit transfer ought to be aware, so as to maintain their own precautions in issuing accurate payment orders. Accordingly, the originator's knowledge of possible automated processing ought to be taken as recognition that the account number is the determinative factor in manifesting the intention as to the beneficiary's identification, regardless of whether the originator's own payment order is issued in writing or in electronic form. It then follows that the obligations of the beneficiary's bank as mandatary or agent are to be delineated pursuant to that newly formulated originator's intention, so that there is no room for an obligation to match beneficiary's name and account number.

[17]   Jurisprudence on this point has not set a clear course. A Quebec case involving an inconsistency between the name and account number identifying the beneficiary is *Koridon Inc. v. JWI Ltd.*[74] Unfortunately, the issue concerning the obligation of the beneficiary's bank to match and ensure that consistency existed between the beneficiary's name and account number was avoided there. In that case, a buyer of goods was instructed by the seller's fraudulent officer to pay the price into a designated bank account identified by the officer as belonging to the seller. In fact the

---

[68] Ibid.

[69] See Thunis, above, n. 17 at 143–4 (for transfers under BF 10,000).

[70] CHAPS Rule 4(f) (Nov. 1999).   [71] No. 7, PC 1998–568, s. 49.

[72] See J. M. A. Berkvens and R. E. van Esch, 'Netherlands', in R. C. Effros (ed.), *Payment Systems of the World*, 241 (New York: Oceana Publications Inc., 1994) at 272. According to a co-author's clarification, if a mismatch between a name and a number is established, advice is given by the clearing house to the beneficiary's bank which is then to decide itself whether the discrepancy is merely a matter of a typographical error, namely, whether this is merely a matter of a misspelling of a name, or whether it is indeed a matter of a named beneficiary who is not the holder of the numbered account.

[73] For a Belgian case holding the originator bound by such a rule, see Thunis, above, n. 17 at 144–7. For the prevailing view to the contrary in Germany, see Schimansky, above, n. 2 at 882–3.   [74] [1988] AQ No. 888 (C.A.Q.).

account belonged to a company controlled by the fraudulent officer. Having attempted to send a payment order identifying the payee as the seller and instructing payment into the designated bank account, the originator's bank proceeded, the next day, and sent an amendment changing the beneficiary's name to that of the company controlled by the seller's fraudulent officer. Payment was carried out accordingly. The buyer successfully defended the seller's action for the price of the goods on the basis of the payment to the company controlled by the seller's fraudulent officer.

No evidence was produced to explain the amendment to the payment order changing the beneficiary's name. The court concluded, however, that this must have happened upon compliance with the fraudulent officer's instructions given either directly to the originator's bank or to the buyer. While the report is silent on the point, this must have occurred following the rejection by the beneficiary's bank of the first payment order, identifying the seller as the beneficiary and instructing payment to an account belonging to the officer's company. The case thus appears to involve a beneficiary's bank[75] that verified the consistency between the name and account number of the beneficiary indicated in the first payment order and that moved on to reject it once it found that the beneficiary's name and account number did not match.[76] However, the judgment is silent on whether this was in discharge of a duty to match name and number fastened on the beneficiary's bank.[77]

In South Africa, the issue was avoided in *First National Bank* v. *Quality* **[18]** *Tyres*.[78] In that case, Senbank was instructed by Philip, a director of Quality Tyres, to provide funds under a credit facility available to Quality Tyres from Senbank, by making out a cheque payable to Quality Tyres and having it deposited at Quality Tyres's account with FNB Parktown branch. The cheque, drawn by Senbank on Trust Bank, and made out payable to Quality Tyres, was forwarded for collection by Senbank to FNB Bree Street branch, which was situated close to Senbank's premises, and with which Senbank customarily did its banking. The cheque was accompanied by a credit transfer form signed by Senbank instructing FNB Parktown branch to credit Quality Tyres' account which was further iden-

---

[75] While the report speaks of a 'banking network' ('réseau bancaire') into which the messages of the originator's banks were sent, such a network must be regarded as a processor acting for the beneficiary's bank.

[76] In the facts of the case, both the seller and the company controlled by the seller's fraudulent officer had accounts with the beneficiary's bank, though in different branches. This, however, did not affect the result.

[77] It is however interesting (though unlikely to be material in determining the law on this point) to note that according to the evidence, in the absence of fraud involving the beneficiary's bank and one seeking to misdirect funds, the seller's president 'found it impossible to believe that any Bank would deposit a sum in which the beneficiary did not correspond to the account'.   [78] 1995 (3) SA 556.

tified in the credit transfer form by number, supplied by Philip. In fact, Quality Tyres had no account with FNB, and the designated account was controlled by Philip personally.

From FNB branch, the cheque and the credit transfer form were forwarded to the FNB's centralized bookkeeping centre. The credit transfer form was processed through a machine which caused the account identified by number to be credited with the amount of the cheque. The cheque was passed through the normal automated clearing process, paid by the drawee Trust Bank and returned to the drawer Senbank. Neither the cheque nor the credit transfer form passed through FNB Parktown branch. At all relevant times, this was the only location where the payee's name and designated account number could be matched.

Ultimately, Philip embezzled the funds so credited to his account. Quality Tyres sued FNB for the loss, purporting to bring the action as a 'true owner' claiming from a collecting bank.[79] The action failed on the theory that in the facts of the case and under general law, ownership in the cheque never passed to Quality Tyres, and always remained with Senbank.[80]

In the course of the judgment, the Court consistently treated the credit transfer form as a deposit slip. Thus, the case was not treated as a credit transfer to the beneficiary, under which the originator's bank paid the beneficiary's bank by cheque. Rather, it was treated as involving the collection of a cheque payable to the payee, which in fact, looks appropriate in the circumstances, notwithstanding the unorthodox form of the 'deposit slip'. Nevertheless, it is noteworthy that had there been no cheque payable to the payee, payment to the beneficiary would have been effectuated by means of a credit transfer executed by a payment order issued by Senbank and instructing FNB to pay into Quality Tyres's account identified by number (designating in fact an account controlled by Philip). The issue of the obligation of the beneficiary's bank, here FNB, to confirm consistency between beneficiary's name and number, would have then arisen.

The issue may however still be addressed in South Africa in *Gilbey Distillers and Vintners* v. *ABSA Bank*.[81] In that case, the beneficiary bank was instructed to make payment into an account identified by number. Allegedly, this account belonged to someone other than the one named in

---

[79] For the action of the 'true owner' against the collecting bank in South Africa see 4.D(iv)(d)(South Africa), above.

[80] But this overlooks the possibility of a constructive delivery of the cheque by Sebank to Quality Tyres. See above, 4.D(iv)(a) n. 80.

[81] Case No. 12698/94 (High Court of South Africa, Cape Good Hope Provincial Division), ¶58, 4 Dec. 1998, *per* Brand and Traverso JJ. I provided expert assistance to ABSA Bank in whose favour judgment was given.

the originator's payment order as executed by the payment order issued by the originator's bank to the beneficiary's bank. Indeed, this raises the very issue under discussion. So far, however, the issue has been avoided, as the case was disposed of on the lack of standing by the originator to sue the beneficiary's bank.[82] At this point, however, the case is under appeal.

One Swiss case[83], discussed previously,[84] appears to be directly to the **[19]** point. A beneficiary's bank received a payment order identifying the beneficiary both by name and account number. In fact, the account did not belong to the named beneficiary. The beneficiary's bank complied with the account holder's instructions and directed the funds to the specified account. Judgment was given against the beneficiary's bank, which wrongfully relied on information emanating not from its sender, but rather, from a customer claiming to be the beneficiary, which in fact was not intended by the originator to receive funds. Rather, the originator was fraudulently induced to make payment to a specified account, misrepresented to the originator as belonging to the named beneficiary, and not the actual account holder. The Court held that a beneficiary's bank is not free to act on the basis of the account number alone, and in doing this, it broke its due diligence as mandatary. Nevertheless, it seems to me that the case falls short of undermining automated processing, since in the facts of the case, the beneficiary's bank acquired knowledge of the inconsistency between name and number, and chose to believe its customer and act on the customer's instructions. Stated otherwise, the case ought not to be taken as fastening on the beneficiary's bank an obligation to match a name and number; the Court merely held that once knowledge of the inconsistency has been acquired, the bank is not free to overlook it. As will be seen below, this is also the position adopted by the drafters of the UCC.[85]

American common law was more decisive. In *Bradford Trust Co. of* **[20]** *Boston v. Texas American Bank*,[86] loss was allocated to the originator's bank. That bank did not follow its own internal procedures to verify the genuineness of an unauthorized payment order. The payment order identified the destination account at the beneficiary's bank by number, as well as by the name of the purported originator. In fact, the numbered account belonged to the impostor's innocent creditor. This negligence of the originator's bank, and not the failure by the beneficiary's bank to notice the discrepancy between name and number, was held to be the ultimate cause of the loss. However, where the originator's payment order is genuine, the standard risk bearer under pre-Article 4A American common law was the beneficiary's bank. The leading case is *Securities Fund Services, Inc.* v.

---

[82] See above, 3.C(xi). [83] BGE/ATF 126 III 20 (1999), n. 8, above.
[84] See (i) s. 6, above. [85] See (iv) s. 22, below. [86] Above, n. 64.

American National Bank & Trust Co. of Chicago.[87] In that case, the beneficiary's bank was required to exercise care so as to notice a discrepancy between the account number and the beneficiary's name. Having failed to do so, it became liable to the originator. The originator could also sue the beneficiary's bank as a third party beneficiary of the undertaking by the beneficiary's bank to deliver funds as directed, as well as the principal who was injured by the negligence of his subagent (the beneficiary's bank).

[21]   It is noteworthy that the Secretariat of the United Nations Commission on International Trade Law (UNCITRAL) took the position that 'the development of a fast, reliable and inexpensive electronic funds transfer system could clearly be furthered by enabling banks to rely entirely upon the account number in the funds transfer instruction'[88] so that 'a bank that entered a . . . credit according to the account number on a funds transfer instruction it received would not be liable even though the entry was made to an account bearing a different name from that on the instruction'.[89] Originally, however, the drafters of UCC Article 4A were reluctant to go all that far. Rather, under the 1987 draft of §4A–207(6), processing based on number alone accorded protection to a beneficiary's bank only in connection with a payment order 'transmitted [to it] by use of a standard machine-readable format', and only towards any sender with notice that 'payment will be made on the identifying or bank account number'. This, however, was an exception to the general rule under the 1987 draft of §4A–207(5), under which the acceptance by the beneficiary's bank by means of payment into the designated account that did not belong to the named beneficiary was invalid.[90]

[22]   Ultimately, the drafters endorsed the UNCITRAL position. As finally adopted, UCC §4A–207(b) deals with the position of a beneficiary's bank receiving a payment order identifying the beneficiary 'both by name and by an identifying or bank account' where 'the name and number identify different persons'.[91] Explicitly declining to treat such a payment order as

---

[87] Above, n. 63.

[88] Secretariat of the United Nations Commission on International Trade Law, *UNCITRAL Legal Guide on Electronic Funds Transfers*, 37 (New York: United Nations, 1987).

[89] Ibid. at 128.

[90] National Conference of Commissioners on Uniform State Laws, *Uniform Commercial Code Article 4A—Wire Transfers* (Chicago: NCCUSL, 28 Sept. 1987, Draft for Discussion Only). For the UNCITRAL position, the early draft of UCC Article 4A, and Pre-Article 4A case law, see H. Koh, 'Liability for Lost or Stolen Funds in Cases of Name and Number Discrepancies in Wire Transfers: Analysis of the Approaches Taken in the United States and Internationally', (1989), 22 Cornell Int. L. J. 91.

[91] Notwithstanding *General Electric Capital Corp. v. Central Bank*, 49 F. 3d 280 (7th Cir. 1995), the provision does not cover a payment order received by the beneficiary's bank identifying the beneficiary by name only, even where the account number has been omitted by the sending intermediary bank due to its own error.

payable to an 'unidentifiable' beneficiary under subsection (a), subsection (b)(1), in the footsteps of UNCITRAL, allows a beneficiary's bank receiving inconsistent instructions to rely solely 'on the number as the proper identification of the beneficiary of the order,'[92] provided that the beneficiary's bank did not know that the name and number refer to different persons. 'The beneficiary's bank need not determine whether the name and number refer to the same person.'[93] The loss thus falls on the originator. However, under §4A–207(c), where a non-bank originator had no notice that payment might be made by the beneficiary's bank solely on the basis of the number, loss is shifted to the originator's bank. Under §4A–207(d), recovery from the person identified by number who was not entitled to receive payment from the originator, is available (either to the originator or to the originator's bank, as the case may be) to the extent allowed under the law of mistake and restitution.

Comment 2 to §4A–207 explains that '[s]ubsection (b) allows banks to utilize automated processing by allowing banks to act on the basis of the number without regard to the name if the bank does not know that the name and number refer to different persons'. The underlying automated processing environment is described in the Comment as follows:

A very large percentage of payment orders issued to the beneficiary's bank by another bank are processed by automated means using machines capable of reading orders on standard formats that identify the beneficiary by an identifying number or the number of a bank account. The processing of the order by the beneficiary's bank and the crediting of the beneficiary's account are done by use of the identifying or bank account number without human reading of the payment order itself. The process is comparable to that used in automated payment of checks.

Indeed, the drafters were quite cognizant of the fact that '[t]he standard format . . . may also allow the inclusion of the name of the beneficiary and other information which can be useful to the beneficiary's bank and the beneficiary'. However, such information 'plays no part in the process of payment'. As a matter of fact, the drafters did not deny that a beneficiary's bank which has both number and name can determine the inconsistency; however, their conclusion was that 'if a duty to make that determination

---

[92] This position is implemented in the USA by interbank electronic networks. See e.g. Section 4.1.4 of the Operating Rules of the National Automated Clearing House Association (NACHA) (2000 ACH Rules), as well as Section 5(b) of Administrative Procedures—Clearing House Interbank Payments System (CHIPS) (1999 CHIPS Rules and Administrative Procedures).

[93] UCC §4A–207(b)(1). No similar protection is afforded under UCC Articles 3 and 4 to a depositary bank that misdirected proceeds of a check on the basis of an incorrect lock box identification number placed on a check that contained the correct name of the payee. See *Continental Airlines, Inc. v. Boatmen's National Bank of St. Louis*, 13 F.3d 1254 (8th Cir. 1994). However, in part, the decision was based on lack of knowledge by the payee (and payer) of the consequences of automatic processing. Ibid at 1260. Cf. UCC §4A–207(c).

is imposed on the beneficiary's bank the benefits of automated payment are lost'. According to Comment 2:

Manual handling of payment orders is both expensive and subject to human error. If payment orders can be handled on an automated basis there are substantial economies of operation and the possibility of clerical error is reduced.[94]

It should be noted, however, that §4A–207(b) is not limited to actual cases of automated processing. 'A bank that processes by semi-automated means or even manually may [nevertheless] rely on number as stated in Section 4A–207.'[95]

No protection is afforded to a beneficiary's bank receiving inconsistent instructions as to the beneficiary's identity and acting on the basis of the name only, unless, under §4A–207(b)(2), the named beneficiary 'was entitled to receive payment from the originator of the funds transfer'.[96] This rule applies regardless of whether processing is done by that bank in an automated manner, by semi-automated means, or manually. Where applicable, protection for payment to the rightful beneficiary is given to the beneficiary's bank under subsection (b)(2), even where it knows that 'the name and number identify different persons'. In effect, under subsections (b)(1) and (2), where a payment order received by the beneficiary's bank identifies the beneficiary both by name and by an identifying number, the beneficiary of the order is the account holder, unless the beneficiary's bank knows that the name and number identify different persons.

Where the beneficiary's bank knows that the name and number identify different persons, however, it may not rely on the number as the proper identification of the beneficiary. In such a case, under subsection (b)(2), 'no person has rights as beneficiary except the person paid by the beneficiary's bank if that person was entitled to receive payment from the originator of the funds transfer'. Otherwise, where 'no person has rights as beneficiary', the rule under subsection (b)(2) is that 'acceptance of the order cannot occur'.

A beneficiary's bank which receives a payment order identifying the beneficiary both by name and number and which pauses then to confirm that they match, notwithstanding the freedom given to it by subsection (b)(1) not to do so, thereby learning of a conflict in the identification, has withdrawn from the territory protected by subsection (b)(1) and brought itself into the area covered by subsection (b)(2). This means that acceptance of the order cannot occur unless payment is made to the person entitled to payment from the originator. Mere payment in reliance on the number is no longer sufficient.

---

[94] Official Comment 2 to UCC §4A–207.   [95] Ibid.
[96] UCC §4A–207(b)(2). In theory, this may even be broader than the intended beneficiary.

The combined effect of §4A–207(a) and (b) is that no person has rights [23] as a beneficiary and acceptance by the beneficiary's bank cannot occur:

(1) where the beneficiary is a non-existent or unidentifiable person; or

(2) unless payment was made to the beneficiary entitled to payment from the originator, where the beneficiary's name and number in the payment order identify different persons, and the beneficiary's bank either paid the named payee, either with or without knowledge of the beneficiary's conflicting identification in the payment order, or knowing of the conflicting identification in the payment instructions, paid into the numbered account.

Where, under subsection (a) or (b)(2), no acceptance occurs, each sender is released from its obligation to pay the payment order under §4A–402(c), and subject to the one-year limitation period under §4A–505, may be entitled under §4A–402(d) to a refund for a payment already made. In practice, the fact that payment was made by the beneficiary's bank to a person other than one 'entitled to receive payment from the originator' may be discovered long after the completion of the funds transfer. Unwinding the transaction may thus be fraught with practical difficulties, particularly in the case of an intervening insolvency by a party required to refund.

Practically speaking, in an Article 4A jurisdiction, a beneficiary's bank receiving a payment order should overlook the beneficiary's name and act solely on the basis of the number identification. However, where the bank knows that the name and the number identify different persons, no acceptance occurs unless it pays the person entitled to payment from the originator. Under UCC §1–201(26), 'knowledge' is 'actual knowledge'. Under UCC §1–201(27), for an organization such as a bank, knowledge is effective for a particular transaction 'from the time when it is brought to the attention of the individual conducting that transaction, and in any event, from the time when it would have been brought to his attention if the organization had exercised due diligence'. Due diligence requires the maintenance of 'reasonable routines for communicating significant information to the person conducting the transaction' as well as 'reasonable compliance with the routines'.[97] It follows that knowledge by somebody at the bank, other than someone processing the payment order, does not taint the bank with knowledge. Furthermore, in an automated processing setting, it is not expected that knowledge of inconsistency between a name and number should be discovered through any interdepartmental communication. Ignorance by those processing payment orders is likely

---

[97] UCC §1–201(27).

to achieve the desired result of lack of knowledge as to any discrepancy between a name and number.

[24] Obviously, subsection (b)(1) will not shield a beneficiary's bank that in purporting to carry out what it believed to be the intention expressed in the payment order rectified both name and number.[98] Arguably, however, subsection (b)(1) may be broad enough to protect a beneficiary's bank that does not act automatically on the basis of the account number, if the bank paid the designated account holder without knowledge of the discrepancy between the name and number. Thus, as discussed,[99] in *Royal Bank of Canada* v. *Stangl*,[100] the beneficiary's bank received a payment order directing payment at a designated branch (hereinafter 'the destination branch') to *Lynwil* International Trading Inc., account no. 916327. This account, however, belonged to another entity, Unitec. Unitec had several accounts at that branch, one of which (no. 627902) was in the name of *Linwell* International. Having consulted Unitec, the destination branch deposited the funds into one of Unitec's accounts. In fact, the intended beneficiary was *Linwil*, a different entity that had no account at the destination branch.

Under the common law, in a non-Article 4A jurisdiction, judgment was given in favour of the intermediary bank against both the beneficiary's bank and Unitec. Unitec failed to assert any restitutionary defence to the action for the recovery of the mistaken payment. Under such circumstances, both the common law and Article 4A warrant the judgment against Unitec. Judgment was given against the beneficiary's bank on the basis of its negligence. Elsewhere, I have argued that inasmuch as it was plausible for the beneficiary's bank to believe that the beneficiary's name was misspelled and not that it referred to someone other than the account holder, this aspect of the decision is not defensible.[101]

At first blush, the application of §4A–207(b) to this situation is unclear. Indeed, the beneficiary's bank might have assumed that 'Lynwil' was a misspelling of 'Lynwell', so that the bank '[did] not know that the name and number refer[red] to different persons', as envisaged by subsection (b)(1). Nonetheless, was payment made in reliance on the number (subsection (b)(1)), or to 'the person [mistakenly] identified by name' (subsection (b)(2))? This may be a question of fact; however, inasmuch as payment was made to the holder of account no. 916327, as instructed in the payment order, and in the absence of knowledge of the discrepancy between the name and number, the beneficiary's bank should be protected under subsection (b)(1).

[25] Article 4A does not elaborate on the duties of a beneficiary's bank which knows that the beneficiary's name and number identify different

---

[98] As in the facts of the Belgian case *Frabelmar*, n. 21 above, discussed in (i) s. 5, above.
[99] See (i) s. 5 above.   [100] Above, n. 19.   [101] Above, n. 20.

persons. Indeed, payment is a perilous course of action for the bank, since it can be misdirected. Non-payment, on the other hand, is quite safe, since no acceptance by mere passage of time can occur for a payment order containing contradictory instructions.[102] An unaccepted order is cancelled by operation of law five days after the payment date of the order.[103]

Whether this also absolves the beneficiary's bank as against its customer, the intended but unidentifiable beneficiary of the payment order, may be a different matter. Arguably, having become aware of the contradictory instructions, a beneficiary's bank might be required by sound banking practices to determine who is, in fact, the rightful beneficiary. Inasmuch as this duty might emerge from the relationship between a banker and customer, it may not be negated by §4A–212, providing for lack of responsibility for unaccepted payment orders, except by express agreement. A beneficiary's bank might be expected, at least, to contact the persons identified as beneficiaries, as well as the originator, the latter possibly through prior banks in the transaction chain, in the absence of direct means to communicate with (or even identify) the originator directly. Clarifications received within the five days prior to the expiration of the order may be treated as an amendment enabling the beneficiary's bank to complete the funds transfer properly.[104]

In the alternative, §4A–212 may be taken at face value. This provision states that, except by express agreement, a bank 'does not . . . have any duty to accept a payment order or, before acceptance, to take any action, or refrain from taking action, with respect to the order'. Furthermore, it may be impractical for the beneficiary's bank to contact the originator and, in any event, information coming from the originator and the beneficiary may not be consistent; particularly, a customer may mislead the beneficiary's bank as to that customer's entitlement as a beneficiary. In the final analysis, no liability should be attached to the beneficiary's bank to reconcile between the inconsistent name and number received by it. Furthermore, the plain language of §4A–212, as quoted above, appears to preclude the fastening of a duty on the beneficiary's bank, running in favour of the intended but unidentifiable beneficiary, even when the latter is its customer, to reject outright a payment order containing a patent inconsistency, instead of allowing it to lapse after five days, notwithstanding the ensuing unnecessary loss of time.[105]

---

[102] Otherwise, for a payment order properly identifying a beneficiary account holder at the beneficiary's bank, acceptance by the beneficiary's bank can take place under UCC §4A–209 (b) and (c), by the mere passage of time, upon the receipt of payment from the sender. See above, 3.C (x) s. 8.   [103] UCC §4A–211(d).

[104] Ibid.

[105] On this point, UCC Article 4A does not follow the position emerging from the Quebec case of *Pollack*, above, n. 9, under which a beneficiary's bank that has not rejected a payment

[26]   Inconsistency between numbers is not dealt with by §4A–207. An example of this is where the beneficiary is identified both by an identifying customer number and a bank account number, each designating a different person. In theory, the inconsistency can be discovered by the beneficiary's bank in the course of the automated processing of the payment order. In practice, however, this is not usually so. In an automated environment, the system will look to a specified message field for an account number. It will detect incomplete or non-existent account numbers, but is unlikely to be programmed to compare an account number to a customer number so as to detect an inconsistency. In any event, two questions arise:

(1) What duties are imposed on the beneficiary's bank upon the discovery of an inconsistency between a customer number and account number? and

(2) If the inconsistency is not discovered, what rules apply?

One can speculate, by analogy to §4A–207(b), that according to the automated processing rationale, payment to the account number, if made without knowledge of the contradiction, is a valid acceptance. However, once it becomes tainted with knowledge of the conflicting instructions, the beneficiary's bank can only accept in favour of the person entitled to receive payment from the originator and, in the absence of knowledge as to who that person is, the beneficiary's bank is advised not to make any payment. One may argue that 'name' in subsection (b) includes 'customer's number', so that the subsection applies directly and not by analogy.

[27]   Where the beneficiary's bank receives a payment order identifying the beneficiary both by name and by an identifying or bank account number, payment by the beneficiary's bank in reliance on the number as the proper identification of the beneficiary, without knowledge of a conflict in the instructions, is effective acceptance under §4A–207(b)(1). As such, it binds every prior sender, including the originator.[106] Nonetheless, such a payment may not necessarily be made to the person entitled to receive payment from the originator. A payment not made to 'the beneficiary of the originator's payment order' within the meaning of §4A–406(a) does not discharge the originator from its debt to the intended beneficiary.

It follows that under these circumstances, the originator ends up paying twice: first, on the acceptance by the originator's bank of the origina-

order improperly identifying the beneficiary is bound to act diligently in endeavouring to identify the beneficiary, even when the latter is not a customer of that bank. See (i) s. 3, above.

[106] UCC §4A–402(c) and (d).

tor's payment order; and second, on the original undischarged debt to the intended beneficiary.

The drafters of Article 4A recognized that this may be unfair for a non-bank originator who was not aware of the risk involved in describing the beneficiary by number and name. It could have been reasonable for such a non-bank originator to assume that on receiving a payment order, a beneficiary's bank ought to match name and number, to determine inconsistency, and to prefer the name, since it is more likely that a mistake would occur in the number. For a non-bank originator, it could thus be unpleasantly surprising to find out that the beneficiary's bank was allowed to rely solely upon the number as the proper identification.

To accommodate such a non-bank originator, §4A–207(c) provides that, upon effective acceptance according to the identifying number under subsection (b)(1), the originator is obliged to pay its payment order under all circumstances, where the originator is a bank. For a non-bank originator to be obliged to pay, two cumulative conditions must exist. First, the non-bank originator must have failed to prove that the person identified by number was not entitled to receive payment from the originator. Second, the originator's bank must prove[107] that the non-bank originator, before acceptance of the originator's order, had notice 'that payment of a payment order issued by the originator might be made by the beneficiary's bank on the basis of an identifying or bank account number even if it identifies a person different from the named beneficiary'. Having proven lack of entitlement on the part of the person identified by number *and* not being on notice as to the automated processing on the basis of the account number, a non-bank originator, but not an originator which is a bank, is not obliged to pay. Subsection (c) goes on to permit 'any admissible evidence' as proof of notice. In particular, '[t]he originator's bank satisfies the burden of proof if it proves that the originator, before the payment was accepted, signed a writing stating the information to which the notice relates'.

Stated otherwise, under subsection (c), where payment by the beneficiary's bank was made on the basis of an erroneous account number, a non-bank originator without knowledge of the possible reliance on the identifying number is not obliged to pay its payment order. It may shift to the originator's bank the loss the originator incurs by virtue of an effective payment under subsection (b)(1) made by the beneficiary's bank to the wrong beneficiary, provided the originator was not advised by the originator's bank prior to acceptance by that bank that the beneficiary's bank may rely on the number as the proper identification.

Whoever bears the loss under subsection (c), namely either the

---

[107] As defined in UCC §4A–105(a)(7), by reference to UCC §1–201(8).

originator or the originator's bank, is entitled, under subsection (d), to
recover from the 'person identified by number ... that ... was not entitled to receive payment from the originator'. The amount paid may be
recovered from that person 'to the extent allowed by the law governing
mistake and restitution'.[108]

While §4A–207 is silent on the point, recovery from the person paid by
the beneficiary's bank should be afforded to the beneficiary's bank to the
extent permitted by the law governing mistake and restitution, where
payment was made in the absence of acceptance by the beneficiary's
bank. This is the case under subsection (a) where, after payment, it is
determined that the identification of the beneficiary in the payment order
referred to a non-existent or unidentifiable person, or, under subsection
(b)(2), the payment order identified the beneficiary both by name and
number, each identified a different person, and payment was not made to
the person entitled to receive payment from the originator, either in
reliance on the name identification, or, where the beneficiary's bank knew
of the inconsistency, in reliance on the number identification.

Effective acceptance under subsection (b)(2) occurs in conjunction with
payment either in reliance on the named beneficiary or with knowledge
of the inconsistent identification of the beneficiary in the payment order,
but either way, only where payment is made to the person entitled to
receive payment from the originator. This situation does not, therefore,
give rise to actions in restitution.

(v) MISDESCRIPTION OF INTERMEDIARY OR BENEFICIARY'S BANK

[28]   Under §4A–208, where a payment order identifies an intermediary or
beneficiary's bank by either number or name and number, a receiving
bank, without knowledge of any inconsistency, may act either on the
number or the name. No obligation is fastened on a receiving bank to verify consistency between number and name of an intended bank. Allocation of loss is then determined under the rules applicable to erroneous
execution.[109]

Briefly stated, where a beneficiary's bank is protected, loss accordingly
falls on the erring sender, to whom recovery against the unintended beneficiary is available under the law of mistake and restitution. In turn, any
prior sender, if one exists, is excused from payment or is entitled to a

---

[108] For defences available under the law governing mistake and restitution, particularly,
good faith change of position and discharge for value, see above, (iv) s. 15, text and n. 65.
[109] Rules contained in UCC §4A–208 relating to the misdescription of a bank are extensively discussed by P. S. Turner, *Law of Payment Systems and EFT* (Gaithersburg, NY: Aspen,
Looseleaf) at § 6.02[B][2].

refund under the money-back guarantee, so that the originator is accorded with funds to discharge the originator's underlying debt to the beneficiary.[110] Against a non-bank sender, good faith reliance on a number is available to a receiving bank only where such a non-bank sender had notice of the possibility of such reliance.

§4A–208 is drafted against the background of automated processing of payment orders by receiving banks. It nevertheless applies regardless of the degree or even the existence of automation in a given case.[111] No direct parallel exists in other legal systems.

(VI) INCOMPLETE PAYMENT ORDER

As indicated,[112] there is a difference between the two following cases. The **[29]** first is of a beneficiary's bank acting under what appears to be the most reasonable interpretation of ambiguous instructions. The other is that of a beneficiary's bank acting arbitrarily under one interpretation of ambiguous instructions, when it is obvious that at least one other reasonable, and materially different, interpretation is equally plausible. No protection ought to be accorded to the bank in the latter case, so long as it is evident that each course of action will benefit another person.[113] This becomes particularly apparent in the case of an incomplete payment order whose blanks may be filled in in several ways.

A beneficiary's bank that chooses not to reject a payment order containing incomplete instructions ought to refer the matter to, and seek necessary information from, its sender. But even this could safely be done only prior to the completion of the transfer. A beneficiary's bank that rectifies an action on the basis of the sender's instructions arriving after completion runs the risk of liability to a third party. In the USA, *General Electric Capital Corp. v. Central Bank*[114] is a case to the point. In that case, the beneficiary's bank received a payment order instructing payment to a customer identified by name only. The beneficiary's bank acted on these instructions by crediting one of the accounts it maintained for that customer. In fact, this was a blocked account under the control of the customer's secured party. The customer requested rectification and instructed the beneficiary's bank to transfer the credit to the customer's

---

[110] For the 'money-back guarantee rule' and loss allocation in connection with the erroneous execution of a payment order, see 3.C (x) ss. 5 and 7 above.

[111] See Official Comments 1 and 3 to UCC §4A–208.   [112] See (i) s. 6, above.

[113] That is, a beneficiary's bank receiving a payment order instructing payment to a named customer, with no destination account specifically identified, will usually be fully protected if it deposits the funds to any account of such a customer.

[114] Above, n. 91.

personal account. The beneficiary's bank complied only upon confirming with its own sender, an intermediary bank in the credit transfer. That confirmation from the intermediary bank was to the effect that the payment order received by it actually identified the customer's personal account as the destination account. This piece of information was overlooked by the intermediary bank in sending its own payment order to the beneficiary's bank. It, however, turned out that the customer, under a security agreement, was required to instruct the originator of that credit transfer to direct payment to the blocked account, but that the customer, in fraud of the secured party, misled the originator to instruct payment to the customer's personal account. It was held that once funds were credited to an account under the control of the secured party, who had a legitimate claim to them, their subsequent unauthorized withdrawal was unlawful against that secured party.[115] Obviously, had the beneficiary's bank sought supplementary information from its sender prior to crediting the account to the blocked account, and had it subsequently credited the customer's personal account on the basis of such supplementary information, it would have been entirely exonerated from liability to the secured party.

[30]　　　Regardless, the beneficiary's bank acts at its peril if, instead of acting prior to completion under the supplementary instructions of the sender, it follows the advice of a third party, claiming to be the intended beneficiary, who was not identified in the payment order received by the beneficiary's bank. The risk is present even when that third party properly identifies the incoming payment order. There is always a danger that the third party correctly guessed the details of the payment order. Alternatively, it may be that the third party's intimate knowledge of relevant details of the incoming payment order stems from the third party's dishonest involvement in the fraudulent origination of the credit transfer, rather than from honest familiarity with the details of a legitimate forthcoming payment. Against a restitution action of an earlier sender, the beneficiary's bank, acting mistakenly, but in good faith upon the guidance of a fraudulent (or even mistaken) third party, may raise the defence of change of position, but this will not necessarily always be successful.

[31]　　　*State Bank of New South Wales Ltd.* v. *Swiss Bank Corporation*[116] was an action of the Swiss Bank Corporation (hereafter: 'Swiss Bank') against

---

[115] *Quaere* whether this is not limited only to the situation where crediting the original account was according to a plausible interpretation of the payment order, as opposed to an altogether erroneous action contrary to the language of the payment order.

[116] (1995), 39 N.S.W.L.R. 350 (S.C. C.A.) (Priestly JA, Handley JA, and Sheller JA), *aff'g Swiss Bank Corp.* v. *State Bank of New South Wales* 50693 of 1989, 1993 NSW LEXIS 7467; BC9301702 (S.C. Com. Div.) (Rogers CJ Comm D) and *Swiss Bank Corp.* v. *State Bank of New South Wales* (1993), 33 N.S.W.L.R. 63 (Com. Div.) (Giles J.). As seen below, the case involved two branches or subsidiaries of each bank, each of whom, for the purpose of considering their actions under credit transfer law, is to be considered as a distinct and separate entity.

State Bank of New South Wales (hereafter: 'State Bank') for the restitution of money paid by mistake of fact. In this case, a 'trusted senior',[117] but unfaithful employee of the Swiss Bank in Zurich (hereafter: 'SBC Zurich'), acting in concert with a fraudster, a customer of the Sydney branch of State Bank (hereafter: 'SBN Sydney'), input an unauthorized payment order, instructing SBC Zurich to transfer $20,004,583.33 in US funds to account 137–327 at the State Bank of New South Wales New York (hereafter: 'SBN NY'). This purported to be in repayment of a fictitious overnight $20,000,000 (US) deposit of SBN Sydney[118] that the unfaithful employee had caused to appear on the records of SBC Zurich.[119] In fact, no such deposit had been made and account no. 137–327 was the defraudster's account in SBN Sydney (and not in SBN New York).

SBC Zurich acted on the unauthorized instructions in good faith and without knowledge of the fraud. It thus issued its own conforming SWIFT payment order directing Swiss Bank in New York (hereafter: SBC NY)[120] to make payment to account no. 137–327 of SBN Sydney in SBN NY.[121] SBC NY[122] followed up with a conforming CHIPS payment order issued to SBN NY instructing payment to SBN Sydney, and omitting any reference to account no. 137–327, or any other account number. On his part, the defrauding customer advised SBN Sydney of a forthcoming payment of $20,004,583.33 in US funds to the credit of that customer's account no. 137–327 in Sydney.[123] SBN Sydney passed on the information to SBN NY, which accordingly accepted the CHIPS payment. Consequently, funds

---

[117] 39 N.S.W.L.R. 350 at 351.

[118] The report describes the 'depositor' as 'State Bank' without specifically identifying it as 'SBN Sydney'. Yet, as will be seen below, payment by Swiss Bank was directed to 'SBN Sydney', from which it is logical to conclude that the 'depositor' was designated by the unfaithful employee as 'SBN Sydney'.

[119] In fact, both the fictitious 'deposit' and the unauthorized payment order were input by the unfaithful employee in one communication, causing the fraudulent deposit to appear on the records of SBC Zurich, and instructing it to repay it upon maturity, with interest, to SBN NY account no. 137–327.

[120] Unfortunately, in that respect, the report is quite confusing, if not altogether misleading, in referring to the recipient of the SWIFT message who acted on it as 'SBN NY' (rather than 'SBC NY'). See 39 N.S.W.L.R. 350 at 353–4. Perhaps the confusion is attributed to the unreported summary of the facts, *Swiss Bank Corp.* v. *State Bank of New South Wales*, 50693 of 1989, BC9203217, 9 Dec. 1992 (Rogers CJ Comm D), inexplicably referring (at 94 and 96) to the addressee of SBC Zurich's SWIFT message who acted on it as 'SBM'. The latter is an unidentified party not participating in the transaction; the reference to it must have been erroneous, and it should have been made to 'SBC NY'. Both the logic of the judgment and the initial summary of the facts by Rogers CJ Comm D unequivocally support the interpretation of the facts as outlined in the text here.

[121] The contents of both the SWIFT and subsequent CHIPS message appear in BC9203217 at 94–9.

[122] See n. 120, above.

[123] It is this aspect which made the misdirection of funds as not exclusively dependent on the unauthorized originator's payment order, so as to fall within the ambit of the present discussion.

were forwarded to the defraudster who withdrew them. Upon the discovery of the error, Swiss Bank sued State Bank in restitution. State Bank's defence of change of position upon payment to the defraudster was rejected, since State Bank acted on the basis of knowledge exclusively derived otherwise than from the payor Swiss Bank.[124] Judgment was thus given for Swiss Bank.

One commentator welcomed the judgment both from 'a purely legal point of view' as well as '[f]or practical reasons'.[125] From the former perspective, the judgment was said to clarify the requirement that to be a good defence against an action in restitution, a change of position must be made 'in reliance on the receipt'. Also, so far as practical reasons are concerned, the result was said to accommodate the processing environment of CHIPS, under which a high volume of transactions is processed daily. Consequently, 'the integrity of the system requires strict and mechanical adherence by receiving banks to the terms of payment messages so that there is no room for discretion in relation to the application of the funds'.[126] However, as explained below, the judgment is not in line with the prevailing current thinking in the law of restitution. Further, the particular litigation was not concerned with the completion of the credit transfer or with banks' obligation thereunder. Yet, both the facts of the case and the Court's analysis serve as a good focal point for discussing the position of a beneficiary's bank receiving incomplete or ambiguous instructions.

[32]   To begin with, it is not all that certain that in the facts of the case State Bank acted exclusively on the basis of information forthcoming other than from Swiss Bank. Thus, SBC Zurich's SWIFT message identified the transferred funds as having been generated from a foreign exchange transaction, which consequently had to be credited by SBN NY to SBN Sydney's foreign exchange account and not for any of its customers. At the same time, SBC NY's CHIPS payment order instructed SBN NY to credit the funds to SBN Sydney's Trade and Overseas (or TOS) account that was used for customer-related transactions.[127] It is immaterial that the reasonableness of SBC NY's conduct in generating the CHIPS payment message was not questioned;[128] what matters for our purposes is that there was a representation to State Bank, forthcoming from SBC NY, as to the possible destination of the funds to customers. Yet, in the final analysis, this may not be enough to justify reliance on customer's information, notwithstanding the fact that it extensively matched with the incoming Swiss Bank message. Ultimately, there was nothing in the information coming from Swiss Bank to suggest in any way whatsoever that payment was to

---

[124] Above, n. 117 at 355–7.   [125] Note, [1996] 2 J.I.B.L. N-23 at N-24.
[126] Ibid.   [127] BC9203217 at 94–9.   [128] Ibid. at 99.

be directed to the defrauding customer. Accordingly, while there was some knowledge derived from the payor, it did not suffice as a basis for the conclusion that funds were to be paid to the defrauding customer.

On the other hand, the lack of information in the CHIPS payment order linking the forthcoming payment to the defrauding customer is attributed to the deletion of the reference to account no. 137–327 by SBC NY. It is thus ironic that it is Swiss Bank's omission which facilitated judgment in its favour; after all, had the account number been included in the CHIPS message, it would have been impossible to argue that State Bank took action on the basis of knowledge exclusively derived otherwise than from the payor Swiss Bank. In any event, the trial judge concluded that by itself, 'deletion was reasonable' since in light of the identification by name of the beneficiary as SBN Sydney, the reference to the account number at SBN NY 'could . . . properly be regarded as immaterial'.[129] Indeed, if SBC NY cannot be faulted for deleting the account number information, it cannot be held responsible for losses precipitated by the deletion.[130]

At first blush, the result appears to be justified on the basis of lack of adequate ambiguity in the payment order sent to and received by SBN NY. This payment order either unequivocally directed payment to SBN Sydney,[131] or at least, due to the destination of the funds to the TOS account at SBN NY, raised a query to be addressed to the sender and not the beneficiary. Indeed, no reliance can be put on information originating from a customer seeking incoming funds to be credited to his account unless three conditions have been met. First, the pertinent payment order instructing the payment of the incoming funds ought to be ambiguous. Second, there ought to be something in the payment order received by the beneficiary's bank to reasonably resolve the ambiguity by identifying that customer as the beneficiary. Third, the information provided by the customer must serve as a mere confirmation to a conclusion the beneficiary's bank could have justifiable reached from the four corners of the payment order itself.

However, in the facts of the case, all this is true only to the extent that attention is focused exclusively on the conduct of State Bank as both the beneficiary and the beneficiary's bank. On balance, this perspective overlooks the initiation of the fraud by an insider within the organization of Swiss Bank.

---

[129] Ibid. at 96.
[130] Nonetheless, due to the common practice of automated processing of CHIPS messages, this aspect of the judgment is not all that convincing. At present, under Section 5(e) of CHIPS Administrative Procedures (in connection with sections 8–10 of CHIPS Rules) above, n. 92, the use of numerical information for identifying a beneficiary in a CHIPS message is explicitly 'encouraged'.
[131] BC9203217 at 94–9.

Moreover, both State Bank's reliance on someone other than the payor as well as, particularly in the facts of the case, its apparent negligence, may not be all that relevant in the context of a defence of change of position against an action for the restitution of a sum of money paid under a mistake of fact. First, unlike estoppel, change of position does not require reliance on an express or implied representation of the payor. Stated otherwise, no sound basis exists for the requirement that change of position must be made 'on the faith of the receipt'. Second, so far as fault is concerned, the better view is that at least as long as it was not the recipient's fault that initiated the chain of events leading to the mistaken payment, change of position is available other than to a recipient to whom more fault is attributed than to the payor.[132] This has been the view under the American common law,[133] with Canada,[134] England,[135] and Australia itself,[136] gradually falling in line. In the facts of the case, State Bank's fault was neither the source of the problem nor was its fault greater than that of Swiss Bank. Consequently, the defence of change of position ought to have been made available to State Bank.[137]

[33]   Allocating the loss to Swiss Bank would have been consistent with *Bradford Trust Co. of Boston* v. *Texas American Bank*,[138] an American pre-Article 4A judgment. In that case, an unauthorized payment order input to an originator's bank by an imposter identified the destination account at the beneficiary's bank by number as well as by the name of the purported originator. In fact, the numbered account belonged to the impostor's innocent creditor. The beneficiary's bank acted on the number alone and thus credited the innocent creditor's account, in breach of what was perceived then to be the duty under the common law. Loss was nevertheless allocated to the originator's bank. That bank did not follow its own internal procedures to verify the genuineness of an unauthorized payment order. This negligence of the originator's bank, and not the failure

---

[132] For these principles, as applied here to the facts of the case, see P. D. Maddaugh and J. D. McCamus, *The Law of Restitution* (Aurora, Ont.: Canada Law Book, 1990) at 231–6.

[133] See American Law Institute, *Restatement of the Restitution, Quasi Contracts and Constructive Trusts* (St Paul, Minn.: American Law Institute Publishers, 1937) at §69.

[134] For the introduction of the defence of change of position in Canada by *Rural Municipality of Storthoaks* v. *Mobil Oil Canada Ltd.* (1976), 55 D.L.R. (3d) 1 (S.C.C.), see Maddaugh and McCamus, above, n. 132 at 233.

[135] The leading case is *Lipkin Gorman* v. *Karpnale Ltd.* [1991] 2 A.C. 548. For the change of position defence in general, see Lord Goff and G. Jones, *The law of Restitution*, 5th edn. (London: Sweet & Maxwell, 1998) at 818–41.

[136] The leading case is *David Securities Pty Ltd.* v. *Commonwealth Bank of Australia* (1992) 175 CLR 353.

[137] For a milder criticism on the case, pointing out its failure 'to make any significant progress' in connection with the defence of change of position, see R. Chambers, 'Change of Position on the Faith of Receipt (*State Bank of New South Wales* v. *Swiss Bank*)', [1996] Restitution Law Review 103.   [138] Above, n. 64.

by the beneficiary's bank to notice the discrepancy between name and number, was held to be the ultimate cause of the loss.[139]

It is indeed acknowledged in the facts of our case that the credit transfer was completed upon payment to SBN Sydney, at least insofar as in relation to the payment order received by SBN NY. This, however, does not affect the restitution action against State Bank, based on the mistaken, albeit completed, payment. Under the preceding analysis, State Bank was to win on the basis of a successful assertion of the change of position defence, notwithstanding the completion of payment, as well as its own negligence.

Under the law of credit transfers, State Bank's negligence may have nevertheless been relevant, if no fraud against the originator's bank had been committed at the initiation of the credit transfer, and if the plaintiff had been an intended beneficiary, rather than the originator's bank. Namely, suppose the payment order addressed to SBC Zurich was genuine and instructed payment into account number 137–327 at SBN Sydney. Suppose this account belonged to one Z to whom the originator was indebted. Further suppose that the message sent by SBC Zurich to SBC NY properly identified the beneficiary's account by number only, as instructed by the originator. However, as in the facts of the case, SBC NY's payment order addressed to SBN NY erroneously instructed payment only to SBN Sydney. On its part, SBN Sydney went on to commit an error of its own by crediting X's account, as in the facts of the case, on the basis of X's representation that payment had been due to it. As explained above, this would have been entirely unjustifiable on the part of State Bank. Finally, suppose X withdrew the funds and disappeared. Under such circumstances, the originator, who remained indebted to Z on the underlying obligation, may have shifted liability over to SBC NY, which committed the first error.[140] Presumably, SBC NY's action against SBN Sydney could have been characterized as an action in restitution,[141] to which SBN Sydney would have attempted to meet by pleading change of position. Indeed, in such a scenario, it was not SBN Sydney's fault which initiated the chain of events leading to the loss. Nevertheless, arguably, SBN Sydney's fault may be greater than that of SBC NY, so it is not impossible for a court to accord restitution to SBC NY against SBN Sydney.

Obviously, had SBN Sydney been instructed to pay into account

---

[139] See (iv) s. 19, above.

[140] In the absence of privity with SBC NY, an intermediary bank, the originator would have recovered from SBC Zurich, as an agent vicariously liable for loss cause by the negligence of a sub-agent. SBC Zurich would have then recovered from SBC NY. For the chain of liability in connection with a default of an intermediary bank, see 3.C(viii)(c) s. 15, above.

[141] In effect, SBC NY is claiming mistakenly making an unrestricted payment instead of a payment subject to restrictions, and thus seeks restitution.

137–127, identified as belonging to Y but in fact belonging to the defraudster, the case would have raised the issue of a beneficiary's bank receiving a payment order containing inconsistency between the beneficiary's name and account number, extensively discussed in (iv), above. However, in the facts of the case, no account number was passed on by SBC NY. As well in SBC NY's payment order, no beneficiary was identified by name other than SBN Sydney. Furthermore, SBC Zurich instructed payment to account 137–127 at SBN NY. Presumably, no such account belonged to the defraudster, and possibly, account 137–127 at SBN NY was non-existent.

In the final analysis, the case involved a situation under which a beneficiary's bank should not have safely acted on the advice of a purported beneficiary. Indeed, and notwithstanding the actual judgment, in the particular context of a restitution action by the defrauded originator's bank, the beneficiary's bank should nevertheless not have been penalized. Yet, reliance on the purported beneficiary to fill in ambiguities is misplaced and could be detrimental.

(VII) CONCLUSION

[34]   In settling once and for all the controversy relating to the duty of the beneficiary's bank to verify the consistency between the beneficiary's name and number, UCC Article 4A introduced great certainty. In eliminating such a duty, Article 4A took full account of modern day automated processing. In thus introducing certainty based on current processing environment, UCC Article 4A constitutes a substantial improvement to the situation in general law jurisdictions.[142] Also, by affording an originator a money-back guarantee in the case of an ineffective acceptance by a beneficiary's bank, irrespective of any theory of liability for breach, Article 4A overcame a great complication existing in those general law jurisdictions regarding the beneficiary's bank as an agent or mandatary for the beneficiary, and thus potentially not liable, either directly or through the vicarious liability of the originator's bank, to the originator.[143]

No similar credit can, however, be given to the Article 4A provision dealing with a non-existing or unidentifiable beneficiary. To a large extent, the provision precipitated preoccupation with linguistics at the expense of a more focused discussion relating to the standard of care required from a beneficiary's bank purporting to carry out payment to the intended beneficiary.[144]

Indeed, other than in connection with inconsistency between name and number under UCC Article 4A, in both general law and Article 4A juris-

---

[142] See (iv), above.   [143] See s. 7, above.   [144] See (iii), above.

dictions, the real issue is the extent to which protection is to be given to a beneficiary's bank that resolved an ambiguity or inconsistency in the payment order contrary to the originator's true intention. The questions are then: the extent to which protection is afforded in general law jurisdictions to a bank acting in an automated processing environment and, in both general law and Article 4A jurisdictions, the extent of immunity given to a bank that exercised due diligence in purporting to identify the intended beneficiary. It is in this latter context that the determination of the standard of care becomes crucial.

While there is no conclusive, universal answer to such questions, one trend of the courts has been to lean too much in the direction of a 'strict compliance' standard, so as to effectively require banks to reject a payment order for any defect.[145] This is quite regrettable; it is contrary to both customer expectations and the fundamental due care obligations of banks. It is also obvious that the interpretation by courts of the UCC provisions has not contributed to clarifying the issue, but, rather, has reinforced this rigidity.[146]

Nonetheless, such a trend is neither conclusive and irreversible nor inevitable. It is not too late for courts in both general law and Article 4A jurisdictions to be faithful to principle as well as to business reality and adopt a flexible approach accommodating smooth processing thereby protecting a beneficiary's bank acting diligently.[147] In the final analysis, among participants in a credit transfer, it is typically the originator who is best placed to eliminate any ambiguity or inconsistency; it is thus only fair to allocate to the originator responsibility for any such ambiguity and inconsistency, at least as long as the beneficiary's bank did not act unreasonably.[148]

[145] See e.g. *Stangl*, above, n. 19, and discussion in (i) s. 5, above.
[146] See (iii), ss. 12–13, above.
[147] See e.g. *Donmar*, above, n. 46, and discussion in s. 11 above.
[148] As in fact was rationalized in *Bradford*, above, n. 64, and see discussion in (iv) s. 20, above.

Index